REFORMATION
EUROPE

REFORMATION EUROPE

Age of Reform and Revolution

SECOND EDITION

DE LAMAR JENSEN
Brigham Young University

D. C. HEATH AND COMPANY
LEXINGTON, MASSACHUSETTS   TORONTO

To Mary W. Jensen, Dale and Jonna Lu Williams, Ross and Marde Brunson, Brad and Kathy Jensen, Bob and Emily Porfiri, Albert and Christine Peters

Address editorial correspondence to:
D. C. Heath
125 Spring Street
Lexington, MA 02173

Cover:
Lucas Cranach: THE LAST SUPPER, from the altarpiece at St. Marien in Wittenberg. Photo by Christoph Sandig/ARTOTHEK.

Published simultaneously in Canada.

Printed in the United States of America.

International Standard Book Number: 0-669-20009-3

Library of Congress Catalog Number: 91-71582

10 9 8 7 6 5 4 3 2

PREFACE

The lessons of history are not always easy to learn, nor are their meanings simple to interpret. One of the banes of our time is the oversimplification and rationalization of history to make it fit preconceived ideas or bolster previously made conclusions. History is the account of human experiences. To be of value, it must be studied and presented both accurately and honestly, critically as well as understandingly, and in context. That is what I have tried to do in *Reformation Europe*, Second Edition, and its companion text, *Renaissance Europe*, Second Edition.

No one is free from bias. To think that one's views are not subjective, and not shaped to varying degrees by one's own cultural, political, and religious frame of reference and experience, is a dangerous form of self-delusion. Yet balance and greater objectivity can be achieved through conscientious endeavor, just as the sharp abrasiveness of prejudice can be smoothed by broadening thought and sympathetic effort.

The challenge of presenting and interpreting a subject so complex and controversial as the Reformation is indeed awesome. Many times in the preparation of this book I have thought, "Only a fool would attempt such an impossible task." Nevertheless, as Erasmus reminds us, Folly may succeed where reason fears to tread. I continue to be motivated by the powerful incentives of wanting to know and wanting to teach others. As I have studied the intricacies of sixteenth-century religious ideas, compared these with the equally conflicting assertions of secular thought, and related them both to the political, economic, military, and artistic events and movements of the time, I have become increasingly conscious of the interrelationship of all human endeavor. That interrelationship will be shown in the following pages, as will the consequences of ideological conflict.

Europeans living in the first decades of the sixteenth century were caught in a great cultural convulsion resulting from the collision of Renaissance optimism, worldliness, and exuberance for life, with the concurrent anxiety over disease, death, and eternal salvation. The Renaissance reconciliation of the spiritual and the mundane was not adequate to calm people's fears about death, nor to ease the pains of life. *Reformation Europe* is partly the story of that dilemma and the desperate struggle to find its solution. It is not an ecclesiastical history but rather a general account of European life and thought during the dynamic 150 years from the beginning of the sixteenth to the middle of the seventeenth century. Yet because of the pivotal nature of the Protestant Reformation, religion came to play a transcendent role in the overall history of the period.

Because of the continuing diversity of religious affiliations and belief, I am aware that not everyone will agree with all of my interpretations and emphases, particularly in those chapters dealing primarily with religious matters. Nevertheless, I have tried to present the knowable facts of this period accurately and to interpret them as objectively and meaningfully as I could.

In this second edition I have expanded and updated the coverage of social aspects of the Reformation. More attention is given to the impact of printing, for example, as well as to the effect of religious upheaval on the common people (insofar as that can be determined), and the effect those people had on the social and religious upheavals. In particular, I have paid significantly more attention to the role of women, to the part they played in the economy of the time and in the spread of Reformation ideas, and, in turn, to the Reformation's effects on women's lives. Other areas of recent scholarship, such as demography, popular culture, and family life, are also emphasized. The significance of humanism in the early Reformation is highlighted, as is the overall impact of the Reformation on political, economic, social, and cultural life. Some of the chapters have been reorganized for greater clarity and continuity, and all of them have been tightened and corrected where necessary.

Suggestions for Further Reading

The short bibliographical essays following each chapter have been rewritten to assist the student in making purposeful selections of the best and most recent additional reading material. I feel that this is better achieved by a limited number of good books, accompanied by brief comments or evaluations, than by long impersonal lists of authors and titles.

To keep these bibliographies as brief and functional as possible, the following criteria have been used: (1) Despite the great amount of important historical literature in foreign languages, only works written in English or translated into English are included. (2) In order to make these bibliographies as current as possible, the most recent works are cited. Those written before 1980 are included only if they have been reissued in later editions or are of unusual value. (3) First priority has been given to full-length, single-author books, although books containing collections of articles are included, and occasionally source documents.

Acknowledgments

I greatly appreciate the suggestions, corrections, and admonitions of those experts who have read all or parts of this book. They include representatives of most of the religious persuasions discussed here, and they have prevented me from many errors that I might otherwise have committed had they not read the manuscript carefully and critically and given me the benefit of their knowledge. Two of the scholar-teachers who read and commented constructively on the text, and to whom I am greatly indebted, are Robert V. Schnucker, Northeast Missouri State University, and Kyle C. Sessions, Illinois State University. I wish to thank my colleagues and a generation or more of students for their stimulation and long suffering, and my family for their continuing support. The editors at D. C. Heath have been a constant help in bringing this project to a successful conclusion, especially James Miller for his valuable, expert advice, and Carolyn Ingalls for her patience and skill in guiding the project through to completion. Having been able to incorporate into this volume some of the information and interpretations gained while doing research in Europe on more specialized studies supported by grants from the Institute of International Education, the Rockefeller Foundation, the National Endowment for the Humanities, the John Simon Guggenheim Foundation, and the David M. Kennedy Center for International Studies at Brigham Young University, I gratefully acknowledge their interest and help.

DE LAMAR JENSEN

CONTENTS

CHAPTER SEVEN

CHAPTER EIGHT

List of Maps

INTRODUCTION
FROM RENAISSANCE TO REFORMATION

T HE DYNAMIC LITERARY AND ARTISTIC RENAISSANCE REACHED ITS CLI-
max during the first three decades of the sixteenth century. By then Florence had already passed its prime. With the death of Lorenzo the Magnificent in 1492, the great age of Florentine preeminence began drawing to a
close. Cristoforo Landino and Piero della Francesca died that same year; and
in 1494, the fateful year of the first French invasion, Pico and Poliziano both
passed away, as did Boiardo and Ghirlandaio. Pollaiuolo followed in 1498,
Ficino in 1499, and Botticelli in 1510. After that the flame of Florentine art
was kept alive for another ten years by Leonardo da Vinci, Raphael, Andrea
del Sarto, and Michelangelo.

The glow of the High Renaissance was brightest in Rome—where Bra-
mante, Sangallo, Raphael, and Michelangelo now amazed the world with their
mightiest creations of classical-Christian beauty—and in Venice, where the Bel-
linis, Giorgione, Carpaccio, and Titian carried Venetian art to its climax in a
blaze of harmonious light and color. However, the rampant Italian (Habsburg-
Valois) Wars, especially the devastating sack of Rome in 1527, contributed to
the rapid deterioration of Roman art, as well as to the decline of Renaissance
letters (especially after the deaths of Machiavelli in 1527, Castiglione in 1529,
and Ariosto in 1533) and the loss of intellectual leadership. The stylish affec-
tation and strained tensions of Italian Mannerism after 1530 clearly reveal the
waning of the Renaissance in Italy.

Nevertheless, beyond the Alps, Renaissance spirit and style began to flourish in modified forms. Indeed, the first two or three decades of the sixteenth
century saw the rapid expansion of Renaissance ideas and expression throughout Europe. In this period, the most successful reconciliations of ancient and
modern thought, classicism and Christianity, scholarship and faith, action and
devotion, were achieved north of the Alps in the humanism of Lefèvre d'Étaples, Guillaume Budé, Jiménez de Cisneros, Juan Luis Vives, Jakob Wimphel-
ing, Johann Reuchlin, John Colet, Thomas More, and especially Erasmus. The
poetic power of Clément Marot and Garcilaso de la Vega was supplemented

1

by the prose distinction of François Rabelais, while the artistic harmonization of the natural and the supernatural was attempted by Albrecht Dürer.

Manifestations of Renaissance classicism, harmony, order, and balance continued throughout the century, providing a thread of continuity with the High Renaissance. These manifestations were particularly notable in the poets of the *Pléiade* during the second half of the century, in the *Essays* of Montaigne, and in the dramatic literature of Shakespeare's England and Cervantes's Spain. They also provide the warp of Baroque architecture in the early seventeenth century, and show up even stronger in the classicism of French painting from Georges de La Tour to Claude Poussin.

By the time the second decade of the sixteenth century drew to a close, however, a new and powerful force had appeared in the form of the Protestant Reformation, a complex movement of such magnitude that no area of Europe or field of thought and activity was unaffected by it. In many ways the Reformation was a repudiation of the Renaissance, a reaction against its humanism, classicism, and secularism, but also—and especially—against its ecclesiastical authoritarianism. The effect of the Reformation on northern art and literature was almost immediate, as the arts were mobilized for the war of religious polemics and propaganda. Humanism was diverted into more sectarian channels, and secular scholarship was converted to confessional apologetics. Political alignments and international relations were altered by religious disputes and wars that profoundly affected economic development and social organization as well as the daily lives of millions.

The Reformation has frequently been described as a repudiation of Renaissance "paganism" and a return to Judeo-Christian theocracy. The Reformation did advocate a renewal of piety and a rejection of the vanity of human pleasures, and it produced the greatest resurgence of biblical theology since the time of the Latin fathers. Many of the religious reformers were uneasy about the humanists' exaltation of worldly things, and saw in this a dishonoring or even degrading of God. The Reformation emphasized instead human corruption and sinfulness. The depravity of human nature was so profound, according to Calvin, "that everything in man—the understanding and will, the soul and body—is polluted and engrossed by lust."

Yet the Reformation also had much in common with the Renaissance and can therefore be understood in part as a continuation and intensification of the Renaissance spirit, especially the spirit of reform. The Renaissance was an age of reformers. They wanted to reform education, correct the errors of medieval scholarship, improve the translations of legal and religious texts, enrich the content as well as style of literature, recover the wisdom of the ancients, recapture the order and simplicity of nature, and renew and refine the relationship between humanity and God by thoroughly reforming the church.

Christian humanists of the early sixteenth century combined all of these endeavors and, by a blending of piety and learning, hoped to effect a revitalization of religion. Indeed, through erudition, reason, and education, these humanists aspired to transform not only the church but also society at large. Erasmus of Rotterdam (1466–1536) was the leading voice of this reform movement. A many-faceted genius, Erasmus had a thorough training in the classic authors as well as in languages and grammar, which he mobilized in the cause of Christian scholarship. The greatest classical scholar of his age, he used his knowledge of Greek and Latin sources to demonstrate the profound effect of ancient culture on Christianity and to use the best in classical civilization for Christian service and improved morality. For Erasmus, erudition was not a pursuit extraneous to a religious life but was rather the very heart of it. He believed not only that the classics had the capacity to inculcate good taste, stimulate sound and clear thinking, and cultivate lucid, accurate, and precise verbal and written expression, but also that their study, along with that of the Bible, would promote greater religious devotion and goodness. This "*pietas literata*" (piety through literature) was the basis of Erasmus's educational philosophy and his religious reformism.

Erasmus was not alone in his devotion to Christian humanism. Many men and women in every country of Europe shared both his enthusiasm for classical culture and his dissatisfaction with the formalism and banality of the ecclesiastical establishment. They, too, wanted to expose corruption and purge the church of its punctiliousness. This movement, of course, opened the way to a crescendo of anticlericalism during the first two decades of the sixteenth century. Led by Erasmus, many other humanists took up their pens to attack clerical abuse and ecclesiastical bigotry. At the same time (and frequently in the same works), the Christian humanists laid the foundation for a positive religious reform, based on biblical scholarship and using the historical and philological study of Greek and Hebrew texts of the Bible as a starting point. In this regard, the religious works of John Colet, Jacques Lefèvre d'Étaples, and Johann Reuchlin stand with Erasmus's Greek and Latin New Testament as evidences of their desire for genuine religious reform.

In a different and even more intense way, the Reformation continued to promote the goals of cleansing and reform—so vigorously, in fact, that reform eventually led to revolution instead of reconciliation. Erasmus wanted to regenerate the church in order to strengthen and unite it; Luther believed it was his duty to correct the church even if that correction destroyed it.

The "Bible revival" was also common to both the Renaissance and the Reformation, since it began even prior to the Protestant emphasis on the written word. Going back to the sources was basic to Renaissance scholarship and humanism, and the transition from late fifteenth-century biblical scholarship to Protestant scripturalism was natural and continuous. Lefèvre d'Étaples's, Reuchlin's, and Erasmus's interest in the Bible was as genuine as Luther's and Calvin's, although perhaps not as theologically profound (Luther thought not, anyway, when he chided Erasmus "to suffer my lack of eloquence, as I in return will bear with your ignorance in those matters").

The long-term relationship between Renaissance and Reformation was both causal and continuous. Both movements were committed to reform; both dealt with people and their relationships to their fellow human beings, to their surroundings, and to God; both gave great impetus to writing and reading, and were reciprocally related to the development of printing; both contributed substantially—although not always intentionally and not immediately—to the development of religious and political freedom. The Reformation also was an important factor in the continued consolidation of the national states in Europe.

Yet, however strong the cords of continuity between the Renaissance and Reformation, the transformation that began in the second quarter of the sixteenth century has altered many aspects of life to the present day. One of the significant characteristics of European society until the sixteenth century was its ecclesiastical unity. The universal jurisdiction of the Roman Catholic church gave a certain homogeneity and uniformity to society and provided a stabilizing influence, despite many distractions and disorders. This religious unity was destroyed by the Reformation, and a drastically different world came into existence. The disappearance of the *Respublica Christiana* caused strains and fissures that resulted in Europewide upheavals. The stability and consonance of Renaissance society gave way to disparity and discord. Tension and uncertainty characterized life throughout much of the sixteenth century, because people were unable to comprehend or accept religious heterogeneity. What began as a religious revival and attempt, in Roland Bainton's words, "to give man a new assurance in the presence of God and a new motivation in the moral life," resulted also in aroused passions, dogmatic assertions, and unbelievable human cruelty.

The pain of religious fracture was accompanied by the stress of political, social, and economic disorder. The consolidation of monarchical power proceeded at an increased pace as the authority of the pope was whittled away and religious war eliminated many of the crown's most dangerous rivals. The new social mobility and the seemingly unpredictable fluctuation of prices further reduced the strength of local and regional rulers. Civil war and inflation, however, were double-edged swords that also reduced many kings to penury and brought violent death to others. Still, the aggrandizement of the state continued, and with the social upheavals of the century providing new bureaucrats to operate the administrative machinery, some monarchs aspired to no less than "absolutism." With the rising tensions of ideological war, international diplomacy also became tinged with sectarian dogmatism, and rulers used religious pronouncements as well as military weapons to attack their enemies.

The bewilderment caused by these religious and social upheavals, and the groping for meaning and direction through the labyrinth of early sixteenth-century politics, are reflected in the *belles lettres* and art of the age, as well as in the polemical pamphlet literature generated by the printing press. Insecurity masked by pontifical pronouncements characterized the religious and political tracts of the time, as traditional values came under attack and the old norms of truth and error collapsed. Long-held notions about the world and nature were likewise challenged, as the authority of popes and priests was questioned. Attempts to comprehend or control the new forces that had been unleashed were awkward and mostly unsuccessful.

In the second half of the century, the anxiety of the Reformation Age seemed to generate even greater assertiveness and fanaticism. Dogmatism replaced doubt, because boldness appeared to be the best response to the cultural malaise. Yet an outward show of confidence was no substitute for genuine solutions to the dilemma. Beneath the veneer of conviction, doubts and unresolved conflicts still lingered. In a seeming attempt to belie their insecurity, people of the early seventeenth century stopped at nothing to prove the superiority of their particular party or sect and to display their personal prowess. Baroque artists overwhelmed the eye with monuments of grandiose proportions, dramatically proclaiming their power and passion, just as soldiers paraded their valor and strength.

The intensity of life (and death) reached a peak in the epoch of the Thirty Years' War (1618–48), the period many scholars call the "Age of Crisis." It was indeed a time of culmination of the forces set loose by the Reformation—a final tempestuous struggle for stability following a century of revolt and revolution. By the second half of the seventeenth century, Europe had come full circle since the High Renaissance. The Age of Reformation finally ended when a new synthesis and resolution was found in the neoclassicism and scientific rationalism of the Age of Reason.

Suggestions for Further Reading

GENERAL

A good overview of early modern Europe may be obtained from H.G. Koenigsberger's handy and clearly written *Early Modern Europe, 1500–1789* (New York and London, 1987). Also stimulating is Henry Kamen, *European Society, 1500–1700* (London, 1984). Useful collections of essays on this period are contained in Steven Ozment, ed., *Religion and Culture in the Renaissance and Reformation* (Kirkville, Missouri, 1989); H.G. Koenigsberger, *Politicians and Virtuosi: Essays in Early Modern History* (London, 1986); and Kaspar von Greyerz, ed., *Religion and Society in Early Modern Europe, 1520–1800* (London, 1984), which consists of challenging essays by seventeen historians analyzing religion as cultural phenomenon, the reform of popular culture and religion, religion and social control, religion and community, and historiography. Harold J. Grimm's classic *The Reformation Era, 1500–1650*, 2nd ed. (New York, 1973) is an older, broad-ranging account of the period, focusing on the religious upheaval and its effects.

THE SIXTEENTH CENTURY

The best general analysis of the age is H.G. Koenigsberger, George L. Mosse, and G.Q. Bowler, *Europe in the Sixteenth Century*, 2nd ed. (New York and London, 1989), in the Longman General History of Europe series, edited by Denys Hay. It is up-to-date, well-written, and authoritative. The Fontana History of Europe series provides outstanding studies of the period in the two volumes by G.R. Elton, *Reformation Europe, 1517–1559* (New York and London, 1963), and J.H. Elliott, *Europe Divided, 1559–1598* (New York and London, 1968). A comparable coverage is contained in the Harper Rise of Modern Europe series: Lewis W. Spitz, *The Protestant Reformation, 1517–1559* (New York, 1985), and Marvin R. O'Connell, *The Counter–Reformation, 1559–1610* (New York, 1974).

Several recent *Festschriften* (commemorative collections of articles) contain a variety of important essays devoted to many aspects of sixteenth-century life and thought. Among these are Peter N. Brooks, ed., *Reformation Principle and Practice: Essays in Honour of A.G. Dickens* (London, 1980); Phyllis Mack and Margaret C. Jacob, eds., *Politics and Culture in Early Modern Europe: Essays in Honour of H.G. Koenigsberger* (New York, 1986); Jerome Friedman, ed., *Regnum, Religo, et Ratio: Essays Presented to Robert M. Kingdon* (Kirksville, Missouri, 1987); E.I. Kouri and Tome Scott, eds., *Politics and Society in Reformation Europe: Essays for Sir Geoffrey Elton on His Sixty-Fifth Birthday* (Houndmills, England, 1987); Claire Cross, et al., eds., *Law and Government under the Tudors: Essays Presented to Sir Geoffrey Elton on His Retirement* (New York, 1988); Sellery Schalk, ed., *Culture, Society and Religion in Early Modern Europe: Essays by the Students and Colleagues of William J. Bouwsma* (Waterloo, Ontario, 1988); and Sherrin Marshall and Philip N. Bebb, eds., *The Process of Change in Early Modern Europe: Festschrift for Miriam Usher Chrisman* (Athens, Ohio, 1988).

THE REFORMATION

Many interesting and challenging studies of the Reformation are available. Steven Ozment, *The Age of Reform, 1250–1550* (New Haven, 1980) not only is a good survey of medieval intellectual antecedents but also provides many insights into the Reformation itself. In addition, see Pierre Chaunu, ed., *The Reformation* (New York, 1990), and James Kirk, ed., *Patterns of Reform: Continuity and Change in the Reformation* (Edinburgh, 1990). Very useful is Heiko A. Oberman's *Masters of the Reformation,* trans. by Dennis Martin (Cambridge, England, 1981), which describes the emergence of the new intellectual climate of Reformation Europe. Some of Oberman's earlier articles are made available in *The Dawn of the Reformation: Essays in Late Medieval and Early Reformation Thought* (Edinburgh, 1986). The most recent, and very incisive, book is Euan Cameron, *The European Reformation* (Oxford, 1991).

The most challenging analysis of doctrine is Jaroslav Pelikan, *The Christian Tradition: A History of the Development of Doctrine, Vol. 4: Reformation of Church and Dogma, 1300–1700* (Chicago, 1984). Other significant studies of Reformation thought include Bernard M.G. Reardon, *Religious Thought in the Reformation* (New York and London, 1981), concisely covering most aspects of Reformation theology including, in addition to the mainstream reformers, Erasmus, the Anabaptists, English thought, and Catholic response; Alister McGrath, *The Intellectual Origins of the European Reformation* (Oxford, 1987), and *Reformation Thought: An Introduction* (New York, 1988), which maintain that religious ideas were the cause and heart of the Reformation. More narrowly focused are John R. Loeschen, *The Divine Community: Trinity, Church, and Ethics in Reformation Theology* (Kirksville, Missouri, 1981), and Timothy George, *Theology of the Reformers* (Nashville, 1988). The attitude of the Reformers toward the application of theology to worship itself, particularly the uses of images, is studied in Carlos M.N. Eire, *War Against the Idols: The Reformation of Worship from Erasmus to Calvin* (New York, 1986).

The new emphasis on social history, led by Robert W. Scribner and others, attempts to divert attention from theology toward sociology. In a very short but persuasive plea for studying the Reformation in its social context, Scribner's *The German Reformation* (Atlantic Highlands, New Jersey, 1986), emphasizes the important role of social groups and classes in the reform movement. This theme also pervades Scribner's *Popular Culture and Popular Movements in Reformation Germany* (Ronceverte, West Virginia, 1988); the works of Norman Birnbaum, *Social Structure and the German Reformation*

(New York, 1980); Kaspar von Greyerz, *Religion, Politics and Social Protest* (London, 1984); Keith Moxey, *Peasants, Warriors, and Wives: Popular Imagery in the Reformation* (Chicago, 1989); and Lorna J. Abray, *The Peoples' Reformation* (Oxford, 1985), which uses Strasbourg as a model. In addition, several excellent collections of essays sharpen the focus on social issues and popular religion. See especially R. Po-chia Hsai, ed., *The German People and the Reformation* (Ithaca, 1988); Kaspar von Greyerz, ed., *Religion and Society in Early Modern Europe* (London, 1984); Peter Blickle, et al, *Religion, Politics, and Social Protest* (London, 1984); and Kyle C. Sessions and Philip N. Bebb, eds., *Pietas et Societas: New Trends in Reformation Social History* (Kirksville, Missouri, 1985).

1 | THE CONDITIONS OF SOCIAL AND RELIGIOUS UNREST

A LTHOUGH THE REFORMATION OF THE SIXTEENTH CENTURY WAS PARTLY the product of intelligent and concerned minds looking at religious tradition and theology in new ways, it was also the result of the sociopolitical circumstances of late-medieval and Renaissance Europe and the collective responses of thousands of ordinary people. The stress of social life and institutions—particularly the community life of the German and Swiss towns, but also the unenviable subsistence of the rural peasants—played a prominent role in the upheavals of the sixteenth century. The economic and technological revolutions that were changing the nature and relationships of governments and society also played a role in those upheavals. The development and spread of printing, for example, had an overwhelming impact in shaping sixteenth-century society and culture, not only for the educated few but for the larger unlearned community as well. The dramatic increase in literacy brought the religious controversies directly and quickly to thousands of people. At the same time, the close involvement of governments in religious affairs helped determine the direction and nature of the evangelical movements.

Sixteenth-Century Society and Life

European life at the beginning of the sixteenth century was not easy. Sickness and death were constant companions of even the high-born and were especially present among the lower classes. Famine, pestilence, and war plagued the daily lives of most of Europe's almost 70 million inhabitants. The first half of the sixteenth century witnessed continual warfare in some parts of the continent, with the principal battlegrounds in northern Italy, eastern and northern France and Flanders, and, after the Reformation began, throughout Germany. Sixteenth-century armies were composed largely of mercenaries, living off both their contracted salaries and the land. Populaces, as a result, suffered disastrously. Mercenaries were frequently uncontrollable rabble who, with their hordes of voracious camp followers, devoured everything that was in their path. Furthermore, technology had greatly increased the destructive power of armies since the Middle Ages.

Famine and pestilence were the natural companions of war, leaving death and misery in their wake. The reiteration of the Dance of Death theme in early sixteenth-century woodcuts and paintings reflects the nearness of the specter of death. Much of this preoccupation with death resulted from the almost yearly encounter with the dreaded plague, which hovered over Europe for more than three centuries, devastating its cities and villages. The plague usually struck during the hot, late-summer months, but its appearance was so capricious, its destructive pattern so unpredictable, that people could only conclude that it was a supernatural manifestation. It was so infectious that it sometimes wiped out entire populations. Burials became the responsibility of the new class of professional gravediggers, who also looted the homes of plague victims and terrorized many of the survivors. Other diseases also ravaged many parts of Europe, particularly typhus, smallpox, scurvy, dysentery, and various respiratory maladies. From the 1490s on, a highly infectious strain of syphilis, probably of New World origin, was added to the list.

Renaissance life was not all sorrow and suffering, however. The economic transition that Europe was then experiencing brought many advantages and opportunities to some people, and slight improvement for most. Above all, this was a society in transition, suffering and enjoying a painful but promising transformation from medieval protective feudalism to modern competitive capitalism. The passage was turbulent and far from complete in the sixteenth century. Some aspects of feudalism had ended or been transformed much earlier, while others were to remain relatively unchanged for centuries yet to come.

Peasants and Rural Life

The peasants' status had altered considerably in most parts of western Europe since the Middle Ages, yet the conditions of their life were not so different. In western Europe, serfdom was almost a thing of the past by the sixteenth century. Most peasants were now free to move about, to compete with others for employment, and to choose their profession. Their new-found freedom, however, was more theory than fact; being without money in a money economy has little to commend it. Most serfs became rural workers, doing what they had always done, except now they worked for a few pieces of money with which they were expected to buy their food and clothing and pay rent on their meager shelter. Under feudalism, the manorial lord was as responsible to his serfs as they were to him. Now the landowner owed his workers nothing but the coins he paid them for their labors.

Some of the peasants were able to do better and acquired landholding rights of their own. Two forms of land tenure emerged out of the old feudal manors: sharecropping and leaseholding. Sharecropping was the most common practice in the sixteenth century and remained the typical form of tenure in France until the nineteenth century. Under this system, the sharecropper worked the soil and harvested the crops for a share of the proceeds, while the

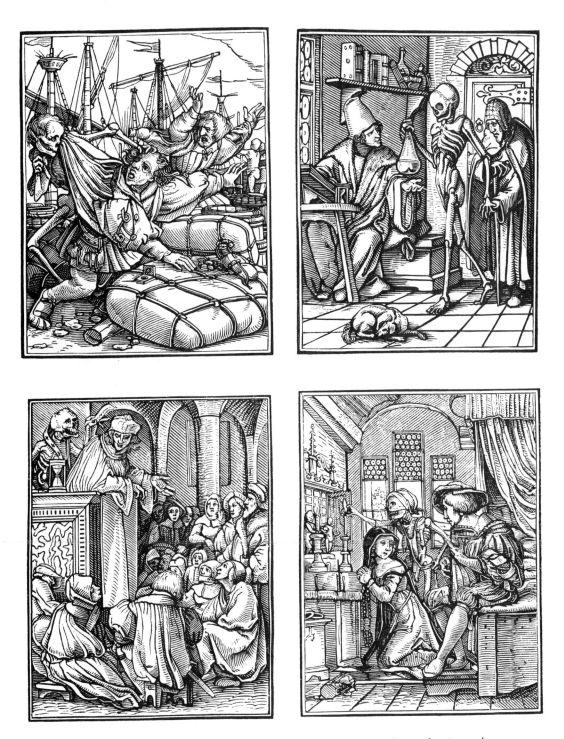

The Dance of Death. *Sudden death was an ever-present reality in the sixteenth century, and the grim image of death descending on unsuspecting individuals in the prime of life was a favorite theme of moralists. These four woodcuts, representative of the genre, are by the great artist Hans Holbein the Younger.*

Peasants at work.   *Even after the crops were in, the peasant's work was never done. Here, representing a typical November day's activity, are a group of villagers pounding dry stalks of flax to separate the long fibers that will be woven into fine cloth.*

proprietor furnished the seeds and tools necessary for producing the goods. The laborers' share rarely was sufficient for them to become self-sufficient. Leaseholders, on the other hand, leased land from a proprietor for a specific number of years and paid the rent in cash. All profits from the cultivation of the land in this arrangement went to the leaseholders themselves. From these profits, they paid rent and other accounts, bought animals and tools, and made improvements on the land. Any surplus was added to their own savings. Obviously this was the better arrangement from the farmer's point of view, but unfortunately, since it required a considerable outlay of money, few former serfs could hope to become more than sharecroppers. Common lands, jointly owned by all of the villagers in the area, were used and misused as pasturage for cattle and sheep. By the early sixteenth century, many of these "commons," as they were called, were being purchased and enclosed by wealthy proprietors for their own purposes, much to the dismay and discontent of the peasants.

Life for the ordinary people of Europe was difficult and dangerous for other reasons as well. Lucien Febvre and others of the *Annales* school of historical interpretation, who have written much about the *mentalité collectif* (collective mentality) of the sixteenth-century commoners, argue quite convincingly that the peasants were prisoners of an environment that they could not control or even understand. Hunger, cold, sickness, and death weighed heavily on the lower classes, and when these scourges were combined with the ravages of war, they dominated the life of the people. Physical insecurity led to mental anxiety and fear. Ignorant of the natural processes governing climate, crops, or personal health, the people were victims not only of physical misfortunes but also of imagined supernatural forces.

Fearful of the fantasies and terrors of nature, the masses sought protection or security in communal association and in the interplay of what Robert Muchembled calls social solidarities, that is, surrounding themselves with successive circles of human support—family, neighbors, various economic associations, and confraternities (lay fellowships to promote common religious rites). Indeed, according to Muchembled, the entire interplay of popular culture functioned as a "system of survival" against the stress and fear of the ominous unknown. The peasants warded off physical threats by participating in various agricultural and religious rites, conjurations, processions, prayers, and Masses to control the elements. Likewise, the lack of physiological understanding of bodily functions such as conception, pregnancy, and childbirth led to an elaborate set of rituals and various "magical" formulas for preserving health during those conditions. Thus ritual and festivity were essential features of the popular culture of the time, giving a brief sense of comfort to those trapped in a hostile world. Of course, these anxieties and the means to reduce them were not limited to the rural population, nor was the inability to distinguish between natural and supernatural forces. These fears and lack of understanding were common to all.

Urban Life   Life in the cities was also stressful, accompanied by new pressures unknown in the Middle Ages. In appearance, the Renaissance towns of northern Europe were not unlike their medieval predecessors, except in their greater number and size. Inside the city walls were concentrated every form of human and animal life known, living in everything from splendid palaces to mud-covered hovels. Streets were narrow, dark, and dirty, and most dwellings were little better. In these jungles of wood, stone, mud, shingle, tile, and rubbish, however, lived increasing thousands of Europe's population. Homes were small and simple, and the street floors were usually used for merchandizing and handicraft. Shops were everywhere, selling shoes, clothing, pots, pans, wine, fish, candles, bread, spices, firewood, meat, and every other item of necessity and luxury.

At the same time, urbanism promoted civic consciousness and identification with the community. Participation in civic events—from the punishment of criminals to theatrical and other cultural displays—was common in European cities. Burghers also took part in the political life of the community through municipal elections to the governing council and through the political activities of the guilds, to which many of the citizenry belonged. A further *esprit de corps* was promoted in cities like Nuremberg, Goslar, and Strasbourg, where citizens came to identify with certain causes or uphold cherished principles against outside influences and pressures. Urban dwellers had increasing opportunities to become aware of ideas and events in other places as the ubiquitous printing press dramatically reduced the informational time lag and as social mobility and civic pride increased.

Frequent popular celebrations and public festivals strengthened this communal spirit and released the tensions and frustrations of urban life (as well as that of rural villages). In addition to the civic rituals associated with birth, marriage, and death, many festivals took place in celebrations of local saints' days and general "holy days," such as Christmas and Easter. The greatest extravaganza of all was Carnival, the pre-lenten season culminating in Shrove Tuesday (Mardi Gras), the day before Ash Wednesday, when Lent begins. Legend linked Carnival with the time when sin was openly revealed so it could be conquered by Lent. This notion was then reenacted by the people. Carnival became a time for indulgence and revelry, when everything that was illegal or immoral was for a brief period condoned. It was a world turned upside-down: women dressed as men and vice versa, social roles were reversed, gluttony ran rampant, immorality was let loose, and fantasy was turned into reality. All aspects of orderly society were mocked, including the church and civil governments. Sometimes the prolonged orgy turned into bloody civil riots as the people worked themselves into a frenzy. Understandably, Carnival was criticized by the churches, both Catholic and Protestant, but with little success.

Other changes were also becoming apparent in the northern cities. The miller and baker were still the pivots of daily life, but the merchants were rapidly becoming the wealthiest and the haughtiest class of society. In no other area did merchants achieve the political power they exercised in central and northern Italy, but they vied everywhere with nobles and princes for luxurious dress and sumptuous living. Imaginative and audacious, successful merchants and entrepreneurs were involved one way or another in every economic enterprise that promised financial profits or social gain. Frequently, rich merchants used their wealth to purchase land or titles, which served to enhance their prestige but, because of fixed rents and spiraling inflation, proved to be poor economic investments. By the end of the century, enough merchants had bought land, titles, and offices to constitute a new nobility that in many ways rivaled the older military aristocracy.

Wealth and the Nobility

Nevertheless, the European nobles were not willing to give up the struggle so easily. Many of them adjusted to the Renaissance monarchy by becoming a part of it rather than continuing their feudal rivalry with the king. Others were geographically far enough removed from the seat of government that they could retain much of their medieval independence. In many cases (Spain being the best example), the monarchy compromised with the nobility by taking over some of their political power but leaving the grandees with landed wealth and prestige. Whereas in early Renaissance Italy the nobles had been effectively constrained from political influence in many of the city-states, by the second decade of the sixteenth century they were openly or covertly in power in all but a handful of those states.

The orders of society.   *Depicted at left are two young nobles, at right two clergymen, and in the center two merchants representing the third estate. Although Renaissance society was less rigid than medieval society had been, social mobility was still very limited.*

The court aristocracy represented the most exclusive level of society and embodied both the cultural tastes of the urban elite and the chivalric code of the landed *noblesse de l'epée* (nobles of the sword). Court society was based on rank and ceremony, for rank was the affirmation of the divine structure of the universe, and ceremony authenticated that rank. Courtiers saw themselves as the civilizing influence on the rest of society and the model for proper manners. Others saw them as representing pomp, artificiality, and disdain for the lives of ordinary people. Yet there was practical value in being at court, for it was there that one found opportunities for patronage and employment and the chance to be in contact with the principal fountainhead of political power.

Elaborate court festivals provided opportunity for further ostentatious display and dramatization of the nobles' role in society. These stylized celebrations drew from church and religious rituals as well as from ancient and medieval triumphs and tournaments. Guests consumed enormous amounts of food at endless banquets and indulged themselves in elaborate theatrical presentations, water spectacles, and armed jousts. One function of such court festivals was to display the "manly" military virtues of the noble class, while modulating their propensity toward violence with "civilized" refinement and manners; the main purpose, however, was to enable nobles to impress one another. Certainly the most pretentious of all these pageants was the 1520 "summit meeting" of Francis I and Henry VIII at the Field of Cloth of Gold, near Calais, with splendidly panoplied tents covered with velvet, satin, and cloth of gold erected for the occasion. The French king's pavilion reportedly stood 120 feet high, with 32 walls surrounded by galleries "covered in cloth of gold with three lateral stripes of blue velvet powdered with golden fleur-de-lis." Not to be outdone, Henry VIII had a splendid palace built of wood and stone more than 300 feet long. The extravaganza brought 12,000 nobles together for two weeks of music, dancing, displays, military competitions, and a continuous consumption of food.

The aristocracy was not without its own problems, however. The loss of political power to the king was not easy for noblemen to take, and when their private lands failed to return sufficient rent to maintain accustomed status, they found themselves in a real dilemma. They could sell part or all of their holdings to an eager merchant. Then what would the nobles do? In some ways as unprepared for competitive economics as the former serfs, they might, as did the serfs, find themselves at the mercy of a rather merciless society. They could always fall back on brigandage and freebooting, but that was not without cost, either. In the end, the frequent argument as to whether the nobles were rising or falling in relation to the middle class is hollow. Some were losing their power, wealth, and prestige; others were not only retaining but actually enhancing theirs. In the total picture of the century, both merchants and nobles—and also the monarchs—increased their status and their strength.

Domestic Life and the Role of Women	By the beginning of the sixteenth century the family was in serious trouble. Marriage had fallen into some disrepute as antimarriage sentiment and misogynist writings spread. Many people avoided marriage out

of fear of its responsibilities and difficulties, but the most influential factor was the church. Teaching that the highest form of godliness could be attained only through celibacy, the church exalted virginity, considering the cloister to be a higher state than marriage. This advocacy of the celebate life had a powerful effect on domestic life. Canon law accepted marriage as a safeguard against fornication and an aid to social stability but not as an intrinsically desirable state. Furthermore, the church raised various impediments to marriage in the form of laws against marriages within certain groups, while custom frowned upon marriages across social lines.

The problem was widely recognized and exposed. Erasmus and the other humanists sharply ridiculed the church's prohibition of clerical marriage, fearing among other things that it inhibited population growth at the very time Christendom was threatened by the advancing Turks. Humanists and reformers also condemned clerical celibacy on the grounds that, instead of elevating the moral level of society, it actually lowered it because of the laxity of morals in the cloisters—a laxity disapproved by the church yet tolerated through the payment of penitential fees. Many of the reformers hoped to correct this situation by setting the family above the cloister. Luther exalted marriage as the foundation of society and a divine institution. In the minds of many Europeans, Catholics and Jews as well as Protestants, the family was not only the

Ladies at needlework. *Upper-class women occupied themselves diligently in managing the household's daily life—often including hours in which the wife, her daughters, and perhaps her widowed mother-in-law would work together with their needles finishing the family's clothing.*

basis of society, it was the focus of the work force, providing the location, motivation, and resources of much of the rural production and urban industries of the time.

Women were an important part of this economic force as they converted domestic skills into money-making enterprises. They worked in virtually every craft from textile piecework to food production. Wives of most craftsmen were business partners with their husbands, marketing their wares as well as assisting in their production. Many also had occupations apart from those of their husbands. Some women belonged to craft guilds, but this was a touchy issue since men viewed it as a threat to their security. Young girls as well as boys became apprentices in many trades, such as shoe- and glovemaking, hatmaking, skinning, bookbinding, silk weaving, and embroidering, mostly under the tutelage of the master's wife. Single women also labored as housemaids, barmaids, innkeepers, small shopkeepers, nurses, street cleaners, carriers, weavers, and even goldsmiths. During the course of the sixteenth century, however, many new restrictions were put on working women. Local governments made laws prohibiting female workers in many of the skilled occupations and regulating their control over financial matters. At the same time, guilds became more restrictive in their attitude toward women artisans.

In the countryside as well as in the cities, the two principal industries employing women labor were carried on in the home. These were cloth manufacturing and the production and sale of food and beverages. Spinning, for example, was almost exclusively women's work. They also carried out nearly all of the preliminary textile-making processes, such as combing and carding. Brewing seems to have been primarily, but not exclusively, a woman's job. In Germany, married women were particularly prominent in this occupation. They also baked bread in the communal ovens, although more of the bakers were men, and women did most of the retail selling. Every village and town had its marketplaces where the women actively sold their wares: bread, beer, fish, poultry, butter, cheese, and all kinds of edibles, mostly processed by themselves, as well as flour, salt, candles, and a variety of cloth and other textile products. Of course, peasant wives and daughters also had to work in the fields alongside the men. After these labors they had many other chores to perform, both inside and outside the house. Obviously the economy of sixteenth-century Europe relied heavily on women, despite the limitations against them.

Economic Conditions

One of the great paradoxes of the early sixteenth century was the amazing increase of wealth and splendor along with growing poverty and apprehension. Folk laments such as "Death and disease stalk us day and night, and there is little hope that we will see ought but taxes and wars from the king" were not uncommon. Yet equally typical is the exultation of Erasmus, who jubilantly exclaimed in 1517, "At the present moment I could almost wish to be young again, for no other reason but this, that I anticipate the near approach of a golden age, so clearly do we see the minds of princes, as if changed by inspiration, devoting all their energies to the pursuit of peace." One is tempted to suggest that the majesty and grandeur of High-Renaissance culture is due partly to a widespread refusal to face the dreary realities of life, or perhaps a hope that its fearfulness could be mitigated through grandiose display and extravagance. People did believe that the Devil might be restrained through the intercession of the saints and martyrs, and that the collection and adoration of religious relics provided protection against the adversary. Why could not the building of splendid churches and the painting of magnificent murals have the same vicarious effect?

Whatever their purposes in building churches and mansions, and in patronizing painters, builders, and sculptors, many people of the sixteenth century had more wealth with which to endow these projects than most of their predecessors had. After 150 years, Europe had fully recovered from the great depression of the fourteenth century and stood now on the threshold of an economic boom. In France and central Europe, land that had been idle since the Black Death was again being cultivated and improved. Swamps were being drained, forests cleared, and new crops planted. The overseas expansion of Europe further accelerated the breakup of the feudal estates, not only by stimulating other economic activities but also by introducing new crops and new demands into the European economy.

Agriculture continued to employ the majority of the population and provided the most important commodities of daily existence. As in times past, wheat, rye, oats, barley, beans, and peas were the principal food crops, with flax and hemp providing important raw materials for clothes, rope, and other necessities. Eventually many root crops, including potatoes, introduced from America, enriched the nourishment of peasant fare and gave the soil much-needed vitality.

In the early sixteenth century, however, agricultural lands in some parts of Europe were rapidly being converted to more financially profitable use. As urban populations increased, so did the demand for food. To supply this need, as well as to make economic gains, farm production became more specialized. In England and Spain especially, the demand for wool caused many proprietors either to "enclose"—fence in—the common lands (hitherto the property of the entire community) to provide more feeding area for sheep or to neglect agriculture altogether and turn over formerly productive soil to pasturage. The wholesale enclosure of farm lands in order to reap profits from wool production not only had harmful effects on agriculture but also destroyed many small tenant farmers and cottagers who depended upon the soil for their survival. So flagrant was this abuse in England that Sir Thomas More was constrained to lament in *Utopia:* "Your sheep . . . that used to be so gentle and eat so little. Now they are becoming so greedy and so fierce that they devour the men themselves, so to speak."

Spanish Sheep Raising   In Spain, although wheat and other food products had to be imported, sheep grazed over thousands of acres of arable land. The peculiar nature of Spanish sheep raising destroyed thousands of additional acres of farmland. Sheep were migratory in Spain, grazing on the arid uplands of León and Soria during the summer months; then in September and October they were driven south into the sunny pastures of Andalusia and Estremadura, where they remained for the winter. Lambs born during the fall were ready for the return migration northward in April, along with all of the older sheep not sold for meat in the south. Shearing took place at clipping stations along the way, and the wool was marketed at the great fairs of Medina del Campo or transported to northern ports for shipment to Flanders and Italy.

The entire operation was organized and tightly controlled by the powerful sheep growers' guild called the *Mesta.* Because of its influence and the favored position it enjoyed with the Castilian government, the *Mesta* was able to obtain many advantages and privileges for its members. Its greatest prestige extended from the third quarter of the fifteenth century to the middle of the sixteenth. During that time, it had no rivals and little opposition. The *Mesta* not only had first priority to pasture lands in both the north and the south but also the exclusive right of passage between the two, even across the cultivated fields of the "dirt farmers." These sheep roads, or *cañadas,* were established by law and protected by salaried *entregadores* against the possible encroachments of disgruntled landowners. This encroachment of sheep on arable land was a factor in the rise of grain prices in the sixteenth century. While passing through uncultivated areas or forests, the sheep were allowed to wander unrestricted to forage for grass. A disastrous by-product of centuries of this practice was

Sheepshearing.   *This miniature from the* Breviaire de Grimani, *by Gerard of Ghent and others, shows sheep being sheared and grain being cut in the month of June. This rare book was left to the Republic of Venice by Cardinal Domenico Grimani.*

widespread deforestation, especially in the highlands of Old Castile and León. Even the herders enjoyed remarkable privileges in Spain because of the *Mesta*. They and their families were given royal protection from local laws and law enforcement officers when passing through towns; they were exempt from all military service; and they were not subject to court summonses or taxes in any but their home towns. The sheepowners themselves were among the wealthiest people in Castilian society.

About a third of their total wool production was sold in local markets to Castilian weavers and clothmakers. The rest was traded abroad, primarily in Antwerp, but also in London, Marseilles, and Genoa. Most of the wool exports from eastern and southern Spanish ports were handled by Genoese merchants who had entrenched themselves in the Spanish economy by the beginning of the sixteenth century.

**Antwerp and Early
Modern Finances**

⸨From the gradual accumulation of great amounts of capital in the early sixteenth century, and from the financial organization and techniques developed to handle it, came the beginning of early modern capitalism⸩ This capitalism was more an attitude toward money than it was a system of economics. Believing that money was the principal standard of wealth, and partly justifying its acquisition by the salutary effect it had upon the entire economy, sixteenth-century entrepreneurs believed in the legitimacy of money per se and in its value to society through reinvestment and circulation. They rejected the medieval notion that money is sterile and substituted a dynamic faith in its infinite fertility. For the successful merchant-capitalist, it usually was. Many techniques of capitalism developed or advanced in the sixteenth century, ranging from funded and interest-bearing floating debts to several kinds of commercial joint-stock partnerships. Particularly in the Netherlands, the international financial network took on some of the appearances of its modern descendant. The financial trading houses (bourses) of Bruges, Ghent, and particularly Antwerp, dealt in bills of exchange, loans, discounts, and notes, and became the year-round financial fairs of Europe.

Antwerp, with its strong connections with the house of Habsburg, became the greatest center of financial activities from the time Portugal made it the

The pleasures of the ice on the Scheldt River.   *This woodcut shows the frozen Scheldt, one of Belgium's major rivers. The residents of Antwerp are enjoying various winter activities on the ice, with the spires of the city rising in the background.*

principal outlet for Eastern spices until the whirlpool of religious war in the second half of the century drew Antwerp into its destructive orifice. Merchants from every country and many cities of Europe, as well as agents and factors of the leading foreign banks, set up shop in Antwerp to trade in coins, bills of exchange, and all forms of credit. By the third decade of the century, Antwerp had become the principal money market of the Habsburg empire, and the chief credit bureau for many other princes and private investors, as the Antwerp bourse became the center of European finance.

Although much of Antwerp's preeminence depended upon the favor of the emperor, upon the Portuguese spice staple, and on the selling of Spanish wool, its prosperity was also closely linked with the English cloth trade. The establishment in Antwerp of the English Merchant Adventurers, principal guild of the cloth-making industry, marked the beginning of a long economic marriage between England and the Low Countries. It was at Antwerp that the English merchant and royal factor, Sir Thomas Gersham, carefully watched over English economic interests and penned the famous aphorism that came to be known as Gresham's Law: "Bad money drives out good." By this observation, Gresham meant that when two currencies of unequal metallic content having the same face value are circulated together, the one with the greater intrinsic worth will tend to be hoarded while the cheaper continues to circulate. Antwerp was also the hub of every kind of international trade, from Baltic grain, Dutch fish, and Gouda cheese to Rhenish wines, Italian silks, and sugar from the Canary Islands. Much industry centered in Antwerp as well, including cloth finishing and dyeing, armaments and metal work, glass-making and papermaking, and especially book publishing.

Lyon, in southeastern France, was another financial capital and the most important for the French crown. Constantly in need of money to carry on his dynastic wars against the Holy Roman emperor, Francis I drew heavily on the Lyon bankers for the credit and cash he needed. After 1494, Lyon became the key to all French relations with Italy, serving not only as the French financial capital but also as the principal news center vis-à-vis northern Italy and the recruiting depot for nearby Swiss mercenaries.

Charles V also made frequent use of Italian and Spanish bankers to support his costly enterprises. He often negotiated loans in Barcelona, but the closest economic ties during the first half of the sixteenth century were with the merchant bankers of Genoa, who financed many of the Spanish enterprises in both the Old and New Worlds, and with the south-German bankers of Nuremberg and Augsburg.

The Fuggers of Augsburg

In the imperial cities of Nuremberg, Rothenburg, Hall, Nördlingen, Regensburg, Ulm, and Augsburg were scores of important banking and trading houses, set up and operated largely by single families or tightly knit corporate groups. Of these powerful financial organizations, the most important were the Nuremberg Tuchers and Imhofs, and the Hochstet-

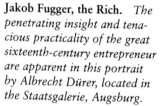

Jakob Fugger, the Rich. *The penetrating insight and tenacious practicality of the great sixteenth-century entrepreneur are apparent in this portrait by Albrecht Dürer, located in the Staatsgalerie, Augsburg.*

ters, Herwarts, Adlers, Welsers, and Fuggers of Augsburg. The financial history of the sixteenth century is largely a history of these families, especially the Fuggers.

The fortunes of this famous family originated in the fourteenth century with the weaver, Hans Fugger, who used his business acumen and modest income to engage in lucrative commercial enterprises and establish the Fugger reputation for honesty and efficiency in financial activities. Branching out from the cloth trade into silks, gems, and spices, the Fuggers established a factory in Venice in 1484, where great profits were gleaned from the Malabar pepper trade and from the spices of the Moluccas. Later the family invested in the newly prospering mining and metallurgical industries of southern and eastern Germany. They were eminently successful in Tyrolean silver mining and, with the Herwarts, controlled a large share of the copper-mining operations in Hungary.

Under the skillful direction of Jakob Fugger (1459–1525), the firm became primarily a banking house, investing less in commercial enterprises while dealing more heavily in international loans to governments and rulers. The Fuggers became deeply involved in making high-interest, short-term loans to the emperors Maximilian I and Charles V on the collateral of Habsburg mining interests and later the silver shipments from the New World. In this capacity, the Fuggers became one of the most important families of early modern history, holding the financial well-being of Europe in their hands. Fugger support of Charles V (half a million gold florins' worth) tipped the scales in his favor against Francis I in the imperial election of 1519. Fugger money was crucial in many other negotiations and most of the wars of the early sixteenth century.

Jakob Fugger, "The Rich," became the sole head of the Fugger firm in 1510 after the death of his two older brothers. Apprenticed as a youth at the *Fondaco dei Tedeschi* (the German Warehouse) in Venice, and gaining experience with his brothers after his father left them the business in 1478, Jakob Fugger quickly revealed an amazingly sophisticated financial skill even before he came to control the family enterprise. Having a virtual monopoly on the Habsburg mining interests, he soon became not only the emperor's chief banker but the financier of many European princes. The transfer of papal income (including annates, dispensations, and indulgences) from Germany to Rome was handled almost entirely by the Fuggers. In fact, Fugger agents located in all of the major cities of Europe provided an international network of financial coordination surpassing even that of the earlier Medici. They also provided a news service unique in its regularity and extent.

From his "Golden Counting House" in Augsburg, Jakob Fugger presided over a financial empire estimated at over 2 million gulden in capital. Yet, unlike the Medici and other Italian financiers, Jakob Fugger participated only indirectly in politics. He never aspired to the kind of political leadership of Augsburg that the Medici exercised in Florence. It was enough for him to know that the greatest princes in Christendom relied upon him for loans or subsidies in order to carry out their projects. His personal compulsion, in true capitalist spirit, was to continue to increase his capital.

Despite his wealth, Jakob Fugger was a nonpretentious man with a strong philanthropic bent. In 1519 and 1520 he constructed a large housing project in Augsburg, known as the *Fuggerei*, where indigent workers (mostly Italian weavers) could live for a few pennies a year. The *Fuggerei* still functions and continues to provide comfortable accommodations to its occupants for a token rent. When Jakob died in 1525, control of the firm passed to his nephew, Anton Fugger, whom he had personally trained for leadership of the bank. Under Anton it continued to expand and by 1546 was worth between 4 and 5 million gulden. Although the firm continued to flourish until the seventeenth century, its too-close association with the Habsburgs, which caused serious capital depletion whenever the Spanish king reneged on his payments or went bankrupt, eventually resulted in financial ruin. In the meantime, national monarchs were coming to dominate the economic, as well as the political, life of Europe as they had never done before.

Statebuilding in France

European politics in the first half of the sixteenth century was dominated by the larger-than-life personalities of Francis I, Henry VIII, and Charles V. The fate of most of Europe's 60 to 70 million people depended to a large extent upon the decisions and actions of these three monarchs.

Francis I about 1525. *This famous Louvre portrait of the French king, by Jean Clouet, shows him at the height of his power (probably prior to the battle of Pavia) dressed in the royal silks and satins.*

⟨The flamboyant and colorful Francis I of France (1515–47) exemplified the "Renaissance prince," combining the military leader with the patron of the arts and literature.⟩ He loved the rigors and glory of war just as he did the excitement of the hunt or the spectacle and grandeur of the tournament. Yet the *roi chevalier* was also the most generous patron of culture in France, building palaces and gardens, inviting Italian artists to France to inspire the arts in his country, and patronizing French men of letters. Francis was brought up by a devoted mother, Louise of Savoy, and a loyal older sister, Marguerite d'Angoulême, later queen of Navarre, who gave him both affection and a feeling for refinement. His counselors often found that the King was more receptive to the advice of his mother, wife, or mistresses than he was to theirs. By nature and tradition, however, Francis I was the typical autocrat, intent on maintaining and aggrandizing the strong state that had been bequeathed to him by his predecessors.

By the time Francis I ascended the throne in 1515, the kingdom of France had made great strides toward a consolidated territorial monarchy. There were still French-speaking lands outside of the royal jurisdiction and many corporate limitations upon the absolute power of the king, but on the whole, Francis I's authority was as full as that of any of his predecessors and encompassed a considerably greater territory. By 1515 all of the great feudal magnates, with

Francis I with his two sons *and members of the royal council. At left, Antoine Macault reads to the king his translation of Diodorus Siculus (1532).*

the exception of the duke of Bourbon, had either been subordinated to royal authority, with their lands incorporated into the national domain, or allied to the king's cause through marriage or mutual affiliation. Francis I had no intention of relinquishing the gains of his predecessors or of becoming anything less than a sovereign. He left no doubt in anyone's mind that he expected to be obeyed *because he was king.* And he never questioned his own right to make and enforce the laws.

Yet it was not his self-pronouncements of absolutism that made Francis I a powerful ruler; it was the loyalty and support of the French nobility that made him appear more absolute than he really was. Such a rapport was not accidental. Francis showered the nobles with honors, positions, and preferments. After the Concordat of Bologna (the 1516 treaty between Francis and the papacy), he gave many of them ecclesiastical benefices. He bestowed pensions, allowances, and rewards on them, and granted them exemption from oppressive taxes. They in turn honored and followed him. Never before had there been such a close kinship between a French monarch and the great nobles. Even in times of uncertainty and disorder, as during the king's captivity in Spain, the nobles remained staunchly loyal to the crown—all but the duke of Bourbon, who refused to knuckle under to the king.

Governmental organization of the various provinces began to take shape under Francis I. The governorship of these territories was either appointed by the crown or sold to faithful nobles who were then expected to administer the laws in accordance with the royal will. Lesser offices were similarly sold, as were many types of privileges and honors, to wealthy merchants and burghers. As many of these offices and privileges became hereditary, a new nobility was gradually created, the *noblesse de robe* ("nobility of the cloak"—named for the magisterial cloak worn by those possessing judicial authority). These newly ennobled families eventually came to dominate the judicial courts of France and also the Parlement de Paris.

Central government likewise took on a new meaning under Francis I. Not many institutional innovations were made, but the authoritarianism of the king made up for the lack of effective administrative organs. Francis was in some ways a medieval monarch, ruling by personal will through the various household offices, from master of the king's household (*Grand-Maître d'Hôtel*) to ushers of the bedchamber (*Valets de Chambre*). His court was a magnificent gathering of the royal household plus the officers of the crown, members of the councils, princes of the blood, and any others invited by the king. Yet in spite of the pomp and sumptuous display of the court, Francis did not neglect the more important organs of government. The Grand Council he had inherited from his predecessors was much too large and heterogeneous a body to serve the needs of an organized state. Instead, Francis selected five or six of his most trusted advisors to meet with him as sort of a royal cabinet, known as the *Conseil des Affaires,* to transact the major business of governing France and dealing with foreign states. This narrowed the real power base and helped shift it from the great nobles to the king. Another step toward the development of a coherent governmental organization was the creation of a central department of finance, administered under the newly created *Trésor de l'Épargne.* This bureaucratization provided Francis with sufficient revenue to enable him to meet the growing expenses of government, even during a time of almost continual warfare, without summoning the Estates General.

The foreign policy of Francis I was both ambitious and aggressive but narrowly based on the obsessive fear of enemy encirclement. Surrounded by hostile powers—Burgundian on the north, Habsburg influence throughout the east, new Aragonese and Castilian threats from the southwest, and the perennial enemy, England, across the channel—Francis I sensed the precariousness of the French position. Only the southeastern frontier was unthreatened by hostile powers. Here, in the political vacuum of Renaissance Italy, lay an

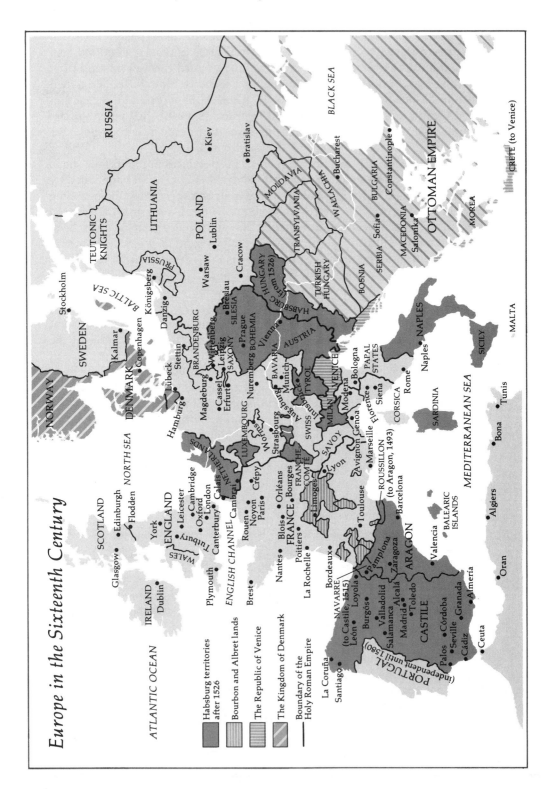

Europe in the Sixteenth Century

opportunity for Francis to take the initiative against his enemies. The opening gesture of his reign was a strike into Italy, where he smashed the Swiss and papal armies sent against him. Yet the battle of Marignano was an illusory victory for France; instead of strengthening the French position, it merely committed France to a continuing succession of costly and increasingly futile campaigns in Italy, leading eventually to bankruptcy. In 1515, however, no one could foresee what lay ahead; the king's strategy seemed to be sound.

Confident that he had won the first round in the struggle with his enemies, Francis moved to forestall their recovery in the second. Only too aware of the consequences should young prince Charles of Burgundy (and since 1516, king of Spain) be elected Holy Roman emperor upon the death of Maximilian, Francis began a campaign to secure the imperial title for himself. The election race of 1519 was intense, vitriolic, and completely corrupt. Francis bribed the electors with money, lands, and favors, but Fugger wealth eventually turned the electors' heads to Charles. Now three of France's four hostile neighbors were ruled by the same person, Charles V, and the fourth by another rival, Henry VIII. For almost half a century, the bitter feud between Habsburg and Valois, with the Tudors playing a significant nuisance role, would dominate the diplomatic and military history of Europe and help determine the course of the Reformation.

English Politics Under Henry VIII

Unlike his shrewd and calculating father, Henry VIII (1509–47) seemed to be outgoing, glamorous, and affable. He was also handsome, robust, and athletic, just like his cross-channel rival, Francis I. In addition, Henry was a competent musician, a fair writer, and well-read both in theology and in the "new learning" of the humanists. He encouraged the growth of good letters in England. Yet Henry was also overbearing and dogmatic, vain and compulsive—traits that drew him into enterprises that often turned out disastrously. He could also be petty and cruel, as his later domestic life would show, and his mercurial personality brought both sorrow and splendor to the country. Few monarchs, however, have been more successful in symbolizing the office and power of kingship. He had no peer in projecting his personal image as monarch and tying the two together in the minds of his subjects. He was a great showman and opportunist, and successfully combined his personal ambition and exalted view of kingship into a symbol of authority that made an indelible impression on his age and on history.

Although no longer able to exert the decisive pressures on the continent that his predecessors once were able to do, the English king nevertheless occupied himself with great aspirations of grandeur and power in Europe. Safely entrenched behind his great moat, the English Channel, Henry VIII was free to become involved or not in European rivalries according to his own pleasure. Of course Henry's pleasures were extravagant, which meant that when he could afford it, he preferred involvement to isolation. Unlike France, England was not threatened by military encirclement and might well have profited from

Henry VIII. *This painting by Joos van Cleve of Antwerp conveys the authority and power that the English king brought to his office.*

a continuation of Henry VII's policy of aloofness. Yet the young hero who ascended the throne in 1509 was restless to win his spurs on the battlefield.

The resources of England in 1509 were considerable. The soil was generally fertile and productive, easily yielding sufficient grains to sustain the population and still leave ample pasturage for the profitable production and export of wool and woolen cloth. England's forests were fruitful and its coastal towns prosperous. Foreign visitors were usually surprised and impressed by the appearance of wealth in England and by the splendor of English dress. Yet the economy of the country was not luxurious enough to support extended wars on the continent, nor were the people very pleased about turning over their earnings to the crown to be used for errant expeditions into France and the Netherlands.

On the other hand, Henry VIII was as aware as were his continental counterparts that an inactive and restless nobility at home spelled domestic trouble as serious as any foreign war. Without a standing army, and with limited resources to raise a mercenary force, Henry was committed to getting along with the English nobles as best he could. Two traditional institutions in particular aided the king: a common system of law for the entire realm, and a widely based parliamentary body generally favorable to the king's wishes. The peculiar history of the English Parliament had contributed to the evolution of medieval knighthood from a military caste into a landed gentry frequently indistinguishable from the middle class. Certainly the English laws of primogeniture had much to do with this change; also, the close association of knights and middle-class representatives in the House of Commons had a profound effect upon both political and social development. In this way the higher nobility of England lost a valuable ally, for without an independent source of wealth or prestige, the gentry, like the bourgeoisie, was predisposed to side with the crown in matters of authority and jurisdiction.

The recently ended Wars of the Roses had been so costly and devastating to the upper baronage that many of them had also become "king's men" rather than risk destruction in futile opposition to the revitalized government. Nevertheless, wealthy and powerful nobles remained; the dukes of Northumberland, Norfolk, and Somerset vied with one another as often as with the king for preferment and advantage. Such illustrious families as the Percys, Howards, Stanleys, and Dudleys were not to be ignored, even by Henry VIII. In England, as in France, the strength of both crown and nobility grew simultaneously, and frequently in collaboration.

The process of statebuilding in early sixteenth-century England, however, was more than a fluctuating counterpoint of kings and lords. Governmental institutions had become increasingly centralized; the potential power of the English king, if fully understood and used, was alarming. "If the lion but knew his own strength," noted Sir Thomas More, "it were hard for anyone to hold him." It became the role of Thomas Wolsey (ca. 1475–1530), Henry's lord chancellor after 1515, to recognize and apply that power.

Thomas Wolsey   Like his master, Wolsey was ambitious and opportunistic, and he knew how to use the machinery of government to the greatest advantage. Wolsey loved the administrative details of kingship that Henry disdained. The two men complemented each other perfectly. With the king's favor, Wolsey quickly became the most powerful man in England in both ecclesiastical and civil affairs. To the bishoprics of Worcester, Salisbury, and Winchester he added the royal chaplaincy, the deanery of Hereford and Lincoln, the bishopric of Lincoln, and finally the archbishopric of York, thus making him the ecclesiastical ruler of territory running from London to the borders of Devon, and from the Dorset coast to Scotland. In 1515 the pope awarded him the cardinal's hat, and three years later he became papal legate in England. As lord chancellor and head of the judicial machinery of government and as the chief minister and personal advisor to the king, Cardinal Wolsey dominated English government—as long as he kept the king's favor. His administrative reforms were not insignificant. He raised the Court of Chancery (for estate and other property disputes) to a regular position alongside the older courts of common law—King's Bench (criminal and crown cases), Common Pleas (cases between subjects), and Exchequer (royal finances)—and shaped the Court of Star Chamber (the king's council sitting in its judicial capacity) into a powerful weapon against the vestiges of feudalism. Wolsey's chief weakness was in the field of finance, where he had great difficulty getting along with Parliament, which did not take well to his browbeating methods, and he failed to appreciate fully the significance of trade to the English economy.

The king's foreign policy, as conducted by Wolsey, was neither nationalistic nor altruistic; it was based upon opportunism and personal aggrandizement. This policy could best be achieved, thought the cardinal, by peace or, in its absence, by playing off one continental enemy against another while making the weight of English intervention decisive on the winning side. Marriage and treaty arrangements before his time had given Henry an alliance with Castile and Aragon, but even a Spanish wife could not prevent him from switching sides in the middle of the diplomatic stream if it promised some material advantage. Nevertheless, the ancient rivalry with France was hard to ignore for very long, and the jealousy Henry VIII felt toward Francis I made Wolsey's frequent schemes to ally England and France grandiose failures. The most colorful and lavish of these attempts was the personal meeting he arranged between the two monarchs at the "Field of Cloth of Gold." Personal animosities, rekindled by Henry's injured vanity (when he was thrown by Francis in a wrestling match!), brought the conference to a sudden end and helped drive Henry back to a new alliance with his nephew, the recently elected Emperor Charles V. The failure of that détente set the stage for a new confrontation with both the emperor and the pope.

The Empire of Charles V

Charles V (1516–56) contrasted significantly in appearance, personality, and character with his rivals Francis I and Henry VIII. Physically, he ran a distant third. With his protruding lower jaw, bulging eyes, and sallow skin, Charles was not likely to inherit the questionable epithet of his father, Philip the Handsome. He was slow and stammering in speech but possessed considerable linguistic ability. His native language was Flemish, and he was also fluent in French and eventually mastered Castilian. He read Latin and conversed haltingly in German and Italian. According to a Spanish anecdote, he "spoke Italian with the ambassadors, French with the ladies, German to the soldiers, English to his horse, and Spanish with God." Charles showed an active interest in humanism and history, was well read in the classics, and proved to be a knowledgeable patron of the arts and sciences. At the same time he was pious and reserved, and took his onerous responsibilities very seriously.

From the moment of his birth in 1500, Charles of Ghent, son of Philip of Habsburg-Burgundy and Juana of Aragon-Castile, was destined to become the pivot around which European politics, diplomacy, and religious controversy revolved. In 1506, at the age of six, Charles inherited all of his father's Burgundian territories, which included by that time Franche-Comté, Luxembourg, and the Low Countries (governed during his minority by his remarkable aunt, Margaret of Austria). In 1516, upon the death of his maternal grandfather, Ferdinand of Aragon, he became King Charles I of Spain, which included Castile, Aragon, Catalonia, Valencia, and the Mediterranean territories of Ma-

Emperor Charles V. *The weight of his vast responsibilities and countless disappointments is reflected in the eyes and face of this portrait of the emperor by Titian.*

jorca, Minorca, Sardinia, Sicily, Naples, and a claim to the duchy of Milan. He also became ruler of the Castilian territories overseas: the Canaries, West Indies, and in a few years the New World empires of Mexico and Peru. When he was barely nineteen his other grandfather, Maximilian, died, leaving him the Austrian inheritances in central Europe and opening the way for his subsequent election as Holy Roman emperor.

Charles V's Piedmontese chancellor, Gattinara (1465–1530), announced, "God has raised you above all the kings and princes of Christendom to a power such as no sovereign has enjoyed since your ancestor Charles the Great [Charlemagne]. He has set you on the way towards a world monarchy, towards the uniting of all Christendom under a single shepherd." That is precisely what worried Pope Leo X the most, and also what made Francis I's election defeat so bitter, and many German princes' apprehensions so real.

Gattinara's imperial ideas not only were more grandiose than those of his young master but also overlooked the realities of sixteenth-century power. Charles may have been, as his titles affirmed, "King of the Romans, Emperor-elect, semper Augustus; King of Spain, Sicily, Jerusalem, the Balearic Islands, the Canary Islands, the Indies, and the mainland on the far side of the Atlantic; Archduke of Austria; Duke of Burgundy, Brabant, Styria, Carinthia, Carniola, Luxemburg, Limburg, Athens, and Patras; Count of Habsburg, Flanders, and

Tyrol; Count Palatine of Burgundy, Hainault, Pfirt, Roussillon; Landgrave of Alsace; Count of Swabia; Lord of Asia and Africa," but he was still hard-pressed to make his actual strength reflect even a fraction of this titular authority. Each of his territories was held by a separate right, and there were no central institutions for collecting taxes, enforcing laws, or fighting wars. Different languages, customs, institutions, traditions, resources, and needs made ruling these widely separated realms next to impossible. The wonder is not that Charles failed to create a "universal empire," but rather that he succeeded in holding his titles as long as he did. He was never free enough of internal disorder and foreign threats to entertain dreams of imperial unification. The emperor's personal attention was required in each of his dominions, yet he was unable to attend a crisis in one part of his patrimony without neglecting two or three others. And always he had with him the Turkish threat, the aggressions of Francis I, the Protestant revolt, and the jealousy of the popes—except for the two years when Adrian of Utrecht, his former tutor, wore the papal tiara.

Spain   No sooner had Charles left Spain in the spring of 1520 to receive the imperial crown at Aix-la-Chapelle (Aachen) than he faced a major uprising of the towns and villages of Castile, known as the revolt of the *comuneros* (commoners). Tacitly supported by the church, the *comunero* revolt repudiated the rule of Charles's regent, Bishop Adrian of Utrecht, and set up a governmental junta headed by the bellicose bishop of Zamora. Some radical voices called for the overthrow of the king, but the predominant cause of discontent was the extent to which Charles had turned over administrative and even religious offices to his Burgundian courtiers and allowed many foreign followers to establish themselves on Castilian lands. Charles's unwise attempt to raise money for his costly journey northward by demanding a grant (*servicio*) from the towns provided the trigger for the revolt. Lack of a unified effort on the part of the towns, clergy, and nobility, however, together with the emperor's promise to curtail foreign exploitation in Castile, undermined the *comunero* strength and brought the junta to defeat by the time Charles met the imperial diet at Worms in January 1521.

In the meantime, a different kind of revolt was spreading in the kingdom of Valencia, causing serious threats to the emperor's rule and setting the temper for a major social upheaval. Organized into a "Christian Brotherhood" (*Germanía*), the populace of Valencia took up arms against the ruling aristocracy and against the tenant Moors in the kingdom. For a year and a half, Valencia was rocked with insurrection and violent class and racial struggle before the newly appointed viceroy, the Castilian nobleman Diego Hurtado de Mendoza, was able to restore order and obedience.

These violent disruptions demonstrated that ruling Spain would not be a simple matter. Yet Charles gradually came to rely more and more heavily upon Spanish manpower, brainpower, and moneypower to control his scattered domains. Governing the separate kingdoms of Spain through their respective institutions and laws, Charles was eventually able to win their cooperation and support. The essential machinery of his rule in Spain was the system of administrative and advisory councils developed by the Catholic Kings.

The financial machinery bequeathed to Charles by Ferdinand and Isabel was efficient for its time and proved to be a valuable asset to the emperor. However, lack of a consistent mercantile policy to gain the greatest value from the New World, along with lingering social prejudices against trade, and the overall scarcity of natural resources, led eventually to economic stagnation and bankruptcy. From the Castilian *Cortes,* Charles was able to obtain a regular tax during most of his reign, but even a dependable income was insufficient for the emperor's extended military commitments, and he was forced to rely heavily upon deficit financing from German, Flemish, and Genoese bankers to produce the large sums he required. Like other monarchs, Charles also sold a form of state bonds or annuities, called *Juros,* that were handled something like a modern floating debt. Before long, however, he had mortgaged the total Castilian income for several years ahead, and the resources of Spain could not keep pace with his enormous expenditures.

The Netherlands   Had it not been for the industrial, commercial, and financial strength of the Low Countries, Charles could hardly have continued his political policies beyond the first decade of his reign. Even more than in Spain, Charles was a personal ruler in the Burgundian Netherlands, where he governed through his household officers and the nobles. Among the Netherlanders, the state-building impulse was very weak, but Charles revealed a proclivity for rational organization. In 1515 he purchased Friesland from Duke George of Saxony; Groningen was next wrested from French protection; Utrecht was secularized and acquired by the emperor in 1524; and finally Gelderland fell under his direct control.

Centralization, however, was resisted by the states and by their representatives in the States General. This body, unlike the *Cortes* of Castile or the Estates General of France, met without the summons of the king and exercised considerable control over both finances and laws. Nevertheless, throughout the reign of Charles V, a working compromise between the states and emperor was possible through negotiation and by the conjunction of mutual interests. As one of their number, Charles was able to deal successfully with the Dutch nobles, although he was usually at loggerheads with the independent-minded burghers and guild members of the towns. As his demand for higher taxes increased, their loyalty became less assured, and by the time of his abdication in 1556, open rebellion had flared up on numerous occasions.

Charles governed his scattered Burgundian and Habsburg lands through his family. During his frequent and extended absences from the Netherlands, the royal authority was represented there by his devoted and capable aunt, Margaret of Austria (who had also served as regent during Charles's minority), until her death in 1530. After that his half-sister, Mary, widowed queen of Hungary, became governor of the Netherlands. Charles was well served by these remarkable women but theirs, like his, was an impossible task, carried out with distinction and dignity but leading ultimately to failure. Before leaving Germany in 1521, Charles reduced his direct administrative responsibilities by awarding the governorship of all the Austrian territories to his younger brother, Ferdinand, who then further extended the Habsburg dynastic interests by marrying the daughter of the king of Bohemia and Hungary. In Spain the emperor's wife, Isabel of Portugal, acted as regent when Charles was away, until her death in 1539, and in 1543 his sixteen-year-old son, Philip, became regent when Charles left for Germany. In Italy, appointed viceroys and governors (usually Castilian) governed Sicily, Naples, and later Milan, in the emperor's name. These appointments were made by Charles himself, and final decisions on all important matters of policy were deferred to him in spite of the insurmountable hardships and delays in communication. This meant that regardless of the separate nature and titles of the emperor's realms, he alone was responsible for whatever unity they might possess. It also meant that without unifying institutions, the empire never really materialized, and each part went its own way, following its own laws and traditions.

Gattinara died in 1530 and with him died the active promotion of a unified empire. Acceptable imperial institutions—especially the meaningful ones like an army, laws, and taxation—could never be created, and Charles came to rely ever more heavily on the functioning institutions and human resources of Castile. To carry out his policies and supervise the machinery of government, he leaned on his two principal secretaries, Francisco de los Cobos, an extremely capable Castilian commoner, and Nicolas Perrenot, seigneur de Granvelle, a middle-class Burgundian functionary, whose specific duties were with imperial affairs. Cobos's responsibilities were Spanish administration and finances, Italian affairs, and the New World. Under his direction, the Castilian bureaucracy reached its peak and from that time on, Spain became the mainstay of the Habsburg empire.

Foreign Policy   Charles V's foreign policy was aimed at preserving intact the inheritance he had received from his predecessors. Since his territories and interests spread halfway around the globe, this meant that he was involved and committed on every front. What appears to be a policy of aggression was really a tenacious attempt not to lose what he already possessed. Fortuitous marriages had given him an empire and a responsibility that he was unwilling to release or compromise. After the initial misunderstanding in Spain, the principal threats to his rule came from three sectors: the Turks, Francis I, and the German Protestants.

The Ottoman Empire, now led by the ambitious sultan, Suleiman the Magnificent, presented the greatest menace since its takeover of Constantinople three-quarters of a century before. Charles faced the daunting challenge of a renewed Turkish threat on two fronts: in the Mediterranean, where his Spanish and Italian territories put him in the direct line of attack by the westward-expanding Turks (after the fall of Rhodes in 1522, he was in great jeopardy there), and in the eastern Habsburg area, particularly in Austria and Hungary, where the enemy was steadily moving up the Danube valley. In August 1526 imperial forces were routed at Mohács, the Hungarian king fell in battle (widowing Charles's sister, Mary), and the Turks moved on to besiege Vienna itself. As titular head of Christendom, Charles called upon Europeans everywhere to take up the banner against the threatening infidel. But the crusading era had passed, and the most that the majority of princes were willing to do was to justify their dynastic rivalries as well as their recurring invasions of Italy as preliminary moves to attack the Turks. To Charles alone was left the defense of Christendom.

The second point of his foreign policy was the containment of France. Here was an obligation that the emperor would have been happy to relinquish, yet he found it to be his most constant occupation. Fear of the emperor and of imperial encirclement drove Francis I to continual aggression in an attempt to break the Habsburg cordon. The rival claims of the two monarchs to territories in Italy (chiefly Milan) and along the borderlands between France and Spain, coupled with distressing French alliances with the sultan and with the Protestant princes of Germany, further dictated Charles's reaction to every French move.

As if his frustrations were not yet enough, Charles inherited a budding religious schism in Germany that was destined not only to handicap his actions on the other two fronts but also eventually to grow to such proportions that Christendom itself was shattered as a result. Again, by the nature of the movement and his commitments, the emperor was forced to a policy of conservative reaction in order to maintain the status quo.

Power, Prestige, and Poverty in Germany

If Spain and the Netherlands were the strong areas of Charles V's empire, Germany was its most volatile. In the opening decades of the sixteenth century, Germany was at a crossroads. Europewide political polarization, coinciding with internal fragmentation, economic tensions resulting from capitalistic expansion and financial relocation, and intellectual and religious upheavals spreading northward from Renaissance Italy, all joined to make Germany "the tinderbox of Europe." Furthermore, a nebulous, but nonetheless genuine, national feeling was generating among Germans of various classes and regions, though it lacked the institutional and historical supports that favored similar sentiments in England and France. It also lacked leadership and direction but not passion. Most of all, it lacked cohesion. Caught in the throes of a recent population explosion, strained by the precipitous rise in prices and the intensification of financial activities, and split by a vicious struggle for power and prestige, the active elements of German society were more a centrifugal force pulling it apart than a unifying pressure holding it together.

Early sixteenth-century Germany, however, was flourishing economically, producing great wealth from its mines and forests and participating, through the Welsers, Fuggers, and several other south-German bankers, in the commercial revolution. The active and direct Welser participation in the conquest of

Activities in a German city. *Scenes of music, astronomy, printing, and woodcarving are among the activities depicted in this woodcut from Hans Sebald Beham's series* The Seven Planets.

Venezuela is only one example of German financial involvement with other parts of Charles V's empire. Yet economic prosperity was no more uniform in Germany than were social or political stratifications. Some areas of northern Germany, for example, were entering a period of serious attrition. As long-range climatic changes caused the herring to migrate from the Baltic into the North Sea area at the end of the fifteenth century, many of the Hansa towns that depended on herring fishing declined sharply, while the Dutch fishing industry was greatly enhanced. Poverty grew as rapidly as prosperity. Previous cleavages and fissures in the social order now became irreparable ruptures.

At the top of the sociopolitical pyramid were the German princes, not only the seven electors who chose the emperor (the king of Bohemia, the margrave of Brandenburg, the elector of Saxony, the count palatine of the Rhine, and the archbishops of Mainz, Trier, and Cologne) but also the two hundred or so other rulers of German states and territories. Bent upon consolidating and fortifying their respective positions, these men paid little attention either to the growing social inequalities or to the rising winds of national feeling. They were more concerned and alarmed by the emperor's attempts to institutionalize the empire and restrict their precious autonomy.

The ruling councils of the free imperial cities were likewise jealous of their independent authority and resisted all attempts to integrate them into a more controllable structure. These imperial cities stood in the same relationship to the empire as the great princes; that is, they were privileged, semiautonomous units owing allegiance to no authority other than the emperor himself. And even their duty to him was remarkably loose, consisting mainly in a formal oath of fidelity and a tacit agreement to give financial support to the empire. For all practical purposes, the city governments of Nuremberg, Magdeburg, Frankfurt, Ulm, Augsburg, and the eighty other imperial cities, were independent agents, free to govern, restrain, or punish their citizens as they saw fit, and strong enough even to defy the emperor at times. The municipal councils, largely made up of the wealthier and more influential citizens, ruled the cities with an iron hand and sometimes extended their jurisdiction beyond the city walls. Once started, the Reformation spread through these imperial cities like fire through a dry forest.

Politically and socially apart from the ruling princes and the imperial cities was a unique group in Germany known as the imperial knights. As medieval tenants-in-chief of the emperor, these lesser barons had occupied a unique position in European feudalism; however, with the decay and transformations of that system, the imperial knights lost most of their wealth and prestige and all of their land. They still had pride and arrogance, however, and they were determined not to be obliterated or fused into the lower classes, whom they despised. From their fortified castles, many of these knights engaged in brigandage and banditry along the trade routes, while others turned to more ambitious and spectacular forms of military adventure. Even so, they were not all bad. Some took their titles seriously and became trusted advisors to the emperor or champions of reform. Ulrich von Hutten was an enlightened and idealistic humanist, Franz von Sickingen became a passionate "warrior for God," and Götz von Berlichingen served as the sixteenth-century model for the eighteenth-century German poet Goethe's champion of the common people.

Always at the bottom of the social ladder, the German peasants were probably no worse off than the farmers and workers of other lands. In the rapidly changing times of the early sixteenth century, however, impersonal forces and avaricious rulers brought them to a very low state. With no protection other than in their own great numbers, the German peasants had on more than one occasion banded together to force concessions from their masters. Seldom had these uprisings been permanently successful, but they had set precedents and established practices that might be revived at any time. Most peasant demands had been moderate and conservative, seeking no more than some of the guarantees and rights they had enjoyed as medieval serfs. In the sixteenth century, they reacted against arbitrary rule, against the restrictions on fish, game, and forest use, against the physical burdens imposed by their lords, and against the injustices of the laws. Yearly their mood grew darker as their chances for redress seemed more hopeless. Sometimes they formed into loosely organized brotherhoods, such as the *Bundschuh,* a peasant confederation that used the common clog as its symbol.

In all of their diversity, the political and social groups of Germany had one thing in common—resentment and even hatred of the papacy. Because the secular power in Germany was unable to resist the encroachments of the church, papal influence was greater there than in any region outside of Italy; at the same time, clerical abuses and corruption seemed to reach a new high. The church not only was the largest landholder in the empire but also exercised greater political jurisdiction there than in any other part of Europe. Political, social, and economic upheavals put Germany in a precarious position in the early sixteenth century. Religion provided an even more explosive ingredient to the volatile mixture.

Erasmus and the Christian Humanists

The most persistent critique of clerical abuses and the most positive program for religious reform came from those active scholars and literary figures known as Christian humanists. Placing less weight on metaphysics than did the medieval scholastics, less stress on asceticism than the mystics, and more devotion to Scripture than the Italian humanists, the Christian humanists emphasized historical study and a "return to the sources," meaning the Bible. One of the goals of the Christian humanists was to reconcile the seemingly conflicting traditions of pagan and Christian cultures, hoping thereby to place greater importance on moral values. They looked at the abuses and corruption of the contemporary clergy with deep concern, and took the lead in denouncing all forms of religious hypocrisy. Believing most people had a natural desire to do good, they felt that broader education and emphasis on common moral values could eliminate abuses and preserve the integrity of Christianity. In a real sense, they were the vanguard of the Reformation.

The leading spokesman of the Christian humanists, and the greatest literary figure of his time, was Desiderius Erasmus (c.1466–1536), a brilliant scholar and tireless writer whose fame spread far beyond the boundaries of his native Netherlands. At an early age he attended school at Gouda, then the grammar school of the Brethren of the Common Life at Deventer. These pious followers of Christ, who sought to imitate the Savior and cultivate a Christ-like spirit of devotion through service and teaching, exerted an indelible impact on the young Erasmus. Following the death of both his parents in 1484, Erasmus studied for three years at s'Hertogenbosch, then entered the monastery of the Canons Regular of St. Augustine at Steyn, where he received the priesthood in April 1492. As a choir monk at Steyn, Erasmus continued to cultivate his intellectual curiosity by reading books in the monastery library. At first he seemed contented as a monk, but he soon began to feel the strictures of monastic life and desired to participate more actively in the world of literature and ideas.

In 1493 fortune seemed to smile on him when he was offered an appointment as Latin secretary to the bishop of Cambrai and sent off to France to study at the University of Paris. His patron also got him released from his monastic vows. Erasmus made a living in Paris by tutoring young students in Latin grammar and rhetoric. This brought him into friendship with the English

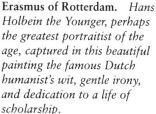

Erasmus of Rotterdam. *Hans Holbein the Younger, perhaps the greatest portraitist of the age, captured in this beautiful painting the famous Dutch humanist's wit, gentle irony, and dedication to a life of scholarship.*

nobleman, Lord Mountjoy, who took an immediate liking to the gifted young teacher and invited him to visit England. There Erasmus began a lifelong acquaintance with Thomas More and other English scholars. Returning to the continent, he entered the most productive period of his creative life, publishing a growing collection of *Adages,* insightfully annotated classical proverbs and sayings; *Colloquies,* delightful dialogues and tales poking fun at the foibles of society; the *Enchiridion* (1503), a penetrating handbook of Christian virtues and practice that summarized his faith and practical theology; editions of Cicero's and Saint Jerome's letters; and a critical edition of Lorenzo Valla's *Annotations of the New Testament.* While living in the home of Thomas More in 1509, on his third trip to England, Erasmus composed his most popular work, *The Praise of Folly* (the Latin title, *Moriae Encomium,* was a play on More's name). Although reportedly written in jest, *The Praise of Folly* had a serious intent and has remained the most enduring of all Erasmus's works. Coaxed from Cambridge in 1514—where he had been professor of divinity and lecturer in Greek—by the printer Johann Froben of Basel, Erasmus began editing the works of Saint Jerome, Seneca, Plutarch, and Cato; published a critical Greek and Latin edition of the New Testament; and wrote a handbook on the education of a Christian Prince, *Institutio principis Christiani,* which he dedicated to Prince Charles, soon to become king of Spain and Holy Roman emperor.

The year Luther nailed his *Ninety-Five Theses* to the castle door in Wittenburg, Erasmus moved to Louvain, in the Low Countries, where he divided his time between the university and writing religious works.

Erasmus's pen was never idle. He had something relevant for everyone. Although a sincere Catholic, he argued for liberalizing the narrow constraints of Catholic worship, defended the use of the vernacular in the Mass, and condemned the pope and his "courtiers" for abandoning their flock. In biting satire and reasoned treatise he spoke out against tedious lawyers, pretentious philosophers, sanctimonious theologians, and impious monks. The goal in his writings, whether erudite or humorous, was to promote a meaningful reform of the church based on reason and Scripture. He viewed his mission as one of cleansing and purifying, through the application of humanistic scholarship to the important sources of the Christian tradition. Hence truth and piety for him were products not of sacraments and rituals but of clear thinking and right living. Erasmus hoped to reconcile both personal and universal conflicts by moderation and balance.

Humanism in France, Spain, England, and Germany

Although he was the most famous, Erasmus was not the only northern humanist who believed in the pursuit of wisdom as a moral good and worked for religious reform. Several French humanists applied their studies to the goal of moral and ecclesiastical improvement. Perhaps the most important of these was Jacques Lefèvre d'Etaples (1450–1536), who was interested in all knowledge, whether scholastic, mystic, or humanistic. He was fascinated by medieval mysticism as well as the ancient occult Hermetic writings, and was strongly attracted to Jewish Cabalism, a mystical tradition supposedly handed down orally from the time of Moses. But Lefèvre's greatest efforts were toward moral regeneration of the church by returning to the basic texts of Christianity. Between 1505 and 1522 he published an impressive number of works in this vein, including editions of some of the early church fathers; the *Quintuplex Psalter,* in which he endeavored to clarify the Book of Psalms; a lengthy commentary on the epistles of Paul; and a new translation, with commentary, of the New Testament. Although he, like Erasmus, remained loyal to the Catholic church, Lefèvre's intellectual wanderings and friendship with many Protestants would make him a leading influence on the prereformers and early Protestants in France.

The leading promoter of humanism in Spain was not in the strict sense a humanist himself. Francisco Jiménez de Cisneros (1437–1517), confessor to Queen Isabel, archbishop of Toledo, inquisitor general, grand chancellor of Castile, and cardinal regent of Spain, was a conscientious and energetic reformer. Having no more tolerance for clerical abuse than for heresy, he instigated and carried out an ambitious program of ecclesiastical reform in Spain. So effective was his reforming zeal that by the time of his death the Spanish church was probably less in need of overhaul than any in Europe. Cardinal Cisneros founded the University of Alcalá to provide a better and more complete education for the Spanish clergy, and a center for biblical scholarship and linguistic studies. He was also responsible for the great Complutensian Polyglot Bible, the first significant attempt to produce the complete Bible in original languages. He completed the New Testament in 1514 and the entire Bible, in six large volumes including a Greek-Hebrew-Aramaic lexicon, in 1522. For this monumental work, Cisneros attracted scholars from all parts of Spain and beyond, including some leading Jewish scholars.

Best known of the Spanish humanists was Juan Luis Vives (1492–1540), a philosopher, teacher, and man of letters, whose scholarly reputation was surpassed only by that of his mentor, Erasmus. Vives's earliest major work, the *Fabula de Homine* (The Fable of Man, 1518) is a penetrating inquiry into human nature, revealing a view of man that is both Platonic and humanistic but even more strongly Christian. His educational reforms were based on the reconciliation of Christianity and humanism, since the primary aim of education, he believed, was to acquire moral goodness, which can be realized through the study of Latin and Greek literature combined with the application of Christian piety. True wisdom, Vives concluded, "consists in judging things correctly, so that we may estimate a thing at its true worth, and not esteem something vile as though it were precious or reject something precious as though it were vile."

In England the most influential champions of Christian humanism were John Colet and Thomas More. The mission that motivated Colet (1466–1519), the brilliant and sympathetic founder and dean of Saint Paul's School in London, was the desire to combine scholarship with piety to produce a balanced and harmonious Christian life. He stood for a simple exegesis of Scriptures as the inspired but simple writings of real-life men. Colet's criticism of the church was that the Gospel had been obscured and perverted by the narrowly allegorical expositions and definitions of the scholastics, and the abuses and ignorance of the clergy.

A more famous humanist, and lifelong friend and admirer of both Colet and Erasmus, was Sir Thomas More (1478–1535). More, a layman and trained lawyer, was an active and wealthy man of affairs who eventually attained the highest political office in the kingdom, next to the king. Son of a moderately well-to-do London lawyer, he was given the best educational opportunities available. Schooled first at Saint Anthony's in London, where he was introduced to Latin grammar and acquired a taste for the classics, he continued his education at Oxford under the auspices of Cardinal Morton. Then he studied law at the Inns of Court and began a promising legal career. His brilliant mind and quick, perceptive personality soon opened many doors of opportunity and challenge. In 1504, at the age of twenty-six, he was elected to Parliament, and later became active in Henry VIII's diplomatic service; in 1518 he became a member of the king's council. In 1523 he was chosen speaker of the House of Commons. For more than four years, he was also chancellor of Lancaster and high steward of both Oxford and Cambridge. In October 1529 he succeeded Thomas Wolsey as lord chancellor of England.

Despite his active public career, More never lost interest in the intellectual, cultural, or spiritual aspects of life. He was a pious and religious man, dedicated to Christianity and to the church. Yet he had no tolerance for heretics, and pursued them relentlessly as lord chancellor. His religious convictions are revealed in many writings, such as *The Supplication of Souls; The Dialogue Concerning Heresies; Confutation of Tyndale's Answer;* and *The Dialogue of Comfort.* His scholarly distinction and urbane humor are best illustrated in his great social satire, *Utopia.* Disturbed by the abuses and corruption of his day, More proposed in the *Utopia* a new social order in which reason, tolerance, and cooperation would replace power, prestige, and wealth as motivating forces. Recent research on More has somewhat tarnished the lustre of his name by emphasizing his political ambitions and religious intolerance, but there is still much in his life and works that makes him a "man for all seasons."

Humanism in Germany differed most from its counterparts in France, Spain, and England in that it exerted a more active reforming pressure on the church within its territory and a more embittered hostility toward Rome, thus providing a breeding ground for greater discontent and social disorder. German humanists tended to be more caustic in their criticism of the church and more aggressive in their reactions to clerical abuse. Some, like Willibald Pirkheimer and Ulrich von Hutten, would quickly cross over to the Lutheran camp, but others would maintain their loyalty to the church while continuing to advocate needed reforms.

The most illustrious of the German humanists was Johann Reuchlin (1455–1522), who was interested in all areas of human knowledge, and during his lifetime mastered many of them. He was an eloquent Latin stylist and one of the most accomplished Greek scholars in Germany. The real passion of his life was Hebrew, particularly the mystical tradition of the Cabala. In 1506 he published a Christian-Hebrew grammar and in 1518 another treatise on Hebraic studies. His interest and enthusiasm in this direction led to many serious controversies with the orthodox Thomists of Cologne and with others who considered his studies not only radical but heretical. His most rabid opponent was a converted Jew named Johannes Pfefferkorn, who had assumed the role of exterminator of Judaism in Germany. Pfefferkorn charged that all Jewish books were wicked and should be destroyed, while Reuchlin defended them as being of religious and cultural worth. The immediate result of the Reuchlin-Pfefferkorn controversy was the publication of a celebrated satire, *Letters of Obscure Men,* written by Reuchlin's humanist friends, Ulrich von Hutten and others. Reuchlin's Hebrew scholarship was not an end in itself, however, but a means to the central aim of most Christian humanists: to cleanse the church of its follies and redirect it toward a simpler and more spiritual course. There was much that needed to be changed.

Social Disorder and Religious Unrest

The church in Germany was a large and powerful institution, fulfilling its role as the conscience of the people and as the civilizer of manners and morals. Its omnipresence was imposing, when not outright intimidating, to most of its "universal" members. Administering the canon law with efficiency and relative speed, the church's legal structure and court system reached into every hamlet of the empire. Parishes established from the Alps to the North Sea and from

France to the plains of Poland brought solace and comfort to frightened souls, education to the curious, hope to the despondent. The parishes also dispensed discipline and collected the ecclesiastical taxes necessary to operate the church. On the higher administrative levels, the ecclesiastics were equally prominent. Some of the greatest German lords were also princes of the church, and three of the seven imperial electors were ecclesiastical rulers.

Despite this impressive structure, Germany was teeming with religious questions and controversies, and corruption ran rampant. Multiple benefices were as common as the Lord's Prayer, and the sale of offices as serious a malediction as it had been in the Middle Ages. Few bishops attended to their clerical duties, while papal legates scandalized the people with their impropriety. Moral depravity, corruption, and turpitude were all equally flagrant. The monks and friars were not noticeably better, charged Erasmus: "In church, when they bray out the psalms they have memorized without understanding, they think they are anointing God's ears with the blandest oil." According to *The Praise of Folly:*

> Equally commendable is the pious effort of the ordinary priests not to fall short of their leaders in holiness. They fight for their tithes in true military fashion, with darts, stones, and force of arms. How keen they are to be able to find what they need in the writings of the ancients to terrify the people and make them believe that they owe even more than their just tithes! . . . But the priests have this in common with the laity: they are not ignorant of the laws of making money, which they look to with an eagle eye.

Many of the moral disorders resulted from the overgrown officialdom of the church, which had created a vast network of vested interest.

Nevertheless, these clerical abuses were not so much new in the early sixteenth-century as they were more conspicuous, more talked and written about, more resented than before. The German humanists were especially critical. Their belligerency is vividly revealed in the satirical *Letters of Obscure Men,* which censured the monks as those:

> who ever yearn to declare others heretics, and stir us up against them, and hold an inquisition concerning heretical pravity on them—yet hold so many benefices, one, six; another, ten; another, twenty or more; and heap up so much money, and sideboards with bottles and goblets—as though they were the sons of counts or princes—and keep harlots or concubines within their doors at a great cost, with chains on their necks, and rings on their fingers, and mantles fit for the wives of knights. Sometimes one of them holdeth three Canonries at one and the same time, and putteth dues in his purse from all three; whence he is able to enjoy many a drinking bout.

The economic, social, and political upheavals of the time were having their effect upon the church as well as upon other institutions and customs. Yet the church hierarchy seemed unable, or unwilling, to adjust to the shifting conditions or to accommodate itself to changing needs. Still claiming universality, the papacy was in fact becoming more narrowly provincial than it had ever been. As succeeding popes paid more attention to expanding the physical frontiers of the Papal States, they lost more of their pastoral interest in the non-Italian church. Beyond the confines of papal territory Christians were considered more as subjects than as "joint citizens with Christ." As the papacy lost touch with the people, especially in the eyes of Germans, making itself a foreign and enemy power, the lesser clergymen also alienated themselves from the sentiment and needs of the people through obsessive grasping for material wealth.

By the beginning of the sixteenth century, there was a widespread cry for reformation of the church—not a doctrinal reformation, but a reform of the legal, economic, administrative, and moral practices of the officialdom. Most of the advocates of reform were as thoroughly opposed to doctrinal deviations and heretical thought as they were to the perversions of the prelates. They wanted reformation, not revolution.

Each segment of German society had its reasons for complaint against the church. The princes objected to papal interference with elections to church offices within their territories, to the frequent bestowal of benefices on foreigners, to papal judicial procedures, and to clerical exemptions from the jurisdiction of German courts. Especially they reacted to the drain of money out of their states into papal coffers. At the same time, the cities resented ecclesiastical encroachments into their jurisdictions, while the common people complained against the moral degradation of the clergy and the abuses that were condoned and practiced. Yet even these violations did not "cause" the Protestant revolt. They were important factors in making it spread among various classes, but the immediate cause of the upheaval was religious.

In the early sixteenth century, Christendom was experiencing a general religious revival on the part of the common people, a craving for meaningful religious expression and satisfaction, a "spiritual thirst" that the church could not always quench. In no place was this revivalism stronger than in Germany. Piety was expressed in a myriad of ways, both institutional and personal, reflecting a deep religious and devotional feeling. The collection and veneration of relics was on the rise. By 1519 Frederick of Saxony was reputed to have owned more than 5000 relics in his famous collection. Pilgrimages, too, were a favorite form of religious expression. Santiago de Compostella in northwestern Spain, Mont Saint–Michael in Normandy, and Wilsnack in Brandenburg were popular shrines of European worshipers. Rome, of course, occupied a special place in Christian hearts, as did far-off Jerusalem, and both cities received record numbers of pious pilgrims in spite of the physical hardships and political risks. The convenient institution of selling indulgences flourished, as did such nonecclesiastical expressions of worship as mysticism and spiritualism.

A predominant characteristic of this revivalism was the strong belief in the imminent coming of Christ as spoken of in both the Old and the New Testaments and elaborated by the twelfth-century abbot, Joachim of Fiore, who had prophesied that the ushering in of the millennial age would be heralded first by the appearance of the Antichrist and a purging of the church by an "emperor-savior." Joachim's apocalyptic prophesies were veiled in mysticism and allegory, thus lending them to various interpretations by later generations. In the early sixteenth century they added fuel to the eschatology of the Second Coming, in which Christ would judge and scourge the earth, punishing the wicked and rewarding the faithful. Thus the fear and apprehension of impending punishment added fervor to pious prayers and devotions. It also reinforced the cults of saints as intercessors with the angry and vengeful God. And what better medium of communication could exist between fallen man and the mighty Savior than his own devoted and compassionate mother? In this state of agitation and guilt feeling, the cult of the Virgin Mary flourished as the pivot of popular religion.

During the late fifteenth and early sixteenth centuries, Germany also experienced a great growth of university activity, in both the increase in student enrollment and the founding of many new schools. In these universities, and in many of the older ones as well, the *via moderna* (modern way) of Occamist thought (deriving its name from the Nominalist philosopher William of Occam, d. 1349)—with its denial of much of medieval Thomism, including the belief that all church doctrines could be proved by reason—prevailing over Saint Thomas's *via antiqua* (the old way). For the Occamists, knowledge rested on an inner experience rather than on a rational or experimental process. It is beyond intellectual power to know God, they said; He must be experienced through faith. The impact of Occamist determinism on German thought quickly became apparent after Martin Luther's initial confrontation with the church.

The expansion of intellectual horizons, along with technological advances, also influenced the dissemination of theological knowledge and made the Scriptures more accessible. Intellectual curiosity and desire for religious understanding made reading the Bible a growing practice throughout Europe. By the opening of the sixteenth century, over 100 versions of the Bible were available in Latin and vernacular editions. Demand for the Scriptures had reached a high pitch when Cardinal Cisneros and Erasmus published their Greek and Latin New Testaments, and shortly thereafter Luther issued his new German translation. With this urgency, there was an accompanying rise in the frequency and amplitude of theological discussion and pamphleteering. The belief by many that the Bible contained the answer to the dilemmas of the time, as well as the key to the understanding of God, provided the theological basis for religious reform.

Suggestions for Further Reading

SOCIETY AND LIFE

No area has received more attention in the past decade than social history. Certainly the most comprehensive description of how people lived and worked in Europe from the Middle Ages to the Industrial Revolution is Fernand Braudel's 3-volume masterpiece (totalling some 2,000 pages), *Civilization and Capitalism, 15th–18th Century* (New York, 1981–84), Vol. I: *The Structures of Everyday Life*, Vol. 2: *The Wheels of Commerce*, Vol. 3: *The Perspective of the World*, all translated by Sian Reynolds. Contrasting in size is George Huppert's excellent little synthesis entitled *After the Black Death: A Social History of Early Modern Europe* (Bloomington, 1986). Other perceptive studies of social life are J.R. Hale, *War and Society in Renaissance Europe, 1450–1620* (New York, 1985); John Walter and Roger Schofield, *Famine, Disease, and the Social Order in Early Modern Society* (New York, 1989); and Piero Camporesi, *Bread of Dreams: Food and Fantasy in Early Modern Europe*, tr. by David Gentilcore (Chicago, 1989), which claims that many ordinary people in the sixteenth century lived in a state of almost continual hallucination because of hunger or from eating bread containing hallucinogenic herbs.

A closer look at peasant life may be seen in Sheldon Watts, *A Social History of Western Europe, 1450–1720: Tensions and Solidarities among Rural People* (Dover, New Hampshire, 1984); David W. Sabean, *Popular Culture and Village Discourse in Early Modern Germany* (New York and Cambridge, England, 1985), revealing the conflict between rural popular religion and official church doctrines; Robert Muchembled, *Popular Culture and Elite Culture in France, 1400–1750* (Baton Rouge, 1985); and Michael Mullett, *Popular Culture and Popular Protest in Late Medieval and Early Modern Europe* (London, 1987). The higher classes are examined in Michael Jones, ed., *Gentry and Lesser Nobility in Late Medieval Europe* (New York, 1986), and Elias Norbert, *The Court Society*, tr. by E. Jephcott (New York, 1984). The movement of rural and urban populations Europewide is studied in Michael W. Flinn, *The European Demographic System, 1500–1820* (Baltimore, 1985), and interpreted for England in Peter Laslett, *The World We Have Lost*, 3rd ed. (London, 1983).

WOMEN AND FAMILIES

Roland Bainton opened the doors to Reformation women's studies with his 3-volume *Women of the Reformation* (Minneapolis, 1971–77). More recently this has become one of the most active fields of investigation, and there is much more to come. Highly recommended are Sherrin Marshall, ed., *Women in Reformation and Counter-Reformation Europe* (Bloomington, 1989); Jean R. Brink, et al., eds., *The Politics of Gender in Early Modern Europe* (Kirksville, Missouri, 1989); Merry Wiesner, *Working Women in Renaissance Germany* (New Brunswick, 1986), a valuable and insightful study; L. Roper, *Work, Marriage and Sexuality: Women in Reformation Augsburg* (London, 1985); Joyce Irwin, *Womanhood in Radical Protestantism, 1525–1675* (Lewiston, New York, 1989); and Katharina M. Wilson, ed., *Women Writers of the Renaissance and Reformation* (Athens, Georgia, 1987). For England see Margaret P. Hannay, *Silent But for the Word: Tudor Women as Patrons, Translators, and Writers of Religious Works* (Kent, Ohio, 1985); Retha M. Warnicke, *Women of the English Renaissance and Reformation* (Westport, Connecticut, 1983); and Mary Prior, ed., *Women in English Society, 1500–1800* (New York, 1985).

Marriage and family are seen in a new light in Steven Ozment, *When Fathers Ruled: Family Life in Reformation Europe* (Cambridge, Massachusetts, 1983), which revises the traditional view of the tyrannical husband and father, and describes Protestant marriage and family life in a more favorable light. Ozment provides a revealing portrait of one sixteenth-century family in *Magdalena and Balthasar: An Intimate Portrait of Life in Sixteenth-Century Europe Revealed in the Letters of a Nuremberg Husband and Wife* (New York, 1986). Other insights can be gained from H. Rebel, *Peasant*

Classes: The Bureaucratization of Property and Family Relations under Early Habsburg Absolutism, 1511–1636 (Princeton, 1983), and Ralph A. Houlbrooke, *The English Family, 1450–1700* (London, 1984).

ECONOMICS

Immanuel Wallerstein's pioneering study of *The Modern World-System* (New York and London, 1974) has had many spin-offs in recent years. One of the more controversial of these, although more directly related to Franklin Mendels's proto-industrialization theory than to Wallerstein's work, is Peter Kriedte, *Peasants, Landlords and Merchant Capitalists: Europe and the World Economy, 1500–1800* (Cambridge, England, 1983), a concise sketch of European economic development in early modern Europe, as seen from a Marxist point of view. Two leading economic historians have given us ground-breaking studies of financial history. Charles P. Kindleberger, *A Financial History of Western Europe* (London, 1984) covers 500 years, but its early chapters give a lucid run-down of early modern finances. The other, Carlo M. Cipolla's *Money in Sixteenth-Century Florence* (Berkeley, 1989), has a narrower scope but some cogent observations about the impact of the influx of New World silver through Spain. Cipolla's *The Fontana Economic History of Europe: The Sixteenth and Seventeenth Centuries* (London, 1974) is still a satisfactory general survey, covering population, technology, rural economy, industry, trade, and finance, supplementing rather than replacing E.E. Rich and C.H. Wilson, *The Cambridge Economic History of Europe,* Vol. IV: *The Economy of Expanding Europe in the Sixteenth and Seventeenth Centuries* (Cambridge, England, 1967). Also see James D. Tracy, ed., *The Rise of Merchant Empires: Long-Distance Trade in the Early Modern World, 1350–1750* (New York, 1990).

STATEBUILDING IN FRANCE

A large sweep of French history is covered in Christopher Allmand, *Power, Culture, and Religion in France, c. 1360–1550* (Rochester, New York, 1989). Howell A. Lloyd explores several features of French history in relation to the development of the state in *The State, France and the Sixteenth Century* (London, 1983). See also the first part of J.H.M. Salmon's *Society in Crisis: France in the Sixteenth Century* (London, 1975). The long wait for an adequate study of Francis I in English has finally been rewarded with R.J. Knecht's *Francis I* (New York and London, 1982), a highly acclaimed and scholarly life of *le roi chevalier.* A briefer introduction, with a few documents, is provided in the same author's *French Renaissance Monarchy: Francis I and Henry II* (New York and London, 1984).

TUDOR POLITICS AND SOCIETY

The best overall study of the period is John Guy, *Tudor England* (New York, 1988), an important book by a leading Tudor scholar. Also useful are Arthur J. Slavin, *The Tudor Age and Beyond: England from the Black Death to the End of the Age of Elizabeth* (Malabar, Florida, 1987); Alan G.R. Smith, *The Emergence of a Nation State: The Commonwealth of England, 1529–1660* (New York and London, 1984); and Joyce Youings, *16th Century England* (London, 1984). Specific features of the age are highlighted in David Loades, *The Tudor Court* (Totowa, New Jersey, 1986); Lacey Baldwin Smith, *Treason in Tudor England: Politics and Paranoia* (Princeton, 1986), which presents a thought-provoking thesis that traitors were driven by the paranoia that was endemic in Tudor society; Michael A.R. Graves, *The Tudor Parliaments: Crown, Lords and Commons* (New York and London, 1985); Roger B. Manning, *Village Revolts: Social Protest and Popular Disturbances in England, 1509–1640* (Oxford, 1988); Diarmaid MacCulloch, *Suffolk and the Tudors: Politics and Religion in an English County, 1500–1600* (New York and Oxford, 1986); and Narasingha P. Sil, *Life of William Lord Herbert of Pembroke (c. 1507–1570): Politique and Patriot* (Lewiston, New York, 1988).

THE AGE OF HENRY VIII

Alistair Fox and John Guy, *Reassessing the Henrician Age: Humanism, Politics and Reform, 1500–1550* (Oxford, 1986) challenges, though not always successfully, many of the long-held assumptions of early Tudor institutions. Some powerful personalities of the age are examined in G.W. Bernard, *The Power of the Early Tudor Nobility: A Study of the Fourth and Fifth Earls of Shrewsberry* (Totowa, New Jersey, 1985), followed by *War, Taxation, and Rebellion in Early Tudor England: Henry VIII, Wolsey, and the Amicable Grant of 1525* (New York, 1986); Barbara J. Harris, *Edward Stafford, Third Duke of Buckingham, 1478–1521* (Stanford, 1986), a penetrating study of the relationship between crown and nobility; and S.J. Gunn, *Charles Brandon, Duke of Suffolk, 1484–1545* (New York and Oxford, 1988), showing how charm might have been a more successful weapon than wealth and rank in Henrician England.

At the center of the Tudor stage was Henry VIII himself, and he continues to attract the attention of biographers and historians. The latest, but not necessarily the best, of a long line of biographies is Jasper Ridley, *Henry VIII: The Politics of Tyranny* (New York, 1985). He sees Henry as a cunning and ruthless ruler whose personality dominated the politics and personalities of his time. A shorter but very valuable study of the king and those around him is David Starkey, *The Reign of Henry VIII: Personalities and Politics* (New York, 1986). Starkey argues that the struggle for power among the king's courtiers is the central feature of national affairs in Henry's reign. Another useful study of crown and court is Helen Miller, *Henry VIII and the English Nobility* (New York and Oxford, 1986), which gives a very negative view of the king. The attempts of Thomas Starkey to regenerate the government and society of England are outlined in Thomas F. Mayer, *Thomas Starkey and the Commonwealth: Humanist Politics and Religion in the Reign of Henry VIII* (New York, 1989). In my opinion, the most insightful study of Henry's mind is still Lacey Baldwin Smith, *Henry VIII: The Mask of Royalty* (Boston, 1971), and the soundest analysis of his politics is J.J. Scarisbrick, *Henry VIII* (Berkeley, 1968).

THE EMPIRE OF CHARLES V

We are still waiting for the ideal biography of Charles V. In the meantime, two older works serve quite well as far as they go: Karl Brandi, *The Emperor Charles V*, tr. by C.V. Wedgwood (London, 1939), from the German point of view, and Manuel Fernández Alvarez, *Charles V: Elected Emperor and Hereditary Ruler* (London and Levitton, New York, 1975), from the Spanish. The very brief Seminar Studies in History volume by Martyn Rady, *The Emperor Charles V* (New York and London, 1988), with nineteen short documents and a convenient bibliography, is a useful little handbook. The institutional processes at the upper level of Charles V's administration are studied in John M. Headley, *The Emperor and His Chancellor: A Study of the Imperial Chancellery under Gattinara* (New York, 1983).

For an overview of the Spanish side of Charles V's empire, and its continuation through the reign of his son, A.W. Lovett, *Early Habsburg Spain, 1517–1598* (New

York and Oxford, 1986) is a good starting point, especially when used in conjunction with John Lynch, *Spain under the Habsburgs,* Vol. I: *Empire and Absolutism, 1516–1598,* 2nd ed. (Oxford, 1981). The insights of J.H. Elliott are always enlightening, and the essays in his *Spain and Its World, 1500–1700* (New Haven, 1989) are particularly cogent. The best analysis of social upheaval in Spain during the first years of Charles's reign is Stephen Haliczer, *The Comuneros of Castile: The Forging of a Revolution, 1475–1521* (Madison, 1981). On the transfer of power from Charles V to Philip II see Mia Rodríguez-Salgado, *The Changing Face of Empire: Charles V, Philip II, and Habsburg Authority, 1551–1559* (New York, 1988).

The Holy Roman Empire was more complex, and its historiography is less focused, but some valuable new interpretations are appearing, especially in German. Recent works in English include Paula S. Fichtner, *Protestantism and Primogeniture in Early Modern Germany* (New Haven, 1989); Gerald Strauss, *Law, Resistance, and the State: The Opposition to Roman Law in Reformation Germany* (Princeton, 1986); Jeffrey C. Smith, *Nuremberg: A Renaissance City, 1500–1618* (Austin, 1988); Kenneth J. Dillon, *King and Estates in the Bohemian Lands, 1526–1564* (Brussels, 1976); Lawrence G. Duggan, *Bishops and Chapter: The Governance of the Bishopric of Speyer to 1552* (New Brunswick, 1978); Steven Rowan, *Ulrich Zasius: A Jurist in the German Renaissance, 1461–1535* (Frankfurt, 1987); and especially Thomas A. Brady, Jr., *Turning Swiss: Cities and Empire, 1450–1550* (New York, 1985), a well-written and suggestive study of the politics, diplomacy, and social tensions of the south-German cities, and why, in the end, they turned not to the Swiss but to the emperor.

ERASMUS AND THE CHRISTIAN HUMANISTS

The best recent studies of Erasmus and his humanist influence are Cornelis Augustijn, *Erasmus: His Life, Works, and Influence,* tr. by J.C. Grayson (Toronto, 1991); J.S. Weiland and W.T.M. Frijhoff, eds., *Erasmus of Rotterdam: The Man and the Scholar* (Leiden, 1988); Marjorie O'Rourke Boyle, *Christening Pagan Mysteries: Erasmus in Pursuit of Wisdom* (Toronto, 1981); Erika Rummel, *Erasmus as a Translator of the Classics* (Toronto, 1985); and Walter M. Gordon, *Humanist Play and Belief: The Seriocomic Art of Desiderius Erasmus* (Toronto, 1990). His theological/spiritual dimension is probed in Richard L. DeMolen, *The Spirituality of Erasmus of Rotterdam* (Nieuwkoop, the Netherlands, 1987); Erika Rommel, *Erasmus' Annotations on the New Testament: From Philologist to Theologian* (Toronto, 1986); and Richard J. Schoeck's brief *Erasmus Grandescens: The Growth of a Humanist's Mind and Spirituality* (Nieuwkoop, the Netherlands, 1988).

On the influence of other Christian humanists, much can be learned from Anthony Goodman and Angus MacKay, eds., *The Impact of Humanism on Western Europe* (New York, 1990); Eckhard Bernstein, *German Humanism* (Boston, 1983); Philip E. Hughes, *Lefèvre: Pioneer of Ecclesiastical Renewal in France* (Grand Rapids, 1984); Maria Dowling, *Humanism in the Age of Henry VIII* (London, 1986); Richard Marius, *Thomas More: A Biography* (New York, 1984); and Louis L. Martz, *Thomas More: The Search for the Inner Man* (New Haven, 1990).

2 | MARTIN LUTHER AND THE GERMAN UPHEAVAL

THE APOCRYPHAL QUIP, "ERASMUS LAID THE EGG THAT LUTHER hatched," contains some truth. The Christian humanists did indeed advocate a reformation of the church. Placing great emphasis on Scripture, they championed the "philosophy of Christ" as the true goal of Christian scholarship, and called for higher moral integrity among the clergy. Erasmus was at the forefront in exposing clerical abuse and in advocating a regeneration of the church by replacing empty ceremonialism with true Christian devotion. Yet there was a basic difference in the thrust of the two reformers, and the ripening Reformation drove them further apart. While Erasmus had no significant argument with doctrine, only with practice, Luther held that doctrine was crucial. It was not so much the abuses in the Catholic church to which he objected, as the Christian humanists did, but the theology of Catholicism itself. For Erasmus, the church should be strengthened by reform. Luther declared that God's truth must prevail regardless of the church. In Erasmus's poignant words, "Luther hatched a bird of quite a different species."

The Nature of the Lutheran Schism

In the complexity of social, economic, and political activities forming the background of religious upheaval, it is easy to lose sight of the theological dilemma that first drove Martin Luther into the monastery and eventually thrust him into the vanguard of religious reform. Time and again he reemphasized the fact that his dispute with the pope was a doctrinal disagreement of fundamental significance, not a simple castigation of the clergy for improper conduct. "Others," he maintained, "have attacked the life. I attack the doctrine." Of course the abuses disturbed him, but his greater concern was with the principles of divine truth. In 1520 he wrote:

> Someone said to me: "What a sin and scandal all these clerical vices are, the fornication, the drunkenness, the unbridled passion for sport!" Yes, I must confess that these are dreadful scandals, indeed, and they should

53

be denounced and corrected. But the vices to which you refer are plain for all to see; they are grossly material, everyone perceives them, and so everyone is stirred to anger by them. Alas, the real evil, the incomparably more baneful and cruel canker, is the deliberate silence regarding the word of Truth, or else its adulteration.

Martin Luther was an outgoing and gregarious person, living, praying, preaching, eating, and drinking with a zest and enthusiasm that infected all who were near him. Quick to anger as well as to laugh, he seemed happiest when in the thick of verbal battle. Frequently he said or wrote what he might later regret; but once uttered, he stoutly refused to retract or retreat. Compromise was foreign to his nature. One contemporary noted that "In company he is vivacious, jocose, always cheerful and gay no matter how hard his adversaries press him. Everyone chides him for the fault of being a little too insolent in his reproaches and more caustic than is prudent for an innovator in religion or becoming to a theologian." At the same time, Luther was a sensitive person, moved by the beauty of God's creations and touched when kindness and love overcame the baser human emotions.

Above all, he was a deeply religious man, and his writings and actions disclose his concern for religious truth as it appeared to him in the Scriptures. His rediscovery of Pauline/Augustinian theology became the foundation of Protestantism as he declared that salvation was not something won or bought through individual good deeds but by the free gift of a just and merciful God. Luther's natural conservatism made him reluctant to deviate from former religious traditions unless explicitly required by Scripture to do so—and then only by persuasion. "I grant that one may preach against the Mass," he declared in 1522, "I grant that one may speak and write against it; but I do not wish anyone to use compulsion and violence, for the faith demands to be free and willing, and must be received without force." Yet he felt compelled by his conscience and interpretation of the Bible to boldly proclaim his views, even when they brought him into a collision course with the papacy itself.

The theological reformation, initiated and led by Martin Luther, was the result of a rediscovery of God, through Christ, in the Scriptures. It was an attempt to go directly to the source of truth and power rather than through the intercession of saints, relics, priests, and popes. It was the realization that the chasm between God and humankind is bridged not by institutional rituals and sacraments but by Christ himself on the cross, and by faith in that atonement. The gradual unveiling of this concept of God-centered religion is the story of Luther's struggle to find salvation in a world filled with sin and corruption. Its realization brought a resounding end to that cherished ideal of the Christian humanists, the religious unity of western Christendom.

Young Martin Luther and His Struggle for Salvation

Luther was born on November 10, 1483, at Eisleben in Upper Thuringia. He was the son of a tough and industrious farmer-turned-miner who held great hopes and ambitions for his son. By peasant standards, Hans Luther was fairly

Martin Luther. *An oil on panel of the reformer, painted by Lucas Cranach the Elder in 1525 or 1526, about the time Luther married Katherine von Bora. It is now located in Bristol, England.*

well-to-do and highly respected for his industry and integrity. He taught his son with an iron hand, while his wife Margarethe imbued the boy with trust in God and in the church. Young Luther's boyhood was spent mostly in Mans-feld, where his family moved in 1484, near the center of one of the largest copper-mining regions of Germany. At the age of fourteen, he went to the great city of Magdeburg to continue his studies. A year later, however, after having some exposure to the school of the Brethren of the Common Life at Magde-burg, his parents sent him to Eisenach, the ancestral home of his mother's family.

Eisenach was located in the western corner of Electoral Saxony, ruled by Frederick the Wise. Just thirteen years earlier, the duchy of Saxony had been divided between Ernest and Albert, the two rival sons of the ruling Wettin duke. To Ernest went the north-south half (from Brandenburg on the north to Coburg on the south and Eisenach on the west) and the office of elector. Albert received the central portion running east to west from Stolpen to Mühlhausen, and the title of duke. The electorate (also known as Ernestine Saxony) passed to Frederick a year after the division, upon the death of his father. Albert ruled ducal (Albertine) Saxony until succeeded by his son George in 1500.

In three years Luther had completed his preparation for the university, and in May 1501 the enthusiastic and impressionable young scholar entered the faculty of arts at the nearby University of Erfurt, one of the leading centers of learning in the Empire. There he was introduced to, and considerably influenced by, the nominalist philosophy of William of Occam and his German disciple Gabriel Biel (d. 1495). This school accentuated the separation between reason and faith (always insisting on the superiority of the latter) and emphasized the omnipotence of God.

Luther was bright and eager to learn. A contemporary recalled that "he began to study earnestly and industriously logic as well as the other liberal and rhetoric arts. . . . Though by nature alert and joyful, he began his studies every morning with prayer and Mass. His rule was, 'Eagerly prayed is half studied.' He never overslept or missed a lecture; he consulted and questioned his teachers in honourable fashion. He studied with his fellow students and whenever there were no lectures he spent his time in the library." In eighteen months he received the bachelor's degree and two and a half years later, at the age of twenty-one, he became a master in the liberal arts. In May 1505, he began the formal study of law, which his father hoped would open the doors of the world to his son. Then suddenly, to the amazement of his colleagues and the chagrin of his father, he abandoned his career and entered the cloister of the Augustinian Hermits in Erfurt.

The perplexing question of why Luther rejected his schooling and entered the monastery has been variously answered. His own assertion in later life, that it was due to a sudden vow taken during a violent thunderstorm, seems likely to have been a catalyst but was not the cause. Luther's deep religious convictions, coupled with his emotional nature, caused him great anxiety when he contemplated the difficulty of achieving salvation in a world of corruption, immorality, and impiety. More specifically, how could he, a hopeless sinner, be accepted by a just God who cannot look upon sin with the least allowance? For a long time Luther had wrestled with this all-important problem without being able to solve it. Finally, in apparent desperation and fear, he renounced the world for the security of the monastery.

Luther flung himself into his new life and routine with enthusiasm, convinced that here he could do the will of the Lord free from the overwhelming burden of sin. "I was a good monk," he later wrote, "and I kept the rule of my order so strictly that I may say that if ever a monk got to Heaven by his monkery, it was I. All my brothers in the monastery who knew me will bear me out." Yet for all his fasting, rituals, prayers, and sanctifying works, Luther failed to receive the inner conviction that he had yet pleased his God. The harder he tried to separate himself from sin, the greater became his awareness of it, and the greater became his fear of God's judgment. In the monastery he found no more relief for his tormented mind than he had in the world. His dilemma became even greater, he tells us, as he came to fear and despise the words *law*, *justice*, and *righteousness*, and to hate a God who would prescribe requirements that were impossible for humans to achieve, then condemn them for their failure.

In the spring of 1507, Luther was ordained a priest and shortly thereafter, upon the recommendation of his superior and patron, Johann von Staupitz, he returned to the University of Erfurt to begin the study of theology. His next five years were spent in study and lectures, both at Erfurt and at the newly created university at Wittenberg (founded in 1502 by the Elector Frederick himself). Luther also went on a mission to Rome in behalf of the Augustinian order, and was shocked by the irreverence of the Roman worship and by the sensuousness of the people. Twenty years later he noted sarcastically:

> When in Rome I was a frantic saint. I ran through all the churches and crypts and believed everything, their suffocating lies and falsehoods. I celebrated several Masses in Rome, and almost regretted that my father and mother were still living, for I would have liked to redeem them from purgatory with my Masses and other good works and prayers. There is a saying in Rome: "Blessed is the mother whose son celebrates a Mass at Saint John's on Saturday." I surely would have liked to make my mother blessed! But there was a great commotion and I could not get near, so I ate a smoked herring instead.

In 1512 Luther completed his theological study at Wittenberg and received the doctorate of theology. Thereupon he became a professor with the theological faculty at the university, lecturing on the Bible. He was at the same time preacher at the Wittenberg convent and the parish church, regent of studies for novices and friars, and vicar of the Augustinian order, which entailed supervising eleven convents.

Luther's continued occupation with intellectual and spiritual matters still seemed to bring him no immediate relief from his mental anguish. At the heart of his dilemma was his conception of the "justice of God" (*iustitia Dei*) as punitive, retributive justice, by which the Lord weighs merit against sins, as a judge decides a case of law. Does God therefore demand what is impossible, namely a life so full of good works that it merits salvation? If so, then how can it be said that he is merciful, or even just? If that is not what he demands, then how is salvation attained?

As Luther prepared and systematically lectured during the next few years on Psalms, Romans, Galatians, Hebrews, and Titus, he gradually came to a different understanding of the meaning and relationship of the terms *justice, mercy, faith,* and *grace,* as he focused his attention more on Christ than on the teachings and traditions of the church. Finally, as a result of prolonged study and reflection, particularly on the epistles of Paul, Luther underwent what he called his "tower experience," and the misfitting pieces of his theological puzzle began falling into place. Here is how he described the experience:

> After I had pondered the problem for days and nights, God took pity on me and I saw the inner connection between the two phrases, "The justice of God is revealed in the Gospel," and "The just shall live by faith" [Romans 1:17]. I began to understand that this justice of God is the justice by which the just man lives through the free gift of God, that is to say "by faith." Thereupon I felt as if I had been born again and had entered Paradise through wide-open gates. Immediately the whole of Scripture took on a new meaning for me.

Thus Luther came to believe that *iustitia Dei* was not punitive justice but really the *righteousness*, or *grace*, of God, by which he bestows faith, and thereby salvation, through Jesus Christ. In other words, salvation is not earned or bought by human works, nor by the intervention of the church, but is given freely by God, through the sacrifice of Christ. He also bestows the power to believe, so even faith does not result from human merit but from divine grace. ⟨This doctrine of justification by grace through faith in Christ, with its corollary, the reliance upon biblical authority, became the twin banners of the Protestant Reformation, and *sola gratia* (salvation by God's grace alone); *solo Christo* (human righteousness is wrought by Christ alone); *sola fide* (by faith alone people receive Christ and his righteousness); *sola scriptura* (only through the Bible is this "good news" revealed) became its popular slogans.⟩

The Road to Reformation

Although Luther's "tower experience" was the significant first step in the Reformation, the event that brought him into open conflict with the prelates and later the pope was the scandalous sale of indulgences, particularly the plenary Jubilee Indulgence, initiated by Pope Julius II (1503–13) and revived by Leo X (1513–21), which was used to obtain funds for the rebuilding of Saint Peter's Basilica in Rome. Indulgences were written remissions of part or all of the temporal punishment imposed for sins that had been confessed to, and absolved by, a priest. These temporal penalties had to be paid, either in this life

The Sale of Indulgences.   *Woodcut by Jörg Breu (ca. 1530) depicts the involvement of pope, cardinals, priests, princes, and bankers in the sale and distribution of indulgences. Papal authorization for the sale is displayed on the banner.*

or in purgatory, and the purchase of an indulgence (drawn on the collateral of the "Treasury of Merit," a kind of spiritual bank account of extra grace earned by Christ and the saints) would supposedly lighten that penalty and might even be applied to sins not yet committed, thus allowing its holder to bypass purgatory altogether. In 1476, Pope Sixtus IV added the final distortion to indulgences by declaring that they could stop the punishment being endured by souls already in purgatory. By Luther's time, indulgences were blatantly trafficked throughout Christendom, usually as a source of ecclesiastical revenue.

Pope Leo's Jubilee Indulgence was not sold in Saxony and many other parts of northern Germany, but in nearby Brandenburg an arrangement was reached between the pope and Albrecht of Brandenburg (younger brother of Elector Joachim) by which Albrecht became archbishop of Mainz in return for promoting the sale of the indulgence in Brandenburg, Magdeburg, and Halberstadt, and allowing half of its proceeds to go directly to Rome. The indulgence was vigorously hawked by the Dominican friar Johann Tetzel (d. 1519) under the watchful eyes of an agent of the Fugger bank, which had advanced the money to Albrecht for the purchase of his benefice—and for his previous acquisition of the archbishopric of Magdeburg and the bishopric of Halberstadt. As more and more of Luther's congregation crossed the border to purchase the papal indulgence from Tetzel, both the Wittenberg professor and the Saxon elector became incensed. "Let them buy good Saxon indulgences with their money," insisted Frederick. But Tetzel had made this particular indulgence highly attractive by promising far-reaching and immediate results. According to Luther, Tetzel's favorite jingle was: "As your money into the coffer rings, a soul from purgatory springs."

The Ninety-Five Theses

Luther's reaction to the indulgence traffic was much deeper than that of the elector, for he felt that indulgences completely reversed the true nature of repentance and that instead of bringing contrition and sorrow, which were prerequisites to forgiveness, they brought arrogance and self-satisfaction. Therefore, he maintained, the people were victims of a great swindle. Finally, angry enough to take a dramatic stand, Luther composed a rebuttal to the sale of indulgences in the form of ninety-five theses, or arguments, which he allegedly nailed to the door of the castle church in Wittenberg on the eve of All Saints' Day, 31 October 1517. The Ninety-Five Theses were intended as a challenge, particularly to the Dominicans, but also to anyone else who cared to debate the issues and propositions suggested by Luther. Among the more pregnant of these propositions, in addition to those directly challenging the validity of indulgences (such as number 32, which declared "All those who believe themselves certain of their own salvation by means of letters of indulgence, will be eternally damned, together with their teachers"), was the affirmation that "The true treasure of the church is the Holy Gospel of the glory and the grace of God" (62), and "Every Christian who feels true compunction has of right plenary remission of punishment and guilt even without letters of pardon" (36).

The controversy might have ended there after perhaps a few disputations with the rival Dominicans had it not been for the transformation that had taken place in mass communications during the preceding fifty years. Copies of Luther's handwritten challenge were soon printed and distributed. A translation was made into German, and the printing of this edition reached many thousands of readers in Saxony and other parts of Germany. In a very real sense it could be said that the Reformation was a result of the invention of printing. Luther's conflicts were no longer a private matter. He had suddenly become the center of a continentwide controversy as the *Ninety-Five Theses* aroused excitement everywhere. Luther followed his *Theses* with a fuller vernacular treatise entitled *Sermon on Indulgences and Grace,* and began another, called *Resolutions.* By then the affair was creating a loud stir throughout Germany. The Dominicans wanted it taken up in Rome where their influence through Cardinal Cajetan was strong. But the Roman curia still seemed unperturbed. Leo X reportedly referred to Luther as some "drunken German who will amend his ways when he sobers up."

The Hearings at Heidelberg and Augsburg

Early in 1518, attempts were made to quiet the Wittenberg professor through the channels of his own order. In April, Johann von Staupitz and other officials of the Augustinian Hermits met Luther at Heidelberg to learn more of the "new theology" of the University of Wittenberg. Some understanding was reached and Luther agreed to complete his *Resolutions* for publication and forward it, together with a special introduction and letter of apology, to the Roman pontiff. The troubled waters seemed to be calming. However, from the direction of Ingolstadt, where the illustrious and brilliant Professor Johann Eck had taken up his pen against Luther a new tempest was rising.

The Luther problem was also beginning to generate political attention. As Emperor Maximilian convened an imperial diet at Augsburg to unite the German princes against the increasing Turkish threat, it became apparent that he was also preparing the ground for the election of his grandson, Charles of Burgundy and Spain, as Holy Roman emperor. Fearing the power and influence of Charles, Pope Leo began to woo Frederick of Saxony toward a declaration of his own candidacy for the imperial crown. This meant that the Luther affair had to be handled very carefully. In September 1518 Cardinal Cajetan offered to give Luther a "fatherly" hearing at Augsburg. What began as "friendly persuasion," however, ended in violent argument. From the beginning, a difference in objectives made conciliation difficult. Cajetan's instructions were to secure from Luther a recantation of his statements and writings; Luther wanted to dispute the issues. The resulting condemnations began to shake Luther from his belief that the Roman curia might accept his clear explanation of the Gospel.

Following the Augsburg interview, Cajetan sent a report of the unfavorable proceedings to Rome, and wrote to Frederick demanding that he take action against Luther. Frederick was "on the spot." It is unlikely that the elector was converted to Luther's new theology, but he was far too wise a prince to follow Cajetan's orders rashly. That would be like killing the goose that laid the golden eggs. Thanks to Luther, Frederick's infant university was receiving more publicity than all the other great centers combined. Therefore, when the decree arrived inviting Luther to appear in Rome to answer charges of doctrinal irregularity, Frederick refused to let him go. Remembering the fate of John Hus under similar circumstances, the elector sent the pope a statement, along with a letter from the Wittenberg faculty, asking that Luther be excused "because of illness and the perils of the way."

In January 1519 Emperor Maximilian died, and Karl von Miltiz was sent as papal nuncio to offer Frederick the coveted Golden Rose as a token for his peacemaking efforts in the Empire. Miltiz was also charged to see Luther and "extirpate this tare and coccle from the fertile field of the Lord." But Miltiz, a fellow Saxon, had other things in mind. Thinking of the feather in his own cap if he should bring about a reconciliation between Luther and the church, Miltiz showered Luther with words of understanding. He agreed that Luther had been misunderstood in Rome and got the latter to agree not to speak out in public again if he were not attacked in public. Miltiz's flattery was disarming but not convincing.

The Leipzig Debate

In the meantime, Luther's associate, Dr. Andreas Bodenstenstein von Karlstadt (ca. 1480–1541), had been challenged to a debate in Leipzig by Johann Eck (1486–1543), the prominent Ingolstadt theologian. When he learned of the challenge, Luther insisted that he accompany Karlstadt and take part in the disputation. For seven days Eck and Karlstadt debated issues before Luther was allowed to enter the arena on 4 July 1519 to defend his infant cause. Luther knew his Scriptures and could handle himself well in debate, but against the shrewd Eck he did not fare much better than Karlstadt did. Instead of debating the indulgence problem, for which Luther was fully prepared, Eck brought up many new issues to which Luther had not given as much thought. Thus Eck was able to draw out of him heretical and near-heretical pronouncements, particularly concerning the authority of the pope and of the councils. Furthermore, Eck persisted in identifying Luther with the Hussites whom everyone agreed were heretics. Nevertheless, Luther defended himself well and made some good points of his own, showing how both popes and councils had at times contradicted themselves.

The Leipzig debate lasted for three weeks, and it turned out to be one of the most important steps on the road to Reformation. In the first place, Eck's identification of Luther's ideas with the condemned doctrines of John Hus exposed Luther for the first time to open charges of heresy. Up to the time of the debate Luther believed, like most Germans, that Hus had been a heretic, yet when Eck succeeded in pinning the label of "Hussite" on him, Luther was obliged to study Hus's writings more seriously. To his amazement, he found that he agreed with many of the Czech reformer's doctrines, and by the end of the debate he was publicly admitting this. Secondly, Luther clarified his own

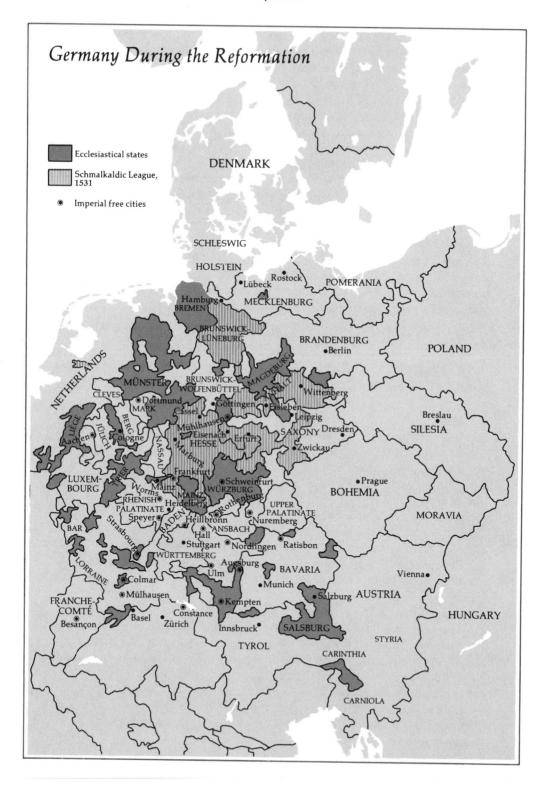

Germany During the Reformation

Ecclesiastical states

Schmalkaldic League, 1531

⊚ Imperial free cities

DENMARK

SCHLESWIG

HOLSTEIN

•Lübeck Rostock•   POMERANIA

Hamburg• MECKLENBURG

BREMEN

BRUNSWICK- BRANDENBURG
LÜNEBURG

•Berlin   POLAND

MÜNSTER BRUNSWICK- MAGDEBURG
WOLFENBÜTTEL ANHALT

CLEVES •Wittenberg

•Dortmund •Göttingen
MARK Cassel• •Eisleben

BERG Mühlhausen• •Leipzig   Breslau•
Aachen• •Eisenach •Erfurt SAXONY Dresden• SILESIA

JÜLICH HESSE
Cologne• Marburg• •Zwickau

NASSAU

LUXEM- •Frankfurt
BOURG •Schweinfurt •Prague

TRIER Worms• Mainz• WÜRZBURG BOHEMIA
RHENISH MAINZ•
PALATINATE Heidelberg• •Rothenburg MORAVIA
Speyer• UPPER

BAR BADEN •Heilbronn PALATINATE
•Nuremberg

Strasbourg• •Hall •ANSBACH
•Stuttgart Nördlingen• Ratisbon•

LORRAINE WÜRTTEMBERG
•Augsburg BAVARIA

Colmar• Ulm• Vienna•
FRANCHE- •Mülhausen •Munich AUSTRIA
COMTÉ •Kempten Salzburg• HUNGARY
•Besançon Basel• Constance
  Zürich• Innsbruck• SALSBURG STYRIA

TYROL CARINTHIA

CARNIOLA

views more fully than he had done before. Now he saw the full implications of his theology, and he realized that his views were not the views of the majority of the church after all. Shortly thereafter, in a letter to his close friend, Spalatin, secretary to the elector, Luther confessed that he must have been a Hussite all along without knowing it. Thirdly, the great publicity of the Leipzig debate brought the Lutheran controversy to the center of the religious stage and made Luther the focus of all the smoldering discontent in Germany. By the beginning of the decisive year 1520, Luther's views were becoming crystallized and popularized. The formative years were past and the time of struggle was at hand.

Confrontation at Worms

Following the Leipzig debate, Luther busied himself with programmatic writing and managed to convince himself that the pope was the very Anti-Christ. He also became acquainted with the humanist Ulrich von Hutten, who tried to talk Luther into joining forces with him and leading a political as well as religious rebellion against Rome. But Luther refused to consider himself anything but a theological leader and recoiled from any association with a political revolution. His principal concern now was "to make room in the world for the free passage of the word of God." This was the motive for his three famous treatises of 1520.

One of these, entitled *Address to the Christian Nobility of the German Nation*, was a strongly worded appeal, in German, to the princes of the Empire against the unjust dominion of the pope. The papacy, Luther charged, had thrown up three walls around itself which must be broken down and destroyed. These walls were the claims (1) that the church is superior to the state, (2) that the pope alone has the right to summon councils, and (3) that the pope alone has the right to interpret Scriptures. The papacy, Luther insisted, must be confined to a spiritual realm, and the church in Germany must be made a German church. He denounced celibacy, monasticism, and ritualism, maintaining that the final authority in matters civil and religious was the Bible. He continued in this way, step by step, to strike at the foundations of papal authority in Germany, calling upon the ruling classes to lead a reform of the church. The seeds fell in fertile soil.

Another, lengthier discourse of the same year was the *Babylonian Captivity of the Church*, written in Latin and addressed primarily to the theologians. It consisted largely of a theological attack against the sacramental system of the Roman church, in which Luther denied the reality or necessity of the Catholic priesthood, and recognized only two sacraments, the Lord's Supper and baptism, as valid testaments of God's grace. "For only in these do we find both the divinely instituted sign and the promise of forgiveness of sins." He allotted baptism to the beginning and course of a Christian life, and the Lord's Supper to its end. "And the Christian should use them both as long as he is in this mortal frame, until, fully baptized and strengthened, he passes out of this world, and is born into the new eternal life."

In November 1520 Luther wrote the third of his treatises, *On the Freedom of a Christian,* and published it along with an open letter to Pope Leo X. In this short but meaningful essay, Luther set forth what he called the true doctrine of salvation and of the Gospel. No other document gives a more succinct or clearcut description of Luther's doctrinal break with the church. In its few pages he set forth the concept of faith, which alone—without works—justifies, frees, and through Christ, brings salvation. He also defined his views on Christian love, which, along with faith, is the fulfillment of God's commandments and the manifestation of Christian freedom. It is obvious that his doctrinal differences with the Catholic theologians were fundamental, and his final plea to the pope for understanding and conciliation is pervaded with confidence and defiance: "And believe me when I say that I have never thought ill of you personally, that I am the kind of a person who would wish you all good things eternally, and that I have no quarrel with any man concerning his morals but only concerning the word of truth. In all other matters I will yield to any man whatsoever; but I have neither the power nor the will to deny the Word of God. If any man has a different opinion concerning me, he does not think straight or understand what I have actually said."

Three months earlier Pope Leo had issued the bull, *Exsurge Domine,* calling worldwide attention to Luther's heresy and threatening his excommunication if he did not retract his stand within six months. On 10 December 1520, in further defiance of the papal authority, Luther burned the bull, along with copies of the canon law, decrees and decretals of the papacy, and other documents of the church, in a ceremonial fire at Wittenberg. One month later, a second papal bull, *Decet Romanum,* verified Luther's excommunication. The breach with Rome was almost complete.

Until now the imperial authorities had taken relatively little notice of Luther. His fight had been with the church, not with the Empire. Yet the nature of the struggle was such that it would inevitably bring Luther into conflict with the political interest of Germany and with the emperor himself. In January 1521 the young newly elected Emperor Charles V met with his first imperial diet in the city of Worms, in southwestern Franconia. The diet was summoned for grave and urgent purposes: to attempt to create a legal system for the Empire; to raise money and troops from Germany to be used against the advancing Turks, and also against the threats from Francis I; and to organize a council of regency to manage affairs in Germany during the emperor's frequent and extended absences. To this diet Martin Luther was summoned to answer the imperial charges of heresy and treason.

The meeting at Worms was one of the most dramatic confrontations in history. Shortly after 4 o'clock on that Sunday afternoon, April 17, Martin Luther was escorted into the bishop's palace next to the Worms cathedral where were assembled the dukes and princes of the Empire, the imperial electors, and the emperor, with many additional servants, scribes, and courtiers. Also present was the papal legate, Hieronymus Aleander. The city was packed with masses of people eager to see the new emperor and to get a glimpse of the now-famous Wittenberg professor who had so boldly defied the pope. Inside, from among the assembled notables stepped the secretary of the elector-bishop of Trier to speak for the emperor and the court. He asked Luther whether he publicly acknowledged authorship of the books and pamphlets lying on the table beside him, and if he would recant what was in them. Luther answered yes to the first question but requested more time to ponder the second before replying. He was granted twenty-four hours.

On the following day, Luther responded with an explanation that since he had written many different kinds of books, they should be judged differently. In some he claimed he had simply discussed religious faith and morals; he would not recant these because to do so would be to repudiate Christ. In others he admitted attacking the affairs of the papists, but only when their unchristian doctrines and wicked example threatened to lay waste the church. To retract these would be to encourage tyranny. Concerning a third category of books, against certain individuals who upheld the evils of the papacy, he admitted that he had been more violent than he ought to have been. "But then," he quickly retorted, "I do not set myself up as a saint; neither am I disputing about my life, but about the teaching of Christ." Thereupon he hurled a challenge to the assembled lords to dispute with him and prove wherein he had erred, citing as he did the words of the Savior, "If I have spoken wrongly, bear witness to the wrong."

When Luther had finished his speech, the imperial spokesman arose and chastised him for speaking in such a manner instead of answering the question. He then ordered Luther once more simply to respond. Luther's reply became the battle cry of the Reformation:

> Since then your serene majesty and your lordships seek a simple answer, I will give it without horns or teeth as follows: Unless I am convinced by the testimony of Scripture or by evident reason (for I trust neither in popes nor in councils alone, since it is well known that they have often erred and contradicted themselves), I am bound by the Scriptures that I have quoted and my conscience is captive to the Word of God. Therefore I cannot and will not recant, since it is neither safe nor right to go against one's conscience. I cannot do otherwise. Here I stand. God help me. Amen.*

The drama, however, was not yet over. The emperor was still to be heard. After reviewing his royal and Catholic lineage, Charles affirmed his determination to hold fast to the church and all its teachings. "For it is certain that a single monk must err in his opinion if he stands against all of Christendom; otherwise Christendom itself would have erred for more than a thousand years." He allowed Luther his safe conduct back to Wittenberg but denounced him as a heretic and called upon the assembled princes to proceed formally against him. Thus the challenge was thrown down and accepted. The point of no return was past.

---

*The "Here I stand" flourish, inserted in German to the Latin text, may have been added at a later date.

The diet was already dispersing when Aleander's draft of an edict was approved, with modifications, by a rump of the diet and issued by the emperor on May 26. The Edict of Worms condemned Luther's doctrines and actions, along with all who aided, condoned, published, or read his views. Yet it was too sweeping a pronouncement to be enforceable. In the meantime, ominous clouds were gathering on the horizon. The Turks were beginning to move westward up the Danube plain and into the Mediterranean; Francis I opened hostilities against the emperor; and the menacing challenge of the *Bundschuh* (an organization of rebellious peasants in southwestern Germany) was becoming louder and more frequent.

The Crisis Years: 1521–25

The period immediately following the Diet at Worms was a crucial one in the development of Lutheran ideas and institutions. Fearing for the safety of his valuable charge, Frederick the Wise whisked Luther away to the fortified castle of the Wartburg overlooking Eisenach. For a year, Luther busied himself there writing sermons, tracts, and commentaries, and translating the New Testament into German. This outpouring of works was partly to compensate for the gnawing doubts that plagued him as he silently reflected on the events of the preceding four years. "At night the devil tempted me mercilessly," Luther confessed, "trying to capture my spirit and mind. I resisted him in faith and confronted him with this verse: 'God, who created man, is mine, and all things are under his feet. If you have any power over him, try it'!" Arising triumphantly after his bouts with Satan, Luther threw himself energetically into his literary output.

Bible translating was not a new thing in Luther's time, but his New Testament was something different and powerful. The vigor of his expression and the clarity of style made his Bible a new revelation in German. It also made Luther's *Hochdeutsch* (High German dialect) the principal literary form of the language from that time on. The other significant thing about Luther's translation was its freedom and looseness. Unhampered by much knowledge of Hebrew history or language, he put the text into the language of Germans, with a natural feel for its emotional and expressive appeal. Undaunted by the dilemma of all translators—who must transform the strange language of one people, of a different era and tradition, into the familiar idiom of another while still maintaining the feeling and ideas of the former—Luther made no attempt at a literal rendition. Instead of transporting the reader to the original text, he brought the original to the reader. Under his hands the Bible became a modern German witness, not an ancient Jewish testament, as understandable in the marketplace as in the cathedral. "When I translate Moses," Luther warned, "I want to make him so German that no one will know he was a Jew." Luther's own mark was indelible in every line.

A new kind of crisis awaited Luther when he returned to Wittenberg. In every revolution, the time comes when its advocates must assess their progress and decide whether the principal aims have been reached, or whether the fight must be continued and intensified. That moment was a crucial one for Luther.

In his absence, many of his followers and those who considered themselves co-leaders had carried out a more thorough and radical reformation in Wittenberg than Luther had envisioned. Karlstadt and others were preaching an apocalyptic gospel, destroying relics, images, and pictures, and mutilating church properties in the name of religious freedom. Under Karlstadt and Gabriel Zwilling, the sacramental ordinances were altered, the Mass abolished, and many other changes implemented. Luther was appalled by this disorder and expelled his overzealous colleagues from Wittenberg. But the problem did not end there. Many Lutheran "converts" resented Luther's conservatism, insisting that the break with Rome must be complete if it was to have any meaning at all. Shortly he was confronted with even more radical revolutionaries in the "Zwickau Prophets" who, claiming to receive direct communication from God, were preaching the overthrow of the unrighteous by the sword, and the immediate establishment of the kingdom of God.

Luther and the Humanists

In those crucial years of rapid change, Luther was not only confronted with dissension from his radical friends, but also with a break with the more conservative reformers. For many years the Christian humanists had criticized the abuses and follies of the church. Most of them had welcomed Luther's entry into the reforming arena and praised the boldness and vigor of his attack on indulgences. But for most of the humanists, Luther had gone too far. It seemed to them that he was not contributing to the strength and unity of the church but was recklessly tearing it down. He had ceased being a reformer and had instead become an enemy of the church. Erasmus had frequently written in favor of Luther, but after 1521 it became increasingly obvious to him that the spirit of Luther's reforms was far different from that of his own. By 1524 the gulf between them had widened irreparably. In his *Essay on Free Will* of September 1524, Erasmus carefully examined the biblical evidence for and against Luther's doctrine of grace, concluding that the Scriptures disagreed with Luther and supported the Catholic tradition of free will and salvation through faith *and* works. He further admonished Luther to be less dogmatic in his assertions and more ready to accept correction! Luther was infuriated by Erasmus's essay. He answered with the strongly worded *Bondage of the Will*, which contained not only a vigorous statement of his views on human depravity, but also a caustic invective against Erasmus himself. Between 1521 and 1525, with few exceptions, humanism became alienated from the Lutheran movement.

One of those exceptions was Philipp Melanchthon (1497–1560), a classical scholar who, from the moment they first met, was Luther's loyal supporter and almost constant companion, yet remained a dedicated humanist all his life. Melanchthon came to Wittenberg in 1518, at the age of twenty-one, to teach Greek and Hebrew, which he had learned at Tübingen. Luther immediately volunteered to teach him the gospel of Christ if he would teach Luther Greek. The exchange was beneficial to both men. Luther's character and strong religious convictions helped determine the subsequent direction of Melanchthon's intellectual pursuits, while the latter's sharp mind and moderating personality provided a leavening influence on Luther, who held Melanchthon in high esteem throughout his life. Some of the value of this partnership can be seen in Melanchthon's *Loci communes* (Commonplaces), published in 1521, the first and most important systematization of Luther's doctrines. It was immediately recognized as a masterful exposition, which Luther himself pronounced worthy of immortality. This work is only one of the countless services Melanchthon rendered to the evangelical cause.

Revolt of the Imperial Knights Despite Melanchthon's conciliatory nature, neither he nor Luther himself could prevent the further alienations and upheavals that occurred in rapid succession after Worms. Hoping to regain some of their lost prestige and political influence, and stimulated by Luther's *Address to the German Nobility,* many of the imperial knights took seriously his exhortation to seize church lands. Under the leadership of Ulrich von Hutten and Franz von Sickingen, some of the knights joined to despoil the lands of the archbishop-elector of Trier. Late in the summer of 1522, Sickingen laid siege to the capital city, but he was unsuccessful in doing more than raising the ire of Trier's neighbors and allies.

The following year, the archbishop, with the Elector Palatine and the Landgrave of Hesse, retaliated in a decisive counterattack. The knights were crushed at Landstuhl, and Sickingen was killed. Hutten sought refuge in Switzerland, where he soon died. This so-called Knights' Revolt was not only a fiasco but also led to further retaliation by several of the princes, who razed twenty-three castles in Franconia alone, and brought an abrupt end to the independent role of the imperial knights in the political and religious affairs of Germany. It also raised fears in some circles that the Lutheran movement was indeed a threat to orderly government and in others the hope that Luther might be counted on to support action against social injustice.

The Peasants' Revolt and the Common Man

Even more serious in its immediate and long-range effects was the so-called Peasants' War of 1524–25. The causes of the uprisings were rooted deeply in the social and economic changes of the time. Part of the problem was a "revolt of rising expectations" as economic conditions gradually improved from the dismal depression and chaos of the late fourteenth and early fifteenth centuries. The slowness of improvement, especially in rural areas, led to frustration as people grew restless and dissatisfied. Furthermore, the decline of feudalism in some areas had placed many of the peasants under serious handicaps, and they now clamored for a return to "the good old days." In other regions, especially southwestern Germany, the worst features of feudalism still prevailed as the powerful local lords and prelates ruled and abused the peasants ruthlessly.

The oppressed farmers of the southwest reacted by demanding use of pasturelands and the common forests, and called for the restoration of ancient Germanic laws and customs. Some of their grievances were put into writing, as in the Twelve Articles of the Swabian peasants. These demanded the right to choose their own pastors; protested the paying of so many tithes, taxes, dues, rents, and forced labor; denounced serfdom and demanded the right to fish, hunt, and cut wood in the common forests; protested the making of new laws; and censured the landowners' seizure of common lands.

More than rural peasants were involved in the massive upheavals of 1524–25. Written grievances from the Black Forest area described the leaders of the movement as "the poor common man (*gemeiner mann*) in town and countryside," while the margrave of Baden referred to them as a "union of the common man," meaning, of course, his restless subjects both urban and rural. In many contemporary accounts the uprising is called a "rebellion of the common man." Luther seems to have used the phrase to mean "simple," "ignorant," or often "misinformed." Regardless of how contemporaries described the participants, they saw the revolt as a more extensive social upheaval than is usually implied by the term *peasant*. So it was, for in some areas the towns were the first to raise the standard of rebellion, and in many cases the urban poorer classes made common cause with their country cousins. For that reason some modern scholars prefer to call this the Revolution of the Common Man, not just the Peasants' War.

In the towns, according to the Swiss historian Peter Blickle, the term *common man* referred to those social groups that were ineligible to serve in the municipal assembly, that is, those underprivileged people without citizenship. He cites remonstrances of the imperial cities demanding more rights, or "rebellion and resistance would grow between magistrates and the common man in the towns." The term also included rural people of the lower classes other than peasant farmers. The key characteristic of this definition of the common man was the lack of political authority. He was "the peasant, the miner, the

The Peasant Bundschuh. *Displaying their familiar banner bearing a peasant shoe with a long lace, a group of peasants menacingly surround a dismounted knight. The* Bundschuh *organization typified the social unrest in rural Germany.*

resident of a territorial town; in the imperial cities he was the townsman ineligible for public office." Thomas Brady notes that the term was used by the
lords for those who should only be subjects. "The Common Man," he writes,
"was not necessarily poor or grievously oppressed—the concept excluded beggars, criminals, and gypsies and other marginal folk—but he had no possibility
for political life except through common action with others of his kind." That
is what happened in 1524–25.

Into this combustible mixture, the torch of religion was thrust. Luther's
open defiance of church authorities gave the people courage and a precedent—
and, they thought, a leader. But the impassioned oratory and violent writings
of Luther's former follower, Thomas Müntzer (1489–1525), was the direct
spark that ignited the peasant protests in Thuringia and Saxony, and fanned
them into a blaze of fanaticism and violence engulfing a large part of Germany.
Believing that the Second Coming of Christ was at hand and that the wicked
must be cut down to prepare the way of the Lord, Müntzer became the passionate leader of the social revolution, making it at the same time an apocalyptic religious conflict intent on wiping out all the enemies of God. Boldly
defying the princes to their faces, Müntzer stirred the commoners to a frenzy
with his fanatical speeches. "Strike while the iron is hot!" he ranted; "Don't
let your swords cool off! Don't allow them to become feeble!" The peasants
were easily excited and soon they were pillaging churches, defying laws, and
repudiating authority.

War first broke out in the Black Forest area of southwestern Germany in
June 1524, where the nobles' despotic rule was particularly galling, and from
there it spread gradually northward and eastward into the rest of Swabia, the
Rhineland, Franconia, Würtemberg, and Thuringia. As the uprisings spread,
they became intensified with religious emotions. Lands were seized and many
monasteries and churches were looted. In a few cases the people demanded
common ownership of all property. Many of the towns cooperated, forcing
some of the nobles to acknowledge the people's grievances and to promise
them reforms.

Luther's reaction to this uniting of social revolution and religious revolt
was consistent with his previous position. He himself had charged the princes
with ungodliness, corruption, and cruelty, and had called on them to end their
oppression of the peasants. But he never advocated nor condoned social revolution. The peasants misunderstood him completely if they thought he would
lead, or even sympathize with, their more violent actions. He had repeatedly
reaffirmed only his theological, not social or political, leadership. He was not
ready for an all-out reform of both church and society at large, even if it was
accomplished according to the word of God (as Müntzer avowed it would be).
Fear of insurrection haunted him incessantly. So alarmed was Luther by the
peasant uprisings that he issued an unfortunate pamphlet entitled *Against the
Thievish, Murderous Hordes of Peasants,* in which he denounced the rebels in
most vitriolic language, encouraging the princes to strike them down without
mercy. "For one cannot argue reasonably with a rebel," he charged, "But one
must answer him with the fist so that blood flows from his nose."

The princes, however, needed no justification from Luther to put down the rebellion ruthlessly. Weakened by internal dissension and lack of leadership, the peasants were no match for the power of princes like the duke of Saxony, the landgrave of Hesse, the bishop of Wurzburg, and the nobles of the Swabian League. At Frankenhausen, near Luther's birthplace, the revolution came to a bloody end in May 1525. A chronicler described the scene in this way:

> Then they advanced towards the peasants and began to fire. The poor people just stood there and sang, "Now we pray the Holy Spirit," as if they were insane. They neither resisted nor fled. Many comforted themselves in Thomas's [Müntzer's] great promise that God would send help from heaven, since Thomas had said he would catch all bullets in his coat sleeves.

The massacre was complete. Müntzer escaped from the carnage but was soon captured and executed. Reprisals and vengeance bathed the countryside in blood following the collapse of the revolution.

Although Luther remained constant in his social views, always accepting the hierarchical order of society, including the rule of the nobility, the peasants believed he had betrayed them. Many denounced him as a traitor. Yet Luther's own charisma and the persuasiveness of his message continued to attract tens of thousands, particularly where no uprisings had occurred or where they had not been repulsed so severely. Nevertheless, after 1525 the evangelical movement came to depend more and more upon the support of the princes and the municipal magistrates, and it was they who carried the Reformation to its logical, political conclusion.

Lutheran Doctrines

The essence of Luther's religious philosophy was a different conception of the relationship between God and humankind. From his view of salvation based on faith grew most of the other doctrines of Protestantism. In his treatise *On the Freedom of a Christian* Luther stated succinctly:

> The Word of God cannot be received and cherished by any works whatever but only by faith. Therefore it is clear that, as the soul needs only the Word of God for its life and righteousness, so it is justified by faith alone and not any works; for if it could be justified by anything else, it would not need the Word, and consequently it would not need faith.

Good works played an important role in Luther's theology, but always as the result of faith, not the cause of it. "Good works do not make a good man," reasoned Luther in an oft-quoted phrase, "but a good man does good works; evil works do not make a wicked man, but a wicked man does evil works." And again: "Our faith in Christ does not free us from works but from false opinions concerning works, that is, from the foolish presumption that justification is acquired by works." In other words, faith frees people by separating works from salvation. Once freed from the continual concern over salvation, true believers could devote their life and thought to doing good out of gratitude to God and not because it would contribute to their salvation. Only then are works of any value.

Thus, faith was not the end of Luther's theology, but its beginning. From faith grows love, which is the active expression of the true Christian's faith. "We conclude, therefore, that a Christian lives not in himself, but in Christ and in his neighbor. Otherwise he is not a Christian. He lives in Christ through faith, in his neighbor through love." God had shown the way by displaying the supreme act of love—the incarnation, life, and resurrection of the Savior. In this regard, Luther strongly emphasized the difference between the Law and the Gospel, a distinction, he maintained, that was the essence of true Christian understanding. Both are God's word, the Law being the Ten Commandments and the Gospel being the "good news" of Christ's atonement. By the Law, God "commands us what we are to do and not to do, and demands our obedience." The Gospel, on the other hand, "does not demand our works or command us to do anything, but simply receive the offered grace."

What, then, is the relationship between salvation and the sacraments? To Luther, a sacrament is not a merit-earning work, but "a mystery, or secret thing, which is set forth in words and is received by the faith of the heart." It is a divinely instituted sign that carries with it the promise of forgiveness of sins—hence, salvation. By this definition Luther held that there were only two sacraments in the church of God: baptism and the Lord's Supper (also called the Sacrament of the Altar, or Communion). Baptism is a sign by which a man born in sin "is there drowned, and a new man, born in grace, comes forth and rises." In his *Small Catechism,* Luther defined the Sacrament of the Altar as "The true body and blood of our Lord Jesus Christ under the bread and wine, for us Christians to eat and to drink." Its purpose, he continued, "is shown us by these words, 'Given and shed for you for the remission of sins'; namely, that in the Sacrament forgiveness of sins, life, and salvation are given us through these words. For where there is forgiveness of sins, there is also life and salvation." Luther denied the Catholic doctrine of transubstantiation, by which, upon elevating the host, the substance of the bread and wine is changed into the body and blood of Christ, leaving the outward appearances (species, or accidents) of bread and wine. But at the same time, he insisted on the real presence of Christ's body and blood in the visible elements, as a continuing testament from God to humankind.

Church and State

In Luther's view, the hierarchical priesthood was not merely unessential; it was prejudicial. What a person needs, he affirmed, is not a priest but a belief. Any true believer is his own priest. Nevertheless, even though this view suggests the invisible nature of the true church (the *Corpus Christi*), Luther came to rely more and more on the educational, disciplinary, and brotherhood features of the visible, organized territorial church (the *Corpus Christianum*). Although he was never fully satisfied with the resulting institutionalization of the prince-controlled churches of Germany, still he left almost all organizational matters to the discretion of the rulers themselves. The result was that the Lutheran churches of Germany, and later of Scandinavia, became state churches in a very literal sense.

Luther's recognition of the authority of the territorial princes in organizational matters was predicated on the hope that once the churches were organized and functioning, they would become largely self-operating, and the exercise of the "priesthood of all believers" would follow the path of divine will. He allowed the congregations the right to call pastors and teachers, and also to raise and administer ecclesiastical revenues. He also hoped the functions of the church would be carried out jointly by the magistrates and the pastors.

But Luther found that even true believers had to be governed, in religious as well as political matters, and to maintain peace and order the arm of the secular state had to be used. Besides, the role of the territorial princes in religious as well as secular matters had become so strong by the sixteenth century, it was impossible for Luther to prevent their active supervision of affairs even if he had wanted to. Beginning in 1527 in Electoral Saxony, magistrates appointed by the rulers for the purpose of coordinating and regulating the form of worship began "visiting" the religious congregations. With the visitation also came the elucidation of laws and the establishment of consistorial courts, which tried all manner of cases, from adultery to theological unorthodoxy. "Our princes do not impose the faith and the Gospel," Luther insisted in his doctrine of the Two Kingdoms, "but they repress outward abominations." In this way he distinguished between the functions of religious and civil authority, and between freedom of conscience, which he allowed, and freedom of worship, which he did not. There was no equivocation in Luther's views on the relationship between church and state. Each, under God, has its legitimate sphere of operation. The church is necessary to comfort and strengthen believers; the state is to protect, supervise, and discipline them.

As far as authority was concerned, Luther found it in Scripture. He considered the Bible to be the "written record of the revelation of God in Christ," containing the central message of Christ's redemption of the world through his own sacrifice. It also contained the authority to speak in God's name. Luther rejected the Catholic view that the Scriptures were supplemented by the traditions and decrees of the church. The Bible itself is sufficient. "All that God has done, particularly all that pertains to our salvation, is clearly put down and noted in Scripture, so that no man may excuse himself." Religious authority, he insisted, comes from the word of God as revealed in the Bible, not from an institutionalized church.

The Consolidation and Growth of Lutheranism

Luther began reforming the religious service in Wittenberg even before his confrontation with the emperor. In place of the Mass, he instituted a daily worship service consisting of Bible reading and preaching. On Sundays, Communion

Katharina von Bora. *Luther's wife Katie, versatile in her talents and genial of nature, became the model Protestant pastor's spouse. This painting by Lucas Cranach the Elder captures the character of this woman of wit and spirit.*

was celebrated, along with a sermon and some of the liturgy of the medieval church, including the Gloria, Halleluja, and the Nicene Creed. German was used in both the liturgy and the singing of hymns, which became a part of the religious service. In this Luther contributed not only his support and encouragement but also his talent by composing several hymns himself, the best known being "A Mighty Fortress Is Our God." During the 1520s he also wrote a number of manuals for instructing the youth and new converts, which were later published as the *Small Catechism*. His so-called *Large Catechism*, a manual for pastors and teachers, contained a rather detailed exposition of biblical texts, and exhortations on the confession, as well as the Ten Commandments, the Apostles' Creed, the Lord's Prayer, and other prayers that were based on earlier catechisms.

In the meantime, Luther's sermons decrying clerical celibacy and encouraging his associates to marry, resulted eventually in his own somewhat reluctant marriage to Katharina von Bora (1499–1550), a former nun, in June 1525. She was twenty-six and he was forty-one. His quip, that he had decided to marry to spite his enemies, may have been partly true, because Luther was less than enthusiastic about entering into matrimony himself. It proved to be a happy and fruitful union, however, and did much to hallow the institution of marriage and the home in Protestant lands. "My wife," Luther wrote, "is compliant, accommodating, and affable beyond anything I dared to hope."

Katie, as Luther affectionately called her, was not only a dutiful wife and companion but also managed their household affairs with efficiency and some degree of shrewdness; tended their orchard and garden as well as managing their farm in Zulsdorf; provided a welcomed gathering place for scores of relatives, friends, colleagues, and students; gave birth to six children (three girls and three boys); and brightened Luther's life with her cheerful disposition. She was also his favorite brewer, and during his frequent illnesses she was not only his helpmate but also his doctor. He acknowledged his love for her and affirmed that "the union of man and woman is a great thing, taking place, as it does, by the law of nature as well as by divine order and arrangement." Elsewhere he declared, "Nothing is more sweet than harmony in marriage—and nothing more distressing than dissension."

Evangelical Education

Closely related to Luther's feelings about marriage and family life was his attitude toward education, which he believed should be available to all children and provided by the state. For this reason he insisted that the cities and villages of Saxony establish schools at public expense. Not all of the magistrates complied with Luther's wishes, but many of them did. Educational reform and the stimulation of schools in Germany were mostly the work of two of Luther's associates, Johannes Bugenhagen (1485–1558) and Philipp Melanchthon (1497–1560).

Melanchthon was a brilliant humanist and teacher. As early as 1528, he drew up a plan for more effective teaching in the Saxon schools by a gradation of instruction according to age or capabilities. He also stressed curriculum reform that would provide more intensive attention to fewer subjects. He likewise rendered service to education in Germany by writing several textbooks, including a very popular Latin grammar. Under his influence many former monasteries were transformed into grammar schools, and he promoted the establishment of schools of higher learning at Eisleben, Nuremberg, and Magdeburg. His advice on educational matters was sought by many towns. It is small wonder that Melanchthon should be acclaimed the *Praeceptor Germaniae* (Teacher of Germany).

Luther and some of the other reformers hoped that through education (including that of girls) a society of pious people would emerge capable of reading the Bible and understanding its precepts. Several of the Protestant princes, such as Philip of Hesse and Ulrich of Württemberg, actively promoted education in their territories by establishing schools and introducing ordinances to promote and regulate primary education. This joint endeavor to educate the young in the essentials of evangelical Christianity as well as civic duty was pursued systematically and vigorously.

Nevertheless, according to the American scholar Gerald Strauss, these efforts were largely unsuccessful. Strauss argues that despite the employment of the most up-to-date (sixteenth-century) teaching techniques, the vast majority of the population, even in those regions receiving the most intensive indoctrination, subsequently displayed both widespread ignorance of the rudiments of

Philipp Melanchthon.
A striking woodcut done by Albrecht Dürer in 1526. It depicts a slightly wild-eyed Melanchthon, rather un-characteristic of this moderate humanist and disciple of Luther.

Protestant religion and a remarkable apathy toward it. He attributes this failure largely to the continuing vitality of the popular religion of the common people, rendering them rather impervious to any religious indoctrination coming from outside their circle. In other words, the moral transformation of society that was to be the end result of Lutheran education did not take place. Other scholars have taken issue with Strauss, some arguing that he failed to recognize that Luther's aim was not to transform society but to correct theological errors. Luther, they claim, was largely indifferent to the way the world received the evangelical gospel. He was essentially a theologian interested only in proclaiming the Truth and correcting the errors that had been promulgated by the Catholic church.

This may have been Luther's position in the beginning, but with each stage of the burgeoning Reformation he took a more active role in order to steer events toward a more favorable resolution—that being to upgrade Christian life by understanding God and promoting His divine will. That is why Luther wrote his catechisms, and the reason he supported the rulers' endeavors to regulate worship within their domains by establishing schools. Whether those endeavors failed or not is still a matter for debate. Luther seemed to be of the opinion that the schools were successful, when in 1530 he wrote, "Our young people, girls as well as boys, are now so well taught in catechism and Scripture that my heart grows warm as I observe children praying more devoutly and speaking more eloquently of God and Christ than, in the old days, all the learned monks and doctors." That the promulgation of the evangelical gospel. did not result in a society of peace and virtue, free from the ravages of war and oppression, is not necessarily an indictment either of the message or of the proselyting and catechizing methods.

The implementation of Luther's doctrines into a political and social world did not come easily, yet it did come. Whatever Protestantism's original attraction as spiritual enlightenment or religious liberation, it soon solidified into a politically definable church. Realizing that he had no way of institutionalizing his precepts, Luther depended heavily on the functioning instruments of the state, and on the princely authority of the secular rulers, first in Electoral Saxony and later in other states where Lutheranism took root. Frederick the Wise died in 1525 and was succeeded as elector by his brother, John (1525–32), who immediately and wholeheartedly accepted Lutheranism. The first non-Saxon ruler to join the evangelical revolt was Albrecht of Hohenzollern, the grand master of the Teutonic Knights, who ruled the territory of East Prussia. His lead was soon followed by Philip, landgrave of Hesse. Within the next three years several more of the princes joined the evangelical movement, including the margrave of Ansbach, the dukes of Lüneburg and Schleswig, the prince of Anhalt, and the count of Mansfeld. At the same time, many of the imperial cities, led by Nuremberg, Strasbourg, Ulm, Constance, Erfurt, and Magdeburg, overturned their ecclesiastical structures and made common cause with the Reformation.

Reformation in the Cities   The evangelical movement set in motion by Luther had some of its earliest and most enthusiastic followers in the cities and towns. Notable is the response of the imperial cities, even though their joining the movement would likely mean alienation from the emperor. Bernd Moeller argued in his seminal book, *Reichsstadt und Reformation*, that the imperial cities found in Lutheranism a religious belief compatible with their "organic" view of the urban community, which held salvation to be a collective matter, just like the community, and that religious reform in the long run would serve to promote unity, stability, and peace. According to Moeller, the dynamic union of ruling authority and alert citizenry provided evangelical preachers with a ready audience. In turn the Reformation gave those cities a renewed awareness of their communal foundations and stimulated a vital participation of the citizens in communal affairs. Furthermore, Luther's principle of "the priesthood of all believers," that is, the idea that every person, or organization, has a divine calling which is equal in the sight of God to the calling of the highest prince or prelate, justified the civil magistery in its supervision of religious matters.

Some recent studies have taken issue with the view that urban religion had a peculiarly communal character, or that fundamental differences existed between cities and country, showing that the phenomenon of the urban Reformation was more complex and varied than Moeller suspected. The reasons for towns turning to the Reformation are as numerous as the towns themselves. In many cases the humanists were the first to pick up on Luther's reform ideas and combine these with insights from classical writers to propose changes in church practices. Often the initial impulse came from the clergy, especially the most educated urban clergy—not as a group but as individual preachers moved by Luther's theological message. Luther's teachings were being propagated by evangelical preachers in imperial Nuremberg under the very noses of the magistrates, and soon the magistrates themselves were among the converts. Many lawyers, city officials, lay leaders in town councils, and even burgermeisters, inclined to the new ideas and influenced the course of events in the 1520s. Among larger groups we find many merchants supporting the Reformation, and always a large number of artisans and shopkeepers. In south Germany the guilds were active in exerting pressure for religious reforms.

Such expressions of collective support for the Reformation were not simply echoes of Luther's evangelism, however. They were inextricably combined with myriad political, social, and economic grievances. These grievances varied from city to city but always figured high among the ingredients of protest. The variety of responses to the established church increased as the Reformation spread. Although Luther lit the match that ignited the German tinderbox, he could not control the direction or intensity of the ensuing blaze. Each reformer gave a distinct emphasis and personality to the movement, and the addition of diverse social, economic, and political causes eventually altered the thrust of Luther's initial protest. In the south-German cities this was particularly noticeable as the magistrates gradually brought religious practice under their own control in what Thomas Brady has called a "domestication" of urban religion.

There were some Catholic holdouts, however. In Nuremberg, for example, the convent of the Sisters of Saint Clare (the Klarakloster), refused to renounce their cloistered life and beliefs and become Protestant. The abbess was Barbara Pirckheimer (known as "Caritas," or Charity), friend of several prominent humanists including Conrad Celtis; she was also sister of the humanist and legal advisor to the Nuremberg city council, Willibald Pirckheimer. A learned woman in her own right, she steadfastly defended the convent against all the Reformation's attempts to close it. Despite the harassment of Lutheran sympathizers, Protestant preachers, and the city council itself, Caritas Pirckheimer and her nuns remained faithful to their vows and to the Roman church until her death in 1532.

The Printing Press and Spread of the Reformation

The transmission of Lutheran ideas was particularly rapid after 1520 as printing presses all over Europe flooded the continent with writings of the reformers. Most of these were short pamphlets and broadsides containing sermons, lectures, debates, and a variety of polemical tracts, as well as more carefully argued doctrinal treatises. Sometimes the writings were crude, even savagely obscene, as mounting passions pushed partisan disagreements into confrontation and conflict. The propaganda value of Protestant pamphleteers quickly exploited the popular press to

Luther's opponents: A Lutheran cartoon of 1521. *From left to right: Dr. Murner, the Alsace cat; Dr. Emser, the Leipzig goat; Pope Leo X, the Antichrist lion; Dr. Eck, the Ingolstadt pig; Dr. Lemp, the Tübingen dog.*

the fullest, vigorously attacking Catholic doctrines, practices, and people. Decades of pent-up anticlericalism found a cathartic release in printed attacks on the monks and bishops. Even the pope was not spared from these virulent assaults. Catholics answered in kind.

Much of the output of the popular press contained explicit illustrations and captions so the message would not be lost on those who could not read. Illustrated broadsheets were a particularly effective form of mass communication. Luther and the Protestant reformers exploited this means of popular propaganda to the limit. The publicists made their messages even more effective by basing their pictures on preexisting imagery that everyone understood. Thus images of monsters and misbirths represented to the common people omens that kindled many fears and apprehensions that could be generously exploited. The pamphlet entitled *The Papal Ass of Rome and the Monk Calf of Freyberg*, for example, composed by Luther and Melanchthon in 1523 and designed in the Lucas Cranach workshop, contained woodcuts depicting two monstrosities: the Papal Ass, an odd-looking dragon of sorts, part animal and part human, representing the corrupted papacy; and the Monk-Calf, an exaggerated image of a freak calf born near Freiberg with a large flap of skin on its back and a bald spot on its head, resembling the cowl and tonsure of a monk. By expressing his message in terms of these portents, Luther sought to give divine sanction to his theology. Such imagery was widely used by both Protestants and Catholics for character assassination as well as to impress their respective ideologies upon a broad popular audience.

More temperate doctrinal treatises introduced and elaborated the new teachings of the reformers, while apologists of the orthodox faith defended the sacraments of the church and the supremacy of the pope. Some treatises addressed the issues of secular authority, the responsibilities of Christians in society, and the role of marriage and family relationships. The impact of this outpouring of printed matter was immediate and profound. Through the facility of the printing press laymen not only became conversant with the religious issues that were being cast abroad, they became participants themselves in the publishing process as they took up the challenge to express their views in print.

The printed word and illustrations were not the only means of communicating ideas, however. Sermons grew in popularity as the momentum of the reform movement increased. They also reached a much larger audience. The common people came into contact with the Reformation mainly through sermons. Indeed, the pulpit had long been the primary medium of mass communication. It was where the majority of public announcements were made and where new ideas were proclaimed. Protestant preachers were especially active in this regard, both as benefice holders and as free-lance preachers. Many proclaimed the word beyond the confines of their local churches, preaching outdoors or in private homes. Wandering preachers were also familiar, moving from village to village and town to town, preaching wherever they found a receptive audience, a practice viewed with suspicion by most magistrates.

Oral dissemination of the new ideas took place on many levels, from private gossip in family circles to informal group discussions in public. The marketplace was a frequent locale for the transmission of such ideas, as were inns, taverns, and workplaces. Sometimes this communication took the form of singing ballads or hymns containing evangelical views. Popular culture as well as popular religion provided the milieu for religious innovation. Festivals were frequently the catalyst for the diffusion of Reformation ideas, especially during Carnival and other ritual celebrations.

Women and the Reformation

The part played by women in the spread of the Reformation is only beginning to receive the attention it deserves. For that reason there are still more questions than answers about this subject, but at least questions are now being asked. As a result of recent research by a number of scholars, we are beginning to discern more clearly both the influence of some women in the spread of Reformation ideas and practices, and in turn the impact of the Reformation on women generally.

Most women's first contact with the Reformation was through their husbands or fathers. Moved by what they saw and heard, some women took Luther's slogan of the priesthood of all believers literally and began to proclaim the word themselves. In the atmosphere of intellectual and religious upheaval that existed in the 1520s and 1530s, it was not unusual to see women as well as men challenging religious authorities and, inspired by the preaching of some of the more enthusiastic reformers, actively promoting the evangelical cause.

Katherine Zell (ca. 1497–1562), the zealous wife and helpmate of the Strasbourg reformer Matthias Zell, preached from the pulpit alongside her husband and devoted all her efforts to further their faith; Sibilla Eisler and Catherine Ebertz were active evangelizers, and in Zwickau, despite admonitions of the city council, several women preached in public, claiming direct illumination from God. Some educated women took up the pen to publish polemical as well as devotional works, hymns, and religious poems. The remarkable noblewoman Argula von Grumbach (ca. 1492–ca. 1563) could not remain silent and actively promoted Protestant doctrines in writing, even though it cost her husband his position. Katherine Zell, Ursula Weide, Justitia Sanger, Olympia Morata, and others also wrote in behalf of their new religion. And in Poland, Regina Filipowska helped lead her husband's tiny congregation and wrote hymns for them to sing.

However, the thought and sight of women preaching the Gospel, or even discussing religion in public, alarmed most men of the time, even those who agreed with the tenets they taught. The magistrates of many German cities, Protestant as well as Catholic, tried to prevent such behavior on the part of women, whose accepted role was to be "chaste, silent, and obedient." Women were more severely criticized when speaking or writing on matters of theology than they were when discussing piety. Since women could not receive formal theological training, the higher realms of dogma were considered to be beyond their capacity. Those who did discuss doctrinal matters claimed divine inspiration for their insights rather than theological degrees. Katherine Zell affirmed that she spoke "not according to the standards of a woman, but according to the standards of one whom God has filled with the Holy Spirit." The strength and directness of her words as well as her familiarity with Scripture are revealed in her answer to those who tried to quiet her by citing Paul's admonition to women to be silent in church. "I would remind you," she retorted, "of the word of this same apostle that in Christ there is no longer male nor female, and of the prophecy of Joel: 'I will pour forth my spirit upon all flesh and your sons and your daughters will prophesy'."

Prohibitive laws did not entirely prevent committed women from transmitting their views and feelings. The most common way to do this was in the home, where devoted adherents of the new faith took up the Protestant challenge to make the home "a seminary for the church." Married women had many opportunities to teach their children and household servants, and frequently other relatives and guests. Reciting catechisms, pronouncing prayers, and singing hymns were among the simple pedagogical methods employed by these women and accepted by sixteenth-century society. Women of higher station of course had greater influence. Elizabeth of Braunschweig, wife of Duke Erich I, for example, was the leading force in bringing that duchy into the evangelical camp despite pressures from the emperor and threats from Catholic states, and Katherine of Mecklenberg is credited with converting her husband, Duke Heinrich of Freiberg, to Lutheranism.

What impact did the Reformation have on the lives of women in general? Scholars working in this field have shown that the effect was great, not just from the new religious ideas but also from institutional and political changes that accompanied the Reformation. Alterations in the marriage institution, the allowance of divorce and clerical marriage, the closing of the convents and secularization of public welfare and charitable institutions, all had an impact on thousands of women. Very important was the increased emphasis given by the reformers to the value and sanctity of marriage, elevating it to a "cooperative relationship of mutual responsibility." Luther was especially ebullient about marriage, calling it a divinely appointed union and blessed estate. The highest calling of women, he claimed, was marriage and motherhood. Man and wife, he taught, "should live together, be fruitful, beget children, and nourish and rear them to the glory of God." Celibacy, on the other hand, he condemned as a foil of Satan. "If the pope had brought about no other calamity than this prohibition of marriage, it would be sufficient to stamp him as the Anti-Christ, who is rightly called the man of sin and the son of perdition." However, regardless of how exalted the state of matrimony, Luther insisted upon the subordinate status of women in that union. The supreme duty of wives was to obey their husbands and bear children!

With the closing of the convents in Protestant states, the number of marriageable women increased, and so did their dilemmas, since not all of them had the opportunity to marry. There was no structure in the evangelical churches comparable to the convents, and no feminine imagery to take the place of the Virgin Mary. Many of the ' liberated" girls—and especially the older women—were without security, or sometimes even a livelihood, in an increasingly hostile environment. Some of those who did not marry returned to their paternal homes, but many had to face the hazards of life without protection or patronage. Some gained employment in charitable institutions, hospitals, orphanages, and cure houses, while others became domestic servants or even day laborers. Under these circumstances it is not strange that illegal prostitution increased, since the public brothels were also closed. The allowing of divorce in Protestant societies probably added to the social disorder, although remarriage was also condoned.

Married women were not only involved in the economic activities of their husbands, they usually shared their religious beliefs as well, rejoicing and suffering with them according to the demands of the time. This frequently meant confiscation or other loss of possessions, exile, hiding, or even death. Wives of successful reformers, that is, those whose territories adopted their form of religion, were more fortunate but not without serious challenges and frustrations as their homes were opened to students (as in Katie Luther's case) or religious refugees, and as they were called upon to provide all sorts of provisions and services. At all times, of course, these women were expected to be models of "wifely obedience and Christian charity," caring for children and managing a household often handicapped by serious economic strictures.

The Habsburg-Valois Wars

As the Lutheran Reformation was sinking its roots into German society, international tensions had escalated into open war. The growing rivalry between Charles V and Francis I drew most of Europe into conflict. These so-called

Habsburg-Valois wars, continuations of the Italian wars begun in 1494, were extremely costly and disruptive in the areas of combat (southern France, the Netherlands, the Rhineland, northern Spain, and Italy); they were also decisive in preventing the emperor from following the policy against Lutheranism that he had proclaimed in the Edict of Worms. Hostilities between the two rulers were deepseated. In addition to the long-standing rivalries over the Burgundian inheritance, the duchy of Milan and control of Italy, and the possession of Navarre, there was the more recent bitterness left by the imperial election of 1519. There was also the mutual suspicion resulting from geography: France cut the Habsburg realms in two, while Francis feared encirclement by the emperor. To some degree there was also an emotional involvement caused by the manifestations of embryonic modern nationalism, mixed with the much stronger drive of feudal family dynasticism.

The first of these Habsburg-Valois wars, from 1521 to 1525, was fought mostly in northern Italy, and ended in a decisive victory for the emperor at the battle of Pavia. The encounter was a dramatic and glorious one for the young Charles V because it resulted in the capture of the French king. Taken to Spain, Francis was required to sign the Treaty of Madrid, by which he renounced all rights and claims to Milan, Naples, and Genoa, ceded the duchy of Burgundy to Charles, and agreed to restore all of the possessions of the duke of Bourbon (who had repudiated his allegiance to the French crown and fought on the side of the emperor). Released after signing the treaty, Francis immediately repudiated the entire agreement on the grounds that it was an illegal transaction forced upon him while a prisoner.

Pope Clement VII (1523–34), alarmed by the imperial victory, and Henry VIII, trying to avoid becoming a mere pawn in the emperor's military policy,

The battle of Pavia, *where, according to Francis I's report to his mother, "All is lost save honor." A Flemish tapestry made from a cartoon by B. van Orley depicts the defeat and capture of the French king.*

joined Francis in the League of Cognac to reopen the struggle the following year. Milan, Venice, and Florence joined in. This time the result, although not so glorious for Charles, was equally disastrous for Francis. For the pope it was catastrophic. In April 1527 the bulk of the Spanish-imperial army in Italy mutinied and put Rome to the worst sack since the days of the Visigoths and Vandals. Clement VII sued for peace, and two years later the French king joined in a general settlement. The Peace of Cambrai (sometimes called the Ladies' Peace because its prime negotiators were Francis's mother, Louise of Savoy, who was regent in France during her son's campaigns, and Margaret of Austria, Charles's aunt and regent of the Netherlands) was a restatement of the terms of Madrid except that Charles withdrew his demand for Burgundy.

At the imperial Diet of Speyer, in 1529, the emperor's representatives tried once more to unify the vulnerable empire against the continuing onslaught of the Turks, and gain support for the war against Francis I. To do this, they demanded the religious submission of all the princes and ordered them to carry out the Edict of Worms. Instead of obtaining unity, however, the emperor reaped rebellion. Six of the rulers who had by that time embraced Lutheranism (Elector John of Saxony, Landgrave Philip of Hesse, Margrave Georg of Brandenburg, Dukes Ernst and Franz of Brunswick-Lüneberg, and Prince Wolfgang of Anhalt), along with fourteen of the imperial cities, defied the emperor by drawing up a written "protestation" against the orders of the Diet of Speyer and affirming their refusal to compromise their religious beliefs. From this protest came the term *Protestant*, in reference to the evangelical movement.

A year later the emperor himself presided at the Diet of Augsburg, where he hoped to heal the German schism. Flushed with victory in Italy, where at Bologna he had finally received the imperial crown from the hands of the pope (eleven years after his election), Charles's hopes ran high for a workable solution to the dangerous situation. He was soon to be disappointed. To the diet came the leading theologians of Lutheranism (except Luther himself, who was still under imperial ban) to present a formal statement of their theological views and those of the Lutheran princes. This Augsburg Confession, written mostly by Philipp Melanchthon, was conciliatory and pacific, attempting to mollify the emperor while defining and maintaining certain crucial doctrinal principles. Rather than healing the breach, the statement ensured its continuation. Melanchthon and his colleagues genuinely sought reconciliation but only under specific conditions, which the papal representative, Cardinal Campeggio, was unwilling to grant. Papal supremacy, he declared, could not be compromised, and no deviation from the accepted dogmas and practices of the Mass, the priesthood, or merit and works would be countenanced. The Augsburg Confession became the manifesto of the religious schism.

The Schmalkaldic League

In February 1531, fearful that the emperor would use force against them, eight of the Lutheran princes and eleven imperial cities met at the town of Schmalkalden, between Saxony and Hesse, to draw up an alliance for their mutual protection. It read, "Now we, solely for the sake of our own defence and deliverance, which both by human and divine right is permitted to every one, have agreed that whenever any one of us is attacked on account of the Word of God and the doctrine of the Gospel . . . all the others shall immediately come to his assistance as best they can and help to deliver him." The event was unparalleled; a large segment of the Empire had in effect not only declared its independence from Rome but had openly renounced its full allegiance to the emperor.

The Schmalkaldic League was saved an immediate test of strength by the menacing reappearance of the Turks, who under the aggressive leadership of Suleiman the Magnificent (1520–66), were once more nearing the gates of Vienna. Charles had little time to weigh alternatives. Early in 1532 he made a truce with the Protestants at Nuremberg, in return for their military assistance, and rushed to relieve Vienna. The Lutheran princes provided men and money, and Charles kept his word to allow them religious toleration until their differences could be settled at a general council. The Ottoman forces withdrew to their Balkan citadels at the emperor's approach, but Charles had no sooner reached Vienna than he received news of a combined Turkish, Arab, and Barbary attack on the Mediterranean coasts of Italy and Spain. For the next three years he waged war in the Mediterranean. At the height of his short-lived success there—the brilliant capture of Tunis in 1535—he learned that Francis I had signed an alliance with the Turks and intended to strike at his back while he was engaged in the Mediterranean.

The third Habsburg-Valois war was reopened by the French king when the Sforza dynasty in Milan came to an end with the death of Duke Francesco in November 1535. With lustful eyes on Milan, Francis marched across the Alps into neighboring Savoy (to which he laid claim through his mother), occupying almost the whole of the duchy within a few weeks. Charles counterattacked into French Provence and Languedoc in order to flank his enemy, after forcing the pope's reluctant support. At the same time Charles ordered a simultaneous attack on the French frontier in the north. Neither offensive achieved its goal, and the war dragged on month after month, with neither side able to gain a decisive victory. The stand-off was finally recognized and a new peace settlement reached at Nice in 1538. Yet Charles probably knew now that a permanent peace with Francis I was impossible, that this would be another truce to be broken as soon as The Most Christian King had caught his breath. While it lasted, however, the emperor could turn again to the threat of the Turks and to the unsolved problems of Germany.

The Schmalkaldic Wars and the Peace of Augsburg

Despite his disillusionment over relations with France, Charles still seemed confident that religious peace could be restored to the Empire and the widening schism healed. He had exerted increasing pressure on Pope Clement VII to summon a general council for that purpose, and now he continued to urge Pope Paul III (1534–49), the successor to the last Medici pope, to respond to Protestant willingness to discuss their differences. Unlearned in theological subtleties, the emperor was hopeful that if the leaders of the two sides could sit down together, they would be able to resolve their differences.

During 1540 and 1541 it seemed as though his hopes might be realized. A series of disputations, or colloquies, among the leading Protestant and Catholic theologians were held at Speyer, Hagenau, Worms, Regensburg, and Leipzig. At the Regensburg (Ratisbon) disputation, even the emperor was present and rejoiced at the early progress made toward mutual understanding and indications of unity. Compromise agreements were reached on some fundamental issues, yet in spite of reciprocal concessions, it soon became obvious that there remained a wide area of disagreement in which no compromise was possible. Besides, both sides had already conceded far more than either Luther or the pope was likely to accept.

Disillusioned by the failure of the colloquies, the emperor reluctantly resolved on war, but again a war not entirely of his own choosing. The Turkish fleet, led by the Barbary pirate, Khair ad-Din Barbarossa, in conjunction with French naval units, was pillaging along the Mediterranean coast when Francis launched an attack against the Low Countries and began preparations for an invasion of Milan. At the same time Suleiman resumed his conquests in Hungary and the Danube valley. Ignoring the Mediterranean threat and leaving the defense of Austria to his brother Ferdinand, the emperor concluded a new alliance with Henry VIII in 1543 and began to clear a widening path into western Germany. On this, his third and last campaign in Germany, Charles struck first at the duchy of Cleves, a recently acquired ally of France, and then, with the aid of English diversion in the west, he turned on Francis, forcing him to terms at the peace of Crépy (September 1544).

Then, with plodding tenacity, Charles returned to the problem of Germany. His confidence that the schism could be healed by a general council of the church was soon dashed to pieces. The Lutheran representatives who attended the opening session of the Council of Trent in 1545 were not in a mood for compromise, and Pope Paul had convinced the assembled bishops that heretics should be crushed. The chasm between the old church and the new church widened.

In February 1546 Martin Luther died, and with him went one of the strongest voices for peace among the Protestants. He had greatly feared a religious war in Germany; now it would come. The emperor had finally decided to solve the religious problem by force of arms. In July he placed Landgrave Philip of Hesse and Elector John Frederick of Saxony under imperial ban, then gave the electoral title to Maurice, duke of Albertine Saxony, and prepared to move against the Schmalkaldic League. What was at first a very modest military force grew to be a sizeable imperial army, composed of German, Dutch, Spanish, papal, and Italian troops, with one contingent of Hungarian infantry. Only skirmishes took place in the fall and winter, but in the spring of 1547 both sides girded for battle. It came at Mühlberg on the Elbe River in Saxony, in the early hours of April 24. When the day was over, the emperor was victorious—and exultant, because the victory was not only decisive, it was won with a minimal loss of life. John Frederick was taken prisoner and forced to surrender his lands as well as his title. Philip of Hesse had decided not to fight, but he was imprisoned anyway. Mühlberg marked the zenith of Charles V's political and military career.

Charles V at the Battle of Mühlberg. *This Titian canvas shows the emperor at the zenith of his power, victorious over the army of the Schmalkaldic League.*

Charles then turned his attention to the religious issue. At the conclusion of the Diet of Augsburg, which had been in session from September 1547 until May 1548, he had drawn up and issued a document known as the *Augsburg Interim*. Its purpose was to establish an interim religious policy for Germany until such time as a general council could resolve the entire religious problem. The *Interim* was essentially a restatement of Catholic doctrines with some rather innocuous concessions to the Protestants. Charles naïvely thought it would be accepted by all parties. In fact, hardly anyone was satisfied. Formal acceptance was given by the princes at Augsburg, but few of them intended to be bound by it. Clergymen on both sides denounced both the document and the emperor. Lutherans in Saxony were especially uncooperative and forced Maurice to agree to further concessions. Accordingly, Melanchthon and Julius Pflug, bishop of Naumburg, worked out a compromise known as the *Leipzig Interim,* which was only slightly more acceptable to the Protestants and was rejected outright by the Catholics. Melanchthon was rebuked by the hardline

Lutherans, who accused him of betraying them in order to win Catholic friends. It was the beginning of the Lutheran schism, between the Gnesio-Lutherans (who claimed to adhere unswervingly to Luther's doctrines) and the Philippists, followers of Philipp Melanchthon, who held that compromise on nonessential matters (*adiaphora*) was acceptable.

Disappointed by the failure of the *Interim,* Charles V received a further setback to his dynastic ambitions when the German electors refused to accept his proposal that the succession to the Empire should pass through his seed rather than through his brother Ferdinand's. Soon the emperor's failures swelled into massive defeat. By 1550 the Schmalkaldic League was alive again, and strengthened by the addition of the margraves of Brandenburg-Küstrin and Mecklenburg, and Duke Albrecht of Prussia. When Maurice of Saxony deserted the emperor, Charles found himself in serious trouble. Maurice had been secretly negotiating with the Protestant princes for some time, and in return for their submission to his military leadership, he agreed to desert the emperor and join the league.

Meanwhile, both Henry VIII and his lifelong rival, Francis I, had died. The new French king, Henri II, was brought into alliance with the Schmalkaldic League. Henri invaded the Empire from the west and quickly seized the vital bishoprics of Metz, Toul, and Verdun. Aware of the magnitude of this new threat, Charles turned to dislodge the French king from his strongholds. However, it was too late to salvage much from the disastrous wars. The emperor was thankful to be able to end the campaign with a negotiated peace.

The religious Peace of Augsburg (1555) marks one of the important crossroads in the history of the Reformation. By its terms, the Lutheran princes were given legal recognition and allowed to retain all of their acquisitions and conquests. Furthermore, it was stipulated that thenceforth the princes of Germany would be free to choose between Catholicism and Lutheranism as the faith for their respective states. This settlement, although recognizing for the first time the split of the church and allowing the legal operation of Lutheranism within the Empire, did not grant religious toleration or freedom. The people did not have the right to choose their religion; only the prince had this prerogative, and only a single religion was recognized within the boundaries of each state. According to Article Ten of the treaty, the prince was the head of the church, with supreme power to determine the religion of his realm and to impose it upon all of his subjects.

The Peace of Augsburg marked a step in the direction of independent and autonomous territorial states and helped ensure the continued decentralization and fragmentation of Germany. If the emperor had envisaged a unified empire, his hopes were now completely destroyed. One month later, disillusioned and exhausted, he relinquished sovereignty of the Netherlands, followed in January 1556 by renunciation of all his Spanish jurisdictions. In September he abdicated the imperial throne and retired to the Jeronimite monastery of Yuste, in southwestern Spain, where he died two years later.

Suggestions for Further Reading

GENERAL: REFORMATION IN GERMANY

Two older surveys that are still very useful are Hajo Holborn, *A History of Modern Germany: The Reformation,* 2nd ed. (New York, 1967), from a Protestant point of view, and Joseph Lortz, *The Reformation in Germany,* tr. by R. Wallis, 2 vols. (New York, 1968), from the Catholic. The urban Reformation, emphasized in Bernd Moeller's *Imperial Cities and the Reformation,* tr. by H.C. Erik Midelfort and Mark U. Edwards (Philadelphia, 1972), is expanded in Steven Ozment, *The Reformation in the Cities* (New Haven, 1975). For studies of specific cities, see Kaspar von Greyerz, *The Late City Reformation in Germany: The Case of Colmar* (Wiesbaden, 1980); Harold J. Grimm, *Lazarus Spengler, a Lay Leader of the Reformation* (Columbus, 1978), about Nuremberg; and Susan C. Karant-Nunn, *Zwickau in Transition, 1500–1547: The Reformation as an Agent of Change* (Columbus, 1987). A valuable study of the Reformation and political succession is provided in Paula Sutter Fichtner, *Protestantism and Primogeniture in Early Modern Germany* (New Haven, 1989).

Specific attention to social and economic issues is given in William J. Wright, *Capitalism, the State, and the Lutheran Reformation: Sixteenth Century Hesse* (Athens, Ohio, 1988); Kaspar von Greyerz, ed., *Religion, Politics and Social Protest* (London, 1984); R. Po-chia Hsia, ed., *The German People and the Reformation* (Ithaca, 1988), containing some very valuable articles; H.H. Robinson-Hammerstein and M.W. Senger, *Reformation and Society in Germany, 1500–1530* (Dublin, 1981); Paul A. Russell, *Lay Theology in the Reformation: Popular Pamphleteers in Southwest Germany, 1521–1525* (New York, 1986); David W. Sabean, *Power in the Blood: Popular Culture and Village Discourse in Early Modern Germany* (Cambridge, England, 1984); and especially Robert W. Scribner, *For the Sake of Simple Folk: Popular Propaganda for the German Reformation* (Cambridge, England, 1981), and *Popular Culture and Popular Movements in Reformation Germany* (Ronceverte, West Virginia, 1988).

LUTHER AND THE REFORMATION

There are now several excellent single-volume studies of Luther to choose from, and Roland H. Bainton's classic *Here I Stand: A Life of Martin Luther* (1950) has been reissued several times. Of more recent works, two stand out: James M. Kittelson, *Luther the Reformer: The Story of the Man and His Career* (Minneapolis, 1986), a reliable and up-to-date biography especially written for the nonspecialist, and Heiko O. Oberman, *Luther: Man Between God and the Devil,* tr. by Eileen Walliser-Schwarzbart (New Haven, 1989), a brilliant biography by a leading Luther authority. Walther von Loewenich, *Martin Luther: The Man and His Work,* tr. by Lawrence W. Denef (Minneapolis, 1986), is a challenging work giving special attention to Luther's theological development. Bernhard Lohse, *Martin Luther: An Introduction to His Life and Work,* tr. by Robert C. Schultz (Philadelphia, 1986) is a shorter overview, presented in a topical format.

An excellent, more detailed study of Luther's early years and break with Rome is provided in Martin Brecht, *Martin Luther: His Road to Reformation, 1483–1521,* tr. by James L. Schaaf (Philadelphia, 1985). Other issues of the period prior to the Diet of Worms are examined in Marilyn J. Harran, *Luther on Conversion: The Early Years* (Ithaca, 1983), which looks at Luther's "tower experience" in light of the concept of conversion in his early thought; Scott Hendrix, *Luther and the Papacy: Stages in a Reformation Conflict* (Philadelphia, 1981), sees Luther's criticism of the papacy centered in the failure of its pastoral duty; and David C. Steinmetz, *Luther and Staupitz:*

An Essay in the Intellectual Origins of the Protestant Reformation (Durham, 1980) points up Staupitz's influence on Luther's early development. On the Diet of Worms see De Lamar Jensen, *Confrontation at Worms: Martin Luther and the Diet at Worms* (Provo, Utah, 1973).

The neglected middle years of Luther's life are brilliantly analyzed in Heinrich Bornkamm, *Luther in Mid-Career, 1521–1530* (Philadelphia, 1983), while the declining years are best studied in Mark U. Edwards, Jr., *Luther's Last Battles: Politics and Polemics, 1531–46* (Ithaca, 1983). Stimulating insights into several aspects of Luther's work are found in James Atkinson, *Martin Luther, Prophet to the Church Catholic* (Grand Rapids, 1983), portraying Luther as the prophet called to assist God in creating "a fuller and truer Catholicity"; Jan Lindhardt, *Martin Luther: Knowledge and Mediation in the Renaissance,* tr. by Fred. Cryer (Lewiston, New York, 1989), incorporating the latest research on Luther, especially from Scandinavia and continental Europe; David C. Steinmetz, *Luther in Context* (Bloomington, 1986), essays showing the contrast between Luther's theology and late medieval thought; and Eric W. Gritsch, *Martin—God's Court Jester: Luther in Retrospect* (Philadelphia, 1983).

LUTHER'S THEOLOGY

Undeterred by the current popularity of social history, theologians continue to summarize, analyze, and categorize the religious thought of Luther. In addition to the classical studies by Bornkamm, Ebeling, Pelikan, and others, much can be learned from more recent analyses, such as Alister E. McGrath, *Luther's Theology of the Cross: Martin Luther's Theological Breakthrough* (New York and Oxford, 1985); Egil Grislis, *The Theology of Martin Luther in Five Contemporary Canadian Interpretations* (Winnipeg, 1985); Johann Heinz, *Justification and Merit: Luther vs. Catholicism* (Berrien Springs, Michigan, 1984), contrasting Luther's *sola fides* with the Catholic doctrine of works and merit; Siegbert W. Becker, *The Foolishness of God: The Place of Reason in the Theology of Martin Luther* (Milwaukee, 1982), showing Luther's objections to Aristotelian ethics; Denis R. Janz, *Luther and Late Medieval Thomism: A Study in Theological Anthropology* (Waterloo, Ontario, 1984), and *Luther on Thomas Aquinas: The Angelic Doctor in the Thought of the Reformer* (Stuttgart, 1989); Franz Posset, *Luther's Catholic Christology According to His Johannine Lectures of 1527* (Milwaukee, 1988), focusing on Luther's mid-career Christology; and Robin B. Barnes, *Prophecy and Gnosis: Apocalypticism in the Wake of the Lutheran Reformation* (Stanford, 1988), which looks more closely at sixteenth-century eschatology in relation to Luther's thought. Useful also are the new printings of Paul Althaus's *The Theology of Martin Luther* (Philadelphia, 1989) and *The Ethics of Martin Luther* (Philadelphia, 1986), both translated by Robert C. Schultz.

Luther's political and social thought are emphasized in W.D.J. Cargill-Thompson, *The Political Thought of Martin Luther* (Hassocks, England, 1984); James D. Tracy, ed., *Luther and the Modern State in Germany* (Kirksville, Missouri, 1986); and Gert Haendler, *Luther on Ministerial Office and Congregational Function,* tr. by Ruth Gritsch (Philadelphia, 1981), a short book showing that Luther favored a balance between ministerial authority and congregational responsibility. Gerald Strauss caused some feathers to fly with his *Luther's House of Learning: Indoctrination of the Young in the German Reformation* (Baltimore, 1978), which argued that the Reformation failed to get through to the general populace, and that a wide chasm continued to exist between the religion of the people and the ecclesiastical establishment. Several aspects of Strauss's thesis have been questioned or strongly criticized in articles by Mark Edwards, James Kittelson, and others. The issue is largely by-passed in Marilyn J. Harran, ed., *Luther and Learning* (Cranbury, NY, 1985), a collection of essays for the 1983 Luther symposium at Wittenberg University, Ohio.

MÜNTZER AND THE PEASANTS' WAR

Much important work has been done on the peasant revolts of 1524–25 in the last ten years, both Marxist and non-Marxist. A seminal book in the latter category is Peter Blickle, *The Revolution of 1525: The German Peasants' War from a New Perspective,* tr. by Thomas A. Brady, Jr., and H.C. Erik Midelfort (Baltimore, 1981), which sees the war as a revolution of the common man. Also see Robert W. Scribner and Gerhard Benecke, eds., *The German Peasant War of 1525: New Viewpoints* (London, 1979). None of the important works of the German Max Steinmetz and others on Thomas Müntzer and the "early bourgeoisie revolution" have been translated. In English the most recent insights are Eric W. Gritsch, *Thomas Müntzer: A Tragedy of Errors* (Minneapolis, 1989); Tom Scott, *Thomas Müntzer: Theology and Revolution in the German Reformation* (New York, 1989); and Abraham Friesen, *Thomas Muentzer, a Destroyer of the Godless: The Making of a Sixteenth-Century Religious Revolutionary* (Berkeley, 1990). For Luther's role see Robert N. Crossley, *Luther and the Peasants' War: Luther's Actions and Reactions* (Jericho, New Hampshire, 1974); Hubert Kirchner, *Luther and the Peasants' War* (Philadelphia, 1972); and Harry Loewen, *Luther and the Radicals* (Waterloo, Ontario, 1974).

MELANCHTHON AND OTHER REFORMERS

Lowell C. Green, *How Melanchthon Helped Luther Discover the Gospel: The Doctrine of Justification in the Reformation* (Fallbrook, California, 1980) challenges the traditional view of Luther's "discovery" of the doctrine of justification in the period between 1513 and 1517, arguing that he arrived at it only after the influence of Melanchthon and others. Further studies of Melanchthon's thought are E.P. Meijering, *Melanchthon and Patristic Thought: The Doctrines of Christ and Grace, the Trinity and Creation* (Leiden, 1983), and Carl E. Maxcey, *Bona Opera: A Study in the Development of the Doctrine in Philip Melanchthon* (Nieuwkoop, the Netherlands, 1980). Mark U. Edwards, Jr., *Luther and the False Brethren* (Stanford, 1975) is a good starting point from which to understand the relationship between Luther and Müntzer, Karlstadt, Oecolampadius, et al. Ronald J. Sider, *Andreas Bodenstein von Karlstadt* (Leiden, 1974) is still basic on Karlstadt, but see Calvin A. Pater, *Karlstadt as the Father of the Baptist Movement: The Emergence of Lay Protestantism* (Toronto, 1984), which views Karlstadt as the precursor of the Anabaptist reformers Grebel, Manz, Hoffman, Menno Simons, and the seventeenth-century Baptists. For others, see James M. Estes, *Christian Magistrate and State Church: Reforming Career of Johannes Brenz* (Toronto, 1982); Robert Kolb, *Nikolaus von Amsdorf, 1483–1565: Popular Polemics in the Preservation of Luther's Legacy* (Nieuwkoop, the Netherlands, 1978); and Susan C. Karant-Nunn, *Luther's Pastors: The Reformation in the Ernestine Countryside* (Philadelphia, 1979), a very brief study of the village pastors in Saxony and Thuringia.

3 | THE EXPANDING REFORMATION

W HAT LUTHER STARTED, OTHER REFORMERS CONTINUED, MODIFIED, altered, and expanded. Once begun, the Reformation soon picked up momentum until most of Germany was affected one way or another. Many dissatisfied humanists, monks, and priests took up the evangelical cross and began expounding the gospel according to Luther's (or their own) interpretation. Among Luther's immediate followers, the most active were Wolfgang Capito, a learned lawyer and theologian who had been councilor to the archbishop of Mainz before becoming a Protestant preacher; Johannes Bugenhagen, a Pomeranian schoolmaster who wrote church constitutions for many of the northern German cities; Martin Bucer, a former Dominican friar who carried the Reformation westward into Strasbourg; Justus Jonas, a humanist student of Luther's at Wittenberg who later taught law and theology there and at the University of Halle; Johannes Agricola, who became court preacher in Berlin to the margrave of Brandenburg; Johannes Brenz, the Lutheran reformer of Swabia; and, of course, Philipp Melanchthon. Religious discussion and disputation became widespread, as the ideas raised by the Wittenberg reformer and others spread to neighboring states and as the printing press quickly carried their words beyond the frontiers.

Lutheranism in Scandinavia and Eastern Europe

Since the Union of Kalmar in 1397, the northern kingdoms of Denmark, Norway, and Sweden had functioned under the rule of a single elected monarch, the king of Denmark. Monarchical centralization, however, had produced neither social nor political unification of the three realms. As the independent power of the Scandinavian nobility increased, the strength of the titular ruler declined. Frequent rebellions and uprisings in the fifteenth century, and the restlessness of the landed barons, indicate that by the opening decade of the sixteenth century the union was on the verge of disintegration.

Scandinavian cultural and intellectual contacts with Renaissance Europe were relatively slight by the time of the Protestant revolt, although a "Biblical humanism" was rather widespread among the upper clergy. Even the ecclesiastical ties with Roman Christianity were lightly held in the Viking lands north of Mecklenburg and Schleswig. That is why the religious winds blowing northward from Germany in the 1520s were felt and appreciated in Scandinavia; they were meaningful and fresh. Scandinavian relations were much closer with northern Germany than with Italy, and it is not surprising that a German religious movement would find a welcome home there. Nor is it strange that the primary instrument of religious revolt in the northern lands was the high nobility and the crown itself.

At the time of Luther's break with Rome, Scandinavia was under the rule of Christian II of Denmark (1513–23), who first opened the doors of reformation by allowing Lutheran theologians to teach at the University of Copenhagen. Christian's authoritarian ways, and in particular his harassment of the nobles, eventually led to revolution. Swedish barons, led by Gustavus Vasa, whose father had been ruthlessly killed by the Danish king, raised the standard of revolt against Danish domination in 1520. Three years later, Vasa was crowned hereditary king of an independent Sweden and a new dynasty was born. Meanwhile, the revolt spread to Denmark, where Christian II was deposed by the Danish nobility and replaced by his uncle, Duke Frederick of Schleswig-Holstein.

During Frederick I's ten-year reign (1523–33), the Catholic foundations of Denmark were eroded by Protestant preachers who poured into the country from Lutheran Schleswig. The most effective of these reformers was the monk Hans Tausen (1494–1561), who had studied at Rostock, Copenhagen, Louvain, and Wittenberg. From his monastery in Viborg, Tausen proclaimed the evangelical message in a barrage of sermons, printed tracts, and pamphlets. Frederick I improved his relations with the Danish nobles by opposing the Catholic clergy, and soon Lutheran preachers were carrying their message to all parts of the kingdom. Three years after his accession, Frederick openly repudiated papal authority and began the introduction of Lutheran liturgy and doctrines into the church services. In 1530 the Copenhagen Confession was published, expressing the faith and beliefs of the Danish Lutherans. This creed, appearing almost simultaneously with the Augsburg Confession, revealed a stronger biblicalism, a less doctrinaire concept of justification, and an even greater reliance upon the state than did the German creed.

The short civil war that followed Frederick's death in 1533 resulted in a further consolidation of Lutheranism in Denmark. Christian III (1533–59), Frederick's son, was already a convert when he came to the throne. In 1539 he consummated the Reformation in Denmark by proclaiming a new evangelical church ordinance, outlining the rules of service and worship and declaring the king to be the supreme authority in all ecclesiastical matters. From Denmark the Reformation spread into Norway under Christian III's tutelage. Catholic services were converted into evangelical communions, and much of the church's property was seized, either by Lutheran nobles or by the crown. The Church Ordinance of Denmark was established there and new bishops installed. Nevertheless, Protestant expansion into Norway was slow and tedious for several years, because it was considered a foreign product imposed on them

Christian II of Denmark, *called "Christian the Cruel" for his harsh treatment of the leaders of the national Swedish party in the "Bloodbath of Stockholm" in 1520, which led to the revolt and independence of Sweden under Gustavus Vasa. Christian was subsequently deposed in Denmark.*

from outside. In the end, however, it met with more resentment than resistance, and by the middle of the century it was difficult to distinguish Norwegian Lutheranism from Danish.

The Lutheranization of Sweden was a slower process, due in part to the greater strength of the Catholic church there and to Swedish resentment of all things Danish. Leadership of the Swedish Reformation came from the new king himself, Gustavus Vasa (1523–60), who opposed the power of the bishops and denied the jurisdiction of the papacy. He was greatly aided by the higher nobles and by the evangelizing of Olavus Petri (1493–1552). Petri not only authored religious books and a number of evangelical tracts, based upon Luther's Reformation writings (Petri had studied at Wittenberg between 1516 and 1518), but also published the first Swedish New Testament in 1526. The following year, at the Diet of Västeras, Lutheran preaching was allowed in Sweden, but it was still another decade before the Swedish National Church was finally established. By the time of Luther's death in 1546, Sweden was fully within the Protestant fold.

Bohemia, Hungary, and Poland

In the eastern kingdoms the spread of the Reformation was sporadic and uneven. Once again it was primarily the nobles, and to a lesser degree the university students, who were most responsible for its propagation. What Protestantism lacked in eastern Europe was the immediate support of the rulers, without whose patronage it could hardly be more than a minority movement. On the other hand, these monarchs were equally loath or unable to suppress reform in the vigorous manner pursued by some of their western counterparts. Consequently, Protestantism and other forms of religious unorthodoxy did prosper, receiving a degree of toleration unknown in western Europe.

Bohemia, the hotbed of religious dissent since the days of John Hus, sheltered many forms of Christian worship, from Catholics, Utraquists (conservative Hussites), and Anabaptists to Lutherans and the Bohemian Brethren of the Unity (*Unitas Fratrum*), together creating a curious and heterogeneous religious spectrum. Since the death of the Hussite king, George of Poděbrady, in 1471, Bohemian politics had been dominated by the Czech upper nobility, who were mostly Utraquist Hussites or nationalist Catholics. Lutheran influence was felt primarily among the lower nobility and within the German communities of Bohemia. But strong Czech antipathy to the Germans prevented the wide acceptance of a religious movement so thoroughly Teutonic in its origins. The fact that Bohemia was part of the Holy Roman Empire tended to balance the Czech dislike of Germans with a corresponding repugnance to Rome. The later success of Calvinism in Bohemia shows that the Czechs were not too averse to Protestantism as long as it did not come from Germany.

In Hungary, however, the Reformation spread rapidly among the Magyar nobles. In the wake of the battle of Mohács in 1526—when the Turks broke through the imperial defensive perimeter, occupying Buda, and driving on to the very gates of Vienna—Protestantism seemed to thrive in the areas not directly occupied by Turkish forces. The Hungarian-Bohemian king, Louis II, had fallen at Mohács, and his brother-in-law, Ferdinand of Habsburg, Emperor Charles V's brother, was elected king of Bohemia, and by a minority of the Magyar lords he was also chosen king of Hungary. However, the Transylvanian magnate John Zapolya, backed by the majority of the Hungarian nobles, challenged Ferdinand's title. While these two neutralized each other, and the Turks carved out a Hungarian state of their own, Lutheranism expanded into the Austrian-controlled regions of Hungary, Slovakia, Transylvania, and parts of Turkish Hungary under the auspices and protection of the barons. As long as the Habsburgs ruled part of Hungary (which they did from 1541 on), the state church there remained Catholic.

In the loosely ruled Polish-Lithuanian Commonwealth, the nobles and townspeople used the Lutheran appeal to oppose their political and clerical enemies. The Jagiellonian dynasty in Poland, although successful in expanding its influence into neighboring territories (reigning in Bohemia from 1471 to 1526 and intermittently in Hungary from 1440 to 1526), was unable to control the powerful magnates who ruled the land and dominated the Polish parliament. Lutheranism's modest success among the lesser nobility was not effectively hindered by the government of Sigismund I (1506–48). Although he remained a Roman Catholic, in 1525 Sigismund permitted the Grand Master of the Teutonic Order to transform East Prussia from an ecclesiastical state into a secular, Lutheran duchy under the Hohenzollern dynasty, subject to Polish suzerainty. Ducal Prussia thereafter served as a conduit for Lutheranism into Poland and Lithuania.

The fate of Protestantism in eastern Europe illustrates the consistency and continuation of the western-European experience expressed in the principle established by the Peace of Augsburg: "*Cuius regio eius religio*" ("Whoever rules decides the religion"). In the sixteenth century, the religion of every state was ultimately determined by the religious preference of its ruler.

Political and Religious Unrest in Switzerland

Sixteenth-century Switzerland was a loose confederation of thirteen small states called *cantons,* nominally still part of the Holy Roman Empire. The six so-called rural or forest cantons of Uri, Schwyz, Unterwalden, Zug, Glarus, and Appenzell were the cradle of Swiss liberty. The governments of these rugged eastern cantons were strikingly democratic for that age, functioning through popularly chosen assemblies. The governing body of the smaller cantons consisted of all the male citizens when gathered, like the ancient Athenians, in open-air assembly (*Landesgemeinde*). Quarrelsome and touchy, the Swiss mountaineers not only disliked foreigners but even had great difficulty getting along with one another. That is why the confederation of cantons was so loosely organized and the government exercised no power except by a unanimous vote of the representatives of the cantons. For all practical purposes, the cantons were completely independent, voluntarily entering into league for the purpose of mutual defense. After the decisive Swiss victory over Emperor Maximilian and the Swabian League in 1499, the confederation continued more as a tradition than a necessity.

In the seven urban cantons of Zürich, Luzern, Bern, Fribourg, Solothurn, Basel, and Schaffhausen, political power was in the hands of narrower oligarchical conciliar governments representing their respective cantons. Even here, however, a large degree of popular political activity existed in the towns. The last of these cantons (Fribourg, Solothurn, Basel, and Schaffhausen) joined the confederation in 1481 and 1501. These newcomers were resented by the older members of the confederation, and only the timely intervention of the saintly hermit, Nicholas of Flue, prevented a civil war. In addition to the thirteen confederation cantons, a number of allied and subject frontier territories owed various allegiances to the confederation. Among these were the southern mountain regions of the Grisons (which included the Valtelline, commanding the Splügen and Bernina passes into Italy); Ticino, just north of Lake Maggiore; and the Valais, which surrounded the Rhône River from its source to Lake Geneva. In the west lay the free city of Geneva and the French-speaking regions of Vaud and Neuchâtel. To the north, between Basel and Zürich, were the jointly administered territories of Aargau and Thurgau.

The unity of Switzerland in the early sixteenth century was not due to its political organization, which in fact exercised no power other than that freely agreed upon by the separate cantons, but rather was based on a common tradition of military enterprise and success. Warlike and hardened, the Swiss warriors willingly sold their services to foreign *condottieri* at high rates to augment the meager economy of their own homeland. More than once the Swiss diet

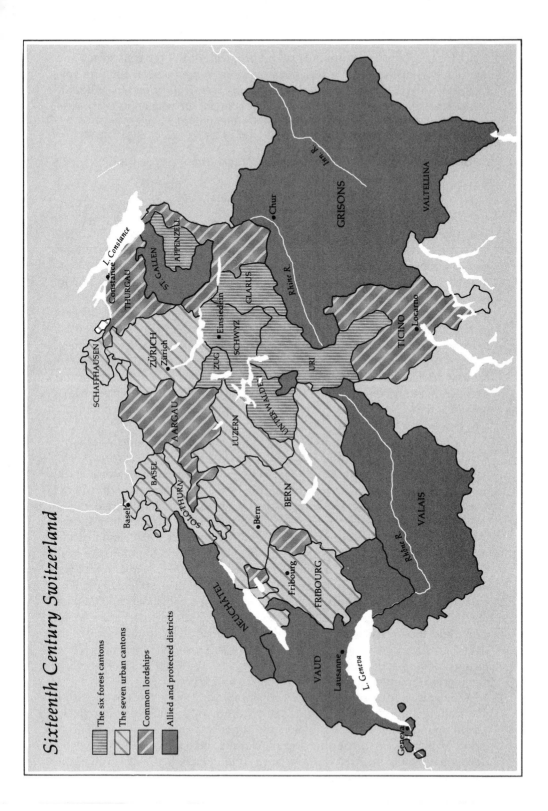

Sixteenth Century Switzerland

The six forest cantons

The seven urban cantons

Common lordships

Allied and protected districts

GRISONS

VALTELLINA

Inn R.

L. Constance

Constance

THURGAU

ST GALLEN

APPENZELL

Chur

SCHAFFHAUSEN

ZÜRICH

Zürich

Rhine R.

Einsiedeln

GLARUS

SCHWYZ

ZUG

AARGAU

URI

TICINO

Locarno

BASEL

LUZERN

UNTERWALDEN

Basel

SOLOTHURN

BERN

Bern

VALAIS

Rhône R.

FRIBOURG

Fribourg

NEUCHÂTEL

VAUD

Lausanne

L. Geneva

Geneva

agreed to restrict or prohibit their traffic in manpower, but in every case the cantons ignored their own restrictions at the very next call for pikemen. Without a common treasury, judiciary, or sovereignty, the Swiss were a conglomerate of warring cantons, rival towns, and pugnacious individuals joined together in the loosest possible way for the purpose of mutual survival and gain.

Nevertheless, to foreign observers they seemed an awesome and threatening power. Machiavelli frequently warned his countrymen to guard against the time when the Swiss would recognize their strength and descend on Italy for themselves instead of as mercenaries for the French, Spanish, or Germans. That was before the battle of Marignano. Any ambitions that some imperial-minded Swiss may have entertained collapsed in the French victory of September 1515. For the next three centuries, Switzerland continued to be the principal exporter of mercenary soldiers, but it never became a unified state acting in its own political interests.

The Swiss Cities

Economically, the towns of the western lowlands, especially Basel, Bern, and Geneva, actively participated in the commerce between Italy and northern Europe. As urban prosperity increased, the governing power became more narrowly oligarchical and tightly aristocratic. Tensions mounted not only among the different cantons but also *within* each of them as the social stratification was strained by the growing prosperity of some and the accompanying destitution of others. Social unrest was particularly noticeable in the urban cantons. With social and economic stress came religious strain. The upper clergy was particularly ingrained in the ruling oligarchies of Basel, Bern, and Zürich. To the disfranchised majorities, these symbols of vested interest and corruption became particularly galling. Many of the prelates were only too prone to parade their wealth as well as exaggerate their power.

Zürich is a good case in point. By the beginning of the sixteenth century, Zürich had become a moderately prosperous trading city, exchanging the products of the south, such as wine, silk, and textiles, for northern grains, iron, and salt. Zürich contributed products of its own artisan industries to this commerce, including textiles, handicrafts, weapons, and armor. For many years, however, Zürich's principal export was mercenary soldiers. Growing unrest in the late fifteenth century resulted in a series of social upheavals that intensified the class cleavages and brought the artisan guilds into a share of the governmental power. After the constitutional reforms of 1498, the guildmasters and wealthy patricians formed an elite that dominated the political life not only of the city (whose population is estimated at between 5,000 and 7,000 of a total canton population of some 60,000) but also of the entire canton.

Zürich was administered by a Great Council of some 200 city fathers, chosen for life by the guilds, and by a Small Council of fifty, selected jointly by the Great Council and the guilds. Leadership and direction of the Small Council, which was reconstituted yearly (although frequently by the same people), was provided by two lifetime mayors and four direct representatives of the guilds. The jurisdiction of the government extended into religious as well as

Zürich in the early sixteenth century. *A view by Hans Leu the Elder, showing the Grossmünster, where Zwingli was People's Priest from December 1518. With its vigorous municipal government, Zürich quickly became the leader of Protestantism in Switzerland.*

civil matters, to the occasional chagrin of the bishop of Constance and more often of the local priests and monks. When Zwingli was appointed by the council to become priest of the Grossmünster in December 1518, it was with a clear knowledge of his open criticism of the practices and many of the beliefs of sixteenth-century Catholicism.

Zwingli and the Reformation in Zürich

Huldrych (Huldreich, Ulrich) Zwingli was born in the rural canton of Glarus, in a tiny town in the Toggenburg valley, on the first day of January 1484, just seven weeks after the birth of Martin Luther. Zwingli's father was a fairly prosperous farmer who provided the best education he could for his sons. Entrusted to the care of his uncle, the vicar of Wesen, when he was only five, young Zwingli soon developed a love of study. His pious uncle taught him the rudiments of Latin and then sent him off to a primary school at Basel, the city that was soon to become closely associated with Erasmus and Christian humanism. At the age of twelve, Zwingli continued his studies at Bern, where he was first introduced to humanism and to the classics. From there he moved to Vienna in 1498. Four years later he returned to Basel, where he obtained the university degree of Bachelor of Arts in 1504 and in another two years the Master of Liberal Arts. Most of his schooling at Basel was Aristotelian, but he could not forget the attachment he had developed for humanism and was drawn as if by a magnet to the refreshing company of the humanist printers, Amerbach and Froben.

Soon Zwingli was in a position to test and apply his training. At the age of twenty-two, he was ordained a priest in order to accept the vicarage of Glarus. For the next ten years, from 1506 to 1516, as parish priest of Glarus, which included the neighborhood villages as well as the town itself, Zwingli looked after his doting flock, teaching them the fundamentals of Christianity, chastising them when necessary, and administering to their many needs. At the same time he continued to read, study, reflect, and write. He taught himself from the Bible, and diligently studied the works of the Greek and Latin Fathers. When Erasmus's *Annotations on the New Testament* was published, he embraced it enthusiastically, as he did the *Enchiridion* and *Adages*. At Glarus, Zwingli censured many of the church abuses and also became an outspoken commentator on Swiss politics, criticizing the exhaustion of manpower through mercenary service in foreign wars. He was particularly critical of the Treaty of Fribourg, which tied the Swiss to French service.

Zwingli's growing reputation as a conscientious, rational, and practical man brought him an additional responsibility in 1516 when he was appointed rector of nearby Einsiedeln, a position he held for two years. Influenced by Erasmus's *New Testament,* which was published in 1516, Zwingli not only deepened and intensified his study of the Bible, especially the Pauline Epistles, but also began to preach more like an evangelical humanist than like a Catholic priest. At the same time, he became more persistent in his criticism of church abuses, particularly of venality and indulgence selling.

At this point in his rising career, Zwingli was offered the coveted post of cathedral priest at the Grossmünster in Zürich, where he was appointed on Saturday, 11 December 1518. On New Year's Day 1519, he preached his first sermon. It was immediately obvious that the enthusiastic prelate, who was also celebrating his thirty-fifth birthday, did not intend to bury his talents under a bushel. His disciple and successor, Heinrich Bullinger, reported the inaugural sermon:

> He praised God the Father, and taught men to trust only in the Son of God, Jesus Christ, as saviour. He vehemently denounced all unbelief, superstition and hypocrisy. Eagerly he strove after repentance, improvement of life, and Christian love and faith. He rebuked vice, such as idleness, excesses in eating, drinking and apparel, gluttony, suppression of the poor, pensions, and wars. He insisted that the government should maintain law and justice, and protect widows and orphans. The people should always seek to retain Swiss freedom. The mistresses of the rulers and lords should be banned.

Zwingli also announced that he intended to preach the Gospel according to Saint Matthew from beginning to end, instead of following the prescribed scriptural expositions set down by church practice.

During his first three or four years at Zürich, Zwingli came under the spell of Luther's evangelical writings, and as he did he moved further from the Christian humanism of Erasmus. Although Luther's influence was apparent in

DVM PATRIÆ QVÆRO PER DOGMATA SANCTA SALVTEM
INGRATO PATRIÆ CÆSVS AB ENSE CADO

Huldrych Zwingli. *This famous painting of the Zürich reformer is by Hans Asper, a follower of Holbein and a strong sympathizer with the Reformation. It was painted in 1531, the year of Zwingli's death.*

some of Zwingli's theological views, his ideas up to the beginning of 1519 were predominantly independent of those of the Wittenberg reformer, and many of them continued to diverge sharply from Luther's. Zwingli resented the inference that he obtained his ideas from Luther and stoutly denied the charge that the Zürich reformation was a mere aping of the Wittenberg revolt. In 1523 Zwingli complained:

> The high and mighty of this world have begun to persecute and hate Christ's teaching under the presence of the name of Luther. They call all of Christ's teaching "Lutheran," no matter who on earth proclaims it. . . . This is now my fate. I began to preach the Gospel of Christ in 1516, long before anyone in our region had ever heard of Luther. . . . For this reason I began some ten years ago to study Greek in order to learn Christ's teaching in the original language. I leave it to others to judge how well I comprehended it. At any rate, Luther did not teach me anything. . . . The papists none the less burden me and others maliciously with such names and say, "You must be a Lutheran, for you preach the way Luther writes." I answer them, "I preach the way Paul writes. Why do you not also call me a follower of Paul? Indeed, I proclaim the word of Christ. Why do you not call me a Christian?"

The first three years of Zwingli's appointment in Zürich passed without undue excitement or conflict. The flavor of the Zwinglian sermons was tightly biblical. By 1522 many in his congregation had come to recognize the superficiality and sham in many church rituals and doctrines while being led to a greater appreciation of what he called the pure Gospel of Christ. Moved by the logic of Zwingli's sermons, some of his parishioners openly defied church practice by eating meat and other prohibited foods during Lent, justifying themselves by "the Word of God which clearly allows the eating of all foods at all times and calls it a teaching of Satan to prohibit food which was created by God." Although he observed the Lenten fast himself, Zwingli defended the actions of the culprits. Shortly afterward, the council issued a mandate that the fast be observed, but it also opened the door to further discussion and the possibility of reform. The result was a great public disputation, held in January 1523, in which this and many other doctrines and practices of the church were openly examined and criticized. The pattern was set, and during the next few years a number of such disputations were held in Zürich, after which the council made a public pronouncement of its decisions. Here was the kind of biblical confrontation Luther had always longed for but never received. In its first edict, dated January 29, 1523, the council declared:

> Master Huldreich Zwingli . . . has in the past been much attacked and accused. Yet no one opposed him after he had stated and explained his articles nor did anyone disprove them on the basis of sacred Scripture. Several times he challenged those who have accused him of heresy to step forward, but no man proved any heresy in his doctrine. Therefore Mayor, Council and Great Council of Zürich, in order to do away with disturbance and discord, have upon due deliberation and consultation decided and resolved that Master Zwingli should continue as heretofore to proclaim the Gospel and the pure sacred Scriptures, until he is instructed better.

During the next two years, with the support of the council (for Zwingli never altered any ritual without government order), the collection of tithes was ended, fasting altered, clerical celibacy denounced, images removed, and other ecclesiastical observances changed. Simultaneously, the council forbade the participation of Zürich troops in foreign military service. Zwingli further repudiated saint worship, transubstantiation, pilgrimages, monasticism, the doctrine of purgatory, and the overriding authority of the pope. In their place he proclaimed the supremacy of the word of God and the brotherhood of all believers in Christ. Finally, in 1525, the Mass itself was abolished.

The Spread of the Swiss Reformation

Although the Reformation in Zürich seemed to be complete, there was cause for apprehension by the ease with which it was carried out. Why, for example, had the papacy remained almost indifferent to the Zwinglian threat while prosecuting Luther to the fullest? Was Zwingli being enticed into a trap that would shortly ensnare him and all those who supported him? Probably not. Although not entirely clear, the pope's actions—or lack of them—may not have been so surprising after all. The Netherlander, Adrian VI, who was pope during 1522 and 1523, was more understanding of the humanists' demands for clerical reform than was his predecessor, Leo X. Adrian was a reformer himself and recognized the need for meaningful and far-reaching reforms within the church. Although he was certainly not sympathetic to heresy, he thought Leo had acted rashly toward Luther, thus helping him become a rebel rather than a reformer.

Adrian's approach to Zwingli seemed to be set to a different gauge. Rather than popularizing the commotion in Zürich by papal pronouncements and bulls, he chose to win rather than force Zwingli's allegiance to the church. Understanding the humanists' dissatisfaction with Luther, the pope appealed to Zwingli's humanism in the hope that he, like Erasmus, could be converted into a defender of the faith against the Lutheran attacks. There was in Zwingli, however, an evangelical activism that was absent from Erasmus. Zwingli was not likely to play the papal role for which Adrian had cast him. We shall never know how successful the pope might have been, for he died on 14 September 1523. Adrian's successor, the Medici Pope Clement VII, was too dependent upon Swiss mercenaries in the Italian wars to risk meddling in their domestic struggles.

The other Swiss cantons, however, were not so indifferent to the innovations at Zürich. The eastern cantons, led by Luzern, Uri, Schwyz, and Zug, formed a league against the rebellious city. As they did, Zwingli's words began to find receptive listeners in neighboring towns. After 1527 ecclesiastical reform spread rapidly. Followers and companions of Zwingli carried his ideas, always with some modifications and differences, into the surrounding cities: Wolfgang Capito and Johannes Oecolampadius into Basel, Berthold Haller and Niklaus Manuel to Bern, Vadianus (Joachim von Watt) and Johann Kessler to Saint Gall, Sebastian Hofmeister to Schaffhausen, and Matthew Zell and Martin Bucer to Strasbourg. Zwingli soon formed a defensive alliance with some of these cantons and with the south-German Protestants, although many of the Swiss towns, even though sympathetic to the Reformation, remained neutral in the ensuing confrontation. The first Kappel War of 1529, which pitted Zürich against the five forest cantons, involved little actual fighting and resulted in a negotiated truce favorable to the continuing spread of reform in western and northwestern Switzerland.

The doctrines taught by Zwingli and his followers were closely related to those of Luther. Both based their theology on the words of the Bible, which they identified with the Word of God. They viewed the Bible as the supreme authority in all matters of faith, morals, ecclesiastical organization, and practice. The essential message of Zwingli's theology, as outlined in his *Commentary on the True and False Religion* (1528) and in other works, was that the reconciliation between righteous God and evil humans was provided by faith and election, through the atonement of Christ. "The election of God is free and gratuitous," Zwingli wrote, "for he elected us before the foundation of the world, before ever we were born. Consequently, God did not elect us because of works."

Zwingli's general conception of the church was not unlike Luther's. Both recognized that not all members of the community are true Christians. While proclaiming the Gospel would convert some, others would never be converted.

Zwingli used the term church in three ways: to signify the invisible church (composed of the elect of God, and known only by him), to identify the visible church of all Christians, and to represent that portion of the visible church congregated to worship and serve God in the correct manner and in the true spirit. Desiring the proper organization and functioning of this church, Zwingli took a much more active role in political and organizational matters than did Luther.

Zwingli was an activist in regard to church-state relations. For him, church and state were not separate entities but only different aspects of the same entity. Both preacher and ruler were obligated to God, who had entrusted them to establish the rule of God in the land. Zwingli's experiences in a self-governing urban society, in which popular opinion and pressure played a large role, caused him to be greatly involved in jurisdictional matters. He felt the need to shape society in conformity with the principles of the reformed religion, and he therefore participated actively in the institutionalization of the church and in guiding that institution in cooperation with the political authority. By persuasion and the skillful direction of popular pressure, he induced the council to initiate the religious changes he advocated, always assuring the government considerable authority in organizational and disciplinary affairs. In this way Zwingli repudiated all non-scriptural Catholic practices, including priestly vestments, the use of musical instruments and hymns in worship, and the "idolatrous" Mass.

Sacramentarianism and the Marburg Colloquy

The issue that most separated the Zwinglians from the Lutherans, and prevented the Swiss and German reformations from presenting a united front against the Catholics, was the doctrine of the Lord's Supper. From early in 1525 Zwingli had interpreted the scriptural phrase "This is my Body," referring to the bread of the Eucharist, to mean "This represents my Body." He accepted the idea that Christ is present "according to His divine nature," and agreed with Luther that the communicant receives Christ's blood by faith. Zwingli, however, believed that the words were meant to be taken in a figurative, rather than a literal, sense. Luther, on the other hand, insisted that they be taken literally, affirming the real presence of the body and blood of Christ "in, with, and under the bread and wine" and declaring that the communicant receives Christ's true body and blood in this sacrament.

Many verbal missiles had passed between the two reformers on this matter when Landgrave Philip of Hesse invited the leaders of the German and Swiss factions to meet in colloquium to resolve their differences and present a united front against the Catholics, and against possible military action by the emperor. In the autumn of 1529, the principal Swiss and German reformers—Zwingli, Oecolampadius, Bucer, Capito, Luther, Melanchthon, Jonas, Brenz, and others—met in the beautiful city of Marburg to conclude some sort of doctrinal agreement and political cooperation. On many issues they were able to reach satisfactory compromises, when they were not in complete agreement.

Devastation of war, *a hauntingly graphic battleground scene by Urs Graf, a Swiss soldier-artist who participated in many campaigns as a mercenary.*

On the doctrine of the Lord's Supper, however, the conference ran into real difficulties. Both sides denied the sacrificial nature of the Catholic Mass and agreed that communicants should be given both bread and wine, but they differed on the issue of the bodily presence of Christ in the sacrament. Zwingli's symbolic interpretation brought from Luther the strongest reaction. "*Hoc est corpus meum*" ("This is my body") he emphatically quoted from the Scripture, and refused to accept any deviation from the literal meaning of these words. Oecolampadius's countertext from John, "It is the spirit that quickeneth; the flesh profiteth nothing," made no impression on Luther. "You have a different spirit from us," he declared. "One side in this controversy belongs to the Devil and is God's enemy."

After the colloquy had ended, Luther proferred an olive branch in the form of a definition describing Christ's body as "essentially and substantively," but not "qualitatively, quantitatively, or locally" present in the Lord's Supper. For Zwingli this formula was still too close to the Catholic doctrine. The Marburg Articles were signed by both parties but they did not agree to do more than be civil to one another. No political alliance was possible without complete doctrinal agreement, Luther insisted; besides, Melanchthon worried about an accord that might prejudice any future Lutheran discussions with the Catholics. So the German and Swiss reformations continued along their separate ways.

In October 1531, the Swiss armies again faced one another. The second

Kappel War was bloody and decisive. The Zürich troops, with Zwingli as their chaplain, met the army of the five forest cantons between Zug and Kappel. The battle was short. The Zürichers were defeated and scattered, and Zwingli was killed. The Catholic cantons made no attempt to alter the Reformation that had already occurred, but they did prevent its further spread eastward. Zwingli was ably succeeded in Zürich by Heinrich Bullinger, but leadership of the Sacramentarians (as the Swiss reformers were called) gradually shifted to Bern and eventually, after the appearance of John Calvin, to Geneva, where the movement merged into Calvinism. In the meantime, a more radical manifestation of religious and social unrest was beginning to appear in Switzerland and was rapidly spreading to surrounding areas, where it became one of the most important movements of the Reformation.

The Anabaptists

The radical wing of the sixteenth-century Reformation took many forms. Indeed, it may be misleading to refer to it in the singular because of the great divergences among its different manifestations. Nevertheless, we can distinguish enough common beliefs and practices among many of the groups constituting that wing to justify the use of some identifying term, such as *Anabaptist*, for a large segment of it. Anabaptism had its beginning in the reading groups at Zürich, led by Conrad Grebel (1498–1526) and others, who protested the religious conservatism and political statism of Zwingli, and carried the Reformation a step further by trying to reconstitute the New Testament church.

For Grebel, a religious reformation carried out by consent of the civil authority was not a reformation at all. He urged Zwingli to restore the Kingdom of God in its biblical purity, a complete restitution (*restitutio*) of the New Testament church without reference either to the medieval church or to the secular state. Lutheran and Zwinglian attempts simply to reform the Roman Catholic church (*reformatio*), using the Bible as authority and guide, were missing the real root of the problem, Grebel believed. Therefore, at the Zürich disputation of 1523, Grebel called for not only the immediate abolition of the Mass but the repudiation of both the church and the council.

The key feature of Grebel's thought was his interpretation of the true church as a voluntary community of believers, freely entered into, upon conversion, through the waters of baptism. From this belief it followed that membership in the religious community was not synonymous with membership in the political state, and participants in the former were not necessarily obligated to the latter. This concept of complete separation of church and state, unlike Catholic or Protestant belief, implied that the commonly recognized duties of paying taxes, bearing arms, and taking oaths were not incumbent upon true Christian believers. Furthermore, since baptism was the covenant through which the convert entered the community of believers, it was obvious that Catholic, Lutheran, or Zwinglian baptism, administered a few days after birth, was considered invalid. The name "Anabaptist" (rebaptizer) was given them by their enemies to bring them under the condemnation of Roman law, which prescribed the death penalty for rebaptizing. Anabaptists, of course, denied that they were rebaptizing; they insisted that infant baptism was not "true baptism." In German-speaking areas, they were referred to as *Wiedertäufer* (rebaptizers) or more derogatorily as *Schwärmer* (fanatics), in the Netherlands, as *Wederdopers*. They usually referred to themselves simply as "Christians," or "Brethren," or "Saints."

Spreading rapidly into all parts of western Europe, the Anabaptist movement appealed especially to those who felt that the Protestant political and scriptural tyranny was as oppressive as the Catholic ecclesiastical tyranny. Its adherents came largely from the urban lower classes, occasionally from the peasantry, and in many cases were strongly motivated by social and economic pressures. Some middle-class elements, especially intellectual ones, appeared very early, but the bulk of the Anabaptist membership was drawn from the peasants, small shopkeepers, day laborers, miners, textile workers, and porters, giving it a strong social flavor and making it especially feared and hated by all of the "respectable" strata of society, whether Catholic or Protestant.

The place of women in Anabaptist society was ambiguous. For most Anabaptists, faith took precedence over marriage vows, especially those taken prior to conversion. Because they taught believers' baptism, the Anabaptists were usually willing to accept single women converts, and even allowed married female believers to leave their non-believing husbands. However, Merry Wiesner points out, these women were expected to remarry soon and "come under the control of a male believer." In some cases, where there were more women members than men, polygamy was condoned or even required. Female prophets and seers were generally accepted in Anabaptist communities. These women were vigorously prosecuted when arrested by the authorities, however, as attested by the large number of female Anabaptist martyrs in Germany. This may account for the low ratio of women to men in the Anabaptist communities. By denying the Catholic tradition of ordination through apostolic succession, the Anabaptists made it easier for women to enter the ministry. And if authority to preach came from divine inspiration rather than through a bishop, then women could claim that right as well as men. Although the Anabaptist insistence on the principle of freedom of conscience for all adult believers seems to have constituted a noteworthy breach in the rigid patriarchalism of the age, there was little inclination to grant women any greater role within the community than they held in sixteenth-century society generally.

The ferocity of the Peasant Wars in Germany during 1524 and 1525 multiplied fears of social upheaval and added vehemence to the attacks on the Anabaptists. However, the Swiss Brethren were not as affected by the disorders in Germany as many thought. Grebel, Felix Mantz (the "Apollo" of the Anabaptists), Wilhelm Reublin, Georg Blaurock (called the "Hercules" of the Anabaptists for his vigorous ministry), Michael Sattler, and other early converts were more directly motivated by religious principles and the purity of the faith than they were by social and political issues, although it may be misleading to separate them too widely. Grebel, originally a disciple of Zwingli, believed that the moral, ethical, and social precepts of Christianity ought to be put into practice instead of only preached. On 21 January 1525, the new movement was born in the home of Felix Mantz in Zürich, where Grebel baptized Georg Blaurock, and Blaurock then baptized others. Door-to-door proselyting added many more converts in Zürich and especially in nearby Zollikon.

As the number of adherents increased, they developed a fuller canon of doctrine that, although not followed uniformly, constituted a recognizable theology and ethic. Believing themselves to be true disciples of Christ, having taken up his cross upon baptism, the Anabaptists did not shrink from its consequences, meeting the inevitable persecutions and trials with devout resignation. They believed in the visible church—a community of "gathered" saints, the literal restitution of the primitive church—and used this as their guide to ecclesiastical organization. They also tried to recreate the social life of the apostolic church. Brotherhood, restitution, and nonresistence in rejecting the symbols and practices of civil government became their tokens of divine discipleship.

At one with Zwingli in their view of the Lord's Supper as a memorial ceremony symbolizing the acceptance of Christ, they refused to adopt either his or Luther's doctrines of salvation, and rejected the Protestant Augustinian view of human depravity. They held that works are the products of faith and that they also stimulate and enlarge that faith. Believing in their individual responsibility and in their own destiny as children and disciples of God, they proclaimed the freedom of the will in spiritual matters and insisted upon complete religious liberty. Sobriety and devotion marked their conduct in Switzerland, and even their bitterest oppressors were forced to admit that they were pious, humble, and patient.

Yet it was not for their behavior that the Anabaptists were persecuted and hunted down by all parties but for their radical concept of the complete separation of church and state, which disrupted the whole structure of politics and society known to the sixteenth century. Furthermore, implicit in their revivalism, even among the more pacific, was the danger of religious and social extremism engendered by their creed and by their social composition. Their religious sanction for political disobedience could not be taken lightly by the guardians of order and status. They were simultaneously feared and hated by everyone. The reward Anabaptists could expect if they were caught was either burning at the stake or the "third baptism" (drowning), which was the fate of Felix Mantz, the first Anabaptist martyr, who was drowned by the Protestants at Zürich in January 1527. Drowning was the usual form of punishment inflicted on Anabaptist women.

Anabaptists in Switzerland and South Germany

The expansion of Anabaptist beliefs and practices into nearby regions of the Empire was rapid after 1525. From Switzerland they spread first into southern Germany and Austria where Michael Sattler, Hans Denck, Hans Hut, Pilgram Marpeck, Balthasar Hübmaier, and others preached, baptized, and endeavored to establish the New Testament church in the face of harsh persecution. Most of them became martyrs for their beliefs and practices.

Michael Sattler (ca. 1490–1527), a former monk become Lutheran, who fled to Zürich in 1525, became an Anabaptist there and immediately devoted himself to the ministry. After being expelled from Zürich, he concentrated his preaching in the duchy of Württemberg. In February 1527, he drew up a set of seven articles that were approved at a conference of Anabaptists meeting in Schleitheim, on the Swiss-German border. These Schleitheim Articles (known also as the Brotherly Union) were the first formal Anabaptist confession of faith. They were concerned with religious practices as well as doctrines: believers' baptism; the ban as a disciplinary measure; the Lord's Supper; separation from evil; the responsibilities and needs of pastors; the use of the sword by secular authority only, not by true Christians; and the forbidding of oaths. Shortly after the Scheitheim conference, Sattler was apprehended by imperial officials, peremptorily tried, and brutally tortured before being burned at the stake. Thirteen other followers, including Sattler's devoted wife, were put to death by the sword and by drowning.

Hans Denck and Pilgram Marpeck were both wandering scholars (as many Anabaptist intellectuals were forced to be). Denck (ca. 1495–1528) taught in Nuremberg, Augsburg, and Saint Gall before identifying himself with the Anabaptists and being baptized by Hübmaier in 1526. Denck, in turn, became an effective missionary throughout southern Germany, where he baptized many others, including the fiery Hans Hut. Denck was, above all, an independent thinker who published several theological works that show him to have been doctrinally on the fringe of Anabaptism, difficult to classify because he was unwilling to be cast in any sectarian mold. Pilgram Marpeck (d. 1556) was a mining engineer from the Tyrol, whose conversion resulted from the teachings and valiant death of Michael Sattler. Marpeck succeeded Reublin as leader of the Anabaptist refugees in Strasbourg; however, after a series of debates with Bucer, he was forced to leave and spent the next twelve years wandering about southern Germany before finally settling in Augsburg. There, while serving as city engineer, he became an influential Anabaptist theologian, even though he was untrained in theology. His most important contribution was his distinction between the Old and New Testaments, holding that only the latter was authoritative for true believers.

Balthasar Hübmaier (ca. 1480–1528) was perhaps the greatest intellectual leader of the early Anabaptists. A former student and disciple of the renowned Dr. Johann Eck, Hübmaier was a brilliant scholar in his own right and a popular preacher. He rose rapidly in the academic community of Ingolstadt to become vice-rector of the university by 1515. Shortly thereafter, he left to accept positions as parish priest in Regensburg and then in Waldshut, on the Rhine. His intense study of the New Testament, however, and subsequent contacts with Zwingli and other Swiss reformers, caused him to change views and he became a reformer himself. By January 1525, he was convinced that infant baptism was wrong, and in April he was baptized in Waldshut by Wilhelm Reublin. Upon resigning his clerical office, Hübmaier was immediately chosen by his congregation to continue as their minister. Later in that same momentous year, he responded to Zwingli's pamphlet against rebaptism with a pow-

Drowning an Anabaptist Woman. *This illustration from a late seventeenth-century Dutch book shows the relatively "mild" form of execution meted out to the first generation of Anabaptists. Many other people were burned at the stake.*

erful little book, *Vom christlichen Tauf der Glaubigen* (Concerning Christian Baptism of Believers), which immediately became the best statement of the Anabaptist view of adult baptism. Arrested and tortured in Zürich, Hübmaier recanted, but soon repented of his weakness and resumed his vigorous promotion of Anabaptism in Nikolsburg in southern Moravia near the Austrian border.

Moravia and the Hutterites
Moravia, under the suzerainty of the king of Bohemia, seemed to be a much more hospitable home for the new movement than was western Europe. It already sheltered other evangelical groups, including many Hussites. Shortly after his arrival there, Hübmaier converted and baptized two of the landed barons, lords of Lichtenstein, who in turn allowed him to preach in their territories. Spectacular results followed. Within a year he claimed as many as 6000 adherents. Hübmaier was not only busy preaching and baptizing; he also continued to write, publishing some seventeen pamphlets during 1526 and 1527. These writings reveal a remarkable knowledge of Scripture and a high degree of literary skill. Equally significant—and unusual for the times—was his vigorous espousal of religious toleration.

Hübmaier was soon joined by the zealous former Müntzerite from Augsburg, Hans Hut, who declared that the time was ripe for divine punishment of the wicked. Hut's eschatological ideas (the conviction that the Second Coming was imminent) included a confusing mixture of nonresistance and revolution. Jakob Wiedemann, another Anabaptist preacher in Nikolsburg who joined forces with Hut, advocated communal ownership of property and goods, and complete nonresistance to secular authority. Hübmaier disagreed with both of them. Unlike many Anabaptists, he accepted the right of the state to use the sword in a righteous cause (such as war against the Turks) and thought even true believers should support that cause. He rejected pacifism as being irresponsible. Their disagreements led to serious dissension among their followers, the Hut-Wiedemann *Stäbler* ("staff-bearers") and the Hübmaier *Schwertler* ("sword-bearers"), as they were called.

Meanwhile, Bohemia had come under the jurisdiction of the Habsburgs after the Battle of Mohács (1526), and Ferdinand I, the emperor's brother, soon took steps to root out heresy in his lands. Hübmaier was arrested, tried, and condemned, then tortured, and on 10 March 1528, burned at the stake in Vienna. A few days later, his wife was drowned in the Danube. Hut was killed a short time after that in an Augsburg jail, leaving Wiedemann and a fragmented remnant of the Nikolsburg congregations.

Soon Wiedemann and his followers were forced to leave Nikolsburg. Partly because of the emergency situation and partly because of Wiedemann's teachings, these outcasts pooled their possessions and money, after the pattern of the primitive Christians in Jerusalem, and closed ranks to form the first communal settlement (*Brüderhof*) at Austerlitz, some forty miles north of Nikolsburg, on the manorial estates of the lords of Kaunitz. The Austerlitz community quickly expanded, as oppressed Anabaptist refugees flocked there from Switzerland, Bavaria, Württemberg, and the Tyrol. With this growth also came discord and dissension, as the delicate experiment all but collapsed in a flurry of disputes. One rival faction, led by Wilhelm Reublin, established itself in Auspitz, halfway between Austerlitz and Nikolsburg.

The Moravian settlements were saved from disintegration by the arrival in 1533 of Jakob Hutter (d. 1536) from the Tyrol, where he had been converted by the preaching of Georg Blaurock. Hutter was the chief pastor of the Tyrolese Anabaptists and brought many of his flock with him on the perilous trek to Moravia. Once there, he united the majority of the groups, and they elected him as their chief elder (*Vorsteher*). Hutter then reorganized the Moravian Brethren into tight-knit congregations with common ownership of all goods, based on the practice of the apostolic church, as reported by the Book of Acts, Chapter 5, in the Bible. Under his charismatic leadership, the Hutterites emerged as an economically viable, socially cohesive, and religiously active community. Missionaries were sent out into all parts of Europe to convert, baptize, and encourage converts to gather in Moravia. After Hutter's execution in 1536, the Hutterites went through perilous times and intense persecution. Nevertheless, they succeeded in maintaining their identity, particularly under the leadership of Peter Riedemann—whose *Rechenschaft unserer Religion* (Account of Our Religion) is accepted even today as the definitive statement of Hutterite faith—to become one of the strongest and most successful survivors of sixteenth-century Anabaptism. From Moravia and Slovakia, the Hutterites eventually spread into Hungary, Transylvania, and the Ukraine. In the nineteenth century, they emigrated in large numbers to North America, always maintaining their close-knit communal lives.

Anabaptists in the Netherlands and Northern Germany

The spread of Anabaptism northward into the Netherlands and northwestern Germany revealed some new features of the Radical Reformation that resulted in their being persecuted with even greater intensity. The first of a succession of extreme apocalyptic preachers to circulate their message of millennialism (the belief that Christ would soon return to begin his thousand-year reign on earth) was Melchior Hoffmann (ca. 1495–1543), a Swabian furrier who had become disenchanted in turn with Catholicism, Lutheranism, and Zwinglianism. After several years of wandering about northern Europe from Friesland to Scandinavia, Hoffmann settled in Strasbourg, where he joined the Anabaptist brotherhood, soon becoming "the Anabaptist Apostle of the North." A zealous man of extraordinary gifts, Hoffmann was an eloquent preacher. Subsequently, at Emden, in East Friesland, he baptized many new converts and continued his ministry throughout the Netherlands. As he did, he became convinced that he was the very Elijah sent to prepare the way for the coming of the Lord, an event he believed was near at hand. Indeed, he prophesied that the Second Coming would be fulfilled in 1533 and that the New Jerusalem was none other than Strasbourg. A staunch pacifist as well as millennarian, Hoffmann returned to Strasbourg to await quietly the "great and dreadful day," and the establishment of the Kingdom of God on the earth. Immediately arrested, he spent the last ten years of his life in prison while his followers, the Melchiorites, continued to spread his eschatology. The seeds he had sown produced fruit in many congregations in scores of cities, each announcing the forthcoming day of wrath.

Some of Hoffmann's successors in the Netherlands were the barbersurgeon Obbe Philips of Leeuwarden; David Joris, a glass painter from Delft; and fanatics like Jan Matthys (Mattijs, d. 1534), a baker from Haarlem, and his disciple Jan Beuckelsz of Leiden (ca. 1509–36). Claiming to be the prophet Enoch, Matthys radically altered Hoffmann's message by declaring that the way must be prepared for the Lord by the extermination of the wicked. Hundreds of ecstatic followers readied themselves for whatever God should require of them. As their enthusiasm mounted, so did the measures of repression taken by civil and religious authorities. When twelve enraptured saints (seven men and five women) ran naked through the streets of Amsterdam predicting the imminent scourges of God, they were immediately seized and brutally butchered by unbelievers.

The Münster Disaster   In the nearby Westphalian city of Münster, the final bizarre episode was played out. Under the aegis of Bernard Rothmann, a Catholic-turned-Lutheran priest, and his collaborator, the merchant and political official Bernard Knipperdolling, Münster underwent a reformation in 1533 that opened the city's gates to all sorts of religious and social innovations. Early the

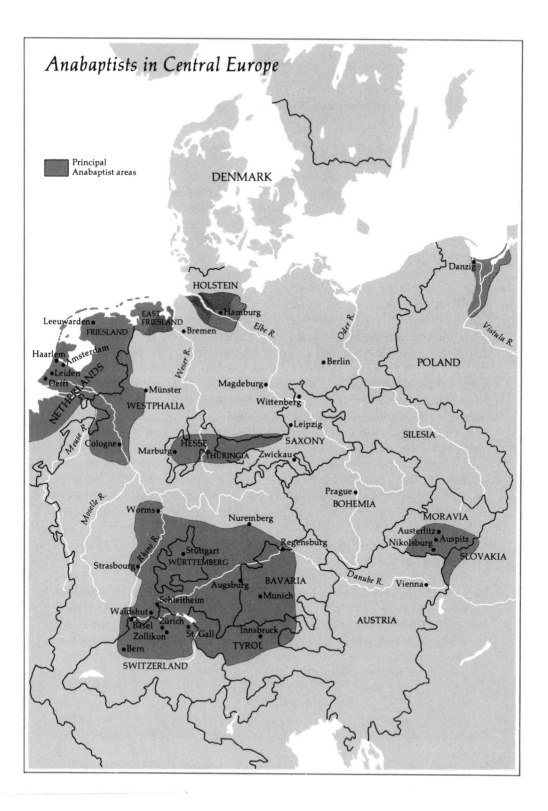

Anabaptists in Central Europe

Principal
Anabaptist areas

DENMARK

HOLSTEIN

Leeuwarden

EAST
FRIESLAND
FRIESLAND

Hamburg
Bremen

Elbe R.

Oder R.

Vistula R.

Danzig

Haarlem
Amsterdam
Leiden
Delft

NETHERLANDS

Meuse R.

Münster

WESTPHALIA

Weser R.

Magdeburg

Berlin

POLAND

Wittenberg

Leipzig

SAXONY

SILESIA

Cologne

Marburg

HESSE
THURINGIA

Zwickau

Prague

BOHEMIA

MORAVIA

Austerlitz
Nikolsburg
Auspitz

Moselle R.

Worms

Nuremberg

Regensburg

SLOVAKIA

Rhine R.

Stuttgart
WÜRTTEMBERG

Danube R.

Vienna

Strasbourg

Augsburg

BAVARIA

AUSTRIA

Schleitheim

Munich

Waldshut
Basel
Zollikon
Bern

Zürich
St. Gall

Innsbruck

TYROL

SWITZERLAND

following year, Rothmann and Knipperdolling were converted to revolutionary Anabaptism by Dutch missionaries sent out by Matthys, who now announced that the New Jerusalem was Münster instead of Strasbourg. In February 1534, Jan of Leiden, Matthys's most enthusiastic convert and disciple, appeared in the "holy city" to help establish the earthly kingdom of God, and a short time later the prophet himself arrived with the bulk of his followers. Soon the municipal council was displaced by a radical tribunal headed by Knipperdolling, and Matthys was able to carry out a complete religious, social, and political revolution. All those who accepted the prophet's leadership were rebaptized; those who refused were expelled from the city. All remnants of worldly vanity and vice were destroyed and a "reign of righteousness" inaugurated. With a restitution of the apostolic church in mind (along with strange overtones of Old Testament Israel), property was communalized and laws established for the "perfection of the saints" preparatory to the coming of the Lord.

The events at Münster caused fear and alarm on all sides. Supported by Catholics and Lutherans alike, and with money and troops volunteered from as far away as Bavaria, the prince-bishop of Münster laid siege to the city. Münster proved no easy nut to crack. Heavily fortified behind their protective walls, and fully prepared now to carry the fight against their enemies, who were therefore, by definition, the enemies of God, the Münster Anabaptists returned blow for blow. On Easter Sunday, 1534, while leading a sortie against the besiegers, Matthys was killed, and the mantle of the prophet passed to the tailor from Leiden.

Under Jan of Leiden, the final phase of the apocalyptic hysteria was concluded. The new "messiah" proclaimed himself king of Zion and the whole world his subjects. Dressed in his robes of state, he issued "divine decrees," while the beleaguered city consumed its last remnants of food. In July, with the reluctant consent of the city elders, he established the practice of polygamy, after the pattern of the Old Testament prophets, in order to provide husbands for the inordinate number of women in the city. He led the way by taking fifteen wives himself, including Matthys's widow. Lashed into a frenzy by their leader, the Münsterites repelled attack after attack mounted by the ecclesiastical and imperial forces. But the outcome was inevitable. After sixteen months of bloody siege, the starving inhabitants finally succumbed to superior strength, reinforced since early 1535 by the army of Philip of Hesse. Few of the Münsterites escaped the bloodbath that followed. Men, women, and children with ruthlessly slaughtered and the leaders tortured to a slow and agonizing death. Knipperdolling and Jan of Leiden were exhibited throughout northern Germany before they were publicly mutilated with red-hot tongs until they were dead. After that their bodies were put into cages and for more than 300 years hung from Saint Lambert's tower in Münster as a warning to all beholders. The empty cages can still be seen hanging from the church's tower.

Dutch Anabaptism went through a period of great stress following the Münster episode. Some of the survivors, and many others who were converted to their militant millennialism, continued to advocate the forceful overthrow of the ungodly by the sword. Others rejected violence of all kinds and, while

Menno Simons *faithfully led the Anabaptists of the Netherlands and North Germany through the crucial years 1536–61, and in so doing set the tone of Mennonite devotion and pacifism.*

insisting on believers' baptism, strict discipline, and austerity, repudiated the millennialism and other practices of the extremists. Somewhere in the middle was the visionary David Joris (1501–56), who tried to mediate between the other factions, proclaiming a fanaticism of his own. Believing that the true followers of Christ are persecuted but do not persecute, he embraced a strange allegorical conception of the Last Days, described in his *Wonder Book* of 1542. He, too, was a prophet of the Apocalypse, the "third David," an ambassador of the Lord, whose ministry was mystic and primarily clandestine. After suffering great hardships in the Netherlands, Joris and a few of his followers escaped to Basel, where he lived the remainder of his life under an assumed identity.

Two of the leaders of Dutch Anabaptism during and after Münster were the brothers Obbe and Dirk Philips. Obbe Philips (ca. 1500–68) had first embraced the messianic message of Melchior Hoffmann, but became disillusioned when he witnessed its results in Münster—and in Amsterdam, where he saw hundreds of his colleagues cruelly killed. In revulsion, he withdrew into a passive spiritualism, much as Hans Denck had done a few years earlier, although his followers, the Obbenites, continued to be a prominent part of Dutch Anabaptism for some time. Dirk Philips (1504–68), on the other hand, remained a staunch defender of the majority pacifist Anabaptists and, with Menno Simons, became one of their leaders. Trained as a Franciscan friar before joining the Anabaptists (he was baptized by his brother), Dirk knew Greek and Hebrew as well as fluent Latin, and became an influential theologian. His collected works, published in 1564, stand next to Menno's in importance for Mennonite doctrines.

The Mennonites   The person most responsible for the survival and rejuvenation of Dutch Anabaptism was the soft-spoken but brilliant Friesland pastor, Menno Simons (1496–1561), who joined the movement only in 1536, several months after the Münster debacle. For twelve years, Menno Simons had been a parish priest but had gradually come to the conclusion that the Mass was a fraud and that many other Catholic doctrines were unscriptural. Then in 1527 he was stirred by news of the execution of Sicke Freerks, the first Anabaptist martyr in the Netherlands. "It sounded very strange to me to hear of a second baptism," Menno Simons related in the account of his conversion. "I examined the Scriptures diligently and pondered them earnestly, but could find no report of infant baptism." Still he made no outward evidence of disaffection with the Catholic church, continuing to gain reputation and stature as a popular preacher. But his conscience would not allow him peace as long as he believed one thing and professed another. The Münster episode caused him even greater soul-searching for he discerned in the Münsterites righteous souls who were led astray by wicked and overzealous leaders. He tried to correct them by preaching and exhortations, but to no avail. When the desperate city finally collapsed and its inhabitants were massacred, Menno Simons felt the full impact of his own dilemma:

> After this had transpired the blood of these people, although misled, fell so hot on my heart that I could not stand it, nor find rest in my soul. I reflected upon my unclean, carnal life, also the hypocritical doctrine and idolatry which I still practiced daily in appearance of godliness, but without relish. I saw that these zealous children, although in error, willingly gave their lives and their estates for their doctrine and faith. And I was one of those who had disclosed to some of them the abominations of the papal system.

The Münster massacre brought Menno Simons face to face with himself, and forced him to the long-avoided decision. In October 1536, he was baptized by Obbe Philips. From that time on, Menno Simons became the popular leader of the Dutch Anabaptists, "the sheep who have no shepherd," he called them, devoting the remainder of his life to the cause of peaceful, evangelical Anabaptism. The force of Menno's leadership was grounded in the strength of his character, especially his devotion and courage, and in the conviction of his beliefs: Christlike morality, peace, toleration, and complete separation of church and state. He taught that true Christianity consists in not only believing in Christ but also living the way Christ taught and lived; faith must be accompanied by works. His view of a living religion called for high morals and the strong personal commitment to a way of life that was in most respects alien to the practices of the time. This meant separating from the worldly social and political order, or as Jesus taught, being *in* the world but not *of* it. For Menno Simons, the focus of a Christian's activity was the church, not the state, because the church, he believed, was the earthly agent of Christ, who was the supreme sovereign.

For seven years he labored in northern Holland, Friesland, and Groningen, shepherding the persecuted Brethren and publishing numerous evangelical tracts and several longer works. His most significant books were the *Foundation of Christian Doctrine* (1539), *The True Christian Faith* (1541), and *Reply to Gellius Faber* (1554). The final eighteen years of his life were devoted to the ministry in northwestern Germany, principally in the duchy of Holstein, where many Anabaptists had fled from the persecution in the Netherlands and Westphalia. Menno Simons's followers, widely known after 1541 as Mennonites, prospered in northwestern Europe despite bitter persecution. At one time they numbered almost one-tenth of the population of the Netherlands. Many of them also migrated eastward into Poland and Lithuania, where they settled in the marshy delta of the Vistula and in the hilly country of Upper Silesia. Wherever they colonized, they followed the admonition of their patron to seek an inner regeneration and renounce the world instead of trying to conquer it. Their modern descendants have found this principle of renunciation increasingly difficult to maintain.

Spiritual Reformers and Mystics

The many varieties of sixteenth-century Anabaptism further emphasize the eclectic nature of the Radical Reformation. Some of the reformers might be identified with several sects or religious traditions, whereas others completely defy classification. A number of these "free-lance" reformers had enough characteristics in common that we can categorize them as "spiritualists." Rejecting the visible organized church as an instrument of tyranny rather than as a medium of salvation, they upheld the freedom of the will in all religious matters and insisted that the spirit had to take precedence over both the letter and the law. They eschewed congregationalism because it required structure and organization, which they believed was inimical to the true spirit of God. They accepted the Bible as a guide to moral and spiritual life but recoiled from the rigidly literal interpretation of Scripture applied by all of the Protestant reformers.

Such an exponent of inner religion, although in some ways very untypical of other spiritualists, was Hans Denck, who has already been discussed as an Anabaptist theologian. Although Denck had been baptized by Hübmaier, and in turn performed baptisms himself, he eventually rejected ceremonialism and scripturalism to such an extent that he found even Anabaptist congregations incompatible with his view of personal freedom and inward salvation. Strongly repelled by the predestinarian limitation of God's love implicit in Luther's doctrine of salvation by grace, Denck maintained that "God compels no one, for He will have no one saved by compulsion." He felt that humanity's God-given free agency allows people to choose either good or evil, to be saved or lost. For Denck, this freedom likewise explains sin, since sin results from the unrighteous application of self-will. Free choice is thus the key to sorrow and damnation as well as to happiness and eternal life. In the attainment of either of these goals, claimed Denck, rituals, ceremonies, and sacraments are of no value whatever. By the same token,

He who thinks that he can be made truly righteous by means of a Book is ascribing to the dead letter what belongs to the Spirit. For that reason, salvation is not bound up with the Scriptures, however necessary and good they may be for their purpose, because it is impossible for the Scriptures to make good a bad heart, even though it may be a learned one.

Expelled from one city after another for his written and spoken views, Denck died of the plague in Basel at the age of thirty-three.

Two other former Anabaptists, devotees of the "inward word" who were strongly influenced by Denck's spiritualism, were Johann Bünderlin and Christian Entfelder. They both loved freedom, but separated themselves from Anabaptist associations when they saw these degenerate into license. In place of an institutional church, they sought "spiritual religion" in a mystical fellowship with God and with other spiritual persons. Above all, they rejected the theological systems and subtleties of both Protestants and Catholics, conceiving Christianity to be a way of living rather than a definition of doctrines. In his own way, despite his messianic eschatology, the Dutch Anabaptist-mystic David Joris was also a spokesman of this inner religion. He sought a mystical union with God through the pure love of Christ, and rejected all creeds, confessions, and outward contrivances.

An even more interesting and controversial figure in the mystical-spiritualistic reformation was the Silesian nobleman Caspar Schwenckfeld (1489–1561). Schwenckfeld had been an early convert to Lutheranism and served for many years as a lay preacher in Silesia. In 1525 he disassociated himself from Luther after a violent disagreement over the Lord's Supper, which Schwenckfeld interpreted in the sense of a symbolic partaking of Christ's spirit through the visible elements of bread and wine, a remembrance of his sacrifice and a rededication to his service. Schwenckfeld placed great emphasis on the celebration of the Lord's Supper, but believing that the true ordinance had been so perverted by men that its sanctity and validity had been lost, he refused to participate in it until God saw fit to reveal further knowledge and authority. He also believed that human nature and God's are compatible, that human beings participate in the divine nature and through a mystical fusion can become divine themselves.

Denying the necessity of a visible church, Schwenckfeld wandered about Europe preaching the inner gospel of freedom and love, which together with belief in personal revelation, constituted the nucleus of his theology. Like most of the spiritual reformers, Schwenckfeld believed Luther had deceived his followers by leading them only halfway to religious freedom. "He led us out of Egypt and guided us through the Red Sea into the desert," said Schwenckfeld, "but there he has left us, wandering at random, and yet trying to persuade us that we are already in the Promised Land."

Another maverick apostle of inward religion who shared many of Schwenckfeld's views was Sebastian Franck (1499–1542), a south-German humanist and priest who was converted to Lutheranism in 1527. Franck soon abandoned evangelical Protestantism because of its capitulation to the secular state and its encrustation with forms and rituals. For him the physical forms were encumbrances to true religion and perverted spirituality rather than promoted it. He conceived of religion as an individual matter between a person and God, not as an organ of the state (as with Catholics and Protestants) nor as a community of believers (as with Anabaptists). Franck believed religion requires no external organization or rituals, for the true sheep are known by their master and they in turn know him, by the inward light. To Franck, this inner light was the Word of God, not the printed word but the spiritual manifestation of God acting through human beings. Consequently, the Book, like the Church, inhibited true Christianity. Franck accused the reformers of substituting a "paper pope" for the Roman pope. For Franck it was entirely the spirit that gives life. His religious position can best be seen in his own testimony:

> Nobody is the master of my faith, and I desire to be the master of the faith of no one. I love any man whom I can help, and I call him brother whether he be Jew or Samaritan. . . . I cannot belong to any separate sect, but I believe in a holy, Christlike Church, a fellowship of saints, and I hold as my brother, my neighbour, my flesh and blood, all men who belong to Christ among all sects, faiths, and peoples scattered throughout the whole world—only I allow nobody to have dominion over the one place which I am pledged to the Lord to keep as pure virgin, namely my heart and my conscience. If you try to bind my conscience, to rule over my faith, or to be master of my heart, then I must leave you. Except *that*, everything I am or have is thine, whoever thou art or whatever thou mayest believe.

Reformers in Italy and Spain

South of the Alps and Pyrenees, the religious controversies of the early sixteenth century were of a different nature from those of northern Europe. Although Renaissance secularism was more apparent in Italy than in any other area of Europe, and the ritualistic vestments of religious orthodoxy were most lightly worn, still the theological, ecclesiastical, and financial center of the church was Rome. Disrespect for many of the church doctrines and practices was widely manifested; and open anticlericalism was expressed on all sides. Nevertheless, such assertions of religious concern were not in themselves prejudicial to the church. Italian humanists had a long tradition of ecclesiastical criticism while remaining staunch in their adherence to Christianity and in their defense of the church against outside forces. They eagerly reproved wayward monks and denounced clerical abuses, but they seldom censured basic doctrines or criticized the organizational concepts upon which the church was established. Therefore, although outwardly it would have appeared at the beginning of the century that the church in Italy was weak, it actually became stronger and more united as a result of the Lutheran threat.

Naples did not harbor the only reformist congregation in early sixteenth-century Italy. Similar circles could be found in Venice, Pavia, Turin, Florence, and Padua. At Ferrara, the popular Duchess Renée, wife of Duke Ercole and daughter of the former French king Louis XII, presided over a court that was not only indulgent of most forms of religious unorthodoxy but gave asylum to many of the religious and social outcasts of northern Italy. Olympia Morata (1526–55) was a close friend of the duchess and well versed in the classics, having been encouraged from an early age by her father. At the age of thirteen she is reported to have given a declamation in Latin on the *Paradoxes* of Cicero. She also wrote poems in Greek. While still at Ferrara, Olympia met and married a young German humanist and physician named Andrea Grunthler. When religious intolerance forced the couple to leave Ferrara, they crossed the Alps to Schweinfurt, where he lectured and practiced medicine and she continued to write, odes and dialogues as well as hundreds of letters to her friends in Italy and Germany. Many of these letters reveal her religious commitment to an interesting evangelical humanism, and her boldness in preaching it.

Lelio Sozzini (1525–62), a Sienese jurist who had been influenced by Anabaptists in Venice, was converted to antitrinitarianism by reading Erasmus's New Testament and by the burning of Servetus. Like some of the spiritualist reformers, Sozzini was forced to travel most of his life—in Italy, Switzerland, France, Germany, Bohemia, and Poland—and consequently attracted few organized followers. His nephew, Fausto Sozzini (1539–1604), inherited most of Lelio's books and some of his disciples and carried them with him to asylum in Poland where, under the protection of the Transylvanian prince Stephen Báthory, antitrinitarianism (Socinianism) flourished.

Jews and the Reformation

It was to Poland also that many thousands of European Jews fled when their lives became intolerable in the West. The Renaissance had been a time of relief and even fulfillment for many of the Jewish inhabitants of Italy. Under the patronage of the Italian despots, many of them not only found intermittent safety but a degree of identification and fulfillment as they participated in the economic and cultural life of the time—although always under the shadow of suspicion and the risk of oppression. In addition to following traditional occupations as goldsmiths, artisans, traders, and especially moneylenders, the cosmopolitan outlook of Italian Jews tended to make them more compatible with the cultural Renaissance, and many Jews in Renaissance Italy achieved a unique and remarkably successful synthesis of Hebraic and Christian-Renaissance cultures. Several distinguished rabbis in Florence examined Latin texts while studying the Talmud and expounding the mysteries of the Cabala; and in Ferrara, Mantua, and Padua lived prominent Jewish scholars of Hebrew and the Bible. They were in demand not only as teachers of Hebrew mysteries but as insightful commentators on Christian texts. This lively intellectual exchange did not lead to a general breakdown of suspicion and intolerance, however, for it was accompanied by a growing pressure to Christianize the Jews.

The drive to convert the Jews led to an unfortunate change of atmosphere. Venice began supporting an important Jewish colony in the early sixteenth century, made up both of refugees of the Italian wars and of German immigrants, reinforced by some Spanish and Portuguese exiles. One of the conditions of settlement in Venice, however, was that all of the Jews must live together in a designated area of the city. In 1516 they were established in a quarter called the New Foundry (*Ghetto nuovo*), hence the term *ghetto* to designate the Jewish quarter. This action is noteworthy not only because it separated Christians and Jews but because it forced Sephardic Jews (those from Spain), with their distinct liturgy, customs, and language, to live with Ashkenazi (German-rite) Jews, who had a very different history and tradition. In spite of the ghetto, Venetian rule was relatively light, and Jews in Venice continued to intermingle with Christians until religious pressures became overwhelming.

In the Holy Roman Empire, which, like Italy, lacked a centralized government, many scattered groups of Jews enjoyed a precarious protection from local rulers and city councils at the beginning of the sixteenth century. The Reuchlin-Pfefferkorn encounter reveals how sympathetic many German humanists were toward the Jews and their literature. The same sympathy seems to have pervaded the early years of the Reformation as well. The emperor Charles V, as a humanist sympathizer, granted the Jews very liberal privileges in the Empire, declaring that no Jew should be physically harmed or arbitrarily deprived of property. This order, of course, like so many imperial decrees, could not be enforced. At the same time, pressure to convert the Jews—or expunge them from the land—grew as religious polemics intensified. As in the past, Jews became the scapegoats of every natural catastrophe or disaster. Now, with the fear and anxiety of the imminent purging associated with the end of the world, accusations of ritual murder increased, as Jews were accused of killing Christian children and drinking their blood in a mystic rite.

As a devoted biblical scholar, Luther was initially attracted to Hebrew studies and was openly favorable toward the Jews, whom he expected to convert en masse. Believing they would respond to his simple and straightforward exposition of the Gospel, he had visions of them flocking to the "pure teachings of Christ." He soundly castigated the popes, bishops, and monks for their rash treatment of the Jews and for doing "nothing but curse Jews and seize their wealth." In contrast, he advocated treating them with kindness and consideration. However, when Luther discovered how tenaciously they held to their traditional religion and customs, refusing to embrace evangelical Christianity just as they had rejected the traditional Catholic faith, he turned on them savagely, blaming their stubbornness and the falsehood of their doctrines for their unfortunate condition. He began writing violent anti-Jewish diatribes advocating not only their expulsion from remaining Christian lands but even the burning of their synagogues and books.

The princes of Saxony and Brandenburg responded by expelling all Jews from their territories. Through the mediation of Joseph of Rosheim, a respected Jewish leader of Alsace, other German rulers were persuaded not to follow suit, and even in Brandenburg the expulsion decree was somewhat modified. Nevertheless, all of the German states adopted restrictions, such as confining the Jews to ghettos and requiring them to wear a yellow badge when outside the ghetto walls. Joseph of Rosheim also succeeded in getting Emperor Charles V to forbid the circulation of Luther's anti-Jewish writings in the Empire. This was a hollow victory, however, since the emperor had already outlawed all of Luther's writings—and to little avail.

The persistent image of the Jews as the embodiment of evil, stoked by the fiery sermons of zealous preachers, prevailed in most of Europe by mid-century. Charles himself ordered the expulsion of Jews from the territory of Naples in 1540 and forbade their migration to the New World. Pope Paul IV reversed the lenient policy of Renaissance popes by renewing all the repressive medieval strictures and adding a few of his own. Jews were to be segregated in ghettos, excluded from the professions (especially medicine), and required to wear a demeaning mark of identification; their commercial activity was restricted, and they were forbidden to own real property. Finally, in 1555 he expelled them from the Papal States, except in Rome and Ancona, where their financial activities made them indispensable.

Actions during the Reformation and Counter-Reformation brought an end to the age of western European Judaism, at least for two centuries. It had had periods of flowering, especially in medieval Spain and Renaissance Italy, but after the middle of the sixteenth century the greater concentration of Jews was to be found in eastern and southeastern Europe, particularly in Poland-Lithuania and, more precariously, within the Ottoman Empire. Here too were the new centers of Jewish literature and thought until the time of the Enlightenment in Europe.

Suggestions for Further Reading

SCANDINAVIA AND EASTERN EUROPE

Not much is available in English on the Reformation in the north, but much good material exists in some of the more general histories such as Michael Roberts' priceless *The Early Vasas: A History of Sweden, 1523–1611* (Cambridge and New York, 1968, 1986), and N.K. Andersen's essay on "The Reformation in Scandinavia and the Baltic," in *The New Cambridge Modern History,* vol. II, 2nd ed. (Cambridge, England, 1990). There is also much useful information in E.H. Dunckley, *The Reformation in Denmark* (London, 1948). The standard work on Petri is Conrad Bergendoff, *Olavus Petri and the Ecclesiastical Transformation of Sweden, 1520–1552* (New York, 1929), but it is very dated. E.E. Yelverton, *An Archbishop of the Reformation: Laurentius Petri* (Minneapolis, 1959) is useful. Brief but insightful and current is Leif Grane, *University and Reformation: Lectures from the University of Copenhagen Symposium* (Leiden, 1982).

For eastern Europe, there are some highlights in Béla K. Király, ed., *Tolerance and Movements of Religious Dissent in Eastern Europe* (New York, 1975). Norman Davies, *God's Playground: A History of Poland, vol. 1: Origins to 1795* (Oxford, 1981) is a good starting point for Poland. David A. Frick, *Polish Sacred Philology in the Refor-*

mation and the Counter-Reformation (Berkeley, 1989) is very specialized and only partially apropos. Three other books are highly recommended: Anatanas Musteikis, *The Reformation in Lithuania: Religious Fluctuations in the Sixteenth Century* (Boulder, 1988); Henry R. Cooper, Jr., ed., *Four Hundred Years of the South Slavic Protestant Reformation* (Bloomington, 1985); and Alexander S. Unghvary, *The Hungarian Protestant Reformation in the Sixteenth Century under Ottoman Impact* (Lewiston, New York, 1989).

ZWINGLI AND THE REFORMATION IN SWITZERLAND

The leading account in English of Zwingli's life and thought is still G.R. Potter, *Zwingli* (New York and Cambridge, 1976), although the new English edition of Ulrich Gäbler, *Huldrych Zwingli: His Life and Work,* tr. by Erik Gritsch (Philadelphia, 1986) is also satisfactory. On Zwingli's thought the best sources are Gottfried W. Locher, *Zwingli's Thought: New Perspectives* (Leiden, 1981), and especially W.P. Stephens, *The Theology of Huldrych Zwingli* (Oxford, 1986), which is a comprehensive and systematic treatment based on the careful reading and interpretation of Zwingli's writings. His views on church and state are well presented in Robert C. Walton, *Zwingli's Theocracy* (Toronto, 1971), and his cultural commitment in Charles Garside, Jr., *Zwingli and the Arts* (New Haven, 1966). Valuable essays are contained in E.J. Furcha, et al, ed., *Prophet, Pastor, Protestant: The Work of Huldrych Zwingli After Five Hundred Years* (Allison Park, Pennsylvania, 1984), and Furcha, ed., *Huldrych Zwingli, 1484–1531: A Legacy of Radical Reform* (Montreal, 1988). Zwingli's attitude toward the poor is discussed in Lee Palmer Wandel, *Always Among Us: Images of the Poor in Zwingli's Zurich* (New York, 1990).

The best study of the covenant theology of Zwingli's successor in Zurich is J. Wayne Baker, *Heinrich Bullinger and the Covenant: The Other Reformed Tradition* (Athens, Ohio, 1980). For the spread of the Reformation to Strasbourg, see especially William S. Stafford, *Domesticating the Clergy: The Inception of the Reformation in Strasbourg, 1522–1524* (Missoula, Montana, 1976); Thomas A. Brady, *Ruling Class, Regime and Reformation in Strasbourg, 1520–1555* (Leiden, 1978); and Lorna Jane Abray, *The People's Reformation: Magistrates, Clergy, and Commons in Strasbourg, 1500–1598* (Ithaca, 1985). Miriam U. Chrisman's innovative *Lay Culture, Learned Culture: Books and Social Change in Strasbourg, 1480–1599* (New Haven, 1983) provides a new perspective on the culture and thought of this period.

THE ANABAPTISTS

A very readable yet scholarly introduction to Anabaptist origins is provided in J. Denny Weaver, *Becoming Anabaptist: The Origins and Significance of Sixteenth Century Anabaptism* (Scottdale, Pennsylvania, 1987). A broader account of the entire Radical Reformation is Michael Mullett, *Radical Religious Movements in Early Modern Europe* (London, 1980), much shorter than George Williams's classic *The Radical Reformation* (Philadelphia, 1962; Kirksville, Missouri, 1991). Twenty-one biographical sketches, edited by Hans-Jürgen Goertz, provide a good introduction to the movement, in *Profiles of Radical Reformers* (Scottdale, Pennsylvania, 1982). Other meaningful essays may be found in James M. Stayer and Werner O. Packull, eds., *The Anabaptists and Thomas Müntzer* (Dubuque, Iowa, 1980); Wilbert R. Shenk, ed., *Anabaptism and Mission* (Scottdale, Pennsylvania, 1984); and Hans Hillerbrand, ed., *Radical Tendencies in the Reformation: Divergent Perspectives* (Kirksville, Missouri, 1988), emphasizing the idea that the so-called Radical Reformation cannot be correctly understood outside the mainstream of the German Reformation. Another valuable collection, this of excerpts from writings about women, plus selections from original sources, is Joyce L. Irwin, ed., *Womanhood in Radical Protestantism, 1525–1675* (New York, 1979). The best social history of the movement is Claus-Peter Clasen, *Anabaptism: A Social History, 1525–1618* (Ithaca, 1972).

VARIETIES AND SPREAD OF ANABAPTISM

The first full-length biography of the early Anabaptist leader, martyr, and author of the Schleitheim Confession, Michael Sattler, is provided by C. Arnold Snyder in *The Life and Thought of Michael Sattler* (Scottdale, Pennsylvania, 1984), a valuable addition to the growing literature on the life and thought of leading Anabaptists. Also see H. Wayne Pipkin and John H. Yoder, *Balthasar Hubmaier, Theologian of Anabaptism* (Scottdale, Pennsylvania, 1989), a comprehensive study of this pivotal figure; and Gustav Roehrich, *Essay on the Life, the Writings and the Doctrine of the Anabaptist Hans Denck*, tr. by Claude Foster et al (New York, 1983). Leonard Gross has given us a vivid picture of second-generation Hutterite life under Peter Walpot, in *The Golden Years of the Hutterites* (Scottdale, Pennsylvania, 1980).

On the Dutch Anabaptists, see especially Cornelius Krahn's comprehensive *Dutch Anabaptism: Origins, Spread, Life, and Thought, 1450–1600* (Scottdale, Pennsylvania, 1981). Valuable analytical studies are presented in Irvin B. Horst, ed., *The Dutch Dissenters: A Critical Companion to Their History and Ideas* (Leiden, 1986). The interaction of religion and society in Münster following the Anabaptist debacle there is studied in detail in R. Po-chia Hsia, *Society and Religion in Münster, 1535–1618* (New Haven, 1984). For the Mennonites, see Cornelius J. Dyck, *An Introduction to Mennonite History*, rev. ed. (Scottdale, Pennsylvania, 1981), also Calvin W. Redekop and Samuel J. Steinter, *Mennonite Identity: Historical and Contemporary Perspectives* (Lanham, Maryland, 1988). On Joris the best is Gary Waite, *David Joris and Dutch Anabaptism, 1524–1543* (Waterloo, Ontario, 1990).

MYSTICAL SPIRITUALISTS AND THE REFORMATION IN SPAIN AND ITALY

The most active area of scholarship in recent years has been directed toward Casper Schwenckfeld and his followers. See especially Horst Weigelt, *The Schwenckfelders in Silesia*, tr. by Peter C. Erb (Pennsburg, Pennsylvania, 1985), covering a broad sweep of history; André Séguenny, *The Christology of Casper Schwenckfeld: Spirit and Flesh in the Process of Life Transformation*, tr. by Peter C. Erb and Simone Nieuwolt (Lewiston, New York, 1987), which claims that Schwenckfeld's spiritualism was more indebted to Erasmus than to Luther. The richest study of Schwenckfeld himself and the development of his ideas is R. Emmett McLaughlin, *Casper Schwenckfeld, Reluctant Radical: His Life to 1540* (New Haven, 1986), which maintains that Schwenckfeld was essentially Lutheran until 1525. A valuable collection of papers is Peter C. Erb, ed., *Schwenckfeld and Early Schwenckfeldianism* (Pennsburg, Pennsylvania, 1986), presented at the 1985 Pennsburg Colloquium on Schwenckfeld.

The basic works on the Spanish and Italian reformers are José C. Nieto, *Juan de Valdés and the Origins of the Spanish and Italian Reformation* (Geneva, Switzerland, 1970); A. Gordon Kinder, *Spanish Protestants and Reformers in the Sixteenth Century* (London, 1983); Jerome Friedman, *Michael Servetus: A Case Study in Total Heresy* (Geneva, Switzerland, 1978); and Anne J. Schutte, *Pier Paolo Vergerio: The Making of an Italian Reformer* (Geneva, Switzerland, 1977). There are useful articles in Joseph C. McLelland, ed., *Peter Martyr Vermigli and Italian Reform* (Waterloo, Ontario, 1981).

JEWS AND THE REFORMATION

For a brief overview of anti-Semitism in the Reformation see Heiko A. Oberman, *The Roots of Anti-Semitism in the Age of Renaissance and Reformation,* tr. by James I. Porter (Philadelphia, 1984), and John Edwards, *The Jews in Christian Europe, 1400–1700* (London, 1988). A brilliant analysis of one virulent form of anti-Semitism, the ritual murder trials, is R. Po-chia Hsia, *The Myth of Ritual Murder: Jews and Magic in Reformation Germany* (New Haven, 1989). On the other hand, Jerome Friedman shows how Hebrew learning and rabbinic tradition became an important ingredient in sixteenth-century Christian theology in *The Most Ancient Testimony: Sixteenth-Century Christian-Hebraica in the Age of Renaissance Nostalgia* (Athens, Ohio, 1983). Several other dimensions of Jewish thought are explored in Bernard D. Cooperman, ed., *Jewish Thought in the Sixteenth Century* (Cambridge, Massachusetts, 1983). André Neher, *Jewish Thought and the Scientific Revolution of the Sixteenth Century,* tr. by David Maisel (New York, 1987), and David B. Ruderman, *Kabbalah, Magic and Science: The Cultural Universe of a Sixteenth-Century Jewish Physician* (Cambridge, Massachusetts, 1988) focus on David Gans and Abraham Yagel. The Jewish story is followed into the seventeenth century in Yosef Kaplan, *From Christianity to Judaism: the Story of Isaac Orobio de Castro* (New York, 1989), the saga of a Portuguese *converso* who returned to Judaism. Very enlightening on the influence of the Jews between 1550 and 1750 are Brian B. Pullan, *The Jews of Europe and the Inquisition of Venice, 1550–1670* (Totowa, New Jersey, 1983), and Jonathan I. Israel, *European Jewry in the Age of Mercantilism, 1550–1750* (New York, 1985). Also pertinent is Myriam Yardeni, *Anti-Jewish Mentalities in Early Modern Europe* (Lanham, Maryland, 1990).

4 | THE RISE AND EXPANSION OF CALVINISM

T HE MIDDLE DECADES OF THE SIXTEENTH CENTURY FORMED A WA-
tershed between the fluid early Reformation period and the hardened
and polarized dogmatism of the age of religious wars. The first half of
the century witnessed continually changing political alignments and the birth
of many new and untried religious doctrines and affiliations. After mid-century, this effervescence gave way to cantankerous certainty and black-or-white
rigidity. In between were the crucial years of decision that set the course succeeding generations would follow. The factors responsible for shaping the
events of this period were numerous and complex; among them was the clash
between the recently arisen militant Calvinism and a rejuvenated Catholicism.
In 1536 Calvinism did not yet exist; by 1562 it had developed such strength
and ardor that it was ready to challenge the greatest kingdoms in Europe.

Reformation and Repression in France

Compared to early sixteenth-century Germany, France seemed to be a country
of tranquility and peace. Yet France, too, had political, economic, and social
problems requiring attention, and there was religious discontent—although its
causes were not as numerous nor its manifestations as great as in Germany.
What is certain is that the position taken by France in the religious fissure
cutting across Europe would greatly affect the direction and final outcome of
the Protestant Reformation.

Politically, France was relatively calm under the benevolent despotism of
Francis I. The authority of the French crown, unlike that of the Holy Roman
emperor, was secure and extensive, and as long as good rapport continued
between the king and the great nobles, there seemed little cause for concern.
The vital factor was the king himself. As long as he remained steadfast in the
Catholic faith there was little danger of a Protestant takeover. Yet how steadfast was Francis? Could he be counted on to uphold the worldwide authority
of the pope as well as support the doctrines of the church, or would he, like
his rival, Henry VIII, desire all power in his own hands, ecclesiastical as well

as political? This question could only be answered with time, but it did seem as though the king's 1515 settlement with Pope Leo in the Concordat of Bologna would provide a suitable *modus vivendi* and prevent the occurrence of a rift between the French crown and the papacy.

The social and economic situation, however, was not so bright. As early as the 1520s, the rise in prices was beginning to be felt by French artisans and wage earners. The costly Italian and Habsburg-Valois wars required the imposition of higher taxes, the burden of which fell heavily upon the lower classes. Social unrest appeared in Lyon among the printers and in Paris among the lesser artisans, retail grocers, and drapers. Francis's fiscal system, which was based more on improving his own means of collecting revenues than on increasing the wealth of his subjects, did nothing to alleviate social unrest. Nevertheless, during the crucial period of the early Reformation, many of these symptoms were not yet apparent; France was riding the crest of unprecedented prosperity. Few Frenchmen in the 1520s were likely to seek economic and social redress in Protestantism.

France, however, was seething with intellectual ferment in the early sixteenth century, just as the Empire was. The literary Renaissance in France and Flanders had a profound effect upon religious and philosophical thought, and the spread of humanism added a moralizing factor to the intellectual ferment. Christian humanism took root quickly in France under the inspiration of Erasmus and his disciples there. It grew particularly fast at Paris and among intellectual circles at Lyon, Orléans, Grenoble, Le Mans, and Poitiers. This moral-intellectual humanism sought to unify and strengthen Christianity through charity, moral regeneration, and a return to Scripture. However, it also led to sharp and sometimes penetrating criticism of existing religious practices, since the Christian humanists were reformers as well as scholars and writers. Nevertheless, in France the censuring of delinquent monks and clerics was not practiced with quite the same relish as it was in Germany. It lacked the deep bitterness and hatred that characterized German anticlericalism.

A more mystical and emotional manifestation of discontent appeared after 1520 in the village of Meaux, a short distance from Paris. Inspiration for the reform movement there came from the beloved old humanist, Jacques Lefèvre d'Etaples, but its active leader was Lefèvre's former pupil, Guillaume Briçonnet (1470–1533), once abbot at the monastery of Saint-Germain-des-Prés and now bishop of Meaux. The Meaux group was composed of deeply religious people who dreamed of a genuine revival of Christian piety and love. This renewal would be effected, they believed, by a return to the truth and love of Christ as revealed in the Scriptures. In 1523 Lefèvre's translation of the four Gospels was published, followed shortly by the Old and New Testaments, as Meaux became the center of religious revivalism in France. However, neither the mild-mannered Christian humanist nor the pious and eloquent bishop intended the slightest infidelity to the church, much less the promotion of religious dissension or turmoil. Implicitly revolutionary, the Meaux "reformers" nevertheless remained staunchly obedient to the church.

Marguerite of Navarre. *The sister of Francis I was an outstanding writer and patron of learning. Devoted to the cause of religious reform, she tried to steer a middle course between Catholicism and Calvinism.*

Less compliant was Briçonnet's friend and confidant, the king's sister, Marguerite of Navarre (1492–1549), who presided over a circle of avant-garde literati and devotees of the New Learning at Nérac, near the Pyrenees. Marguerite was a remarkable and talented woman who not only contributed greatly to the literary Renaissance in France with her own writings, notably the *Heptameron,* but was also an avid student of the Bible. She disliked the rigidity of scholastic theology and denied the supernatural powers of the priesthood. She was in agreement with Lefèvre and the Christian humanists who emphasized the moral teachings of Christ, and came very close to the Protestant conception of faith and love. Nevertheless, the queen of Navarre was scarcely more likely to lead a genuine religious revolt in France than were Lefèvre and Briçonnet. For all three of them, regeneration had to come from within the heart and soul of each believer; it could not be accomplished through institutional or doctrinal innovations.

The first winds of real religious revolt were felt in France from the printing and circulation of Lutheran pamphlets and tracts. In the weeks following the Leipzig debate, Luther's message began to penetrate the Gallic lands. By 1523 many of his writings were circulated and read by French intellectuals. Small groups of Lutheran sympathizers began to appear in Paris; at Meaux among the more reform-minded followers of Bishop Briçonnet; in several cities of

Picardy; in Châlons, Vitry, and Metz in eastern France; and in the south from Grenoble to Bordeaux. The most enthusiastic translator and interpreter of Luther to the French was Louis de Berquin, an aristocratic friend of Lefèvre and Marguerite, who became one of the first martyrs of French Protestantism.

The principal instruments for the control and suppression of doctrinal irregularities in France were the Parlement de Paris and the Sorbonne. Following the papal condemnation of Luther, the Parlement de Paris began to crack down on Protestant literature and on persons involved in distributing it. The zeal of the Parlement, however, was largely nullified by the patronage of the king, who not only looked favorably upon the intellectual activities of the reformers but rather fancied himself a discriminating and knowledgeable humanist.

The first hardening of the crown's attitude toward the reformers came during Francis I's captivity in Spain following the disastrous battle of Pavia in February 1525, when the king's mother, Louise of Savoy, ruled as regent. At the instigation of the Sorbonne and the Parlement de Paris, Lutheran books were burned, the group at Meaux was scattered, and some Protestant converts were executed. However, a degree of tranquility was reestablished with the return of the king, who needed the continued friendship of the Lutheran princes of Germany in his foreign policy. Then suddenly in the autumn of 1534, the peace was broken by the Affair of the Placards: on the morning of 18 October, people in Paris and many other cities of France awoke to find walls and doors plastered with tracts against the church. Believing now that a widespread Protestant conspiracy was afoot, the government took repressive action. In 1540 the Edict of Fontainebleau created machinery within the Parlement de Paris for prosecuting heresy. However, it succeeded only in driving the movement underground.

In the meantime, a new spirit and intensity was infused into French Protestantism after 1536 by the publication of John Calvin's *Institutes of the Christian Religion* and the subsequent introduction of Calvinist theology and organization. With the entrance of Calvin, a new stage in the Reformation began.

John Calvin and the Institutes of the Christian Religion

John Calvin was born 10 July 1509 at Noyon in Picardy, the son of Gérard Cauvin (Calvin), a successful notary and fiscal secretary of the bishop of Noyon, and Jeanne Lefranc of Cambrai. Young Calvin possessed a brilliant mind that he trained assiduously at school and by avid reading. When he was only twelve, his father used his ecclesiastical connections to obtain a cathedral chaplaincy for him, to which were later added other benefices that helped pay for the boy's education. At the age of fourteen, Calvin entered the Collège de la Marche at the University of Paris where he began his humanistic studies under the distinguished Latinist, Mathurin Cordier. Shortly thereafter, he transferred to the celebrated Collège de Montaigu where his father hoped he would receive a solid foundation in theology and enter the priesthood. At Montaigu (satirized by Erasmus for its stale eggs and equally stale theology), Calvin first came to associate with other great minds of the day, including

Guillaume Cop, Guillaume Budé, and François Rabelais. There he developed a deep thirst for knowledge.

Early in 1528, at the age of eighteen, he was awarded the Master of Arts degree, and appeared to be intent on continuing the study of letters. Then suddenly, due in part to a quarrel between his father and the bishop of Noyon, and partly to the elder Calvin's feeling for law, young Calvin was sent to the renowned university at Orléans to begin the study of law. At Orléans, and subsequently at Bourges, Calvin was a student of Pierre de l'Etoile, the foremost teacher of jurisprudence in France, and attended lectures by the great Italian law reformer and teacher, Andrea Alciati. At the same time, he studied Greek under the German scholar Melchior Wolmar, who is known to have had Lutheran leanings.

In 1531 Calvin's father died and the eager young student returned to Paris where, at the Collège Fortet, he resumed his devotion to humanist letters and scholarship. How deeply he immersed himself in the classical authors is reflected in his first publication, a penetrating *Commentary on Seneca's Treatise on Clemency,* a book that exhibits remarkable learning in classical literature and philosophy. Stoicism appealed to many of the Christian humanists, who admired Seneca's love of truth and his implied belief in the unity and equality of humanity. Calvin was particularly sympathetic with the Stoics' belief in the existence of a supernatural and overriding providence. He emphasized this point in his *Commentary* and used it as a springboard to insist on the supremacy of natural and divine law. His interest in Seneca and other ancient authors was not just a passing fancy for Calvin. Humanism did not remain the only focus of Calvin's thought after his religious conversion, yet his humanistic and legal training continued to influence both the elegance and power of his Latin style and the methodology of his biblical exegesis.

Although we know little about Calvin's activities between 1531 and 1534, and almost nothing about his religious and intellectual struggles during that time, it is apparent that he was experiencing a vital intellectual change. Unlike Luther, Calvin seldom wrote about himself, and when he did it was cryptic and reserved. In the preface to his *Commentary on the Psalms,* which he wrote in 1557, he reveals only that he experienced a "sudden conversion." It is apparent that his soul was still troubled when he returned to Paris in 1531. He traveled regularly between Noyon, Paris, Orléans, and Bourges; obtained the law degree in 1532; participated in Parisian Bible study groups in 1533; and may have taken part in the Affair of the Placards in 1534.

The outward turning point took place when Calvin's friend, Nicholas Cop, son of the royal physician and recently elected rector of the university, was forced to flee the city because of a Protestant-sounding rectorial address he delivered at the opening of the fall session. Cop criticized the Sorbonne theologians and emphasized the role of grace in salvation, while minimizing works. Although the precise relationship of Calvin to this address is unclear, it is evident that he was acquainted with its contents before it was presented—if indeed he was not its co-author—and that he approved of the ideas it contained. Warned that his life was in jeopardy, Calvin escaped from the city, never to return again except in disguise. It was during his exile of the next two years, terminating in Basel, that Calvin wrote the most important book of the Protestant Reformation.

Almost from the moment of its publication in March 1536, the *Institutes of the Christian Religion* was the strongest weapon of the Reformation against the Roman church. Written in clear-cut, humanistically styled Latin, the *Institutes* was at once a comprehensive and well-proportioned catechism of Christian doctrine, a manual for church organization, and a scholarly synthesis of Protestant thought. It contained a bold preface addressed to Francis I, calling upon the king to take serious note of its contents and to reject the superstitions of Catholicism. "Seeing that countless folk in this realm hunger and thirst after Christ, but that very few know Him," Calvin charged, "seeing also that the fury of some iniquitous persons has been raised in your realm . . . and that every way is closed to righteous teaching, I should like this book to confess the faith of the persecuted believers."

This first edition of the *Institutes* contained six chapters, dividing the presentation into the headings Law and Decalogue, Faith, The Sermon, True Sacraments, False Sacraments, and Christian Liberty (that is, the church and state), with the emphasis throughout on worship, morals, and administration. Later editions lengthened the work to some eighty chapters, yet its unified impact remained unchanged. In 1539 Calvin added themes of Pauline-Augustinian theology, devoting a special chapter to predestination and divine election, and included a chapter on the Christian life. In 1541 he assured his position at the vanguard of French literary creation by publishing an elaborate version of the *Institutes* in French, an immediate landmark in the evolution of French prose. The final, definitive edition was published by the well-known French publisher Robert Estienne in 1559. In it can be seen the justification for John T. McNeill's conclusion that "It is not Calvin's logic but the vigor of his rhetoric and his rarely matched power of communication, under the sway of religious conviction and emotion, that constitute him, through the *Institutes,* one of the makers of the modern mind."

Despite the maturity of his *Institutes,* Calvin had much schooling ahead of him when he made the decision to devote his life to the service of God. From Basel he set out for Italy, where he visited the talented and refined duchess of Ferrara, Renée of France, daughter of Louis XII and sister-in-law to Francis I. Calvin knew of her sympathy with the Reformation and that her court was a haven for Protestant refugees. For the time being, Renée could do little to help the young reformer, but she did become a loyal follower, and after the death of her husband, Ercole d'Este (d. 1559), she joined the Calvinist Huguenots in France. In the meantime, en route to Strasbourg from Paris (and Noyon, where he had returned to arrange the estate of his father and to persuade some of his relatives to join him in exile), Calvin was forced by the renewed hostilities of the Habsburg-Valois war to detour to the south, where he passed through the city of Geneva. Here his life took a new and unexpected turn that was to have the greatest significance for the future development of Protestantism.

Calvin's first reaction to Farel's entreaty was negative, but when the fiery preacher insisted that it was God's will that he stay, Calvin submitted. He was deeply motivated by the conviction that he was "called" to serve. The first position he occupied was "Reader in Holy Scripture to the church in Geneva." Later he was assigned to preach and participate in ecclesiastical reorganization. A three-pronged campaign to reform the religious worship, elaborate a clear-cut and meaningful doctrinal basis for the church, and clean up the moral life of the city, was launched in November 1536. Under the watchful eyes of Calvin and Farel, the remnants of Catholic ritual were eliminated and the Mass was replaced with simple services of prayers, sermons, and psalms sung to homey melodies. Two months later, Calvin submitted his reform program in the form of *Articles Concerning the Government of the Church,* also a *Confession of Faith and a Catechism,* which were abstracted from his *Institutes.* He proposed to make the Confession mandatory for all citizens of Geneva by public profession and oath, in order to differentiate between those who "preferred to belong to the kingdom of the popes rather than the kingdom of Christ." He also insisted that the church have the right to examine the worthiness of its members and to discipline impenitent sinners. After considerable discussion and hesitation, the councils accepted both the Articles and the Confession.

Calvin's attempt to reform and regulate the lives of the Genevans, however, met with opposition from the people. Disorder and violence resulted. There was so much dissension, in fact, that the magistrates began to renege on some points in the program, and by July they rejected Calvin's plan for church discipline, fearing it would challenge their own authority. Now Calvin locked horns with the councils. He demanded that church authority only should determine the prerequisites and conditions of church fellowship, and that the means of spiritual discipline should be exercised by the church. The magistrates, on the other hand, insisted that discipline, including the supervision of public morals, had always been and should remain a prerogative of the civil government.

The gulf widened after February 1538 when several of Calvin's opponents were elected to the Little Council. A crisis then developed when the Council of Two Hundred decreed that the Lord's Supper should be celebrated in the Bernese manner, with unleavened bread. Calvin protested that the council had no such authority, but was answered with an edict forbidding him from interfering in affairs of state and later banning him from preaching at all. Riots and demonstrations ensued. On Easter morning, 1538, Calvin defied the ban and not only preached a sermon at Saint Peter's, in which he denounced the council's action, but refused to distribute the sacrament to anyone. The next day, both Calvin and Farel were expelled from the city, leaving it with their curse.

The two companions went first to Bern, then to Zürich, and finally to Basel, where they hoped to remain in peace at this well-developed center of Protestantism. However, Farel soon accepted a call from his former parish at Neuchâtel, and Calvin was invited by Martin Bucer, the leader of the Reformation at Strasbourg, to join him in that imperial city. Calvin hesitated, as he had when Farel summoned him to Geneva, but in like manner he submitted to Bucer's insistence that it was divine will that called him.

Strasbourg, Calvin, and Martin Bucer

Strasbourg was a busy and prosperous commercial city located at the cross-roads between Germany, France, Switzerland, and the Netherlands; it was an open mart of ideas as well as goods. By 1538 it had become one of the most flourishing centers of the Protestant Reformation. Under the political leadership of the venerable Alsatian, Jakob Sturm, Strasbourg had undergone many momentous yet relatively peaceful modifications since the first introduction of Lutheranism there in 1521. The real architect of Reformation in Strasbourg was Martin Bucer (1491–1551) who, with his companions and followers, Matthew Zell and Wolfgang Capito, established a broadly based Protestant worship in Strasbourg that allowed a compatible home for Lutherans, Sacramentarians, and even some Anabaptists. During the first thirty years of the Reformation, Strasbourg remained an island of toleration in a sea of persecution and oppression.

Bucer, a former Dominican friar—whose supportive wife, Wibrandis Rosenblatt, had previously been married to the Swiss reformers Johannes Oecolampadius and Wolfgang Capito before their untimely deaths in 1531 and 1541—was a theological moderate, able to reconcile the divergent doctrines of Luther and Zwingli, and even to win a degree of cooperation from Catholics. Flexible and willing to compromise, he built up in Strasbourg a religious community that was unique in its Protestant eclecticism and in its determination not to be led into extremism. Calvin's initial contact with Bucer reaffirmed him in many of his theological assumptions. Both of them abhorred the ritualistic relic worship of the Catholic church; and both maintained that true worship primarily meant an encounter with the Bible, involving prayer, sermon, and psalm singing as the essential ingredients. Anything in the religious service that tended toward superstition, or that might distract from the Bible sermon, should be abandoned. The gospel was composed of spirit and law, the former revealed in the sovereignty of God and the latter in the Bible as a pattern of life.

In his new role as pastor of the colony of French refugees in Strasbourg, Calvin was able to clarify and expand his doctrinal views while closely observing the operation of Bucer's orderly and disciplined ecclesiastical government. He also learned much about the organization and functioning of schools as he saw the foundations for the Strasbourg gymnasium laid by the distinguished Lutheran humanist and educator, Johann Sturm (no relation to Jakob), and observed its productive growth under Sturm's capable rectorship. Calvin was appointed lecturer in Holy Scripture in Sturm's school and contributed enthusiastically to his educational objective of producing young men who were "pious, learned, and able to express themselves well."

Calvin's entire experience at Strasbourg was one of learning and fulfillment. Early in 1539 he participated with a Strasbourg delegation at the Congress of Frankfurt, summoned by Emperor Charles V to settle the problem of religious schism. Here, and in subsequent meetings at Haguenau, Worms, and Regensburg, Calvin came into intimate contact with German Protestantism and became personally acquainted with Melanchthon, whom he admired greatly even though he disagreed with him on some doctrines. Their mutual humanist orientation gave them much in common. During the next two years at Strasbourg, Calvin found further personal fulfillment in marriage to Idelette de Bure, widow of a former Dutch Anabaptist, and in the production of an impressive repertoire of writings. He translated, modified, and published Bucer's Protestant liturgy; compiled a book of psalms with musical notation; answered Jacopo Sadoleto's appeal to the Genevans to return to the Catholic fold with the crisp *Reply to Cardinal Sadoleto,* a brilliant defense of Protestantism; wrote his lengthy *Commentary on the Epistle to the Romans* and the *Short Treatise on the Lord's Supper*; and published the first French edition of the *Institutes.*

The relative tranquility of Calvin's life in Strasbourg was not destined to continue. For months, delegates from Geneva had been trying to persuade him to return to Switzerland and resume his pastorate in the city that had banned him three years before. Calvin hesitated. "I would rather suffer a hundred deaths than bear that cross on which one must perish a thousand times daily," he claimed. The very thought of returning to Geneva terrified him. Yet changes had come about in Geneva during the three years of his absence. Civil disorder and chaos had continued at an accelerated pace after the expulsion of the French pastors. Rival factions arose to deepen the social and religious upheaval. As they did, the Catholics reopened their assault, threatening to regain the city for Rome. In the process, the governing councils had been reconstituted and were now composed of men predominantly favorable to Calvin. It was this new Genevan government that persuaded him to return. "My timidity suggested to me many reasons for excusing myself from again willingly taking upon my shoulders so heavy a burden," he later confided. "At length, however, a solemn and conscientious regard to my duty prevailed with me to consent to return to the flock from which I had been torn; but with what grief, tears, great anxiety and distress I did this, the Lord is my best witness." On 13 September 1541 Calvin, now age thirty-two, arrived in Geneva and presented himself to the magistrates, receiving from them his appointment as pastor of the Saint Peter parish, a substantial salary, and a large house (on what is now Rue de Calvin) for himself, his wife, and his stepdaughter.

The Church in Geneva

Organization

Calvin had been called to restore order in the church in Geneva, and he wasted no time in getting at it. His first step was to draw up a constitution for regulating and governing the church. The *Ecclesiastical Ordinances of the Church of Geneva* was submitted to the Little Council for its approval, and after two months of serious discussion, disagreement, and some compromise, the councils granted their endorsement and presented the *Ordinances* to the general assembly of citizens for ratification. Calvin had to back down on several points and to agree to an article specifically stipulating that civil matters lay outside the jurisdiction of the ministers. Yet the church was still allowed greater jurisdictional autonomy than it had in any area where the Lutheran and Zwinglian reformations had occurred. With certain qualifications, the administration of ecclesiastical discipline was given to the church, supported by the civil magistrates, of course. This was the issue that had driven Calvin from Geneva three years earlier, and it continued to be the most delicate question after his return.

The *Ecclesiastical Ordinances* established four orders of offices: pastors, teachers, elders, and deacons. The primary functions of the pastors (ministers) were to preach the word, administer the sacraments (baptism and the Lord's Supper), and admonish the worshipers. New pastors were to be chosen by the ministers and the magistrates, and presented to the people for their "common consent." Pastors had to take an oath to serve God, keep the Ecclesiastical Ordinances, and maintain and obey the civil laws. The calling of teachers (doctors) was to "instruct the faithful in sound doctrine." Prospective teachers were presented to a committee for examination after being chosen by the ministers and the magistrates. Provision was made for the establishment of schools, and specifically for "a college to teach the children, so as to prepare them for the ministry as well as for the civil government." Elders (presbyters) were laymen whose primary responsibility was to maintain order and discipline. They were chosen by the Little Council, upon the advice of the pastors and subject to the approval of the Council of Two Hundred. The deacons were delegated to assist the pastors, specifically to help the poor, comfort the sick, and care for the widows and orphans.

The principal organ for administering disciplinary correction was the Consistory, a committee composed of twelve elders and five pastors, presided over by one of the syndics of the Little Council. Theoretically, the elders and pastors were not authorized to "constrain," but only to "hear the parties and make remonstrances." However, since the Consistory had a secular as well as ecclesiastical composition, the charge to "take care of the life of everyone, amiably to admonish . . . and to apply brotherly correction" was interpreted and applied very broadly. Indeed, the Consistory often acted with extreme zeal in supervising the moral life and daily behavior of the citizens as well as their doctrinal orthodoxy, becoming in practice a highly active ecclesiastical police. Cases involving violations of the civil law or requiring more severe punishment than excommunication were turned over to the councils for interrogation (which usually included torture) and judgment.

Calvin, meanwhile, devoted himself single-mindedly to making the church in Geneva the Protestant model of Christianity. Daily sermons, lectures in theology, and religious instruction for children on Sundays were all part of his educational effort to reform the religious life of the people. When he returned from Strasbourg, he quickly drew up a new catechism, patterned after Bucer's catechism of 1534, and in 1542 he published a new liturgy. He also found time to write his *Defense of the Sound and Orthodox Doctrine of the Slavery and Deliverance of the Human Will* (in which Calvin vigorously attacked the doctrine of free will), against the Catholic theologian Albert Pighius; a commentary on the epistle of Jude; and the first of many editions of his *Treatise on*

Relics. At the same time, Calvin put great emphasis on schools in Geneva and supported the establishment of the Collège de la Rive with Sebastian Castellio, a Savoyard humanist turned Protestant, as its director. A few years later, Calvin established the famous Geneva Academy. Theodore Beza, a French scholar teaching in nearby Lausanne, was chosen to be its first rector.

The Struggle for Control

Despite his strong personality and leadership (or because of it), Calvin's authority did not go unchallenged. Many Genevans resented the rigid attitude and actions of Calvin and the other ministers, and became increasingly outspoken against them. A crisis developed in 1546, when Pierre Ameaux, a member of the Little Council, charged Calvin with preaching false doctrine and rashly called him a wicked man. Calvin demanded not only an apology but pressured the council into forcing Ameaux to march through the streets in disgrace, dressed only in a shirt and carrying a torch. The public impression of seeing a member of the governing magistracy thus humiliated for having insulted the pastor of Saint Peter's was indelible. Discontent mounted.

Shortly thereafter, François Favre, father-in-law of Ami Perrin, an even more influential member of the Little Council, was excommunicated by the Consistory for immoral conduct. Favre's daughter, Perrin's wife, defied the Consistory and found herself in exile, too. Thereupon, Perrin charged the Consistory with malice and incompetence, and accused Calvin of exceeding his authority. The affair became more involved when Perrin returned from a diplomatic mission to France and it was discovered that he had, without authorization, entered into negotiations with the French king. Perrin was arrested but was shortly acquitted and reinstated in office. The anti-French hatred then focused on Calvin who, through a French refugee, had also been in communication with the court of France.

The two factions (the "old Genevans" led by Perrin, and Calvin's partisans—mostly French and some Italian refugees) faced one another in the conciliar elections of 1548. The Perrinists, or "libertines" as Calvin called them, were victorious, and for the next five years the struggle between councils and Consistory over the nature and extent of ecclesiastical authority continued. Only the deepening theological rifts and common fear of heresy caused them to close ranks and work more or less in harmony after that.

Beginning as early as 1543, Calvin had a falling out with Sebastian Castellio (1515–63) over the canonical status of the Song of Songs in the Old Testament. This, plus Castellio's insistence on drawing a distinction between essential and nonessential doctrines, and his vehement criticism of the pastors, led to his dismissal from the school and, in 1545, banishment from Geneva. Thereafter he became an outspoken critic of Calvin's regime and especially of his theological intolerance. In response to Calvin's support of the death penalty for heresy, Castellio wrote the treatise *Whether Heretics Should be Persecuted* (1554), in which he championed the cause of religious toleration. "Killing a man is not defending a doctrine," he reasoned, "it is merely killing a man."

Calvin and his followers (increased by the influx of French refugees from Henri II's persecutions) paid no attention to Castellio's blasphemies. But theological dissension did not end. A more disruptive dispute issued from Calvin's doctrine of double predestination. Jerome Bolsec (d. 1584), a physician and recent convert to Calvinism, asserted that Calvin's rigid predestination theology made God out to be the author of sin. Calvin emphatically denied this in his *Community on the Eternal Election of God* (1551), and branded Bolsec "an accomplice of Satan." Arrested and held for trial, Bolsec was finally banished from Geneva for life. Others, like Jean Trolliet, whom Calvin refused to accept as a pastor, also reacted negatively to predestination. In 1552 Calvin published another important treatise, *On the Eternal Predestination of God*, against his old antagonist Albert Pighius. After some browbeating by Calvin, the council finally declared that henceforth "no one may dare to speak against the said book [Calvin's *Institutes*], nor against the said doctrine [of predestination]."

The most serious theological confrontation reached its climax in 1553 when the outspoken Spanish anti-Trinitarian, Michael Servetus, was apprehended and tragically put to death in Geneva. Far from damaging Calvin's reputation or his position, however, the action taken against Servetus actually strengthened it, because all of the leading reformers—in Geneva and elsewhere—agreed that Servetus's denial of the Trinity was not only heretical but blasphemous and seditious. Following the execution of Servetus, Calvin's prestige increased, and he was looked upon as the Saint George of Protestantism who had slain the dragon of deceit and perversion. Obviously, Reformation Europe took theology very seriously, and Calvin's resolute biblicalism and theocentricity played a particularly decisive role in the history and character of Reformed Protestantism.

Calvinist Theology

The heart of Calvin's theological system, the core of which he acquired from Luther, was his belief in the transcendent majesty and absolute sovereignty of God. Knowledge of God, Calvin affirmed, is "the entire sum of our wisdom" and "the chief end of human life"; not just an abstract or mental knowledge but a knowledge of him in relation to us, a knowledge that "induces us to look to him for all good and return praise to him." Yet how can such a knowledge be attained? Through the twofold revelation of creation and Scripture, Calvin replied. The earth and all its creatures testify of God the Creator, and also that he remains the absolute master and controller of the universe. More directly, we know God through Jesus Christ, who is found in the Scriptures. The Bible (Old Testament as well as New) is the only authority for our knowledge of God and reveals all that we should and can know about him, and teaches us to put our trust in him and walk in fear of him.

Yet Calvin insisted that the essence of God is inscrutable, and that an infinite chasm separates the divine from the human. Through the Fall, all mankind became corrupted and spiritually deformed. Mortals are perverse and

John Calvin. *Austerity and firmness are engraved in the facial lines of this portrait of Calvin by a Master of the French School, around 1550.*

worthless in the sight of God. "For, though we are composed of a soul and body, yet we feel nothing but the flesh, so that to whatever part of man we turn our eyes, it is impossible to see anything that is not impure, profane, and abominable to God." The Mosaic Law itself, as Luther also taught, is a mirror of sin, revealing the total corruption and depravity of mankind. The Law also manifested that God had not abandoned man and, although fallen and utterly incapable of doing good or of contributing one whit to his salvation, he could be rescued by another. "The Law was given," Calvin wrote in the *Institutes*, "to nurture the hope of salvation that they should have in Jesus Christ."

The only mediator possible between majestic God and wretched man was the God/man, Jesus of Nazareth, the Redeemer, and it was his atoning death on the cross that made reconciliation possible. Therefore, through the redemptive grace of Christ and the gift of faith received from the Holy Spirit comes a spiritual union with Christ. This union brings about a regeneration, or sanctification, and the believer is "born again," becoming a new creature in Christ and the inheritor of salvation. This state results, Calvin emphasized, not from any human merit or effort but from faith in Christ. "He will be said to be justified by faith who, being excluded from the righteousness of works, appropriates by faith the righteousness of Christ, being clothed wherewith he appears before the face of God not as a sinner, but as righteous."

There was a catch, however. The justifying grace of Christ is not for everyone. It is only for those whom God preelects. In his 1537 *Catechism*, Calvin explained:

> The seed of the word of God takes root and grows fruitful only in those whom the Lord, by his eternal election, has predestined to be his children and heirs of the heavenly kingdom. To all the others who, by the same counsel of God before the constitution of the world, are reprobate, the clear and evident preaching of the truth can be nothing else but an odour of death in death.

Hence, God's word germinates only in the "elect," those whom he has already chosen for salvation even before their creation; only on them does Christ's redemption have any effect. The rest, in what Calvin himself called that "horrible decree," are predestined to perdition. "Eternal life is foreordained for some, and eternal damnation for others," Calvin explained in the *Institutes*. "Every man, therefore, being created for one or the other of these ends, we say, he is predestinated either to life or to death." God being just, the latter receives only what he deserves. And the elect deserve no better, but God's mercy intervenes in their behalf. "If we ask why God takes pity on some, and why he lets go of the others and leaves them, there is no other answer but that it pleased Him to do so." God's will cannot be thwarted or questioned.

This is Calvin at his most rigid and impersonal. Recent scholarship has drawn attention to the other side of Calvin's complex personality, his more humanistic, freedom-loving tendencies that made him respected, even loved, by his closest followers. Yet it was his inflexible determinism and theological dogmatism that gave dynamic form and direction to his movement. There is no doubt that Calvin's doctrines, as well as the man himself, were full of paradoxes, but to a large extent they were the paradoxes of his own time. "Like other great figures of his century," writes William Bouwsma, "he was peculiarly sensitive to the subtleties and contradictions of the human condition and can tell us much about it. He could also be singularly practical about coping with its difficulties."

The Outward Church

For Calvin, as for Luther, Zwingli, Bucer, and the other Protestant theologians (but not the Anabaptists), the invisible church of God consisted of the elect of all times and places, and was known only to God. Besides this invisible congregation there exists an outward church, the visible community of Christian believers grouped together for worship and communion. This visible church is composed of the gathered elect, but may also shelter some reprobates, wolves in sheep's clothing, who are undetected by human discernment, but "The eyes of God see who will endure to the end." According to Calvin, a true Christian church exists where the pure word of God is preached and believed, and where the sacraments are administered according to the institution of Christ. Its members are those who profess Christ by confession, example, and participation in the sacraments.

The purpose and function of the church, in addition to providing fellowship, orderly discipline, and effective charity, is to give to corrupt and fallen mankind an external aid by which faith may be engendered and grow. Through the preaching of the word, faith is awakened in those to whom this gift is given, and by the administration of the sacraments spiritual life is communicated to the elect, thereby promoting their sanctification.

Calvin defined a sacrament as the testimony of an external sign confirming God's grace toward us. Like the other reformers, he recognized only two sacraments, baptism and the Lord's Supper. Baptism was the sign of the remission of sins. It was also an evidence of faith and the means to profess Christ through membership and fellowship in the church. The Lord's Supper was a confirmation of God's grace. Calvin rejected transubstantiation, and the Mass as a sacrifice, but at the same time he disagreed with Luther's concept of ubiquity and real presence, and also opposed Zwingli's symbolism. Calvin believed that Christ was "truly and efficaciously" present in the Lord's Supper, but in a spiritual sense, and through the mysterious intervention of the Holy Spirit, the communicant partakes spiritually of Christ's body.

Church and State

The final chapter of the *Institutes* treats the subject of civil government and how civil and spiritual government are related. Calvin's words are emphatic in distinguishing between the two realms of church and state. "Whoever knows how to distinguish between body and soul, between this present fleeting life and that future eternal life, will without difficulty know that Christ's spiritual Kingdom and the civil jurisdiction are things completely distinct." Each institution has its domain of jurisdiction and its separate functions. The trouble comes in defining where the boundary between them lies.

It is the duty of the state to maintain peace and order, Calvin stated, and this involves preventing "idolatry, sacrilege against God's name, blasphemies against his truth, and other public offenses against religion. In short, it provides that a public manifestation of religion may exist among Christians and that humanity be maintained among men." This is because the magistracy, as well as the ministry, is ordained by God. They are both extensions of God's will and cannot, therefore, be entirely separate. They are "distinct in function but inseparable in being." Magistrates must make and enforce laws, collect taxes, and even wage war. But they should also "do justice and righteousness," Calvin quoted from Jeremiah. And if they don't? Calvin insisted that rulers must be obeyed, regardless of their faults and failings. In his *Commentary on Romans*, he reiterated that "We ought to obey them . . . for it belongs not to a private individual to take away authority from him whom the Lord has in power set over us." And again in the *Institutes*:

> We owe this attitude of reverence and therefore of piety toward all our rulers in the highest degree, whatever they may be like . . . Therefore, if we are cruelly tormented by a savage prince, if we are greedily despoiled by one who is avaricious or wanton, if we are neglected by a slothful one, if finally we are vexed for piety's sake by one who is impious and sacrilegious, let us first be mindful of our own misdeeds, which without doubt are chastised by such whips of the Lord.

Calvin's advice, then, was: obey and suffer.

Yet what if obedience to the ruler requires one to disobey God? "Fear God and honor the king," Daniel enjoined, and Calvin emphasized the sequence; God must be obeyed first, and always. "Sometimes," Calvin conceded, God "raises up open avengers from among his servants [Moses against the tyranny of Pharaoh, for example], and arms them with his command to punish the wicked government and deliver his people." Thus, constitutional magistrates might, under certain circumstances, overturn intolerable governments. In such cases, support and obedience should then be given to those magistrates.

Thus we see in Calvin's political philosophy—whether the government be a city-state or a monarchy, a republic or a despotic ruler—cautious conservatism and a reluctance to disturb the status quo. But it also contained a latent justification for political resistance and even revolution. This would be used in the next seventy-five years to justify armed rebellion in France, the Netherlands, Scotland, and England.

The Calvinist Appeal

The Christian life, according to Calvin, consists in overcoming the flesh and glorifying God. Regeneration brings with it the implantation of faith and the desire to overcome the flesh, to withstand suffering and tribulation, and to meditate upon life and death. The renunciation of self and of all things worldly is the first step in the process of sanctification. "There is no mean between these two extremes: either the earth must be despised by us, or it will hold us bound in an intemperate self-love." Nevertheless, contempt for this life is not an end in itself; it is, rather, a measure for the full realization of divine glory and salvation.

In practical terms, regeneration and justification resulted in action, and it was in dynamic action that Calvinists distinguished themselves for the next century or more. "If God is for us who can be against us?" was their motto. Whatever their profession or occupation, it was a divine calling, to be fulfilled with diligence, efficiency, and thanksgiving. The shackles of sin and destruction had been cut by the Savior; human energies could be directed to the single pursuit of carrying out his will. Only God knows who the elect are, but surely those who sincerely confess the faith, participate in the sacraments, and live exemplary and upright lives should be counted among the Church of Christ. Although the elect would live moral lives, morality itself was not a sign of election, Calvin warned, nor was material prosperity. Yet even though the marks of the elect are indistinguishable to the flesh, they are revealed spiritually to the recipient. The sheep will know their master. This conviction was the active faith that could move mountains. The Calvinists refused to recognize defeat or failure, for God's will was theirs. And to be most effective in whatever enterprise, they had to be disciplined, single-minded, and united. Calvin's strict moral code was a practical rule.

Calvin stressed mutual responsibility. Talents and gifts as well as material goods ought to be shared, and community concern for everyone's welfare should replace both greed on the one hand and sloth on the other. In Geneva, poor relief was institutionalized under the jurisdiction of the deacons, and all citizens were encouraged to participate in productive labor according to their skills, or "calling." Furthermore, all callings were deemed of equal dignity in the eyes of God. All vocations were equal in status, and hard work was expected of everyone, as were thrift, honesty, and dedication.

The social effects of this Calvinist ethic are apparent but not always easy to distinguish. Ever since the first publication of Max Weber's *Protestant Ethic and the Spirit of Capitalism,* in 1904–1905, it has been customary to equate Calvinism with "middle-class values" and with the rise of capitalism. In this equation, more facts have been assumed than proven. Nevertheless, patterns of affiliation did occur that allow us to venture some generalizations about the social appeal of Calvinism.

The first point worth noting is the very wide spectrum of people who were attracted to the Reformed church movement, or Calvinism. Some were converted by the straightforward call to follow Christ; some by the logic and intensity of Calvin's entire biblical theology; others by the vigor of his commitment, which gave them confidence and security in the assurance of their divine election; still others liked the devotion and camaraderie engendered by common goals and strong organization. Even though the social composition of Calvinist communities was varied, its adherents shared a dedication to the doctrine of calling, and to other principles that gave them both collective strength and personal commitment. In other words, the dynamic nature of the Calvinist ethic attracted active people to its ranks, especially in the cities where printing and literacy were important factors in the spread of Protestantism.

Many urban shopkeepers and artisans joined Reformed congregations in the first years after Calvin began preaching, and throughout the century they provided the numerical backbone of the movement, constituting from 50 to 60 percent of most Calvinist congregations. Other urban social orders showing a strong affinity for Calvinism were lawyers, notaries, and clerks of various kinds. In commercial centers like Lyon, Montpellier, Basel, Heidelberg, Amsterdam, and London, a great many merchants were Calvinists. A surprising number of city notables and magistrates were also adherents, even in places where Calvinism was not in the majority.

Although the appeal of Calvinism was strong in the cities, it was not without its adherents in the country as well. Some peasant farmers and independent leaseholders were sympathetic to the fresh religious winds blowing across western Europe; but on the whole most peasants remained loyal to the Catholic church. Not so with the landowners—the rural gentry and lesser nobility. For a multitude of economic and military reasons, many of the landed aristocracy were attracted to Calvinism, especially in France, but also in the Rhineland and the Low Countries. The strong affiliation of French nobles and their non-noble dependents with the Huguenots after 1559 played a vital role in the subsequent civil wars in that country. Calvinism also became an increasingly important factor among the English and Scottish gentry during the second half of the sixteenth century, as they challenged the old nobility and the religious establishment.

**Women and
Calvinism**

The position of women in Calvinist worship was complex. Calvin was generally hard on women, chastising them for their vanity in dress, adornments, and immodest behavior; condemning them for frivolity, talkativeness, gossip, and affected piety; and even blaming them for many of the sins of men. "There have been too many examples of how men, otherwise inclined to behave virtuously, have been debauched and turned from the right way by women," he charged. "When a youth is not deceived and the devil does not apply the fagot, he can remain chaste and pure; but when a shameless and wanton woman entices him, it is all over for him." Even more devastating was Calvin's blanket condemnation of women's mental as well as moral inferiority. Wives, by nature and divine ordination, he insisted, are inferior and subordinate to their husbands. He saw the subjection of a wife to her husband as a guarantee of their subjection to the authority of God. Of course Calvin denied any authority to females in ecclesiastical functions, claiming that in the early church "a woman was not allowed to speak in church, and also not to teach, to baptize, or to offer." And he rejected government by women as "an unnatural monstrosity," yet such a government might be sometimes imposed on a nation by an angry God to punish the people for their sins, in which case it should be borne with patience, like any tyranny.

Nevertheless, Calvin strongly advocated marriage, not only as a safeguard against sexual sin but as an honorable and desirable institution founded on love and instituted by God. Indeed, it was *the* calling for women. Of his own wife he wrote, following her death in 1549, "I have lost the best companion of my life, who, if our lot had been harsher, would have been not only the willing sharer of exile and poverty, but even of death. While she lived, she was the faithful helper in my ministry. From her I never experienced the slightest hindrance. During her illness she never spoke about herself and never troubled me about her children. Her greatness of spirit means more to me than a thousand commendations." He recognized that women and men were intended to be companions, and that in the eyes of God they are equal. This spiritual equality meant that both male and female are created in the image of God, and that salvation is not determined by sex. Calvin also believed in religious education for girls, and approved of women reading the Bible, in private. He condoned female singing in church, for which he was criticized by the Genevan council.

The conversion of women to Calvinism seems to have been in part a ramification of the general movement toward independence that was manifesting itself in the street and in the marketplace, despite increasing efforts on the part of men to forestall it. Natalie Davis has noted three characteristics of female adherence to Calvinism. First, there seems to be no evidence that wives were either more aggressive or less aggressive than their husbands in embracing the reformed faith. Second, a large number of widows and self-employed women—midwives, merchants, dressmakers, and so on—were numbered in the Calvinist ranks. Third, relatively few highly educated women in the city became converted. Like the men, Calvinist women belonged neither to the bottom nor the top of society. They came largely from families of artisans, merchants, and professional people. The patronesses of the literary world, however, generally remained Catholic, in name and association at least. This did not hold true, however, for many noblewomen and leaders, such as Jeanne d'Albret, Catherine de Bourbon, Eléonore de Roye, and Louise de Coligny, who were faithful, even zealous Protestants.

Another exception was the remarkable Marie Dentière, one-time abbess in Tournai, who was expelled from the convent because of heresy. She then found her way to Geneva, where she became an activist not only in the Reformed church but also in the cause of feminism. In 1538 she published a *Letter to the Queen of Navarre* (Marguerite d'Angoulême, sister of Francis I), containing a spirited "Defense of Women" against the defamations of ecclesiastical authorities, which caused a stir in Geneva because of its criticism of the pastors. Urging women to speak up about religious matters and to speak and write about the Scriptures, she wrote, "If God has done the grace to some poor women to reveal to them by His Holy Scriptures some good and holy thing, dare they not write about it, speak about it, and declare it, one to the other?"

The Spread of Calvinism

Calvinism was better equipped for international expansion than was Lutheranism. Thanks to Calvin's concise and adroit *Institutes,* and his systematic exposition of the gospel in other works, Calvinism was more intelligible and orderly than the evangelical movements of Germany. It had a particularly strong appeal to those who desired a complete theological and ecclesiastical system to take the place of the Roman Catholicism they had known. At the same time, Geneva provided active leadership for Calvinist expansion and served as a model for other Calvinist and semi-Calvinist cities like Amsterdam, Edinburgh, and Montauban. The founding of the Genevan Academy in 1559—patterned after Johann Sturm's school in Strasbourg—and its rapid growth likewise influenced the spread of Calvinism. Many of the leaders of the Reformed Protestant movement in Europe received their training at the Genevan Academy. The many book publishers in Geneva also provided a steady flow of Protestant propaganda into neighboring cities and towns even after Calvin's death in 1564.

With Calvin's own personal courage and total dedication as their lodestar, committed followers soon carried the message of Christ into the surrounding countries. From Geneva, Calvin's religious and social ideas quickly spread into the other cantons of western Switzerland, and then throughout Europe. Few countries were unaffected by Calvinism's growth, and in several it became the crucial factor in their religious and political development.

France
Calvin's most persistent proselytizing efforts were directed toward his native France. Conversions to his ideas began there shortly after the first edition of the *Institutes* was issued. When the French version was published in 1541, its effects were immediate. Francis I died in 1547 and responsibility for public order

Henri II. *This Louvre painting of the French king by François Clouet shows him in 1557 or 1558 after ten years of vigorously combating the growth of Calvinism in France.*

and defense of the faith rested with his twenty-eight-year-old son, Henri II. The new king was a less inspiring leader than his illustrious father had been, although, according to the Venetian ambassador, "He has great natural kindness, so much so that you cannot rank any prince, no matter how far back you go in the past, above him," and "He has a good mind . . . and is bold in all that he does." Henri II, however, was unfamiliar with affairs of state and leaned heavily on the constable, Anne de Montmorency (male despite his name). When he was fourteen, Henri had been married to Catherine de' Medici as a pawn in his father's Italian diplomacy, but his constant companion was the influential Diane de Poitiers, a well-read and capable woman who not only wrote poetry and poignant letters but had a pragmatic sense of politics and took an active part in public affairs. In religious matters, Henri II was more orthodox than his father, and less inclined to be lenient with dissenters, reformers, or heretics. Upon his ascension to the throne, he created the *Chambre Ardente* (the "Burning Chamber"), a special criminal committee of the Parlement de Paris to suppress heresy. Popular resentment forced its dissolution three years later, but in that time it tried over 500 separate cases.

In the meantime, beginning in 1555, or perhaps earlier, Calvin secretly dispatched highly trained pastors to France for the purpose of preaching the gospel of Christ and organizing the French sympathizers into cadres of devoted congregations prepared to serve the Lord. The leading voices of the ministry in France were Pierre Viret (1511–71) and Calvin's close friend, disciple, and successor, Theodore Beza (1519–1605), the man who represented and spear-headed Calvinism in France for the next forty years. By 1559 the trickle of missionaries had become a torrent and, under Beza's vigorous leadership, France underwent a dramatic religious change, symbolized by the meeting of the first national synod of the French Reformed church in Paris. The promulgation of the French Confession of Faith, also in 1559, is a landmark in the rapid spread of Calvinist Reformed Protestantism. By this time, its organization was complete on all levels, from the local congregations in many of the cities of southern and southwestern France (with some scattered also in the northwest), through district colloquies representing numerous consistories, to the provincial synods, and finally to the national synod in Paris. This phenomenal growth of Calvinism in France was in part due to the natural affinity of the French for a Reformation leader who was genuinely their own. Luther would always remain a foreigner in France, and so would Zwingli and the Anabaptists.

Other conditions and events also contributed to the rapid expansion of Calvinist congregations in mid-sixteenth-century France. Stronger than the social and economic strains that influenced many to abandon their traditional views and vows was the deep longing for a more personal involvement in religion and a more meaningful and direct communication with God. In the early years of the Calvinist expansion, this religious attraction brought many people from all walks of life into the Protestant community. Immediately following the Peace of Cateau-Cambrésis in 1559, when Europewide peace seemed to be assured, thousands of nobles from almost every region of France swelled the Huguenot ranks until, according to fairly reliable estimates, nearly one-half of the French aristocracy could be counted on their side. The economic dislocation of the French nobles perhaps accounts for many of these conversions, but a great number of the highest rank, even princes of the blood who had no economic worries, also joined the spirited saints. Perhaps they saw the opportunities in Calvin's doctrine of church and state. Whatever their motives, this influx of nobles into Huguenot ranks supplied an already volatile mixture with an explosive fuse. By 1562 France was ripe for civil war.

The Netherlands Calvinism was carried into the Netherlands by French refugees of the persecutions of Henri II and by ministers sent directly from Geneva. Progress was slow at first, because of the religious repressions of Charles V, but it quickened after 1555 when the emperor abdicated and his son, Philip II of Spain, became ruler of the Lowlands. This was not because Philip lifted the burden of religious oppression established by the emperor, but rather because his subjects were less inclined to obey the offensive rules of this foreign-born prince than they had been to abide by those of his Flemish father.

The logical dogmatism of Calvin's theology, with its biblical humanism and its ethical emphasis, appealed to many devotional Dutch who respected their Erasmus but also yearned for greater involvement than the illustrious Rotterdamer had provided. Above all, they respected and employed Calvinist organizational structure, and soon flourishing congregations similar to those of Geneva and France were springing up from Arras to Groningen. With its greatest strength in the French-speaking provinces of Artois, Namur, Hainaut, and southern Flanders and Brabant, a Belgic Confession of Faith was drafted in 1561. This confession was of great importance in the religious history of the Netherlands, providing the basic catechism for the later Synod of Dort and the standard for the modern Dutch Reformed churches.

Germany

As might be expected, Calvinism moved northward and eastward through Germany almost as early as it did into France and the Netherlands, although without as much immediate success. Its growth in the Rhineland, however, was rapid after 1555, following the Peace of Augsburg (although no allowance was made for Calvinism in that agreement) and the accession of Frederick III as elector and Count Palatine of the Rhine. By 1560 Frederick was himself a convert to Calvinist doctrines, and from that time on, the spread of the Reformed church was encouraged throughout the Palatinate. In the Rhineland, however, Calvinism was of necessity broader and more eclectic than in either France or Scotland, and it was more subservient to the control of the prince. That is as it should be, maintained Thomas Erastus, the elector's physician and professor of medicine at the University of Heidelberg, whose view that the state should rule supreme over the church came to be known as "Erastianism."

In 1563, Calvinist pastors and professors, including Zacharias Ursinus (1534–83), who had been brought to Heidelberg by the elector to assist in formulating a statement of belief, drew up a remarkable and influential confession of faith. It was appropriately known as the Heidelberg Catechism. Less dogmatic than previous Calvinist statements of faith, thus accommodating most of the Sacramentarians and Melanchthonian Lutherans, the 129 questions and answers of the Heidelberg Catechism soon became the doctrinal guide of Reformed churches throughout the Empire, and with the second Helvetic Confession of 1556, written by Heinrich Bullinger at Zürich, formed the theological basis of most Calvinist congregations east of the Rhine.

Elsewhere in the Holy Roman Empire, Calvinism spread more slowly, but with increasing penetration, for the rest of the century. It was introduced into Nassau and neighboring Hesse, and later Anhalt, by missionaries from the Palatinate, and into Wesel and Cleves by Dutch refugees. Early in the next century, Calvinism was adopted by the Hohenzollern electors of Brandenburg. In the meantime, sons of Czech noble families returning from universities in the Rhineland, Switzerland, and Alsace brought Calvinism into Bohemia. In 1575 a Bohemian Confession was drafted at Prague, and thereafter a growing number of Czech nobles embraced the Reformed faith, adding spirit as well as strength to Czech opposition to the emperor. Nevertheless, Calvinist penetration into the Empire was sporadic and ineffectual compared to its success in the West. The heavy hand of the Habsburgs and the solid power of the Lutheran princes prevented the development of anything more than a few scattered congregations.

Eastern Europe

Further east, in Poland and Hungary, the story was different. Here the landed nobility, hostile both to German influences and Roman rituals (and to the Polish king), were strongly attracted by the orderly radicalism of Calvinist theology. They were similarly impressed with the presbyterian form of government, in which strong authority rested with the lesser magistrates, and which had a graded system of representative ecclesiastical bodies. Under noble and gentry patronage, Calvinism grew rapidly in Poland during the 1550s. Even on the national level, there was sympathy and sometimes enthusiasm for it. King Sigismund II (1548–72), last of the Jagiellonian dynasty, was initially sympathetic to the reform movement, and the Lithuanian chancellor-prince, Nicholas Radziwiłł, openly avowed Calvinism. In December 1556, the most zealous Polish reformer, John à Lasco (Jan Łaski), who had been in the West since 1523, returned to his homeland and began an enthusiastic effort to unite the Polish Protestants into a national church. His failure was due in part to the inability of the Polish nobles to rally around a single Protestant doctrine and to the lack of active support by the crown. After Łaski's death in 1560, both antitrinitarian and Anabaptist ideas (some introduced by exiles from Calvin's Geneva) won a considerable following among the Polish and Lithuanian nobility. The Catholic Counter-Reformation, though, was also picking up momentum, and Poland became one of the prime targets of its Jesuit shock troops.

In Hungary, and especially in Transylvania, where John Zapolya's rule (1526–40) was unchallenged except when he forgot that he reigned by the grace of the Turkish sultan, religious heterodoxy was already of long standing. Catholics, Moslems, Lutherans, Unitarians, and Greek Orthodox all lived in precarious harmony. Calvinism experienced a similar growth and vitality there as the Magyar nobles, like the Polish landlords, welcomed Calvinist doctrines and organization. So successful was the Calvinist expansion east of the Danube that the city of Debrecen proudly called itself the "Hungarian Geneva." Throughout the principality of Transylvania, a remarkable degree of religious toleration was allowed and radical doctrines gained a firm foothold. In 1557 its diet called for a national synod to settle religious differences peacefully, while the Unitarian court preacher Francis David (d. 1579) eloquently defended freedom of conscience for everyone. As a result, in 1568 the Diet of Torda proclaimed religious liberty throughout the jurisdictions of the Transylvanian prince. Such toleration did not last, however, and after Prince John Sigismund Zapolya died in 1571, the various faiths had to fight for survival.

Scotland and England

The Reformation in Scotland began in the early 1500s with humanist criticisms of church practices and clerical abuse, but the Catholic church retained its control until after mid-century. Lutheran ideas began penetrating the country in the 1520s, and in 1526 Tyndale's English New Testament was introduced there. Soon many voices were raising the cry for religious reforms, and the burning of Patrick Hamilton in 1528 only increased their number and volume. The martyrdom of another Protestant zealot,

George Wishart, in 1547 introduced a strong new voice when Wishart's friend and admirer, John Knox (ca. 1505–72), joined the chorus of protestors.

Son of peasant parents who schooled him in self-reliance and tenacity, Knox studied at Saint Andrew's University and subsequently became a papal notary and a tutor. He was also ordained to the priesthood some time before 1540. After Wishart's death, Knox renounced his clerical vows and joined the band of Scottish Protestants who boldly called themselves the Lords of the Congregation. Captured by the French in 1547, Knox was condemned to the galleys, where he toiled at the oar until his liberation by the English two years later. In the England of King Edward VI (1547–53), he became a popular preacher; but on the accession of Mary Tudor to the throne in 1553, this prophet of Protestantism fled to the continent, where he came under the pervasive influence of Calvin. In Geneva he was pastor of the English exiles and became completely imbued with Calvin's spirit and theology.

In 1559 Knox returned to Scotland to resume the battle in earnest against Catholicism and against the political rule of the French regent, Mary of Guise, widow of King James V. He had already launched the first salvo of the civil war three years earlier with the publication of his *First Blast of the Trumpet against the Monstrous Regiment of Women,* which not only attacked Mary but reveals his attitude toward women rulers generally. From this point on, he never wavered in his determination to Protestantize the kingdom. Led by Knox's passionate preaching, nobles joined with commoners to oppose the established order and eject the queen-regent from power. The Scottish revolt was closely linked with both English and continental politics as French reinforcements arrived to support the regent, and English forces, reluctantly sent by Queen Elizabeth, were dispatched to intercept them. The death of the regent in 1560 resulted in the Treaty of Edinburgh, and left the field open to Knox and his followers. The government was reorganized, a parliament summoned, a Scottish Confession of Faith proclaimed, and a complete ecclesiastical overhaul accomplished. By the end of August 1560, the Mass had been abolished, papal supremacy overthrown, and the Roman church replaced by the Reformed Kirk of Scotland, with a directing board of presbyters and a national consistory.

With the return of Mary Stuart from France (where she had been left a widow by the death of her husband, King Francis II) in 1561, the Scottish Reformation seemed to be in jeopardy. Knox again mounted his pulpit at Saint Giles, drew his pen, and entered the battle. Boldly he proclaimed the right of rebellion against idolatrous (meaning Catholic) rulers. In his *Appellation,* employing Calvin's doctrine of resistance, but without Calvin's judiciousness, he had already appealed to the Scottish nobles to depose their Catholic regent. Now he enlarged his appeal to include not only the nobles and magistrates, "but also the whole bodie of that people, and to every membre of the same," calling upon them to kill the idolatrous queen as they would have killed any idolator in the days of Moses. In a face-to-face confrontation with the queen herself in August 1561, Knox reaffirmed that when princes exceed their bounds "they may be resisted, even by power."

Reformation monument in Geneva. *This modern landmark shows Calvin flanked by his colleagues and followers Guillaume Farel, Theodore Beza, and John Knox.*

Knox might not have needed such vehemence to conquer Scotland for the Reformed cause, since Mary was her own worst enemy. By 1568 her entangled private life so compromised her public rule that she was no longer able to maintain either her throne or her esteem. With the Queen of Scots removed, there were no further obstacles to the Reformation, although a determined minority of Catholic nobles continued to work for her rehabilitation, and innumerable highland parishes operated a hybrid form of Catholic-Protestantism for many decades. Nevertheless, it was John Knox, with his powerful preaching, who made the Scottish Reformation succeed. "He was the one person as 'God's trumpeter,'" notes his biographer, Stanford Reid,

> who seemed capable of maintaining and strengthening the morale of the forces which were seeking to make the Reformation successful. He was above all else the one who, when the clouds seemed darkest and the outlook most threatening, was able to keep his faith and stimulate those threatened with defeat to action and achievement.

The influence of Calvinism in England was slight until Edward VI's reign when Calvinist writings began to enter the country and increasing contacts were made between English Protestants and Calvinist-leaning continental reformers. During the restoration of Catholicism under Mary Tudor (1553–58), many English Protestant preachers and scholars, as well as Knox and the continental theologians who had settled in Edwardian England, fled to the continent to avoid persecution or death. The more direct impact of Calvinism came only when Queen Mary died in 1558 and many of the Marian exiles returned to England. In the religious controversies of Queen Elizabeth I's (1558–1603) first years, some of the exiles joined with other dissenters to protest the overly ritualistic establishment of the Anglican church. Out of these protests came the beginnings of English Puritanism.

To understand the impact of Calvinism in England, as well as the development of the Anglican church and Puritanism, however, we must look more closely at the political and religious struggles that were taking place in that island kingdom from the beginning of Henry VIII's reign to the death of Queen Mary. Only then can we distinguish and appreciate the unique nature of the English Reformation.

Suggestions for Further Reading

THE EARLY REFORMATION IN FRANCE

For the general background of reform in France, R.J. Knecht, *Francis I* (New York, 1982) is very useful, and Mark Greengrass, *The French Reformation* (Oxford, 1987) provides a good brief introduction. More specific insights may be gained from Donald R. Kelley, *The Beginning of Ideology: Consciousness and Society in the French Reformation* (Cambridge, England, 1981), and James K. Farge, *Orthodoxy and Reform in Early Reformation France* (Leiden, 1985), a study of the faculty of theology of Paris, 1500–1543. On the most influential pre-reformer see Philip E. Hughes, *Lefèvre: Pioneer of Ecclesiastical Renewal in France* (Grand Rapids, 1984). Of related interest to the early Reformation are Francis M. Higman, *Censorship and the Sorbonne* (Geneva, Switzerland, 1979), a bibliographical study of books censured by the Faculty of Theology at Paris between 1520 and 1551; and Raymond A. Mentzer, Jr., *Heresy Proceedings in Languedoc, 1500–1560* (Philadelphia, 1984).

CALVIN: GENERAL

The most penetrating study of Calvin to date is William J. Bouwsma, *John Calvin: A Sixteenth Century Portrait* (New York, 1988), which sees Calvin as a person of his time, and analyzes his complex personality as a paradox between his humanism and dogmatism. Also significant and wider-ranging is Alister E. McGrath, *A Life of John Calvin: A Study in the Shaping of Western Culture* (Oxford, 1990). These works now supersede all previous biographies, although something can still be learned from François Wendel, *Calvin: The Origins and Development of His Religious Thought*, tr. by Philip Mairet (New York, 1963), and T.H.L. Parker, *John Calvin, a Biography* (London, 1975), a handy brief life. There is also much in Ronald S. Wallace, *Calvin, Geneva and the Reformation: A Study of Calvin as Social Reformer, Churchman, Pastor, and Theologian* (Edinburgh, 1988). Some useful articles are contained in B.A. Gerrish and Robert Benedetto, eds., *Reformatio Perennis: Essays on Calvin and the Reformation in Honor of Ford Lewis Battles* (Pittsburgh, 1981); E.J. Furcha, ed., *In Honour of John Calvin, 1509–1564* (Montreal, 1987); and Robert V. Schnucker, ed., *Calviniana: Ideas and Influence of Jean Calvin* (Kirksville, Missouri, 1988).

CALVIN'S THEOLOGY AND SOCIAL THOUGHT

T.H.L. Parker's perceptive studies of Calvin's Commentaries are very useful in understanding Calvinist thought. See his *Calvin's Old Testament Commentaries* (Edinburgh, 1986) and *Commentaries on the Epistle to the Romans, 1532–1542* (Edinburgh, 1986), which complement his earlier *Calvin's New Testament Commentaries* (1971). These may be followed with Thomas F. Torrance, *The Hermeneutics of John Calvin* (Edinburgh, 1988), though somewhat difficult for the nontheologian to follow, and Suzanne Selinger's provocative *Calvin Against Himself: An Inquiry into Intellectual History* (Hamden, Connecticut, 1984), which analyzes how Calvin's interpretation of Luther was influenced by his own psychological condition and the contemporary social environment.

Calvin's reaction to that environment is further assessed in John B. Leith, *John Calvin's Doctrine of the Christian Life* (Louisville, 1989); Jeannine E. Olson, *Calvin and Social Welfare: Deacons and the Bourse française* (London, 1989), which argues that Calvin's theological belief in charity as a response to love of God and neighbors was supported by his actions, as evidenced in his founding and generous backing of a welfare fund in Geneva known as the Bourse française; and Elsie Anne McKee, *John Calvin on the Diaconate and Liturgical Almsgiving* (Geneva, Switzerland, 1984). Her *Elders and the Plural Ministry: The Role of Exegetical History in Illuminating John Calvin's Theology* (Geneva, Switzerland, 1988) examines Calvin's use of texts to support his division of the ministry into the four offices of pastor, teachers, elders, and deacons. Other features of Calvin's thought are covered in Mary Potter Engel, *John Calvin's Perspectival Anthropology* (Atlanta, 1988), and Harro Höpfl, *The Christian Polity of John Calvin* (New York and Cambridge, England, 1982), which looks at Calvin's views on government within the context of Geneva; and Stephen Strehle, *Calvinism, Federalism, and Scholasticism: A Study of the Reformed Doctrine of Covenant* (Bern, 1988).

On women in Calvinism see Jane Dempsey Douglas, *Women, Freedom, and Calvin* (Philadelphia, 1985), as well as the appropriate sections of Bonnie S. Anderson and Judith P. Zinsser, *A History of Their Own: Women in History*, 2 vols. (New York, 1988), and especially Natalie Zemon Davis, *Society and Culture in Early Modern France* (Stanford, 1975), chaps. 3 and 5.

THE SPREAD OF CALVINISM

The international scope of Calvinism is underlined in the articles in Menna Prestwich, ed., *International Calvinism, 1541–1715* (New York and Oxford, 1985), also W. Stanford Reid, ed., *John Calvin: His Influence in the Western World* (Grand Rapids, 1981). A limited and somewhat doctrinaire look at the spread of Calvinism into France is Henry Heller, *The Conquest of Poverty: The Calvinist Revolt in Sixteenth Century France* (Leiden, 1986), in which the author tries to tie the Reformation in France to social and economic distress there. A very different approach is taken in Robert M. Kingdon, *Geneva and the Coming of the Wars of Religion to France* (Geneva, Switzerland, 1956) and its sequel, *Geneva and the Consolidation of the French Protestant Movement* (Madison, 1967), which focuses on the dispute between lay and clerical factions in French Protestantism. For Calvinism in the Netherlands see Phyllis M. Crew, *Calvinist Preaching and Iconoclasm in the Netherlands, 1544–1569* (New York, 1978), and Keith L. Sprunger, *Dutch Puritanism: A History of English and Scottish Churches of the Netherlands in the Sixteenth and Seventeenth Centuries* (Leiden, 1982). For a study of the German theologian who founded the German Reformed Church, see Derk Visser, *Zacharius Ursinus: The Reluctant Reformer—His Life and Times* (New York, 1983).

CALVINISM IN SCOTLAND AND ENGLAND

A good, wide-ranging study is Ian B. Cowan, *The Scottish Reformation: Church and Society in Sixteenth-Century Scotland* (New York, 1982). More limited in scope but a more in-depth monograph and reference work is Michael Lynch, *Edinburgh and the Reformation* (Edinburgh, 1981). Two excellent studies of Knox are W. Stanford Reid, *Trumpeter of God, a Biography of John Knox* (Grand Rapids, 1982), and Richard G. Kyle, *The Mind of John Knox* (Lawrence, Kansas, 1984). A closer look at the theology of the Reformation is Richard L. Greaves, *Theology and Revolution in the Scottish Reformation* (Grand Rapids, 1980), and at economic factors is Gordon Marshall, *Presbyteries and Profits: Calvinism and the Development of Capitalism in Scotland, 1560–1707* (Oxford, 1980). For England see R.T. Kendall, *Calvin and English Calvinism to 1649* (Oxford, 1979), and John Patrick Donnelly, S.J., *Calvinism and Scholasticism in Vermigli's Doctrine of Man and Grace* (Leiden, 1976). Lutheran origins of the Scottish Reformation are assessed in James E. McGoldrick, *Luther's Scottish Connection* (Cranbury, New Jersey, 1989).

5 | THE ENGLISH REFORMATION

D URING THE EARLY YEARS OF THE ENGLISH REFORMATION, THE PRI-
mary motivation and decisions came from the government, although a
growing undercurrent of religious protest greatly influenced later stages
of the Reformation. To understand and appreciate this fact, we must remember
that the religious authority in England had been, even before Henry VIII's time,
subordinate to the political authority of the crown. English bishops were not
supreme in their dioceses, and the numerous immunities and privileges exercised by them were understood as grants from the king, not marks of their
own sovereignty. Yet the church still owed part of its allegiance to Rome, and
as long as it did, the power of the king was compromised. It remained for a
monarch of Henry VIII's caliber to terminate that compromise and establish a
national church within an autonomous state.

Clergymen, Reformers, and Humanists

Even though English bishops were not sovereign lords, as were many of the
prelates of the Holy Roman Empire, their conduct frequently gave the impression that they were. The English clergy had succeeded in accumulating great
wealth in lands and money, and paraded that prosperity in ostentatious dress
and extravagant display. They were perhaps less guilty of simony and absenteeism than were the German clergy, but some were not averse to ignoring
canon law or Christian morality if it led to material gain. At any rate, they
were accused of venality, avarice, and corruption by reform-minded humanists
and writers of the time. In their dichotomous role as servants of both king and
pope, they naturally tended to respond more quickly and vigorously to the
power closest at hand.

Resentment and reaction resulted from this condition. The laity was offended by the suffragan bishops (auxiliary bishops with administrative and
episcopal responsibilities but no jurisdictional functions) who "filled in" for
ecclesiastical officeholders while the latter were engaged in the king's business,
and they chafed under the burdensome financial obligations imposed upon

them by the church. Ecclesiastical courts were notoriously corrupt in early sixteenth-century England, adding greater hopelessness to the situation. "These are not the [shep]herds," charged Simon Fish in his caustic *Supplication of Beggars,* "but the ravenous wolves going in [shep]herds' clothing, devouring the flock." It was not just the laymen who criticized the clergy. "Everywhere throughout town and countryside there exists a crop of oafish and boorish priests," charged William Melton, chancellor of York Minster, "some of whom are engaged on ignoble and servile tasks, while others abandon themselves to tavern-haunting, swilling and drunkenness."

Nevertheless, clerical conditions are not an accurate measure of spirituality or devotion. In England in the early decades of the sixteenth century, there was also a deep craving for spiritual expression. Not only did church attendance and other forms of religious observance increase, so did the more inward expressions of religious feeling and devotion, and the continued activity of heretical groups like the Lollards.

Lollardy was born in the late fourteenth century out of the influences of John Wyclif's (ca. 1320–84) religious teachings, especially his emphasis on the preaching role of the clergy rather than its sacramental function, and his insistence that the Bible (in the vernacular) should be available to everyone. The Wyclif Bible initiated the ground swell of Reformation biblicalism. Although Lollardy appears to have declined in importance during much of the fifteenth century, it did not cease entirely to influence many people in England. By the end of the century, there is evidence of some renewed vigor and growth, especially among the laborers and urban tradesmen, and among women. To a large extent, the longevity of Lollardy was due to its association with the family, in which maternal influences were very strong. This persistence of family religion helps account for the internal vigor of clandestine Lollardy despite vigorous persecution by the authorities. Yet it was not confined to family circles, for beliefs were shared with neighbors and friends, again especially by women. In fact, recent evidence suggests that in some areas—notably in Kent—a female proselyting network existed and that women were active also in distributing Lollard literature.

By the end of the century, there is evidence of some renewed vigor and growth, especially among the common laborers and urban tradesmen. By the opening of Henry VIII's reign, Lollard "cells" existed in many parts of England but especially in Buckinghamshire, Essex, Kent, Berkshire, and the Midlands. According to Foxe's *Book of the Martyrs,* the incidence of Lollard executions increased notably in the early sixteenth century. Since the Lollards believed in predestination, divine overlordship, and the authority of the Scriptures, while rejecting papal supremacy, transubstantiation, clerical celibacy, monasticism, and the worldly wealth of the clergy, it is not surprising that they were feared and despised as dangerous heretics by sixteenth-century church authorities. Lollard circles were among the first to embrace evangelical writings when these spread to England in the 1520s.

Meanwhile, other forces and ideas were beginning to act upon the religious orthodoxy of early sixteenth-century England. Mysticism, for example,

Sixteenth-Century England

which was so widespread on the continent in the late Middle Ages, also exerted influence in the English church, especially in the devotional writings of Walter Hilton and Richard Rolle. The deep asceticism of the Carthusian Brothers, reinforced by the circulation of both continental and native devotional literature, stimulated an increasingly personal worship that, although never contrary to the institutional church, functioned largely without regard to it. The same can be said of the *devotio moderna*, whose influence was not confined to the continent.

Christian humanism also encouraged a more critical attitude toward the clergy. To devout English humanists like John Colet and Sir Thomas More, the essence of true worship was morality and spirituality, not ecclesiastical observances or theological definitions. In his 1511 Convocation Sermon to the assembled prelates, Colet boldly charged them to reform the English church "because that nothing hath so disfigured the face of the Church as hath the fashion of secular and worldly living in clerks and priests." Erasmus's accusation also reverberated across England as well as the continent: "What point is there in your being showered with holy water if you do not wipe away the inward pollution from your heart? You venerate the saints and delight in touching their relics, but you despise the best one they left behind, the example of the holy life." However, we must not misunderstand these Christian humanists. They intended their criticism to reform the church, not to disrupt or destroy it. Colet's closing admonition to the clergy was, "Go ye now in the spirit that ye have called on, that, by the help of it, ye may in this your council find out, discern, and ordain those things that may be profitable to the Church."

Tyndale and the Cambridge Circle

Most of the English humanists recoiled from Luther's theological position. Nevertheless, after 1520, Lutheran books and ideas became increasingly noticeable in certain English circles, many of them distributed by the young scholar and bookseller Thomas Garrett. The first and most important of these Protestant cells was at Cambridge, where a growing body of interested students and clerics met regularly at the White Horse Inn to read and discuss the doctrines of the Wittenberg reformer. From this early coterie came many of the later leaders and martyrs of English Protestantism, including William Tyndale, Miles Coverdale, Hugh Latimer, Thomas Cranmer, John Frith, Nicholas Ridley, Robert Barnes, Thomas Bilney, and Matthew Parker. Through them, Lutheran and other evangelical writings were smuggled into England and secretly distributed. Better educated and usually coming from a higher rung on the social ladder than the contemporary Lollards, these men represented a more serious threat to the religious establishment, for what they received from the continent in the biblical theology of Lutheranism was a formidable weapon.

Among these scholars was William Tyndale (ca. 1492–1536), a student and master of ancient and classical languages, who became passionately interested in the Scriptures and in making them more available to a wider reading public. In London, Tyndale began his translation under the fruitful patronage of the wealthy merchant Humphrey Monmouth. Forced to flee to the continent in 1524, Tyndale went directly to Wittenberg and a year later began the publication of his New Testament at Cologne. Immediately, copies of the new English text were distributed in England, despite rigorous attempts by the authorities to prevent their circulation. Tyndale's translation was at once majestic and simple, erudite yet emotionally stirring. Strongly influenced by Lutheran ideas, its publication was a landmark in the development of English Protestantism. With Coverdale's subsequent Old Testament translation, it formed the Great English Bible of 1539. But Tyndale did not put down his pen when the New Testament was finished. He also became the principal instrument of Protestant propaganda in England, flooding his homeland with translations of Lutheran pamphlets and writing many moving and militant tracts of his own. Tyndale was one of the great religious pamphleteers of the age and the beginning bridge between the continental Reformation and Henrician England.

In one way or another most of the Cambridge circle helped promote Protestantism in England and strongly affected the outcome of the English Reformation. And most of them paid with their lives. Thomas Bilney (ca. 1495–1531) was a mild Erasmian cleric whose religious orthodoxy was unjustly challenged by Cardinal Wolsey. After recanting and spending a year in the Tower of London, Bilney was again charged with heresy and burned at the stake in 1531. A similar fate awaited the brilliant young John Frith (1503–33), who assisted Tyndale in translating the New Testament and published several tracts, including one against Thomas More's *Supplication of Souls*. Upon returning to England in 1532, Frith was arrested and imprisoned for heresy, then burned at the stake on 4 July 1533, at the age of twenty-nine. Dr. Robert Barnes (d. 1540), a prior of the Augustinian friars, was a serious reformer who fell afoul of the authorities because of his theological indiscretions. Escaping to the continent, he met Luther and in 1531 returned to England as a dedicated Lutheran. Still, he got along fairly well until the promulgation of Henry VIII's rigid Six Articles in 1539, under which he was arrested and burned to death the following year.

Not all of the Protestant martyrs were men. One of the most outspoken members of the London circle was Anne Askew, a well-educated Lincolnshire gentlewoman who had been turned out of the house by her husband because of her "religious heresies." In London she became an active promoter of the Bible and Bible reading before she was arrested early in 1545 and subjected to several interrogations. In each of the inquiries the examiners, including the bishop of London, were no match for her clear thinking, constancy, and wit. After that she was tortured on the rack "'til the bones were almost plucked asunder." When she was taken to be burned some months later, her body was so limp it had to be chained to the stake to keep it from sagging. Many others preceded and followed her.

Hugh Latimer and Nicholas Ridley fared better and escaped the stake until much later. Latimer (ca. 1485–1555), although a zealous, reforming preacher, managed to maintain a close relationship with the king until his opposition to the Six Articles, which cost him a stint in the Tower. In 1535 he was made bishop of Worcester, although he resigned that post in 1539. Under Edward VI he resumed his preaching, for which he was arrested when Mary came to the throne, and in 1555 he was burned at Smithfield, along with Ridley and Cranmer. Ridley (1500–55) was chaplain to Henry VIII and canon of Canterbury before becoming bishop of Rochester in 1547. He helped Cranmer compile the Prayer Book of 1549 and a year later succeeded Edmund Bonner as the prestigious bishop of London. After Mary's accession, Ridley's career (and life) came to an abrupt end. Matthew Parker was another member of this circle, whose low-key prelature under Henry, Edward, and Mary, preserved him for the highest ecclesiastical office in the realm under Elizabeth.

Another personality who also helped bring about (more unwittingly than the others and in a very different way) the religious revolt in England was Henry's lord chancellor, archbishop of York, and papal legate in England, Cardinal Thomas Wolsey (ca. 1475–1530). As an outstanding man of affairs and a capable organizer, Wolsey had been the king's principal assistant for many years and had given his master devoted and skilled service. Wolsey, though, was ambitious and used his office to bully the English clergy—not only the lowly parish priests but the bishops and higher prelates as well. As cardinal archbishop of York, he stood next to the archbishop of Canterbury in the English hierarchy; as permanent papal legate *a latere* (with wide powers), he represented the Holy See directly and thus overruled all other ecclesiastical authorities in the nation. Whatever his ultimate intentions (probably the papacy itself), Wolsey's administration of papal affairs in England made himself and the pope so hated by the English clergy that they were much less adverse to supporting Henry's break with Rome than they might otherwise have been.

Henry VIII and the Divorce Controversy

The unique factor in the English Reformation was not clerical corruption, Lutheran influences, or Wolsey's administrative tyranny, but the personality and ambition of the king. Henry VIII was not unacquainted with the Scriptures and had more than a superficial knowledge of canon law. Indeed, he fancied himself to be something of a theologian in his own right, although he customarily deferred to the theological interpretations of his bishops. In 1520 Henry rose to the defense of the church against the attacks of Martin Luther, particularly against his *Babylonian Captivity of the Church*. So vigorously did Henry uphold the Catholic sacraments that Pope Leo X, in gratitude for the king's "pious labours in defense of the faith of Christ," bestowed upon him the title "Defender of the Faith." Relations between England and the papacy had been amicable ever since the first Tudor monarch seized the throne some forty years earlier. This friendship had at times been strained by the fluctuating power struggle over the domination of Italy, but after the papal accession of Clement VII in 1522, and Wolsey had moved England from the imperial camp into an alliance with Francis I, it seemed that both Wolsey's and Clement's dreams were attached to the same star. When Charles V's armies sacked Rome and imprisoned the pope, Henry appeared destined for the role of defender of the

Henry VIII. *This portrait by Hans Holbein reflects the egotism and determination that characterized Henry's clash with the church in the 1530s.*

papacy as well as the faith. After 1527, however, Charles V, not Clement VII, made the decisions in Rome, and when Henry's whims called for the annulment of his eighteen-year marriage to Catherine of Aragon, Charles's aunt, a major confrontation was in the offing.

Just when or why Henry VIII first decided he wanted a divorce we will probably never know. What is clear is that during the years 1527 through 1533, the divorce issue (technically an annulment case, though commonly referred to, even then, as a divorce) was the center of English diplomatic and domestic affairs. Henry's own confession that he had sinned in marrying Catherine in the first place, and that as a consequence God was punishing him by depriving him of a son, although probably not the motive for the divorce, was his justification for it. After several miscarriages, his wife had given birth to six children, but three of them were stillborn and two others died in infancy. Now she was beyond the age of childbearing. The only child to survive was Mary, a frail girl of eleven. Being a narrowly religious man, Henry began to believe what the preachers and the Scriptures had said about the curse on a man who marries his brother's widow. Catherine had been married to Henry's brother Prince Arthur only a short time when he died. Later, a dispensation from Pope Julius II legalized her marriage to Henry. Now King Henry VIII avowed that the marriage violated Leviticus 20:21 (which declares that anyone

Catherine of Aragon.
Daughter of Ferdinand and Isabel, sent to England at the age of sixteen as a pawn in Ferdinand's political schemes, Catherine was married to Prince Arthur for a short time before becoming Henry VIII's first wife and popular queen of England. Portrait by Michael Sittow.

marrying his brother's widow would be childless), and he was therefore living in sin. However, he reasoned, if he could witness to God his repentance by repudiating his wife, the Lord might respond by continuing his line.

And then there was Anne Boleyn! A lady-in-waiting to Queen Catherine, and sister to Henry's former mistress, Anne Boleyn was destined to play a role in history far greater than her own modest talents or abilities might suggest. Nor did she possess ravishing physical beauty. The Venetian ambassador, in fact, considered her rather homely. "Madam Ann is not one of the handsomest women in the world," he reported to the Doge, "she is of middling stature, swarthy complexion, long neck, wide mouth, bosom not much raised, and in fact has nothing [to recommend her] but the English King's great appetite, and her eyes, which are black and beautiful." She also had a clever mind and more than the usual amount of ambition for a lady-in-waiting. Before 1527 Henry had fallen in love with her. Had she wished, she might have served as his mistress, but her own aspirations to the throne and Henry's desire for a legitimate male heir combined to make marriage a necessity. Before that could take place, though, the king had to lawfully dispose of his current wife.

To Chancellor Wolsey fell the task of solving "the King's Great Matter." In normal times, securing a pronouncement from Pope Clement to the effect

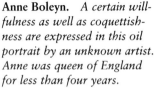

Anne Boleyn. *A certain will-fulness as well as coquettish-ness are expressed in this oil portrait by an unknown artist. Anne was queen of England for less than four years.*

that Julius's dispensation was out of order and void would not have seemed unlikely. The pope, however, was now a virtual prisoner of Catherine's nephew, Charles V, and in no position to defy the emperor. Wolsey hoped to strengthen his master's position by a stronger alliance with France, offering Catherine's daughter, Mary, as wife to Francis's son. Like much of Wolsey's policy, it missed the mark. When France and Spain agreed to the Peace of Cambrai in 1529, Wolsey was left holding the bag—in this case a black portfolio containing Henry's orders to obtain a papal commission giving Wolsey authority to dissolve the marriage. The pope refused, ordering instead a committee headed by Cardinal Campeggio, cardinal protector of the English nation at Rome, to hear the case. In March 1529 the court finally convened, but four months later it was no nearer a decision than it had been at the beginning. Catherine's steadfast denial that her marriage to Arthur had ever been consummated deprived Henry of his only legal case, unless the papal dispensation allowing the marriage could be proven inadequate or unauthorized. This Clement could not do without seriously weakening his own authority. In October he removed the case to Rome, and it became obvious to Henry that his policy of persuasion had failed. So had his servant who was supposed to have carried it out. This failure was to cost Wolsey his position, his fortune and, indirectly, his life.

Wolsey's lament as he lay on his deathbed at Leicester Abbey, that "Had I served my God as I have served my king, He would not now abandon me to my enemies," was doubtless true. Yet Wolsey fell victim to his own success. As long as the ships of state and church ran a parallel course, he could maintain his prominence with a foot in each. Still, for all of his power and pomp, he was not the supreme commander of either vessel, and when it became advantageous for the king of England to alter his course, Wolsey was sacrificed to the sea. His collapse was as colossal as it was sudden, for it was not just the defeat of a man; it was the end of a system, medieval in structure and scope, which for centuries had bound together the destinies of the English state and the Roman church.

The Break with Rome

Sir Thomas More was named lord chancellor to succeed Wolsey in October 1529, but Henry was developing other means to fulfill his desires. More accepted the chancellorship on the condition that he would not be called upon to intervene in the divorce issue, an affair he thoroughly disliked. The king therefore made plans for an assault on the pope that would not require the aid of his lord chancellor. One month after Wolsey was discharged, Henry summoned Parliament. Remembering the strong anticlerical feelings of the last two parliaments, Henry hoped to use this base to strengthen his position against the pope. The plan worked marvelously. Pent-up resentment against the clergy, fed by decades of slothfulness and abuse, was released in the House of Commons in a series of anticlerical bills attacking the financial, judicial, and administrative prerogatives of the church in England. Wolsey's demoralization of the upper clergy now began to show as the bishops in the House of Lords did almost nothing to defend the church against the Commons' attack. Henry remained aloof, only reminding Pope Clement that his English subjects were growing restless but that he, the king, could keep them in line—especially if the pope saw fit to grant his divorce. The emperor's presence, however, still counted for more than Henry's pretense. Clement did not budge.

For two years the situation changed little. Negotiations continued, and tensions mounted. The marriage question was presented to the universities of Europe for their opinion, but their replies were indecisive and contradictory. In the meantime, seeing that his policy of pressure had been no more successful than his previous attempts at persuasion, Henry was forced either to concede defeat or launch a direct assault on the pope. Given the king's personality and ego, the first alternative was probably never considered.

Cranmer and Cromwell   Into the inner councils of English government now came two men who soon became the chief agents in fulfilling the king's will. These were Thomas Cranmer (1489–1556), who was named archbishop of Canterbury after the death of William Warham in 1532; and Thomas Cromwell (1485–1540), Wolsey's former secretary, who since his master's fall, had become a member of Parliament and, in 1530, of the Royal Council. From 1531 on, Cromwell rose rapidly in the king's estimation until he occupied all of the key positions, from chancellor of the exchequer, principal secretary, and master of the rolls to lord privy seal. Cromwell was an administrative genius, capable of handling an enormous amount of business, both consequential and trivial, with ease and efficiency. Unlike Wolsey, he had no commitment, either ceremonial or personal, to the ecclesiastical church—although he was a religious person with a reserved predilection for Protestantism. Furthermore, he was unencumbered by the cardinal's colossal egotism and love of display. That is not to say that the new minister was devoid of pride or of self-esteem, but he gratified them in a different way. Where Wolsey had been demonstrative and affected, Cromwell was cool and calculating, content to have his ideas win whether he received the credit or not. Cromwell also had a much clearer intellectual grasp of the nature of sixteenth-century power and of the underlying forces that were most useful at the time. In Machiavelli's sense, he was a man of *virtù* (valor and decisiveness). He not only saw what he wanted, he recognized the means for achieving it and accepted the consequences that it would bring. His was a logical and unemotional mind, a fitting instrument for carrying out the king's volcanic will.

The new archbishop was a different sort of person. Mild and soft-spoken in temperament, Thomas Cranmer was a scholar by profession. He was Cambridge trained—a colleague of Barnes, Latimer, Ridley, and the others of the White Horse Inn days—and would probably have preferred the sheltered life of a professional chair of theology had he not been catapulted into public affairs by "the King's Great Matter." It was Cranmer who first proposed that the marriage issue be resolved by canvassing the learned opinion of the continent, and Cranmer himself was sent abroad to help present the king's case to the universities. Cranmer was sympathetic to the king's cause and none too enamored with the dictates from Rome. Here was a prelate who could be counted on to follow the king's command and at the same time persuade others in the church that the king's wishes were right.

In 1531 Henry struck. First he declared the papacy guilty of violating the English Statute of Praemunire, which prohibited appeals to Rome or the sending of legates (in this case Wolsey) into the country without royal consent. He followed this with the announcement to the English clergy that they stood equally guilty, because they had accepted Wolsey as the papal legate. Without accessible recourse, the clergy submitted to the king's bludgeoning and accepted his self-designation as "Protector and Only Supreme Head of the Church and Clergy in England," with only the vague limitation, "so far as the laws of Christ permit."

In Parliament, Cromwell now took the lead in advancing the king's case. His solution to the impasse was as simple as it was extreme—that is, remove the pope from England and let Canterbury grant the divorce. With a single stroke, the Gordian knot was cut. Early in 1532 an act was passed forbidding all future payments of annates to Rome. If the pope refused to relinquish his right to the annates and withheld consecration, said the bill, the newly appointed archbishop would be consecrated without papal sanction. This statute was followed by an even more resounding defiance of pope and clergy.

Henry VIII Triumphs over Pope Clement. *A woodcut from Foxe's* Actes and Monuments *(1569) shows Henry trampling on the prostrate pope.*

The House of Commons made supplication against the entire order of church government and ecclesiastical courts in England. This supplication, severely criticizing and condemning the legal and administrative structure of the church, was presented to the convocation of bishops for their reply. At first the clergy resisted, upholding their ancient right to make and judge ecclesiastical laws. Finally, under pressure from the king, they submitted unconditionally to his demands, aggreeing that the canon-making power of the church must be subordinated to the lawmaking power of the crown and Parliament. Thenceforth no new ecclesiastical ordinances would be enacted without license from the king, and those already in existence must be submitted to a royal committee for approval or rejection. This submission of the clergy took place on 16 May 1532. On 17 May, Sir Thomas More resigned as lord chancellor. His attempt to "guide policy indirectly, so that you make the best of things, and what you cannot turn to good, you can at least make less bad" (*Utopia*, Bk. I), proved unsuccessful. Now he hoped only to live out the remainder of his life in peace and solitude at Chelsea. He was soon to discover that in Henrician England there was no safety in silence. One must either submit to the monarch's will or else suffer his displeasure, with its inevitable results.

The final step in the repudiation of Rome was the promulgation of an act in restraint of appeals to the Papal See. With the enactment of such a law, there would be no further need to beg or beat the pope to grant the annulment. Authority for such an action would reside in England. Again Thomas Cromwell prepared the bill and led its debate through the Commons. Before the bill was ready, however, Henry's marital affairs took a new turn. In January 1533, he learned that Anne Boleyn was pregnant. Until the statute against appeals could be enacted, he could not repudiate his wife and declare Anne his queen. Nevertheless, Henry could not run the risk of having a male heir born out of wedlock, so on 25 January he secretly married Anne Boleyn. In the meantime he charged his new archbishop of Canterbury with the responsibility of pronouncing officially on his divorce from Catherine. In March the Statute of Appeals was passed. The last of the papal controls in England was ended. Shortly thereafter, Archbishop Cranmer opened ecclesiastical hearings on the king's case. One month later the solemn decision was handed down that the king's marriage to Lady Catherine "is null and absolutely void, . . . thus separated and divorced they are free and immune from every bond of matrimony in respect of the said pretended marriage." On 28 May Cranmer pronounced the king's marriage to Anne Boleyn "good and lawful." Four days later, Anne was crowned queen of England.

Reign by Statute and Terror

The English people were surprised by the king's actions, and more than a little disappointed. Catherine had been a good queen and was sincerely loved by her subjects. Henry, however, was king! His subjects respected and obeyed his will. There were some quiet murmurings against his divorce and new marriage, but little love was lost for the papacy. Henry's defiance of the pope was greeted with general but subdued acclaim. Where signs of grumbling and discontent appeared, the crown moved quickly, as it did against the Holy Maid of Kent.

Some notoriety had become attached to a simple peasant girl named Elizabeth Barton, a victim of epilepsy and of unscrupulous exploiters. Widely known as the Holy Maid of Kent because of her mystical experiences involving frequent religious utterances and prophecies made while in a trance, she began to be used for political purposes by some Canterbury monks. Directing her prophecies now toward the king's matter, she proclaimed that he would die within six months if he put away Queen Catherine for another woman. Fearing that her ravings might have a dangerous effect on the credulous people, Henry had her arrested and, under the pressure of torture, made her and her accomplices publicly confess their fraud. In April 1534, they were all executed at Tyburn. The case of the unfortunate Maid of Kent illustrates the steps Henry was willing to take to stifle all opposition.

Beginning to sense the magnitude of his strength, Henry anticipated the pope's excommunication with a barrage of parliamentary enactments, making the breach with Rome complete. The Heresy Act established a new definition of the heresies for which the death penalty was pronounced, and laid down the procedures to be followed, thus placing control of religious doctrines entirely under civil jurisdiction. The act also removed the denial of papal supremacy from the list of infractions punishable by death. This was followed by a new Act of Submissions giving statutory sanction to the previous promises extracted from the clergy, just as a further Act of Annates confirmed the earlier financial decree. A new Appeals Act made the king's Court of Chancery, rather than the papal curia, the final court of appeals, and an Ecclesiastical Appointments Act transferred all clerical appointments from pope to king. In the final session of the 1534 Parliament, an Act of Supremacy was added declaring the king, this time without further qualification, "The only supreme head in earth of the Church of England." This was accompanied by a Succession Act, which defined and confirmed the succession through the issue of Anne Boleyn (even though she had not yet produced the desired male heir), and a Treason Act, which more clearly defined a number of punishable deeds, including now the denial of the king's ecclesiastical supremacy.

The enactments of the Reformation Parliament were indeed significant in the constitutional as well as the religious history of England. The king and Parliament had in effect not only legalized Henry's moral actions and repudiated the authority of Rome, they also established the autonomous sovereignty of the English government—a government composed of both king and Parliament and based on the sanction of statutory law. Just how unrestrained this new Renaissance monarchy could be only time would tell, but it lost no time in demonstrating that it meant business.

Among those few who steadfastly opposed this conception of rule—who maintained that neither an act of Parliament nor a decree of the king could nullify the law of God—were the bishop of Rochester, John Fisher, and Henry's former lord chancellor, Sir Thomas More. Neither Fisher nor More had openly opposed the king in his confrontation with the Papal See, but all of England knew how they stood on the divorce issue and where they placed their ultimate allegiance. Neither of them denounced the king now, but the royal lion was uneasy with even a single dissenting voice. And Thomas More's was not an ordinary voice. He was admired and respected by all Catholic Christendom. With Erasmus he stood as a symbol of the humanist's harmonization of the religious and secular life. Now, however, a choice had to be made. Henry deeply feared his former lord chancellor. More's influence could be dangerous if used against the king. It was not enough that he remain silent on the King's Great Matter; he must be made to proclaim his support of his master. More's loyalty to both church and country had been unquestioned; now loyalty to Rome meant treason to England.

For refusing to take the oath attached to the Act of Succession, which demanded not only the acceptance of Henry's marital actions but also the negation of papal supremacy, Fisher and More were arrested and sent to the Tower. More's distinguished and eloquent self-defense before a special tribunal of judges was his last public service. Perjured evidence by the solicitor-general, Sir Richard Rich, resulted in a conviction of treason. Upon notification of the death sentence, More is reported to have made the simple but pregnant declaration, "I do nobody no harm, I say none harm, I think none harm, but wish everybody good. And if this be not enough to keep a man alive, in good faith I long not to live." He was beheaded in London on 6 July 1535. Fisher had been executed two weeks earlier, and before that three Carthusian monks and two priests. Three more Carthusians were tortured and put to death in July. The lesson was clear: no one stands in the way of royal revolution with impunity.

The Henrician Reformation Completed

Thomas Cromwell's role in the English Reformation did not end with the parliamentary sessions of 1534, nor with the consolidation of the king's supremacy in 1535. In the developments of these years, during which the Tudor government revolutionized its role in ecclesiastical affairs and institutionalized its new position by statute, Cromwell was the primary instrument of the king's will. Carefully yet confidently, he worked out the details of the governmental overhaul, merging the active strength of Parliament with the majesty of the crown to create a concept of centralized power that was unique in Europe at the time. Now his skill was needed to solve another vital problem of Renaissance rule—finance.

The treasury left by his frugal father had been squandered by Henry VIII before his reign was two years old. Wolsey had tried all of the known schemes for raising revenue, but they were not enough. The extravagant tastes of both minister and king, and their expensive involvement in continental diplomacy and war, kept the exchequer continually dry. Parliaments were summoned, forced loans extracted, excises demanded, payments to Rome curtailed, but still there was not enough money for the costly operation of government.

Dissolution of the Monasteries

By the Act of Supremacy, the crown was accorded the right to "visit, repress, redress, reform, order, correct, restrain, and amend" all abuses and heresies discovered in the church. With the newly granted title of vicar-general, Thomas Cromwell now began the implementation of these statutory rights. He ordered a visitation of all churches and monasteries within the realm, with specific instructions to collect information on the value and income of every benefice. The results of this survey were compiled and used as a basis for the next step in his financial plan, the dissolution of the monasteries and the confiscation of monastic lands. Parliament was then presented with an exaggerated picture of monastic irresponsibility and delinquency, based upon the results of the commission's reports. In March 1536 a bill was passed ordering the dissolution of all monasteries, nunneries, abacies, and priories with an annual income of less than £200. The charge of inefficiency in the operation of these smaller establishments, along with the corruption of their occupants, was used to justify their suppression. These holdings now became the property of the crown to do with as the king saw fit, according "to the pleasure of

Almighty God and to the honour and profit of this realm." Almost 400 religious houses were thus closed and their income reverted to the king.

In the next three years, those establishments that had escaped the first purge were also gradually devoured by the crown. In April 1539 a second Act of Dissolution was sent through Parliament, legalizing the confiscations that had taken place since 1536 and confirming the "free and voluntary" gifts of "divers and sundry abbots, priors, abbesses, prioresses, and other ecclesiastical governors and governesses," to the king.

Not everyone took the monastic confiscations with the equanimity suggested by the words of the dissolution statute. The people of the north country, already in bad humor over new taxes imposed upon their woolen industries, the increase of rents, and the general disrespect in which they were held by the king, began to seethe with discontent. In Lincolnshire a motley army of nobles, gentry, yeomen, monks, and priests demanded repeal of the Act of Dissolution along with other unwelcomed acts of the government. The revolt, soon to be known as the Pilgrimage of Grace, gained momentum as it spread into Yorkshire, Lancashire, and East Riding. At Doncaster, late in October 1536, the pilgrims sent the king their demands, summarized in five articles, calling for an end to the suppression of monasteries, relief from the new and burdensome taxes, the dismissal of heretical bishops, and the deposition of Thomas Cromwell. They also asked for the summoning of a new and "free" parliament. Henry flew into a rage when he received the demands. Defiantly, he ordered the earls of Shrewsbury and Suffolk and the duke of Norfolk to move against the rebels. By December the "pilgrims" were willing to listen to some compromising promises by the duke of Norfolk, and they soon disbanded without achieving their goals. Not one to forgive and forget, Henry VIII had the leaders of the rising put to death and many of the recalcitrant abbots and monks hanged at their abbey gates.

The Pilgrimage of Grace was the only consequential protest against the Henrician Reformation. Through all the turmoil of the five years of religious upheaval in England, the majority of the people were surprisingly apathetic. There had been no great devotion to the Roman allegiance, while for years the growing strength of the government had won the acceptance and support of the people. That the crown should one day assume the same jurisdiction over ecclesiastical matters that it already exercised in the political realm was not really too surprising. And since religious doctrine and worship changed very little under Henry (his Six Articles of 1539, for instance, reaffirmed the doctrines of transubstantiation, clerical celibacy, and oral confession), most people were indifferent to the matters of higher ecclesiastical jurisdiction. A few years later, Giovanni Micheli, the Venetian ambassador in England, observed that "the English regard and practice their religion only insofar as it relates to their duty as subjects of the king. They live as he lives and believe as he believes; indeed, they do everything he commands." Micheli exaggerated when he proposed that "they would accept Mohammedanism or Judaism if the king believed it, and told them also to believe in it," but he was quite correct in seeing that the position of the king was of paramount importance in the religion of the people. The last phase of Henry's managerial revolt, the suppression of the monasteries, was accepted, if not enthusiastically at least effectively, by the people of England. What dissatisfaction it aroused was more than balanced by the tighter allegiance it brought from other beneficiaries, nobles, and gentry, who received church lands as gifts from the king, and from wealthy speculators, who were able to purchase them outright.

The Last Decade of Henry's Rule

With Cromwell at the helm, the government of Henry VIII became a more effective instrument of royal administration than it had ever been before. Few totally new institutions were introduced in the 1530s, but the entire structure was overhauled and streamlined. The Privy Council, for example, emerged as the pivotal instrument of administration, while the financial machinery and the civil service were drastically reorganized. Cromwell's reorganization was based on a system of administrative and judicial councils staffed by crown appointees from all classes. Finally, the embodiment of absolute legal authority in the statutory power of the "King in Parliament" did much not only to enhance the role of Parliament in the English government but also to increase the

Thomas Cromwell, *by an unknown artist, after Hans Holbein, shows the secretary with the critical, hawklike look of a bird of prey. Actually, Cromwell was more a builder than a predator, and contributed creatively to the development of the English state.*

effective strength of the king by providing him with the sanction of law and of public support.

Cromwell was also the motivating force behind the Great Bible of 1539, a remarkably successful revision of Tyndale's, Coverdale's, and John Rogers's English translations, put together by Miles Coverdale, who skillfully edited the work and superintended its printing, begun in Paris and concluded in England. Cromwell not only sponsored the project of an authoritative English Bible but also saw it through publication and urged the bishops to provide a copy in every church and to exhort the laity to read it. Ultimately, the effect of the open Bible extended far beyond its immediate religious impact. Once appetites were whetted and indulged, they could not again be easily repressed. Under Cromwell's guidance the English Reformation turned an important corner.

Yet in spite of Cromwell's administrative genius, he was unable to ensure his own survival in the wilderness of Tudor politics. The royal supremacy he had helped create was no guarantee against his own destruction. His fall illustrates the continuing volatility of the politicoreligious situation, and emphasizes the disruptive role played by rival factions, both religious and political. Cromwell's strongest enemies at court by the time of the second Act of Dissolution were Thomas Howard, third duke of Norfolk, who was then lord treasurer and since 1533 earl marshal of England, and his conservative colleague, Stephen Gardiner, bishop of Winchester and secretary to the king prior to Cromwell's elevation to that post in 1533. Norfolk and Gardiner represented the old guard of aristocratic privilege and strongly resented the rapid elevation of upstarts like Cromwell and Cranmer. Furthermore, the noticeable Lutheran leanings of the archbishop of Canterbury, and Cromwell's more subtle sympathies with some Protestant views, brought these two under suspicion of heresy. The reaffirmation of Catholic doctrines in the Six Articles illustrates the rising tide of theological orthodoxy under Henry VIII following the break with Rome, and exemplifies the growing influence of the Norfolk-Gardiner faction in the government.

As early as 1538, Cromwell found himself caught on the horns of a dilemma. In order to satisfy the king's personal whims, and at the same time placate the powers partly responsible for the success of Henry's fight with the pope, Cromwell would have to play the contradictory roles of friend to the emperor and ally to the Lutheran princes. At the same time, he was forced to act against Protestant tendencies at home while guarding against the revival of papalism. Tensions at home and abroad were further aggravated by the king's continuing marital problems. Early in 1536, after repeated failure to present Henry with the male heir he desired, Anne Boleyn lost the king's favor. She had given birth to a daughter, Elizabeth, in 1534, but after frequent miscarriages it seemed apparent to Henry that God was still unplacated, or else his wrath was kindled anew over the king's marriage to Anne. His mistress-turned-queen would have to be cast off. Besides, he had already grown tired of her. This time no involved divorce suit would be needed. Anne was charged with infidelity to the king, which in the sixteenth-century scheme of things meant treason as well. She was convicted on perjured and circumstantial evidence, and beheaded within a fortnight. Two days later, Cranmer declared the marriage invalid from the first (which, if true, should have nullified the charge of adultery by which she was killed), and nine days after that Henry married Jane Seymour. His third wife was a peace-loving lady of the court with a good mind and a pleasant disposition. It was her lot to give the king his long-awaited son, Edward, born 24 October 1537; but it was not given to her to bask in the rewards of her effort. She died a few days after the birth.

The Fall of Cromwell

A new rapprochement between Spain and France in 1538 suggested to Henry and his minister the feasibility of a closer relationship with the Protestant princes of Germany. Representatives of the Schmalkaldic League had already urged the king to support their cause. In order not to lose the foreseeable advantages of some sort of German alliance, Cromwell proposed and negotiated a treaty with the duke of Cleves, custodian of the lower Rhineland, sealed and guaranteed with a marriage alliance between Henry and the duke's only daughter, Anne. Thus Anne of Cleves became the unwitting pawn of Cromwell's diplomacy and the unfortunate victim of Henry VIII's caprice. But Henry was in no mood to be tricked into supporting Lutheran heretics. He not only renounced the treaty with Cleves, he also repudiated his wife after a five-month marriage and charged Cromwell with deceit and treason. The duke of Norfolk's return from an embassy to France with a tenuous promise of friendship from the French monarch in exchange for a guarantee that Cromwell would be removed sealed the vice-regent's fate. Further charges of heresy instigated by Cromwell's enemies in Parliament only added thinly veiled evidence to bring him to trial. The evidence was never required. Cromwell was arrested for heresy and treason, and executed without trial on 23 July 1540.

The six-and-a-half remaining years of Henry's reign were almost disastrous for the island kingdom. Still determined to play the lion's role in Europe, if not by arbitration then by war, Henry once again plunged his armies into the Habsburg-Valois conflict. With all the fanfare and color of the Middle Ages, he sent 40,000 men under Norfolk and Suffolk to invade northern France, as agreed upon in a newly signed treaty with Charles V, and soon followed in person to accept Francis's surrender. Yet the fortunes of war were not so easily turned. After two years of partial and indecisive action, the English held only Boulogne. Although many towns had been burned, great losses of life were suffered on both sides, and the king had spent over a million and a half pounds (seven times the average annual income of the crown), yet won nothing significant. Furthermore, the attack on France was preceded by a renewal of the chronic war with the Scots, who had revived their alliance with France. Again the cost was staggering, reaching nearly a million pounds before the end of 1546. A Scottish army under King James V had been defeated at Solway Moss in November 1542, and the king himself died three weeks later; but Henry's ensuing arrogance lost him the conclusive victory that might have followed, and led to further involvement and expense.

Without the help of a Cromwell, or anyone approaching his ability as a manager and financier, Henry was forced to resort to the age-old expedients of forced loans, increased taxes, sale of crown lands (mostly confiscated monastic properties), and sale of benefices. The financial predicament was not helped by the growing inflation that forced prices steadily up and the value of money down. When the king died in January 1547, he left a country weakened by financial mismanagement and reckless foreign involvement, with a religious reformation still far from complete, and a government rife with factions and cliques poised to spring at one another's throats as soon as the king's heavy hand was removed.

The Reformation Under Edward VI

On the death of the fifty-seven-year-old monarch, the throne of England was left to Henry's haughty nine-year-old son, Edward VI (1547–53), whose overrated opinion of himself and of his ability might be expected from Henry's heir. The real control of England, however, resided now in a council of regency headed by Edward's incompetent uncle, Edward Seymour, duke of Somerset (1500–52). The new lord protector was the brother of Henry's third wife and had risen rapidly in the king's service after that marriage resulted in a royal heir. The Seymours were latecomers to the English peerage, but then so were most of the Tudor lords. Somerset's prominence in the royal service was assured when the execution of Henry's fifth wife, Catherine Howard, brought the duke of Norfolk and all the Howards to disgrace. The poet Henry Howard, earl of Surrey, holds the dubious distinction of being the last execution of Henry's reign, and his father, Thomas Howard, the venerable duke of Norfolk, escaped hanging only by the death of the king. Somerset himself had already shown some distinction at arms in the recent wars with Scotland, and held the offices of lord treasurer and earl marshal. His tempestuous young brother, Thomas Seymour, became lord admiral in 1547; but his indiscretions soon led to his own execution, and contributed to Somerset's fall. Somerset, a self-serving manager of government affairs, was incapable of coping with the complexities of administration caused by the machinations of the various factions.

The single achievement of Somerset's regency was his supervision of the rapid protestantization of the English Reformation. Regardless of Henry VIII's theological orthodoxy, an undercurrent of Protestantism continued to influence the English church and many of its patrons during the 1540s, some of whom were sheltered by Henry's sixth and only surviving wife, Catherine Parr (1512–48). A very intelligent woman, with noticeable Protestant leanings, Catherine assuaged the suspicions of her imperious husband while providing encouragement to the reformers. She also provided what has been called (perhaps with some exaggeration) a manifesto of reform, a gem of devotional writing called *Lamentation of the Sinful Soul*, reminiscent of Marguerite of Navarre's *Miroir de l'âme pérchereuse* (Mirror of a Sinful Soul) and Vittoria Colonna's *Rime religiose* (Religious Poems). It is quite possible that Catherine's

Catherine Parr. *Henry VIII's sixth and last wife was the daughter of a high royal official and had been twice widowed before marrying the king. She was a capable woman of great tact, considerable learning, and deep religious faith.*

influence on subsequent reform in England through her circle of friends may have been greater than is usually recognized.

When Henry died in 1547, only one member of the Privy Council was strongly Catholic in outlook, and he was quickly discharged. With this more favorable climate to beckon them, many continental reformers, especially Zwinglians from western Switzerland and the Palatinate, came to England, and reformation writings became more numerous. Soon many Protestant doctrines were being absorbed into the English church. Archbishop Cranmer now was given the green light to introduce the kind of religious liturgy that he had favored for a long time, but that he had been careful enough not to propose while Henry VIII was king.

Cranmer had been influenced in his views of the Lord's Supper by his former colleague at Cambridge, Nicholas Ridley, who favored a middle position somewhere between Luther's real presence and Zwingli's symbolism. Cranmer's own views had gone through several changes, and by 1547 he was ready to make some major changes in the Mass. He was even more interested in compiling an English Prayer Book and modifying the outmoded forms of the liturgy. He also defended popular Scripture reading against its conservative opponents led by bishops Gardiner and Bonner. The undercurrent of Protestant and independent opinion that had been growing in England for decades was now filtering to the surface and being shaped by people like Ridley, Latimer, Richard Cox, Sir John Cheke, and especially Archbishop Cranmer.

Edward VI. *Henry VIII's act would have been hard for anyone to follow, but young Edward had neither the maturity, moral character, nor physical strength to lead the nation. His weakness is reflected in this portrait attributed to William Scrots.*

The Edwardian Reformation, like the Henrician, was carried out largely by acts of Parliament. In the first year of Edward's rule, Parliament completed the monastic dissolution by assigning to the crown all remaining chantries (foundations providing money for Masses to be said for particular people), free chapels, colleges, hospitals, guilds, and fraternities. It also enacted the Order of Communion, which directed that the sacrament should be administered in both kinds, thus opening the path to a rejection of transubstantiation, and allowed the celebration of the rite in English. An Act of Uniformity followed in 1549, authorizing Cranmer to draw up a new prayer book and liturgical guide for the English church. This first Book of Common Prayer was also published in 1549. The principles upon which it was constructed were drawn partly from Zwinglian and Calvinist services and partly from native sources. Consolidation, emphasis upon instruction of the laity, and simplification were its guidelines. Wherever Scripture did not specifically prescribe a change, however, the ceremony was left in its Catholic form. Permission for the clergy to marry was granted by parliamentary enactment, and an order was issued that all images "of stone, timber, alabaster, or earth, graven, carved, or painted," should be defaced and destroyed.

The rapid swing of the English Reformation toward Protestant doctrine and practices after 1547 owed much to the influx of continental theologians in Edward's reign, largely at the invitation of Cranmer. Martin Bucer arrived in 1549, becoming Regius Professor at Cambridge, where he completed his *De*

Archbishop Cranmer. *This painting of Thomas Cranmer depicts the Archbishop of Canterbury in old age, not long before he was burned at the stake. He was clean-shaven until 1547 when, in memory of Henry VIII, he resolved never to shave again.*

regno Christi (On the Reign of Christ). Peter Martyr Vermigli (1500–62) was appointed professor at Oxford, and Bernardino Ochino (1487–1564), the one-time head of the Capuchins and now a wandering Protestant preacher, received a stipend at Canterbury. Valérand Poullain, who had succeeded Calvin as pastor of the French congregation in Strasbourg, settled in England a short time later and soon became involved with the English Protestants; while the Flemish Calvinist Jan Utenhove and the Pole Jan Łaski organized the congregations of foreign refugees in London. The Scottish reformer John Knox also arrived in England in 1549 and for three years was a preacher at Berwick and Newcastle.

England's protestantization was not threatened by the kingdom's political instability—provided the sickly Edward VI remained alive. But three years after the reign began, Somerset found himself deeply in trouble. Faced with two major uprisings—one in Cornwall and the other, known as Kett's rebellion, a more serious peasant revolt against the gentry in Norfolk, where mounting poverty and social dislocation caused by sharply rising prices led to open defiance—Somerset was forced into attempting emergency remedies. Early in 1551 his archrival, John Dudley, earl of Warwick, struck. Having outmaneuvered the protector in gaining the ear of the king, Warwick not only won for himself the new title and honor of duke of Northumberland but also persuaded Edward to undercut his uncle when charges were brought against him in council. In October 1551 Somerset was arrested for treason and lodged in the Tower. Three months later, he was beheaded amid the sorrowful but unprotesting gaze of the London spectators. Northumberland now became the virtual ruler of England.

**The
Northumberland
Interim**

John Dudley (ca. 1504–53) had come a long way
since that day in August 1510 when he had watched
the execution of his own father (on charges trumped
up by the new monarch, Henry VIII). Perhaps he felt
some brief pangs of remorse as he harried Somerset
to the block on equally flimsy evidence, but there is no record of any such
"weakness." The new duke of Northumberland was as devoid of compassion
or sympathy as any ambitious nobleman in the Tudor court. Early in life he
had demonstrated his physical prowess and his aptitude for military service.
Knighted on the field of battle at Calais when he was twenty-one, Dudley rose
through many military and civil assignments to become deputy governor of
Calais, lord high admiral, governor of Boulogne, lord lieutenant of the English
army that invaded Scotland in 1547, and a privy councilor. It was he who led
the next campaign against Scotland in 1549 and who crushed Kett's rebellion
in that same year. He was ruthless, uncompromising, and grimly ambitious.
Yet he was a strong and able administrator, capable of making some headway
against the spiraling economic crisis and of bringing the royal administration
out of some of the chaos it had been entangled in for a decade. Had he not
been so avaricious, and had the king not died so soon after Northumberland
took power, some of the tumult of the next decade might have been avoided.

Without real religious convictions of his own, Northumberland was un-
harmed by the revolutionary steps that had been taken toward Protestantism
during Somerset's protectorate. He simply attached himself to the protestantiz-
ing movement and pushed it forward with increasing speed. Cranmer was in-
structed to compile a new Prayer Book in 1552, and a new Act of Uniformity
made the English worship compulsory. Although not a radical departure from
the previous version, the liturgy of the 1552 Prayer Book was unmistakably
Protestant. The words of the Communion, "Take and eat this in remembrance
that Christ died for thee, and feed on him in thy heart by faith with thanksgiving," are close to the Zwinglian form, yet they reflect a definite determination to avoid aping the continental Reformation too much and to create a
distinct Anglican liturgy, soberly rejecting both Roman Catholicism and radical Protestantism.

A year later, Cranmer's final formulary of faith, known as the Forty-Two
Articles, was published. It, too, was an attempt not only to express a moderate
Protestant theology but also to denounce explicitly the polar positions of the
Catholics on the one hand and the Anabaptists on the other—a reflection of
the increasing concern over the spread of Anabaptist ideas in England during
the late 1530s and the 1540s. The articles affirmed justification by faith alone;
declared that "predestination to life is the everlasting purpose of God"; defined
the sacraments (of baptism and Communion) as "effectual signs of grace"; and
emphasized the sole authority of the Bible. At the same time they explicitly
denied transubstantiation, the Mass as a sacrifice, purgatory, the invocation of
saints, the primacy of Rome, and the infallibility of general councils. And while
condemning Millenarianism, free will, and other Anabaptist doctrines, they
also affirmed, in good Erastian fashion, the royal supremacy and admonished

obedience to the civil magistrates. It was clear that during Edward's short reign, and under the guidance of Thomas Cranmer, the English Reformation had finally become Protestant. Calvinist influences were particularly noticeable in the Forty-Two Articles, but above all the Anglican confession was broadly eclectic, drawing its doctrines from native as well as several continental sources.

In the meantime, the physical health of the young king could no longer keep pace with his precocious mind. When it became evident to those nearest the king that his days were numbered, Northumberland began stacking the cards that he hoped would ensure his own continued power and bring him even greater glory. Only weeks before the king's death, Northumberland persuaded him to put aside the succession of his two older half-sisters, Mary and Elizabeth, in favor of Northumberland's own daughter-in-law, the hapless Lady Jane Grey (Dudley). This beautiful and talented girl was the sixteen-year-old daughter of Henry Grey, duke of Suffolk, and granddaughter (on her mother's side) of Henry VIII's sister. Therefore, as cousin to Edward VI, she was in line of succession to the English throne, but only if Mary and Elizabeth were disinherited. Scarcely a month before the king's death, Northumberland arranged with the equally ambitious duke of Suffolk the marriage of Suffolk's daughter to Northumberland's son, Guilford Dudley, knowing that if Lady Jane became queen the real power could be controlled by Northumberland. Had this plot to place Lady Jane on the throne succeeded, Northumberland would still have had to deal with her father, but that was a problem that could wait.

For nine tense days after the announcement of Edward's death on July 8, the reluctant Lady Jane was queen. Yet Northumberland's plot to control England through his daughter-in-law had no hope of success because it was without legal sanction and without popular support. As soon as the people realized what had happened, they rallied to the support of Queen Mary. Northumberland's fate was assured, and so were young Dudley's and Lady Jane's. They were both beheaded on 12 February 1554, unfortunate victims of others' greed.

Queen Mary and the Catholic Restoration

With the crown now secured and peace restored, Queen Mary I began the religious reorientation of England. There had never been any secret of the fact that Catherine of Aragon's daughter was Catholic, or that she intended to return her country to its former allegiance to Rome. But there was hope that it would be done gracefully and without submission to outside influences. Vested interests also demanded that the political, economic, and religious benefits of the Reformation be retained. To accomplish this, tact, patience, moderation, and unusual wisdom would be required. Unfortunately, Mary was deficient in all of these. The fact that she was a woman did not help her either. In a patriarchical society that was not accustomed to having a female ruler, her task was doubly difficult.

Although she was honest, devoted, and sincere, and at the beginning of her reign had the popular support of her people, Mary lacked the political judgment necessary to accomplish her ambitious project. The least egocentric of any of the Tudor monarchs, she was also wanting in the flexibility and practicality that allowed Elizabeth to adjust to new situations and to ride the troughs of adversity until they became waves of opportunity. Mary had learned little about the practical nature of politics during her years of suffering and sorrow. She had only become more deeply embittered over her father's treatment of her mother, and more devoted to the idea of restoring England to the Catholic fold. That she was wantonly cruel or vindictive is a popular notion that is without factual support, although her zealous and intolerant dedication to "the cause" led her to actions that are unjustifiable. Certainly the epithet "Bloody Mary," with all of its implications, is unfair to her, and has been abandoned by most serious historians. Perhaps it would be better to think of her as the tragic queen, for from her own viewpoint as well as from England's, her reign was a tragedy.

Seeing the handwriting on the wall, most of the foreign Protestant theologians in England and some of their English disciples fled back to the continent. Joining earlier refugees in Zürich, Strasbourg, Frankfurt, Wesel, and Emden (they were not welcome in the predominantly Lutheran areas), some of these so-called Marian exiles also established new English settlements in Switzerland at Aarau, Basel, and Geneva. A violent schism in the English and Scottish communities at Frankfurt in 1555 resulted in the separation of the more radical faction led by John Knox and their migration to Geneva, where the enthusiastic Scot was their pastor. Knox's *First Blast* was published at Geneva in 1556 under Calvin's watchful eye. Aimed as much at Mary Tudor as it was at the Scottish regent Mary of Guise, it awakened in some English minds new alternatives to both Marian Catholicism and Edwardian Protestantism.

For the moment, however, Mary Tudor was succeeding in her plans to restore the old faith. The restoration of Catholicism in England, like its expulsion, was accomplished by joint actions of crown and Parliament, a surprising fact when it is realized that the composition of the Marian Parliament was not radically different from the Edwardian and Henrician Parliaments before it. Some key positions in both church and state were overhauled, however, and that made a great deal of difference. First, the treason acts of her brother and father were replaced with pre-Reformation laws, and the Edwardian legislation pertaining to church doctrines and worship was repealed. Cardinal Reginald Pole (1500–58) was brought back to England from his Roman exile to direct the more delicate operation of undoing the Henrician acts, and to represent the papacy when its full powers were restored. Gradually throwing caution to the winds, the Restoration Parliament finally established full reconciliation with Rome and restored the rights and authority of the Holy See over the church in England. Less enthusiasm was shown for Mary's proposal to return the confiscated monastic lands to the church, however. Wisely, Pope Julius III, the gentle and conciliatory pontiff who had succeeded Paul III in 1549, was willing to compromise. In return for full reestablishment of papal authority in

Mary I. *Mary Tudor, as seen in this portrait by Antonis Mor, was an essentially tragic figure, driven to extreme methods in her frustrated desire to restore the Catholic faith in England.*

England, the pope confirmed the secular possession of all properties formerly held by the church. He could have done little else since the gentry and nobles who now owned the lands were not likely to give them up without a fight.

Open hostility to Mary at home did not begin until she made the unfortunate mistake of marrying the emperor's son, Philip of Spain. After their marriage, Philip lived in England with Mary for some months, until it seemed apparent that she could not become pregnant. By this time it was also clear that the English public detested the queen's Spanish husband. It may seem strange, and certainly it must have been a surprise to the queen, that her subjects, who were so placid about resuming their papal allegiance, were so violently opposed to such an alliance with Spain. Yet the evidence of her poor judgment lies not only in seeking the marriage—after all, she was half Spanish herself and England's foreign policy had been consistently allied with Spain's for half a century—but in persisting in it even after the wide dissatisfaction of the country had been manifested. Henry VIII's aggressive involvement in continental affairs had taught the English a lesson that they were not soon to forget—namely, that it was costly, dangerous, and promised little advantage to be allied with Spain, especially if that involvement made England a subordinate rather than an equal partner.

The immediate result of the marriage was to stir some of the more volatile of the queen's subjects to open rebellion. In Kent in the southeast, in the Midlands, and sporadically in the Welsh marches, demonstrations and protests became more frequent and more violent. Led by the impulsive Sir Thomas Wyatt, son of England's leading poet and boon companion of another, the disturbances began taking on the appearance of a full-scale rebellion against Mary's rule. In the end, the Wyatt Rebellion collapsed of its own misguidance, but the execution of Wyatt, Suffolk, and others did not restore harmony to the realm.

It soon became obvious that more than parliamentary statutes and royal decrees were needed to fulfill Mary's dream of a repatriated and united England. Catholic restoration had been formalized, but not yet fully accepted. The loudest voices of opposition now came from the remaining Protestant bishops and pastors, who protested both the reunion with Rome and the reinstitution of Catholic doctrines. Against these dissenting voices the queen turned her wrath. Some of the ministers—John Hooper, bishop of Gloucester; Nicholas Ridley, former bishop of Rochester and London; Hugh Latimer, former bishop of Worcester; and even Thomas Cranmer, archbishop of Canterbury (until he was replaced by Cardinal Pole), along with hundreds of lesser men and women—were put to death by fire. Many managed to go underground and survive, while some 800 others escaped to exile in Switzerland and Germany. The reverberations of Mary's persecutions were Europewide.

Through its alliance with Spain, England was soon drawn into the widening arena of European politics. The final phase of the chronic Habsburg-Valois wars began in 1557. The original antagonists, Charles V and Francis I, were now gone from the scene. Their sons, Philip II of Spain and Henri II of France, while no less willing to accept a humiliating defeat, had noticeably less enthusiasm for the struggle per se. The last major campaign of the war resulted in two great Spanish victories, one against the papal forces in Italy (the quarrelsome Pope Paul IV having entered the war on the side of France in 1557), and the other against the French at Saint Quentin in northern France. The only French victories were at the expense of the Empire and of England as the French successfully defended Metz, Toul, and Verdun, while driving the English from Calais, the last English relic of the Hundred Years' War. Financially and psychologically exhausted, both sides sued for peace.

The Treaty of Cateau-Cambrésis, ending the wars in 1559, marks a watershed in the political-military history of the century. By its terms, Spain was recognized as the predominant power in Italy, and France was left to pursue its interests in the northeast. England's humiliating loss of Calais eventually turned to its favor, for it helped provide the justification for a new orientation of policy based on control of the sea. However, it was not for Queen Mary either to recognize or exploit the new European balance that emerged from Cateau-Cambrésis. Her death came, like her life, in the midst of sorrow, on 17 November 1558, shortly after hearing the news of the fall of Calais. Mary's death marked the close of the short-lived restoration of Catholicism in England, but not the end of the broader Catholic revival that was now gaining momentum in much of Europe.

Suggestions for Further Reading

GENERAL

Not only has the volume of literature on the English Reformation grown during the 1980s, some of it seems to have increased in polemical intensity. The interpretation expressed in A.G. Dickens, *The English Reformation* (New York, 1964)—that English Protestantism, growing out of the Lollard background, provided a widespread popular support for Henry VIII's attack on clerical jurisdiction and repudiation of Rome—had challenged the earlier view that the English Reformation was essentially a revolution from above, a political move directed by the king himself without much help or hindrance from the people. In *The Reformation and the English People* (Oxford, 1984), J.J. Scarisbrick in turn challenges Dickens, arguing that the people were very conservative and clung to their old ways as long as possible. Downplaying anticlericalism and popular discontent, he maintains that the Reformation actually reduced the role of the laity, enhanced clerical prerogatives, and strengthened the power of the crown. A similar tack is taken by Peter I. Kaufman in *The "Polytyque Churche": Religion and Early Tudor Political Culture, 1485–1516* (Macon, Georgia, 1986). He maintains that the church and state were inseparably linked and that the traditionalism of the laity helped the church "promote both spirituality and solidarity in the community." He further argues that the participation of clerics in secular government did not necessarily imply a revolution in the church's religious role, or that anticlericalism led to reformation. A broader view of church-state relations is Leo F. Solt, *Church and State in Early Modern England, 1509–1640* (New York and Oxford, 1990). Another revisionist account, Christopher Haigh, *The English Reformation Revised* (New York and Cambridge, England, 1987), shows that the Reformation was slow developing in England, that it was more an act of state than the result of popular revolt, and that the "reformation of conversion" lagged behind the "official reformation." In a similar vein, Patrick Collinson, *The Birthpangs of Protestant England: Religious and Cultural Change in the Sixteenth and Seventeenth Centuries* (New York, 1988), suggests that the influence of Protestantism was more conservative than revolutionary.

LOLLARD AND PROTESTANT IMPACT

The literature on Lollardy and early Protestantism in the English Reformation is varied and at times penetrating. Some of the most useful works are: Donald D. Smeeton, *Lollard Themes in the Reformation Theology of William Tyndale* (Kirksville, Missouri, 1986); Anne Hudson, *Lollards and Their Books* (Ronceverte, West Virginia, 1985); Margaret Aston, *Lollards and Reformers: Images and Literacy in Late Medieval Religion* (London, 1984); James E. McGoldrick, *Luther's English Connection: The Reformation Thought of Robert Barnes and William Tyndale* (Milwaukee, 1979); and Philip E. Hughes, *Theology of the English Reformers* (Grand Rapids, 1980). Another approach to the English Reformation is provided by Thomas F. Mayer, *Thomas Starkey and the Commonweal: Humanist Politics and Religion in the Reign of Henry VIII* (New York and Cambridge, England, 1989); and Robert Whiting, *The Blind Devotion of People: Popular Religion and the English Reformation* (New York, 1989), looks primarily at the diocese of Exeter. Joseph W. Martin, *Religious Radicals in Tudor England* (Ronceverte, West Virginia, 1989), emphasizes the role of the Anabaptists and other radicals. John N. King demonstrates in *English Reformation Literature: The Tudor Origins of the Protestant Tradition* (Princeton, 1982) that even fiction writing reflected and was used to promote the ideas of the Reformation.

Some noteworthy studies of the conditions and impact of the Reformation in different parts of England include Diarmaid MacCulloch, *Suffolk and the Tudors: Politics and Religion in an English County, 1500–1600* (New York and Oxford, 1987); John F. Davis, *Heresy and Reformation in the South-East of England, 1520–1559* (London, 1983); Margaret Bowker, *The Henrician Reformation: The Diocese of Lincoln under John Longland, 1521–1547* (Cambridge, England, 1981); and Christopher Haigh, *Reformation and Resistance in Tudor Lancashire* (Cambridge, England, 1975). The key role of London, where the new faith was both vigorously promoted and fiercely resisted, is emphasized and clarified in Susan Brigden, *London and the Reformation* (New York and Oxford, 1990). Some useful essays on women and the religious issues are found in Margaret P. Hannay, ed., *Silent But for the Word: Tudor Women as Patrons, Translators, and Writers of Religious Works* (Kent, Ohio, 1985).

THE BREAK WITH ROME AND ITS CONSEQUENCES

The divorce controversy and Henry's marriage to Anne Boleyn were central to the king's confrontation with Rome. The most satisfactory biography of Anne is E.W. Ives, *Anne Boleyn* (Oxford, 1986), the result of exhaustive research, reasonable interpretation, and readable prose. Some are comparing it favorably with Garrett Mattingly's classic *Catherine of Aragon* (Boston, 1941). Retha M. Warnicke, *The Rise and Fall of Anne Boleyn* (New York and Cambridge, England, 1989) is fascinating reading about the entire Boleyn family. The most penetrating studies of Cromwell are Sir Geoffrey Elton's *Policy and Police: The Enforcement of the Reformation in the Age of Thomas Cromwell* (New York and Cambridge, England, 1972, 1985), and *Reform and Renewal: Thomas Cromwell and the Common Weal* (New York and Cambridge, England, 1973). For other key participants see Philip E. Hughes, *Faith and Works: Cranmer and Hooker on Justification* (Wilton, Connecticut, 1982), and Brendon Brandshaw and Eamon Duffy, eds., *Humanism, Reform and the Reformation: The Career of Bishop John Fisher* (New York and Cambridge, England, 1989). Recent studies of Thomas More include J.A. Guy, *The Public Career of St. Thomas More* (New Haven, 1982); Jasper Ridley, *The Statesman and the Fanatic: Thomas Wolsey and Thomas More* (London, 1982), complimentary to Wolsey but critical of More; Richard Marius, *Thomas More: A Biography* (New York, 1985), which depicts More as a committed and passionate man, though not always *com*passionate when dealing with heretics; and especially Louis L. Martz, *Thomas More: The Search for the Inner Man* (New Haven, 1990).

The most useful works on the dissolution of the monasteries and its aftermath are still Joyce Youings, *The Dissolution of the Monasteries* (New York, 1971); David Knowles, *Bare Ruined Choirs: The Dissolution of the English Monasteries* (New York, 1976); and Christopher Haigh, *The Last Days of the Lancashire Monasteries and the Pilgrimage of Grace* (Oxford, 1969). For the Henrician parliaments see Stanford E. Lehmberg, *The Reformation Parliament, 1529–1536* (Cambridge, England, 1970), and *The Later Parliaments of Henry VIII, 1536–1547* (Cambridge, England, 1977). G.R. Elton's *Tudor Revolution in Government*, 2nd ed. (Cambridge, England, 1973) sparked a long and heated controversy over the nature of the political changes brought about by the break with Rome and the acts of the Reformation Parliament. The most recent barrage of criticism and revision is found in Christopher Coleman and David Starkey, eds., *Revolution Reassessed: Revisions in the History of Tudor Government and Administration* (New York and Oxford, 1986), a volume of polite but vigorous challenges to Sir Geoffrey's views, some by former students.

THE REIGN OF EDWARD VI

The standard account of Edward's reign remains W.K. Jordan, *Edward VI, the Young King: The Protectorship of the Duke of Somerset* (Cambridge, Massachusetts, 1968) and *Edward VI, the Threshold of Power: The Dominance of the Duke of Northumberland* (Cambridge, Massachusetts, 1970). Somerset's incompetent regency is assessed in M.L. Bush, *The Government Policy of Protector Somerset* (London, 1975), while E.E. Hoak focuses on the royal council in *The King's Council in the Reign of Edward VI* (Cambridge, England, 1976). Also see the related chapters of David M. Loades, *The Tudor Court* (Totowa, New Jersey, 1987). The Northumberland regency is the focus of Barrett L. Beer, *Northumberland, the Political Career of John Dudley, Earl of Warwick and Duke of Northumberland* (Kent, Ohio, 1973). Much attention has been given to the social unrest and popular disorders in Edwardian England. See Julian Cornwall, *Revolt of the Peasantry, 1549* (London, 1977); Stephen K. Land, *Kett's Rebellion: The Norfolk Rising of 1549* (Totowa, New Jersey, 1978), and now Barrett L. Beer, *Rebellion and Riot: Popular Disorder in England during the Reign of Edward VI* (Kent, Ohio, 1982). The Suffolk involvement in the succession is clarified in Alison Plowdon, *Lady Jane Grey and the House of Suffolk* (New York, 1986).

QUEEN MARY I

Jasper Ridley's *The Life and Times of Mary Tudor* (London, 1975) contains some interesting insights, but the most thorough and reliable analysis is David M. Loades, *The Reign of Mary Tudor: Politics, Government and Religion in England, 1553–1558* (London, 1979). The same author has recently provided a brilliant biography in *Mary Tudor: A Life* (Cambridge, Massachusetts, 1989). A handy brief account, with some documents, is Robert Tittler, *The Reign of Mary I* (New York, 1983). The first comprehensive account of the Marian parliaments is Jennifer Loach, *Parliament and the Crown in the Reign of Mary Tudor* (New York and Oxford, 1986), while the House of Lords is scrutinized in Michael A.R. Graves, *The House of Lords in the Parliaments of Edward VI and Mary I: An Institutional Study* (Cambridge, England, 1981). David M. Loades examines the religious conflicts of the reign in *The Oxford Martyrs* (New York, 1970), and the unsuccessful Wyatt and Dudley uprisings in *The Two Tudor Conspiracies* (Cambridge, England, 1965).

6 | THE CATHOLIC REFORMATION AND COUNTER-REFORMATION

T HE CATHOLIC RESPONSE TO THE CHALLENGE OF PROTESTANTISM HAS traditionally been called the Counter-Reformation, meaning, of course, counter to the Protestant Reformation. Particularly after the appearance of Calvinism, a strong reaction did develop, reemphasizing Catholic dogma, reasserting the liturgical ceremonies of the church, and relying even more heavily upon the hierarchical structure to combat the Protestant threat. In this struggle, the papal Index, the Inquisition, and the Society of Jesus were its key instruments; the Council of Trent was its most important guide.

Yet another and very different kind of influence was also permeating the Catholic church in the sixteenth century. This was a vigorous reform from within, dedicated to the revitalization of religious life through the improvement of gospel teachings and the application of moral truths to daily life. The same desire for devotional expression and direct contact with God that motivated Lutherans, Calvinists, and Anabaptists acted also upon devout Catholics and caused them to seek spiritual rebirth in faith, prayer, and religious observance. Indeed, the demarcation line between Catholic reform and Protestant reformation was sometimes very thin. The various internal responses to the problems and abuses that afflicted Christianity brought about significant changes and reforms within the church. The culmination of this reform movement was also reached in the Jesuit Order and in the reforming decrees of the Council of Trent.

Catholic Reformers in Spain and Italy

The Catholic Reformation took place on many levels and in several countries. It was especially meaningful in Spain and Italy where an unrelenting individualism combined with a strong ecclesiastical commitment gave the church a dynamic quality that it lacked in Germany and the north.

Spain

By the beginning of the sixteenth century, the Hispanic kingdoms under Ferdinand and Isabel had already experienced a religious reformation of considerable depth. The queen herself was largely responsible for infusing her religious zeal into the minds and hearts of her Castilian subjects. Early in their reign, Ferdinand and Isabel attacked the problem of ecclesiastical abuse on the highest levels, and brought the church in Spain under closer crown control than existed in any other country. Before the conquest of Granada (1492), the Catholic Kings secured from the papacy a grant of royal patronage (*Patronato Real*) over the churches of that kingdom, making the crown the supreme ecclesiastical authority. This concession was eventually enlarged to include the whole of Spain and, with even wider powers, Castilian territories in the New World. Crown domination of the church did not automatically solve all ecclesiastical problems, but it did eliminate many of the papal abuses practiced in other countries and provided meaningful support to clergymen who advocated reforms within their respective jurisdictions. Under the guidance of her confessors, Hernando de Talavera and Francisco Jiménez de Cisneros, Isabel launched a general attack on absenteeism, pluralism, concubinage, and other abuses of the clergy, and set herself the task of raising the intellectual as well as the moral standards of the church in Spain.

Isabel's principal confidant after 1492, and the most effective reformer of the Spanish church, was Cardinal Francisco Jiménez de Cisneros (1436–1517), primate of Spain, grand inquisitor, founder and patron of the University of Alcalá, governor of Castile, and for a time vicar of the Holy Roman Empire. Strangely, however, Cisneros spent the first forty-eight years of his long life (he lived to be eighty) as a relatively colorless priest in the bishopric of Sigüenza. Then, after a sudden spiritual experience, he renounced the world to become an Observatine Franciscan and spent the next ten years as a penitent hermit until he was plucked from obscurity by the queen, who saw in him a faith and devotion to duty that could be employed in a greater service to the church. Starting with his own Franciscan order, Cisneros began a reforming program dedicated to rooting out all forms of vice and corruption. It soon carried over into the Dominicans, Benedictines, Jeronimites, and Cistercians.

Before his death, in the year Luther wrote his *Ninety-Five Theses*, Cisneros's reforming zeal had penetrated into almost every avenue of religious life in Spain, among the secular clergy as well as the orders. Under his influence, the religious practices of Spain were tightened, though not necessarily narrowed, for his patronage of culture and learning was no less pronounced than his zeal for spirituality. He founded the University of Alcalá in 1508 to improve the quality of clerical education, and his fathering of the great Complutensian Polyglot Bible was a landmark in the history of both erudition and reform of the church (and of the art of printing). It represented a significant reconciliation of divergent elements for the greater glory of the church that he served.

Meanwhile, at the convent of La Piedrahita in Valladolid, the raptures and prophecies of Sor María de Santo Domingo were starting to be noticed as they became a source of inspiration for an increasing number of her followers. This pietistic movement found favor and support from Cardinal Cisneros. He provided a refuge for her after her trial at Valladolid in 1509–10, and through his instigation much of what María said while in trance was written down and made available as the *Libro de la Oración* (Book of Prayer). This book was dedicated to Adrian of Utrecht, later Pope Adrian VI. Father Castillejo, a Dominican professor at Valladolid, concluded that "that frail woman knew more than all the scholars in the kingdom because her science came from the Holy Spirit." She was not the only female reformer supported by Cardinal Cisneros. He was also impressed by the early pietism of Isabel de la Cruz, later teacher and founder of the *Alumbrados*.

María de Cazalla, another friend and early associate of Isabel de la Cruz, was an admirer of Erasmus and a staunch advocate of inward spiritual enlightenment. Largely self-taught, she became a knowledgeable, well-read person, and through her brother the bishop of Alcalá, a close friend of Cardinal Cisneros, she was acquainted with the intellectual life of the university. At Alcalá she developed a view of the true love of God as selfless love for its own sake, without conditions or expectations. Gathering a sizeable group of devotees from among the intellectuals and also the common people, María Cazalla became an outstanding preacher and leader of Catholic reform, based on a mixture of *Alumbrado* mysticism and Erasmian Christian humanism. These teachings got her in trouble with the religious authorities, and after the deaths of her brother and Cardinal Cisneros, she was arrested by the Inquisition. Two years of imprisonment, interrogation, and torture, however, failed to produce any evidence of heresy, and she was finally set free, "without recanting anything or incriminating anyone."

Others continued the reform movement: Pedro Ruiz de Alcaraz, the leading disciple of Isabel de la Cruz; Juan de Avila, a former student at Alcalá, who tirelessly preached the message of God and reform throughout Andalusia; Juan Ciudad, who founded the lay order of Juan de Dios (or Fathers of Charity), dedicated to service in hospitals and asylums; Tomás de Villanova, the eloquent and charitable "New Apostle of Spain," who became the archbishop of Valencia and was later canonized; and that dauntless humanist-theologian professor at Salamanca, Fray Luis de León (1527–91). Advocacy of reform also developed in the private Bible-reading groups in the larger cities. Some of these spiritual *Alumbrados* maintained only tenuous ties with the church—Juan de Valdés left it entirely—while others maintained a close relationship with the hierarchy, hoping to harmonize their spirituality with institutionalized worship.

The Spanish Inquisition

The manifestations of piety and devotion erupting in early sixteenth-century Spain also had sources other than simple spiritual dedication. Springing from the bowels of this same spiritually fecund country were some of the most unsavory and destructive elements of the entire religious revival. The Spanish Inquisition, a monument to human cruelty, intolerance, and racial discrimination, also grew out of the political, social, and religious atmosphere of Spain. The religious energy pouring forth in the age of Ferdinand and Isabel, and continuing through the sixteenth century, carried Spanish ingenuity and creativity to some of the greatest heights and lowest depths.

The Spanish Inquisition was largely the result of antisemitism. At least the justification of its establishment was to investigate the sincerity of Jewish converts to Christianity. These New Christians, *conversos* as they were called, or more derisively, *marranos* (meaning "dirty"), were suspected of falsely accepting baptism in order to protect their political positions and economic privileges while secretly continuing to hold Jewish beliefs and practice Jewish rites. By the second half of the fifteenth century these crypto-Jews composed a large percentage of Spanish society at all levels, and were perceived as a serious social threat. Indeed, their penetration extended through the middle class occupations of merchant, tax-gatherer, doctor, and even clergy, and many had married into the aristocracy. In an effort to ferret out these "false Christians" a full-time investigating committee was proposed by the Catholic Monarchs. Authorized by papal bull in 1478, it provided for the appointment by the crown of two or three priests as inquisitors into the religious orthodoxy of all baptized Christians.

The new institution began its operations in 1480 in Seville, where the *converso* danger was believed to be most serious. The first *auto-de-fe* (literally "decree or act of faith," meaning the public announcement of the sentence imposed by the Inquisition, usually followed by the public execution by the secular authorities of those sentenced) was held in February 1481, when six people were burned at the stake. Subsequently, tribunals were set up throughout Castile and the office of inquisitor general was established in 1483, with the appointment of Tomás de Torquemada. A few months later his jurisdiction was extended into Aragon as well. The threat of judaizing *conversos* was all but eliminated by the 1530s, as thousands were committed to the flames. Yet the Holy Office did not cease its operations with this "success." A new threat was now perceived in the growth of Protestantism. The fear of Lutheranism fueled the inquisitorial machinery for another half century at least. Although Protestantism never became a major threat in Spain, the popular feeling was that it would have been if it were not for the alert and aggressive actions of the Inquisition. After mid-century its victims were mostly Moriscos and Old Christians suspected of heresy or other dangerous forms of religious or racial unorthodoxy. Thus the Inquisition continued its long and infamous existence (though never again as vigorously as during its first fifty years) perceived as the guardian of Spanish culture and life.

Italy   Italy did not experience the electrifying spontaneity and unity of the Spanish religious revival, but it did produce a number of deeply pious and devoted reformers, such as Battista da Crema (d. 1534), a devout Dominican who preached personal reform. Another was Gasparo Contarini (1483–1542), a distinguished Venetian senator and diplomat who also attained wide recognition as a humanist scholar and man of letters. Born just three weeks before

Luther, Contarini studied philosophy, philology, and natural science at the renowned University of Padua, and occupied a distinguished post there before entering a life of public service. From 1520 to 1525, he was Venetian ambassador at the imperial court of Charles V, during which time he attended the Diet at Worms and witnessed the early spread of Lutheranism in Germany. In 1528–30 he occupied the same diplomatic position at the papal court. Common sense, consideration, and the desire to reconcile opposing viewpoints made him both a successful diplomat and a deeply respected individual. His ability to compromise gracefully and skillfully was recognized by everyone with whom he dealt.

Contarini was also a very religious person and as loyal to the church as he was to the republic. It was to help cleanse the church of its appalling abuses that he wrote many tracts and books calling for meaningful reforms and moral rejuvenation. The most penetrating of these was *De officio episcopi* (On the Office of Bishop), written in 1516, a year before Luther's *Ninety-Five Theses*, in which Contarini listed in detail the faults of the clergy—as he, a layman, perceived them—and then outlined the attributes he thought a deserving bishop should possess. His deep concern over religion, particularly the problem of salvation, led him to an experience similar to Luther's. Like that of the German reformer, Contarini's resolution of the problem convinced him that confidence in Christ was the only answer to his dilemma; he believed human works are powerless to bring salvation. Instead of leading him to oppose the church hierarchy, however, Contarini's belief convinced him that reformation must come from within.

Gasparo Contarini. *This Venetian humanist was trained as a scholar and served Venice as a diplomat before turning to the cause of Catholic reform. Appointed a cardinal in 1535, he attempted unsuccessfully to define a formula on justification that would be acceptable to both Lutherans and Catholics.*

It also gave him a greater understanding of Luther's theology and a stronger desire to heal the schism and restore unity to the church. This was still his hope when he was made a cardinal in 1535, and when he advocated the convening of a general council to reunite the fractured church. Contarini's best opportunity to effect such a reconciliation came at the Regensburg Colloquy of 1541, when he represented the Catholic party in a last attempt to settle the religious cleavage peacefully. Contarini and his Lutheran counterpart, Melanchthon, who shared many of his religious views as well as his conciliatory temperament, were able to reach a compromise agreement on some significant points of doctrine, such as justification by faith, but the conference failed when both the Catholic and Lutheran parties repudiated their efforts.

Another example of devotion and commitment is Gian Matteo Giberti (1495–1543), son of a Genoese admiral. Although he had, since age twenty, occupied positions of trust and importance under both Pope Leo X and his cousin, Clement VII, he desired nothing more than to serve God in the simplest way possible. Following the sack of Rome in 1527, Giberti appealed to the pontiff to release him from his onerous duties and responsibilities as papal secretary and datary (principal minister) and allow him to return to his diocese of Verona, over which he presided as bishop. It was here, during the last sixteen years of his life, that Bishop Giberti set the standard for enlightened and progressive religious reform, as he embodied the ideal described in Contarini's *De officio episcopi*. He attended to the responsibilities of his see with devotion and efficiency, personally carrying out reforms of the orders, attacking the problems of absenteeism and lethargy, and infusing a more spiritual atmosphere into its administration. He founded orphanages, almshouses, and schools, hostels for outcasts, associations for the relief of the poor, and a study circle for the promotion of learning among clerics.

Reformed and New Religious Orders

The influence of men like Contarini and Giberti was considerable, but they were faced with an almost insurmountable task. The extent of clerical abuse in early sixteenth-century Italy was enormous. Fortunately, awareness of these difficulties had also reached a peak, and sensitivity to problems usually results in solutions to them. One effect of this situation was a general spirit of revival among the religious orders and brotherhoods. Hardly an order was unaffected by this spirit during the first two decades of the century, and many of them experienced major changes or reorientation. Similar movements of regeneration had occurred before among the monastic congregations; but in each case after a period of renewed religious vigor, the zeal of rejuvenation burned out and decline set in. The monastic reform movements of the early sixteenth century were unique, therefore, not in their nature but in their extent and ultimate effect.

Among the old monastic orders, the Benedictines experienced the earliest revitalization. From Montserrat, near Barcelona, to Bursfeld in Germany, Benedictine abbeys and monasteries renewed their ancient covenants and attempted to restore their former discipline and rituals. In Italy this spirit was particularly manifested at Modena, Perugia, and Venice under the brilliant guidance of Gregorio Cortese, abbot of San Giorgio Maggiore, whose humanistic influence was also felt among the dedicated monks of Monte Cassino, the monastery between Rome and Naples that suffered such devastation in World War II. The Camaldolese, an eleventh-century offshoot of the Benedictine order, underwent further rejuvenation in 1510–12 under the radical reforms instituted by the Venetian noble, Paolo Giustiniani.

Reform within the Augustinian order caused considerable commotion in Germany, where Johann von Staupitz's attempt to bring the entire province of Saxony under the strict Observantine rule led to loud protests and prompted Luther's famous journey to Rome in 1510. Tranquility was restored largely through the leadership of Giles of Viterbo, the versatile and talented disciple of Plato, Augustine, and Marsilio Ficino, who was vicar-general of the Augustinians from 1507 to 1517. Much of Giles of Viterbo's reforming influence in Rome resulted from his sensational sermons. In 1512, during the hotly disputed Lateran Council, he almost persuaded Pope Leo X to adopt a broad program of reform for the entire church. Giles was not punished for his outspoken proposals for reform; instead, in 1517 he was promoted to cardinal.

The most frequently reformed of the mendicant orders was the Franciscan. Due to the extreme simplicity and abject poverty of the founder of the Friars Minor, Saint Francis of Assisi, it was easy for its members to fall away from the strict rule of the order. It also invited more self-sacrificing members to attempt a return to the principles and discipline of Saint Francis, thus fragmenting the order into numerous divisions.

The most successful of all these Franciscan revivals began in the early sixteenth century with the efforts of a simple Franciscan peasant to observe the letter of the rule. Matteo da Bascio had no intention of founding a new order when he approached Pope Clement VII in 1525 for permission to preach to all the world and to wear a coarse robe and a strange-looking four-pointed hood (*capuchia*), which he maintained was the authentic habit of Saint Francis. Clement gave him verbal approval, which was promptly denied by superiors of the order. Matteo and his companion, Ludovico da Fossombrone, would have been imprisoned had it not been for the intervention of Caterina Cibo, the duchess of Camerino. Through her mediation, a papal bull was issued in July 1528 officially authorizing their simple reform program. The name Capuchin, by which they have subsequently been known, was a derisive nickname applied to them and their followers because of their square hoods. The Capuchins, pledged to a revival of the simple and austere life and service of Saint Francis, appealed greatly to the masses and became the popular symbol of religious fundamentalism. Rejecting the subtleties and sophistries of the theologians, the Capuchins ministered to the humble, downtrodden, and sick, and in so doing exercised a great influence in keeping the common people loyal to the Catholic church.

The sixteenth century saw the rapid growth of a number of confraternities or religious brotherhoods, similar to pre-Reformation movements of lay piety, with wide-ranging social as well as religious functions. Most of these confraternities were lay associations, but could also include clerics or even women and children. Their prime purpose was to provide proper funeral services and burial for their members, and see that they were remembered after death, but they carried out many other functions as well. Some founded hospitals and orphanages, provided dowries to help poor girls contract respectable marriages, organized religious instruction, or even patronized art and music. Sometimes they overlapped with activities of other social groups, such as trade or craft guilds, but they usually paid more attention to personal piety.

The Oratory and the Clerks Regular   Symptomatic of the varied approaches to reform advocated in the early sixteenth century were several brotherhoods devoted to regulating and spiritualizing the lives of the laity and the secular clergy. The earliest and most important of these was the Oratory of Divine Love, founded in Genoa in 1497, under the inspiration of the remarkable Caterina Fieschi, better known as Saint Catherine of Genoa, and brought to Rome early in the pontificate of Leo X. This informal organization of laymen and clergy emphasized the harmonization of culture and faith, the New Learning and theology, and advocated reform through personal sanctification, prayer, frequent confession, and performing works of charity and service. Its members were sympathetic to Erasmus's Christian humanism and were also advocates of personal piety. An exemplary life, they believed, would have a greater influence for good than a hundred sermons. Units of the Oratory were established at Milan, Verona, Vicenza, Padua, Lucca, and Florence, as well as Rome. Some of the high church prelates associated with the Oratory and a great many of the advocates of reform, including Giberti, Contarini, Gaetano Thiene (Saint Cajetan), Gian Pietro Carafa (the future Pope Paul IV), Jacopo Sadoleto, the humanist bishop of Carpentras in southeastern France, and Luigi Lippomano, were numbered among its members.

Closely related to the Oratory of Divine Love were three so-called orders of "clerks regular," that is, organizations of secular priests who took vows similar to the monastic and mendicant orders. These groups were intended to provide the opportunity and means for members of the ordinary clergy to follow a more regulated devotional life without abandoning their normal pastoral duties. This movement to bring the seculars and regulars closer together, to reconcile the active with the contemplative life and reveal to the people a living example of the gospel in action, was extremely popular in the early years of the Catholic Reformation.

The earliest of these orders was the Theatine, an active and influential brotherhood founded in 1524 by two leading associates of the Oratory of Divine Love, Gaetano Thiene and Gian Pietro Carafa. Two more contrasting personalities could hardly be imagined—the first a meek and gently persuasive monk from Vicenza, the other a tempestuous and brilliant Neapolitan bishop—but both were dedicated to the cause of church reform. From the outset, the Theatines were extremely effective as a "nursery for leaders" among the more reform-oriented clergy, and soon spread into neighboring countries, although like the Oratory, the order never sought or claimed large numbers of adherents. Contarini, Cortese, and Giberti were associated with it, as were the bishop of Feltre, Tommaso Campeggio, and the English reforming cardinal, Reginald Pole. Spiritual regeneration on the upper levels of the church hierarchy was the goal of the Theatines. Their method involved study, meditation, preaching, and works of charity. Their degree of success may partially be measured by the fact that soon anyone advocating spiritual reform in the church was referred to as a Theatine.

The two other orders of clerks regular were rather different from the Theatines in both their objectives and methods. The Somaschi were first organized as a body of pious laymen, with their headquarters in the village of Somasca near Bergamo in the Milanese, by the Venetian soldier Girolamo Miani. Although his followers began their ministration to victims of the imperial invasion of 1526–27 immediately after the war ended, it was another forty years before the Somaschi were officially recognized by the papacy. In the meantime they performed valuable work among the orphaned, sick, and outcasts, and were revered by the masses.

The Barnabites were founded in 1530 by the twenty-eight-year-old Cremona nobleman, Antonio Maria Zaccaria, who had left the study of medicine for the priesthood. With two companions, one a lawyer and the other a professor of mathematics, he set out from the church of San Barnaba in Milan to repair the moral, physical, and spiritual damage left by the peninsular wars. Unlike the Theatines, the Barnabites proselyted energetically and spread rapidly from Milan into all of Italy and soon beyond the Alps into France, Spain, Germany, and Bohemia. They founded female auxiliaries in Italy and in the missions, to stimulate the work of regeneration and education among girls.

Yet despite the charitable works of the Theatines, Somaschi, and Barnabites, and many other new religious orders whose fervor for reform was manifested throughout Italy and Europe, all of the orders subordinated external actions and theological propagation to inner sanctification and personal mortification. In this respect, they were much like the Brethren of the Common Life, or more perhaps like the earlier mystics, in their emphasis on prayer, devotion, and spiritual communion with God. This characteristic, however, is not true of two other orders founded before mid-century, whose commitment to inner sanctification was not an end in itself but the means to a very practical and pragmatic goal of promoting Catholicism in the world.

The Ursulines   Angela Merici of Brescia (1474–1540) was a remarkable woman whose sense of divinely inspired mission led her to found one of the most important new orders. Orphaned at age ten, Angela became a Franciscan terciary when she was thirteen and began living a life of austerity. When she was twenty-three, she had a vision in which she was told that she would found a religious congregation that would be devoted to the education of youth. After the death of her guardian uncle, she began her lifetime career of service and teaching. In 1535 she founded the Company of Saint Ursula, concerned primarily with educating young girls, the first teaching order of women to be established. The rule she wrote for the Ursulines was designed to achieve results in the lives of people, not simply promote piety. Although she described her nuns in the traditional Catholic language as brides of Jesus and potential queens in heaven, the order she created was different. The Ursulines observed the canonical hours, took vows of chastity and submission, but were not cloistered. The nuns usually taught in the homes of their pupils. They wore simple dark clothes instead of a distinctive habit, and were recognized for their work rather than for what they wore.

Seeing her order as a bulwark against ignorance, the deceits of the Devil, and a protection from the "trickery of worldly people," from "heretics and evil men," and "idle women," Angela devoted the rest of her life to the work of teaching. In so doing she set the pattern for future education of young girls in the church. Not until after her death, however, was the order formally recognized by Pope Paul III, and then with some alterations. First the nuns were required to wear a habit, and with the tightening of controls characteristic of the Counter-Reformation church later in the century, they became a cloistered order under the authority of the male ecclesiastical hierarchy. In 1612, under Pope Paul V, the rule written by Angela Merici was discarded and the Ursuline nuns were required to follow the Augustinian rule.

Ignatius Loyola and the Society of Jesus

In 1512, using Henry VIII's magnificent expeditionary force as a decoy, Ferdinand of Aragon conquered the Basque kingdom of Navarre and attached it to the Aragonese crown. Nine years later, during a lull in the Habsburg-Valois duel, while the newly elected Emperor Charles V presided at the Diet of Worms and his Aragionese and Castilian nobles were occupied in suppressing the revolts of the *Comuneros* and the *Germanía,* a French army under the Count de Foix crossed the Pyrenees with the intention of recovering Navarre. The key to the defense of Navarre was the fortress of Pamplona, garrisoned by a single company of infantry commanded by a thirty-year-old Basque nobleman from Loyola in the province of Guipuzcoa.

Iñigo López de Recalde, whom we know as Ignatius Loyola (1491–1556), was a career soldier, born and raised among the hardiest and most willing fighters of Spain, whose pride in nobility and valor at arms appeared to destine him for a life of military exploits and glory. However, Loyola's military career was suddenly cut short when a French musket ball ripped through his leg, shattering tendons and bone. This experience was the first of many traumatic episodes in his life. At the time, it could only have seemed to him the end of everything. What value is a crippled soldier to anyone? Without hope of full recovery, and haunted by the illusive vision of what might have been, Loyola occupied his mind during his long months of convalescence by reading—not the books of his youth on chivalry and romance, but for the first time he hesitatingly opened the covers of religious writings. When he did, he opened the

Ignatious Loyola. *The founder of the Society of Jesus is seen here in a remarkable work by Montañez.*

door of a new life—a life of which he had scarcely been aware. Among these books, he chanced to read a Spanish adaptation of Voragine's *Golden Legend,* now called *The Flower of the Saints,* and a Castilian translation of Ludolf of Saxony's tender *Life of Christ.* The impact of these devotional writings on his mind was profound. A change came over him; a new vision of his life's work appeared, as it had to Luther, Calvin, and Menno Simons. This was Loyola's "Tower Experience." He would now become a soldier of God.

His decision was made, his will was firm, but he had no idea yet what God wanted him to do. Many possibilities went through his mind, and they must have all whispered to him that first he must prepare himself. One does not change from a soldier to a saint overnight. So for the next twelve years, Loyola doggedly devoted himself to preparation for his new life's work. At the secluded Benedictine monastery of Montserrat, outside of Barcelona, he laid down his arms of war and took up the garb of a pilgrim. In a cave at nearby

Manresa, he fasted, prayed, and read García de Cisneros's *Exercises of the Spiritual Life*. He remained there a year, until he became convinced that it was not a life of seclusion and self-mortification that the Lord was preparing him for, but one of action and service. He was to be an instrument for converting both Christian and heathen to God.

Out of Loyola's hermitage at Manresa came another instrument for religious reform, a tiny book of scarcely 100 pages, called the *Spiritual Exercises*. This was to become the most poignant handbook of the Catholic Reformation, and the most effective weapon of Counter-Reformation. Emerging from Loyola's own experiences at Manresa, the *Spiritual Exercises* is a practical training manual of the will, designed, like manuals for training the body, to develop the user's fullest potential. It proceeds from the proposition that through self-discipline and contemplation, the human mind can be lifted to a union with Christ and to total obedience to his commands. The book also illustrates the continuity of the mystical with the practical in Loyola's mind, and anticipates the marriage of idealism and realism in the Jesuit order. In fact, most of the elements that were later to characterize the Jesuits—renunciation of self, striving for results, a sense of the practical and possible, militant missionary effort, submission to iron discipline, and unquestioning obedience—are all evident in the *Spiritual Exercises*.

In 1523–24 Loyola made a pilgrimage to the Holy Land, returning convinced that the church had need not only of willing hands but also of educated minds. Conscious of his own deficiencies, Loyola began the arduous process of education. For four years he traveled, preached, and studied at the universities of Salamanca, Alcalá, and Barcelona; three times he was apprehended by the Inquisition, accused of being a secret *Alumbrado,* or even a Lutheran. Then in 1528, at the age of thirty-seven, he entered the Collège de Montaigu at the University of Paris, just as Calvin, eighteen years younger, was leaving. For the next six years, this serene and resolute middle-aged student pursued his studies, gradually mastering the fundamentals and intricacies of philosophy, arts, and grammar. Lacking the intellectual brilliance of Calvin or the literary genius of Erasmus, he was unimpressive as a student except for his unswerving determination to prepare himself adequately for the work ahead. Loyola's greatness lay in his character, not in his intellect.

On the day of the Feast of Assumption, 15 August, 1534, at the Benedictine chapel of Saint Denis in Montmartre, Paris, the forty-three-year-old Loyola and a tiny circle of six devoted followers (one Basque, three Castilians, one Portuguese, and one Savoyard, ranging in ages from nineteen to twenty-eight) took solemn vows of poverty and chastity and resolved to dedicate their lives to the ministry, either as missionaries to the heathen or in whatever other capacity they were called upon by the pope to serve. Thus was born the Society of Jesus, less than a year after Nicholas Cop and John Calvin were expelled from the university and just two months before Paris was shaken by the Affair of the Placards. Neither Loyola nor his disciples seem to have taken the slightest note of these events, unaware that the order's future role would be shaped in part by the consequences of those occurrences.

Loyola was now approaching the next major turning point in his life. As agreed in their vow, the companions made their way to Venice, where they hoped to take passage to the Holy Land and begin their ministry. War, however, raged in the Mediterranean, as the Barbary corsair and now Turkish admiral, Khair ad-Din Barbarossa, ravaged the coasts of Italy and Charles V launched his great counterattack against Tunis. After a year, the patient missionaries were still unable to sail for Jerusalem; they spent six months in a preaching tour through eastern France, Switzerland, and southern Germany, and six more months performing hospital service in and around Venice. At Vicenza in 1538 Loyola decided to abandon the Palestinian venture and submit to the will of Pope Paul III. In the meantime the tiny band had more than doubled its size, and counted now among its numbers the nephew of Cardinal Contarini and the secretary to Cardinal Pole. Still it was another two years before opposition to the Society could be constrained enough to assure its survival. Finally, in September 1540 the papal bull *Regimini militantis Ecclesiae* officially established the Society of Jesus. Wary at first, the papacy eventually discovered that it had created the finest weapon yet forged for the defense of the church and the promulgation of papal policy.

Jesuit Organization, Aims, and Methods

The legendary hierarchy of Jesuit structure was not apparent in the early youth of the order, although Loyola's hand was always present as it gradually took shape. Originally the society needed little government; but as its numbers grew, a stronger control from the center became necessary. Loyola began drafting a constitution shortly after the order's establishment in 1540, but the instrument was ten years in forming and did not become the binding law of the society until after Loyola's death. Obedience at all levels was demanded and received, yet individual initiative and flexibility were also manifested and encouraged—indeed, rewarded—so long as they did not go counter to the established doctrines and canons of faith, or to the orders of superiors.

As it eventually developed, the Jesuit organization did resemble the pyramidal structure of a military command. From its closely regulated and disciplined two-year novitiate through the scholasticate (an extended period of education usually lasting from nine to ten years), the tertiate (a third level of traineeship), temporal and spiritual coadjutors, then the "Professed of the Three Vows," and finally the exclusive governing body to the lifetime general at the top, the organization was tight and effective. The general made all nominations to important posts in the society and thus represented a degree of centralized authority unknown in the other religious orders of the time. The influence of Loyola was nowhere more strongly felt than in this organizational structure, and its continuance was assured by his election as first general of the order, a post he held until his death in 1556. He was succeeded by the *converso*, Diego Laynez, a Jewish Castilian merchant's son who joined Loyola at Paris and was one of the original seven founders. His tenure lasted from 1556 to 1565.

A unique feature of the Jesuit organization was the existence of an inner core of the most highly trained and disciplined members, constituting the small governing body of the society under the general. These men were set off from the rest by their profession of a fourth vow, of direct personal obedience to the pope. It was this fourth vow that seriously hindered acceptance of the Jesuits by the Spanish and French monarchs, and others who had reason to fear too close a subordination to the papacy. Paradoxically, for many years the popes in turn distrusted the society because they feared it would be dominated by the king of Spain. The Jesuits also clashed with the Spanish Inquisition over its *limpieza de sangre* (purity of blood) campaign, which Loyola and his followers repeatedly opposed. Until 1593 *conversos* were freely admitted to membership in the society, and Loyola fought courageously against the Inquisition's infectious racism.

In all of their activities, the Jesuits emphasized efficiency, moderation, and practicality. They wore no distinctive habit because it might reduce the efficiency, and therefore the results, of their activity. Means were always subordinated to ends. Personal asceticism was practiced in moderation, because it was obvious to them that a person weakened in body by excessive devotions, however exalted in spirit by the humbling experience, would be less effective than one in full health. A successful warrior for Christ, they reasoned, needs physical strength, just as any other soldier does. If he is half dead from fasting, prayers, and vigils, he is no good to anyone, including God. In the confessional, Jesuits were taught to give the sinner the benefit of the doubt. "Send no one away dejected," Loyola advised. "God asks no one the impossible." It is small wonder that they became such popular confessors, especially to Catholic rulers.

The major aims of the Jesuit order were threefold: to educate and spiritually train the youth of the church; to propagate the faith among the heathens and infidels; and to uphold the doctrines and carry the fight against Protestantism. The first two of these were initiated immediately; only in the second decade after their foundation did the Jesuits become seriously engaged in the Counter-Reformation.

To carry out the first of their objectives, the Jesuits established schools throughout the continent. The Jesuit system was highly organized, and discipline was firm but not unkind. Academic competition was encouraged within the framework of authoritative texts and under close supervision. All aspects of education, recreation, and exercise as well as academics and religion, were integrated into the scheme set forth in the *Ratio Studiorum* (Plan of Studies), which combined the principles of both scholasticism and humanism as it guided the student through the steps of grammar, humanities, and rhetoric, to composition, oratory, and philosophy. Memorization played a key role, as did uniformity, long-range practicality, and purpose. Jesuit methods of teaching were also carried over into the universities, where they placed emphasis on thorough scholarship and sound reasoning. Jesuit professors were soon vying with the Dominicans for the highest academic posts, and by the end of the century they were among the most prominent educators in Europe.

Jesuit Missionaries Overseas

The Jesuits' second objective, propagation of the faith, carried them to all parts of the world. Francis Xavier (1506–52), the first and closest companion of Loyola and one of the original seven at Montmartre, was the first to receive an important overseas call from the pope. By the middle of the sixteenth century, Christianity had made some progress in the Portuguese eastern empire, particularly where outposts had been established in India. At Goa an episcopal diocese had been created as early as 1534. Not until the arrival of the Jesuits, however, did a real impetus and zeal grip missionary activities in Asia.

Early in 1540 the king of Portugal, having already heard of the eager new proselytizing order organized by Loyola, appealed to Pope Paul III for religious help in the East. Francis Xavier had just turned thirty-five when he was called to what became his life's labor. He accepted the assignment without hesitation. In November 1541 he embarked from Lisbon; six months later he arrived in Goa, full of enthusiasm for the uncharted venture ahead. After a year among the Portuguese colonists and traders of Goa, he ministered among the pearl divers on the coast of Travancore and journeyed to Madras and Cape Comorin. For the time spent in this ministry Xavier had great success, baptizing

Jesuit missionary received by Akbar. *From a miniature of Nar Sing in an Akbar-nama manuscript of 1605.*

thousands of converts in a matter of months, mostly Hindus of the lowest caste. From India, Xavier sailed further eastward to Malacca, Amboyna, and points along the Malay Peninsula. At Malacca in 1548 he chanced to meet a Japanese refugee named Hashiro, whom he converted to Christianity and gained as a devoted friend. From this friendship came the inspiration to carry the gospel to Japan. In August 1549, Xavier and his companion landed at Kagoshima after a terrible voyage across the pirate-infested, typhoon-plagued waters of the South China Sea, and began an event-filled two and a half years in the land of the Rising Sun.

Japan and China   Xavier and his tiny party encountered numerous problems. Politically, Japan was almost in chaos as the great feudal lords (*daimyos*) defied the decadent Ashikaga shogunate and spread civil war and disorder throughout the land. The emperor was a figurehead with no real power. For centuries, Japan had been ruled by military dynasties of *shoguns* (*sei-i tai-shōgun*, meaning "barbarian-conquering generalissimo"), whose office had become hereditary by the end of the twelfth century. The Ashikaga dynasty (1338–1568) ruled from Kyoto, but its authority rested precariously on a shaky coalition of *daimyo* families who controlled most of the country and held many subordinate offices and titles. Constant feuds among all of the *samurai* (the warrior class) and intense rivalry for control of power kept the country in a state of continual warfare.

There was turmoil in religious matters, too, as the various branches of the Buddhist priesthood vied with one another for domination. Xavier quickly observed that the lords seemed to favor the Zen sect, and he made every effort to cultivate the friendship and respect of the nobles as well as the young Zen students. His diligence did not go unrewarded, and when he left Japan late in 1551, he had made several hundred scattered converts. The field was a difficult one, however, not only because of the language barrier and the Jesuit's inability to penetrate or fully understand the subtleties of esoteric Buddhism, but also due to the Japanese cultural and intellectual dependence upon China. This realization, that Christianity would succeed in Japan only after China had been converted, convinced Xavier that he should preach to the Chinese.

In 1552 Francis Xavier set out once more from Goa, this time as part of an official embassy to China from the Portuguese governor. The expedition never got beyond Malacca, however, and the dauntless missionary was forced to proceed on his own. Knowing of the Portuguese trading post at Canton, Xavier embarked once more from Malacca across the South China Sea. He got as far as the island of Shang ch'uan (Shangchuan), at the mouth of the Canton River, before he was stricken with fever and died in December 1552. An outstanding missionary career was ended, but his pioneering work set the pattern for others to follow.

For the next thirty years, Christianity flourished in Japan under the missionary efforts of the Jesuits. Three hundred churches were built in that time and over 300,000 members claimed. Yet the time of harvest was about to end.

For a decade the fate of the Jesuit mission was in jeopardy, as the political situation deteriorated further and internal feuds between Jesuits and other missionaries turned the people against them. From the beginning of the Tokugawa dynasty at the end of the century, and for the next fifty years, the Christians of Japan suffered a purge comparable in violence and intensity to the Roman persecutions of fourteen centuries earlier. For all practical purposes, Christianity was dead in Japan for another 250 years.

In China, initial results were more moderate and more lasting. Of the many Jesuits to follow Saint Francis Xavier, none was more devoted or more successful than the Italian, Matteo Ricci (1522–1610). One of the most distinguished graduates of the Jesuit college in Rome, Ricci was an accomplished mathematician, astronomer, humanist, and theologian. He was also a talented painter. His first assignment in the East was as a teacher in Goa, where he further busied himself acquiring the fundamentals of the Chinese language and learning the history, religions, and customs of the people. He was better prepared to influence the Chinese than any Westerner had ever been. Finally he was granted permission by the emperor to embark upon his mission, but for many years he was allowed to go no further inland than Canton (Guandong). Meanwhile Father Ricci's fame began to spread, as favorable observers carried word of his intellectual and personal achievements from village to village. Eventually he was allowed to move to Nanchang (Nanzhang), then to Nanking (Nanjing), and finally, late in his life, he was summoned to the imperial capital at Peking (Beijing). Ricci was instrumental in converting thousands of Chinese to Christianity, and at the same time, he succeeded temporarily in opening the door to subsequent Jesuit missions. In doing this, he won such respect of both the Chinese people and ruler as few Westerners have ever duplicated.

Jesuit Missions in America and Europe

Elsewhere in Asia and Africa, Jesuit success was less pronounced, ranging from sporadic conquests in southern India to disaster in Mozambique. In the New World, the Jesuits met with general good fortune and some marked achievement. This was especially true in Brazil and later in Paraguay, where they separated the native Guaranis from all contact with the Spanish colonists and established separate colonies where the Indians could be Europeanized and Christianized without the negative influences of Spanish governmental and social exploitation. Over 100,000 natives were thus organized into Jesuit fiefs, supervised and defended by the Jesuit fathers. The transformation of the Indians was amazingly successful, so much so that two centuries later these colonies still existed and prospered.

In all of these examples of Jesuit missionary enterprise overseas, the purpose and emphasis was on evangelizing and converting non-Christian people to the Gospel of Christ. In Europe, Jesuit activities were directed first toward schools and the education of Christian children and adults in the principles and observances of the church, and then, as the threat of Protestantism increased, especially from active Calvinism, Jesuit missionary endeavors were turned more toward the repression of heresy. The Jesuit mission to Germany and eastern Europe was remarkably active and was responsible for winning back sizable areas to the Roman allegiance and in preventing the further expansion of Protestantism. Among the more successful Jesuit missionaries in Germany was Saint Peter Canisius (1521–97), a devoted Dutchman who spent almost his entire life in missionary efforts to restore Catholicism in the Holy Roman Empire and improve the quality of Catholic devotion. He served with equal dedication as a teacher, rector, confessor, theologian, and diplomat. Farther east, in Poland, a successful Catholic revival was ushered in following the opening of the Jesuit mission there in 1564; and the combination of Jesuit schools, the supervisory genius of Cardinal Stanislaus Hosius, and Protestant rivalries helped restore Catholicism to large areas of Poland and immunize it against further conversion to Protestantism.

Papal and Imperial Reforms

Although the Renaissance popes generally resisted reform and looked upon spiritual matters in a uniquely political way, it would be incorrect to conclude that they were all oblivious to the problems that seemed so apparent to their contemporaries. Even Alexander VI and Julius II were aware of the dangers of clerical abuse and indolence, and took some meager steps to control it. Both of these pontiffs, though, were too occupied with political and military affairs to give proper attention to the grave matters of religion and morals.

During the pontificate of Leo X (1513–21), it was recognized at the very highest echelons that there were serious problems of corruption in the church that might need correction if the papacy were not to find itself in serious difficulties. This recognition was most boldly admitted in the controversial Lateran Council of 1512–17, which recommended a stricter adherence to canonical rules in selecting and conferring ecclesiastical benefices and in granting dispensations. The council also suggested that members of the papal curia adopt a more virtuous rule of life. Still the recommendations given by this council were timid and half-hearted. Furthermore, the pope did not follow them with actions.

The first real shake-up in papal policy came with the selection of Adrian of Utrecht as pope in 1522. Adrian VI was both an austere, pedantic priest and a humanistically inclined scholar and reformer. He had been Charles V's tutor for many years, and at the time of his elevation to the pontifical chair served as the emperor's regent in Spain. As the first non-Italian pope since the Great Schism, Adrian represented to the culture-loving Italians a renunciation of the Renaissance. According to his rival, Cardinal Gonzaga, Adrian's election was a mistake resulting from the physical and mental exhaustion of two weeks of bickering and dispute during the conclave. It is more likely, however, that the subtle influence of the recently elected emperor, and the impeccable moral stature of Adrian at a time when the papacy could use an improved image, account for his election. Upon learning of his elevation, the new pope immediately issued an order that thenceforth cardinals were not authorized to promise or give vacant offices to anyone. When he arrived in Rome, he announced a new and radical policy in respect to the life of the curia, and particularly to the activities of the cardinals, whom he expelled from the Vatican and sent out to do the work they were supposed to do.

This interlude, however, was brief. Early in 1523 the pope died, and Rome breathed a sigh of relief. Giulio de' Medici, cousin of the previous pope, Leo X, and son of Lorenzo the Magnificent's brother who was murdered in the Pazzi conspiracy, received the papal tiara as Pope Clement VII (1523–34). For a time, at least, the threat of a radical papal reform was ended. Clement was without major vices, but equally free of noteworthy virtues. Although he was knowledgeable and appreciative of Italian culture, he was not so exclusively devoted to "enjoying the papacy" as was his cousin. Clement was well-meaning and honest but unable to cope with the intricacies and dangers of European politics or with the rapid growth of Protestantism. The historian Francesco Guicciardini, advisor to the pope and governor of the Romagna, believed the cause of Clement's many misfortunes was his chronic indecision. Guicciardini had worked for him long enough to know whereof he spoke.

In the meantime, Charles V grew increasingly convinced that religious unity could be restored if moderate Catholics and moderate Lutherans would only sit down together and discuss their problems and differences. The emperor's faith in the decisions of a new general council was shared by many of his humanist advisors, including his chancellor, Gattinara, who was an ardent devotee of Erasmus. After 1529 Charles put increasing pressure upon the pope to call a council, but Clement procrastinated, hoping the need for one would go away. His dilemma was magnified by his awareness of the dangers involved in exposing the church, and himself, to conciliar criticism. The nightmare of the Council of Constance still haunted Reformation pontiffs.

Pope Paul III and a General Council

The emperor's conciliar entreaties found more receptive ears in the next pope, Alessandro Farnese, Pope Paul III (1534–49), not because his fears of a council were less but because he was more conscious of the problems in the church and aware of the dangers of leaving them uncured. Under Pope Paul the papacy took its first meaningful steps toward a major churchwide reformation. By temperament and training, Paul III would have preferred the pleasure-loving life of a Renaissance patron—in fact his expenditures for building and art surpassed those of Pope Leo X—but Paul was an old man when he became pope. His worldly cardinalate had taught him many things about people and about the church; he recognized the corruption in high places and appreciated the necessity of reform at the very top. He believed in reform because it was needed and also because without it the church would become even more vulnerable to the twin threats of Protestantism and the Turks. During his fifteen-year pontificate, the Catholic Reformation reached its zenith.

No sooner had he taken control of the papacy than he began to overhaul the curia and the college of cardinals. While encouraging Francis I's repression

Pope Paul III, by Titian. *In his patronage of arts and letters, as well as his nepotism, Alessandro Farnese was a typical Renaissance pope. Yet he was also the pope who initiated the most serious religious reformation of the curia and prepared the way for the Council of Trent.*

of Protestants following the Affair of the Placards, supporting the emperor's attempts to reduce the Schmalkaldic League, and taking the first decisive papal action against the rebellious Henry VIII, the pope also laid down a hard line for the cardinals. They were to clean up their own affairs and put their ecclesiastical houses in order. New bureaus were established to supervise improvements in the morals and conduct of the Roman clergy and to investigate administrative practices in the Papal States. Most important, a number of new cardinals were added to the college, many of them men with long-standing reputations as reformers or advocates of reform. Included among these clergymen were John Fisher, the bishop of Rochester who was at that very time being sentenced to death by Henry VIII; his countryman, Reginald Pole; Jean du Bellay, bishop of Paris; Gian Pietro Carafa, cofounder of the Theatines; Jacopo Sadoleto, the humanist bishop of Carpentras; and most significant of all, the eminently respected Venetian, Gasparo Contarini.

At the outset, Paul III concluded that a general council was inevitable; but he also resolved that before such a council could be summoned, Rome, the papal curia, and the whole hierarchy of officialdom would have to be reformed. "When our own house is cleansed, we more easily take in hand the cleansing of others," read the August 1535 bull, *Sublimis Deus,* creating a reform commission for Rome. In the meantime, another important body was created to function as a precouncil committee of inquiry for the purpose of learning the areas most in need of attention prior to convening the general council. This commission of nine eminent reformers—including such capable persons as Gregorio Cortese, the reforming Benedictine abbot of San Giorgio Maggiore; Bishop Giberti of Verona; and the newly created cardinals Contarini, Carafa, Sadoleto, and Pole—began, under the chairmanship of Contarini, an intensive investigation into the conditions of the church.

In the spring of 1537, the commission submitted its report to the pope. The findings were not surprising, but the forthright manner in which they were reported was remarkable, to say the least. In its preface, the commission charged that the root of all the corruption and abuse in the church was the papacy itself, that is, the unwarranted exaggeration of papal authority and the flagrant misuse of a divine trust for the purpose of aggrandizement and power. From this basic fault, as from the Trojan horse, springs the multitude of abuses that have brought the church to the brink of disaster, they charged. In succeeding sections, the report outlined the nature of these abuses in vivid frankness, from simony, greed, extortion, immorality, and deceit to nonresidence, slothfulness, and incompetence. It recommended more care in making appointments to office, regulation of the monasteries, and sharp restrictions on dispensations and graces.

The first step toward churchwide reformation had been taken, the cause of disease located and diagnosed. Yet how willing would the physician be to operate on himself? On the other hand, was this really the correct diagnosis? Certainly corruption and immorality contributed to the disenchantment of thousands of believers and to the total revulsion of many others, and needed to be corrected if the church was to survive as an institution. Were these ills, however, the primary cause of schism? Religion consists of both morals and doctrine. Catholics, no less than Protestants, found existing moral practices reprehensible and took steps to correct them. The separation between the two came from their disagreement about theology, not about morality. While condemning abuse, and even chastising the pope, most of the Catholic reformers were unwilling to compromise on their doctrinal views. On these grounds, the schism grew wider as the two sides confronted each other with doctrines and dogmas.

Counter-Reformation: Inquisition and Index

As the 1540s approached, the prospects for religious reunion seemed good. Not since the excommunication of Luther and the subsequent imperial ban twenty years before had the situation been more favorable to solution. The pope made plans for the upcoming council and acted on some of the more moderate proposals of the precouncil inquiry, but the most needed reforms were not forthcoming. How could they be? If the disposal of exemptions, dispensations, and licenses were curtailed as the commission admonished, or the sale of indulgences reduced, where would the papacy secure its much-needed revenues? Besides, once the council was convened and the Lutherans made aware of the reforms already carried out, there would be no further need for concern. Here Pope Paul made the same error as Charles V in believing that all that was necessary to bring Protestants back to the fold was for Catholics to put their own moral house in order. Neither emperor nor pope understood the complex nature of the Protestant revolt.

To help crush the plague of heresy and strengthen the church's powers of repression, Pope Paul III introduced the papal Inquisition in 1542. Inquisitions had been set up by the papacy in the Middle Ages for ferreting out heresy and crime, although none of these had remained as a permanent ecclesiastical institution. The Spanish Inquisition was established in 1478, but it had become an organ of the Spanish government over which the Roman church had little jurisdiction or control. Furthermore, it was as much an instrument of social and racial persecution as it was an institution for guarding religious orthodoxy. The Spanish Inquisition was the model Cardinal Carafa now proposed to the pope for the creation of a Roman Inquisition. This so-called Holy Office of the Universal Church was endorsed in July 1542 by the bull *Licet ab Initio*. Carafa and Pope Paul III hoped to use it to centralize and modernize the machinery for the suppression of heresy and thus make that machinery more effective throughout the church. Six cardinals were appointed as inquisitors, with Carafa, of course, as inquisitor-general, with power to try heresy cases originating in Rome and to function as a court of appeals from subordinate bodies established throughout Italy. Like the Spanish inquisitors, the cardinals were authorized to imprison suspects, confiscate property, and employ the secular arm to extort confessions or to carry out punishment.

Another measure taken up by the papacy to enforce religious conformity was the Index of Prohibited Books. Censorship was certainly not new to either Catholics or Protestants, but it was not until the mid-sixteenth century that it was institutionalized. In 1559 Carafa (now Pope Paul IV) published the *Index Librorum Prohibitorum*, an elaboration of the list of "dangerous and unholy" books he had issued while he was inquisitor-general. This papal Index, which continued now on a permanent basis, listed three categories of prohibitions, from heretical authors like Luther, Zwingli, Calvin, Knox, and Beza, whose complete writings were condemned, to such books and pamphlets as *The Prince, Pantagruel,* and the Koran that were listed as "unwholesome" in doctrine, either totally or in part. This Index was reissued in 1561 by Pope Pius IV with a number of Carafa's titles left out. In 1564 a second list, known as the Tridentine Index, was published following the discussion and recommendation of the project by the Council of Trent. It is difficult to determine the actual effectiveness of the papal Index. Although a number of book-burning spectacles scarred the country, judging from the characteristics of human nature and the prevalence of resistance to intellectual authoritarianism, it might not be an unwarranted guess that the Index provided many otherwise orthodox Catholics with a convenient bibliography of desirable and subversive reading matter.

The author of both Inquisition and Index, and the leading force of the Counter-Reformation, was the energetic reformer-turned-pontiff, Gian Pietro Carafa, elected pope in 1555 at the age of seventy-nine. As Pope Paul IV (1555–59), he launched a frontal attack not only on the laxity of religious practice in Rome but also on any approach to doctrinal accommodation with the Protestants. Self-righteous, dogmatic, and violent, Paul IV alienated many of his former friends (in fact, he imprisoned some of them), and by his uncompromising methods made any closing of the religious schism next to impossible. Early in his short but tempestuous reign, this Spanish-hating Neapolitan sought to purge Italy of Spanish domination by embroiling the papacy once more in dangerous international politics, oblivious to the disaster that had befallen Clement VII. Siding with the French, as had his Medici predecessor, Pope Paul tried to use the Habsburg-Valois rivalry as a lever of papal politics. The results were almost identical. The appearance of a powerful Spanish army before Rome, commanded by the hardened duke of Alba, made the pope change his mind about political involvement. After this show of Spanish force in 1557, Paul IV returned to the policy of neutrality that had generally been followed by the papacy since 1527. Still, he disliked Spaniards and everything that smacked of Spain, including Loyola and the Society of Jesus. Had the Jesuit founder not died in 1556 and been succeeded by a more compromising general, Diego Laynez, it is likely that the pope would have abolished the order. Paul IV's pontificate, more than any other, marked the transition from Reformation to Counter-Reformation; from an emphasis on humanism, piety, and unity, to dogmatism, austerity, and conformity.

The Council of Trent

Even after Pope Paul III had conceded the need for a general council and had received the strong admonitions of the precouncil commission, it was not easy to obtain agreement as to time, place, and purpose, nor was it universally felt that the Lutherans should be invited to attend, as Charles V insisted. The emperor preferred meeting in Germany or Spain; the pope wanted the prelates to come to Italy, where his influence would be greater. Francis I and the French bishops were opposed to a general council at all, believing their cherished Gallicanism would be less endangered by separate national councils.

Finally, in March 1545 an assorted group of four legates and cardinals, four archbishops, thirty-one bishops, five generals of orders, and fifty theologians and canonists assembled in the ecclesiastical city of Trent on the southern slope of the Austrian Alps. Here between Germany and Italy the most important council since Constance, one hundred and thirty years earlier, convened—again to end a schism, combat heresy, and reform the church in head and members.

From the outset, struggles of interests and ideals threatened to disrupt the entire conference. The papal curia, with support from most of the Italian bishops, hoped to impose a stronger centralizing influence on the church by first solidifying doctrines and presenting a united front against the Protestants, and then attacking the problems of internal reform. The Spanish, on the other hand, opposed the papal pretensions with claims for conciliar jurisdiction reminiscent of fifteenth-century conciliarism. With the emperor, they proposed that papal and curial reforms should be discussed and legislated first, with theological clarifications postponed until later. This stance appealed also to the smaller group of moderate bishops who advocated some degree of doctrinal conciliation with the Lutherans. Finally, council members agreed to handle the subjects of reform and doctrine concurrently, although in fact reform was hardly mentioned in the first assembly while doctrinal matters were given considerable attention. To the papal advantage, the council also decided that voting (unlike that in the fifteenth-century councils) would be by head rather than by nation and that proxy votes would not be allowed.

During its protracted debates, the council considered and made emphatic pronouncements on a number of important theological issues. One of these was the question of the relative weights of Scriptures and church tradition as the authority for doctrine and the guide to practice. The delegates agreed that the two were of equal importance, with the additional stipulation that only the church had the right to interpret the Scriptures. The doctrine of original sin was studied next, and the council reaffirmed Saint Thomas Aquinas's declaration that human nature was not totally corrupted by the Fall. The sacrifice on the cross earned redeeming merit that is transmitted to man through the sacrament of the Holy Eucharist. In a further repudiation of Protestant doctrine, the prelates rejected justification by faith alone as inadequate, for faith also requires hope and charity, they declared—in other words, good works. Divine grace (and Christ's merit) is imparted through the sacraments, when administered by the authorized clergy, and can be accepted or rejected by the recipient. Acceptance of that grace constitutes a good work as well as an act of faith, both of which are essential for salvation.

Plague and the resumption of war in the Empire forced the council to adjourn to Bologna in March 1547, just prior to the imperial victory at Mühlberg. The emperor's refusal to recognize the legitimacy of the Bologna meeting, with its handful of Italian prelates, however, forced its termination in 1549.

Not until 1551 was it possible for Julius III (1550–54), Pope Paul III's successor, to reconvene the council for its second meeting. Attendance was more sparse than in 1545. French delegates were absent for political reasons (because the pope failed to support Henri II in his war with the emperor), and few German and Spanish prelates attended either. Again the pope and the Italian bishops held sway. A Protestant contingent arrived in 1552 to present a statement and propose the acceptance of the sacrament in both kinds in the celebration of the Lord's Supper. Hope arose in some of the more ecumenical minds that this assembly might yet restore unity to the church. That dream quickly evaporated when the Catholics refused to rescind their previous pronouncements or listen to the new Protestant proposals; and the latter, for their part, disavowed any council presided over by papal legates. Resumption of the Schmalkaldic war and the defeat of the emperor in 1552 caused the council to be dismissed again after accomplishing little more than reaffirming the Catholic doctrine of transubstantiation.

Not until ten years later did the Council of Trent reconvene for its last assembly. This time 270 voting delegates, with additional thousands of retainers and observers, converged on the tiny alpine city. The new pope, Pius IV (1559–65), was mild-mannered and moderate in contrast to the terrible Paul IV, who had died in 1559, but Pius was as devoted as anyone to strengthening the church against its enemies and to asserting the power of the Roman curia. The several rulers who had influenced the first sessions at Trent, particularly Emperor Charles V, were now dead. In their place were younger potentates whose political duels allowed the pope to play off one faction against the other and thus dominate the final sessions of the council.

The Spanish delegation, led by the archbishop of Granada, opposed any changes in doctrine or ritual that had already been settled at previous sessions. At the same time, Philip II called for a thorough reform of the papacy, including a reduction of its powers, and enjoined his representatives at Trent to promote needed churchwide reforms. The imperial representatives of Emperor Ferdinand I wanted some doctrinal concessions to be made, in the hope of placating the more moderate Lutherans and preserving the uneasy Peace of Augsburg. Peace was of paramount importance to the Empire. The French also feared any hard-line doctrinal definitions that might excite the Huguenots and feed their latent hostility. Catherine de' Medici preferred a national council in France; but since that attempt had failed, she hoped the cardinal of Lorraine, the spokesman of the French delegation, could prevent the council at Trent from upsetting the precarious balance of powers in France.

Pius IV, however, had his own ideas for the council. Skillfully, he saw to it that each national interest was served sufficiently to placate, if not fully satisfy, its representatives without at the same time alienating its opponents. He could then continue to promote what he considered to be the best interests of the curia and the church. As a result, between January 1562 and December 1563, many fundamental reforms were enacted, such as the abolition of indulgence hawkers, a better definition of the responsibilities of priests and bishops, and the establishment of theological seminaries in every diocese. The embarrassing practices of simony and pluralism were also condemned, clerical residence enforced, higher educational requirements demanded, and unlicensed preaching forbidden.

In the meantime, the major doctrines of Catholicism were reaffirmed and reemphasized, while the premises of Protestantism were emphatically denounced. The definition of the Mass as a renewal of Christ's sacrifice was confirmed, along with communion in one kind (bread) for the laity ("Christ being whole and entire under either species"); clerical celibacy and apostolic succession were upheld; indulgences were approved if not sold for "evil gain"; and belief in purgatory, the treasury of merit, and the invocation of saints were

The Council of Trent. *A Titian drawing of the final meetings of the Council of Trent, convened in the church of Santa Maria Maggiore.*

endorsed. By the close of the Council of Trent, the lines of doctrinal demarcation were more clearly and sharply drawn than ever. Henceforth any deviation would be quickly condemned. The clear-cut pronouncement contained in the canons and decrees of the Council of Trent was the Catholic declaration of war against Protestantism. It also marked the victory of thirteenth-century Thomist scholasticism (after Saint Thomas Aquinas) over biblical humanism.

Furthermore, the supremacy of the pope over any or all of the bishops, and over a general council of the church, was recognized, not only in the canons and decrees themselves but also in the creed entitled "Profession of the Tridentine Faith," issued by Pope Pius IV in 1564 and sworn to by all the church after that time. Philip II's quip, "I sent bishops to Trent and they came back parish priests," is an obvious exaggeration, but it is true that episcopal subordination to papal authority was a reality after Trent. The long papal fight against conciliarism had been won. What the Council of Constance had decreed in 1417 about conciliar supremacy was now nullified by the Council of Trent in 1563. The pope was supreme within Catholic Christendom.

In the end, after inauspicious beginnings and amid continuous conflict, the Council of Trent achieved many of its goals. It was in fact the most significant event in the Catholic Reformation and one of the pivotal points in the entire history of the church. It established the framework and pattern of the Roman Catholic church from that time until Vatican II 400 years later. More immediately, it marked both the climax of the crusade for reform within the church and the effective beginning of the Catholic recovery and renewal. Those who had hoped the council would end the schism and unify western Christianity were disappointed; instead, doctrines became hardened, more dogmatic, and exclusive. Yet within its smaller purview, the church would now be better organized, more aware of its limits, and able to demand a stricter adherence to its doctrines and forms.

The Counter-Reformation Papacy and Tridentine Revival

The Council of Trent had done more than institutionalize Catholic opposition to Protestantism and enact a few overdue reforms. During the final sessions especially, under the skillful management of Cardinal Morone, president of the council, some serious overhauling of religious practices was undertaken, and a new spirit of confidence and aggressiveness was initiated. The popes after Trent took the lead in setting the mood and direction of this reform.

Its direction was not toward innovative or novel experiments, however, but rather toward a careful attention to maintaining and strengthening the church without altering its basic form or changing its doctrines. The "Tridentine spirit" was a *reaffirmation* rather than a *reformation*. Yet in making such a reaffirmation, emphasis was shifted from the sensual preoccupations of the Renaissance popes to more spiritual and conscientious concerns, and the whole mood and character of the papacy was altered. Papal activity became more religious as popes assumed a more direct supervisory authority over bishops and other clerics. Pluralism and absenteeism were thereby reduced rather than simply condemned, as in the past. The curia itself became more clerical. Training was improved by the initiation of the seminary system, first in Rome and then throughout Europe. Graduates of these seminaries became more effective priests and better representatives of the church. The papacy also led the way in promoting missionary efforts overseas, although in these endeavors the monarchs of Spain and Portugal played the key role. A significant example of papal reactivation is the way Counter-Reformation popes regained control of their own organs of government, reorganizing papal finances and for the first time exercising meaningful control over the Papal States. Finally, the papacy established an unprecedented control over the liturgy of the church, giving it a uniformity it had never possessed, by issuing a new Roman Catechism, Missal, and Breviary, and by publishing a new, definitive edition of the Vulgate Bible.

Pius IV set the tone of the Counter-Reformation papacy not only by convening and spearheading the final sessions of the Council of Trent but also by setting an example of piety and work. His successor, the austere and dedicated reformer, Michael Ghislieri, Pope Pius V (1565–72), continued to promote the Tridentine spirit with his own pious and single-minded devotion, which brought him eventual canonization, a distinction achieved by relatively few popes. Pius V's careful selection of cardinals for their worthiness and ability had a profound long-range effect on the makeup of the cardinalate. Gregory XIII (1572–85), although less saintly himself, continued the revitalization of the curia by promoting the seminaries, recodifying canon law, reforming the inaccurate Julian calendar, and especially by reorganizing the papal diplomatic network and machinery. Papal nuncios after Pope Gregory's reforms became "ambassadors for God," not just diplomatic representatives of another principality. Finally, Sixtus V (1585–90) represents the reassertion of papal authority in political as well as ecclesiastical affairs, and as such seems to mark a return to the Renaissance papacy. Sixtus, however, asserted his power with a much clearer recognition of religious ends than his earlier predecessors had, and his rule was accompanied by a genuine patronage of piety and honest administration.

Saints and Sinners   The ramifications of this new breed of papal leadership were felt in many ways, especially in a more general Catholic religious awakening and revival of spirituality. Trent and the Counter-Reformation revival made religion more meaningful to millions. Clerics with ability and character began to rise to the top instead of being trampled under by more ambitious and unscrupulous men. A vivid example of the new type of prelate (although nepotism was also responsible for his advancement) is Saint Carlo Borromeo (1538–84) of Milan, worthy and gifted nephew of Pope Pius IV, and one of the towering figures of the Counter-Reformation. Created cardinal and called into the curia as secretary of state when he was only twenty-one, Cardinal Borromeo became one of the leading exemplars and motivators of reform in Rome. After the death of Pius IV in 1565, Borromeo returned to his diocese of Milan, of which he had been archbishop since 1559, and carried out a thorough reform there, conscientiously attending to the business of being a bishop and administering to the needs of his flock. He gave everything his personal attention, not only the vast programs of hospital, school, and seminary promotion but also the daily needs of the simplest peasant. It is not surprising that the name of Carlo Borromeo became synonymous with the highest moral and intellectual ideals of the time and that he was subsequently sainted by the church.

Cardinal Borromeo also actively promoted institutions for sheltering and reforming former prostitutes. Such asylums were already familiar in sixteenth-century Italy, but they received new impetus during post-Tridentine times. Other establishments were created to prevent girls and women from turning to prostitution in the first place. These houses showed especial concern for such "high risk" groups as orphans, widows, women with serious marital problems, women displaced from convents, and the vagrant poor. Inmates participated in religious observances and carried out various kinds of handwork as well as charitable functions. Unlike most convents, however, these "alternative orders" housed females primarily from the lower classes, both those who entered on their own wishes and those who were sent by their families or by the civil or religious authorities, and provided them with both refuge and opportunities to become respectable and reasonably happy individuals.

Sainthood came to many who were less prominent than Pope Pius and Cardinal Borromeo but who in their own ways contributed to the rejuvenation

"San Carlo Borromeo," detail from the painting by Daniele Crespi. *A nephew of Pope Pius IV, Borromeo served as cardinal-archbishop of Milan after 1560 and advised the pope closely during the final session of the Council of Trent.*

of Catholicism. One of these was Saint Angela Merici, founder of the Ursulines. Another pious reformer and founder of a new religious order was Saint Philip Neri (1515–95) who endeavored through "prayerful action" to get people to live more sanctified lives. Neri was born in Florence but spent most of his life in Rome, where he organized a confraternity to care for the sick and needy. This eventually grew into the Congregation of the Oratory, whose function, much like the earlier Oratory of Divine Love, was to provide a more devotional religious experience for the secular clergy and laymen. Neri's own simple piety, humility, and sense of humor made him one of the most popular citizens of Rome in the second half of the sixteenth century.

Neither piety nor humility appeared in the Counter-Reformation writings of the scrappy Antwerp schoolmistress/poet Anna Bijns (1493–1575). There was humor, however, at least a kind of vituperative wit, in her allegorical refrains against Luther, "the wolf in sheep's clothing," and his followers. Proclaiming herself the "avenging angel of the insulted [Catholic] faith," she placed the blame for the evils of her day directly at the feet of the reformer:

> *If Luther had kept his tongue behind his teeth,*
> *For such cruel action there'd surely be no need.*
> *And now he plans to wash it off his hands*
> *As Pilate did with our Savior's death.**

---

*Translated by Kristiaan P. G. Aercke, in *Women Writers of the Renaissance and Reformation*, ed. by Katharina M. Wilson, Athens, Georgia, 1987, p. 371. © by the University of Georgia Press. Used by permission.

Militant and impetuous, Anna Bijns could scarcely support the slow-moving reforms of the Council of Trent. Her solution to the problem was more extreme: "Cut off the rotten limbs ere the whole body decays." The three collections of Anna's Counter-Reformation poems were republished eight times during her life.

Spain produced its share of saints, none more revered or more remarkable than Saint Teresa of Avila (1515–82). Her response and contribution to the Catholic religious awakening was deeply personal yet in a sense universal. A member of the Carmelite convent in Avila, Teresa experienced a religious conversion that led eventually to experiences of spiritual ecstasy, which she wrote about in *Las Moradas* (The Mansions) and *Libro de su vida* (Book of Her Life). Yet Saint Teresa did more than feel and relate her spiritual experiences; she tried to help others meet God and have their own lives transformed. She was also an active reformer in her own right, starting a new, "discalced" (barefoot) Carmelite order whose object was to seek personal communion with Christ. She was totally loyal to the church, yet her mysticism and reforming zeal brought her under suspicion of the Inquisition. Throughout her busy years, she was able to reconcile the active and contemplative life in a way that few, if any, others have achieved.

Saint Teresa's leading disciple, San Juan de la Cruz (Saint John of the Cross), left to posterity some of the finest illustrations of poetic devotional writing, including the moving *Ascent of Mount Carmel*. In Saint Francis Borgia, third general of the Jesuit Order, Spain nourished another individual of personal virtue and idealism who was capable of promoting those traits in active public life. Saint Teresa's profound influence on the visionary artistic genius, El Greco, also underlines the close relationship between religious thought and visual art in the sixteenth century.

The Art of Reformation and Counter-Reformation

The culture of the middle years of the sixteenth century, the age of the Reformation and Counter-Reformation, was expressed in lively artistic production, though generally of lesser quality than that of either the High Renaissance that preceded or the Baroque that followed it—even though it contained elements of both. In some areas, art degenerated into a form of religious propaganda, with artists like Hans Beheim and others bombarding Germany with religious cartoons, some of them very crude and even obscene. Some of the works of Peter Vischer, Lucas Cranach, and Hans Holbein, however, achieved some artistic distinction, and Albrecht Dürer's copper engravings and woodcuts are remarkable.

Lucas Cranach the Elder (1472–1553) was the most capable and prolific propagandist of the Reformation. A devoted Protestant and friend of Luther, Cranach was attached to the court of electoral Saxony and produced innumerable paintings and woodcuts featuring likenesses of Luther (see pages 55 and 74), and caricatures of his Catholic contemporaries (see page 79). Hans Holbein the Younger (1497–1543), the best portraitist of the time, has given us indelible images of the leading Reformation figures, especially at the court of Henry VIII where Holbein spent the last decade of his life (see pages 41, 165, and 426). The master of German art was Albrecht Dürer (1471–1528), a native of Nuremberg, raised in the best tradition of native craftsmanship, which he hoped to elevate to the status of princely art. His paintings have much in common with the High Renaissance art of Italy, especially with the Venetians Bellini and Giorgione (see page 23), but his greatest achievements were in graphic art, which he raised to an unsurpassed level (see page 76). Many of Dürer's works reflect the impact the Reformation and its ensuing religious dilemmas had on the artist's mind.

After Dürer's death the quality of German art declined rapidly, a decay that is usually attributed to the Protestant Reformation with its de-emphasis on human will and outward works. Ecclesiastical art decayed first in Protestant lands where the reformers criticized the idolatrous use of images and looked with suspicion on religious paintings, and where the market for secular art was still very limited. Economic depression also played a part as the means for the patronage of artists dried up.

One exception to the generally dismal state of northern art during the Reformation was the Low Countries, where the Burgundian tradition of patronage continued under the Habsburgs, and where some individual artists perpetuated the traditions of the Van Eycks, Van der Goës, and Bosch. By far the most important of these was Pieter Bruegel the Elder (1525–69). Like his Flemish predecessors, Bruegel sought to depict the reality and beauty of ordinary objects and people through painstaking rendering of the minutest details (see page 257). Yet he also mastered the essential lessons of Italian art—the harmony of form, space, and color—which he then rendered in his own unique terms. His subject matter ranged from biblical episodes, to pastoral landscapes and peasant merriment, to scenes of brutal war and bloodshed. His most famous paintings are of bucolic peasants, but the most vivid is a panorama of the great dilemma of human life, called the *Triumph of Death*. In front of a barren landscape of burning cities devastated by war and pillage Bruegel depicted a chaos of people caught in their activities of music and merriment by Death, who overturns the dining table, assails the priests and kings, mows down the peasants with his scythe, slaughters the soldiers, and drowns many trying to escape. Those who remain alive are driven toward a giant trap-like coffin, guarded by armies of skeletons. Yet Bruegel accepted the certainty of death with a stoic dignity that is reflected in his final paintings, *The Harvesters* (see page 349) and *Hunters in the Snow*, depicting man's simple bondage to the earth. In these paintings Bruegel showed peasants at work and returning from the hunt, interacting with nature to achieve internal peace.

Mannerism   The most fertile soil of artistic production was still Italy, where in the decades immediately following the sack of Rome (1527), a style of painting recognized as *la maniera italiana*, or Mannerism, developed, particularly among the disciples of Michelangelo, Raphael, and Andrea del Sarto. To most sixteenth-century observers, *maniera* meant "stylishness," and reflected such attributes as grace, refinement, sophistication, and virtuosity. However, to achieve these

Tintoretto, "The Last Supper." *This remarkable canvas reveals some of the symbolism, dramatic effect, and suspended tension characteristic of Mannerist art.*

characteristics, many artists resorted to distorted idealization, elongation of figures, and various techniques to heighten emotion and tension. Virtuosity succumbed to eccentricity; sophistication gave way to agitation. Some modern critics have referred to this style as "Counter-Renaissance," but in fact most of the Mannerist characteristics are elaborations and exaggerations of classical Renaissance style rather than its negation. Yet there is also something of a revolutionary nature in this art, a shocking of classical sensitivities by violating or exaggerating traditional techniques and heightening the sense of emotional stress. Unresolved tension is a prominent feature of Mannerist art and is most likely a reflection—conscious or subconscious—of the insecurity and suspense produced by the Reformation and Counter-Reformation. Even in nonreligious themes, the tension is present, sometimes even foreboding.

Early examples of Mannerist art may be seen in the Florentine followers of del Sarto: Jacopo Pontormo (1494–1556), whose paintings show a restlessness that emphasizes his eccentricity, and Rosso Fiorentino (1494–1540), who used color and composition to create strong emotional response. The nervous suspense of Raphael's *Transfiguration* was carried much further by his assistants Giulio Romano (1499–1546) and Francesco Parmigianino (1503–40). The latter's elongated figures give a feeling of instability and a sense of exaggerated elegance. The same might be said of Angelo Bronzino's (1503–72)

Benvenuto Cellini's salt-cellar. *Executed in 1540 for Francis I, this work in solid gold and enamel is a masterpiece of the Renaissance goldsmith's art.*

many portraits of famous contemporaries, or of Francesco Primaticcio's (1504–70) decorations at Fontainebleau where he, Giulio Romano, and Rosso Fiorentino introduced Italian style into French architectural decoration. A second generation of Italian Mannerists thrived in Florence under Francesco Salviati (1510–63) and Giorgio Vasari (1511–74)—who is more noted for his enthusiastic history of the artists of his time than for his own paintings—and in Venice under Jacopo Bassano (1518–92) and Jacopo Tintoretto (1518–94). Tintoretto used extravagant perspective and dramatic color to create moods of emotion and inspiration. Frequently he chose his subjects from the most dramatic episodes of biblical and early church history.

The most flamboyant maverick of Mannerism was the goldsmith-sculptor Benvenuto Cellini (1500–71). In his virtuosity, eccentricity, and penetration Cellini represented Mannerism, but he was too individual to fit into any categorical definition, however broad. In the classical balance of his works he is more a product of the High Renaissance; indeed, his hero and mentor was Michelangelo. Cellini's life, however, reflected nothing of the classicism of his art. He was unpredictable, cantankerous, and egocentric. His remarkable *Autobiography* reveals a boastful yet frank person, energetic and capricious, yet uniquely gifted artistically. During his relatively long and tumultuous life he created some of the finest examples of sixteenth-century art, including an exquisite salt cellar which he made for Francis I; a bronze sculpture of *Perseus and Medusa;* and a bronze bust of Duke Cosimo I de' Medici.

The Impact of the Reformation—Protestant and Catholic

The tensions and exaggerations of Mannerist art emphasize the contradictions and anxiety of life during the age of the Reformation and Counter-Reformation. Many of the issues raised by the early reformers were not yet resolved, even though a spate of solutions were offered. Indeed, this diversity was part of the problem—the relative unity of religious belief and practice had been replaced by a confusion of conflicting creeds and confessions. Where *could* truth be found? Was it in the traditions and authority of the Mother Church, or in the Holy Bible, or in the spiritual manifestations revealed directly to men and women? What *were* the answers to the great dilemmas of life and death? What *was* the nature of human beings, and how could that nature be reconciled with an all-wise, all-powerful, all-righteous deity? For many, the proffered answers to these and other probing questions brought conviction, and in the face of death, even tranquility. Yet these answers also seemed to justify taking the lives of others, when the shoe was on the other foot.

Was the only legacy of the Reformation conflict and upheaval? Without doubt it did aggravate these states, but it also bequeathed much more. Above all, the Reformation ended the unity of Latin Christendom and ushered in an era of religious diversity. It altered the conduct of religious life for Protestants and Catholics alike, and changed the organizational structure of the church. Liturgies, ceremonies, and rituals were reshaped—more in Protestant worship than in Catholic, but even in the latter the church of the 1560s was very different from the church of the 1510s. In the lands that adopted the Reformation the changes were revolutionary. These lands overthrew the papal hierarchy, rejected canon law, converted the Mass to a simple celebration of the Lord's Supper, and made the sermon the central feature of the worship service. The Protestant program of reform revolutionized ecclesiastical practice at all levels, greatly simplifying religious life and giving secular life more meaning. The degree to which ecclesiastical revolution altered personal beliefs and habits is harder to assess and is still being argued by scholars today, but it seems quite likely that formal religion did have some impact on popular religion, even though many things changed very little on the local level. And, as has been pointed out, the transformations in the religious landscape did have a profound social impact as well as cultural.

Sometimes the result was unfortunate, as in the artistic atrophy in Germany, or the apparent impetus to witch hunts and other superstitions. Yet who can deny the positive religious dimension in the great creative works of Rabelais, Marot, Garcilaso de la Vega, Marguerite of Navarre, Hans Sachs, even John Foxe and Edmund Spenser; and, of course, the reformers from Luther to

Loyola? The gradual creation of a Protestant cultural and social identity, with its own customs and myths, created a new outlook on private life as well as a different perspective of cosmic purpose.

Although the Reformation was not primarily a political movement, and the reformers hoped to avoid civic confrontation if possible, it nevertheless was pregnant with political implications and profoundly influenced the issues and balance of power for some time to come. Traditional enmities and alliances based on dynastic or other interest factors did not change overnight, but religion now became one of the important ingredients adding to international tensions, especially in the second half of the sixteenth century. Often religious fissures coincided with older political or economic disputes to increase the intensity of conflict. Even when the religious lines did not correspond at all to political divisions this complication of issues did not necessarily contribute to stability. We would probably be most correct in saying that the overall impact of the Reformation in the sixteenth century was ambivalent. By mid-century it was still too early to assess its long-range effects.

Suggestions for Further Reading

GENERAL

The last 325 pages of Erwin Iserloh, Joseph Glazik, and Hubert Jedin, *Reformation and Counter Reformation*, tr. by Anselm Biggs and Peter Becker, vol. 5 of the *History of the Church*, ed. by Jedin and Dolin (New York, 1980), give a sympathetic account of the Counter-Reformation, as does Louis Chatellier, *The Europe of the Devout: The Catholic Reformation and the Formation of a New Society* (New York, 1989). I think Marvin R. O'Connell's *The Counter Reformation, 1559–1610* (New York, 1974) is also a very good general history. Jean Delumeau's revisionist *Catholicism from Luther to Voltaire: A New View of the Counter-Reformation*, with a critical introduction by John Bossy (Philadelphia and London, 1977) should also be consulted. The most provocative recent study is A.D. Wright, *The Counter-Reformation: Catholic Europe and the Non-Christian World* (New York, 1982). Two very short accounts are N.S. Davidson, *The Counter-Reformation* (Oxford, 1987), and Michael Mullett, *The Counter Reformation and the Catholic Reformation in Early Modern Europe* (New York and London, 1984). John C. Olin, *Catholic Reform from Cardinal Ximenez to the Council of Trent, 1495–1563* (New York, 1990) contains a brief study of Loyola and his illustrative documents.

More specialized works that probe various aspects of the Catholic Reformation are Peter I. Kaufman, *Augustinian Piety and Catholic Reform* (Macon, 1982); Barbara McClung Hallman, *Italian Cardinals, Reform, and the Church as Property, 1492–1563* (Berkeley, 1985), which traces the patterns of accumulation and distribution of church property and money during the Reformation; and Christopher F. Black, *Italian Confraternities in the Sixteenth Century* (New York and Cambridge, England, 1989), a broad, pioneering study of the Catholic organizations. The Counter-Reformation culture of post-Anabaptist Münster is analyzed in R. Po-chia Hsia, *Society and Religion in Münster, 1535–1618* (New Haven, 1984).

CATHOLIC REFORMERS AND NEW ORDERS

An interesting study of reforms in Venice is Christopher Cairns, *Domenico Bollani, Bishop of Brescia: Devotion to Church and State in the Republic of Venice in the Sixteenth Century* (Nieuwkoop, the Netherlands, 1976). Also see Barry Collett, *Italian Benedictine Scholars and the Reformation: The Congregation of Santa Giustina of Padua* (New York and Oxford, 1985), which examines the development of religious thought within the Italian Benedictines from 1470 to the 1560s. Special attention is given to Benedetto da Mantova and Giorgio Siculo. Informative and thought-provoking also is Peter Matheson, *Cardinal Contarini at Regensburg* (New York and Oxford, 1972). Although somewhat dated, Richard M. Douglas, *Jacopo Sadoleto, 1477–1547, Humanist and Reformer* (Cambridge, Massachusetts, 1959) is a solid study of an important Catholic reformer. Also see Francesco C. Cesareo, *Humanism and Catholic Reform: The Life and Work of Gregorio Cortese, 1483–1548* (New York, 1990).

LOYOLA AND THE JESUITS

A reasonably reliable account, dealing with politics and culture as well as religion, is J.C.H. Aveling, *The Jesuits* (London, 1981). The most exacting and original study of the Jesuits in recent years is A. Lynn Martin, *The Jesuit Mind: The Mentality of an Elite in Early Modern France* (Ithaca, 1988), based primarily on source materials located in the archives of the Society in Rome, especially correspondence between Jesuits in France and the generals in Rome. Jesuit schools are analyzed, particularly their relationship to humanist education, in Aldo D. Scaglione, *The Liberal Arts and the Jesuit College System* (Philadelphia, 1986). On the greatest of the Jesuit missionaries see Georg Schurhammer's mammoth 4-volume *Francis Xavier: His Life, His Times,* tr. by M.J. Costelloe (Rome, 1973–82). Volume 4 (1982) on Xavier's labors in Japan and China, 1549–52, is the shortest volume at 713 pages. An extraordinary narrative about a remarkable missionary is Jonathan D. Spence, *The Memory Palace of Matteo Ricci* (New York, 1984).

INQUISITION AND INDEX

A surge of interest in the Inquisition, Roman as well as Spanish, has resulted in a number of useful studies that have greatly enlarged our perception of this institution. Edward Burman, *The Inquisition: The Hammer of Heresy* (Willingborough, England, 1984) is not as successful in this regard as Edward Peters, *Inquisition* (New York, 1988), which is a learned and balanced history. Two more recent books bring together assorted papers on Inquisition research. The first, *The Inquisition in Early Modern Europe: Studies on Sources and Methods* (DeKalb, Illinois, 1986), edited by Gustav Henningsen and John Tedeschi, is a useful collection of on-going research, with several studies offering descriptive summaries of available archival resources. The other, Stephen Haliczer, ed. and tr., *Inquisition and Society in Early Modern Europe* (Totowa, New Jersey, 1987), is a more eclectic collection, mostly of interpretative essays. Two volumes by Paul F. Grendler, the leading authority on the Roman Inquisition and papal censorship, are valuable contributions: *The Roman Inquisition and the Venetian Press, 1540–1605* (Princeton, 1977), and *Culture and Censorship in Late Renaissance Italy and France* (London, rpt., 1981). Brian Pullan, *The Jews of Europe and the Inquisition of Venice, 1550–1670* (Totowa, New Jersey, 1983) is valuable. For the Spanish Inquisition see especially Henry Kamen, *Inquisition and Society in Spain in the Sixteenth and Seventeenth Centuries* (Bloomington, 1985), a lucid summary up-dating his seminal

The Spanish Inquisition, published twenty years earlier. Angel Alcala, ed., *The Spanish Inquisition and the Inquisitorial Mind* (Highland Lakes, New Jersey, 1987) is an uneven collection containing some enlightening essays. Two other important works are Stephen Haliczer, *Inquisition and Society in the Kingdom of Valencia, 1478–1834* (Berkeley, 1990), and William Monter, *Frontiers of Heresy: The Spanish Inquisition from the Basque Lands to Sicily* (New York, 1990).

THE COUNCIL OF TRENT AND THE COUNTER-REFORMATION PAPACY

The standard work on the Council (only the first two volumes are available in English) is Herbert Jedin, *History of the Council of Trent*, tr. by Ernest Graf, 2 vols. (London and St. Louis, 1957–61). This may be supplemented with the same author's *Crisis and Closure of the Council of Trent* (London, 1967). The complexities of imperial politics during the Counter-Reformation is partially unraveled in Robert Bireley, *Religion and Politics in the Age of Counterreformation: Emperor Ferdinand II, William Lamormaini, S.J., and the Formation of Imperial Policy* (Chapel Hill, 1981). Also see his *The Counter-Reformation Prince: Anti-Machiavellianism or Catholic Statecraft in Early Modern Europe* (Chapel Hill, 1990). Many aspects of the Tridentine church are revealed in a recent collection of essays commemorating the death of Carlo Borromeo, edited by John M. Headley and John B. Tomaro, *San Carlo Borromeo: Catholic Reform and Ecclesiastical Politics in the Second Half of the Sixteenth Century* (Washington, D.C., 1988). Broader in scope is Paolo Prodi, *The Papal Prince, One Body and Two Souls: The Papal Monarchy in Early Modern Europe*, tr. by Susan Haskins (New York and Cambridge, England, 1988), which is concerned with the relationship between spiritual and temporal authority in the Papal State from the mid-fifteenth to the mid-seventeenth centuries. The impact of the papacy beyond western and central Europe is studied in Kenneth M. Setton, *The Papacy and the Levant, Vol. 4: The Sixteenth Century from Julius III to Pius V* (Philadelphia, 1984), and Oskar Garstein, *Rome and the Counter-Reformation in Scandinavia*, 2 vols. (Oslo, 1963–1980), Vol. I, 1539–83; Vol. 2, 1583–1622.

SANTA TERESA AND SAN JUAN DE LA CRUZ

John M. Headly and John B. Tomar, eds., *San Carlo Borromeo: Catholic Reform and Ecclesiastical Politics in the Second Half of the Sixteenth Century* (Washington, D.C., 1988), contains 15 essays on Saint Carlo Borromeo's life, work, and influence on the Catholic church. There are a number of commendable works on Saint Teresa. See especially Stephen Clissold, *St. Teresa of Avila* (New York, 1982); Margaret A. Rees, ed., *Teresa de Jesus and Her World* (Leeds, 1981), papers from a conference at Trinity and All Saints College; and Jodi Bilindoff, *The Avila of Saint Teresa: Religious Reform in a Sixteenth Century City* (Ithaca, 1989). Catherine Swietlicki, *Spanish Christian Cabala: The Works of Luis de León, Santa Teresa de Jesús, and San Juan de la Cruz* (Columbia, Missouri, 1986) emphasizes the mystical side of some of the Spanish reformers. Useful studies of San Juan de la Cruz include Gerald Brenan, *St. John of the Cross: His Life and Poetry* (Cambridge, England, 1973); Richard P. Hardy, *Search for Nothing: The Life of John of the Cross* (New York, 1982); José C. Nieto, *Mystic, Rebel, Saint: A Study of St. John of the Cross* (Geneva, Switzerland, 1979), a valuable analysis; and George H. Tavard, *Poetry and Contemplation in St. John of the Cross* (Athens, Ohio, 1988).

ART OF THE REFORMATION AND COUNTER-REFORMATION

By far the best study of northern Reformation art is Carl C. Christensen, *Art of the Reformation in Germany* (Athens, Ohio, 1980). Also see Henry-Russell Hitchcock, *German Renaissance Architecture* (Princeton, 1981); Ruth Mellinkoff, *The Devil at Isenheim: Reflections of Popular Belief in Grünewald's Altarpiece* (Berkeley, 1988), containing interesting iconographic discoveries; and Werner Schade, *Cranach: A Family of Master Painters,* tr. by Helen Sebba (New York, 1980). Five fresh interpretations are presented in Jeffrey C. Smith, ed., *New Perspectives on the Art of Renaissance Nuremberg* (Austin, 1985).

The standard work on Mannerism is Arnold Hauser, *Mannerism: The Crisis of the Renaissance and the Origin of Modern Art,* tr. by Eric Mosbacher, 2 vols. (London, 1965), but also see Jacques Bousquet, *Mannerism: The Painting and Style of the Late Renaissance,* tr. by Simon Taylor (New York, 1964), and J.K.G. Shearman, *Mannerism* (Baltimore, 1967). For specific aspects and individual artists, see Janet Cox-Rearick, *Dynasty and Destiny in Medici Art: Pontormo, Leo X, and the Two Cosimos* (Princeton, 1984); David Rosand, *Painting in Cinquecento Venice: Titian, Veronese, Tintoretto* (New Haven, 1982); Francis L. Richardson, *Andrea Schiavone* (New York, 1980); John Pope-Hennessy, *Cellini* (New York, 1985); and T.S.R. Boase, *Georgio Vasari: The Man and the Book* (Princeton, 1979). Also insightful is James V. Mirallo, *Mannerism and Renaissance Poetry: Concept, Mode, and Inner Design* (New Haven, 1984). For Pieter Bruegel see Timothy Foote, *The World of Bruegel* (New York, 1968), and Walter S. Gibson, *Bruegel* (New York, 1977).

7 | FRANCE DURING THE WARS OF RELIGION

THE PEACE OF CATEAU-CAMBRÉSIS, ENDING THE HABSBURG-VALOIS wars in 1559, marked a watershed in the history of sixteenth-century France. It was a negotiated, not a dictated, peace, because the Habsburg-Tudor allies were as economically and militarily exhausted as was France. Despite the indecisiveness of the wars, the peace seemed to offer some hope of tranquility. Yet that elusive tranquility was already being disturbed before the ink on the treaty was dry. Economic crisis, social disturbance, and religious fanaticism made the situation in 1559 tenuous at best. In France the breakdown of monarchical authority invited additional disaster. The civil wars that erupted there in 1562 grew and spread to become a Europewide conflict pitting the polarized forces of international Protestantism and revitalized Catholicism against one another in bitter war. All of Europe was the battlefield of the so-called Wars of Religion, but the most decisive arena was along the Atlantic seaboard: the English Channel, the Netherlands, and France.

French Government and Administration

The monarchy in France was well established and popular long before the religious upheavals of the sixteenth century threw traditional allegiances and affiliations into disorder. Nevertheless, the power of the French king was far from absolute. In the second half of the sixteenth century, the king summoned the Estates General five times for purposes of remedying economic ills, healing the growing religious schism, and giving general advice; and the assembly took seriously its right to lecture the crown on its business. It also met on three other occasions, but the representation of the three estates was so small that these assemblies are not usually counted as Estates "General." The role of the provincial estates continued to be important, especially to the finances of France, for these were the bodies that sanctioned (or refused) the levy of *aides* and taxes, and in some provinces even determined the amount of the *taille*. The estates of Brittany, Normandy, Burgundy, Dauphiné, Provence, and Languedoc assisted in the ratification of treaties and exercised considerable influence over the legislation and administration of their respective provinces.

Still the theoretical power of the crown in France was greater than that of any other western monarchy, even though its effectiveness was seriously curtailed in the second half of the century. The administrative machinery had only slightly changed from the time of Francis I. The Royal Council, functioning in its various capacities as Privy Council, Council of State, or Council of Finances, advised the king on all matters on which he sought their advice, while the *Conseil des Affaires,* a small group of men enjoying the king's greatest confidence, continued to meet in the king's apartments to discuss with him important matters of state and to provide him with their confidential advice on these affairs.

The most important officials in the royal administration were the chancellor, custodian of the seals of state and head of the judicial structure; the superintendent of finance, chief financial officer under the crown; and four secretaries of state. The French secretaries of state carried out many functions of royal government, from the king's private clerks to advisors and supervisors of foreign affairs. Under Henri II and through the remainder of the century, the division of responsibility among the four secretaries was geographical rather than topical. For this purpose France was divided into four quarters with one secretary in charge of domestic correspondence and affairs in each sector and also foreign matters involving countries adjacent to France in that particular direction. The distribution of assignments varied, but they continued to combine both domestic and foreign affairs. After 1574, when Henri III became king of France, Nicolas de Neufville, seigneur de Villeroy, became the dominant figure in the secretariat and one of the most important men in the entire administration.

The role of the Parlement de Paris gained in importance during the century, but it remained primarily a judicial and administrative organ of the crown. As an instrument of royal authority, it gave legal sanction to decrees of the crown by formal registration in the minutes of the parlement, and helped curtail the activities of some of the unruly nobles. As a judicial organ, the Parlement de Paris stood next to the king as the highest tribunal in France. During the disastrous days of the League, the parlement tried to pursue a nonpartisan course based on what it believed to be the best interests of the country and not of the particular factions that were tearing one another apart, but it succeeded only in barely preserving its own existence until better days arrived.

Provincial supervision and law enforcement were still in the hands of the great nobles. Although the magnates were now mainly crown-appointed governors rather than independent rulers, some of them had become almost as powerful as their ancestors had been. Governorships were subdivided into units administered by local officials with judicial and executive authority from the crown. The chief judicial bodies in the provinces were still the provincial parlements, which exercised jurisdiction over a wide range of cases.

In the final analysis, the abilities a monarch and his chief officials could exercise in person, rather than the bureaucratic institutions at their disposal, counted most in sixteenth-century government in France, as in other countries. Structures, procedures, and organs of administration existed, sometimes in a very sophisticated hierarchy, but they seldom functioned in fact as they did in theory. The personal relations among people with power was still of paramount importance. During the second half of the sixteenth century, especially, the institutions of French government faltered and sometimes failed entirely. As a result, bizarre forms of private allegiance and patronage, sometimes called bastard feudalism by modern historians, arose among powerful nobles and their clients, and among those of other classes and orders. Occasionally these new relationships became institutionalized and developed into powerful affiliations that, as in the case of the Catholic League, aroused such great emotional and ideological feelings that they mushroomed into serious threats to the monarchy and to the very life of the nation.

The Crisis of the French Crown

Among the festivities that followed the signing of the Treaty of Cateau-Cambrésis was the celebration of the marriage alliance linking the former foes in "perpetual peace" by holy and political matrimony. Philip II, king of Spain, having lost his second wife, Mary Tudor, took as his third wife Elizabeth of Valois, daughter of the French king. The solemn ceremonies climaxed in a great tourney, with the king of France himself eagerly participating. The excitement and frivolity, however, suddenly turned into tragedy. In the final course of the day, Henri II was struck in the eye with the splintered butt of his opponent's broken lance. A few days later he died an agonizing death.

The throne of France now passed to Henri's sickly fifteen-year-old son, Francis II (1559–60). Although of legal age to rule, Francis had neither the intellectual capacity nor the strength of character to control the centrifugal forces that were now unleashed. Dominated by his wife's uncles, Duke Francis of Guise and his brother, the cardinal of Lorraine, the king was unable to do more than survive for eighteen months before he followed his father to the grave. Francis's nine-year-old brother, Charles, was the next to occupy the French throne (1560–74). Frightened by the whole affair, and with little to recommend him anyway except a fair complexion and a "round pretty face," Charles IX was content to remain in the protective custody of his mother, Catherine de' Medici. Plagued with chronic ill health and jealous of his more robust and competent younger brothers, Charles did little more than preside over the first painful rounds of governmental disintegration. His humiliation was ended only by his death in 1574.

The third of Henri II's sons seemed to have come from a different stamp than his brothers. Most loved by his mother, yet the least dominated by her, Henri III (1574–89) also possessed greater natural endowments than the others. Robust and highly intelligent, he had commanded the royal army in its victories over the Huguenots at Jarnac and Moncontour when he was only eighteen. Through the caprices of Polish politics and the constant maneuvering of his mother, Henri was elected king of Poland in 1573. He was uncomfortable there, however, feeling like an exile in a strange world. A year later when his brother died, Henri escaped from the royal castle in Cracow and fled across

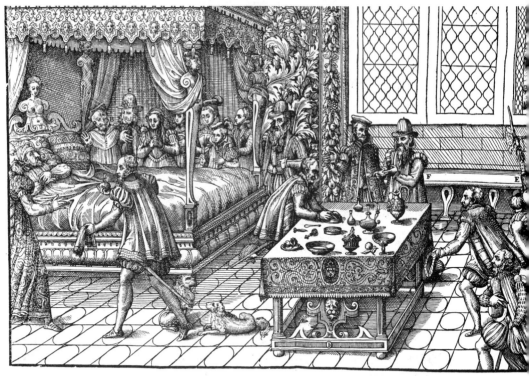

The Death of Henri II *attended by the court physicians and surrounded by members of the court and his family. From Jean Perrissin,* Histoires diverses qui sont memorables *(Geneva, 1570).*

Charles IX of France. *This portrait of the king at about fifteen years of age, by François Clouet, shows a remarkable resemblance to his mother, Catherine de' Medici.*

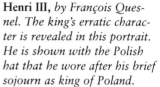

Henri III, *by François Ques-nel. The king's erratic charac-ter is revealed in this portrait. He is shown with the Polish hat that he wore after his brief sojourn as king of Poland.*

the frontier, with the Poles in hot pursuit. He was twenty-three when he be-came king of France. The next fifteen years saw the continuing decline of the monarchy as this promising ruler turned out to be the greatest blight of all on the Valois name. Completely untrustworthy, dissolute, and perhaps psychotic, Henri III dissipated his reign in alternate orgies of wild debauchery and abject penance. His homosexuality scandalized many. Distrusting the queen mother as much as the other crown officials, he surrounded himself with lap dogs and perfumed palace playmates, upon whom he bestowed the choicest titles, hon-ors, and lands. Henri III was preceded to the grave by his ambitious younger brother, Francis, duke of Anjou, leaving the throne to be fought over for an-other five years before the Huguenot king of Navarre, Henri of Bourbon, was crowned Henri IV in 1594.

Catherine de' Medici

In the meantime, the one stabilizing influence of the decadent Valois monarchy was the queen mother, Catherine de' Medici (spelled Médicis in French). Born in Florence in 1519, the daughter of Lorenzo the Magnificent's grandson, Catherine was orphaned at the age of twenty days. Maturing quickly in the chaotic years of the Italian wars and the early Habsburg-Valois conflicts, Catherine at fourteen married the duke d'Orléans (Henri II) as a pawn in Francis I's alliance negotiations with Pope Clement VII,

Catherine de' Medici. *This portrait, done by an anonymous painter, seems to show the heavy load of responsibility and frustration that Catherine carried as queen mother of chaotic France.*

her uncle. Catherine's experience as wife of the dauphin of France was not an easy one. Although Henri appreciated her and treated her with respect, his heart belonged to another woman, the vibrant and intelligent Diane de Poitiers, who was almost twenty years his senior. Henri bestowed upon Diane all of the favors and riches he possessed. Catherine repressed her jealousy and bided her time. For ten years their marriage was barren. Court gossip had it that she would soon be put away. Then Catherine's star began to ascend. In the next twelve years, she gave birth to ten children, seven of whom lived. After Henri's death, Catherine shaped her public policy around these children.

Catherine de' Medici was an intelligent and capable woman, alert to the intellectual and cultural influences of the time, and responsive to their manifestations in France. In outward demeanor she was always graceful, dignified, and courteous; in more intimate company she was charming and amiable. Brantôme, who knew her, described her as "Rich and of very fine presence; of great majesty, but very gentle when need was; of noble appearance and good grace." The Venetian ambassador, Giovanni Correr, was impressed by her physical strength and enthusiasm: "She has a strong and vigorous constitution, and there is no one in the court who can keep pace with her when walking. She takes a great deal of exercise, which gives her an appetite. She eats well and of all things indifferently. . . . Her industry in affairs causes a general wonder and astonishment. No step, however unimportant, is taken without her."

At the same time, Catherine was politically ambitious, even unscrupulous. She would stop at nothing to assure the ascendence and success of her children, even though she showed them little affection. Her possessive maternalism was the greatest flaw in her character, and contributed immeasurably to her own and her children's misery, and to the misfortune of France. Nevertheless, Catherine's concern was not just for her children. She was equally devoted to the success and tranquility of her adopted country, but was never able to convince the French people of that. To them she was always a foreigner, the Italian "shopkeeper's daughter." Another obstacle stood in her way, a barrier that made it impossible for her to achieve the success of which she might have been capable—her sex. In addition to the general dislike of female rulers, France was shackled with the Salic Law, which forbade succession in the female line (at least everyone thought it did). The Venetian ambassador summarized French opinion when he reported: "It is sufficient to say that she is a woman, a foreigner, and a Florentine to boot, born of a simple house, altogether beneath the dignity of the kingdom of France." Besides, Catherine de' Medici was not the queen, only the queen mother (and twice regent, for a total of 12 years) but she made the most of it, acting as surrogate for her ineffectual sons. Many accepted her authority, however reluctantly, as the only alternative to total political chaos.

Catherine's motives were usually honorable, yet her ability was insufficient to cope with the forces and personalities tearing France apart after 1559. She hoped to balance and appease the various forces and preserve the integrity of the crown, but the intensity of religious fanaticism, along with her own maternal vulnerability; forced her into taking the kind of extreme actions she herself abhorred. Her son-in-law and rival, Henri of Navarre, later expressed a sympathy for her that we can concur with:

> But I ask you, I ask you what a poor woman could do, left by the death of her husband, with five little children on her arms, and two families in France who were thinking to grasp the crown—ours and the Guises. Was she not compelled to play strange parts to deceive first one and then the other, in order to guard, as she has done, her sons, who have successively reigned through the wise conduct of that shrewd woman? I am surprised that she never did worse.

Social and Economic Upheaval

The mid-century financial crisis that forced Henri II into bankruptcy and brought the Peace of Cateau-Cambrésis caused serious damage to the French economy. Recovery was irregular during the 1560s and early 1570s because of recurring civil war. In 1573, following the Saint Bartholomew's Day Massacre, another economic setback occurred, followed by similar crises in 1586–87, 1589–91, and 1597. As the intensity of the wars increased, so did the frequency of financial failure. The potential agricultural resources of France were impressive even then, but other factors, some of them uncontrollable, combined to make this an unsettled period for the French economy.

One upsetting feature was the price revolution that gnawed away wages, profits, and investments. Not yet as extreme as in Spain, the inflation in France nevertheless caused great distress. Especially severe increases occurred in grain prices, which rose erratically throughout the century. Regional price fluctuations within the country caused shifts in the normal movement of labor. Seasonal French workers from Languedoc, for example, went to Spain, where they could get higher wages, then returned to France to spend them. Relatively few, however, were able to take advantage of the situation in this way. Most workers came out on the short end of the price-wage squeeze.

With the movement of silver from Spain into France and the general reverse migration of gold, along with the seasonal fluctuations, French currency became highly unstable, especially during the latter phases of the civil wars. As in the rest of Europe, France employed two monetary systems: a money in which people actually made transactions (that is, hard currency) and a theoretical money of account, used in reckoning balance sheets. The latter was intended to control, or at least modulate, the effects of the variable moneys of exchange. In the course of the late sixteenth-century, even the money of account, the *livre tournois*, fluctuated and devaluated until it was finally abandoned in 1577. For the rest of the century, the *écu* and the *teston* served both as circulating coins and as moneys of account. The French monarchy fueled this financial chaos by regularly lowering the precious-metal content of its coins, a practice that had repercussions for credit as well as for the value of hard money. Not until 1602 was this "monetary anarchy" ended by the forceful intervention of Henri IV and the duke of Sully.

Trade and Industry   French trade also declined drastically after its mid-century high. Shipping and shipbuilding were encouraged by Henri II, but during the reigns of his three sons they were both neglected. The erratic policies of the crown with regard to import and export regulations also tended to depress trade. Grain was only reluctantly exported from France in the sixteenth century, and then only when there was a great surplus. Prohibitions on the export of wool and textiles continued into the reign of Henri IV. Some imports of manufactured goods were also limited. Nevertheless, in 1585 Henri III tried to force northern merchandise en route to Spain and Italy to pass through the customs house at Lyon to be taxed. Some English and Flemish merchants reacted by avoiding France altogether, carrying their wares either directly by sea or overland through Luxembourg, Franche-Comté, and Savoy.

France was favored with many good harbors, however, both on the Atlantic and the Mediterranean, and continued to occupy a position of some importance in international commerce. Rouen, for example, was a trading center not only for overland traffic but also for seagoing cargoes moving in all directions. Saint Malo on the Brittany coast was the chief port of the cloth trade with Spain as well as for the fisheries of the North Sea. It was also the base for the most persistent pirates of the Atlantic. Nantes, to the south, was the closest rival of Saint Malo in cod fishing and in trade with England, since Le Havre only began its rise to importance after 1572 when it ceased being a pawn in the civil wars. La Rochelle was a more vulnerable port but, along with Bordeaux, provided the trading outlet for the salt, wine, and cereals of central

France. The Mediterranean was dominated by Marseille, the chief port of all France in terms of volume and value of trade, an indication of the direction of French commerce in the sixteenth century. The Levant trade was considered vital to the national interest and was protected by the heaviest armed galleys in the French service. By treaty agreement with the Turkish sultan, merchants of other European countries could trade with the Ottoman Empire only under the protection and flag of France.

Active government involvement both aided and hindered the industrial development of France. However, the dislocation of populations, the stagnation of commerce, and the insecurity of industrial enterprise during the religious wars caused an alarming constriction of industrial output. Manufacturing was encouraged in many fields, especially glassmaking, linen cloth production, tapestry weaving, silk cloth and velvet making; and paper manufacturing and printing. But the attempt by the crown to supervise and control the guild system resulted in serious conflicts with the whole artisan class. A royal ordinance of 1581 laid down uniform rules for handicraft guilds and made membership in them compulsory. However, the later Valois were no more able to enforce such regulations than their predecessors had been. At the Estates General of 1576, Jean Bodin, spokesman for the third estate of Vernandois, advocated a program of rational government controls based upon the protection of French manufacturers against foreign imports and the export of salt, wine, and wheat, the "inexhaustible mines of France." Yet the country had to wait another ninety years, until the coming of Colbert, before a comprehensive system of state mercantilism developed in France.

Agriculture and the Plight of the Peasants
In the meantime, agriculture had its own problems. During the first half of the century it had prospered. New land was brought under cultivation and productivity was generally high. The costs of Francis I's and Henri II's wars, though, weighed heavily on the French peasants, and the physical devastation and disruption of the civil wars brought havoc. Much of the agricultural land was deserted, and the rural proletariat was left without income and without rights. Many estates passed into the hands of the bourgeoisie as aristocratic proprietors abandoned or sold them and dedicated themselves to the military crusade against their religious rivals. Some of the lesser nobles already felt squeezed by inflation by midcentury. Their situation did not improve with time. Rents were frequently fixed, yet their actual value declined as prices rose. Having been deprived of their traditional occupation by the Peace of Cateau-Cambrésis, many of these lesser nobles turned to privateering and freebooting; some gave their allegiance to greater lords; others joined the spirited and active Huguenots, among whom they could retain their coveted rank and pursue the activity they knew best.

One advantage the nobles continued to demand, and receive, was exemption from the principal royal tax, the *taille*. The burden of this levy fell principally on the peasants. The entire third estate, from cotters to cabinetmakers, had to pay it, but the wealthy and influential burghers usually could finagle exemptions of one kind or another. Sometimes whole cities obtained extensive tax relief, but when they did it usually meant that other regions had to make up the difference. Under Henri III taxes increased alarmingly. Although the *taille* supplied approximately half of the royal revenue, it was not the only source of income; *aides* and other sales taxes, customs duties, and the *gabelle* (salt tax) also accounted for a large share, but not enough. The crown was almost continually in financial distress during the civil war period and resorted to heavy borrowing, forced loans, and even confiscation to meet its rising expenditures. The relatively frequent summoning of the Estates General by Francis II and Henri III was partly an effort to solve the chronic financial crisis. That it was generally unsuccessful may be attributed to the failure of the monarchy itself than to the inadequacy of economic resources.

The peasants of France, as elsewhere, were handicapped by many uncontrollable factors of nature as well as by the seignorial regime. Life for the lower classes was always fragile, as hunger, cold, and disease weighed heavily upon them. When combined with the recurrent wrath of war these scourges often dominated the life of the humble folk (*menu peuple*, as they were called in France), who made up more than 90 percent of the population. Death always lingered near, not only from brigands and beasts but also from malnutrition. Agricultural techniques and tools were pitifully inadequate, and knowledge of agronomy and plant science were rudimentary at best. For most of the masses, fever, scurvy, tuberculosis, and dysentery and other gastrointestinal diseases were always present, and devastating epidemics of cholera, typhus, and plague usually accompanied war and famine years.

Peasants of course depended on the vicissitudes of nature for their livelihood, and the means at their disposal to understand, let alone control, the elements of climate and weather were nil. Unable to distinguish between the natural and the supernatural, the popular mentality took an animist view of this confusing and menacing world, which they believed to be ruled not by coherent laws but by the caprice of incorporeal beings who dominated the world. These demons and their earthling agents, sorcerers and witches, were thought to control the forces of nature. To combat these evil spirits and bring rain when it was needed, or to prevent frost, storms, or the plague, people relied heavily on religious rites of conjuration, processions, and special prayers and Masses. They also participated in other kinds of ritualistic magic and incantations, sometimes superficially camouflaged in religious ritual. Some rural groups even engaged in ritual combat against the unseen forces of evil. Likewise, relics, talismans, and magic potions were all weapons in the peasants' continual struggle against the uncertainties of nature.

Religious Schism

The deterioration of French administration under the unhappy rule of Catherine de' Medici and her sons, and the accompanying stagnation of the French economy, was both a cause and effect of the heightened religious rivalry of the period. These factors, with the desperate feuding of noble families, produced half a century of turmoil and devastation unequaled since the middle decades of the Hundred Years' War.

The polarization and intensification of religious conflict in France after 1559 was due in part to the uncompromising nature of militant Calvinism and Counter-Reformation Catholicism. Calvinism expanded rapidly in France after mid-century, especially among the urban populations of the south and southwest, and most noticeably among the artisan class. Many things about Calvinism seemed to appeal to these skilled laborers, but particularly impressive to them was the clear and confident logic of the doctrine of election and the cohesive effectiveness of Calvinist organization. As a part of the congregation of the saints, these capable and socially involved citizens could indulge their penchant for reform while maintaining strong group ties within their social order and with the larger "body of Christ."

Their own almost unanimous declaration of religious motivation should neither be ignored nor misunderstood. Great skepticism is voiced today as to the sincerity of their religious pronouncements, but it must be remembered that the sixteenth-century conception of religion was a much broader, yet narrower idea than it is in the twentieth century. It included many considerations that we would now regard as distinctly political, social, or perhaps even economic, while at the same time frequently excluding some ethical and other behavioral patterns that we call religious. This was especially true of Calvinism, in which political fibers were intimately interwoven with spiritual and theological threads to produce a social fabric that was political, economic, and devotional, yet at the same time thoroughly religious.

The rapid military-aristocratic infiltration into Calvinist ranks after 1559 did not alter the basic orientation of the Huguenots as much as it increased their power and significance. Always both aristocratic and radical, Calvinist thought now became even more threatening to the conservative Catholic government. The sense of mission that Calvinism infused into its members also appealed to these unemployed soldiers, who felt it was their particular calling to reform the government of France. Catholics, of course, took alarm at this rapid growth of Protestantism.

Political and Religious Factions

On the higher political levels, the interaction of politics and religion was equally involved. The natural rivalries among the great lords and the princes of the blood were intensified by the Reformation. Four major factions were involved in the struggle for power and supremacy. Surpassing all others in ambition and arrogance was the family of Guise, latecomers into the French aristocracy from neighboring Lorraine, where they had outgrown their local boundaries and volunteered themselves to the service of Francis I. The duke of Guise, victor of the siege of Calais and defender of Metz, and his brother, the cardinal of Lorraine, were the leading scions of the house during the first troubled years following the death of Henri II. With their younger brothers—the cardinal of Guise, the duke of Aumale, the marquis of Elboeuf, and the duke of Longueville, and their sister Mary (wife of King James V of Scotland and mother of Mary Queen of Scots)—the Guises were able to exert an unusually powerful influence on the throne, especially when it was occupied by young Francis II, husband of their niece, Mary Queen of Scots. The Guise faction stood at one extreme in the power struggle, placing allegiance to its own dynasty and to international Catholicism higher than duty to either the nation or the Valois monarchy.

Also Catholic, but more moderate and always loyal to the king, was the house of Montmorency, headed by the venerable old soldier and constable of France, Duke Anne de Montmorency (1493–1567). This was an old French family, but only in the reign of Henri II had it been raised to the pinnacle of power that it exercised under the great constable. Montmorency's reputation suffered seriously with his defeat at Saint Quentin in 1557, and his influence declined after the death of his royal benefactor. His sons, however, continued to play a leading role in the political and military affairs of France.

The third faction imposing itself upon the French crown was the house of Châtillon—three members of it at least—nephews of Montmorency, who embraced the Reformed religion and became active supporters of the Huguenots. The most prominent of these was Gaspard de Coligny (1519–72), admiral of France and effective leader of the politicomilitary wing of French Protestantism until his assassination in 1572. Coligny had been raised in the king's service, and was always a loyalist, but he was also devoted to the cause of securing freedom of worship for the Reformed faith, which he embraced. He was supported and strengthened in this resolve by his courageous wife, Charlotte Laval. Coligny continued to be a leading voice in the councils of government until his persistent efforts to enlist the support of Charles IX in favor of the Dutch Protestants brought him into conflict with the queen mother.

Finally, at the opposite extreme from the Guise was the house of Bourbon, princes of the blood who stood next to the Valois in the royal line of succession. Antoine of Bourbon, who was also prince of Béarn and king of Navarre, vacillated between Protestantism and Catholicism, depending upon the immediacy of external pressures and the extent of foreseeable advantages. Yet his wife, Jeanne d'Albret (1528–72), daughter of Marguerite, that other indomitable queen of Navarre, took her Protestantism and her heritage very seriously. Willful, courageous, and stubbornly resolute, the queen of Navarre championed the cause of the Protestants in France. "Your feeble arguments do not dent my tough skull," she defiantly responded to the papal legate, Cardinal Armagnac, "I am serving God and He knows how to sustain his cause." With this same toughness, following the death of her husband, Jeanne d'Albret turned her southern kingdom of Navarre into a Protestant enclave and vigorously supported the Huguenots until her own death in 1572. She passed on to her illustrious son, Henri of Navarre, her religious devotion and her determination to oppose those forces that threatened to prolong the disruption of France. The most vociferous and pugnacious of the Huguenot leaders was the king of Navarre's younger brother, Louis of Bourbon, prince of Condé (1530–69). An implacable enemy of the duke of Guise as well as an impassioned foe of Catholicism, Condé was the active agent of Huguenot military organization and also the most aggressive proponent of the use of force in opposing the Catholics.

Clearly, multiple forces of dissension and decay were at work to destroy the domestic tranquility of France and upset its preeminence in European affairs. Political, economic, social, and religious grievances, along with personal ambitions and incompetence, each thrust itself into the precariously balanced French society, throwing it into such disarray that almost half a century passed before it was able to recover its former position and strength.

Catherine de' Medici and the French Civil Wars

As early as March 1560, a number of hotheaded Huguenot nobles, condoned but not led by Condé, were ready to unleash their pent-up frustrations by plotting to kidnap the king, kill the Guises, and advance the Bourbons to the throne. The conspiracy of Amboise was discovered, however, and retaliation was harsh. Nine months later, Guise domination seemed to be ended when the death of Francis II brought the nine-year-old Charles IX to the throne and allowed Catherine de' Medici to begin exercising her influence as royal regent. A series of toleration edicts in 1561 and early 1562 evidenced her attempt to reconcile the contending forces in France and bring about what we would call a deescalation of tensions. Meanwhile, the leaders of the contending parties were meeting together in a vain effort to reach a more-or-less permanent solution to their differences. The queen mother and her equally conciliatory chancellor, Michel de l'Hôpital, hoped to avoid a confrontation, from which there would be little hope of withdrawal without bloodshed. For more than a year, Catherine succeeded by conciliation and diplomacy in staving off the conflict. Yet the schism in France could not be healed without fundamental compromise, and neither side would relinquish any of its considered principles.

In March 1562, the duke of Guise, with a small detachment of soldiers, massacred a Huguenot congregation at Vassy, near Châlons, and the half century of civil war began. The Protestants were not unprepared for combat, and before the month had ended Coligny and Condé were at the gates of Paris with a formidable Huguenot army. Desperately, Catherine de' Medici committed her fate to Guise and his associates. Month by month the bloody duel continued as central France turned into a battleground of advancing and retreating armies. In spite of significant reinforcements from German Calvinists and mercenaries, the Huguenots were gradually driven southward, and after a decisive defeat at Dreux they began negotiations for peace. The Peace of Amboise (March 1563) ended only the first phase of the conflict, however, serving as a mere truce between even more destructive encounters yet to come. That truce was broken in the fall of 1567 and hostilities opened again. Once more the Huguenots pushed to the environs of Paris and once more the city held as the shifting tide of victory went to the royal forces. This time the peace lasted only a few months before the third civil war erupted in August 1568.

The Saint Batholomew's Day Massacre. *This sequential engraving shows Coligny at left on horseback being wounded by a gunshot. At right he is depicted later being killed in bed and then thrown out of the window.*

The Massacre of Saint Bartholomew's Day

By 1572 it finally appeared that both sides were willing to end their bloodletting. The Peace of Saint Germain was consummated in a great celebration in Paris on Saint Bartholomew's Day, August 24. The highlight of the festivities was the marriage of Marguerite of Valois, sister of the king, and young Henri of Navarre, thus uniting the two warring parties. For the occasion, thousands of Huguenots were in Paris, including their leader, Coligny (Condé had fallen three years earlier). For some time, Catherine de' Medici had been concerned over the Huguenot refusal to put down their arms. She was even more disturbed by the susceptibility of her son, the king, to the strong influence of Coligny, who was now advocating French intervention in the Netherlands to assist the revolutionaries there against the king of Spain.

The combination of personal jealousy and her fear that Coligny's proposal would lead France into a disastrous war with Spain persuaded Catherine to abandon her usual levelheadedness and resort to violence. She convinced herself that the safety and security of France depended upon Coligny's removal. Henri of Guise (son of the former duke who had been murdered in 1563, allegedly at Coligny's instigation) was only too willing to carry out the bloody deed. What began as a quiet murder, however, turned into a national disaster. The assassins botched their assignment, severely wounding the admiral but not killing him as they intended. The Huguenots reacted spontaneously to this treachery by demanding punishment of the culprits and threatening to retaliate in kind. As far as Catherine de' Medici was concerned, the situation was critical, and in the face of this crisis she panicked, issuing, instead of an apology, an order for the extermination of all the Huguenot leaders in Paris. After that the frenzied mobs took over. Two or three thousand persons were slain in Paris before the night was over, and several times that many died in the provinces, where the carnage spread like a forest fire. The true extent of the massacre will probably never be accurately known, but the horror of the event will live as a testimony to the inhumanity of people who allow the base passions of fear, hatred, jealousy, or rampant ideology to displace reason and humanity.

For the moment, it appeared that the massacre of Saint Bartholomew's Day had ended the wars of religion. Yet now, more than ever before, the French Calvinists believed they had a cause to uphold. Their leaders were dead or in prison (Henri of Navarre and his cousin, Prince Henri of Condé, were detained in Paris), but their spirit was not broken, and their numbers not as decimated as was thought. Within weeks after the massacre, the Huguenots took up their swords to avenge the deed. They no longer employed the fiction that it was the house of Guise rather than the king whom they were fighting; they openly denounced and attacked the decadent Valois monarchy.

Huguenot theorists and pamphleteers, from Theodore Beza and François Hotman to Hubert Languet and Philip du Plessy-Mornay, eagerly set forth their views. Hotman's *Francogallia* (1573) maintained that the current arbitrary monarchy was a breach in the continuity of French constitutional history, whose Frankish roots were based on the principle of elective monarchy and a "common council of the Nation" to uphold the fundamental freedoms of the people. Beza's *Right of Magistrates* (1574) claimed that sovereignty rested not with the king but with the community, and that it was the right and duty of "inferior magistrates" to assume the leadership in resisting an unworthy or tyrannical ruler. The anonymous *Vindiciae contra Tyrannos* (Vengeances Against Tyrants, 1579) justified the Huguenot rebellion on grounds of the crown's disobedience to God. It denounced the king's perfidy and declared the right of national rebellion. The ruler had severed his contract with God, it claimed; the countercontract between the people and their king was consequently annulled. In the hearts of many Huguenots, from this point on, the true king of France was no longer Charles of Valois but Henri of Navarre who, three months after the massacre, escaped from Paris, renounced his short-lived reconciliation with the Catholic church, and assumed the leadership of the Huguenots.

In 1574 the sickly Charles IX died and was succeeded by his twenty-three-year-old brother, Henri III. The war was resumed a year later and continued until a truce was reached in April 1576. The Peace of Monsieur, ending the fifth civil war, sent a sudden shock through the Catholic body of France. The liberality of that agreement was without precedent in the sixteenth century, giving concessions to the Huguenots that almost put Protestantism on an equal legal footing with Catholicism. The direct result of this step toward religious toleration was the founding of various Catholic leagues for the purpose of combating Protestantisn and preserving the traditions of the Catholic monarchy. The leagues were at first loosely organized and had little actual strength, but they eventually grew into the great Catholic League which became, under the leadership of Henri of Guise, a powerful organization in France and, through its diplomatic alignments with Spain and the papacy, an instrument of international consequence.

In the meantime, the duke of Anjou, younger brother of the French king and only remaining heir of the Valois dynasty, suddenly died in June 1584, and a new phase of the religious wars began, both in the Netherlands and in France. Now Henri of Navarre, next in the line of succession, according to the Salic Law, seemed on the threshold of victory.

Politiques and the Catholic League

Anjou's death had immediate and long-lasting results. Now that the Huguenots stood to gain the throne of France, their attitude toward monarchy in general, and toward the French throne in particular, began to change. In the pamphlet literature of the late 1580s, the Protestant writers took a new position. Abandoning their previous criticism of the monarchy, the Huguenots now became its staunchest defenders—not of the decadent monarchy of Henri III, but of the theory of monarchical government as it had developed in France.

Huguenot political philosophy after 1584 was approaching that of the *politiques,* the "center party" that was desperately calling for an end to the religious wars. The *politiques* emerged during the early 1570s in protest against the continuing civil upheavals that were tearing the heart out of France. Not advocates of religious toleration by conviction, the *politiques* nevertheless believed that religious coexistence was preferable to mutual annihilation through religious war. Religious confessions, they maintained, should be subordinated to the political well-being of the nation. In their anxiety to deemphasize the religious issues in favor of political considerations, they exalted the position of the king higher than anyone previously had dared. As the wars continued, the *politiques* became more favorable to royal absolutism.

The most vigorous statement of the *politique* position was Jean Bodin's *Six livres de la République* (Six Books of the Commonwealth, 1576). In this important book, Bodin (ca. 1529–96) declared that the monarch is not limited by religious bodies, Catholic or Protestant, or by representative assemblies such as the Estates General, or even by the noble magistrates. Sovereignty rests solely in the monarch himself. The king is not subject to statutory law or to the declarations of magistrates, Bodin contended. The king is above them all, and he alone determines policy and decrees what is to be law. Now, with the possibility of Henri of Navarre succeeding to the throne of France, it became easier for many Frenchmen, especially those of moderate Catholic or Protestant persuasion, to accept this doctrine of absolute monarchy, particularly in its full exposition by Pierre de Belloy after 1585. Belloy's affirmation that the king is the direct image of God on earth leaves little room to doubt the extent to which the *politiques* were willing to promote royal power in order to end the civil wars.

As long as Henri III still lived and ruled, however, the factional and religious schism widened. After 1584 the theoretical position formerly occupied by the Huguenots was taken by the extreme Catholic leaguers who, fearful over the prospect of a Protestant becoming king of France, strongly opposed the theory of absolute monarchy. Basing their arguments for limitations of the king's power on the ancient motto, *une foi, une loi, un roi* ("one faith, one law, one king"), the League pamphleteers flooded France with religious arguments for maintaining a Catholic crown and opposing the possible succession of the Huguenot king. They even argued for popular sovereignty, but of course what they meant by "popular" was Catholic. Yet it was due more to the complete incompetence of Henri III that France succumbed briefly to the dominance of the League than it was to the cogency of League political theory.

The War of the Three Henries	In December 1584, representatives of the Spanish king and of the Catholic League signed a formal pact of assistance, known as the Treaty of Joinville. In the following year, the League frightened Henri III into

submitting to its leadership in a major military offensive against the Huguenots. The resulting so-called War of the Three Henries (for Henri of Guise, Henri of Valois, and Henri of Navarre, the latter being assisted by two more Henries, the prince of Condé and the duke of Montmorency-Damville) turned France into a complete political, economic, and religious chaos.

In the autumn of 1587, Navarre planned a two-pronged attack against royal and Guise forces with the aid of English money, Swiss mercenaries, and a large invading force of German *landsknechts* from the Palatinate. At Coutras, near Bordeaux, the flower of the royal army, commanded by one of the king's minions, was all but annihilated by Navarre's mercenaries. Meanwhile in the northeast, the duke of Guise scattered Navarre's invading German-Swiss army with an inferior force of his own followers. Piqued by Henri III's treachery in not providing him with royal troops, Guise capitalized on his great popularity in Paris to make a new show of force against the king. Coordinated through the Spanish ambassador and the strong League organization in Paris, Guise entered the capital on 9 May 1588, in direct defiance of the king's orders. Three days later, following a massive demonstration by Guise admirers, known as the Day of the Barricades, the king was forced to flee to Chartres for safety. Guise was now king of Paris! With the sympathetic announcements of other cities, principally in the north, the League affiliates became the virtual rulers of the northern half of France.

When confirmation of the defeat of the Spanish Armada reached France, Henri III took new courage. He peremptorily dismissed his chancellor and secretaries of state, selected a new staff he could trust, and made preparations for the Estates General that was to meet at Blois in September. By Christmas he reached the climax of his newfound courage, when he had the duke of Guise and his brother, the cardinal of Guise, murdered. The reaction from Paris and other League cities was immediate and violent. Henri was denounced as a traitor and a tyrant. Every Catholic pulpit rang with curses and condemnations. Instead of regaining control of his realm, he now reaped open revolution. In desperation the king fled to the camp of his former foe, Henri of Navarre, and together they prepared an attack on Paris. Before success could be achieved, however, Henri III was in turn struck down by an assassin. Navarre immediately declared himself king of France as Henri IV, but half of the country was still in the hands of the Catholic League.

Determined to prevent the Huguenot king from mounting the throne of Catholic France, the League announced the accession of the aged cardinal of Bourbon, uncle of Henri IV but an associate of Guise and the League, as King Charles X, and invited Philip of Spain to support their cause. The duke of Parma was called from Flanders to lead a Spanish crusade. Quickly marching south, he lifted Navarre's siege of Paris in the summer of 1590, and a year later again frustrated Henri's attempt to take the city by force. The turning point had been reached, however. Parma perished in this last campaign. No commander in Philip's pay could adequately fill his boots. The League, too, gradually broke up as its allegiance split between Paris and the rest of France. In 1593 Henri IV further undercut the League by announcing his reconversion to Catholicism. Paris, he thought, was "worth a Mass." A few months later he entered the capital in triumph. The *politiques,* the Bourbons, and the concept of absolute monarchy emerged victorious.

Recovery Under Henri IV

Henri IV's five-year struggle to win the crown of France did not end in total victory. Ahead still lay years of trial and floundering before the Bourbon monarchy would rule a prosperous and unified kingdom. The degree of recovery and regeneration achieved by Henri IV is a measure of his administrative skill and his ability to unite the dissident factions of the nation in a common cause.

Henri IV was an energetic king who approached every task with the same zest he displayed in pursuing the wild stag or in making love to court ladies. As proudly stated by one of his contemporaries, "His nature is stirring and full of life, like a true Frenchman." He did indeed have a passion for activity and display reminiscent of Francis I, although he lacked the Renaissance king's refinement and devotion to art and letters. Twenty years of civil war had revealed Henri's courage and aggressiveness in battle, his magnanimity in victory, and his practicality and resolution in defeat. It had also displayed his sensuality in the pursuit of pleasure and his passion for gallantry and display. The famous white plume he wore into battle was a symbol of his bravado. And yet, in the

Henry IV. *The Roi Gallant is colorfully portrayed in this painting from the French School, now located in the Musée de Peinture, Grenoble, France. It captures both his flair and magnanimity.*

words of a modern expert on his reign, "This scruffy, odoriferous squire from the Pyrennes once in power showed himself to have a masterly grasp of the problems of his day."

By 1595 Henri had plenty of problems. France was desperately divided on political, religious, and social issues. The League was still strong and active in Brittany and Burgundy; moderate Catholics and *politiques* resented the ultramontanism (militant papalism) of the Jesuits; Huguenots were disillusioned and perplexed by the king's religious betrayal; the *noblesse d'épée* (the traditional sword-bearing nobles) distrusted the *noblesse de robe* (the newer judicial and magisterial class); the burghers were irate over the exorbitant price of food; and throughout west-central France, the peasants openly revolted against the landowners and tax gatherers. At the same time, the government floundered hopelessly in debt, remained at war with Spain, and compromised precariously with the papacy. Pope Clement VIII called for the extermination of the Protestants as a prerequisite for the king's absolution; the Huguenots demanded recognition and protection. The Bourbon dynasty itself was not secure. After twenty-one years of marriage to Marguerite of Valois, Henri still lacked a legitimate male heir. He sought a divorce so he could marry again, but the pope was reluctant to concede without an assurance of the king's faithfulness to the church.

Henri confronted his dilemmas calmly and confidently, and circumstances favored him. Fearing that an obdurate stand by Clement VIII might result in the kind of confrontation that had driven England from the Roman allegiance sixty years earlier, Jesuits in Rome persuaded the pope to grant the king both absolution and the divorce. Henri, with appropriate counterassurances of service to the church, proceeded next to end the schism in France by uniting the nation in a common cause, expulsion of the Spaniards. To assure his success, Henri negotiated for English military and financial assistance. He also successfully bribed several of the Catholic nobles who had been fighting for the League to join him in the liberation of France. One by one the rebel commanders either laid down their arms or committed their forces to the king's service. The last to surrender was the duke of Mercoeur, who held out in Brittany until March 1598.

The Treaty of Vervins and the Edict of Nantes

Finally, in May 1598, weary from years of struggle, the dying king of Spain agreed to the terms of the Treaty of Vervins. In his own alliance with Elizabeth, Henri IV had agreed not to make a separate peace with Spain. Yet France was as exhausted by the war as was Spain. Henri's costly subsidies had made victory as expensive as defeat, and he was therefore as anxious for peace as was Philip. The Treaty of Vervins restored the status quo between France and Spain roughly to that agreed upon at Cateau-Cambrésis. According to Henri it was an "*heureuse et aimable paix*" ("a happy and kind peace"); to the chief Spanish negotiator it was "*muy a propósito*" ("very timely").

Two weeks before the Treaty of Vervins, Henri IV took a major step toward reducing the internal stresses by issuing the Edict of Nantes, giving a large measure of religious and civil liberty to the Huguenots. By the terms of this edict, French Protestants were allowed freedom of conscience and were permitted to exercise their religion in all of the towns where they had been permitted to worship in previous treaties, plus many additional cities. They also gained a right to freely exercise their religion in the lands of Huguenot nobles. The edict declared the Huguenots eligible for public offices and guaranteed that they could use schools and other facilities on an equal basis with Catholics. Bipartisan judicial tribunals were established to give them fair treatment under the law. They also obtained some seventy-five fortified towns, including La Rochelle, Montpellier, and Montauban. The Edict of Nantes was a solid coup for Henri IV, because although many of his newfound Catholic friends were disturbed by the liberality of the act and some of the Huguenots were disappointed because it was still less than they had hoped and fought for, he won the support of many more by issuing it.

The Duke of Sully and Economic Reform

With the war ended and the Huguenots placated, Henri could now turn his attention to other vital problems—finances, government administration, and foreign affairs being among the most pressing. In his task he was ably assisted by several men who proved to be capable administrators and thoughtful servants. Among these were the Huguenot nobleman and financier, Maximilien de Béthune, duke of Sully,

whom Henri made superintendent of finances; Chancellor Pomponne de Bellièvre, a devoted and long-time servant of the French monarchy; and Secretary
of State Villeroy, a moderate Leaguer during the early 1590s who had previously served Henri III and Charles IX as secretary of state.

Sully's role in the centralization of French government under Henri IV was
especially large, involving military, naval, and foreign affairs as well as economic matters. It was as Henri's aggressive and hard-working finance minister
that Sully made his greatest mark on French history. Employing the old financial machinery that had served the Valois for more than a century, Sully instigated ruthless monetary reforms, established a bureaucratic order of sorts, and
introduced such efficiency into the corruption-ridden system of "farming out"
the collection of taxes to local agents that royal revenues were more than doubled in ten years. At the same time the government debt was drastically reduced, and for the first time in over a century an impressive surplus accumu-
lated in the royal treasury. Sully removed previous restrictions on grain export,
reintroduced silkworm cultivation into southern France, and reclaimed many
thousand acres of farmland. This active promotion of agriculture prompted
Henri's promise of a chicken in every peasant's pot every Sunday (a promise
that remained far from fulfilled, however).

Sully applied the same devotion to order and systematic attention to detail
in his assignments as director of communications, superintendent of fortifications and buildings, and grand master of artillery as he did to the superinten-
dency of finance. Some of his achievements in road construction, canal building, fortification, and military-naval construction were equally impressive.

Sully's ruthlessness, however, brought him into heated debate in the Council of State and particularly into confrontation with Chancellor Bellièvre, custodian of the laws and legal machinery of France. Their most serious disagreement was over the *Paulette,* Sully's proposal that the age-old selling of offices
be institutionalized into a regular system of royal revenue. By this system, purchased offices became hereditary and their tenure made secure upon the payment of an annual fee to the government. This practice, which added much to
the royal coffers during ensuing reigns, thus assisting the Bourbon rulers in
realizing their claim to absolute power, also curtailed that power by depriving
the king of complete authority over a large number of administrative offices.
The abuse of legalized venality remained until the French Revolution as one of
the legacies of the reign of Henri IV.

At the same time, Bellièvre's arguments for the rule of law helped establish
a tradition of order and legal procedure in France that carried the monarchy
through a period of centralized personal rule without allowing that rule to
become totally arbitrary. Through the traditional operation of the overlapping
judicial system, even Louis XIV was somewhat limited in his exercise of
absolutism.

Under Henri IV, French foreign policy again became consciously oriented
toward reducing the Habsburg influence in Europe. After the Peace of Vervins,
Henri pursued an active diplomacy intended to weaken Spanish power on all
fronts by supporting those states that were at war with Spain, and by strengthening the French influence through alliances with Spain's rivals. Toward this

end, Henri successfully negotiated a treaty with the grand duke of Tuscany (with an accompanying marriage to the grand duke's niece, Marie de' Medici), gained the friendship of the duke of Savoy, and concluded an alliance with Venice by 1607.

In his memoirs, Sully attributed to Henri a "Grand Design" to neutralize Habsburg power and establish an era of peace through protective alliances and a system of European councils dealing on different levels with local, national, and international affairs. There is no reliable evidence that Henri ever had such an orderly conception of international organization, but he did fear Habsburg power and geared his diplomacy to counter it. The death in 1609 of the duke of Cleves-Jülich, and that duchy's subsequent occupation by an imperial army, was the catalyst that made Henri openly anti-Habsburg, a cause institutionalized by then in the Protestant Union. In February 1610, Henri IV joined the Union to oppose the Habsburg action and to promote the candidacy of the Protestant elector of Brandenburg to the vacant duchy of Cleves-Jülich. At that crucial moment, however, an assassin's knife cut short Henri's own life, ending his brief and turbulent, yet uniquely successful, reign. When the aggrandizement of France and the French crown was resumed by Richelieu fourteen years later, it was along the lines already begun by the illustrious monarch, still lovingly revered by Frenchmen as "Henri le Grand."

The Cultural Conflict in France

The half century between the death of Henri II and the assassination of Henri IV was a period of cultural as well as social and political upheaval. The disorder and bloodshed of the religious wars could not help but affect French writers and artists—in a negative way, for the most part. Still, artistic creativity went on in spite of the civil wars, producing unique and lasting monuments to human sensitivity and intelligence at the same time that a large share of society was demonstrating the depravity and ruthlessness to which humanity could descend.

The principal patron of music, arts, and literature in France for almost half a century was the queen mother, Catherine de' Medici, whose opulent figure sailed through court life, in Wyndham Lewis's picturesque phrase, "like some stately galleon of the Indies run, armed and arrayed, riding majestic and enormous with full-bellying sails amid a fleet of skiffs and cockboats." Under her ubiquitous touch, the tone of court life was set. Catherine loved music. She employed hundreds of court musicians to give concerts regularly at the Louvre palace or wherever the court resided. Catherine was likewise attracted to the dance. Throughout her reign, even during the worst days of the civil wars, the Valois court was the scene of magnificent and elaborate balls sponsored by the queen mother.

Less needs to be said about French art of the period. Painting, especially, was at a low ebb. The best of the French painters were Antoine Caron, Jean Cousin, and François Clouet (see pages 150 and 232), whose classical miniatures, court portraits, and chalk drawings are familiar to every visitor to the

Louvre. Under Henri IV a minor tradition of French art, known as the Second School of Fontainebleau, emerged near the end of the religious wars. The surprising restraint and balance of this art, along with the transitional classicism of French sculpture and architecture, point unmistakably toward the great flowering of classical art in France during the seventeenth and early eighteenth centuries. The architectural trend that began under Francis I was continued by Pierre Lescot (designer of the Louvre) and his talented disciples, Philibert de l'Orme (or Delorme) and Jean Bullant, and became increasingly classical in tone by the incorporation of graceful statuary produced by sculptors Jean Goujon and Germain Pilon.

Poetry of the Pléiade

By 1559 all of the great figures of French Renaissance poetry were gone. Marot died in 1544; Marguerite of Navarre's brilliant career ended in 1549; Rabelais is believed to have died in 1553; and Saint-Gelais lived only until 1558. In the meantime a new generation of poets with a new school of poetic purpose and scope arose. Its nucleus was made up of seven variously gifted young poets, led by Joachim du Bellay and Pierre de Ronsard, who referred to their school as the *Pléiade* (after the seven tragic poets of ancient Alexandria). The declared purpose of the *Pléiade* was to introduce a broader and more exalted conception of poetry than had previously existed in France, and to make French the supreme vehicle of this lofty poetic literature. In his defense of the French language against the dominance of Latin, Du Bellay opposed the cultural subjection to Italy and advocated a fuller cultivation of French by promoting its embellishment and expansion through the addition of new words and the adaptation of old words and phrases to new uses. However, due perhaps to its propensity to draw themes from classical literature instead of from life, or its inability to resolve the conflict between its admiration for the classics and its rejection of classical Latin, the *Pléiade* as an expanding school of poetic method did not continue much beyond the lives of its original founders. Nevertheless, it did propel French poetry into a position of preeminence and leadership at a time when everything else in France seemed to be in decline.

Joachim du Bellay (1522–60) was a nobleman from Anjou and cousin of the powerful and influential Bishop Jean du Bellay, Francis I's energetic diplomat and literary patron. Du Bellay's prominence as a poet was established in 1549 and 1550 with the publication of *L'Olive* (The Olive), a collection of 115 love sonnets delicately written in the Petrarchan style. His real poetic genius was not revealed until eight years later, however, when two more books of sonnets, *Les Antiquités de Rome* (Antiquities of Rome) and *Les Regrets* (Yearnings) were published in Rome, where he had gone in the suite of Bishop du Bellay on a diplomatic mission for Henri II. The deep nostalgia he felt for France—especially for his native Anjou—and his profound disappointment with Rome gave a personal and poignant melancholy to these verses that freed Du Bellay from the influence of Petrarch and immediately established his position as the French master of the sonnet. Shortly after his return to France, Du Bellay died, at the age of thirty-seven.

His closest friend and associate among the poets of the *Pléiade* was Pierre de Ronsard (1524–85), a gifted humanist-poet from neighboring Vendôme. Ronsard was the son of a lesser nobleman who had served the French monarchs well in the Italian wars and had given his son an early taste for letters, although he advised the boy to make the church his profession so he might have adequate income for a respectable and comfortable life. As a page at the court of Francis I, Ronsard visited Scotland and Germany before he began the active study of letters under the humanist-poet Jean Dorat. Imbued with an appreciation of Greek literature, Ronsard published his *Odes* in 1550, after the fashion of the ancient poet Pindar, and followed these two years later with *Amours*, inspired by his noble but unrequited love for Cassandra Salviati. Other lyric poems followed rapidly, and by 1560 Ronsard was widely recognized as the Prince of Poets. His works are impressive in their number and variety, and include love poems, political poems, elegies, and masquerades; odes to nature, youth, love, and art; as well as sonnets, songs, and one unfinished epic. Ronsard became court poet to Charles IX, but his disenchantment with court life and his rejection by Hélène de Surgères, one of Catherine de' Medici's maids of honor, led to his withdrawal from court and his subsequent denunciation of the Valois monarchy.

Energy and passion mark the poetry of Pierre de Ronsard, whether describing the beauty of a rose or the eloquence of a classic poet. He reveled in the discovery of the long-lost poetry of ancient Greece, and eagerly grasped the succulent lines of Pindar, Horace, and Homer "like a man strolling for his pleasure through a vineyard, taking great clusters of purple grapes with both hands." He understood the ancients well enough to appreciate their love of harmony and to contribute in his own works toward a harmonization of those divergencies sharpened by the Wars of Religion. In its universal appeal to understanding and love, Ronsard's poetry had a tranquilizing effect at a time when it was most needed. It was lyric poetry at its very best, stimulated by passions both personal and universal.

Ronsard's political poems reveal the social cleavages and conflicts of those unsettled times. In them he counseled and praised the king, reminded the court of its duties, and called the people to arms against the threat of Huguenotism. As civil upheavals became chronic and the court became a den of debauchery and frivolity, however, Ronsard found the courtly life incompatible with his own love of nature, freedom, and sincerity. His view of the good life was not the life of a courtier:

> Let him who will laboriously cling
> To the uncertain favor of a king;
> For me, I'd rather feed on naught but bread,
> Drink with a cupping hand from a brook's bed,
> Play on the country lawns, or lie and dream,
> Or make my verses by a murmuring stream,
> Watch in a cave the Muses dance by night,
> Or hear the pell-mell noise in the last light

> *Of sheep and oxen from the haughs returning.*
> *How happier I, in these dear fields sojourning,*
> *To plant and sow, heart-whole and fancy-free,*
> *Than sell myself to a king's slavery!**

It is well that he felt that way because in Henri III's reign, a new court poet had caught the fancy of both king and court. His name was Philippe Desportes (1546–1606), a lucid and fluent draper's-son-turned-poet from Chartres. Desportes's rise to popularity and fame was rapid, and his facile pen entertained and flattered courtiers and courtesans for the next thirty years. The subtle charm of his courtly songs and sonnets (some of which are direct translations and plagiarizations from Italian poets) and his delicately polished love poems were not without poetic merit. His best works are lucid, gay, and (noted Arthur Tilley) "mixed with a spice of malice." In Elizabethan England his influence was almost as great as Ronsard's. Yet the liberties Desportes took with the language by the almost indiscriminate use of Italianisms and pedantic phrases went beyond the *Pléiade's* aim of literary enrichment toward a Baroque embellishment. A similar exaggeration of verbal ornamentation marked the work of Desportes's counterpart at the court of Henri of Navarre, the imaginative Protestant poet Guillaume de Salluste, seigneur de Bartas.

The French Academies

The *Pléiade* has been regarded as the informal association that led directly to the establishment of formal academies for the promotion of literature, art, and science. The first of these was the *Académie de Poésie et de Musique* (Academy of Poetry and Music), established by royal letters patent issued by Charles IX in 1570. The leader and moving force of this academy was the poet Jean-Antoine de Baïf, who was also associated with the *Pléiade* and hoped to effect a closer union between poetry and music. Indeed, the aim of Baïf's academy was to harmonize all of the arts and emphasize their moral value. "The production of the measured poetry and music was valued," wrote Frances Yates, the leading authority on the French academies, "chiefly on account of its 'effects' on the hearers, as a means to a further end which one might characterize as moral reform and mystical aspiration." This is a renewal of the classical notion that the effect of uniting poetry and music was that it made men wise and good by producing a true harmony of the soul.

It is impossible to say with certainty how long this institution continued to function, probably into the mid 1580s, but, in the meantime, another academy, known as the *Académie du Palais* (Palace Academy) was founded by order of Henri III. This new association, or extension of the older academy, placed more emphasis on rhetoric and philosophy (both natural and moral) than on poetry and music. The leader of the Palace Academy was Guy du Faur de Pibrac, a renowned poet, orator, and moralist. The speeches and debates of

---

*Translated by Morris Bishop in *Ronsard: Prince of Poets* (Ann Arbor, 1959), pp. 191–92.

the academy featured an amalgam of Platonic and Aristotelian moral and intellectual virtues, and focused on how these could help achieve a reign of justice, in both government and individual lives. The relationship between politics and ethics thus became a common theme in the academy, extending as well to the harmonization of the sciences, mathematics, art, and religion.

The most spectacular artistic efforts of the academies were achieved in the magnificent court festivals of Catherine de' Medici. These extravaganzas combined theater, ballet, poetry, and painting, with jousts, combats, and masquerades to produce dazzling effects intended not only to demonstrate the unity of the arts and sciences, but also to distract attention from the dismal conditions of the country. These lavish entertainments mobilized all of the artistic and scientific skills of the time.

Several female writers were active in late sixteenth-century France, including Jeanne Flore and Marguerite Briet de Fournet, both authors of impressive prose romances, and especially Louise Labé (1525–66), *La belle cordière,* who not only composed love sonnets, elegies, and dialogues but was an outspoken libertine, encouraging women to lift their minds above their distaffs and spindles. Many of them did. Following Louise Labé's advise, Madeleine Neveu des Roches (ca. 1520–87) became active in the mid-century literary renewal in Poitiers. She educated her daughter, Catherine, in a similar vein and the two became writing companions, composing many sonnets and dialogues together. In the 1570s they established a salon which attracted many scholars and poets—even suitors, for Catherine remained unmarried. When the royal court resided in Poitiers in 1577, bringing with it the luminaries of the Palace Academy, the des Roches ladies composed poems in honor of the king, his wife Louise of Lorraine, and the queen mother. Some of Catherine des Roches's feminist dialogues may have emanated from the lively debates over the role of women in society that took place in the salons and the academies.

The *Essays* of Montaigne	Prose writing of every kind flourished during the almost half-century of civil war, much of it associated with the conflict itself. This was the great age of po-

litical and religious pamphleteering, of Protestant-Catholic polemics and satire, and even of rich devotional literature in both prose and poetry. It was also the age of memoir writing and of contemporary historiography. The rich commentaries left by Brantôme, La Noue, Monluc, L'Estoile, Castelnau, Du Plessis-Mornay, Tavannes, La Place, Palma Cayet, Davilla, La Popelinière, de Thou, d'Aubigné, Bodin, Sully, and many others, have irregular literary merit—and some must be used with caution as historical sources—but they are invaluable personal accounts of sixteenth-century life and activities.

One genre of literature, the essay, reached its zenith in divided France under the gifted pen of Michel de Montaigne (1533–1592). No one before his time, and scarcely anyone since, has been able to employ this literary form so successfully to analyze human nature, both healthy and ill, and prescribe therapy for the human condition. Montaigne's positive skepticism offers a striking

Michel de Montaigne. *The famous essayist, advocate of tolerance and self-mastery, and mayor of Bordeaux, is portrayed here by an artist of the French School.*

antidote to the extremist utopias of his day by urging us to cultivate the higher human qualities with which we are all endowed, control the baser ones, and leave divine pronouncements to God. In the fury of the religious wars, Montaigne emerged as a spokesman of the middle way, of classic moderation, of Renaissance reconciliation. "It is much easier to go along the sides, where the outer edge serves as a limit and a guide, than by the middle way, wide and open," he admits in his Essay on Experience, "but it is also much less noble and less commendable. Greatness of soul is not so much pressing upward and forward as knowing how to set oneself in order." Be yourself! was Montaigne's plea, and allow others to be themselves, "for in truth you cannot be other than what you are." "We seek other conditions because we do not understand the use of our own, and go outside of ourselves because we do not know what it is like inside. Yet there is no use our mounting on stilts, for on stilts we must still walk on our own legs. And on the loftiest throne in the world we are still sitting only on our own rump."

Montaigne's early training was classical and legal. Son of a prosperous merchant of Périgord and mayor of Bordeaux, who imbued his son with a love and taste for classical literature and taught him to read, write, and speak Latin before he could use French, Montaigne furthered his education at Bordeaux and Toulouse before becoming a magistrate in the Parlement de Bordeaux. After the death of his father and his dearest friend, Etienne de La Boétie, Montaigne retired from office and began the composition of his *Essays*, the first two books of which were published in 1580. The next year and a half was spent in an extended trip across southern France, Switzerland, Germany, and Italy, where he sought out especially the mineral baths of these regions in hopes of alleviating the ailments of his middle age. His *Travel Journal* is one of the most fascinating and revealing travel accounts of the time. He returned to become mayor of Bordeaux for two terms, and by 1588 had completed the third and last book of *Essays*.

The importance of Montaigne's *Essays* in world literature can hardly be exaggerated. They have influenced and in some ways shaped every great thinking writer from Shakespeare, Pascal, and Rousseau to Emerson and André Gide. Their universality provides food for thought in any generation, and is a special source of insight in times of turbulence and unrest—in times like Montaigne's, and our own.

Popular Culture and the Wars of Religion

Although literacy increased throughout the century, to a large extent the printed word was transmitted to the lower classes orally by the literate people (churchmen, scholars, or anyone educated) reading aloud to those who could not read. This created a much larger public than might be thought. In France during the second half of the sixteenth century, although literacy remained low even in the towns, and ownership of books was still a privilege of only a few, a large "popular" market had come into existence, especially in the urban centers.

What did they read, or have read to them? High on the list were prayer books, especially primers, containing a calendar of canonical hours and meditations, as well as prayers; lives of the saints; martyrologies; collections of sermons; and hymn books. Also very popular were almanacs, giving detailed astrological information, prognostications, and useful data about farming, including flood calendars, cooking recipes, medical advice, and notices of markets and fairs. Many other "how to" books gave advice and tips on a wide variety of activities from how to cauterize a wound or build a barn, to how to fence or make cosmetics. Another form of literature widely circulated were the so-called *livres bleus* (blue books) or chapbooks (pamphlets containing popular ballads, poems, stories, and religious devotions) sold throughout the towns and villages by peddlers. Broadsheets, as we have already seen in Reformation Germany, were also widespread in France, where news of comets, deformed births, executions, and anything unusual or bizarre was welcomed. Accounts of the wars, past and present, were avidly read, especially the vivid descriptions of massacres and slaughter, as were more literary works, such as prose romances, tales of knight errantry, and comic stories. The sixteenth-century taste for violence in literature has a remarkably modern ring.

Perhaps too great an effort has been made to separate and differentiate "popular" culture from "elite" culture. Many features of peasant belief and activity were shared by their more affluent and privileged "superiors," especially in the fifteenth and early sixteenth centuries. Even the chapbooks and broadsheets, supposedly aimed at the common people, were read and enjoyed by many of the upper class as well. Almanacs and prognostications, so valuable

"The Peasant Wedding Feast," *by Pieter Bruegel the Elder. The vigorous realism of his paintings of the lives of ordinary sixteenth-century men and women has made Bruegel's works important visual documents. Bruegel himself was an educated, religiously undogmatic man, and his works display considerable satire and moralizing.*

to the peasant farmers, were also relied on by the bourgeois, as were books of hours and religious manuals, breviaries, and missals. Rogier Chartier has suggested that a better way to distinguish between popular and learned culture is not *what* was read but *how* it was read; that is, how it was perceived and understood by the reader, or listener. He also reminds us that there was a wide range of reading abilities, attitudes, and levels of imagery, making it difficult to categorize particular kinds of literary culture.

Nevertheless, the literary and oral culture of the ordinary people contained distinctive features, and these distinctions became even more pronounced in the late sixteenth and the seventeenth centuries as the nobility consciously separated themselves and their courtly culture from the culture of the lower classes. The Counter-Reformation clergy considered popular culture to be too closely tied to pagan rituals and produced anti-Christian behavior. Even the bourgeoisie tended to distance themselves from the beliefs, practices, and language of the ordinary people. By the beginning of the Wars of Religion, the poets of the *Pléiade* had rejected popular literary and musical forms, such as ballads, rondeaux, virelais, and farces, as they adopted more classical forms. During the reign of Henri III, the culture of the French court, with its academies and festivals, became even more removed from the people. By the beginning of the seventeenth century, the new aristocratic ideal of the gentleman, or man of honor (*honnête homme*) was making the old chivalric romances obsolete. The gap between courtly and popular culture in France widened.

Suggestions for Further Reading

FRANCE IN CRISIS

The best general accounts of sixteenth-century France are Robert Mandrou, *Introduction to Modern France, 1500–1640: An Essay in Historical Psychology*, tr. by R.E. Hallmark (London, 1975), and J.H.M. Salmon, *Society in Crisis: France in the Sixteenth Century* (New York, 1975), the second half of which covers the period of the religious wars. Also see Salmon's *Renaissance and Revolt: Essays in the Intellectual and Social History of Early Modern France* (New York and Cambridge, England, 1987). The first part of Robin Briggs, *Early Modern France, 1560–1715* (Oxford, 1977) deals briefly with this period. Some of the nature and implications of the crisis in France are revealed in the essays of N.M. Sutherland, collected as *Princes, Politics and Religion, 1547–1589* (London, 1984). Despite the upheavals of the time, this was when the conception of the state as a substantive entity emerged, according to Howell Lloyd, *The State, France, and the Sixteenth Century* (London, 1983), while Donald R. Kelley, in *The Beginnings of Ideology: Consciousness and Society in the French Reformation* (New York and Cambridge, England, 1981), sees it as the time of ideological awareness. A closer examination of life and government in the provinces gives understanding of the broader picture in France. See, for example, Philip Benedict, *Rouen during the Wars of Religion* (New York and Cambridge, England, 1981), and Jonathan Dewald, *The Formation of a Provincial Nobility: The Magistrats of the Parlement of Rouen, 1499–1610* (Princeton, 1980).

CATHERINE DE' MEDICI AND THE GOVERNMENT OF FRANCE

There still is no satisfactory biography of Catherine de' Medici in English, although useful insights may be gained from Jean Héritier, *Catherine de Medici*, tr. by Charlotte Haldane (New York, 1963); N.M. Sutherland's brief *Catherine de Medici and the Ancien Regime* (London, 1966); and from the older work of J.E. Neale, *The Age of Catherine de' Medici* (London, 1957). The modern popularizations by Irene Mahoney, *Madame Catherine* (New York, 1975) and Mark Strage, *Woman of Power: The Life and Times of Catherine de' Medici* (New York, 1976), are well-written and interesting but do not take the place of more scholarly studies. On Catherine's sons, see Victor E. Graham and W. McAllister Johnson, *The Royal Tour of France by Charles IX and Catherine de' Medici* (Toronto, 1979); Keith Cameron, *Henri III, a Maligned or Malignant King?* (Exeter, England, 1978); and especially Mack P. Holt, *The Duke of Anjou and the Politique Struggle during the Wars of Religion* (New York and Cambridge, England, 1986).

The nature and function of the government can best be studied in J. Russell Major, *Representative Government in Early Modern France* (New Haven, 1980); Sarah Hanley, *The Lit du Justice of the Kings of France* (Princeton, 1983); and Robert R. Harding, *Anatomy of a Power Elite: The Provincial Governors of Early Modern France* (New Haven, 1978). Also very valuable are Roland Mousnier, *The Institution of France under the Absolute Monarchy* (Chicago, 1979) and David Parker, *The Making of French Absolutism* (New York, 1983), both of which cover more than the sixteenth century. For specific institutions and personalities, see N.M. Sutherland, *The French Secretaries of State in the Age of Catherine de Medici* (London, 1962); Edmund H. Dickerman, *Bellièvre and Villeroy: Power in France under Henry III and Henry IV* (Providence,

1968); and on the municipal level, Barbara Diefendorf, *Paris City Councillors in the Sixteenth Century* (Princeton, 1983).

SOCIAL AND ECONOMIC

The changes in noble status in the late sixteenth and early seventeenth centuries is analyzed in Davis Bitton, *The French Nobility in Crisis, 1560–1640* (Stanford, 1969). A perceptive explanation of those changes is provided in Ellery Schalk, *From Valor to Pedigree: Ideas of Nobility in France in the Sixteenth and Seventeenth Centuries* (Princeton, 1986), which challenges the view that birth always determined noble status, arguing that nobility was initially thought of as a profession rather than an inherited title, and not until the late sixteenth century was it based primarily on birth and gentility. Kristen B. Neuschel, *Word of Honor: Interpreting Noble Culture in Sixteenth-Century France* (Ithaca, 1989) provides yet another way of looking at the aristocracy. The up-and-coming bourgeois gentry are treated in George Huppert, *Les Bourgeois Gentilshommes: An Essay in the Definition of Elites in Renaissance France* (Chicago, 1977). Urban forces are examined analytically in Philip Benedict, ed., *Cities and Social Change in Early Modern Times* (London, 1989).

The working classes are studied in James R. Farr, *Hands of Honor: Artisans and Their World in Dijon, 1550–1650* (Ithaca, 1988); Robin Briggs, *Communities of Belief: Cultural and Social Tensions in Early Modern France* (New York and Oxford, 1989), which deals with the tensions between the upper and lower classes; and Emmanuel Le Roy Ladurie, *The French Peasantry, 1450–1660* (Berkeley, 1987). Le Roy Ladurie's *Carnival in Romans: A People's Uprising at Romans, 1579–1580,* tr. by M. Feeney (Harmondsworth, England, 1981) is also very revealing, while Daniel Hickey, *The Coming of French Absolutism: The Struggle for Tax Reform in Dauphine, 1540–1640* (Toronto, 1986) analyzes the actions of various groups and individuals for tax reform. Eight significant essays by Natalie Zemon Davis, the leading American authority on sixteenth-century French social history, are published in *Society and Culture in Early Modern France* (Stanford, 1975). Also see her fascinating insights to peasant family life in *The Return of Martin Guerre* (Cambridge, Massachusetts, 1983).

CATHOLICS, HUGUENOTS, AND THE WARS OF RELIGION

Some of the problems of the French church are underlined in Frederic J. Baumgartner, *Change and Continuity in the French Episcopate: The Bishops and the Wars of Religion, 1547–1610* (Durham, 1986). Attempts to reform that entrenched bureaucracy are revealed in Joseph Bergin, *Cardinal de La Rochefoucauld: Leadership and Reform in the French Church* (New Haven, 1987). Also see Barbara Diefendorf, *Beneath the Cross: Catholics and Hugenots in Sixteenth-Century Paris* (New York and Oxford, 1991). Two scholarly accounts of the Huguenots are George A. Rothrock, *The Huguenots: A Biography of a Minority* (Chicago, 1979), and N.M. Sutherland, *The Huguenot Struggle for Recognition* (New Haven, 1980). Nancy L. Roelker's outstanding *Queen of Navarre: Jeanne d'Albret, 1528–1572* (Cambridge, Massachusetts, 1968) looks at some of the personal imperatives underlying the early civil conflict. On the wars themselves see David Buissert's brief *The Wars of Religion* (New York, 1969) and Julien Coudy, ed., *The Huguenot Wars,* tr. by Julie Kernan (Philadelphia, 1969), a useful collection of sources. The political and diplomatic struggles leading to the St. Bartholomew's Day massacre are reviewed in N.M. Sutherland, *The Massacre of St. Bartholomew and the European Conflict, 1559–1572* (New York, 1973), while the repercussions of that tragedy are analyzed in Robert M. Kingdon, *Myths About the St. Bartholomew's Day Massacres, 1572–1576* (Cambridge, Massachusetts, 1988).

A handy summary of Huguenot political thought, including abridged versions of Hotman's *Francogallia,* Beza's *Right of Magistrates,* and the anonymous *Vindiciae contra Tyrannos,* are included in Julian H. Franklin, *Constitutionalism and Resistance in the Sixteenth Century* (New York, 1969). The position of the *politiques,* as expressed in the writings of Bodin, is presented in Franklin's *Jean Bodin and the Rise of Absolutist Theory* (Cambridge, England, 1973). League theory is analyzed in Frederic J. Baumgartner, *Radical Reactionaries: The Political Thought of the French Catholic League* (Geneva, 1975). The best recent work on the League is in French, especially by Elie Barnavi and Robert Descimon, but see De Lamar Jensen, *Diplomacy and Dogmatism: Bernardino de Mendoza and the French Catholic League* (Cambridge, Massachusetts, 1964), and various articles by David Bell, Barbara Diefendorf, Mark Greengrass, Robert Harding, and J.H.M. Salmon.

HENRI IV AND THE RECOVERY OF FRANCE

The transition from the Valois dynasty to the Bourbon is the theme of the nine essays in Keith Cameron, ed., *From Valois to Bourbon: Dynasty, State and Society in Early Modern France* (Exeter, England, 1989). Mark Greengrass, *France in the Age of Henri IV: the Struggle for Stability* (New York, 1984) probes the background and analyzes the problems of French government and society during the wars of religion, and the resolution of some of these under Henri IV. The best biography of "*le vert galant*" is David Buisseret, *Henry IV* (London, 1984), which emphasizes the period after 1593, when Henri was crowned. Other aspects and personalities of the reign are examined in David Buisseret, *Sully and the Growth of Centralized Government in France, 1598–1610* (London, 1968); Raymond F. Kierstead, *Pomponne de Bellievre: A Study of the King's Men in the Age of Henry IV* (Evanston, 1968); and Richard Bonney, *The King's Debts: Finance and Politics in France, 1589–1661* (New York and Oxford, 1981). Peter Clark, ed., *The European Crisis of the 1590s* (Winchester, Massachusetts, 1985) contains a couple of useful essays on France. Much broader than its title suggests is Roland Mousnier, *The Assassination of Henry IV* (New York, 1973), which has many insights into Henri's reign.

FRENCH CULTURE, ELITE AND POPULAR

Ronsard and the poetry of the *Pleiade* have been studied from many angles; see in particular Malcolm Quainton, *Ronsard's Ordered Chaos: Visions of Flux and Stability in the Poetry of Pierre de Ronsard* (Manchester, England, 1980); Isidore Silver, *Ronsard and the Hellenic Renaissance in France* (Geneva, 1981); Ullrich Langer, *Invention, Death, and Self-Definition in the Poetry of Pierre de Ronsard* (Saratoga, California, 1986); and Margaret M. McGowan, *Ideal Forms in the Age of Ronsard* (Berkeley, 1985), which demonstrates the sixteenth-century preoccupation with images of princely power. Natalie Zeman Davis's unique *Fiction in the Archives: Pardon Tales and Their Tellers in Sixteenth-Century France* (Stanford, 1987) offers original insights into the culture and thought of the time. A new issuing of Frances Yates's classic *The French Academies of the Sixteenth Century* (New York and London, 1988) should be welcomed by everyone. Also see Robert J. Sealy, *The Palace Academy of Henry III* (Geneva, Switzerland, 1981).

Studies of Montaigne never cease. I still like Donald M. Frame's *Montaigne: A*

Biography (New York, 1965) and *Montaigne's Essays: A Study* (Englewood Cliffs, New Jersey, 1969) for the fundamentals, but interesting new interpretations are provided in Malcolm Smith, *Montaigne and the Roman Censors* (Geneva, Switzerland, 1981); M.A. Screech, *Montaigne and Meloncholy: The Wisdom of the Essays* (London, 1983); James J. Supple, *Arms versus Letters: The Military and Literary Ideals in the Essais of Montaigne* (New York and Oxford, 1984); Patrick Henry, *Montaigne in Dialogue* (Stanford, 1987); and Michael G. Paulson, *The Possible Influences of Montaigne's Essais on Descartes' Treatise on the Passions* (New York, 1988). Some good essays are contained in Keith Cameron, ed., *Montaigne and His Age* (Exeter, England, 1981).

The most penetrating cultural study of France is Robert Muchembled's *Popular Culture and Elite Culture in France, 1400–1750*, tr. by Lydia Cochrane (Baton Rouge, 1985). Popular culture is insightfully dealt with in Robert Mandrou, *Introduction to Modern France*, cited above. Also useful are Michael Mullett, *Popular Culture and Popular Protest in Late Medieval and Early Modern Europe* (London and New York, 1987), and several of the chapters in Steven L. Kaplan, ed., *Understanding Popular Culture* (Amsterdam, 1984).

8 | SPAIN UNDER PHILIP II

FOR SPAIN, THE SECOND HALF OF THE SIXTEENTH CENTURY WAS AN AGE of assertiveness and fulfillment. Under Emperor Charles V, Spaniards felt somewhat like stepchildren. The Habsburg alliance had thrust them into Europe and into worldwide political involvement. Spain's importance to the emperor was obvious, but what was the empire's significance to Spain? Did it enhance or impede Spanish economic, political, and cultural development? Castilians as well as Aragonese, Valencians, and Catalans could not avoid feeling that they were sometimes exploited for the benefit of Austrian or Burgundian interests. With the accession of Philip II, Spain had its own ruler again. Government policies would be for Spanish (the Aragonese and Catalans hoped that would not mean simply Castilian) interests, not foreign. The "coming home" of the Spanish king in 1559 ushered in a new era of political and cultural vigor.

Yet the Age of Philip II had negative as well as positive features. Spaniards no longer had to be so concerned with German affairs, yet they were still trapped in the deepening impasse with the Low Countries, the steady deterioration of relations with the English, the growing seriousness of shortsighted economic policies, the repressive effects of the Inquisition, and the mounting burden of far-reaching political and military commitments. The greatest legacy the emperor might have left his son—but did not—was a Spain cut free from the Burgundian as well as Austrian heritage, and without the lingering memory of an imperial dream. In many ways this was the golden age of Spain, but it was also the gestation period of Spanish decline.

Philip II, the Ruler and the Man

The most powerful monarch of the late sixteenth century was Philip of Spain, Habsburg ruler of the rich Burgundian Netherlands, Luxembourg, and Franche-Comté; king of Naples and master of Sicily, Sardinia, Corsica, the Balearic Islands, and Milan; king of Aragon, Castile, and all of the Castilian territories overseas. These dominions had all passed to Philip as the inheritance of his illustrious father, Emperor Charles V. Even with ideal conditions, the effective governing of such a disparate and far-flung empire would have been nearly impossible; yet conditions in sixteenth-century Europe were far from ideal, and the temperament and personality of the king imposed additional handicaps.

Philip became the ruler of Spain in January 1556, at the age of twenty-nine, following his father's abdication of the Spanish, Burgundian, and imperial crowns. Philip inherited a great many titles, honors, and territories, but he also inherited a Pandora's box of troubles: war with France in the Low Countries and in Italy; conflict with Pope Paul IV; discontent in the Burgundian territories; threats from the Turks; murmurings in Aragon; trouble with the Neapolitans; and from every side the crescendo of "Luteranismo" all combined to disturb the tranquility of Philip's succession. Only Savoy seemed to be consistently friendly toward the new monarch, and even then first appearances were deceiving.

Modern opinion of Philip II contrasts widely, from the terse conclusion of John Lothrop Motley, "If there are vices—as possibly there are—from which he was exempt, it is because it is not permitted to human nature to attain perfection, even in evil," to R. Trevor-Davies's affirmation, "Those who knew him best recognized him as truthful, devout, frugal in his own living and generous towards others."

The Spanish king was just as controversial to his contemporaries. Luis Cabrera de Córdoba, Philip's long-time servant, warrior, and chronicler, emphasized the king's dignity, grace, judgment, and justice; while his father's secretary, Francisco de los Cobos, became eloquent over his devotion to duty, prudence, virtue, and gravity, "accompanied by a natural majesty and authority which is terrifying." On the other hand, another secretary, the talented but unpredictable Antonio Pérez, wrote in his *Relaciones* (1594) that Philip was a tyrant in every sense of the word; and William of Orange, Philip's bitterest enemy after 1576, accused the king of blasphemy, tyranny, incest, and murder.

Nevertheless, we are not left entirely to the mercy of conflicting partisans to make some meaningful evaluation of Philip II. Many "detached" observers also left their impressions of the monarch, and the bulk of personal papers, official and private correspondence, as well as diplomatic reports from which evidence may be drawn, is mountainous. Although we can never probe the inner recesses of his private thoughts, we can learn a great deal about the Catholic King.

In the first place, there is little disagreement over Philip's outward characteristics and appearance. He was reserved, shy, solitary, and serious; tended toward melancholy; and possessed almost inhuman patience and composure. At the same time, he was always courteous and soft-spoken, to servants as well as to nobles, and unemotional in his meting out of justice or in his reception of personal misfortune. His notorious cautiousness (which his advocates referred to as prudence and his enemies as pretense) contributed to the solemnity of his decisions, but also multiplied the time required to make them. Philip was slightly built, short but erect, fair-haired, blue-eyed (inflamed and swollen from

Philip II. *This familiar painting of the king around 1579 when he was fifty-two years of age has traditionally been attributed to Sánchez Coello. More recently it has been tentatively attributed to Sofonisba Anguisciola, from Cremona, who worked at the Spanish court at that time and painted other portraits of the king and his family.*

long hours of reading by candlelight), with the pronounced prognathous jaw of the Habsburgs and the thick lower lip of his Burgundian ancestry. He had asthma most of his life and in his later years suffered from kidney stones, arthritis, and gout. His pallid complexion attested to his lack of outdoor activity, for unlike most contemporary rulers and nobles, Philip seldom hunted and never participated in tourneys, jousts, or combat.

Under this cold, impassive exterior lay deeper traits that must be recognized if we are to understand the man and his reign. It is seldom that we are privileged to glimpse this aspect of Philip's life, but in his letters to his daughters we can recognize a very tender love and a deep paternal concern for his children. Those close familial bonds must have made the frequent personal tragedies even more onerous, and surely contributed to his introversion. The successive deaths of his mother, father, sister, four wives, one daughter, and four sons cannot but have had their effect on his personality. Philip's overriding sense of responsibility for his kingdoms made his unhappy relations with his erratic and psychotic son, Don Carlos, the most tragic. Contemporary rumor and modern fiction has it that Philip killed Don Carlos, but the evidence allows us to conclude no more than that he confined the unbalanced youth to a secluded portion of the palace for "the public welfare of these Kingdoms," and there he died six months later.

Philip was also sensitive to the world of art and scholarship, not only as a royal patron and advocate but also as a connoisseur. At the Escorial palace, he assembled one of the finest collections of contemporary paintings in Europe. He also supported the universities and patronized learning in many forms, including the study and writing of history, for which he had a particular fondness. He established the Academy of Sciences, the Academy of Mathematics, and the Archives of Simancas. Possessing an alert mind, a retentive memory, and an unswerving devotion to Spanish culture, Philip set the tone and flavor of Spanish scholarship and art for half a century.

His influence on Spanish government was even greater. His own sense of duty and prerogative, as well as his almost ruthless legalism, made him arbitrary and despotic, but it also brought dignity to government service. Austerity and formality were keynotes of Philip's reign. By nature he was both cautious and frugal. On the positive side, these attributes brought an end to the ostentatious Burgundian court of Charles V and instituted a thriftiness that had not been known since the days of Ferdinand and Isabel. Yet these traits also contributed to the stagnation that was to characterize Spanish economy and administration.

Philip took his kingly duties very seriously. He was hard-working to the extreme, partly because he distrusted his subordinates (frequently for good reason) and partly because he felt it was his responsibility to work hard. He was meticulous about every detail of government and administration, a characteristic that was both his weakness and his strength. He complied with his father's final injunction to handle every detail of government himself and not rely on subordinates. The obvious result was a coagulation of administration. Every official document not only passed through his hands, but was carefully read and frequently annotated by him. "*Bien es mirar a todo*" ("It is best to keep an eye on everything") was his oft-repeated rule. The resulting slowness of Spanish administration became notorious. One of Philip's faithful ambassadors expressed the wish "that death might come by way of Madrid for then we would certainly live to a good old age." It is little wonder that the objective of Philip's domestic rule, as well as his foreign policy, was to preserve the status quo.

The Government of Spain

The structure of Spanish government under Philip II was essentially the same as that his father had inherited from Ferdinand and Isabel. Philip found, just as the emperor had, that the various states and territories comprising his inheritance had no intention of relinquishing their individual relationship to the sovereign in favor of some higher concept of empire, or even of nationhood. To understand Spanish government in the sixteenth century, it is necessary to discard the traditional clichés about centralization and monolithic power, and remember that Philip reigned in his different realms by separate rights of inheritance. His authority in Brabant derived not from his being king of Castile, but from his succession as duke of Burgundy and Brabant. Castilian laws had no effect in Aragon, and the financial system of Flanders was unrelated to that of Naples. Philip's titles and honors were separately bestowed and his power separately exercised.

Some of Philip's subjects cooperated more than others; but in almost every instance, they religiously guarded their particular liberties and legal *fueros* (privileges and exemptions) against the real and imagined encroachments of the ruler, just as they resisted his attempts to increase their financial burdens. Philip did succeed in expanding royal power, but the basically fragmented nature of his empire continued throughout his reign. Ultimate decisions and responsibility rested with him alone, but his actual ability to implement and enforce his will was limited by the impediments of communication and travel, the lack of an adequate bureaucracy, the inefficiency of personal rule, and the restrictions of legal traditions.

Nevertheless, Philip II achieved considerable success in administering his far-flung empire, and he attained a surprising degree of unity from his Iberian territories. To do this, he concentrated his administrative machinery in Castile, the largest of his territories, and bestowed the bulk of his political patronage on Castilians. The resulting Castilianization of Spain had detrimental effects on the eastern kingdom of Aragon, where it was deeply resented, but Philip had very little choice if he hoped to administer the country effectively. The population of Castile in the middle of the sixteenth century was approximately 6 million, while that of the combined Aragonese territories was less than 1 million. Furthermore, the Catalan prosperity of the fourteenth century and the Valencian affluence of the fifteenth had both disappeared, leaving Castile as the economic base of Philip's empire as well as its political center.

Councils and Secretaries   The system of administrative councils developed by Ferdinand and Isabel and extended by Charles V was continued and further expanded by Philip II. The largest of these bodies, and the only ones authorized to discuss matters involving all of Philip's territories, were the Council of State (*Consejo de Estado*), drawn largely from the Castilian upper nobility, which advised the king on matters of state and foreign policy; the Council of War, which was composed of the same councilors plus military experts; and the Council of the Inquisition, made up of five members plus the inquisitor-general. In the councils of State and War the great magnates vied for position and influence and successfully cancelled out any real power that the council might have exercised.

At the beginning of Philip's reign, the two leading factions were represented by the prince of Eboli, Ruy Gómez de Silva, a Portuguese grandee who had come to Spain with Philip's first wife; and the crusty warrior Fernando Alvarez de Toledo, third duke of Alba. The capable Burgundian cardinal, Antoine Perrenot de Granvelle, son of the emperor's minister, was a member of the council and influential advisor to the king, as was Don Juan de Zúñiga, who also served as ambassador to Rome and viceroy of Naples. Philip, however, did not trust any of the nobles for very long.

In addition to these three advisory bodies, Philip inherited four other councils whose responsibility was to govern the various parts of the empire, appoint viceroys, oversee finances, and serve as final courts of appeal for the territories they represented. The most important of these was the Council of Castile (sometimes referred to as the *Consejo Real,* or Royal Council). Unlike the Council of State, this compact body was composed mostly of university-trained jurists (*letrados*) whose knowledge of law and experience in public affairs qualified them to serve in this capacity. Because of the unique position of Castile in the Spanish empire, the Council of Castile was assisted in its function by lesser councils that dealt with particular aspects of Castilian administration. The other administrative organs were the Council of Aragon, the Council of Italy, and the Council of the Indies. In each of these the *letrados* occupied the leading roles. The councilors of Aragon were required by Aragonese law to be natives of Aragon, Catalonia, or Valencia (Castilians being specifically forbidden). After the acquisition of Portugal in 1582, a Council of Portugal was created, and in 1588 a similar body was formed for Flanders. The actual administration of these territories was carried out by governors and viceroys appointed by the crown in consultation with the appropriate councils. In most cases these vice-rulers were chosen from among the Castilian upper nobility, for Philip found that the magnates were less troublesome to him when they were on foreign assignments than when they were at home.

Liaison between the councils and the king was provided by written reports (*consultas*) from the president of each council and by the footwork of Philip's secretaries. During the first twenty years of his reign, Philip's principal secretaries were the Aragonese functionary, Gonzalo Pérez, who had served the emperor for many years, and his ambitious son, Antonio Pérez. The latter, an ambitious courtier, was also an able administrator who rose to great prominence through his ability and the favor of the king. Royal patronage, though, was a capricious tool even when employed with caution and tact, and Pérez possessed neither of these. Partly as a result of his incriminating the king in the Escobedo murder in 1578 (by which Pérez eliminated one of his more dangerous political rivals), Pérez lost favor with the king, was removed from office, and was placed under arrest. His subsequent removal to Aragon and his involvement in the Argonese rebellion of 1591 are part of the continuing story of Spanish separatism.

After the fall of Antonio Pérez, the position of chief secretary went to his rival, Mateo Vázquez, a mediocre Corsican cleric who shared secretarial responsibilities with Gabriel de Zayas. Juan de Idiáquez, a Basque functionary, handled most foreign correspondence, particularly with the northern countries, and was also secretary, then a member of the Council of State. Cristóbal de Moura was minister-secretary for Portuguese affairs and advised the king on finances and Castilian affairs. The count of Chinchón was secretary and treasurer general of Aragon and Italy. A small, informal committee of the secretaries (with either Granvelle or Zúñiga), and known as the *Junta de Noche,* met in the royal palace to study dispatches from the ambassadors and the various governors and viceroys. This group made recommendations to the king, but he, of course, was under no obligation to follow them.

The Cortes of Castile and Aragon

The desires and opinions of numerous corporate groups, municipalities, and even individuals, were heard through the parliamentary *cortes*. The Cortes of Castile, which met twelve times during Philip's reign, was not an active partner in legislation as the Parliament of England was, but it did play a more prominent role than the French Estates General. Exercising tangible restraints on the crown through its power of petitioning, the Cortes was the principle forum for political discussion, and frequently made fruitful protests against the king's policies. It also had some say in financial matters. Although Philip was not dependent upon the Cortes to vote direct taxes, he did rely increasingly on its *servicios*, which were "voluntary" grants of money by the Cortes. To obtain such subsidies the crown was forced to listen to the grievances of the *procuradores* (members of the Cortes, elected by the larger cities), though it was not required to act on them. For most of Philip's reign the Cortes of Castile was a subservient tool of the government. Nevertheless, Philip tried to avoid confrontations with the cortes of his realms as much as he could. Their strength and influence had declined considerably since the preceding century, but even Philip II did not ignore them altogether. He summoned the Cortes of Castile with surprising frequency, although it seems evident now that he did so more to preserve the appearance of constitutionalism than to recognize their rights.

With Aragon the case was different. The Cortes of Aragon was a much more active and important body than that of Castile. It could be and occasionally was summoned without royal sanction, and it continued to uphold the medieval Aragonese *fueros* (liberties). These liberties, consisting of a maze of feudal privileges and mutual obligations, were religiously defended by the Aragonese nobles and the Cortes, as well as by the *Justicia*, an official appointed to see that the laws of Aragon were not violated and to protect subjects against arbitrary rule. The Cortes of Aragon was composed of four estates: clergy, grandees, gentry or knights, and towns. Unlike the Cortes of Castile, it insisted that no new taxes could be imposed without its consent, and redress of grievances had to precede the granting of revenue. It is undoubtedly true that Philip allowed the Cortes of Aragon their say not because he was unable to force their submission (the Aragonese revolt of 1591, for example, was suppressed in quick order), but because he felt it was not worth the effort and expense to do so, given the relatively minor contribution of Aragon to the Spanish economy. Still, Philip was apprehensive enough over the Aragonese to prefer the more subtle expedient of ignoring their Cortes than to meeting it on a regular basis, even though this meant giving up important revenues.

The Spanish Overseas Empire

Spanish administrative policy in the New World was similar to that practiced in Naples, Sicily, Milan, or Aragon. Philip was sole ruler, spokesman, and protector, but administration had to function through some sort of bureaucracy.

The Council of the Indies had administrative jurisdiction of the American territories just as the Council of Italy did in Naples and Sicily. It proposed the names of colonial officials for the king's appointment, drafted laws for the organization and administration of the colonies, and supervised all ecclesiastical matters under the *patronato real*. The Council of the Indies sat as a court of last resort in civil suits appealed from the colonies and had primary jurisdiction in cases originating in Spain. From time to time, it sent officials known as *visitadores* to examine the administrations of viceroys, and arranged for the hearings (*residencias*) of colonial officials at the conclusion of their tour of duty. In this capacity the council also supervised the jurisdiction of the Indians.

Delegated authority from the crown and the council was granted to the viceroys, who governed the colonies in the king's name and administered the laws established for that purpose. In both New Spain (Mexico) and New Castile (Peru), the viceroy was the chief civil and military officer, supervisor of justice, economy, and the church, and protector of the Indians. Although his enumerated powers were great, and distance and lack of communication tempted some of the holders of that office to independent actions, most of the forty-one viceroys of colonial Peru and sixty-two of New Spain were hard-working and loyal servants of the crown, who fulfilled their obligations as far as circumstances and their own personal limitations allowed. Just to make sure, Philip kept their terms of office relatively short, and dispatched frequent *visitadores* to check up on their administration.

The colonial *audiencias,* microcosms of the Council of Castile, also helped keep the viceroys in check. *Audiencias* were composed of peninsular Castilian jurists chosen by the king and the Council of the Indies, and were ultimately responsible to the crown in all judicial matters. This lack of trust in the viceroys is frequently criticized by modern writers as an example of Philip's duplicity and his reluctance to share the reins of government with others. This allegation is no doubt true, but given the general unreliability and independence of the aristocracy, and the extent of their influence and power in sixteenth-century Spain, it seems likely that the king was justified in his distrust more times than not. At any rate, we might think of the system as a less sophisticated form of "checks and balances." Whatever it is called, it was, like all of Philip's administration, a characteristically divided authority with the responsibilities and powers of one office counterbalanced, or even nullified, by the authority of another. In this way Philip prevented the overambitious grandees from dominating Spanish government while at the same time making the best use of their talents and resources.

It was particularly important for the crown to maintain a tight hold on the New World territories, because they accounted for a sizable share of the revenues of Castile. To protect these valuable cargoes on their return voyages to Spain, Philip inaugurated an annual convoy system in 1564–66. Under this system, two fleets left Seville in the spring, one (*la flota*) landing at Nombre de Dios on the Isthmus of Panama to trade with Peru, and the other (*los galleones*) docking at Vera Cruz and there selling goods and taking on cargo from Mexico. The following spring both fleets, laden with silver and other products

Table 8–1 Spanish Convoys, 1576–1600

Year	Outward to New World		Return to Spain	
	Number of Ships in Convoy	Tonnage	Number of Ships in Convoy	Tonnage
1576	62	21,049		
1577	45	14,470	61	17,359
1578	36	11,025	45	12,190
1579	48	14,880	51	13,765
1580	43	15,081	52	14,860
1581	42	15,146	44	13,221
1582	67	19,470	37	9,210
1583	46	11,860	74	18,580
1584	75	22,840	85	20,723
1585	51	16,805	82	19,823
1586	107	29,510	58	14,625
1587			93	29,149
1588	103	28,707	9	3,750
1589	87	17,835	80	18,391
1590	92	22,670	2	300
1591	30	5,730	28	2,680
1592	54	10,350		
1593	90	22,905	56	15,567
1594	114	26,219		
1595	33	8,310	81	23,102
1596	81	22,495	55	14,648
1597	80	21,988	27	3,330
1598	57	13,357	67	19,360
1599	67	19,665	28	8,050
1600	67	19,710	102	27,977

Source: Huguette and Pierre Chaunu, *Séville et l'Atlantique, 1504–1650* (Paris, 1956), Vol. VI, pp. 406–407. © 1957 by École des Hautes Études en Sciences Sociales, Paris.

of the Indies, would rendezvous at Havana and return to Spain via the Bahama Straits and the Azores. Table 8–1 shows the size of the convoy system during the last quarter of the century. Voyages of single ships (and there were many, especially after 1585) are not included.

The addition of English pirates to the French and Dutch raiders caused Philip to attach to these treasure fleets the naval squadron that usually policed the waters between Cape Saint Vincent and the Canaries, and escort them part of the way to and from the New World.

Although the great age of the *conquista* was past by the time Philip II mounted the thrones of Castile and Aragon, much consolidation was yet to be carried out and rich new areas yet to be explored and conquered. The fabled land of Florida, for example, described by Cabeza de Vaca during his quixotic quest for the fountain of youth as "the richest country in the world," was still an unknown and forbidding land in 1556. During the next ten years, both the Spanish and French established settlements along the Florida coast. The latter, a colony of Huguenots planted by Admiral Coligny but without support from the French government, was annihilated in 1565 by a garrison from the Spanish colony at Saint Augustine. The great South American pampas opened to Castilian settlement during Philip's reign, particularly after the permanent founding of Buenos Aires in 1580, and the active colonization of the southern Andes began. Indecisive war continued against the determined Araucanian Indians of Chile, but Spanish consolidation in the Bolivian highlands meant more economically than all of the rest of the South American settlements combined.

Economics and Society

Philip II inherited serious financial troubles when he ascended the Spanish thrones in 1556. With royal credit seriously overextended and the government's ability to repay its debts hampered by the renewal of the Habsburg-Valois wars, Philip took the drastic expedient of declaring state bankruptcy. France followed suit and two years later Portugal also repudiated its debts. The financial crisis of 1557–59, which afflicted all of Europe, was the first in the all-too-familiar cycle of boom-and-bust that has characterized the economy of the last four centuries.

Spanish recovery from this mid-century crisis was hampered by a number of factors, but particularly by the spiraling inflation that had been disrupting the Spanish economy since the 1530s or earlier. The influx of bullion from the New World, particularly of silver after the opening of the Guanajuato and Potosí mines, outran the increased production of goods, resulting in a decline in the value of money and an accompanying inflation of prices. Other factors, such as the rapid rise in wool prices and the shift of population from the country to the towns, contributed more inflationary pressures to the Spanish economy. Vast expenditures on war did nothing to alleviate the problem. During the first half of the century, the general level of prices in Spain more than doubled, and by the end of Philip's reign, it had quadrupled. The consequences of this inflation were varied. In general, creditors were affected adversely and debtors favorably, but this did not always hold true, since interest rates also climbed and other means were usually found to augment creditor incomes. As purchasing power declined, all those who depended upon fixed salaries found themselves caught in a disastrous wage-price squeeze that they could neither control nor stop.

Despite this gloomy picture of the sixteenth-century Spanish economy, favorable features should not be overlooked. With the rising price of wool and the legal privileges enjoyed by the *Mesta* guild, sheep raising continued to flourish, producing enviable profits for owners and merchants alike. Other livestock production, particularly of horses, cattle, and pigs, also continued at an active rate. The price revolution likewise favored other forms of agriculture, including grain, olives, and wine. On the whole, however, Spanish agriculture

The "Silver Mountain" at Potosí. *The huge silver mine at Potosí (in modern Bolivia) was one of the great sources of the silver coinage that poured into sixteenth-century Spain. The Indians who worked the mines died in enormous numbers. At the far left and right the ore is being transported by llamas.*

failed to keep pace with the needs of the time; before long, cereals and other foods had to be imported to meet the demands of a growing and increasingly urbanized population.

Landowners and Peasants

The principal beneficiaries of Spanish landowning were the church and the wealthy noble families, who controlled the great landed estates upon which the rural workers eked out their living. The landed aristocrats were doubly blessed in sixteenth-century Spain, since they not only raised rents to compensate for the declining value of money but also profited from the rise in agricultural prices. At the same time, they possessed, by right of their nobility, exemption from direct taxes and were able to avoid many of the indirect levies as well. This wealth helped assuage the resentment they felt over their loss of political power as the monarchy became less dependent upon them. In Castile especially, the political influence of the nobility in the higher echelons of government was drastically reduced under Philip II. Yet as the nobles' power declined, they became increasingly jealous of their economic status and their private prerogatives.

Most of the inhabitants of the land, however, were not nobles, either grandees or the lesser-born hidalgos, but commoners: peasant farmers, herdsmen—including swineherds, goatherds, *vaqueros* (cowboys), and shepherds—miners, and itinerate laborers. In general, as in France and the rest of Europe, their lot was difficult. Rarely did their income allow them more than a subsistence life, and when famine or plague struck they suffered horrendously. In some ways they were even worse off than their counterparts to the north. Most of the Spanish land consisted of *señoríos* (manors) on which living conditions were very hard and the powers of the overlords great, although the severity of their enforcement varied considerably. Whereas France experienced a rather steady evolution from medieval tenure to true ownership, in Spain very few peasants had freehold property.

Because of the long urban tradition in both Castile and Aragon, most peasants also congregated in towns and villages, thus giving a decided agrarian orientation to the life and economy even of urban locations. In Andalusia the great *latifúndias* (large landed estates) owned by a few aristocratic families were cultivated by migrant agricultural workers, who lived in the towns and hired out seasonally to work in the fields. Farmers and artisans were neighbors, part of the year at least, and shared many of the successes and failures of both the urban and rural economy. And they both paid taxes, burdensome at all times, devastating in time of war. They were also subject to the caprices of nature and had many of the same superstitions about it.

Interestingly, peasants shared some of the attitudes of the nobles as well. To a surprising degree, even though they were at opposite ends of the social ladder, the lower classes affirmed the same ideals of chivalry and "honor" as the nobles did, and as unlikely as it was, they even yearned for nobility. Like the warrior class, the peasants identified with the crusading spirit nurtured during the centuries of the reconquest; they too were heirs of the legacy of El Cid. Through the mouth of Don Quixote, Cervantes commented on the social mobility in Spain in an overstatement that was perhaps not entirely facetious: "There are two kinds of classes in the world: those who derive their descent from princes and monarchs, and whom time undoes bit by bit until they are totally ruined; and others who take their beginnings from the common people and rise from rank to rank until they become great lords; the difference being that some were what they are no longer, and others are what they once were not." It may not be too surprising, observes Henry Kamen, that the lower classes should have considered themselves as good as their betters.

Castilian peasants seem to have been more physically mobile than many others. Perhaps this was due to the heavy tax burdens, or because the local or regional economies required workers to move around in order to make a living. Shepherds of the Mesta guild migrated with their flocks semiannually over great distances. Swineherds and goatherds moved too, but not as far. Military service attracted many commoners as well as a large number of hidalgos. For both groups the pay was attractive, and it was the most likely way to realize that honored state of nobility for which they longed. Of course the hazards were also great, especially for the armies sent north to Flanders. Military levies came frequently, and usually caused great hardship to both country and towns, for they were always followed by shortages of labor and increases in taxes. Wage earners were also afflicted by the chronic inflation of the time that ate away fixed incomes and devoured any possible savings. Only the more enterprising merchants and better-off burghers were able to turn the unstable commercial situation into profit.

Castilian Commerce

The New World trade was the most spectacular economic activity of sixteenth-century Spain. The imagination and jealousy of a whole continent was stimulated by the Spanish silver traffic. Table 8–2 gives the value of treasure imports during the half-century of Philip's reign. The immediate impact of the New World bullion on the Spanish economy was felt mostly in Seville and the surrounding regions of Andalusia. Seville quickly became a boom town, tripling in population in less than fifty years, as the riches of America attracted thousands of immigrants from other regions of Spain. For a time this stimulus brought unprecedented prosperity to the south, but it was a temporary prosperity based on wealth merely passing through, not on production. Castile shared in Andalusian affluence by providing ships, cloth, and credit to the Sevillian merchants.

Castilian commerce flourished not only between Seville and America, but also internally and between Castile and northern Europe. The principal products of the home market were textiles, salt, olive oil, and grain, while raw wool, oil, wine, ceramics, silk, leather, iron, and Toledo steel were exported to Italy and the north. From America came sufficient supplies of sugar, dyes (particularly cochineal and indigo), and hides for reexport abroad, and of course the gold and silver of the New World passed through Spain as through a sieve to purchase the manufactured goods and cheaper textiles of northern Europe.

Castilians themselves engaged actively in this international trade from their business houses in Seville, Medina del Campo, and Burgos, and from their

Table 8–2   New World Treasure Imports to Spain, 1556–1600 (In Ducats)

1556–1560	9,598,798
1561–1565	13,449,043
1566–1570	16,969,459
1571–1575	14,287,931
1576–1580	20,702,329
1581–1585	35,249,534
1586–1590	28,599,157
1591–1595	42,221,835
1596–1600	41,314,201
Total	222,392,287

Source: Earl J. Hamilton, *American Treasure and the Price Revolution in Spain, 1501–1650* (Cambridge, Mass.: Harvard University Press, 1934), p. 34. Reprinted by permission.

scattered factories abroad. Yet they never created a truly mercantile class. Whenever a Castilian merchant prospered sufficiently to allow him to purchase land and a title of nobility, he usually abandoned his trade and became a gentleman. Such a case is the Castilian family of Simón Ruiz, who established an impressive financial empire directed from Medina del Campo. Having obtained his start from the wool trade, he expanded his business into an international exchange of cloth, wool, and credit, ultimately becoming the leading native banker in Spain. Unlike the Medici and Fugger dynasties, however, the Ruiz preeminence lasted only one generation before the business was abandoned for land. Other Spanish merchants flourished in northern Castile, particularly at Burgos, but they never gained the wealth, reputation, or influence of their German, Dutch, and Italian rivals.

**Industry and
Internal Revenue**

For a time it appeared that the industrial development of Spain might keep pace with its growing demands. Stimulated by the American market, the Castilian textile industry prospered, until the growing inflation priced Spanish goods out of the market and poor production methods and lack of skilled labor reduced their quality below that of competitors. Manufacturers in Granada and Murcia, however, responded to the growing demand for luxury products, maintaining silk production and the manufacturing of silk cloth at a high level throughout the century. The market for Spanish leather and leather goods continued to stimulate this industry, which was supplied now from the New World with an almost limitless number of hides at a low cost. Meanwhile, the Biscayan coast to the north was experiencing a veritable industrial revolution as iron ore, mined in the mountains of Guipúzcoa, was shipped abroad from Bilbao and employed in the expanding shipyards of San Sebastián, Bilbao, and Santander.

Yet serious problems plagued the Spanish economy even during this half-century of prosperity. Inflation ate up much of the increased revenues, and the overextension of Spanish foreign commitments and wars, particularly after 1580, more than offset the wealth from the New World. The principal sources of crown income during Philip's reign were taxes (levied particularly heavily on the Castilian population), dues and subsidies paid by the church, and the crown's share, usually one-fifth, of the American silver imports. Although the American treasure was impressive, it never amounted to more than 20 percent of the royal revenue (in the peak year of 1598) and usually made up only 10 to 12 percent. This amount was less than the 15 to 20 percent received from the various ecclesiastical sources, which included the *cruzada,* a papal subsidy originally granted to fight the Moors and Turks, and now a direct imposition on the laity; the *subsidio,* a tax on clerical incomes; the *tercios reales,* or royal tithes; and the *excusado,* a tax on parish property.

The largest share of crown income, however, came from direct and indirect taxes imposed on the people of Castile. The *alcabala,* a sales tax amounting to 10 or more percent of the price of goods, and exacted each time a transaction was made, was the largest single tax in Spain but far from the only one.

There were direct levies on Castilian cities, export taxes on the shipment of wool, customs duties on the Biscayan ports, and royal monopolies on everything from salt to playing cards. In the 1590s an additional exise tax, called the *millones,* was initiated to make up the deficits between income and crown spending. Its long-range effect was to further crush the poor, who had no way of evading it. From time to time the Castilian Cortes also voted additional *servicios* that likewise fell heavily on the shoulders of the masses. Even so, with its ever-growing commitments and involvements around the world, the crown had to borrow extensively at very high rates, mostly from Genoese and other foreign bankers, on the collateral of the annual treasure fleets—and still the income was inadequate. In 1575 the government declared bankruptcy for the second time, and twenty-one years later followed the same expedient again, with disastrous consequences for both the crown and its creditors.

Spain's heavy dependence on foreign bankers had damaged the Spanish economy ever since the early years of Charles V. With most of the state bonds (*juros*) in foreign hands, the bulk of the American silver went directly to these creditors instead of remaining in Spain. Furthermore, the failure or inability to create a solid economic base, either in agriculture or industry, meant that the country continued to be a victim of inflation without realizing any of its accompanying benefits. Its economy remained precariously perched on the unpredictable passage of American silver through Spain into the accounts and pockets of foreign merchants and bankers. Thus, the neglect of agriculture as population shifted to the cities; the increase of rents and taxes in order to "beat" the price inflation; the disastrous displacement of the Moriscos after 1571; and the exorbitant cost of military escalation in the Netherlands, Portugal, England, and France had disastrous effects on the Spanish economy.

Spain and the Church

Basic to the entire life, thought, and administration of Spain, in the New World as in the Old, was the Roman Catholic church. We have seen how Christianity prevailed over Islam in the *reconquista,* and how a religious reformation within Spain had placed the church there in a nearly impregnable position by the time of the Protestant Reformation. The conquest of the New World and the Spanish victories over the Valois and the Turks had been won in union with the church. Not only were the Spanish people devoutly Catholic but also their rulers were active defenders of the traditional faith. The zeal of Ferdinand and Isabel had earned them the title "Catholic Monarchs," and Charles V took an early lead in the campaign against Lutheranism. The emperor's religious orthodoxy was passed on to Philip II.

Philip took immediate steps to abate any doubts concerning his religious position when he returned to Spain from the peace settlements of 1559. He moved quickly against the small active groups of Protestants in Valladolid and Seville, and demonstrated his determination to fight heresy by the *auto-de-fe* of October 1559, in which six men and six women were burned at the stake, including the long-time nun Marina de Guevara, who was charged with Lutheran beliefs and interrogated over a period of sixteen months. Likewise, Philip acted vigorously against the militant Calvinism that seemed to be spreading throughout his Burgundian territories and Italy.

Although the repression of heresy was perhaps the most spectacular, and the most unfortunate, feature of Spanish Catholicism, it was not the most characteristic. More fundamental was the deep personal attachment of the Spanish people to the ideology and rituals of the Catholic church, although practiced in different ways and individualized according to local traditions. This attachment was not feigned but rather a deep and genuine commitment, born in a common crusading effort against North African invaders and nurtured through centuries of cooperative activities and joint endeavors. As a result, sixteenth-century Spaniards had a rapport with the church that was unique even in that age of religious activism. They were also zealously and fanatically committed to its defense. It was entirely natural, therefore, that Spain should provide such a fertile soil for the spread of the Counter-Reformation and that its Catholic King should become the champion of Catholicism throughout Europe.

Philip's devotion to the church was genuine, just as his sense of duty to his kingdom was. In his mind the two were synonymous; duty to God encompassed duty to kingdom. That is why it is meaningless to try to separate and differentiate Philip's political and religious motives. We may classify the results from our point of view as political, economic, religious, or personal, but to him they were all the same. Nothing happened, he believed, without God's action or sanction; he was God's tool for bringing about the divine will. As king of Spain, Philip believed he possessed a mandate to serve as guardian of the church, and that guardianship applied to all of its aspects, religious or otherwise.

This coalescence of church and state in Philip's mind is perhaps nowhere more cogently portrayed than in his building of the Escorial. That great and somber structure was undertaken to provide not only a royal court and chambers for the operation of government, but more particularly as a place of religious repose, as a monument recognizing God's hand in the Spanish victory over the French at Saint Quentin in 1557, and as a sacred mausoleum to house the remains of his beloved father, Charles V. It also became the permanent memorial to Philip II as a patron of literature and the arts.

Philip's identification of the interests of Spain with those of the church does not imply that he always saw eye to eye with the pope on matters of religion and politics. As a matter of fact, he had frequent disagreements with Pius V and Gregory XIII over ecclesiastical authority as well as political policy, and when Paul IV and Sixtus V occupied the papal throne, Spanish-papal relations were outright hostile. Philip was ready to submit to God's will and to devote himself to the interests of the church; but who spoke God's will, and who represented the interests of the church? Philip was not so naïve as to fail to recognize that the pope's judgment was not always sound, and that the pontiff might pursue a course that was not for the best good of the church. Further-

El Escorial. *This palace-church-mausoleum, planned by Philip II and designed and built by Juan Herrera and Francisco de Mona, symbolizes the austerity and rigidity of Philip's reign as well as his personal piety.*

more, the possibility existed that the pope might have personal ambitions (just as Sixtus accused Philip of having) that were detrimental to the church. Moreover, since both the Spanish king and the Roman pope were temporal rulers of sizable Italian territories that bordered on one another, it is not surprising that Spanish-papal relations were far from friendly during much of Philip's reign.

The Morisco Uprising and Islamic Threat

Another religious problem plagued the early rule of Philip II. Thousands of Moriscos (nominally Christian Moors) living in the southern provinces of Spain continued to revert to Islamic practices and worship while outwardly observing Christian rituals and belief. This violation of law seemed to Philip a real danger, not only as a religious problem but also as a genuine political threat from menacing "subversives" who might at any time open the gates to invasion from North Africa. In January 1567, a royal order, intended to break down the Morisco allegiance to Islam, was published. Instead it brought open rebellion in Granada. By the early months of 1569, the Moriscos were a formidable threat, and as Arab reinforcements arrived from Algiers and other Moslem lands, the rebellion spread across Spain. In 1570, though, the tide of war began to shift as Morisco towns and strongholds were gradually retaken by Spanish arms. By 1571 the revolt was completely broken. To avoid a possible future outbreak, the Moriscos of Granada were uprooted from their homes and transplanted to other parts of Castile and Aragon.

The Morisco uprising was not the only worry Philip had from the Islamic south and east. Since the Turkish capture of Tripoli in 1556, Moslem forces had dominated the eastern Mediterranean. The great Ottoman sultan Suleiman the Magnificent, after overrunning the Balkans, had led his janissaries (elite troops largely composed of captured Christians) to the very walls of Vienna, and had then turned to conquer North Africa. In 1565 Suleiman's corsairs besieged the island of Malta. Europe seemed to lie at their mercy.

With the accession of Pius V to the papal throne in 1566, however, came renewed pressure for a crusade against the infidel. The ill-advised decision of the new sultan, Selim II (who succeeded Suleiman that same year), to conquer the island of Cyprus became the catalyst for a temporary uniting of the Mediterranean states against this latest Turkish attack. Venice called upon the pope to solicit aid from the European states. With the Dutch revolt in temporary

The Battle of Lepanto, *7 October 1571, was the last major encounter of two galley fleets. The Turkish defeat was decisive, but was not followed or exploited to best advantage by the Christian forces.*

abeyance and the Morisco war favorably terminated, Philip finally agreed to join the Holy League on condition that Spain lead it. Don Juan of Austria (1547–78), Philip's twenty-four-year-old half brother, was chosen to command the Christian fleet.

Late in September 1571 the allied armada reached Corfu and on October 7 virtually the entire Turkish fleet was sighted in the Bay of Lepanto on the Gulf of Corinth. The ensuing battle is one of the landmarks of naval warfare. The two mammoth fleets were of approximately equal size, numbering over 300 vessels each, mostly heavy war galleys and galleasses, and carrying, in addition to their sailors and rowers, some 30,000 soldiers. Don Juan ordered an immediate and massive attack against the Turkish galleys. For three hours the struggle raged, and when the Battle of Lepanto ended, the Turkish force had been crushed. Catholic Europe rejoiced at the defeat of the infidel, and Don Juan became the hero of the day—but only for a day.

Foreign Involvements of Philip II

The Morisco revolt and the naval war with the Turks were closely connected with a vital phase of Philip's foreign policy. Indeed, with the widespread dynastic and religious commitments he had, it would be difficult to point out a single affair or situation in Europe that did not affect the foreign policy and relations of the Spanish monarch. The real focal point of foreign affairs after 1571, however, was the Atlantic seaboard. Here, centered around the key Spanish provinces of the Netherlands, was enacted the crucial interplay of politics among the fluctuating powers of England, France, Spain, and Scotland that was to decide the religious and political fate of Europe.

During the first two decades of his reign, Philip's greatest efforts were to conserve and maintain the territories, jurisdictions, and powers he had inherited. Preserving the status quo in an age of change, however, requires vigorous and decisive action, both of which were rare in the "Prudent King." What has sometimes been mistaken for Spanish aggression and political ambition was often inertia or reaction to a changing situation.

Germany and France

Philip's least complicated field of foreign involvement was with the Holy Roman Empire, where his uncle, Ferdinand I (Charles V's brother), reigned as emperor from 1558 until his death in 1564; he was succeeded by his sons Maximilian II (1564–76) and Rudolph II (1576–1612). Ferdinand and Maximilian provided some support to Philip as they stood in the main line against Turkish aggression by land, but their lenient policy toward Protestantism within the Empire, and especially Maximilian's flirtations with Lutheranism, caused Philip more than a little apprehension during the middle years of his reign.

The peace concluded between Spain and France in 1559, marked by the marriage of Philip II to Elizabeth of Valois, continued precariously through the next thirty years, although not without many dangers and crises. It was broken then only by the rising tensions and excesses of religious conflict. As long as France refrained from molesting the Spanish Netherlands, and as long as the French king could battle the Huguenots on more than equal terms, Philip could afford to remain aloof from affairs in France and watch the French weaken and paralyze themselves by their civil wars. Philip was apprehensive about the policies of his mother-in-law, Catherine de' Medici, however, and continually urged her to take stronger and more decisive action against the Huguenots. Finally, when the Dutch revolt got out of hand and the French Protestants became a real threat, Philip intervened directly in France.

Scotland and England Closely connected with affairs in France were Philip's relations with Scotland, which was experiencing a civil and religious upheaval that pitted the Catholic monarchy of Mary Stuart against the determined opposition of John Knox and the Scottish Protestants. In the revolution that followed and eventually drove Mary from the throne, Philip was faced with a major dilemma. He had no sympathy for the Scottish Reformation, but to assist Mary would be to play directly into the hands of France and the house of Guise, Mary's ambitious relatives on the continent. Philip's policy, therefore, was to remain aloof, supplying both sympathy and encouragement to the Scottish Catholics but avoiding any action that would involve him in a hopeless cause, at least until the mid-1580s, when a changing situation invited his intervention.

Philip's relations with England were even more involved. For at least two centuries, the intercourse between England and the Iberian kingdoms had been predominantly friendly, and during the half-century of Habsburg-Valois wars, Henry VIII had usually been an ally of the emperor. When Philip ascended the thrones of Spain in 1556, he had already been king consort of England for two years. Mary's death in 1558, however, obscured the direction of English policy. Philip's first move was a proposal of marriage to the new monarch, Elizabeth, but the cautious and astute Tudor queen shrewdly rejected the offer, not because she had received a better one but because she wished to avoid closing the door on an avenue of diplomacy that offered such great possibilities for the Virgin Queen. During the first thirty years of Philip's reign, relations with Elizabeth fluctuated with the shifting pattern of international affairs. Hostilities might have opened a number of times had it not been for the determination on the part of both rulers to preserve the peace in spite of growing public antipathy. While Philip delayed and vacillated, Elizabeth flirted with Habsburg, Valois, and Scottish Protestants alike and grew stronger as the stakes mounted higher. When war finally came in the late 1580s, Philip discovered that he had waited too long.

Portugal He did not make the same mistake in Portugal. Relations with this seagoing nation to the west had been fairly calm since a practical delineation of their respective colonial spheres had been worked out early in the century. This did not mean, of course, that there were no more clashes between them on the high seas and in the New World. There still was "No peace beyond the line." Yet the Spanish and Portuguese rulers were able to arrange many peninsular differences to their mutual satisfaction, and developed a number of close marital ties. Philip's policy reached a crucial point in 1578 when the Portuguese king, Sebastian I (1557–78), was killed at the battle of Al Kasar al-Kabir in North Africa, while making an ill-timed and poorly planned attack on the Moors. The Portuguese crown passed to Sebastian's great uncle, the aged Cardinal Henry, who was not expected to live long and had no heirs to succeed him. Philip's claim to the throne, through his mother, Isabel of Portugal, was better than most of the seven who announced their rights of succession. In Portugal there was much opposition to Philip's claim but little unity against him. Through the work of Philip's ambassador in Lisbon, and the influence of the duke of Medina Sidonia with the Portuguese nobles, Philip was able to win the support of the principal grandees and the high clergy. When Cardinal Henry died in 1580, Philip sent an army under the duke of Alba into Portugal to back his claim with appropriate power. The Portuguese Cortes accepted the *fait accompli,* and Philip added Portugal to his list of crowns.

Still, the key to Philip's foreign policy, especially after 1567, was to be found in the Netherlands. He could not permit this rich territory to slip from him or fail to have it contribute its share to the support of his empire. Therefore the attitude and participation of the European states in the complex upheaval in the Netherlands determined Spanish attitude and policy toward those states.

William of Orange and the Revolt of the Netherlands

The Spanish Netherlands was not only the richest part of Philip's empire but also during this period the most prosperous area of Europe. The southern, Walloon (French-speaking) provinces of Artois, Hainaut, Namur, and the predominantly Flemish-speaking provinces of Flanders and Brabant, with cosmopolitan Antwerp as their greatest commercial and financial center, were the area of a flourishing textile industry and were engaged in active trade with all of Europe. The Dutch-speaking northern provinces, especially Holland and Zeeland, were predominantly fishing and trading communities that were becoming more prosperous through their expanding commerce.

From the beginning of Philip's reign, the problem of governing these provinces was challenging. Communication between Spain and its Burgundian territories was slow and arduous, and the growing distrust between the king and his subjects made their differences even greater. Furthermore, the nobles of the southern provinces were very independent and jealously guarded their feudal privileges and freedoms against any encroachment from outside. Under Charles V they were generally loyal, partly because they considered the emperor to be one of them, since he had been born in Ghent and had grown up in Flanders and Brabant. But Philip was a foreigner, and although he did not drastically alter his father's policies, the Netherlanders did not have confidence in him. Many factors led to their estrangement, and the eventual revolt, civil war, and revolution involved religious, social, economic, and political issues as well as personal animosities.

Margaret of Parma, *about forty years of age, by the Flemish master Antonis Mor. Margaret, Philip II's half-sister (the natural daughter of Charles V) and the wife of Ottavio Farnese, duke of Parma, faithfully served as regent in the Netherlands until 1568.*

Philip sensed the looseness of his hold on this vital area of his inheritance and gradually moved to strengthen his control. His intention was to pattern Spanish government in the Netherlands after that already functioning effectively in Italy. Yet Flanders, Holland, and Brabant were not like Naples, Sicily, and Milan. As Philip shifted the burden of rule from his capable regent, Margaret of Parma, and her advisory councils—Privy Council, Council of Finance, and Council of State—to the special committee dominated by Philip's favorite, Cardinal Granvelle, the nobles became aroused and belligerent. Still hoping to avoid an open conflict, Philip conceded to many of their demands, including the removal of Spanish troops from Flanders and the recall of Granvelle. He would not retreat in religious matters, however.

In the meantime, religious dissension in the Low Countries continued to spread despite early action by Charles V to stamp out heresy. Philip did not intend to mitigate the laws enforced by his father. In 1564 he added to them the decrees of the Council of Trent. The breaking point was reached when Philip sponsored a much-needed ecclesiastical reorganization in the Netherlands. The structure that had existed for centuries was cumbersome and awkward, and for that reason was preferred by the nobility of the Lowlands because it perpetuated their privileges and gave them considerable freedom of action. This situation ended when Philip created fifteen new bishoprics, corresponding roughly to the existing political divisions, and put them under the three new archbishoprics of Cambrai, Utrecht, and Malines (the last was the primate see, awarded to Granvelle himself). The nobles resented this encroachment and began to resist Spanish rule.

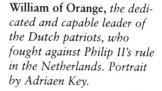

William of Orange, *the dedicated and capable leader of the Dutch patriots, who fought against Philip II's rule in the Netherlands. Portrait by Adriaen Key.*

The leaders and spokesmen of this aristocratic resistance were several knights of the Golden Fleece, including the count of Egmont (1522–68), stadholder (lieutenant) in Brabant and Artois; the count of Hoorn (1518–68), admiral of Flanders and stadholder of Gelderland and Zutphen; and especially William of Nassau, prince of Orange (sometimes known as William the Silent) (1533–84). William was descended from wealthy noble families of the Rhineland and southern France, and his subsequent acquisitions and military successes had made him one of the richest and most influential men in the Netherlands. He also held the official position of stadholder of Holland, Zeeland, and Utrecht. In religion William was no zealot—by 1560 he had already changed his affiliation three times—but political and other considerations had made William's cause the cause of the Dutch Protestants, and together with many members of the lesser nobility, they opposed the Spanish rule in the Netherlands.

In August 1565 petitions were sent to Philip II asking for a relaxation of religious persecution. Philip replied with an order insisting that all measures for the suppression of heresy be maintained. Thereupon, William of Orange, Egmont, and Hoorn withdrew from the Council of State and became the nucleus of an organized opposition. In April 1566 a large body of the lesser nobility presented a request to the regent asking that the king abolish the antiheretical edicts and turn over the religious problem to the States General, which represented all of the provinces. At this interview one of the royal counselors is reputed to have referred to the rowdy group of petitioners as *ces gueux* ("these beggars"). The chance remark was seized upon by the leaders of the group, who knew the value of a striking label, and it became the rallying cry for opposition throughout the Lowlands.

In the summer of 1566, iconoclastic riots began in southern Flanders and spread rapidly northward through the other provinces. Images, pictures, and stained-glass windows were smashed, Catholic churches desecrated, and ecclesiastical property destroyed. Aroused Protestants were taking matters into their own hands. In response to these riots, Philip decided to send the stern and hardened duke of Alba to maintain order and suppress the activities of the Beggars. Alba's long march northward from Genoa across the Alps and on through Franche-Comté, Lorraine, and Luxembourg to the southern Netherlands, along what came to be known as the Spanish Road, took four months, but it was obvious from the discipline, equipment, and caliber of these 10,000 veteran Spanish and Italian infantry that the Spanish king meant business.

The Duke of Alba's Regime Alba arrived in Brussels in August 1567 with almost supreme powers to govern and suppress heresy. He immediately established military control of Brussels and garrisoned the nearby cities of importance. Next he seized Egmont and Hoorn on charges of being associated with the Beggars, and set up a special tribunal, called the Council of Troubles (known popularly as the Council of Blood), which ignored the numerous exemptions and privileges enjoyed by the nobility and made everyone subject to the same laws. For the next eight months, Brussels witnessed a veritable reign of terror as the council swiftly took action against "heretics and traitors." The climax was reached in June 1568, when both Egmont and Hoorn went to the scaffold. Shortly thereafter, Margaret, humiliated and disillusioned by Alba's ruthlessness, resigned as Philip's regent and returned to her home in Parma. Alba now received the title as well as the authority of regent and governor general.

Success, however, brought disaster to Alba as he further antagonized the middle-class interests through his tightening political control, and especially by his financial policy. In 1569 he forced the States General to sanction a permanent sales tax, similar to the Spanish *alcabala*. The effect of this new levy was disastrous. Such a tax might be tolerated in the simple agrarian economy of Castile, but not in the industrial and commercial economy of the Netherlands. Now merchants and many commoners joined nobles and Calvinists in protest against the rigors of Spanish rule. William of Orange fled northward and took refuge in Holland and Zeeland, where for the next four years, with the help of Huguenots from France and mercenaries from Germany, he harassed the duke relentlessly. Yet William staunchly maintained that he was not disloyal to Philip but was only opposing the unconstitutional rule of the duke of Alba.

Unexpected help came from daring Dutch privateers and freebooters known as the "Sea Beggars," who, from scattered bases in the north, and especially from Dover and other English ports provided by Queen Elizabeth, marauded the coastal towns and crippled the meager Spanish shipping. In 1572 they even defeated a Spanish fleet in the Zuider Zee. Eventually, Queen

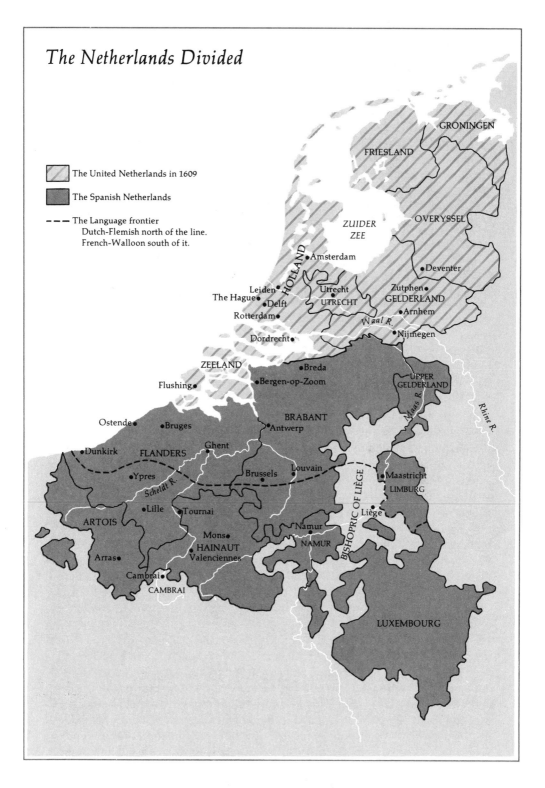

The Netherlands Divided

The United Netherlands in 1609

The Spanish Netherlands

— — — The Language frontier
Dutch-Flemish north of the line.
French-Walloon south of it.

The Sea Beggars Capture Brill *in April 1572 and establish control of the waterways in and out of the Netherlands.*

Elizabeth reversed her policy and closed her ports to the raiders. Forced to seek other bases for their attacks, the Sea Beggars audaciously seized the fortified city of Brill, at the mouth of the Maas, and a few days later they held Flushing, dominating the mouth of the Scheldt. Soon they controlled the whole labyrinth of waterways and islands along the central and northern coast, ensuring the safety of the northern provinces against Spanish attack.

Nevertheless, with the news from France of the Saint Bartholomew's Day massacre in the late summer of 1572, the situation seemed to be reversing. Free now from the Huguenot threat on his southern flank, Alba turned his troops toward the rebellious provinces of Holland and Zeeland, which from 1572 to 1576 were fighting against or almost in isolation from the rest of the provinces, giving the revolt more the appearance of a civil war. Yet it required more than military strength to make headway against an elusive enemy whose ally was the sea. The weapon had not yet been devised that could oppose the flood of an opened dike.

William of Orange rode the crest of the rebel success to become commander-in-chief of the armies of Holland, Zeeland, Friesland, and Utrecht, and in Holland the title of governor and regent with "absolute power, authority, and sovereign command." Soon after, he married the daughter of the French Duke of Montpensier, Charlotte de Bourbon, who had abandoned monastic life to become a Protestant and fled to the Low Countries. She not only made his home a relatively tranquil refuge (it also housed his children by two previous marriages and a good number of other relatives), but assisted him in the administration of his estates and sustained him in times of failure. He confessed that he was able to endure mainly because God had given him such a wonderful wife.

In 1573 Philip recalled the duke of Alba and turned to a more conciliatory policy in the hope of ending the costly war. Alba was replaced as governor general by Don Luis de Requesens (1528–76), grand commander of Castile, who arrived in Brussels in November. Among other things, the new Spanish policy called for the abolition of the hated sales tax and a general pardon and amnesty for all Netherlanders, except heretics. The pardon was predicated, however, on the condition that the Dutch put down their arms and submit unconditionally to the authority of the king. This they refused to do, so Requesens was forced to continue the repression begun by his predecessor. In October 1574 Leiden became the symbol of Dutch determination as it not only broke a long Spanish siege but also commemorated the victory by founding the University of Leiden, the first Protestant university in the Low Countries.

The Pacification of Ghent	When Requesens died of typhus in 1576, he was replaced by Philip's young half-brother, Don Juan of Austria, the victor of the battle of Lepanto. Don

Juan's governorship began tragically with a mutiny of Spanish and Italian troops and the ensuing "Spanish Fury," in which the rich and proud city of Antwerp was subjected to a devastating sack. Only four days after the Antwerp disaster, delegates of most of the Netherlands provinces, meeting in Ghent, concluded an agreement with Holland and Zeeland, ending the civil dispute with them and proposing the common settlement of their religious and financial problems under the leadership of William of Orange. By this Pacification of Ghent (8 November 1576) the provinces vaguely recognized their loyalty to the Spanish crown but at the same time suspended all edicts against heresy and demanded that Spanish troops be withdrawn. Three months later, the States General negotiated with Don Juan a Perpetual Edict, in which the governor general agreed to the Pacification of Ghent but with the guarantee that Catholicism would remain in the provinces. Holland and Zeeland refused to accept this edict and walked out of the States General. Don Juan was unable to live up to his part of the agreement, anyway, and by the end of the year the States General declared him an enemy of the country. With reinforcements from Spain, he reopened the fighting in the southern provinces when he suddenly died in October 1578 at the age of thirty-two. His two years as governor general were no more successful than his predecessors' had been, and the Spanish position was still precarious.

The Birth of the Dutch Nation

The task of pacifying and controlling the rebels now fell to Philip's young nephew, Alexander Farnese (1545–92), duke of Parma and son of the former regent. As a statesman, diplomat, and soldier, Parma was perhaps the ablest man in Philip's service. The hour was very late to save much from the confused

Alexander Farnese, Duke of Parma. *Philip II's most successful commander and able statesmen in the Netherlands was his nephew, the son of Margaret of Parma. Portrait by Otto Van Veen.*

situation. Nevertheless, by force of arms and the skillful use of diplomacy, plus the help of long-standing antagonisms between Walloons and Flemings, Catholics and Protestants, and rival noble families, Parma soon succeeded in drawing the Walloon states and many of the cities of Brabant and Flanders into a formal union for "the maintaining of order, good government, and the Catholic Church"—in other words, reaffirming their loyalty to Philip II. This Union of Arras was concluded early in January 1579. William quickly countered by organizing the northern states of Zeeland, Holland, Utrecht, Gelderland, Overyssel, Friesland, and Groningen into the Union of Utrecht, which also stood for law, order, and protection, but *not* for the Catholic Church. Each province in the northern union was to preserve its separate identity, but they should work together "as if they were but one province." The Netherlands was now divided into two mutually hostile camps with very little hope of reconciliation. William of Orange's dream of some sort of federal state composed of all seventeen provinces ruled by the States General was ended.

The Union of Utrecht, with its smaller geographic size and streamlined States General, intensified negotiations that had previously been initiated with the duke of Anjou (1554–84), brother of the king of France, hoping to secure the much-needed military and financial means to carry on the war against Spain. In September 1580 an agreement was reached between Anjou and the States General by which Anjou, to the chagrin and protest of his brother Henri III, agreed to furnish money and men to the "United Provinces" in return for their recognition of his protectorship of the liberties of the Netherlands and virtual sovereignty over the northern Low Countries—except in Holland and Zeeland, where William of Orange retained his special status as governor and regent with "full authority and power as sovereign and overlord." Despite this confusing exception, after the States General had declared Philip II formally deposed by the Act of Abjuration in July 1581, Anjou was considered Philip's successor as count of Holland and Zeeland.

Detained by his courtship with Elizabeth of England, Anjou finally reached the Netherlands early in 1582 and immediately made himself unpopular with the Dutch, not only because of his religion but also because of his disagreeable character and manners. Disregarding his treaty agreements, Anjou tried to seize control of Antwerp by force in January 1583, but this "French Fury" was a costly failure that seriously curtailed his credibility and caused the Dutch to cast their eyes elsewhere for a protector. Less than a year later, the States of Holland and Zeeland offered William of Orange the ancient title of count. Before he could be inaugurated, however, William was struck down by an assassin, motivated by Philip's offer of a reward for his head. This occurred just one month to the day (10 July 1584) after Anjou had died.

Strange as it may seem now, the States General did not yet consider the possibility of exercising sovereignty itself. The Dutch fight against Spain was not considered a war of independence. Having denied the sovereignty of the Spanish king, they quickly began a search for a new sovereign. Turning to the king of France, they offered to swear an oath of loyalty and obedience to Henri III, "to take refuge in, and to throw themselves into, the arms of His Majesty so that they be joined to the kingdom of France from which they, or most of them, were separated in the past, and be ruled and defended as his very humble vassals and subjects *on certain reasonable conditions.*" Not wanting to become involved in Dutch affairs, seeing what a thorn they had been in the side of the Spanish king, and fearing such involvement would surely mean war with Spain, Henri III quickly refused the Dutch offer.

English Involvement in the Netherlands

The States General turned next to Queen Elizabeth, thereby opening another strange episode in the story of the emerging Netherlands. Charles Wilson has correctly noted that "The Netherlands struggle was not merely a local matter or even simply a civil war. It was part of a vast international and intercontinental dispute involving France and England as well as Spain." The delegation sent to England in July 1585 was prepared to offer Elizabeth sovereignty of the Netherlands "on reasonable conditions." If she refused, they were authorized to ask her to become their "perpetual protector" (by which they meant something very close to sovereign). If she refused this, they were to ask for at least military assistance.

Not wanting to become involved in war with Spain either, Elizabeth accepted only the third alternative. She was leery of taking on the burdens of the Netherlands, and particularly loath to rule the unruly Dutch. Yet the Low Countries were vital to English trade, and she needed a friendly state across the channel for England's own protection. Aiding the Dutch was not a new venture for Elizabeth. She had frequently given them financial assistance, both directly and by interdicting the Spanish payship carrying money for Alba's soldiers. English military intervention had also taken place and had been an important ingredient in the relief of Leiden in 1574. Yet in every case, Elizabeth had been very careful not to let such intervention look official and to withdraw it whenever it brought diplomatic difficulties with Philip.

Now, egged on by her advisors, Elizabeth agreed by the Treaty of Nonesuch (October 1585) to send a military force of some 6,000 men under command of her favorite, Robert Dudley, earl of Leicester (ca. 1532–88), with the misleading title of lieutenant-general. Leicester's authority was left vague, although the treaty specified that he should restore authority and "reform the financial and military situation." More precise arrangements would be worked out with the States General. Worried that Leicester might involve her too far in Dutch affairs, Elizabeth specifically forbade him to accept any further commission than general of the English army. In February 1586, however, the States General designated him governor and captain general, with "full power and absolute command in the matter of the war and all matters concerned with it." Furthermore they granted him "full and absolute power in the aforesaid Provinces in the matter of civil government and justice, such as the Governors General of the Netherlands have in all times legally possessed, and particularly in the time of Charles V of beloved memory." Leicester was now in an extremely ambiguous position. Elizabeth wanted to avoid the appearance of Dutch protectorship, yet her representative was now hailed with higher titles than any that Philip II's lieutenants had ever possessed. She did not want Leicester to appear as her governor, and was furious at his failure to follow her orders. The States General, however, had carefully explained that it was they who made the appointment, not Elizabeth. By so doing they accepted, for the first time, the fact that they possessed sovereignty themselves. It was the beginning of an independent Dutch nation.

Leicester campaigned awkwardly in the Netherlands for a year and a half, interfering in matters he should have left alone and alienating many of his erstwhile friends. He was withdrawn by the queen in partial disgrace in August 1587 and never returned. Forced finally to rely upon their own resources and leadership, the seven United Provinces gradually evolved a loosely organized government, in which power was shared between the States General itself and the representative (called advocate general, later grand pensionary) of Holland, by far the most populous of the seven provinces. After 1586 that representative was Jan van Oldenbarneveldt (1547–1619), a lawyer and a man of considerable moral leadership, who advocated the theory that after the abjuration of Philip II, sovereign power reverted to the several provinces themselves (not to the States General). Military administration was in the hands of Maurice of Nassau (1567–1625), William's son. Maurice succeeded in creating a military machine that successfully assured the independence of the United Provinces from Spanish rule. In 1609 a twelve-year truce with Spain all but recognized that independence.

Meanwhile, the prince of Parma succeeded in consolidating Spanish power in the southern provinces. After his death in 1592, he was replaced as governor by Archduke Albert (brother of Emperor Rudolf II and of Philip II's fourth wife, Anna of Austria), who in 1598 married Philip's eldest daughter, Isabel Clara Eugenia, and received the southern provinces (modern Belgium) as a dowry. Since there were no heirs, however, these reverted to the Spanish crown in 1621.

The Golden Century of Spanish Literature

It must be obvious to even the most casual observer of sixteenth-century Iberia that here was a land of contrasts, a culture of paradoxes. A greater discrepancy can hardly be imagined than that existing between the wealth of Seville and the poverty of an Aragonese village, or between the arrogance of a Castilian lord (even an *hidalgo,* the lowest rung of the noble ladder) and the lowliness of a Murcian peasant. The appearance of Spain's greatest fictional characters, Don Quixote and Sancho Panza, symbolizes not only the physical, economic, and social dichotomy of the country but its profound intellectual and cultural paradoxes as well. Nevertheless, the century beginning with Philip II's ascension and lasting until the death of Philip IV (the *siglo de oro*—Golden Century) witnessed a cultural flowering in Spain that was without equal in all of Spanish history.

The literary expression of the *siglo de oro* took many forms, but it was most creative and influential in the theater and the novel. Four great names mark the transition of Spanish drama from an off-beat and highly suspect rival of classical and religious morality plays to a legitimate and popular genre of literary and dramatic art. These artists were Lope de Rueda (1510–65), a talented and energetic Sevillian author-playwright who started the renaissance of drama in Spain; Lope de Vega (1562–1635), its most prolific and creative genius, whose 500-odd existing comedies and plays are among the most charming, witty, action-packed, and expressively realistic of any period; Tirso de Molina (1571–1658), who brought realism, emotion, and a feeling for the dramatic to its golden-age peak, and created, in Don Juan, one of the most colorful literary characters of all time; and Juan Ruiz de Alarcón (ca. 1581–1639), the most polished and reserved dramatist of the age. These masters of Spanish drama raised Spain to the front rank among the nations of Europe in dramatic literature and theatrical production.

Cervantes and Don Quixote

The novel, which had been pioneered in Spain, reached its zenith in the *siglo de oro* with Miguel de Cervantes Saavedra (1547–1616), whose *Don Quixote* is universally recognized as one of the greatest literary masterpieces of all time. Ostensibly an attack on the medieval chivalric literature still popular in sixteenth-century Spain, *Don Quixote* did much more than lay knight errantry to rest. It perfected the novel of chivalry and made it compatible with literary realism, thus climaxing two traditions—the medieval romance and the sixteenth-century picaresque novel. Cervantes's greatest achievement was the magnificent reconciliation not only of divergent literary genres but also of the dichotomies and contradictions of the Spanish character. In the ingenious knight from La Mancha and his imperturbable squire (one ridiculously sublime and the other sublimely ridiculous) are symbolized the extreme opposites of ethereal idealism and mundane reality, a paradox of human nature as well as a characteristic of contemporary Spain. Don Quixote epitomizes the eternal and epic spirit of the visionary, a man of such lofty ideals and noble intentions that his eyes were blinded to the hard and mundane "facts of life." To him windmills appear as four-armed giants, a flock of sheep as an invading army, and the shaving basin of a traveling barber as the golden helmet of Mandrino. Don Quixote's earthy, crude, fat, and totally devoted squire tried in vain to make his master see and accept the realities as they were, but without success.

Yet in the end, after adventures that took the two inseparable companions to every corner of Spain, something of each wore off on the other. "After all, what is reality?" mused Sancho after their adventures were over. Could it be that his master was no more mad than he himself was? Is it possible that a dream world might in fact be as real as any other? For his part, Don Quixote laid his body to rest with the belief that Sancho, through his simple satisfactions, had already found the riches and comforts that had meant so much to him when he did not have them. Both were right, yet both were wrong. Cervantes leaves us with the conviction that there is something of both Don Quixote and Sancho Panza in all of us, and that both should be welcomed and harmonized, for they are indispensable. No great enterprise is ever achieved without the dual forces of vision and work.

That is not all that attracts us to *Don Quixote*. Cervantes himself lives in its pages as though he were clothed in the same rusty armor riding his own scrawny nag. He was a man who knew life in its coldest and most brutal forms. After 1570 he was a soldier, serving in the battle of Lepanto, where he was seriously wounded. He was later captured by Moorish pirates and spent five years in prison and slavery in Algiers before being ransomed in 1580 and returned to Spain. He was three times imprisoned for debts. His family life was a failure. Yet his spirit was never subdued nor his vision blurred. Self-educated, except for a brief schooling in Madrid under the humanist Juan López de Hoyos, Cervantes possessed both imagination and conviction—and a feeling for Castilian prose that has rarely been matched. He began writing *Don Quixote* while in prison, but the somber walls could not contain either his imagination or his humor. Even if there were nothing deeper in *Don Quixote* than its fast-moving and delightfully hilarious episodes, it would still be a literary masterpiece. Other Spanish prose of the period—even Cervantes' own *La Galatea* (Galatia), a pastoral romance published in 1580, his picaresque *Novelas ejemplares* (Exemplary Novels, 1612–13), and *Viaje del Parnaso* (Journey from Parnassus, 1614)—pale in comparison.

Nevertheless, other novel forms continued to flourish during the Golden Century as Spanish writers added to their productivity and reputation. The picaresque novel, for instance, was given even greater stature in 1599 with the publication of Mateo Alemán's *Guzmán de Alfarache,* a strikingly realistic picture of late sixteenth-century Spanish life as encountered by the rogue-hero; and Francisco de Quevedo's *La vida del buscón* (Life of the Cheat). Quevedo (1580–1645) was the greatest satirist of the age, occupying the role in seventeenth-century Spain that Voltaire was to play in eighteenth-century France. Reacting strongly against the individual and national decay that he perceived about him, Quevedo satirized his times and his countrymen unmercifully in witty caricatures, and in more serious works of satire mixed with moral philosophy, such as *Los sueños* (Dreams). Disillusioned by the baseness and corruption of mankind, Quevedo found solace only in a sort of Christianized stoicism that became typical of many seventeenth-century Spanish thinkers.

Lyric poetry of the Golden Century found its greatest exponent in Luis de Góngora y Argote (1561–1627). Góngora's purpose was to lift Castilian verse to heights undreamed of in the past. Addressing himself to the cultured elite of Spain, Góngora believed that the natural beauty and sonorous rhythm of Castilian could be enhanced even further by adopting Latinisms and by embellishing it with rare words and phrases. He succeeded mostly in drawing a curtain of obscurity between poetry and all but a handful of Spanish readers. His style, referred to variously as *culteranismo* (cultism), because of its narrow clientele, and *Gongorismo,* because of its obscurity and extravagance, is a literary manifestation of Baroque embellishment.

Spanish Art

Pride in Spanish greatness, and in the mother church that was in part responsible for that eminence, produced in the visual arts a blossoming that was never again equaled in Spain. As in all great art, that of the Spanish Golden Age was varied and even divergent, defying simple definitions and contradicting facile comparisons. It was born of many traditions and influences, and produced creations of variable beauty. The strongest foreign flavor was, of course, Italian. During the reign of Charles V, the Italian domination of Spanish art was almost complete, except for the extentuating influence from Flanders. By midcentury, Italian Mannerism, with its strained tensions and its didactic religious emotionalism, had become international. With the spread of the Italian *maniera* into German, Flemish, and Spanish schools of art, it developed greater variety itself and more adaptability to the national and individual peculiarities of these areas.

In painting, the assimilation of Mannerism by Spanish realism during the reign of Philip II produced striking results in the art of Luis Morales and El Greco. Morales, the most elusive of all Spanish painters, "groped for that profoundly mystical expression which evokes religious contemplation." He did so, however, with a consciousness and attention to reality that sets him off from many other Mannerist painters, especially from his more famous follower, El Greco. Morales's deep mysticism, seen as a continuing attachment to Gothic style, reveals the important link between the medieval church and the Spain of the Counter-Reformation.

El Greco Domenikos Theotocópoulos (1541–1614), known as El Greco (The Greek), was the greatest exponent of sixteenth-century Spanish Mannerism. Born in Crete, of Byzantine and Hellenic heritage, El Greco received his early artistic education in Venice from Titian and Tintoretto, and in Rome came under the influence of the later Mannerists. Sometime before 1577, El Greco settled in Spain where he resided for the next thirty-seven years in Toledo, the city of contrasts described by him as that "Rocky mass, glory of Spain, and light of her cities." Toledo had been, until very recently, the political capital of Spain and was still the primate see of the Spanish church. A former center of Moorish life and power, Toledo retained much of its Islamic color and fascination while giving the outward appearance of drab monotony and harsh austerity. Perhaps it was the lively prosperity of the Toledo steel-blade industry or the silk-cloth trade that attracted El Greco, or maybe it was the cultural appeal of the great university, with its literary and artistic preeminence, or even the sumptuousness of the richly adorned churches and cathedral. It might have been the mysterious allure of the narrow, winding streets running like silent corridors through the massive complex that stood as a somber monastery overlooking the arid plain below. Whatever the magnet that drew El Greco to Toledo, he soon became as completely Castilianized yet as distinctively individual as the city that had absorbed him. He became the visual spokesman of Counter-Reformation Spain, the personification of ecstatic mysticism.

El Greco's eclectic yet highly individualistic style was well suited to represent the religious idealism and the physical stresses of sixteenth-century Spain. His characteristically elongated and contorted figures, sometimes placed in unnatural or even grotesque positions, rendered in eerie shades of yellow and green nervously contrasted with livid pinks and blues set against turbulent grays, suggest his deep spiritual involvement. Yet it was an involvement fraught with contradictions and contrasts ranging from agony to ecstasy. Sometimes this opposition is seen in a disparity between his pictures, but more often it is revealed in the movement and intense antithesis within a single work. In *Philip II's Dream* (sometimes known as the *Adoration of the Name of Jesus,* or as the *Allegory of the Holy Alliance*), for example, may be seen the entire range of human emotional responses, from the horrors of hell to the ecstasy of heavenly adoration. The *Martyrdom of Saint Maurice* similarly runs the entire emotional gamut, and the *Burial of Count Orgaz* combines sadness, grief, and remorse with wonderment, devotion, and triumph. The unresolved tensions produced by the religious upheaval and frequently represented in Mannerist art, is effectively portrayed in the feeling of impending doom in the *View of Toledo* and also in the *Laocoön.*

El Greco's mystical qualities are best portrayed in his spiritualization of figures and of nature, "like visions," says Miguel de Unamuno, "like dreams of the natural world, rather than as copies or transcriptions of it." For it was the spiritual life that El Greco responded to most, and that inner life "penetrates the substance of the painting, and itself becomes the painting." Saint Teresa's ecstatic vision of the ethereal realm provides a synopsis of El Greco's

El Greco's "View of Toledo" *reflects some of the emotional power and unresolved tension of El Greco's Mannerist style.*

painting. "I see a white and a red of a quality one finds nowhere in nature," she wrote, "and yet they are nature itself, and life itself and the most perfect beauty imaginable."

El Greco's style, however, did not coincide completely with the tastes of Counter-Reformation Spain. What was catharsis for the artist was agitation for some of his viewers. Philip II was disturbed by El Greco's asymmetrical, violent, and emotional canvases. The king preferred the quiet symmetry and cold solemnity of the Escorial, designed by Juan de Herrera (1530–97) (see page 279) and the reserved, even austere, realism of a younger generation of Spanish painters. One of these was Francisco Ribalta (1565–1638), a Valencian painter whose grim and sober realism, coupled with a dramatic use of light and shadow, more nearly coincided with Philip's tastes. With Ribalta, and his Sevillian contemporaries Francisco Herrera the Elder and Francisco Pacheco, the first truly Spanish school of painting arose. Among its achievements was the notable development of court portraiture by Alonso Sánchez Coello and his disciple, Juan Pantoja de la Cruz. Sánchez Coello learned his art from the Flemish master (Antonis Mor), who, along with Titian, were Philip II's favorite court painters until their deaths in 1576 (see pages 185 and 284).

The king also employed women artists. One of these was Caterina van Hemessen, who had been commissioned to paint several religious scenes as well as portraits and miniatures for Margaret of Parma in the Netherlands, then followed her to Spain in 1568. Philip also invited Marietta Robusti, the talented daughter of Tintoretto, to come to the Spanish court, but her father refused, arranging for her to be married instead. Four years later she died in childbirth.

The most successful woman painter in Spain was Sofonisba Anguissola (ca. 1530–1626), daughter of a remarkable noble family of Cremona, Italy. Sofonisba was the most gifted of six sisters who were all encouraged by their father to study painting. Philip II rewarded her generously, granting her a tidy pension and a position as lady-in-waiting to the court. There she produced portraits of the king and his family as well as other major figures (see page 265). Van Dyck later remarked that he had never learned so much about painting in so short a time as he had from her.

Late sixteenth-century sculpture gradually moved from the classical restraint of Leone and Pompeo Leoni's Escorial statues to the unique early Baroque polychrome (multicolored) crucifixes and emotional sculpture of Gregorio Fernández of Valladolid (ca. 1576–1636) and Juan Montáñez of Seville (see page 201). Realistically carved and elaborately painted wood sculpture, its roots deeply embedded in the popular religious art of Spain, reflected the Spanish penchant toward morbid involvement in religious worship. The emotional appeal of these ultrarealistic images—principally of the crucified Christ and the mourning Mary, fashioned with eyelashes and wigs of real hair, polished and painted with rich colors, and costumed in the finest fabrics—was direct and intense, heightened by the intuitive sympathy of the people with the personalities thus portrayed.

Suggestions for Further Reading

GENERAL

The indispensable book on early modern Spain is still J.H. Elliott, *Imperial Spain, 1469–1716* (London, 1963; New York, 1964), to be supplemented by the appropriate chapters of his *Europe Divided, 1559–1598* (New York, 1969), and essays in *Spain and its World, 1500–1700* (New Haven, 1989). Similarly informative is Henry Kamen, *Spain, 1469–1714: A Society of Conflict* (New York, 1983), which sees Spain as a nation thrust into an imperial role for which it was not adequately equipped. Also see Kamen's very brief *Golden Age Spain* (Atlantic Highlands, New Jersey, 1988). A.W. Lovett, *Early Habsburg Spain, 1517–1598* (New York and Oxford, 1986) is a very useful study of the reigns of Charles V and Philip II, more up-to-date than John Lynch, *Spain Under the Habsburgs, Vol. I: Empire and Absolutism, 1516–1598* (New York, 1964, 2nd ed., 1981), which is still very good.

PHILIP II AND SPANISH GOVERNMENT

The most informed biographies of Philip are Peter Pierson, *Philip II of Spain* (Levittown, New York, 1975) and Geoffrey Parker, *Philip II* (Boston, 1978). They are both lucidly written. Also see the valuable essays dealing with Philip and Spanish government in H.G. Koenigsberger, *The Habsburgs and Europe, 1516–1660* (Ithaca, 1971) and *Politicians and Virtuosi: Essays in Early Modern History* (London, 1986), especially "The Statecraft of Philip II." The transition of power from Charles V to Philip II is analyzed in M.J. Rodríguez-Salgado, *The Changing Face of Empire: Charles V, Philip II, and Habsburg Authority, 1551–1559* (New York and Cambridge, England, 1988). The most important study of government under Philip II and his son is I.A.A. Thompson, *War and Government in Habsburg Spain, 1560–1620* (London, 1976). For a closer look at some aspects of that government see A.W. Lovett, *Philip II and Mateo Vázquez de Leca: The Government of Spain, 1572–1592* (Geneva, Switzerland, 1977). The best account of Philip's leading advisor, general, and governor is William S. Maltby, *Alba: A Biography of Fernando Alvarez de Toledo, Third Duke of Alba, 1507–1582* (Berkeley, 1983). David Goodman, *Power and Penury: Government, Technology and Science in Philip II's Spain* (New York and Cambridge, England, 1988) refutes the assumption that Spain contributed very little to scientific development during Philip's reign.

SOCIETY AND ECONOMICS

Spanish social history has become a very active field of investigation in recent years. A couple of the best works on rural society are David E. Vassberg, *Land and Society in Golden Age Castile* (New York and Cambridge, England, 1984), and Michael R. Weisser, *The Peasants of the Montes* (Chicago, 1976). On urban life, see especially James S. Amelang, *Honored Citizens of Barcelona: Patrician Culture and Class Relations, 1490–1714* (Princeton, 1986), which shows how the Catalan feudal aristocracy merged with the urban oligarchy to form a civic ruling class; Linda Martz, *Poverty and Welfare in Hapsburg Spain: The Example of Toledo* (New York and Cambridge, England, 1983), a critical study of the conditions of the poor in Toledo; Mary Elizabeth Perry, *Crime and Society in Early Modern Seville* (Hanover, New Hampshire, 1980); Richard L. Kagan, *Lucrecia's Dreams: Politics and Prophecy in Sixteenth-Century Spain* (Berkeley, 1990), a case study of the treatment of deviance; and Ruth Pike, *Penal Servitude in Early Modern Spain* (Madison, 1983), which looks at forced labor as a punishment for criminals. Also see her earlier *Aristocrats and Traders: Sevillian Society of the Sixteenth Century* (Ithaca, 1972). The student community is insightfully analyzed in Richard Kagan, *Students and Society in Early Modern Spain* (Baltimore, 1974).

A close look at the printing industry in Clive Griffin, *The Crombergers of Seville: The History of a Printing and Merchant Dynasty* (New York and Oxford, 1989), not only provides insights into Spanish industry and trade but also into culture and Spanish reading habits. David R. Ringrose, *Madrid and the Spanish Economy, 1560–1850* (Berkeley, 1984) traces the interactions between the capital and its hinterland over a period of 300 years. Carla Rahn Phillips, *Ciudad Real, 1500–1750: Growth, Crisis, and Readjustment in the Spanish Economy* (Cambridge, Massachusetts, 1979) is a valuable study of an important city. Helen Nader, *Liberty in Absolutist Spain: The Habsburg Sale of Towns, 1516–1700* (Baltimore, 1990), focuses on the importance of municipal government in Spain and the consequences of the practice of selling towns their independence as a fund-raising scheme.

THE SPANISH OVERSEAS EMPIRE

Broad coverage of the Spanish Empire are provided in Lyle N. McAlister, *Spain and Portugal in the New World, 1492–1700* (Minneapolis, 1984); Colin M. MacLachlan, *Spain's Empire in the New World* (Berkeley, 1988), a stimulating book which focuses on the political ideology of Spanish colonial government; and James Lockhart and Stuart Schwartz, *Early Latin America: A History of Colonial Spanish America and Brazil* (New York and Cambridge, England, 1983). Two good regional studies are Peggy K. Liss, *Mexico under Spain, 1521–1566* (Chicago, 1974), and Murdo J. MacLeod, *Spanish Central America: A Socioeconomic History, 1520–1720* (Berkeley, 1984). Other, more specialized studies include Amy Buchnell, *The King's Coffer: Proprietors of the Spanish Florida Treasury, 1565–1702* (Gainesville, 1981); Louisa Schell Hoberman, et al., eds., *Cities and Society in Colonial Latin America* (Albuquerque, 1986); François Chevalier, *Land and Society in Colonial Mexico,* tr. by Alvin Eustis (Berkeley, 1982); Keith A. Davies, *Landowners in Colonial Peru* (Austin, 1984); and Anthony Pagden, *Spanish Imperialism and the Political Imagination* (New Haven, 1990). The human level of Spain's colonial rule is examined in Ralph H. Vigil, *Alonso de Zorita: Royal Judge and Christian Humanist, 1512–1585* (Norman, Oklahoma, 1987). The role of the overseas church in Mexico is the focus of Robert Ricard, *The Spiritual Conquest of Mexico: An Essay on the Apostolate and the Evangelizing Methods of the Mendicant Orders in New Spain, 1523–1572,* tr. by Lesley Byrd Simpson (Berkeley, 1982); John F. Schwaller, *Origins of Church Wealth in Mexico: Ecclesiastical Revenues and Church Finances, 1523–1600* (Albuquerque, 1985), and the same author's *The Church and Clergy in Sixteenth-Century Mexico* (Albuquerque, 1987). Stafford Poole's *Pedro Moya de Contreras: Catholic Reform and Royal Power in New Spain, 1571–1591* (Berkeley, 1987) looks closely at the life and work of one of Philip II's important appointees.

RELIGION AND THE CHURCH

An outstanding account of the role of religion in Spanish life is William A. Christian, Jr., *Local Religion in Sixteenth-Century Spain* (Princeton, 1981), as is his *Apparitions in Late Medieval and Renaissance Spain* (Princeton, 1981). Also very enlightening is Maureen Flynn, *Sacred Charity: Confraternities and Social Welfare in Spain, 1400–1700* (Ithaca, 1989). For good studies of the saints Teresa of Avila and Juan de la Cruz, see Stephen Clissold, *St. Teresa of Avila* (London, 1979), and Richard P. Hardy, *Search for Nothing: The Life of John of the Cross* (New York, 1982). Catherine Swietlicki, *Spanish Christian Cabala: The Works of Luis de León, Santa Teresa de Jesús, and San Juan de la Cruz* (Columbia, Missouri, 1986) is very stimulating. On Spanish Protestantism see A. Gordon Kinder, *Spanish Protestants and Reformers in the Sixteenth Century* (London, 1983); on the Inquisition, Henry Kamen, *Inquisition and Society in Spain in the Sixteenth and Seventeenth Centuries* (Bloomington, 1985); Stephen Haliczer, *Inquisition and Society in the Kingdom of Valencia, 1478–1834* (Berkeley, 1990); and William Monter, *Frontiers of Heresy: The Spanish Inquisition from the Basque Lands to Sicily* (New York, 1990).

FOREIGN AND MILITARY AFFAIRS

Surprisingly, foreign affairs are still very much neglected in recent scholarship on Spain. One must rely on a handful of articles in Spanish journals and a very few in English. There has been no major book on Spanish diplomacy under Philip II since De Lamar

Jensen, *Diplomacy and Dogmatism* (Cambridge, Massachusetts, 1964), but see vol. 2 of Fernand Braudel, *The Mediterranean and the Mediterranean World in the Age of Philip II* (New York, 1973) for some relevant comments. Military and naval matters have been better served. See in particular Geoffrey Parker, *The Army of Flanders and the Spanish Road, 1567–1659* (Cambridge, England, 1972); Joseph O'Callaghan, *The Spanish Military Order of Calatrava and Its Affiliates* (London, 1975); Paul E. Hoffman, *The Spanish Crown and the Defense of the Caribbean, 1535–1585* (Baton Rouge, 1980); Ellen G. Friedman, *Spanish Captives in North Africa in the Early Modern Age* (Madison, 1983), which deals with the human casualties of the long conflict between Spain and Islamic north Africa; and Jack Beeching, *The Galleys at Lepanto* (New York, 1983). For a broader view of military changes see Geoffrey Parker, *The Military Revolution: Military Innovation and the Rise of the West, 1500–1800* (New York and Cambridge, England, 1988).

Several good books on the Spanish Armada have been published since the pioneering, Pulitzer Prize-winning *The Armada*, by Garrett Mattingly (Boston, 1959), notably Bryce Walker, *The Armada* (Alexandria, Virginia, 1981), a richly illustrated book, and David Howarth, *The Voyage of the Armada: The Spanish Story* (New York, 1982). The greatest stimulus, however, has come from the 400th anniversary commemoration in 1988. See Colin Martin and Geoffrey Parker, *The Spanish Armada* (London, 1988), which uses underwater archeology to come up with some novel theories about Armada guns; also Colin Martin, *Full Fathom Five: Wrecks of the Spanish Armada* (London, 1975). The most refreshing new interpretation is Felipe Fernández-Armesto, *The Spanish Armada: The Experience of War in 1588* (New York and Oxford, 1988). The military/naval aspects are analyzed in Peter Padfield, *Armada* (London, 1988), and Peter Kemp, *The Campaign of the Spanish Armada* (Oxford, 1988). Also see Duff Hart-Davis, *Armada* (London, 1988), and Roger Whiting, *The Enterprise of England: The Spanish Armada* (New York, 1988). The official catalogue of the international Armada exhibition held at Greenwich and Belfast is a magnificent book written by M.J. Rodriguez-Salgado and the staff of the National Maritime Museum, entitled *Armada, 1588–1988* (London, 1988). Medina Sidonia's role is carefully analyzed in Peter Pierson, *Commander of the Armada: The Seventh Duke of Medina Sidonia* (New Haven, 1989).

THE REVOLT OF THE NETHERLANDS

The best overall account of the revolt, its causes, nature, and consequences, is Geoffrey Parker, *The Dutch Revolt* (Ithaca and London, 1977), although Pieter Geyl's *The Revolt of the Netherlands, 1555–1609*, 2nd ed. (London, 1966), has many valuable insights. Also see the penetrating articles in Geoffrey Parker, *Spain and the Netherlands, 1559–1659* (London, 1979). The latest analysis is Alastair Duke, *Reformation and Revolt in the Low Countries* (Ronceverte, West Virginia, 1990). Important regional and municipal studies include James D. Tracy, *A Financial Revolution in the Habsburg Netherlands: Renten and Renteniers in the County of Holland, 1515–1565* (Berkeley, 1985); and more recently, *Holland under Habsburg Rule, 1506–1566: The Formation of a Body Politic* (Berkeley, 1990). C.C. Hibben, *Gouda in Revolt: Particularism and Pacificism in the Revolt of the Netherlands, 1572–1588* (Utrecht, 1983); Charles R. Steen, *A Chronicle of Conflict: Tournai, 1559–1567* (Utrecht, 1984); and Richard Reitsma, *Centrifugal and Centripetal Forces in the Early Dutch Republic: The State of Overyssel, 1566–1600* (Amsterdam, 1982). Some Elizabethan involvement in the Dutch revolt is discussed in Jan Albert Dop, *Eliza's Knights: Soldiers, Poets, and Puri-*

tans in the Netherlands, 1572–1586 (Alblasserdam, the Netherlands, 1981), and G.D. Ramsay, *The Queen's Merchants and the Revolt of the Netherlands* (Manchester, England, 1986).

SPANISH LITERATURE AND ART

On Spanish Golden Age literature in general, see Paul J. Smith, *Writing in the Margin: Spanish Literature of the Golden Age* (New York and Oxford, 1988); Kathleen McNermey, *The Influence of Ausiàs March on Early Golden Age Castilian Poetry* (Amsterdam, 1982), which identifies the impact of Catalan literature; B.W. Ife, *Reading and Fiction in Golden-Age Spain* (New York and Cambridge, England, 1985); and Peter W. Evans, ed., *Conflicts of Discourse: Spanish Literature in the Golden Age* (New York, 1990). The role of drama and the theater in Spain, and its comparison with England is ably presented in John Loftis, *Renaissance Drama in England and Spain* (Princeton, 1987); Walter Cohen, *Drama of a Nation: Public Theater in Renaissance England and Spain* (Ithaca, 1988); and Melveena McKendrick, *Theatre in Spain, 1490–1700* (Cambridge, England, and New York, 1989). The picaresque novel is briefly examined in Francisco Pico, *The Spanish Picaresque Novel and the Point of View* (New York and Cambridge, England, 1984), and Helen H. Reed, *The Reader in the Picaresque Novel* (London, 1984).

For a closer look at the greatest Spanish writer, one may consult William Byron, *Cervantes: A Biography* (New York, 1978); Melveena McKendrick, *Cervantes* (Boston, 1980); Alban K. Forcione, *Cervantes and the Humanist Vision* (Princeton, 1983); and three very interesting studies by John G. Weiger that analyze the role of the reader in Cervantes's major novel: *The Individuated Self: Cervantes and the Emergence of the Individual* (Athens, Ohio, 1979), *The Substance of Cervantes* (New York and Cambridge, England, 1985), and *In the Margins of Cervantes* (Hanover, New Hampshire, 1988). Also very penetrating is Stephen Gilman, *The Novel According to Cervantes* (Berkeley, 1989).

On Spanish art see in particular Richard G. Mann, *El Greco and His Patrons* (New York and Cambridge, England, 1986); Antonio Palomino de Castro y Velasco, *Lives of the Eminent Spanish Painters and Sculptors,* tr. by Nina Ayala Mallory (New York and Cambridge, England, 1987); and M. Haraszti-Takacs, *Spanish Genre Painting in the Seventeenth Century* (New York, 1983).

9 | ENGLAND UNDER ELIZABETH I

E NGLAND ROSE TO UNPRECEDENTED PROMINENCE IN THE SIXTEENTH century under the astute guidance of Elizabeth Tudor. This was not the beginning of European involvement for the island kingdom. Indeed, the reign of Elizabeth was a period of relative retreat from continental affairs. Yet in this very withdrawal, marked by cautious conservatism and semicommitment, the English began to discover hidden strength in their insularity as they embarked on a new course of maritime activity that eventually carried them to the pinnacle of power and eventually to the establishment of a global colonial empire.

In the meantime, the immediate channel ahead seemed full of shoals and hazards for the little kingdom of less than 4 million people when Mary Tudor died in November 1558 and Henry VIII's second daughter ascended the throne. For nearly half a century, England had been a pawn in the emperor's European wars. During the last five of those years, the English state had been tied tightly to Spanish policy. How would England's twenty-five-year-old queen cope with the might of France without succumbing to the overlordship of Spain? How would she meet the perennial problem of the northern frontier? And how would she, a Protestant—and a woman at that—avoid civil upheaval in a Catholic country dominated by men? With little knowledge of finances or law, could she guide Parliament or improve the disastrous economic condition of the majority of her subjects? No one knew, least of all Elizabeth. England's young queen, however, was already a veteran of the Tudor political jungle. She had the gift of adroitness and a strong instinct for survival. Her mark on English history would be indelible.

Elizabeth the Queen

It is not easy to speak with assurance about the character of Elizabeth Tudor. The queen defies simple categorization and has escaped consensus for over four centuries. Veiled fastidiously beneath the cloak of queenship, she is almost as hard to know as Philip II—and generally for the same reasons. Elizabeth

Elizabeth I. *This "Sieve Portrait," attributed to Cornelius Ketel, captures both the regal queen and the enigmatic woman who ruled England for forty-five years.*

Tudor purposely concealed her own feelings from public inspection or even private perusal, and she masked her true intentions behind a flurry of contradictory declarations.

Nevertheless, many things about her can be and are known. Her appearance, for example, is spread before us in hundreds of portraits and likenesses from contemporary artists. They do not all agree perfectly in details, but they convey the visage of a regal, strong-willed, intelligent, and vain woman, possessing, in Horace Walpole's anecdotal description, a "pale Roman nose, a head of hair loaded with crowns and powdered with diamonds, a vast ruff, a vaster farthingale, and a bushel of pearls."

Verbal descriptions of the queen abound in the documents of the time. On the eve of her accession, the Venetian ambassador saw her as "a young woman, whose mind is considered no less excellent than her person, although her face is comely rather than handsome, but she is tall and well formed, with a good skin, although swarthy; she has fine eyes and above all a beautiful hand of which she makes display." At the zenith of her reign, she was portrayed by an admirer in the following terms: "Of stature mean, slender, straight and amiably composed; of such state in her carriage as every motion of her seemed to bear majesty; her hair was inclined to pale yellow, her forehead large and fair, a seeming seat for princely grace; her eyes lively and sweet, but shortsighted; her nose somewhat rising in the midst; the whole compass of her countenance somewhat long, but yet of admirable beauty, not so much in that which is termed the flower of youth, as in a most delightful composition of majesty and modesty in equal mixture." André Hurault, the French ambassador to Elizabeth, described the queen near the end of her reign thusly:

> As for her face, it is and appears to be very aged. It is long and thin, and her teeth are very yellow and unequal, compared with what they were formerly, so they say, and on the left side less than on the right. Many of them are missing, so that one cannot understand her easily when she speaks quickly. Her figure is fair and tall and graceful in whatever she does; so far as may be she keeps her dignity.

A few months later Paul Hentzner, a jurist from Brandenburg, visited the queen at Greenwich, and described her in these words:

> Next came the Queen, in the 65th year of her age (as we were told), very majestic; her face oblong, fair but wrinkled; her eyes small, yet black and pleasant; her nose a little hooked, her lips narrow, and her teeth black, (a defect the English seem subject to, for their too great use of sugar); she had in her ears two pearls with very rich drops; her hair was of an auburn colour, but false; upon her head she had a small crown, . . . her bosom was uncovered, as all the English ladies have it till they marry; and she had on a necklace of exceeding fine jewels; her hands were slender, her fingers rather long, and her stature neither tall nor low; her air was stately, her manner of speaking mild and obliging.

Her contemporaries, especially those who knew her intimately, frequently attested to the queen's domineering will and haughtiness, but they also praised her intelligence, charm, and wit, which she could display or suppress as the situation demanded. She was courageous in face of the greatest odds, yet did not resort to snap decisions that might later prove more venturesome than sound. In fact, her irresolution seems to have aggravated her councilors more than any other trait. In this too she bears comparison with the Spanish king. She was determined, to the point of stubbornness, yet she freely exercised the proverbial feminine right to change her mind. She carried the policy of moderation by indecision and vacillation to its extreme.

Elizabeth was thrifty, even parsimonious, in an age of prodigality, insisting that state expenditures be kept within the crown's income. When it came to spending for the royal wardrobe, pageantry, and pomp, however, the queen was unrestrained. She believed in the mystique of the Renaissance monarchy, in the idea that the people vicariously identified with their monarch, and that in a mysterious way even her lavish dress and display became personalized in each of her subjects. Through their queen, even the most poverty-stricken peasants enjoyed wealth and luxury when her presence was visible. That is why Elizabeth contrived so many extravagant progresses and processions through the provinces, cities, and villages of the south and the midlands. Being seen in her radiant glory by the people of England not only gratified her own yearning to strut but it also enhanced the public image of the monarchy and thus satisfied the requirements of successful "domestic propaganda"—what today we call public relations.

The principal fact about Elizabeth was her sex, and she used that fact as skillfully as any female ruler ever had. She was a master of the calculated art of self-presentation, creating titles for herself or allowing her subjects to confer upon her names associated with heroines of the past such as Astraea, the Greek goddess of justice; Cynthia or Artemis, the moon goddess; Diana, the Roman goddess of chastity and of hunting; and Deborah, the Israelite prophetess and judge. Nothing illustrates this better, or was more carefully cultivated, than her effort to replace the Virgin Mary in the affection of her subjects with the image of the Virgin Queen—a "natural mother . . . unto you all." This cult of the Virgin Queen was actively promoted in contemporary writing as well as in her progresses, and helped fill the void in the popular imagination left by the Protestant dethroning of the Virgin Mary, thus encouraging a deeper loyalty to the queen. It has been noted by Carole Levin and others that many symbols used to represent Elizabeth as the Virgin Queen, such as the star, moon, rose, ermine, and pearl, were symbols appropriated from the iconography of the Virgin Mary, and that images of the queen were treated in England almost like religious icons. Many English Protestants took the coincidence of Elizabeth's birthday with the Catholic feast of the nativity of the Virgin as an omen that in God's sight Queen Elizabeth and the Anglican Church had replaced Marian Catholicism.

Elizabeth also took advantage of her femininity in another way. From the moment she began to reign, or perhaps sooner, she employed every device to

woo her Englishmen and win their indispensable support. Late in life she remarked that she had maintained the good will of her people as though they
were all her husbands, "for if they did not rest assured of some special love to
them, they would not yield me such good obedience." Skillfully using courtship
and the rules of chivalry as a political tool, she let ambitious courtiers know
that the romantic adoration of her person was always helpful in obtaining
favors or advancement. Indeed, she made much political profit by taking advantage of male ego as she variously rewarded the attempts of courtiers and
suitors to please her. At the age of 70 she was still dancing with them and
demanding their homage and fealty. Her many youthful courtships led some
to doubt her virginity, and her scandalous association with Robert Dudley,
whom she created Earl of Leicester, gave gossipers a heyday. Yet through it all,
Elizabeth was in control of the situation, astutely using both rumor and truth
to her advantage while revelling in the attention and love shown her by adoring
subjects.

Yet her sex was also a handicap, since being an unmarried female ruler
put her outside the traditionally perceived role of women as wives and moth-
ers. The psychological ramifications of this fact were important for her to overcome. And she did so ingeniously. Monarchs were thought of as male, and the
ascension of a female ruler was viewed with distrust if not alarm. John Knox
wrote in his *First Blast* that to elevate a woman to the throne was "repugnant
to nature" and it "defiled, polluted and profaned the throne of God." Calvin
offered his opinion "that as it is a deviation from the original and proper order
of nature, it is to be ranked, no less than slavery, among the punishments con-
sequent upon the fall of man."

Elizabeth, however, could reap the best of both worlds and did not hesitate
to identify herself with the male role as well as the female. On many occasions
she presented herself to the nation as both woman and man, queen and king.
Especially in times of crisis she emphasized her "manly" qualities to reassure
her subjects that they were led not by a "frail" woman but a courageous king.
Her most noteworthy androgynous speech was to her army at Tilbury as they
awaited the assault of the Spanish Armada. "I know I have the body but of a
weak and feeble woman," she declared, "but I have the heart and stomach of
a king, and of a king of England too; and think foul scorn that Parma or Spain,
or any prince of Europe should dare to invade the borders of my realm; to
which rather than any dishonor shall grow by me, I myself will take up arms,
I myself will be your general, judge, and rewarder of every one of your virtues
in the field." [spelling modernized]

Most of Elizabeth's officers and advisors hoped she would fulfill her primary female function of having a male heir, so the normal image of the monarch could be restored. That is why the queen's marriage became such a vital
issue in both domestic and foreign affairs. Pretending to accede to the wishes
of her councilors, she sent her ambassadors to gather information about foreign suitors, flirting with them or their agents when they arrived, as she did
with her own courtiers, and always holding out the prospect of favor. She
claimed to dislike such negotiations; however, the Spanish ambassador

thought otherwise. "I do not think anything is more enjoyable to this Queen than treating of marriage," he wrote to his master, "although she assures me herself that nothing annoys her more. She is vain, and would like all the world to be running after her." Still, she always evaded the final commitment and remained the "Virgin Queen."

The nobles and men of affairs, however, were not always so easily placated. Keeping them loyal and docile with the minimum cost to the exchequer taxed Elizabeth's wiles to the limit. It taxed some of the aristocrats' pocketbooks, too. Yet, above all, she was a clever woman who not only was a good judge of character and ability but also knew how to keep the loyalty of those she chose to serve her. By the judicious use of favors, office, and affection, she won the hearts as well as the hands of even her most overmighty subjects.

The pervading feature of the queen's political personality was her desire to rule. Administration interested her intensely, and she loved to plan and plot. Her skill in domestic and international negotiation was admired by friends and feared by foes. She possessed natural political acumen, as witnessed in her handling of the protracted marriage negotiations, although she was not gifted with deep political imagination. Elizabeth lacked the philosophical mind that could speculate on the nature and theory of politics. Instead, she made the most of the situations and institutions at hand. Whatever her motives, by a combination of cautious diplomacy and careful propaganda, she achieved a degree of national unity that was unique in the Europe of her time and had no comparison in England for many years to come.

English Government Under Elizabeth

Elizabeth made few structural alterations in the government of her predecessors, yet during her reign the foundations of that government underwent vital changes. Next to the queen as the central organ of rule was the Privy Council. This body remained essentially unchanged by Elizabeth except for the reduction of its size to more manageable proportions. At the beginning of her reign, the council was reduced to twenty members, carefully chosen by the monarch herself, and by the end of the century it had only nine or ten. Even with these reduced numbers, the average attendance at meetings of the council was seldom more than half of the membership. Faithful service was therefore given by such stalwarts as Sir William Cecil, principal secretary and lord treasurer; Sir Francis Knollys, vice-chamberlain of the household; Lord Howard of Effingham, lord chamberlain; Sir Nicholas Bacon, lord keeper of the Great Seal; Robert Dudley, earl of Leicester; Sir Francis Walsingham, principal secretary from 1573; and Sir Christopher Hatton, lord chancellor after 1587.

The work of the Privy Council included the full range of administrative, advisory, and judicial business presented to it by the queen. The council also drafted bills and pronouncements to be presented to Parliament, and steered them through the treacherous shoals of parliamentary debate. When these bills became law, the councilors supervised their enforcement. One of the council's judicial duties was to sit as the Court of Star Chamber hearing cases involving breaches of the public order and the violation of royal decrees. As such, it was a separate institution with a different clerical staff and the addition of the chief justices of King's Bench and Common Pleas as judges, but composed otherwise of the same privy councilors who sat as the queen's advisors on foreign and domestic policy. In all of their activities, the councilors were responsible, individually and collectively, only to the queen.

Within the Privy Council, yet separate from it, was the office of principal secretary of state, created by Thomas Cromwell. The office had grown during the middle years of the century, as it had in France and Spain, from the position of royal scribe to confidant and advisor to the crown. Correspondence with ambassadors was written and received by the secretary of state, who was privy to the most confidential matters of state. Indeed, the vital problem of national security—both the preservation of domestic law and order and the defense of the kingdom against foreign powers—was the direct responsibility of the principal secretary during Elizabeth's reign. Sir William Cecil (1520–98) was principal secretary from 1558 to 1572, and gave the office a distinction and authority that it was to carry throughout the reign. When Cecil was made Lord Burghley and treasurer in 1572, Sir Francis Walsingham (1530–90) became principal secretary, a post he vigorously magnified until his death eighteen years later. During Walsingham's tenure, Tudor England faced both its greatest threat from abroad and its most serious challenge from within. Much of Elizabeth's success in foreign affairs and in maintaining relative domestic tranquility is due to Walsingham's vigilance. Robert Cecil, Lord Burghley's son, occupied the office from 1596 to 1612.

The Elizabethan Parliament

The largest and most controversial organ of English government in the sixteenth century was the Parliament. As in the past, Parliament was summoned and dismissed by the crown at the royal pleasure. It had few privileges or guarantees of its own, and its rules of procedure depended on the will of the queen. Important matters of state, such as the succession, including the vital issue of the queen's marriage, religious matters, and foreign policy—and especially relations with Mary Queen of Scots—were outside the realm of parliamentary debate unless authorized by the queen herself. Under Elizabeth, the primary function of Parliament was to vote money and taxes for the operation of the government and pass laws to ensure the nation's preservation and stability. It is easy to understand why Parliament was summoned for only thirteen sessions, averaging ten weeks each, for a total of less than three years, during Elizabeth's entire forty-four-year reign.

Nevertheless, raising money was not an insignificant function. The financial situation in late-Tudor England was difficult. The expenses of government, patronage, and war were increasing, yet Elizabeth hoped to keep taxes at the lowest level possible in order to avoid the civil disorders that had resulted on the continent from high taxation. The greatest part (50 to 60 percent) of the annual government revenue came from the rents of royal lands, remaining feudal dues, customs duties, benefices, and judicial fees. Another 10 to 20 percent resulted from the sale of crown lands and from "prizes" taken at sea, leaving approximately 20 to 40 percent that had to be raised from parliamentary subsidies and taxes.

Firm moderation was the keynote of Elizabeth's relations with Parliament. During most of her reign it proved successful. At times the MPs (Members of Parliament) became obdurate, but the queen's pragmatic political skill usually produced favorable results. When charm or reason did not succeed, the queen resorted to more forceful means to win their support: the royal veto, royal interventions to stay bills that Parliament was prone to dismiss, and, as a last resort, the imprisonment of recalcitrant MPs. The Privy Council also played a key role in the crown management of Parliament, as did the speaker of the House of Commons, who for all intents and purposes, was a crown appointee. Nevertheless, as government demands were made for higher and higher taxes in the 1590s, Parliament became increasingly stubborn about granting the queen's wishes. To help finance the costly war in Ireland, no fewer than four subsidies were asked for in the final session of 1601, and were granted only after Parliament had exacted equally costly concessions from the crown in prerogatives and privileges.

In recent studies, Sir Geoffrey Elton argues that Parliament had not yet acquired a major role in English politics by Elizabeth's time, and that the House of Lords still occupied a more important place than the Commons, even though the latter did process more bills. Nevertheless, by the end of Elizabeth's reign, the lower house had become a stronghold of both wealth and power as the successful landed gentry steadily swelled its size and strength. It likewise became the center of outspoken opposition as Puritan divines and laymen, many of whom were also wealthy squires, took up their calling within the Commons as "God's heralds to a wicked and perverse government." These factors contributed to the growing hostility between Commons and crown, and led to more frequent claims by the former of violated privileges and usurped powers. Elizabeth was able to control this undercurrent of unrest and continue giving the impression of parliamentary cooperation to the end of her reign. Her successor, however, being unwilling and unable to continue the deception, reaped the rewards of parliamentary discontent.

Patronage

Just as was the case in France and Spain, the Elizabethan government in England had difficulty enforcing its will beyond a limited range, even with the local development of the lord lieutenants and justices of the peace. The inadequacies of transportation and communication severely limited governmental control beyond the area within a single day's travel. Furthermore, the salaried civil service, through which modern governments are able to make their will felt in all parts of the realm, was small, underpaid, and relatively untrained in the sixteenth century. With so feeble a bureaucracy, unofficial patterns of patronage interlinked the administrative functions of the country in a fluctuating semifeudal system of patron, client, and suitor. The whole system was a mixture of administrative institutions and personal loyalties among secretaries, administrators, and clients, the last being paid not by a fixed salary schedule but by gratuities, some of which, by their amount or method of use, might appear to us as bribes. They frequently appeared so to contemporaries, also. Any system of clientage runs the risk of corruption, for the line between a gift and a bribe is a very fine one. Yet without adequate money to finance a bureaucracy and insufficient knowledge of more modern administrative machinery, Elizabeth can hardly be faulted for failing to use a system that had not yet been invented.

In the Elizabethan structure, the queen was the custodian of a vast treasury of patronage. At her disposal were offices and honors of all kinds, peerages and knighthoods, posts in the military services and in the church, royal lands, charters, pensions and annuities, licenses, and monopolies. These positions and honors could be made available, both directly and through the intermediation of the privy councilors and courtiers, to the thousands of suitors presenting themselves at court, or to others through an elaborate petition system, either as gifts from the queen to enhance the love and loyalty of her subjects and encourage their service, or as payment for services already rendered. Donors had no guarantee of worth, and suitors had no assurance of success. Edmund Spenser must have known the uncertainty and treachery of the suitor's role when he wrote:

> *Full little knowest thou that has not tried*
> *What Hell it is in suing long to bide;*
> *To lose good days that might be better spent;*
> *To waste long nights in pensive discontent;*
> *To speed today, to be put back tomorrow;*
> *To feed on hope, to pine with fear and sorrow;*
> *To have thy Prince's grace, yet want her Peer's;*
> *To have thy asking, yet wait many years;*
> *To fret thy soul with crosses and with cares;*
> *To eat thy heart through comfortless despairs;*
> *To fawn, to crouch, to wait, to ride, to run,*
> *To spend, to give, to want, to be undone.*

With all of its vices and corruption, the Elizabethan patronage system did provide a valuable link between the government and the various strata of English society, thereby assisting that government in its vital function of preserving law and order at home and resisting foreign aggression.

The Religious Settlement

To all of Europe in 1558, England was an enigma. Its new monarch had been coyly noncommittal on both religious and foreign-policy matters, and her decisions in these areas would determine the future role of England in Europe. Mary Tudor might have prevented the religious dilemma had she disinherited Elizabeth and allowed the Catholic Queen of Scots to become the next ruler of England. This action, however, would plainly have sacrificed English independence to Franco-Scottish domination, a price too high to pay even for religious continuity. Besides, the new queen had made no previous commitments to either Catholic or Protestant, and since she had been outwardly friendly to both parties, there was no certainty that she would favor Protestantism over Catholicism. Actually, there was less concern in England over the entire problem than there was on the continent. Three major changes in religious affiliation in the past twenty-five years had left the English people rather insensitive to the subtleties of ecclesiastical argument.

Elizabeth's religious views were as ambiguous as were her matrimonial intentions. She apparently held no strong opinions, and if she did, she carefully masked them behind political actions and professions of piety. Even after severing her Roman allegiance, she allegedly kept a crucifix and lighted taper in her private chapel, "to confound the Puritans and keep Catholic expectations alive." She seems to have preferred an English Catholicism, with supremacy in the crown rather than in the pope, as did her father. Yet Elizabeth was obviously more interested in securing her reign and guaranteeing its stability than she was in doctrinal polemics and religious crusades. Therefore, moderation and expediency in religious matters became the principle of her reign, and her compromise settlement was calculated to bring the greatest amount of religious and political stability to the realm. Her decision to separate once more from the Roman church was dictated by political considerations (although there is no reason to deny that she thought those political factors coincided with her religious convictions), for she rightly feared that a continuance of the Roman obedience would eventually lead to involvement in the Catholic cause throughout Europe. And Elizabeth was not so well equipped to bear the crusader's cross as was Philip II.

Two important acts of Parliament legislated the Elizabethan Settlement: the Act of Supremacy and the Act of Uniformity. The first of these repealed most of Mary's religious legislation and designated Elizabeth "Supreme Governor of the Realm," in spiritual as well as in temporal affairs. This terminology was intended to be less offensive to Catholics than Henry's and Edward's "Supreme Head of the Church." The administration of ecclesiastical affairs was placed in the hands of a Court of High Commission, which acted in the name of the crown. Obedience to the act was provided through an oath taken by all holders of civil and ecclesiastical office. Punishment for its violation was severe, including in certain cases, death, since refusal to take or abide by the oath was interpreted as a crime of high treason.

The Act of Uniformity restored the general liturgy and doctrines of Edward VI's reign. The *Book of Common Prayer* of 1552, revised by the insertion of some phrases to make it more acceptable to Catholics, was republished and made compulsory throughout the kingdom. Its ambiguities were designed to render it palatable to Protestant and Catholic alike. Images, crucifixes, and other trappings of Catholic worship were retained, including the vestments of the clergy, but these soon came under the sharp criticism of the more radical reformers and some returning Marian exiles. In 1562 the crown and a convocation of the clergy accepted a new Anglican confession of faith, known as the Thirty-nine Articles. This confession was a revised version of Thomas Cranmer's Forty-two Articles, with three of the more anti-Catholic items removed. Again the ambiguity was intentional, making the confession acceptable to those of both reformed (Calvinist) and evangelical (Lutheran) conviction.

It used to be thought that Marian exiles, returning to England after having spent much of Mary Tudor's reign in safety abroad, played a major role in pushing English Protestantism in a more radical direction. Recent studies, however, have diminished the importance of these exiles. They came back deeply divided in their opinions, and generally they found themselves viewed with suspicion, even disdain, by English Protestants who had "stuck it out" during Mary's regime. After their return, many of the exiles attained positions in the established church.

Elizabeth's choice of leaders to effect the religious settlement indicates her desire to follow a middle course of compromise and concession, particularly evident in her selection of Matthew Parker, a moderate Protestant devotee of royal authority and order, as archbishop of Canterbury, and Sir William Cecil as principal secretary. Like his queen, Cecil believed the old religion was not only corrupt but also irrelevant, and committed himself wholly to the Reformation. Yet he was not a fanatic. "He viewed Protestantism in coolly secular terms," observes one Elizabethan scholar, "and its most attractive features to him were its rejection of a foreign ecclesiastical jurisdiction." Nevertheless, Cecil's religious conviction was genuine, and he actively promoted it.

Yet fortune—seeming to smile on Elizabeth during the early months of her regime as both the militant Protestants and Catholics were caught unawares by Mary's death and unprepared to capitalize on the succession—is a capricious mistress to serve. The Elizabethan Settlement was a precarious balance at best, predicated on the assumption that religious emotions could be held in check by the compromise arrangement and by deemphasizing religion in government. The settlement profited from the peculiar conjunction of external events and conditions in 1559. The immediate threat of a Franco-Scottish invasion, the patronizing policy of Philip II, and the anticipation of profit from the high-level negotiations going on at Cateau-Cambrésis, all drew attention away from religious matters at a crucial moment when the forces of Reformation and Counter-Reformation might have brought civil war to England. Nevertheless, for many years the situation remained unstable and precarious.

Puritans and Papists   By the early 1570s, the queen's reign was apparently secure. She had weathered the storms of war with Scotland, the tirades of the returned Scottish exile John Knox, the intrigues of Mary Queen of Scots, civil upheaval in the northern counties, excommunication by the pope, and the threat of invasion from France. Nevertheless, the religious situation grew more serious with each passing year. The settlement itself was not as satisfactory as Elizabeth hoped it would be, and factional disputes became increasingly bitter. Disagreements arose over clerical vestments, use of the chalice, and the precise form of the communion service. Catholics became disillusioned by the unmistakable Protestantism of the English church, while the radical elements and native "puritan" reformers advocated a drastic and more fundamentally Protestant Reformation. Finding it difficult to maintain a church that was all things to all people, Elizabeth gradually came to take more frequent and forceful measures against the extremism of both Puritans and Papists.

Puritanism grew rapidly in the English church after the first decade of Elizabeth's rule. Disillusioned by the religious settlement, which they referred to as "a crooked halting betwixt two religions," the nonconformists increased their efforts to modify and evangelize the Anglican church. Puritan preachers enthusiastically expounded biblical teachings on salvation and morality, and zealously castigated Catholics for their lingering ritualism and their stubborn devotion to Rome. The Puritans' influence in Parliament increased during the 1570s, and their voices were even more loudly heard in the cause of European Protestantism as international tensions rose in the 1580s. The Puritan attack—amounting in some circles to demands for outright separation rather than just religious reform—reached a crescendo by 1583 when Archbishop Parker died. His successor, John Whitgift, ably led the counterattack against Puritanism and succeeded in containing its more radical manifestations until his death in February 1604, eleven months after the queen's. From the first, Elizabeth treated these outspoken clerics with disdain and even contempt, for they represented the very religious sectarianism she hoped to avoid. Yet even the queen gradually succumbed to much of the Puritan advice, particularly in foreign policy, as it became increasingly apparent that a greater threat to English unity and independence came from the Catholics than from the Puritans.

In the period immediately following the religious settlement, Catholics were treated with decided deference by the Elizabethan government. The queen herself was solicitous toward them, especially when they conformed outwardly to the Anglican worship and demonstrated devotion to the crown. Yet the great majority of the approximately 150,000 Englishmen who by 1570 still gave their allegiance to Rome were deeply committed Catholics, unwilling to compromise their religious principles to further Elizabethan expedience. As Puritan influence in Parliament increased, so did the severity of anti-Catholic legislation. And as prosecution under these laws mounted and the stream of English Catholic refugees to the continent swelled, hard-core Catholics struck back. The Jesuits made England a prime target for their missionary efforts, and in 1586 William Allen (created cardinal in 1587) gave English Catholicism a new surge by establishing a seminary at Douai, in the Lowlands, for the precise purpose of training priests and missionaries for the English episcopate. Other seminaries were adapted to this purpose in Reims, Valladolid, and Rome, and the river of English Catholic refugees was matched by a counterflood of Catholic missionaries. One of the least known yet most dedicated of these was Doña Luisa de Carvajal y Mendoza (1566–1614) from Spain, who devoted the last years of her life to the ministry in England. She was not only a great comfort to many imperiled and encarcerated Catholics, but strengthened many others in their faith and converted a goodly number of Protestants.

The crisis, which came in the 1580s, proved even more decisively that the settlement could withstand the most serious threats and still maintain, in general, the principle of balance and compromise. The death roll of some 200 Catholic clerics and laymen executed in England between 1570 and 1590 might belie such a statement. Yet the fact that both Papists and Puritans continued to subsist in England after the crisis of the 1580s, and that many shades of theological divergence could still be accommodated within the bounds of the Anglican church, says much for the viability of the Elizabethan Settlement.

Elizabethan Foreign Policy

Elizabeth's foreign policy, like her dealings in government and religion at home, was determined by political expediency and characterized by caution, ambiguity, and concealment of her true feelings. From the outset of her reign, she was faced with the traditional enmity of France and Scotland, probable hostility from Rome, and at best the uncertain friendship of Spain. In Germany Elizabeth was viewed with suspicion and distrust; in much of Italy she was regarded as a usurper and heretic. Elizabeth met these challenges with forthright indecision, to the chagrin and frustration of her advisors. As with her marriage policy, which the queen used to great advantage in foreign affairs, Elizabeth retreated from any situation that would commit her to an inflexible course or that would force the hand of her enemies.

The queen did have general goals and objectives, however. She hoped, for one thing, to prevent any possible alliance between Spain and France, since a league between these two giants, even a progressive *rapprochement,* would seriously endanger the independent position Elizabeth wished to occupy in European affairs. Her cautious attempts to weaken Spanish and French positions in the Netherlands and elsewhere without inciting the wrath of those rulers seemed timid and cowardly to some of her more enthusiastic ministers. Yet Elizabeth was always the prudent queen. And she had other reasons for not wanting to give open aid to the Dutch rebels. Rebellion is a fearful word to most rulers; to Elizabeth it had a particularly repulsive ring. She disapproved of disobedience to authority on principle, and she disliked the radicalism of the Netherlands' reformers in particular. Nevertheless, she was not above supporting such a movement if it could be used in her favor without undue risks. Hence her attitude toward the revolt in the Netherlands and the Huguenot uprising in France was one of open aloofness and clandestine support. She courted the favor of all European princes, but carefully avoided "entangling alliances" that would force her into a hazardous involvement with any major power.

In this regard, Elizabeth's attitude was closely paralleled by that of her principal secretary, Sir William Cecil, Lord Burghley. During the first half of her reign, it was Cecil's voice that asserted the greatest influence in Elizabeth's councils and in the formulation of foreign policy. Objective and cautious like his queen, Cecil was nevertheless capable of concerted action, and even of undertaking hazardous ventures, if the stakes and odds seemed favorable. Thus

William Cecil, Lord Burghley.   *As principal secretary and lord high treasurer, Cecil was, next to the queen, the most powerful voice in the government during Elizabeth's reign.*

he persuaded the queen to take decisive action in Scotland in 1560, possibly averting a French occupation, and leading to the establishment of a more stable relationship with France. Sometimes, however, Lord Burghley led the "dove" faction in the Privy Council, advocating a limited role or nonintervention in neighboring troubles and avoiding the risk of confrontation with rival states.

The "hawks" were led by the more flamboyant figure of Sir Robert Dudley, fifth son of the infamous duke of Northumberland, who rose rapidly in the queen's service to become a Knight of the Garter, master of the queen's horse, privy councilor, and earl of Leicester. As the queen's "favorite" and constant companion, Leicester seemed (until 1564) to be front runner in Elizabeth's game of mock matrimony. Gradually, however, he came to assume a more constant political role as the queen's personal ardor cooled. Leicester continued to appeal to Elizabeth's other self, however, and in spite of her carefully cultivated dignity and decorum, "she liked to flirt with the faintly improper, mildly to scandalize the Spanish ambassador or Puritan zealots." Leicester appealed to these instincts, yet neither yielded to them excessively nor allowed them to interfere with national policy. In the Privy Council, Leicester's venturesome activism became the antidote to Cecil's cautious conservatism. Soon Leicester became the leading spokesman of the Puritan party in the government and the advocate of a pro-French foreign policy, particularly in support of the Huguenot cause.

Until the mid-1570s, Elizabeth's own dilatory nature dictated a policy of prudent noncommitment. After the queen's excommunication in 1570 and the mounting Catholic intrigues and Spanish plots, Elizabeth was under increasing pressure to intervene in the Netherlands revolt. That pressure increased in 1573 with the appointment of Sir Francis Walsingham as principal secretary. Being an ardent Puritan, and a Francophile too, Walsingham was convinced that Elizabeth's policy of playing for time and avoiding commitments was wrong if not outright dangerous. He advocated, along with Leicester, an open alliance with the Huguenots of France, intervention in the Netherlands in behalf of the rebels, and even war with Spain. To Walsingham, foreign affairs were not a matter of diplomacy and finesse for the purpose of gaining political friends, but a general conflict between Protestantism and Catholicism for control of Europe. Walsingham soon became the champion of the anti-Spanish faction in England and the mastermind of an intelligence network operating in almost every court in Europe. Through these diplomatic and espionage agents, Walsingham was able not only to thwart every attempted plot against the queen after 1573 but also at the same time to help prepare the ground for more direct English involvement abroad.

After 1576 English relations with both France and Spain were largely determined by the revolt in the Netherlands. Early in that disturbance, the rebels were encouraged and goaded on by English pamphlets circulated in Flanders and by English-subsidized agitators helping to stir up religious and political discontent. After Alba arrived in the Netherlands, Elizabeth secretly continued to aid the malcontents by grants of money and by making English coastal facilities available to the enterprising Sea Beggars. She refrained from an open show of hostility against the Spanish occupation army, however, for fear of encouraging French intervention. Yet reluctantly and hesitatingly, Elizabeth was drawn steadily into the whirlpool of conflict by a combination of political, economic, religious, and personal crisis. Spanish truculence, maritime rivalry, Puritan pressure, Catholic plots, French impotence, and Dutch persistence all combined to bring England into active military participation in the Netherlands by 1585. Peace did not return again to England until after Elizabeth's death eighteen years later.

Elizabeth and Mary Queen of Scots

In the meantime, much of the international tension of the late sixteenth century, especially between 1571 and 1587, revolved around the person and symbol of Mary Stuart, queen of Scotland and claimant to the throne of England. Mary was a very different sort of person from her cousin Elizabeth. Her youth had been spent at the cultured French court, where she had learned to dance, sing, converse, and develop the arts of femininity. She possessed a more vivacious and emotional temperament than did Elizabeth but lacked the English queen's prudence and objective skill in practical politics. Mary was a woman first, a queen next; Elizabeth was a ruler always. Of greatest importance to European developments of the late sixteenth century was Mary's deeply religious convictions and her staunch Catholicism. Her family heritage, her early French environment, and the Protestant disorders in Scotland all contributed to her religious character.

In 1561 her husband, King Francis II, died and Mary returned to Scotland to assume her duties there. During the regency of her mother, Mary of Guise, the Scottish reformers had abolished the Mass, rejected papal authority, and adopted a Protestant confession of faith. Soon the Scottish kirk—as the native church was called—was organized with its structure of presbyteries, synods, and assemblies, making the Reformation there almost complete. Now, with Mary's return, the Protestants feared that a bloodbath was imminent. To their surprise, though, Mary pursued a policy of religious and political conciliation, and further disarmed the Protestant nobility by including them in her council of state and by reviving a congenial and cultured court life.

With peace established at home, Mary next turned to the problems still pending between herself and Elizabeth. One of the most serious of these was the matter of succession to the English throne. The Treaty of Edinburgh (1560) had avoided the mention of Mary's claims. She now demanded that official acknowledgment be made of her true right as heir presumptive to the English throne. Elizabeth was willing to admit this to Mary privately but would not declare it publicly for fear of losing her own political position at home and abroad. A meeting of the two sovereigns was planned for the autumn of 1562 in Nottingham, where it was hoped an agreement could be worked out. The sudden news of the massacre at Vassy and the beginning of the civil wars in France, however, caused a postponement and then cancellation of the meeting. A new phase of Anglo-Scottish relations began.

The question of the English succession came to a focus in the affair of the queen's marriages. Mary was an eligible and valuable prize in the political schemes of countless European princes and aspiring nobles. Charles IX of France and the Habsburg archduke of Austria were both candidates for the Scottish queen's hand. At one time, her own preference seemed to favor Don Carlos of Spain, the inscrutable son of Philip II. Elizabeth feared any Scottish alignment with the royal houses of Europe and was therefore greatly relieved when the illness of Don Carlos eliminated him as a contender. So anxious was Elizabeth to prevent Mary's conjunction with another European power that she offered her own suitor, Robert Dudley, for a husband. The burlesque con-

Mary Queen of Scots. *Beautiful, headstrong, and misguided, Mary Stuart was at the center of European diplomacy and intrigue, yet spent the greater part of her life as a political prisoner of the queen of England.*

tinued until 1565, when the Queen of Scots married Henry Stuart, Lord Darnley. From the Scottish Catholic point of view, Darnley appeared to be a likely choice. His religious orthodoxy was unchallenged, his claim to the English throne was almost as good as Mary's, and he was, according to James Melville, "the properest, and best proportioned long man that she had ever seen." Yet he was also a contentious egotist, incapable of becoming an intelligent courtier, let alone a king.

Mary's decision was disastrous. Protestants resented the marriage, which resembled an alliance against them, and soon civil war was raging again. The murder of Mary's private secretary, David Rizzio, in a plot concocted by Darnley and carried out by his hired assassins, put the monarchy in serious jeopardy. Mary's subsequent estrangement from her husband and her romantic involvement with James Hepburn, earl of Bothwell, did little to strengthen her position in Scotland. On the night of 9 February 1567, Darnley himself was murdered, and Mary sealed her own fate when she not only refused to make charges against Bothwell, the principal suspect, but shocked public opinion by marrying him three months later. Soon much of Scotland had taken up arms against the queen and, led by the fiery Protestant nobles, forced her surrender and abdication in the summer of 1567. The following year she fled to England.

Elizabeth's dilemma at this turn of events was obvious. The Scottish nobles demanded Mary's return to Scotland. If Elizabeth refused, it could mean war;

if she acquiesced, she would be admitting a diplomatic defeat; if she granted the asylum requested by the Scottish queen, there was danger of English discontent at home and the possibility of Stuart-led conspiracies against the throne. Elizabeth's ultimate decision was to imprison Mary in England, where she remained in "protective custody" for the next nineteen years, a constant source of anxiety and threat to Elizabeth. Mary's imprisonment regained for her the sympathy and support of Catholic Europe that she had lost by her foolish amours, and it cost Elizabeth unending apprehension and distress. When the last of many abortive plots to overthrow the English government and place Mary Stuart on the throne was unearthed by Walsingham's ubiquitous spies, Mary's involvement was too direct even for Elizabeth to overlook. Mary's implication in the Babington Plot of 1586 led the ill-fated Scottish queen to the block at the age of forty-four.

Socio-Economic Activity and the Maritime Clash with Spain

As in other countries, social life in Elizabethan England was organized on a class basis, with the greater nobility—the royal family and hereditary peers—at the top, and the rest of the gentry, knights and squires, rounding out the "gentleman" class. Beneath the gentry were the yeomen, small freeholders who, with the tenant farmers, constituted an amorphous rural middle class between the lesser gentry and the peasants. Copyholders—those who could show in court the "copy of court roll" certifying the conditions by which their serf forebears had acquired title to some land—were also tenured farmers, able, with some enterprise and luck, to rise to yeoman status or even above. Nevertheless, class distinctions in Elizabethan society were less rigid than they were on the continent and often seemed to count less than local loyalties and interests. That is why the persisting debate over whether the aristocracy was on the rise or decline needs to be considered within a regional, local, or even individual context.

English towns were of course composed of a wide assortment of classes and crafts. In the larger port cities and London, wholesalers and merchants pursued their trades, while cloth manufacturers and other industrialists provided merchandise for export. In the towns and villages throughout the country craftsmen and artisans turned out products of domestic need. Sixteenth-century England also had many propertyless laborers—plowmen, herdsmen, and others working for a small yearly or daily wage—and a large population of vagabonds, beggars, and derelicts of every type. These unemployed poor, congregating mainly in towns and cities such as London, York, Norwich, and Bristol, created a major problem that was met with piecemeal attempts at rehabilitation in "houses of correction." The increasing incidence of famine in the 1590s, followed by food riots and general disorder, focused national attention on the problem and eventually led to the enactment of the Elizabethan Poor Law of 1601, which provided government funds to supplement private charities and insure that no one would starve to death.

Contrary to common opinion, the Elizabethan Age was not a time of general economic prosperity. Agrarian problems were chronic throughout the sixteenth century, caused partly by the population growth and partly by the continued conversion of agricultural land into pasturage for the grazing of sheep. The enclosure movement, and other features of the transition from feudalism to an enterprise economy, was accompanied by serious social and economic disturbances. Great estates were won and lost, while thousands of rural laborers were displaced, swelling the already overcrowded streets of London. Industry, especially the manufacture of woolen cloth, had experienced some expansion in the early decades of the century, accompanied by greater financial fluidity and a boom in cloth exports; but the financial collapse of 1552, followed by almost thirty years of recurring slumps and depressions alternating with sprees of spiraling prices, did nothing to promote confidence or stability in the English economy.

The Elizabethan government did little to solve any of the basic economic problems, either by long-range planning or by adjustments in the tax structure that would alleviate the burden on the poor and the middle class. Elizabeth's only solution to the government's dilemma of low revenues and high expenses was to apply strict economizing methods to all expenditures and keep financial speculation to a minimum. As lord treasurer, Burghley stressed frugality and solvency in order to conserve the nation's limited resources; but as prices and expenses rose after the mid-1580s, the government turned more frequently to parliamentary subsidies and higher taxes. Both Parliament and the people complained.

Expanding Trade   England's balance of trade was also unfavorable during the early part of Elizabeth's reign. Depending almost entirely upon the export of woolen cloth to outlets in Flanders, England's commercial balance was more than offset by the heavy import of wine, salt, canvas, wood, and linen from France; wine, oil, and even wool from Spain; silks, velvets, taffetas, and other luxury cloths from Italy; and various naval stores and cordage from the Hansa towns. Nevertheless, the direction of English trade did undergo some dramatic changes in the course of Elizabeth's reign. Until the second half of the sixteenth century, England took almost no interest in oceanic commerce. Trade was exclusively with western Europe, primarily with the Low Countries. By mid-century, however, the growing demand for widening economic contacts gave rise to maritime activity in four new directions: northeast to Russia; into the Venetian and French-dominated Levant; via Africa to the Far East; and westward across the Atlantic.

Interest in the Russian trade and the projected commerce via the North Cape to China was stimulated by the founding of the Muscovy Company in 1555. Year after year, the Muscovy Company and the Merchant Adventurers of London sent out expeditions to penetrate the northeastern waters in the hope of reaching Cathay (China). The names of Willoughby, Chancellor, Borough, Pet, and Jackman are memorials to this English attempt to shorten the sea route to Asia via the arctic north. Such projects were not entirely in vain, for a lively if limited trade was established with Russia.

The London merchants also looked longingly at the lucrative Levant trade with the Ottoman Turks. Using tin and various war supplies needed by the Turks as bargaining strength, the English were successful in breaking the French-Venetian trade monopoly by 1578 and entering into a commercial agreement with the Turks for extensive trade in the eastern Mediterranean. At the same time, English traders intensified their activity along the Barbary Coast and along the Grain, Ivory, Gold, and Slave coasts of west Africa as far south as the Niger River.

Meanwhile, the unknown northwest also beckoned to English seamen to disclose its icebound secrets. Between 1576 and 1578, Martin Frobisher, influenced by the geographer, mathematician, and magician, Dr. John Dee, and financed by Elizabeth and others at court, made no less than three voyages into the frigid waters north of Labrador, returning with nothing more valuable than a cargo of fools' gold. John Davis made three more attempts to penetrate the northwest in 1585–87 and reached as far as 73° north latitude, but failed to locate the elusive passage to Asia.

Growing out of this search for a northwest passage were the slaving, colonizing, and privateering ventures of Gilbert, Hawkins, Raleigh, and Drake into the Atlantic and the New World. One of the heaviest investors in the northwest passage enterprise was Sir Humphrey Gilbert, a Devonshire aristocrat who became interested in schemes for colonizing the northern coast of America. In 1578 Gilbert received a royal patent to discover and settle "such remote, heathen and barbarous lands not actually possessed of any Christian prince." In 1583 he made an ill-fated attempt to plant a colony in Newfoundland but drowned at sea on his return voyage. Gilbert's patent rights passed to his half-brother, Sir Walter Raleigh, who made numerous unsuccessful attempts to colonize the New World. His most famous efforts were at Roanoke Island, just north of Cape Hatteras in present-day North Carolina, and in the Orinoco delta region of Guiana (now Venezuela). The former enterprise was costly in money and in lives, and ended in failure; the latter cost Raleigh his own head.

Francis Drake and the "Sea Dogs"   From early in Elizabeth's reign, adventuresome Devon seamen began harassing Spain on the seas and in the colonies of the Spanish Main. One of the earliest of these "Sea Dogs," as they came to be called, was John Hawkins of Plymouth. In 1562 Hawkins began his notorious slave trade between Africa and Spanish America. Technically his enterprise was illegal, but Spanish settlers in the West Indies were eager to buy his valuable cargoes and made little protest about them. The Spanish government, however, refused to look with impunity upon this violation of their trading monopoly. In the autumn of 1568, as Hawkins's six-ship expedition lay at anchor in the harbor of San Juan de Ulloa, a Spanish flotilla moved into the bay and opened fire on the English vessels. Two of the ships managed to escape and return to England, carrying with them the news of the Spanish treachery, but the rest were sunk or captured. Peace was preserved between the two countries in Europe, but the

Sir Francis Drake. *This engraving attributed to J. Hondius shows the famous Elizabethan seaman shortly after his circumnavigation of the globe.*

incident at San Juan de Ulloa marked the opening of a sea war that continued for the next thirty-five years.

San Juan de Ulloa also marked the debut of the most illustrious seamen of the Elizabethan era. Francis Drake (1543–96) commanded one of the ships that escaped from the ambush and lived to revenge the event many times over. For the next twenty-eight years, he carried on a relentless personal vendetta against the king of Spain. In 1571 Drake was again in the West Indies, this time looking for plunder, not trade. Early the next year, he sacked the port of Nombre de Dios and ambushed the caravan bringing the Peruvian treasure overland from Panama. Drake returned to Plymouth in 1573 after two years of raiding and plundering the entire Spanish Main from Porto Bello to Trinidad. Late in 1577 he sailed from England on the most famous of his voyages, a three-year enterprise that saw him pillage the Spanish ports of Peru, capture the valuable treasure ship between Lima and Panama, sail northward along the Pacific shore as far as Vancouver Island, then plunge westward across the uncharted Pacific to the Moluccas. After taking on a cargo of spices, Drake continued his memorable voyage across the Indian Ocean, around the African cape, northward along the familiar Slave Coast, and finally back to England.

Drake's circumnavigation stimulated the English imagination and spirit perhaps more than any other event of the time. Soon other English seamen were venturing into the unknown seas and taking part in daring free-lance operations against Spanish shipping and trade. A short time later, Thomas Cavendish completed a similar privateering voyage around the world. None of the English trading, exploration, or colonizing ventures had been so successful as these direct attacks against the Spanish Empire. When war finally came, the English seamen were reaching the pinnacle of their strength and vigor.

England and the Spanish Armada

The precise time of Philip's decision to send an invading force against England is unknown, but it is certain that rumors of some such move had been in the wind for many years before the Armada was actually launched. Some of the king's military men and diplomats had favored "The Enterprise" for some time, as had the Eboli faction in the king's council. Since 1570 English Catholic exiles had been clamoring for Philip to "liberate" England by force. Pope Gregory XIII, too, had encouraged Philip in the venture. Yet the more cautious Spanish monarch was reluctant to take such a decisive step, especially since he knew he did not have the sea power to guarantee its success. Nevertheless, as the frictions between Spain and England mounted in the early 1580s, and as Elizabeth's aid to the Dutch became more frequent and decisive, Philip was forced to reevaluate his policy. He was assured by his advisors and by the English refugees that the populace of England would rise against the hated queen as soon as the Spanish "army of liberation" arrived.

After acquiring the Portuguese fleet in 1580, a seaborne invasion became feasible for the first time, although it still required several years of shipbuilding before that possibility could be more than a dream. In the meantime, other events hastened Philip's decision and strengthened his assurances of success. In 1583 the marquis of Santa Cruz, commanding the Spanish Mediterranean squadron, soundly defeated a French fleet assembled in the Azores for the purpose of recovering Portugal. Flushed with the spoils of that victory, Santa Cruz advised the king to follow through with a direct seaborne offensive against England. Philip was interested, but what would be required in ships, men, and supplies for such an enterprise? Other proposals were offered: military and naval support for the Scottish Catholics, who would willingly overthrow James VI, then march on England; massive intervention in Elizabeth's Irish War; an all-out push in the Netherlands with seaborne reinforcements from Spain; a cross-channel invasion of England from Flanders. Still Philip waited. He had more plans than he had money, and more advisors than soldiers.

Through 1584 and most of 1585, nothing was done. Then the situation became critical. A definite move had to be made soon or it would be too late. Philip's alliance with the French Catholic League (31 December 1584) might help ensure French neutrality at least and possibly assist in a positive way by securing a French port for the Armada's use. Elizabeth's decision in 1585 to give full assistance to both the Dutch rebels and the French Huguenots, and her direct intervention in the Netherlands with an English army persuaded Philip to make his move. The revolution in the Netherlands could never be repressed as long as England actively supported it. Besides, Philip reasoned, he would be carrying out God's will because heresy would be overthrown in England and the kingdom brought back to the Catholic fold. In January 1586 the king ordered Santa Cruz to submit his plan. It called for a gigantic fleet of no less than 150 fighting ships, plus cargo carriers and smaller vessels, bringing the total to 500 ships, 64,000 soldiers, half that many sailors, and more than 1,500 guns. The cost of such an Armada was calculated at nearly 4 million ducats. Santa Cruz's estimate was fanciful, but Philip intended to come as close to it as he could. God would make up the difference!

In the meantime, the duke of Parma submitted his own plan for the enterprise, less costly and quicker to prepare, but equally difficult to carry out. He proposed sending a force of 30,000 crack troops from Flanders (his own army plus fresh reinforcements) across the channel in barges under cover of darkness. He would need a fleet from Spain only if something went wrong, or to decoy the English. To make his plan work Parma required three conditions: absolute secrecy, the assurance of French neutrality, and backup in the Low Countries after his departure. Although none of these could be guaranteed, it was too late now to turn back.

Every corner of Philip's possessions bustled with activity. Money had to be raised, soldiers mustered and organized, sailors recruited, ships built, supplies stockpiled, guns founded and moved, powder and cannonballs acquired, and operational plans laid—all with speed and secrecy. Nevertheless, word of the Armada was out even before Philip himself had decided what the plans would be. Soon it was obvious that he could not muster the force Santa Cruz talked about. A compromise was made. The troops sent from Castile would rendezvous with Parma's army in Flanders and be escorted across the channel by the Armada. The fleet would then cover the landing and prevent the English navy from interfering in the operation. It was to be primarily a military campaign, not a naval encounter.

Even Spanish resources were inadequate for the Armada's needs, and Santa Cruz was loath to sail with insufficient strength. Some of the trouble was of his own making because he lacked the organizing talent to coordinate and assemble the diverse elements of the enterprise. Time and again Philip ordered the fleet to depart, only to learn that it was not yet ready. The repeated delays were costly in money, resources, and precious time. Suddenly, in the afternoon of 29 April 1587, Sir Francis Drake, now England's national hero, appeared in Cadiz harbor, opened fire on the Spanish ships, and was not driven off until he had sunk, burned, or captured some thirty Spanish vessels. Drake followed this audacious "singeing of the king of Spain's beard" by a foraging run along the Portuguese coast, further ensuring that the Spanish Armada would not sail in 1587.

Then, in February 1588, Santa Cruz died, leaving the Armada without a commander and still only half prepared to sail. The duke of Medina Sidonia (1549–92), captain general of Andalusia and the first grandee of Castile, was appointed. He accepted the commission with great reluctance but set to work preparing the fleet for departure. For the first time the Armada had an organizer and administrator at the helm. By May the fleet was ready to sail from Lisbon; not the 100,000 tons Santa Cruz had naïvely requested, but still a formidable armada of seventy-three fighting ships (built around the nucleus of twenty galleons and fifty-three converted merchantmen, galleasses, and oar-driven galleys), with another fifty-seven cargo vessels and small pinnaces, totaling some 58,000 tons; 20,000 soldiers, 10,000 seamen; and over 2,000 guns. It was a considerably larger force than Santa Cruz had had ready at the time of his death.

Before the Armada had been at sea a week, it was struck by a devastating gale, which scattered the fleet and damaged some vessels beyond repair. It was the end of July before 124 of the original 130 ships could be reassembled at La Coruña and made ready to resume their course northward.

Awaiting the Armada was Lord Admiral Howard of Effingham with a formidable English fleet of over 190 sails, ranging in size from the mammoth 1,100-ton *Triumph* (a royal galleon commanded by Martin Frobisher) to tiny pinnaces and flyboats used for reconnaissance and courier service. Contrary to the popular notion, the first-line warships were equal in number and size to the Spanish, if we are correct in the method of translating sixteenth-century English and Spanish weights. If the Spanish galleons looked bigger, it was because of their huge fore and aft castles used for boarding when two ships were locked in hand-to-hand combat. Thanks to the advanced ideas of John Hawkins who, as treasurer of the Navy, had supervised the rebuilding and repairing of the queen's navy since 1577, the English galleons were longer and more slender, allowing greater broadside fire power, and had smoother sailing characteristics, since the castles were reduced and the waist decked over. The English also introduced a drastic change in gunnery technique by emphasizing the long-range culverins capable of throwing a shot of nine to seventeen pounds for distances up to 2,000 yards. Their intention obviously was to stay upwind and out of range of the Spanish heavy guns while steady pounding the Armada from a distance.

During the first two weeks of August, the great drama was played out as the European millions waited anxiously for news of the clashing leviathans. From Lizard Point on July 30, past the Eddystone Rocks, Portland Bill, the Isle of Wight, and on to Calais Roads on August 6, the encounters were all indecisive. The long-range bombarding by the English culverins turned out to be far less effective than had been expected. The *San Juan de Portugal*, commanded by Juan Martínez de Recalde, the Spanish vice-admiral, took the heaviest pounding when Recalde tried to entice Drake, Hawkins, and Frobisher into close combat. "Though he had withstood the fire of at least eight English galleons and great ships for more than an hour," wrote Garrett Mattingly, "the worst that happened to him was a moderate casualty list and two cannon balls lodged in his mainmast." The only Spanish casualties in those first days of fighting were due not to English gunnery but to a collision between two of the

The Spanish Armada, *from an unknown artist, showing the encounter at Gravelines on 29 July 1588. The English fireships can be seen bearing down on the Armada.*

larger galleons and an explosion on board another. The lord-admiral had prevented the Armada from landing along the southern English coast (which it never intended to do anyway), but he had not inflicted much damage on it and had not prevented its steady progress up the channel.

When the Armada reached Calais, Medina Sidonia learned the alarming news that Parma could not reach the coast with his army. There would be no rendezvous and no embarkation! Then, while the fleet lay at anchor on the night of August 7, the English loosed eight awesome fireships against the Armada. The resulting panic caused by the "hellburners" broke up the massive formation, and many of the ships scattered for safety. On the following day, Drake and Lord Howard led their squadrons against the enemy before it was able to regroup for the attack. This battle, off Gravelines (near Dunkirk), became the final engagement of the two fleets and, although the English victory was not as complete as the lord-admiral would have liked, he did inflict serious damage on the Spaniards and forced them finally to break off the fight. Since the English were near their home ports and could prevent the Armada from returning to its lost rendezvous, Medina Sidonia had no choice but to continue northward around Scotland, Ireland, and back to Spain. On the homeward marathon, the battered fleet, manned by sick and dying crews, met the full fury of the North Sea storms and the inhospitable Irish coast. Eventually the majority of the ships limped back to Spanish harbors, but less than half of them ever sailed again.

Recent scholarship, published on the 400th anniversary of the Armada, has presented a more objective assessment of the campaign than was previously available and has confirmed the fact that the two fleets were well matched except for the greater maneuverability of the English ships and the superiority of English gunnery. Colin Martin and Geoffrey Parker have argued that the Armada's failure to inflict much damage on the English was due to the Spanish inability to reload and fire as rapidly as the English gunners could. This they explain by the inexperience of the Spanish crews and the suggestion that the Spanish guns were mounted on large two-wheeled, land-based type carriages with long trails that made it almost impossible to move and reload while the ships were in action. There are problems with this theory, but whatever the outcome of the continuing gunnery debate it is instructive to know that major mistakes occurred in the English tactics and execution as well as the Spanish, and that the failure of the Armada marked neither the end of Spanish sea power nor the beginning of English domination.

The war between England and Spain did not end with the Armada; it only began, and for another sixteen years it wore on. In 1589 Drake led a counter-invasion, the "English Armada," against Spain. Its twofold mission was to destroy the remnants of the Spanish Armada and land an expeditionary force in Portugal. It was as unsuccessful as the Spanish venture had been. Of its 25,000 men and 120 ships, nearly half were lost. The crucial test of the Spanish imperial defense came in 1595 when Drake, Hawkins, and Thomas Baskerville led an English expedition to the West Indies, intent on capturing the Spanish treasure fleet and devastating its American bases. The venture turned out to be a more serious failure than the one six years before. Not only were many of the ships lost but also both Hawkins and Drake died before the fleet returned to England. The following year another English fleet, under Lord Howard, the "Armada victor," sailed into Cadiz. The town was sacked but the victory was hollow, for the fifty or more loaded merchantmen they had intended to capture were burned by the commander of the Cadiz garrison, who was none other than the duke of Medina Sidonia. Philip retaliated with two more armadas, one late in 1596 and the other in 1597, but violent storms drove them both from the English Channel. The naval war was still a standoff, incredibly expensive but profitless for both England and Spain, by the time the two monarchs passed from the scene at the turn of the century.

The Elizabethan Age

The last two decades of the sixteenth century and the first fifteen years of the seventeenth were truly a golden age in English literature and drama. The cultural Renaissance had been slow in reaching Britannia, and in the plastic and pictorial arts, England was still far behind. But its belated manifestations in literature were varied and special. The influences from the continent were great on English writers of the time. Boccaccio, Castiglione, and Machiavelli were translated and eagerly read; Tasso was a contemporary favorite; Spanish novels and plays, and French chronicles, essays, and poems were enthusiastically absorbed. Still, the flowering of English Renaissance letters was primarily a native growth, germinating from the depths of genuine feeling and personal experience.

Literature Exuberance, pride, and energy characterized Elizabethan literature. This was an age of heroic exploits, and it produced a literature of epic proportions. Proud of their achievements under the magnificent queen, Elizabethan writers magnified their deeds and glorified their doers. Even in the 1590s, indeed especially then—when the accomplishments were no longer so spectacular, when war was less heroic and more burdensome, when economic crisis followed crisis, when parliamentary frustration with the queen's conservative policies and autocratic methods bordered on defiance and rebellion, when the earl of Essex did flout the queen and rebel against the crown, when Queen Elizabeth herself had become cantankerous and petty—ebullient words continued to pour forth from pens that were caught up in the mystique and glory of the Elizabethan Age.

Historical writing was naturally popular. Chronicles and histories gratified the proclivity for self-pride and stimulated patriotism. Furthermore, they were conceived and written in the conviction that history is useful, that it supplies keys to understanding present events and shaping future needs. "It being the end and scope of all Historie," wrote Sir Walter Raleigh, "to teach by example of times past, such wisdome as may guide our desires and actions." Raleigh, like his compatriots, also believed that the unfolding of history was divinely ordained and that it is the historian's task to reveal the intervention of providence in human affairs. The best of the Elizabethan historians was William Camden (1551–1623) who, along with John Stow, Walter Raleigh, Francis Bacon, and others, was responsible for a veritable revolution in the writing of critical history. Camden's *Britannia* (1586), a detailed description of England, and his *Annales of the Renowned Princes Elizabeth* (1615) are monuments of historical scholarship. The same indefatigable devotion to research and careful writing are revealed in Richard Hakluyt's *Principal Navigations, Voyages, Traffics, and Discoveries of the English Nation,* which tell the remarkable saga of English naval exploits.

Elizabethan literary prose was a natural outgrowth of the development and glorification of the English language in the second half of the sixteenth century. Yet it was slow in maturing. Nothing comparable to Montaigne's *Essays* or Cervantes's novels was produced in the affectedly elegant prose of Elizabethan England. Still there is evidence of stylistic improvement in such works as Roger Ascham's *The Schoolmaster* and Sir Philip Sidney's *Arcadia,* and certainly in Richard Hooker's *Laws of Ecclesiastical Polity.* Even John Lyly, whose 1578 *Euphues: The Anatomy of Wit* (from which comes the word *euphuism,* meaning affected elegance) stagnated the language with elaborately structured sentences and rhetorical elaborations, but did break free from the conventions of medieval romance and demonstrated the versatility of the English language.

Some of the most useful religious works came from the pens of several pious women writers like Anne Wheathill, who tried "to spread God's Word while reassuring herself and her readers that she was not overstepping the bounds of feminine decorum," in the words of her recent biographer Elaine Beilin. Another was Anne Locke Prowse, who translated the *Sermons of John Calvin*, and in her dedication of that work to the Duchess of Suffolk wrote a sermon of her own. And Lady Elizabeth Tyrwhitt, governess of the Princess Elizabeth prior to her succession to the throne, wrote pious verses and prose meditations. Of special note are three of the five daughters of Sir Anthony Cooke and Anne Fitzwilliam Cooke, whose home was a haven of classical and scriptural learning. The second daughter, Anne, was an intelligent, pious, and strong-willed person who might have gone far in public service had she not been a woman. As it was she made available, among other works, two important weapons in the arsenal of the English church: a translation from the Latin of Bishop John Jewel's *Apologia Ecclesiae Anglicanae* (In Defense of the Church of England), and a translation from Italian of nineteen sermons by Bernardino Ochino. In 1556, Anne married Sir Nicholas Bacon, later lord keeper of the Great Seal, and gave birth to the renowned Francis Bacon. Anne's older sister, Mildred, became wife of William Cecil, Lord Burleigh; the next younger sister, Elizabeth (first Lady Hoby, then Lady Russell), translated a radical French tract into English; and Katherine, the fourth of the Cooke sisters, who married the diplomat Sir Henry Killigrew, was a Hebrew scholar and also wrote religious verses.

Poetry

The crowning glories of the Elizabethan Age were poetry and drama. George Gascoigne, perhaps the best known English author after Thomas Wyatt and Henry Howard, wrote fictional prose narratives and prose comedy as well as poetry and blank verse satire. His first book of poetry was entitled *A Hundredth Sundrie Flowers*. The greatest English poet since Chaucer was Edmund Spenser (1552–99). Strongly influenced by Platonism, Puritanism, and the friendship of Gabriel Harvey, a notable Cambridge scholar and patron, Spenser began writing sonnets, pastoral romances, and lyric poems at an early age. In the service of the earl of Leicester, he came into the influence of that romantic and spirited courtier, Sir Philip Sidney, to whom he dedicated his *Shepherd's Calendar* in 1579. There was hardly a form of poetic expression that Spenser had not tried by the time he entered the Irish service of Lord Grey in 1580. In Ireland he wrote the first three books of his masterpiece, *The Faerie Queene*, a strangely allegorical and exotic romance, set in medieval Arthurian England, yet providing a poignant commentary on the political, religious, and social conditions of his own day. Taken as a whole, *The Faerie Queene* is a remarkable Renaissance synthesis of chivalric honor, Christian devotion, Protestant piety, courtly love, Platonic philosophy, medieval pageantry, and modern patriotism. Yet in this, as in all of Spenser's works, there runs a strain of pessimism, a disillusioned idealism with regard to his contemporary world. It might not be incorrect to say that the best poet of Elizabethan times was the least at home in those times.

Yet Spenser was not the only poet of stature. The illustrious Philip Sidney (1554–86), that spontaneous and beloved courtier-adventurer-soldier-diplomat-poet, who was the grandson of the duke of Northumberland, godson and namesake of the Spanish king, nephew of the earl of Leicester, and brother-in-law of Sir Francis Walsingham, might well have become an even greater writer had he not been killed at the age of thirty-two while fighting with Leicester's army in the Netherlands. His *Astrophel and Stella* carried the sonnet to new heights, a genre that was also enhanced by Shakespeare, Samuel Daniel, and Michael Drayton. Sydney's first biographer was his lifelong friend and fellow poet Fulke Greville, whose collection of short poems, called *Caelica*, place him as one of the leading Elizabethan poets. Around Sir Walter Raleigh there also gathered a coterie of courtiers and poets paying homage to the queen and exploring new ideas with daring and zest. Shakespeare referred to them as "The School of the Night."

The Elizabethan Age gave rise to some noteworthy women poets as well, despite the obstacles they had to overcome. One of these was Isabella Whitney, from a family of lesser gentry in Cheshire, who wrote religious poetry vindicating the virtuous life and offering advice to her readers on moral and spiritual matters. Anne Dowriche was another writer who saw herself more as a teacher of religious values than as a poet. Her principal poem was *The French Historie*, based on Jean de Serres's *Commentaires* on the French religious wars, which she said she wrote for "the glorie of God, the edifying of his [the Protestant] Church, and the salvation of the soules of God's chosen." A similar goal motivated the Scottish Elizabeth Colville's *Ane Godlie Dreame*, narrating her own dream of Christ guiding the Christian pilgrim to the heavenly city.

The best of the women poets was Mary Sidney, Countess of Pembroke (1561–1621) and talented sister of Philip Sidney. While still anchoring her writings in religious piety, Mary Sidney marks something of a turning point in the development of women writers in England, both in terms of her wider circle of readers and the innovative variety and depth of her lyrical style. Her works include translations (most notably of Petrarch's *Triumph of Death* and Philippe du Plessis Mornay's *A Discourse of Life and Death*), elegies (including one to her brother), pastoral dialogues, and a metrical version of the Psalms. Fluent in both French and Italian as well as Latin, and skilled in music and embroidery, she joined the court of Queen Elizabeth when she was 14, and two years later married the Count of Pembroke. After the death of her brother, she became something of a patroness of promising young poets.

Shakespeare and the Elizabethan Theater

More than any other form of Elizabethan literature, drama expressed the emotional energy and the intellectual versatility of the time. The conjunction of revived classical drama with English allegorical and morality plays of the schools and court (and under the influence of the Spanish stage) gave birth to a whole new attitude toward drama in general and toward the theater in particular. George Peel, Robert Greene, and Thomas Kyd were the most skillful writers of English drama in the 1570s and early 1580s. They founded romantic comedy as a dramatic form and initiated what came to be called romantic tragedy—the mingling of love and aspiration with conspiracy, murder, and revenge. The earliest and most popular of these "revenge plays" was Kyd's *The Spanish Tragedy,* first produced in the early 1580s. In the meantime, Elizabethans were rapidly becoming addicted to the cult of the stage, a public amusement with "safety-valve" merit for the pent-up tensions and "bad humors" of society. In 1574 Leicester was responsible for the organization of an actors' company, and two years later the first public theater was built. From then on, creating drama also meant playwriting, staging, and acting. Soon music was blended to produce a virtual symphony of the arts, for this was the heyday of the madrigal, and of the great English madrigal composers Morley, Wilbye, Weelkes, and William Byrd. No more beautiful lyrics have ever been written for solo voice accompanied by the lute than those by John Dowland.

Christopher Marlowe (1564–93) struck the real chord of Elizabethan drama: "poetic conviction" harmonized with "rhetorical excitement." His spirit of defiance and independence, set in the framework of a majestically simple story and told in eloquent and powerful blank verse, excited Elizabethan audiences. His first great success was *Tamburlaine,* written in 1586, when he was twenty-two, followed by *Doctor Faustus* in 1588 and *The Jew of Malta* a year later. The potency of all Marlowe's plays was anticipated in *Tamburlaine,* a study of the lust for power and the personal mastery of one's own destiny, a play in which moral inducements are surmounted by self-confidence and ambition. *Doctor Faustus* is an intellectual Tamburlaine, seeking a nonmaterial empire and revealing even more profoundly the contradictions in humanity. Marlowe died suddenly in 1593, at the unripe age of twenty-nine, soon after completing his dramatically moving chronicle play, *Edward the Second.* Had Shakespeare died at the same age, we would have only his *Henry VI* and *Richard III.*

The years just following the Armada were the heyday of the English drama, with plays of all kinds pouring from the pens of both established and aspiring authors. One of the latter was William Shakespeare (1564–1616) of Stratford-upon-Avon, son of a well-to-do yeoman glover. He was a professional actor when he appeared in London in 1592, and already enough of an author to arouse the jealousy of Robert Greene, who called him "an upstart crow, beautified with our feathers." By the time of Marlowe's death, Shakespeare had attained almost complete mastery of his literary medium, and with an ease that seems to defy human limitations. He was a universal genius, combining technical proficiency with a remarkable ability to put experiences into poetic language, and possessing unusual understanding of human psychology. Building on the tradition of Marlowe and his predecessors, Shakespeare carried the public theater to an all-time high in poetic drama.

Shakespeare's earliest plays were the histories, *Henry VI,* Parts I, II, and III, and *Richard III,* based on the recently published chronicles of Raphael Holinshed. Next came the farcical and romantic comedies, *The Taming of the Shrew, Comedy of Errors, Two Gentlemen of Verona,* and *A Midsummer*

William Shakespeare. *This steel-engraving portrait appeared on the title page of the First Folio, the first edition of his collected plays, published in 1623.*

Night's Dream. The romantic tragedy of *Romeo and Juliet* was written in 1596, followed by six more histories (*Richard II, King John, Henry IV,* Parts I and II, *Henry V,* and *Julius Caesar*), and several more witty and dramatic comedies, including the lyrical *Merchant of Venice, Much Ado About Nothing, Love's Labour's Lost, As You Like It, Twelfth Night,* and *The Merry Wives of Windsor.* From these delightful plays have come some of the most enduring literary characters of all time, including Shylock, Rosalind, Malvolio, Falstaff, the irrepressible Bottom, and of course Romeo and Juliet.

At the turn of the century, when he was still a young man of thirty-six, Shakespeare began to write more deeply dramatic poetry, pessimistic and profound in meaning, tragic in plot. The queen was approaching sixty-seven and had been ruling England for forty-two years when Shakespeare completed his *Hamlet,* a poetic paradox of guilt and justice, revenge and remorse, unveiling "the tragedy of moral frustration" in the realization that the past can never be undone. Three years later Shakespeare produced the second of his great tragedies, *Othello,* the classic story of innocence producing evil and of justice demanding murder to placate anguish and satisfy honor. *Othello* was followed shortly by *King Lear,* another universal moral-tragedy rich in imagery, poetic drama, and human insight, and *Macbeth,* the dramatic portrayal of the progressive consumption of a human soul by the psychological consequences of an evil deed. Shakespeare's "tragic period" ended in 1607–08 with the completion of *Antony and Cleopatra* and *Timon of Athens*. Even his comedies of this period, *Troilus and Cressida, All's Well That Ends Well,* and *Measure for Measure,* are bitter problem plays showing human behavior at its worst.

Shakespeare's final plays—mostly romances dealing in various ways with the same elements of good and evil, innocence and guilt, corruption and restoration—are constructed in the unreal atmosphere of mythology and folklore, allowing remorse or sorrow to be alleviated and even reversed rather than hopelessly endured. The principal plays of this final period are *Pericles, Cymbeline, The Winter's Tale,* and *The Tempest.* In each of these, Shakespeare abandoned the direct probing of the tragic paradoxes of human nature and tried to present, through poetic symbolism, the potentialities of life and love.

Through all of his insights into human character, Shakespeare was always the supreme master of his medium, the English language, a literary vehicle that was still in the process of transition, and which he helped to change and develop. His last play was *Henry VIII,* and tradition maintains that he personally spoke the prologue for it at its premier in the Globe theater in June 1613. If that is true, he also witnessed the fire that gutted the Globe during the first performance of that play. Three years later Shakespeare died–again according to tradition—on the day of his birth, April 23, just three days after Cervantes's death. The Elizabethan Age had passed.

Suggestions for Further Reading

ELIZABETH I

A very good summary of the Elizabethan Age—political, religious, legal, social and economic—is D.M. Palliser, *The Age of Elizabeth: England Under the Later Tudors, 1547–1603* (New York, 1983). Biographies of the queen continue to appear. One of the more controversial is Jasper Ridley, *Elizabeth I: the Virtue of Shrewdness* (New York, 1987), which, like the same author's *Henry VIII,* attributes much more to the skill and independence of the protagonist than most historians do. Conversely, Christopher Haigh sees the queen as more rigid and vain, especially in her later years, in *Elizabeth I* (New York, 1988), a small but very provocative book. For a further elaboration of his revisionist views, see the same author's *The Reign of Elizabeth I* (Athens, Georgia, 1984), a collection of essays by some of the current leading Elizabethan scholars. Carolly Erickson's *The First Elizabeth* (New York, 1983) is a popularization but contains some suggestive insights. Even more laudatory and lucidly written is Christopher Hibbert, *The Virgin Queen: Elizabeth I, Genius of the Golden Age* (Reading, Massachusetts, 1991). An avowedly feminist approach is provided in Susan Bassnett, *Elizabeth I: A Feminist Perspective* (New York, 1988). Elizabeth W. Pomeroy shows that much can be learned from pictures in *Reading the Portraits of Queen Elizabeth I* (Hamden, Connecticut, 1989).

POLITICS AND GOVERNMENT

Wallace T. MacCaffrey, *Queen Elizabeth and the Making of Policy, 1572–1588* (Princeton, 1981) continues the penetrating and persuasive analysis of Elizabethan government begun in his *The Shaping of the Elizabethan Regime* (1968). Broader in scope is Alan G.R. Smith, *The Emergence of a Nation State: The Commonwealth of England* (New York, 1984), which looks at the years from Henry VIII to the Civil War. David M. Loades, *The Tudor Court* (Totowa, New Jersey, 1987) examines the development of the court from the reign of Edward IV through the death of Elizabeth. Lacey Baldwin Smith, *Treason in Tudor England: Politics and Paranoia* (Princeton, 1986), evaluates the Tudor paranoia about internal conspiracy, which was especially noticable during the Elizabethan period. *Patronage in Late Renaissance England* (Pasadena, 1983) contains papers edited by French R. Fogle and Louis A. Knafla. Also instructive is Richard C. McCoy, *The Rites of Knighthood: The Literature and Politics of Elizabethan Chivalry* (Berkeley, 1989). The Elizabethan Parliaments have been freshly scrutinized by Sir Geoffrey Elton in *The Parliament of England, 1559–1581* (Cambridge, England, 1986). The result is quite different from the picture described by Sir John Neale forty years ago. Also see Michael A.R. Graves, *Elizabethan Parliaments, 1559–1601* (London, 1987), and D.M. Dean and N.L. Jones, *The Parliaments of Elizabethan England* (Cambridge, Massachusetts, 1990). Political life away from the court is studied in Diarmaid MacCulloch, *Suffolk and the Tudors: Politics and Religion in an English County, 1500–1600* (Oxford, 1986).

The impact of individual politicians and courtiers is revealed in Robert K. Faulkner, *Richard Hooker and the Politics of a Christian England* (Berkeley, 1981); L.M. Hill, *Bench and Bureaucracy: The Public Career of Sir Julius Caesar, 1580–1636* (Stanford, 1988); David Howarth, *Lord Arundel and His Circle* (New Haven, 1986); Narasingha Sil, *The Life of William Lord Herbert of Pembroke (c. 1507–1570): Politique and Patriot* (Lewiston, New York, 1988); Alan Kendall, *Robert Dudley, Earl of Leicester* (London, 1980); and Derek Wilson, *Sweet Robin: A Biography of Robert Dudley, Earl of Leicester, 1533–1588* (London, 1981).

PAPISTS, PURITANS, AND ANGLICANS

The Elizabethan Settlement is freshly examined in Norman L. Jones, *Faith by Statute: Parliament and the Settlement of Religion, 1559* (London, 1982), which provides a convincing alternative to Neale's traditional Puritan interpretation of the Settlement. Also see Winthrop S. Hudson, *The Cambridge Connection and the Elizabethan Settlement of 1559* (Durham, 1980). The broader religious society is examined in detail in Richard L. Greaves, *Religion and Society in Elizabethan England* (Minneapolis, 1981); Leo F. Solt, *Church and State in Early Modern England, 1509–1640* (New York, 1990); and in Patrick Collinson, *The Religion of Protestants: The Church in English Society, 1559–1625* (New York and Oxford, 1984). The same author's *Archbishop Grindal, 1519–1583: The Struggle of a Reformed Church* (Berkeley, 1979) is also informative, as is G.J.R. Parry, *A Protestant Vision: William Harrison and the Reformation of Elizabethan England* (New York and Cambridge, England, 1987). On the English clergy see Rosemary O'Day, *The English Clergy: The Emergence and Consolidation of a Profession, 1558–1642* (Leicester, England, 1979), and Felicity Heal, *Of Prelates and Princes: A Study of the Economic and Social Position of the Tudor Episcopate* (New York and Cambridge, England, 1980).

Catholic politics and thought are studied in Arnold Pritchard, *Catholic Loyalism in Elizabethan England* (Chapel Hill, 1979); E.E. Reynolds, *Campion and Parsons: The Jesuit Mission of 1580–81* (London, 1980); David Lunn, *The English Benedictines, 1540–1688: From the Reformation to Revolution* (New York, 1980); and Peter Holmes, *Resistance and Compromise: The Political Thought of the Elizabethan Catholics* (New York and Cambridge, England, 1982).

Puritanism continues to attract many scholars, the dean of whom is Patrick Collinson. See the reprint of his *The Elizabethan Puritan Movement* (New York and London, 1982), and *Godly People: Essays on English Protestantism and Puritanism* (Ronceverte, West Virginia, 1984). Other excellent studies are Peter Lake, *Moderate Puritans and the Elizabethan Church* (New York and Cambridge, England, 1982); the same author's *Anglicans and Puritans: Presbyterianism and English Conformist Thought from Whitgift to Hooker* (Boston, 1988); Margo Todd, *Christian Humanism and the Puritan Social Order* (New York and Cambridge, England, 1987); and John Morgan's penetrating *Godly Learning: Puritan Attitudes Towards Learning and Education, 1540–1640* (New York and Cambridge, England, 1966). C.M. Dent describes the development of Protestant doctrine and discipline at Oxford in *Protestant Reformers in Elizabethan Oxford* (New York and Oxford, 1983). On Puritan theology see Dewey D. Wallace, Jr., *Puritans and Predestination: Grace in English Protestant Theology* (Chapel Hill, 1982); James T. Dennison, Jr., *The Market Day of the Soul: The Puritan Doctrine of the Sabbath in England* (Lanham, Maryland, 1983); and John R. Knott, Jr., *The Sword of the Spirit: Puritan Responses to the Bible* (Chicago, 1980).

SOCIAL AND FAMILY

Social history of the Elizabethan period is receiving renewed emphasis, resulting in some very interesting publications. For a good overview, see J.A. Sharpe, *Early Modern England: A Social History, 1550–1760* (Baltimore, 1987), as well as A.L. Rowse, *Court and Country: Studies in Tudor Social History* (Athens, Georgia, 1987), a collection of assorted biographical sketches, and *Eminent Elizabethans* (Athens, Georgia, 1983). The role of English universities in the scientific revolution is defined in Mordechai Feingold, *The Mathematicians' Apprenticeship: Science, Universities, and Society in England, 1560–1640* (New York and Cambridge, England, 1984). A fascinating book on royal tournaments during the sixteenth and early seventeenth centuries is Alan Young, *Tudor and Jacobean Tournaments* (Dobbs Ferry, New York, 1987). Life in Elizabethan London is the focus of Steve Rappaport's *Worlds Within Worlds: The Structures of Life in Sixteenth-Century London* (New York and Cambridge, England, 1989), which sees London life as being more stable than it is usually depicted. For contrasting views see John McMullan, *The Canting Crew: London's Criminal Underworld, 1550–1700* (New Brunswick, 1984), and J.A. Sharpe, *Crime in Early Modern England, 1550–1750* (New York, 1984). The actions of ecclesiastical courts in sexual disputes is the subject of Martin Ingram's *Church Courts, Sex and Marriage in England, 1570–1640* (New York and Cambridge, England, 1988).

Women and family life are receiving much more attention now. See in particular Ralph A. Houlbrooke, *The English Family, 1450–1700* (New York, 1984), which examines the family in the light of economic, religious, political, and demographic developments of the time. Also illustrative is Alice T. Friedman, *House and Household in Elizabethan England* (Chicago, 1988), which draws on a wide range of sources to portray an Elizabethan country house (Wollaton Hall) and the Willoughby family who lived in it. More general is Kathy Lynn Emerson, *Wives and Daughters: The Women of Sixteenth Century England* (Troy, New York, 1984). Also see Suzanne W. Hull, *Chaste, Silent and Obedient: English Books for Women, 1475–1640* (San Marino, California, 1982), and Susan Cahn, *Industry of Devotion: The Transformation of Women's Work in England, 1500–1660* (New York, 1987).

FOREIGN POLICY

P.S. Crowson, *Tudor Foreign Policy* (London, 1973) is still standard, but many new insights can be learned from R.B. Wernham, *Before the Armada: The Growth of Tudor*

Foreign Policy (London, 1973), and especially *After the Armada: Elizabethan England and the Struggle for Western Europe, 1588–1595* (New York and Oxford, 1984), which meticulously describes England's role in the European conflict of the late 80s and early 90s, based on the English State Papers, of which Wernham is a master. Also see his shorter and more readable *The Making of Elizabethan Foreign Policy, 1558–1603* (Berkeley, 1980). On specific arenas see E.I. Kouri, *England and the Attempts to Form a Protestant Alliance in the Late 1560s: A Case Study in European Diplomacy* (Helsinki, 1981); Humphrey Drummond, *Our Man in Scotland: Sir Ralph Sadler, 1507–1587* (London, 1969); Charles Wilson, *Queen Elizabeth and the Revolt of the Netherlands* (Berkeley, 1970); Albert L. Rowland, *England and Turkey: The Rise of Diplomatic and Commercial Relations* (New York, 1968); and Herbert Lom, *Enter a Spy: The Double Life of Christopher Marlowe* (Totowa, New Jersey, 1980). The personal and political relationship of Queen Elizabeth and Mary Queen of Scots is presented in Alison Plowden, *Elizabeth Tudor and Mary Stewart: Two Queens in One Isle* (Totowa, New Jersey, 1984). Michael Lynch, ed., *Mary Stewart: Queen in Three Kingdoms* (Oxford, 1988) is a compilation of nine scholarly studies. The best analysis of Mary's reign and her role in European politics is Jenny Wormald, *Mary Queen of Scots: A Study in Failure* (London, 1988).

TRADE AND MARITIME ACTIVITY

Eric Kerridge, *Trade and Banking in Early Modern England* (Manchester, England, 1988), emphasizes the London-centered domestic market as a key to English trade. N.J. Williams, *The Maritime Trade of the East Anglican Ports, 1550–1590* (New York and Oxford, 1988) carefully documents one important dimension of English trade. David B. Quinn and A.N. Ryan, *England's Sea Empire* (Winchester, England, 1983), is an important book focusing on the development of English naval power, external trade, and the early attempts at colonization. Also highly recommended are Kenneth R. Andrews, *Trade, Plunder and Settlement: Maritime Enterprise and the Genesis of the British Empire, 1480–1630* (New York and Cambridge, England, 1984), and Kenneth R. Andrews, et al., eds., *The Westward Enterprise: English Activities in Ireland, the Atlantic, and America, 1480–1650* (Liverpool, 1978). On Drake see Norman J.W. Thrower, *Sir Francis Drake and the Famous Voyage, 1577–1580* (Berkeley, 1984), essays commemorating the anniversary of Drake's circumnavigation; Mary Frear Keeler, ed., *Sir Francis Drake's West Indian Voyage, 1585–1586* (London, 1981), Hakluyt Society documents; and Warren L. Hanna, *Lost Harbor: The Controversy over Drake's California Anchorage* (Berkeley, 1979). On Raleigh and the Roanoke settlement see John W. Shirley, *Sir Walter Raleigh and the New World* (Raleigh, North Carolina, 1985); David B. Quinn, *The Lost Colonists* (Raleigh, North Carolina, 1984); David B. Quinn, *Set Fair for Roanoke: Voyages and Colonies, 1584–1606* (Chapel Hill, North Carolina, 1985); and Paul E. Hoffman's very valuable *Spain and the Roanoke Voyages* (Raleigh, North Carolina, 1987). A brief biography of Raleigh is Steven W. May, *Sir Walter Ralegh* (Boston, 1989). On the Armada see Suggestions for Further Reading following Chapter 8.

LITERATURE OF THE ELIZABETHAN AGE

One of the most successful attempts to analyze the interplay between Elizabethan literature, culture, and politics is Heather Dubrow and Richard Strier, eds., *The Historical Renaissance: New Essays on Tudor and Stuart Literature and Culture* (Chicago, 1989). Poetry and the visual arts from Philip Sidney to mid-seventeenth century are related in Norman K. Farmer, Jr., *Poets and the Visual Arts in Renaissance England* (Austin, Texas, 1984). On Sidney himself see Richard C. McCoy, *Sir Philip Sidney: Rebellion in*

Arcadia (New Brunswick, 1979), and for Spenser, Anthea Hume, *Edmund Spenser, Protestant Poet* (New York and Cambridge, England, 1984). Robin H. Wells, *Spenser's Faerie Queene and the Cult of Elizabeth* (Totowa, New Jersey, 1983) has some interesting things to say about the queen. For Christopher Marlowe see Millar MacLure, *Marlowe, the Critical Heritage* (Boston, 1979).

On women writers and popular culture, essential books are Elaine V. Beilin, *Redeeming Eve: Women Writers of the English Renaissance* (Princeton, 1987); Retha M. Warnicke, *Women of the English Renaissance and Reformation* (Westport, Connecticut, 1983); Margaret P. Hanney, ed., *Silent But for the Word: Tudor Women as Patrons, Translators, and Writers of Religious Works* (Kent, Ohio, 1985), and *Philip's Phoenix: Mary Siney, Countess of Pembroke* (New York, 1990). Popular culture is treated in Leonard R.N. Ashley, *Elizabethan Popular Culture* (Bowling Green, 1988), and Laura C. Stevenson, *Praise and Paradox: Merchants and Craftsmen in Elizabethan Popular Literature* (New York and Cambridge, England, 1985).

The jewel of Elizabethan literature was drama. For a good introduction see Walter Cohen, *Drama of a Nation: Public Theater in Renaissance England and Spain* (Ithaca, 1985); Michael Hattaway, *Elizabethan Popular Theatre* (London, 1982); C.L. Barber, *Creating Elizabethan Tragedy: The Theater of Marlowe and Kyd* (Chicago, 1988); James C. Bryant, *Tudor Drama and Religious Controversy* (Macon, Georgia, 1984). Steven Mullaney, *The Place of the Stage: License, Play, and Power in Renaissance England* (Chicago, 1988), talks about the paradox of popular theater in an authoritarian society. Countless questions about plays and the people who attended them are answered in Andrew Gurr, *Playgoing in Shakespeare's London* (New York and Cambridge, England, 1987). Many insights into Shakespeare's plays and the lives of Elizabethan women may be found in Lisa Jardine, *Still Harping on Daughters: Women and Drama in the Age of Shakespeare* (New York, 1983).

Books about Shakespeare continue to pour off the presses. Some recent ones having special merit are M.M. Resse, *Shakespeare: His World and His Work* (New York, 1980); John R. Brown, *Discovering Shakespeare: A New Guide to the Plays* (New York, 1981), which provides useful helps, as does Stanley Wells, ed., *The Cambridge Companion to Shakespeare Studies* (New York, 1986). Interesting topics are treated in David M. Bergeron, *Shakespeare's Romances and the Royal Family* (Lawrence, Kansas, 1985); D.G. Thayer, *Shakespearean Politics: Government and Misgovernment in the Great Histories* (Athens, Ohio, 1983); Robin H. Wells, *Shakespeare, Politics and the State* (London, 1986); and Stephen Greenblatt, *Shakespearean Negotiation* (Berkeley, 1988). E.A.J. Honigmann, *Shakespeare's Impact on His Contemporaries* (Totowa, New Jersey, 1982), shows Shakespeare's influence on his time, and Arthur McGee, *The Elizabethan Hamlet* (New Haven, 1987), presents the play as the original audiences would have seen it.

10 | ECONOMIC AND SOCIAL CRISIS

T HE CENTURY FROM 1550 TO 1650 WAS A PERIOD OF GREAT ECONOMIC and social disorder as well as political upheaval. It was an age of enormous discrepancy between the living standards of the rich and the poor, and a time of social uncertainty for all classes. Great wealth was harvested from the mines and forests of the New World as well as from the spices, silks, and precious gems of southern and southeastern Asia. Still the overall economy of Europe alternated between boom and bust, seemingly without relation to the influx of riches from overseas. The extreme contrasts of opulence and poverty attest to the continuing dependence upon capricious nature and to the avariciousness of people.

Historians commonly speak of the sixteenth-century price revolution and of the economic crisis of the seventeeth century. Yet we still know relatively little about either phenomenon. The primary obstacle to a full understanding of these problems is the shortage of reliable data. Wage and price statistics are scarce and usually questionable; population figures are at best subjective guesses; trade and business records, although more accurate, are very incomplete. Nevertheless, more documentary sources exist than have hitherto been used, and the current interest in this phase of European history is resulting in the publication of many useful studies, each of which throws a little more light upon this subject.

A Century of Inflation

The so-called price revolution of the sixteenth and early seventeenth centuries was a Europewide phenomenon, although it affected different regions at different times and with varying intensity. The degree of inflation also depended upon the commodity and the price index used—that is, whether calculated in nominal prices (moneys of account), or in terms of bullion or some other unit of financial measure.

Whatever the unit of measure used, however, it is evident that prices were beginning an abnormal increase in most areas of Europe by the early part of the sixteenth century, and by mid-century this price rise, especially of wool and grain, was having its effect upon social and economic conditions. The upswing in the European economy was well pronounced by 1565, after a shaky recovery from the financial crisis of 1557–60, and in the second half of the century it reached serious inflationary proportions. By the 1560s Europeans were conscious of the effects of inflation, and increasingly curious about its causes. The Salamanca scholar, Martín Azpilcueta de Navarra, was perhaps the first to associate the inflation with the influx of precious metals from the New World. In 1568 Jean Bodin, in France, also declared that the abundance of gold and silver was primarily responsible for the increasing prices, along with monopolies and royal extravagance. His antagonist, Jehan Malestroit, maintained that it was only the inflation of moneys of account and the debasement of the coinage that gave the appearance of a rise in prices.

It is true that the moneys of account did not correspond exactly with the inflation in terms of bullion, but by either measure a real inflation was taking place. Wheat prices, for example, calculated in terms of the price of silver, started their upward surge in western and Mediterranean Europe, where they were already much higher than in Poland and eastward, shortly after the beginning of the sixteenth century. By mid-century, Spain, southern France, and Italy showed the sharpest price increases. These reached their climax in France around 1590–94, during the war of the League; in Spain, especially Andalusia, between 1580 and 1595; and in Italy from 1590 to 1600. In northern Europe the inflation of wheat prices did not reach its peak until the second and third decades of the seventeenth century, in Germany between 1620 and 1640, in the Netherlands around mid-century, and in England not until after 1660. In Italy, France, and Spain, inflationary cycles recurred so frequently that grain prices remained high until mid-century and beyond. This was especially true in Castile, where the irresponsible use of copper coins artificially inflated prices until 1679. Spain was the victim of alternating, and sometimes simultaneous, inflation and depression during much of the early seventeenth century.

Wine prices tended to follow wheat prices in most areas, but continued to rise in the seventeenth century when other prices were dropping. This was particularly true in northern Europe where the demand for wine was more recent. The price indexes of other commodities, from armor to wool, show similar but never identical patterns of inflation, with regional and seasonal fluctuations and cyclical deflations. Throughout this period, foodstuffs were the goods most subject to inflation.

Another general trend in the century between 1550 and 1650 was the devaluation of the moneys of account. The value of the French *livre tournois,* for example, declined almost regularly during this period, except for the years 1557–1602, when accounts were reckoned not in *livres tournois* but in gold *écus,* which were actual coins of circulation. The Spanish *maravedí* held its value better than any other moneys of account until 1619, when it began a precipitous fall that did not stop until 1680. These devaluations obviously had a great effect on the price level at any given time. There was also a steady demand for precious metals, especially during the periods of sharpest inflation but, strange as this may seem, in deflationary times too.

In addition to the circulation of coins, many kinds of nonmetallic money, based on credit, became common. Bills of exchange were one form of "ghost money," as were state loans, bank notes, bonds, promissory notes, and several forms of directly transferable paper money. Various means of manipulating the currency value of these instruments had the effect of distorting prices in many localities and in general contributing to price fluctuations and crises. Thus it can be seen that the much-talked-about but seldom understood "price revolution" of the sixteenth century was in fact a very complex phenomenon of interrelated causes.

Wages and Prices Wages and wage movements are difficult to calculate for this period. The sources themselves are incomplete and untrustworthy, and extremely hard to analyze and evaluate. Moreover, even when a nominal wage can be determined, its real value is questionable unless we know the cost of living at the particular time and place, and how expenditures were distributed. Simplified and arbitrary indexes for this purpose have been suggested, but at best they give us only an approximation of the truth. Nevertheless, working as best we can from insufficient data, both statistical and literary, it is possible to reach some meaningful conclusions about wages and their pattern of change. First of all, there seems little doubt that the price-wage separation grew more extreme during the last half of the sixteenth century. In many cases, nominal as well as real wages fell, while prices continued their irrevocable rise. In almost every case where wages did rise, they rose at a slower rate than prices, thus increasing the hardships and poverty of wage earners.

The first victims of this price-wage deviation were, of course, the agricultural laborers and the salaried workers of the cities and towns. These unpropertied and unskilled people had no way of coping with the price-wage spread, so as the cost of living mounted, their living standard and subsistence level were forced ever downward. Although they were the most unfortunate victims of the inflation, they were not the only ones. Anyone with a fixed income was subject to the same pressures. Landowners, especially those who because of governmental decree could not raise rents, were also caught in the same price-wage spiral that plagued peasants and workers. These conditions forced many of the lesser nobility, particularly in France and in other parts of the continent, into bankruptcy. Likewise, some of the Spanish industrialists, who were unable to compete with foreign firms, were hard pressed to make ends meet, and many of them were out of business before the end of the century.

On the other hand, inflation had beneficiaries as well as victims. Many of the well-to-do landed gentry and some of the upper nobility who could raise their land rents were able to keep pace with the inflation and sometimes even outrun it. More often the merchant entrepreneurs succeeded in using the financial situation to their advantage by setting high-enough prices on marketable goods to offset the devaluation of the currency. Among agricultural enterprisers, the wool growers were the most fortunate in this respect. High demand, government protection, and increasing production enabled them to make the best of the economic situation.

Peasant life and work. *This illumination from a Flemish* Hours of the Virgin *illustrates some of the many activities of rural men and women in the sixteenth century.*

Individuals were not the only ones affected by the inflation. Government policies and actions were likewise shaped by it. In order to meet the growing demands of administration and war, with a spiraling inflation eating up the value of currency, governments resorted to higher and higher taxes. New tolls and tariffs were added to older levies, making the burden unbearable for many of the impoverished peasants. Frequently, the taxes could not be collected, or they were still insufficient for the needs, and governments were forced into increased borrowing from foreign bankers. They floated loans with the banking houses of Genoa, Augsburg, Antwerp, Amsterdam, and London, at inordinate rates of interest, some of which were repaid and some not.

By the early years of the seventeenth century, warning signs of a major recession were beginning to show. The economy was no longer able to expand at the rate it had in the sixteenth century. About 1619–20, although earlier in some places, the economic collapse began. As silver imports from the New World fell off drastically in the 1630s and 1640s, the situation worsened. Governmental issuing of vellum (paper) money artificially inflated prices in some countries just as depression was beginning. It was further staved off by the outbreak of the Thirty Years' War, which sporadically stimulated prices and thus averted a full-scale economic "bust" until mid-seventeenth century. But the war strained fiscal policies to their limit and resulted in financial burdens that contributed significantly to the political disorders and revolutions of the 1640s. Deflation and depression followed in the wake of the price revolution, resulting in financial collapse in the 1650s.

International Trade and Banking

Trade

Commercial expansion tried to keep pace with the price revolution. This expansion and the increased circulation rate of money undoubtedly helped feed the inflation. The Mediterranean was still an area of active trade in the early seventeenth century, even though it had ceased being the center of European commerce. Several Mediterranean producers shipped silk from Messina eastward to Constantinople and westward through many ports to northern markets. Other textiles and raw wool also took these routes, as did alum, hides, sugar, wines, olive oil, salt fish, and all kinds of spices. As the Mediterranean became more dependent upon northern Europe for its food and other essentials, the configuration of that commerce changed. On the opposite side of Europe, the Baltic trading area was not as diverse or as extensive as the Mediterranean, but many commodities of food, clothing, and building materials traversed the region in the ships of the Hanseatic League. Danzig (Gdánsk) was the eastern terminus of the vital grain trade, and salt fish made up a large part of Baltic commerce, which was increasingly carried in Dutch ships. The inland trade of central Europe depended heavily on the Rhine and Danube waterways, where traffic was heavy the year around with all kinds of minerals, clothing, and food products. This area was also serviced by the *Hohe Landstrasse,* the overland highway system from Frankfurt eastward through Erfurt, Leipzig, and Dresden to Poland. Of growing importance because of overseas trade, and linking the Mediterranean, Baltic, and central European trading areas, was the Atlantic seaboard, where a lively commerce flourished in salt herring, grain, and textiles, in addition to overseas products. A favorable location and aggressive enterprise made the Dutch the undisputed leaders of this carrying trade.

The vigorous Dutch commerce in domestic and foreign goods produced unheard-of wealth for the merchants and middlemen of that tiny but prosperous land that had successfully won independence from Spain by 1609. The Dutch built a great fleet of merchant vessels, from small fishing yawls and fast whale-hunters to huge East Indian galleons, which was estimated by contemporaries to have numbered in all over 15,000 ships. The backbone of the Dutch carrying fleet was the long, flat-bottomed, mass-produced *fluyt,* capable of carrying large cargoes with relatively small crews. The *fluyt* was a specialized vessel, designed and used exclusively for cargo carrying, particularly in the northern and coastal waters, where the danger of pirate attacks was minimal. The heaviest traffic was in grain, fish, lumber and forest products, copper, iron, tin, and furs carried from Baltic and North Sea ports; and in wines, olive oil, fruits, wool, silk, and salt from the south. These products were either sold to eager buyers at the year-round Dutch fairs or else converted into finished cloth, food, and beverages in Dutch mills and refineries. Either way, the industrious entrepreneurs and merchants made money because they were capable of dealing in large volume and total delivery from raw material to producer and then to consumer. Richard Dunn described the process in his *The Age of Religious Wars* as follows:

> They [the Dutch] would sail a fleet of flyboats [*fluyts*] into the Baltic laden with herring (which Dutch fishermen had caught off the English coast) and return with all of the grain surplus from a Danish island, or with twenty thousand head of lean cattle to be fattened in the Holland polders. They would buy a standing forest in Norway for timber, or contract before the grapes were harvested for the vintage of a whole French district. They would buy shiploads of undyed cloth, crude Barbados sugar, and Virginia leaf in England; have the cloth dyed, the sugar refined, and the tobacco cut and wrapped by Amsterdam craftsmen; and sell the finished commodities all over northern Europe at prices the English could not match. Foreign merchants found it worth their time to shop in Amsterdam because there they could buy anything from a precision lens to muskets for an army of five thousand. The exchange bank eased credit; marine insurance policies safeguarded transport. And no merchant could feel a stranger in a city where the presses printed books in every European tongue, and the French and English language newspapers were more lively and informative than the gazettes printed back home.

Augmenting this trade were the great Dutch fishing fleets, the prime suppliers of salt herring, haddock, cod, and whale oil to the markets and tables of Europe. Even more colorful and complex, though hardly more profitable, was the Dutch international trade in Asian spices, tea, cotton, silk, and porcelain, and in American sugar, tobacco, dyestuffs, and furs.

Although dominated by the Dutch between 1609 and 1660, the commercial revolution of the sixteenth and seventeenth centuries was not a Dutch monopoly. The English were particularly active after the beginning of the seventeenth century, when English cloth exports were becoming more diversified and the demand for overseas products stimulated English trade in Asia, the Middle East, and America. The gradually increasing productivity of European industries, the stimulation of purchasing power by the influx of New World bullion, and the continued refinement of banking and other credit facilities combined with technological innovations and improvements in shipping and shipbuilding to create a Europewide interest and activity in commerce. Still small-scale in relation to modern world trade, the commercial revolution brought Europe out of the subsistence economy of the medieval world and carried it into the industrial era of recent times. Viewed in the context of the limitations of sixteenth- and seventeenth-century transportation, the achievements of early modern ocean commerce seem almost miraculous. Overland transportation was slow and primitive in comparison. The great innovation in Renaissance travel was made in ocean-going ships. The revolution in shipbuilding and oceanography, which accompanied and made possible the overseas expansion of Europe, continued through the sixteenth and early seventeenth centuries. The rapid development of the caravel, *nao,* galleon, and *fluyt* ship designs made worldwide navigation and commerce, for the first time in history, not only possible but commonplace.

Joint-Stock Companies
This commercial revolution also stimulated remarkable developments in financial organization and capitalism. The most successful form of commercial organization in the seventeenth century was the joint-stock trading company, or corporation. Through the joint-stock company, large amounts of capital could be concentrated for the purpose of commercial or other economic enterprise. The huge investments necessary to outfit and send large cargo fleets to the East Indies could thus be supplied from the resources of corporations whose operating capital was contributed by thousands of people buying shares in the corporation. This characteristic was of great importance, for it marked a significant difference between seventeenth-century corporations and the *ad hoc* joint-stock companies of the early Renaissance, which sold shares in a particular enterprise rather than in a continuing corporation. Profits were returned to the shareholders annually in proportion to the amount of their investment.

Regulated and joint-stock companies developed rapidly during the early seventeenth century, a development that stemmed partly from English precedents. The Merchant Adventurers Company was an example of the transition from Renaissance to early modern corporations. Operating as a confederation of independent merchants, though governed by company rules and regulations, the Merchant Adventurers were the principal instruments of English cloth shipping in the sixteenth century. The Levant Company of 1581 gave birth to the more permanent English East India Company of 1600. Shares in that company were transferable, as in modern corporations, and policy control was vested in a board of directors elected by the stockholders. An important factor in the company's financial success was its monopolistic privileges, granted and maintained by government charter.

Even more successful, and certainly more powerful, was the Dutch East India Company, which opened the Spice Islands and all of southeast Asia to Dutch exploitation. While establishing its bases in the East, fighting wars, and exploring unknown oceans, the company also made money. Some idea of its enormous economic success can be judged by the fact that in more than 200 years of operation, it paid dividends to its stockholders at an average of about 18 percent per year! "It is no wonder," noted Sheperd Clough, "that the shareholders settled back to live comfortably on their incomes, and left control to the directors." These two corporations are only the leading examples of scores of successful (and some unsuccessful) joint-stock trading companies that were organized during the early seventeenth century.

Banking
Closely related to the financial operation of these companies were accompanying developments in banking and exchange. The seventeenth-century center of this activity was Amsterdam, which succeeded Antwerp and preceded London

The **Amsterdam stock exchange**, *built by Hendrick de Keyser in 1607, as seen in a panel by Job Berckheyde. This was the center of Dutch economic action in the first half of the seventeenth century.*

as the financial capital of Europe. Family banks, such as the Welsers and Fuggers, were no longer capable of providing the multiple services required by the more sophisticated commercial capitalism of the seventeenth century. Besides, most of these merchant princes of the Renaissance had now been broken by defaulted loans to spendthrift governments. The success and expansion of Dutch trade and the concentration of moneys of all denominations and species in Amsterdam made the development of adequate banking and credit facilities imperative. By 1600 the combination of multiple currencies in Amsterdam and the relative depreciation of Dutch coinage had attracted hundreds of money-changers and private banks to the city, giving rise to widespread speculations and abuses. To remedy these abuses, the city created the Bank of Amsterdam in 1609. Patterned after the municipal Rialto Bank of Venice, the Bank of Amsterdam was a deposit and transfer institution intended to eliminate the coinage confusion by controlling moneychanging and to facilitate large- and small-scale commercial operations by providing safe deposit and exchange facilities. Since most of the merchants became depositors in the bank, it provided a convenient and rapid means of paying debts, transferring credit, and exchanging capital with no more effort than a few bookkeeping entries. For 210 years, the Bank of Amsterdam served the needs of the city and of expanding commercial capitalism. Equally useful was the Amsterdam Bourse, or Exchange, which began as a goods exchange early in the century and gradually shifted to the trading of stocks. By 1620, the Amsterdam Exchange had become the center of the international business world.

Mercantilism

Seventeenth-century statesmen grew increasingly aware of the importance of international trade and expanding business to the successful growth of national states. The doctrine associated with this adaptation of economic policy and practice to the aggrandizement of the national state has been called mercantilism (since the publication of Adam Smith's condemnation of it in 1776). Variously defined and irregularly applied, mercantilism frequently means different things to different people. We can usually agree, however, that it did have to do with the ways seventeenth-century governments reacted to and made use of economic resources in the conduct of national affairs. Indeed, where mercantilism was most fully operative, it is fair to say that the major consideration of government was the development and exploitation of wealth for the purpose of increasing national power.

The English navigation laws, for example, were attempts to protect the national shipbuilding industry and carrying trades from the overwhelming competition of the Dutch. Similarly, national production, markets, and raw materials were protected by prohibitions against foreign trade with a nation's colonies and against the marketing of colonial wares outside the mother country. Colonial expansion, the merchant fleet, and naval power were all considered part of the protectionist system. Mercantilism also promoted a favorable balance of trade, by which wealth flowed into a country because it sold more goods abroad than it purchased. This insistence upon raising exports and lowering imports was an important facet of the mercantilist monetary system. It is also seen in what we call bullionism—that is, the equating of bullion with basic wealth and the belief that the accumulation of it, through balance of trade, protection, or whatever method, was essential to making the country prosperous and therefore powerful.

At first glance, it would appear that the Netherlands was out of step with the rest of Europe with regard to mercantilism. Dutch industries were primarily premercantilist, that is, dominated and tightly regulated by local guilds. Commerce, on the other hand, was a national enterprise and was therefore allowed an unusual freedom of operation, although this policy was contrary to mercantilist doctrine. Bullion was exported without alarm, except by a minority of more orthodox mercantilists, and import and export duties were kept at a low rate. However, three facts must be kept in mind before labeling the Dutch nonmercantilists:

First, the government and the great merchants were one and the same. Allowing wide political and economic powers to the East India Company was not inconsistent with the mercantilist practice of tight government control. The company's successes were the government's successes. More completely and effectively than any other state, the government of the Netherlands was in the money-making business.

Second, dealing as they did in volume trade, and also having a favored competitive position because of the volume and its accompanying lower prices, it was to the government's advantage to keep impediments to trade at a minimum. Because of their huge commercial fleet and worldwide operations, the Dutch were in the unique position of not having to enact many protective tariffs against foreign competitors or regulate the flow of overseas trade. When this position was threatened in the latter part of the century, the Dutch also enacted legislation to protect themselves against the competition of other nations.

Third, the Dutch were extremely protective of their fleets, providing heavily armed escorts in regions such as East India and Brazil, where naval competition was keen. They went to war as readily to protect their economic advantage as other nations did to promote theirs. Dutch diplomacy was likewise mobilized to the needs of commercial interests. Furthermore, government monopolies granted to trading companies, such as the East India Company, were as rigidly maintained and guarded as were similar mercantilist subsidies in other countries. The conclusion seems apparent, therefore, that the variations from mercantilism in Dutch practice do not prove that the Dutch were not mercantilist but rather that mercantilism itself was many-faceted. Whatever the methods used, every state came to recognize the significance of economic strength and the importance of controlling it for the benefit of national power.

The Crisis in Agriculture

In the seventeenth century, as in the sixteenth, the European economy was still tied to agriculture. The methods, means, and quantity of agricultural production had changed very little. The inefficient two-field and three-field rotation of crops was still practiced in most of Europe in the seventeenth century, as it had been in the thirteenth. Cultivating techniques remained essentially unaltered; harvesting methods were still primitive; yields per acre were consistently low. Tied to cereal crops for its subsistence, much of Europe remained dependent upon the Baltic countries for cereal grains. In many agricultural areas, the margin between life and death was always very slim. When crops failed, from drought, rain, or winds, starvation and famine usually followed.

Yet some progress was made in agriculture during the late sixteenth and early seventeenth centuries, even though, unlike commerce, it could hardly be called a revolution. Some local improvement in economic conditions resulted from the higher grain prices of the sixteenth century, which stimulated some increase in cultivated acreage. In this area, as in other examples, the principal beneficiaries of higher prices were the successful grain speculators, some of whom made great profits from the European grain trade. In most cases, the slightly increased production was more than eaten up by increased population. As long as agricultural methods remained essentially unchanged, yields continued to be insufficient. Some improvements in techniques were practiced in the Netherlands, where the use of clover as a fallow crop improved the soil fertility while providing a much-needed cattle food. The use of animal fertilizers expanded only slightly until a later day when the rudiments of soil chemistry were known and the oxygen-nitrogen cycle was better understood.

Farm labor. *A well-known harvest scene by Pieter Bruegel the Elder shows peasants at work in the fields in mid-summer.*

The expansion of food and beverage crops, and the introduction of new ones, had some beneficial effects on European agriculture. Vine cultivation continued to spread, particularly toward the east, and in Champagne in northeastern France, opened a new era in the taste for and production of wine. In Portugal, Valencia, and the Po Valley of Italy, rice was raised for the first time, with moderate success. The discovery and exploitation of the New World provided the greatest stimulation to the cultivation of new crops, although in most cases Europeans were slow to appreciate either the nutritional or economic value of these products. Corn (maize) from America was introduced into Europe early in the sixteenth century but did not catch on until the seventeenth century, and then only on a limited scale in northern Portugal, northwestern Spain, southern France around Toulouse, and in the Po Valley of Italy. The potato was also brought to Spain from America but was only slowly adopted as a food crop in Europe. Most people were suspicious of this new vegetable, which resembled the poisonous nightshade, and they were slow to discover the best ways to prepare it. It was eaten as a human food only in times of extreme famine. In Ireland it first curtailed famine among the destitute peasants in the early seventeenth century but did not become a staple there before the late eighteenth century. Tomatoes and red peppers were introduced and grown in parts of southern Europe, but not in the north. Beans also came from America; one variety appears to have been brought into France from Canada by Jacques Cartier, and from there they gradually spread to the Netherlands and across the channel to England.

Yet even with these and other new stimuli to food raising in Europe, agriculture remained backward and seriously underproductive until well into the eighteenth century. Even the fantastic profits resulting from sheep raising in the sixteenth century accrued to a relatively few among Europe's 70 to 80 million population. Livestock production, especially horses, increased in the early seventeenth century, and selective breeding led to some improvements in cattle strains. These gains, however, were offset by increased deaths from the shortage of winter feed and from the wholesale destructions of the Thirty Years' War.

The growing market economy of the sixteenth century and early seventeenth centuries accelerated the process of dissolving local manorial farming in western Europe and converting some farms into viable economic units. The rise in farm prices, especially of grains, worked to the advantage of landowners and even some tenant farmers. Many landowners converted more of their cultivatable land into cash crops and used the income to climb the all-important social ladder. At the same time, sharecropping and tenant farming continued to free the peasants from social servitude while subjecting them to new economic encumbrances. In eastern Europe, where large estates and rigid serfdom remained the pattern of life, the peasants were yoked with both burdens. The most oppressive features of tenant farming in western Europe came from the heavy imposition of taxes and from the devastations of war, which usually more than offset the increased agricultural incomes.

Industrial Development

Industry, like agriculture, was generally underproductive relative to the population. The reason for this underproductivity is obvious. The theory of static demand handicapped any large-scale market expansion, and primitive manufacturing techniques prevented the adequate supplying of even the available sixteenth-century market. Production was further hampered by the weight of an antiquated guild system. Although not as crude as farming techniques, manufacturing was still primarily by hand and, like agriculture, was geared to providing essential clothing, shelter, and food for sustaining life. These methods of production were barely adequate to supply the needs of the growing European population.

Nevertheless, changes were taking place in early modern industry. Indeed, the improvements in mining and metallurgy in England between 1560 and 1640 were such as to prompt at least one eminent historian to refer to this period as the first industrial revolution. Even if we reject this extreme assessment, we must agree that, given the rudimentary methods available to seventeenth-century industry, the volume and variety of manufactured products was amazing, and in many cases their quality was high. Most industries were not as concentrated as they would later become, because they were based on the system of domestic manufacture (cottage industry). Coarse cloths and even fine fabrics were produced in homes and small shops from Córdoba to Danzig and from Cheltenham to Bari. Some steps in the textile-manufacturing process, such as fulling and dyeing, were performed in large-scale combined operations rather than in scattered cottages. Yet these, too, could be found throughout the country. In like manner, sawmills, distilleries, tanneries, printing presses, and soapworks were distributed widely, even though frequently organized on a fairly large-scale factory system. Government monopolies on the manufacture of tapestries, glass, gunpowder, saltpeter, soap, and bricks further contributed to the early development of centralized industries, which in turn meant increased production and stimulation for improved manufacturing techniques.

The technological progress of this period was not great, but it was sufficient to invalidate the myth that no advancement took place until the Industrial Revolution of the eighteenth century. In the textile trades, several developments are worth noting, among them improvements in the loom that enabled operators to increase their output of figured fabrics (the Jacquard loom), and the introduction of a ribbon loom from Danzig near the end of the sixteenth century. A frame knitting machine was invented by a Nottingham clergyman, William Lee, in 1589, but fear of unemployment among hand knitters caused Queen Elizabeth to prohibit its use. Lee took refuge in France, where he was received with equal suspicion. Fifty years later, the stock loom was developed in France and employed in Louis XIV's stocking factory at Château de Madrid. The knitting industry grew rapidly in France after the middle of the seventeeth century. Glass-making experienced rapid growth, both for building and for glassware, as illustrated in Antonio Neri's famous textbook, *L'arte vetraria* (The Glassmaking Art, 1612). The techniques of grinding glass for lenses were improved by Galileo, Torricelli, and others, and contributed to the invention and improvement of the telescope and the compound microscope. Government prohibitions against the burning of wood (because of the fear of timber shortages) in the growing English glassworks industry led to the use of coal-burning glass furnaces. This, in turn, helped stimulate the demand for coal mining in England after 1615.

Mining and Metallurgy   The English coal industry, which for 300 years was without rivals, had its beginning in the late sixteenth and early seventeenth centuries. In this period, coal came into wide use throughout England and Scotland, not only in the glass, earthenware, dyeing, brick, soap, sugar, and brewing industries, but also as a domestic fuel. By 1650 nearly 530,000 tons of coal were shipped from Newcastle per year, an increase of over 1,500 percent in 80 years. In the same period, the consumption of coal in London increased by 2,000 percent. Air pollution was no stranger to seventeenth-century London. The belching black smoke from brick kilns, glass furnaces, soap houses, sugar refineries, and thousands of domestic fireplaces gave London the appearance of a modern smog-laden metropolis. Yet even the plague of air pollution was followed by benefits and changes that had profound effects upon future life, such as using coke made from coal in the smelting of iron ore. The process, which was slow in developing but proved to be the basic ingredient in the mass production of quality iron and steel, was apparently first discovered during the English Civil War in connection with the drying of malt for the manufacture of beer. Solutions to other difficulties, such as water drainage from the ever-deepening mine shafts, and the transportation of coal out of the mines and overland to its destination, were part of the later Industrial Revolution.

The expansion of the iron industry paralleled, but in the seventeenth century was not yet dependent upon, the mining of coal. Charcoal was the principal fuel of the iron industry, and the waterwheel was the chief source of power. Metallurgy expanded rapidly but was increasingly plagued by the shortage of timber, as shipbuilders and ironmasters vied with one another for the forests. The greatest stimulation to iron production came from war. Not only did the size of armies increase with the Thirty Years' War, but the use of artillery, cannonballs, firearms, and armor multiplied even more. By early in the seventeenth century, Sweden was fast becoming the leading producer and exporter of iron and steel. Rich deposits of iron ore, coupled with vast timber resources, made Sweden a natural metallurgical center. Encouragement and support from the government of Gustavus Adolphus and the steady demand from Swedish armies in Germany greatly stimulated the production of these metals. By the outbreak of the English Civil War, England itself was a heavy importer of Swedish iron.

Other metals also prospered as wood slowly gave way to metal in the manufacture of bolts and nails, bearings, pipes, and machine parts, and was replaced by glass, bronze, and pewter in household utensils and construction. Bronze, brass, and other copper alloys were widely used in industry, from heavy gun and bell founding to intricate clockworks and precision instruments. In this regard, one of the greatest achievements of the early seventeenth century was the invention and manufacturing of the instruments and apparatus that were in part responsible for the revolution in science. New tools enabled scientists to discover new microcosms and macrocosms, which in turn sharpened and broadened their knowledge of the world. Tin was used in making pewter, and was one of the principal metals in typecasting, along with lead and bismuth or antimony. Lead was employed in construction, both for roofing and for decorative work, and for casting bullets and gunshot. For a long time it had been the essential material for joining and reinforcing stained-glass windows. Varying percentages of copper, brass, tin, lead, and zinc were usually alloyed with silver or gold in coinage.

All of this activity must not blind us to the fact that the European economy in general, and agriculture and industry in particular, were in serious trouble by the mid-seventeenth century. The flourishing English coal industry, Dutch commercial expansion, and Swedish iron and copper production were exceptions rather than the rule. In southern France, Spain, all of Italy, most of Germany, Denmark, Bohemia, and Poland, industry was either relatively static or declining by the third decade of that century. Markets were drying up; the population growth was ending; the supply of New World bullion was rapidly dwindling; prices were falling in many areas; profits were becoming rare. The outbreak of the Thirty Years' War perhaps postponed the inevitable depression, and government devaluation and manipulation of coinage created artificial inflation for several decades. Economic recession, however, was apparent on every side by the 1630s. It was particularly acute in the Mediterranean area, where Italy declined from its once-proud position of industrial and financial center of the world to an economic backwater. The wealth expended in the great Baroque palaces and sculptures was drawn from the bottom of the economic barrels, and from the tithes and taxes from other parts of the Christian world. Relatively little new wealth was being produced. Similarly, Spain fell victim to economic exhaustion and was no longer able to support the extravagant court life and the over-committed foreign policies of its government. By the 1640s even Spain's most productive colonies were more burdens than assets. Underdeveloped and neglected, Spanish industries could not provide for domestic needs, let alone make profits from foreign exports. The sixteenth-century "boom" had temporarily broken the subsistence cycle with rising prices, expanding markets, and growing population. By the middle of the seventeenth century, though, the era of inflated prosperity was over.

Population and Plague

The economy of Europe was closely linked with the size, density, and movement of population. Although vital statistics for this early period are scattered, it is possible to compile some meaningful population figures (of varying reliability) from numerous sources, ranging from church and parish records, chantry surveys, and muster rolls, to contemporary chronicles and diplomatic papers. Taking all of these into account, along with the estimates of modern

Table 10–1   Estimated Populations of Europe, in Millions
(Listed in Order of Density in 1600)

Country or Area	1500	1550	1600	1650
Italy	11	12	14	13
Netherlands (North & South)	2	3	4	5.5
France	15.5	17	17.5	18.5
England, Wales, and Ireland	4	4	5.5	6
Germany and Bohemia	13.5	15.5	18	16
Switzerland	1	1	1.5	1.5
Portugal	1.5	2	2	2
Spain	7	8	9	8
Scotland	1	1	1.5	1.5
Hungary	1.5	2	2.5	2.5
Poland-Lithuania	3	3.5	4.5	4.5
Scandinavia	1.5	1.5	2	2
Totals	62.5	70.5	82.0	81.0

demographic historians, it seems safe to estimate that the population of Europe did increase by some 20 million during the course of the sixteenth century (from approximately 62.5 million in 1500 to around 82 million in 1600). This growth leveled off by 1620, and by mid-seventeenth century, a net decrease was evident in most of Europe, especially in war-torn and plague-ridden Germany. Table 10–1 shows the approximate populations of the various parts of Europe between 1500 and 1650. Not surprisingly, the era of rapid population growth also coincided with the century of economic expansion and vitality, and economic recession accompanied the ensuing period of population decline. The ravages of war, famine, and plague during the 1620s, 1630s, and 1640s caused the greatest loss of population during that period.

A wide variety of evidence indicates a close correlation between the sixteenth-century price rise and the increase in the population. In fact, economic historians now generally give more weight to population growth as a causal factor in the price revolution than to the traditional view of bullion imports from the New World. Contemporary chronicles, travelers' accounts, and ambassadors' reports are almost unanimous in their agreement over the increasing populations in the sixteenth century. Growing pressure for land, increased demand for food, and the expansion of cities provide further evidence of the population rise. By the beginning of the seventeenth century, several writers, including Sir Walter Raleigh, were advocating war as a necessary control for the surplus population. Similar and more humane justifications were made for colonial emigration, as many believed the population saturation point was being reached.

Italy

In some respects, and in certain areas, these fears may have been justified. The greatest concentration of population was still in central and northern Italy, where the density approached 120 per square mile in 1600, with a total population of around 14 million for the entire peninsula. Here, where the Renaissance recovery had begun early in the fifteenth century and then been arrested during the chronic Italian wars, a population surge in the second half of the sixteenth century caused a serious strain on land and urban space, despite the violent epidemic in northern Italy in 1575–77. Yet the remarkable population growth in sixteenth-century Italy did not continue long into the seventeenth. Tied as it was to the Spanish economy, Italy suffered many of the same setbacks and depressions that were both the cause and result of demographic decline. Then, in 1630, northern Italy was struck by the worst outbreak of bubonic plague since the Black Death of 1348–50. The mortality rate was almost incomprehensible. Some cities lost a third to a half of their inhabitants; deaths in Verona were reported to have reached 60 percent of the population; Mantua lost nearly 70 percent of its people to plague, siege, and sack. Some of the rural districts were struck almost as hard. Twenty-six years later, central and southern Italy felt the full impact of pestilence as the plague left death and devastation in its wake.

The Netherlands

The population explosion in the sixteenth-century Netherlands was likewise spectacular, almost rivaling that of northern Italy for population density and far outstripping the rest of Europe. By 1609 there were over 110 inhabitants per square mile in the United Netherlands, and its population continued to grow during the seventeenth century. This is even more remarkable in view of the fact that for the last half of the sixteenth century and much of the 1620s and 1630s, this area was the scene of almost continuous warfare. The demographic picture of the Netherlands was further complicated by the spate of migrations, north and south as well as east and west. Religious rivalries accounted for much of this movement after 1581, as Protestants moved northward into Holland and Zeeland, and Catholics flocked southward into the Spanish Netherlands. Some areas were virtually depopulated by these migrations and by war, but not for long. Decline in one area was counterbalanced by rapid growth in another. Immigration from northern France in the late sixteenth century and from Germany during the Thirty Years' War accounted for some of the continued population increase. A steadily rising birthrate also had its effect. Perhaps it was the optimism and stimulation engendered by the successful Dutch conquest of its environment and the equally successful defense of its independence that provided the momentum for a dynamically growing population during most of the period.

Central Europe

Central Europe (Lorraine, Burgundy, and Franche-Comté, with the adjoining Rhineland region of western Germany from the Low Countries to Switzerland) was another area of dense population. There were only a few large cities between Antwerp and Basel, however. The largest, Cologne, claimed no more than 30,000 inhabitants at a time when Venice could count at least 120,000, Milan 100,000, and Naples 200,000. Most of the people here lived in thousands of villages and towns spread over the farmlands of Champagne and Lorraine, and scattered along the deep Rhineland valleys. The population of this region was always in flux. The migrations of ancient peoples, the journeys of medieval and early modern merchants and tradesmen, the frequent dislocations caused by war, and the unpredictable movements of religious exiles had made this a melting pot in the center of the continent, an ever-changing yet never-changing kaleidoscope of human movement and settlement. Strasbourg, representing the steadfastness and vitality of Reformation Europe, was the provincial town-become-cosmopolitan-city that best symbolizes the history and the demography of this region.

France

In all parts of France, the population grew quickly, especially during the first half of the sixteenth century, before the religious wars began their devastations. Growth was particularly rapid in the large cities—Lyon, Marseille, Rouen, Bordeaux, and Paris. Provincial towns and villages were harder hit by the Wars of Religion than were the cities, but accompanying famines and disease were widespread throughout France. Recurring plagues during the last forty years of the sixteenth century further impeded population growth. The eventual conclusion of the religious wars under Henri IV, however, saw an unmistakable demographic upswing, which apparently continued favorably during the next half century, except for the plague-famine-war casualties of 1628–38, and the disease and drought years of 1648–53.

England

The population pressure was as great in much of sixteenth-century England as it was on the continent, especially during the Elizabethan era. Although small in comparison with France, Germany, Italy, and even Spain, England also felt the growing pains of increasing population, rural dislocations, urban transformation, and the proliferation of unemployment, vagrancy, and displacement. Several features of English and European life in the seventeenth century impeded the previous pattern of growth but did not entirely prevent a slow increase in population between 1600 and 1660. The worst of these impediments was the familiar plague, whose almost yearly outbreaks in England were particularly severe in London in 1603, 1625, 1636–37, during most of the 1640s, and in the Great Plague of 1665, the latter terminating in the Great London Fire of 1666. These epidemics were punctuated or accompanied by poor harvests, severe depression in the 1620s, and civil war in the 1640s, although the war may not have been as costly in lives as is usually claimed.

Germany

Sixteenth-century Germany experienced very rapid population growth. Contemporary chronicles confirm the evidence of tax and clerical records that populations in some areas, such as Hesse and the western Tyrol, were approaching saturation levels before mid-century. Swabia and Bavaria were also heavily populated, and all of Westphalia showed significant growth in the second half of the sixteenth century. This population pressure in western Germany led to a new, and not the last, *Drang nach Osten* (Movement to the East) to settle lands in the vast regions to the east. Such migrations were partly responsible for the demographic rise in Poland and in other sparsely populated areas of eastern Europe.

By the early years of the seventeenth century, however, the population surge in Germany was coming to an end. Serious and prolonged economic crisis in some parts of the empire led to population leveling by the 1620s or before. Then came the Thirty Years' War, with its tens of thousands of military and civilian victims. The devastation left by the soldiers was only a small part of the destruction caused by the war. Hunger, starvation, disease, and plague followed the armies. Typhus, dysentery, smallpox, and cholera ravaged the countryside after every military campaign. In 1624–30 and 1634–39, the dreaded plague struck in all of its grim ferocity, laying complete waste to some regions and almost depopulating others. Hardest hit by the combinations of war, famine, and plague were Mecklenburg, Pomerania, and Brandenburg in the north, the upper Palatinate, Hesse, Thuringia, Franconia, and middle Bohemia in the central regions, and the lower Palatinate, Trier, Württemberg, Alsace, Breisgau, and Swabia in the south. Some of these areas lost as many as 50 percent of their inhabitants by 1650. The total population decline of the Holy Roman Empire during the first half of the seventeenth century appears to have been in the neighborhood of 15 percent.

Spain
In sixteenth-century Spain the upward swing of population was as unmistakable as it was in the other countries. Although it remained sparsely populated in relation to the rest of western Europe, an overall increase of some 25 percent (30 percent for the kingdom of Aragon) suggests a very dynamic and expanding population. In the second half of the century, however, many fluctuations and migrations make it difficult to establish a demographic pattern with much certainty. It appears that the overall population continued to grow, although very erratically and perhaps not as rapidly as in the previous decades, resulting in a relative shift in population from the north to the south. This growth was accompanied, as it was in many parts of Europe, by a movement from the country to the cities, and was particularly noticeable in Seville, where the surge began before mid-century and caused the population to triple within fifty years (from 50,000 in 1535 to 150,000 in 1588). Cadiz also experienced a rapid growth as it became the chief rival of Seville in the New World trade.

Perhaps more remarkable was the growth of Madrid from a tiny pastoral town of no more than 4,000 inhabitants in 1530 to over 60,000 at the close of Philip II's reign. The reason for Madrid's rise is not to be found in bullion from the New World or in the configuration of the Castilian economy, but rather in the fact that Philip chose Madrid as his capital and in 1561 established his court there. As both the geographic and political center of Spain, Madrid soon attracted not only the court and its official followers but also all the appendages that surrounded and stifled sixteenth-century governments. By 1660 the population of the capital was approaching the 100,000 mark. Elsewhere in Spain, however, the seventeenth century was a time of serious population decline. Toledo had lost half of its population by 1618 (according to a petition of that date from the university), and Burgos, Segovia, Valladolid, and Medina del Campo experienced similar losses. Emigration to the Americas, the expulsion of 275,000 Moriscos from Spain in 1609, chronic warfare involving Spanish arms, the recurring famines of 1597, 1618–20, 1628–30 and the pestilential epidemic of 1599–1600, which may have killed over a million people in Castile alone, were among the causes of the Spanish decline in the seventeenth century.

In summary, it appears that after a century or more of population growth throughout Europe, only the countries of the Atlantic seaboard—England and the Netherlands, and to a lesser degree France—continued to grow during the first half of the seventeenth century. The Mediterranean areas and the Holy Roman Empire experienced heavy population losses coinciding with their economic and political decline. High infant mortality, poor and unsanitary living conditions, crop failures, low economic productivity, the increased scope and destructiveness of wars, with their inevitable aftermath of famine and disease, and the last annihilating waves of the plague, were the primary impediments to continued population growth. Not until the middle of the eighteenth century did the population of these Mediterranean and Germanic areas again reach their 1600 levels.

Towns into Cities

An important part of the demographic history of the sixteenth and early seventeenth centuries was the rapid development and expansion of towns. This growth, of course, does not compare with modern urbanization. By 1660 some 80 percent of the population of England still lived on the land or in small villages and hamlets adjoining their farms. Yet the picture was changing noticeably. A century earlier, less than 10 percent of the people had lived in cities of over 5,000 inhabitants. This movement from the country to the city was apparent in every part of Europe, from the already urbanized centers in Italy and the Lowlands to the sparsely settled plains of Spain.

In 1500, with the exception of Paris and Constantinople, the only large cities (those exceeding 100,000 population) were in Italy. Naples, Venice, Milan, and possibly Genoa were all in this category, and Florence approached it, with 80–85,000 inhabitants. At the same time, Bologna, Verona, Palermo, and Messina each numbered in the vicinity of 50,000 or more. During the sixteenth century, Italian cities continued to grow at an impressive rate. By 1600 Naples was a giant city of nearly 300,000. Venice, "the metropolis of all Italy," according to Sansovino's 1581 guidebook, reached 170,000 by 1563, but lost some 25–30,000 in the plague of 1575. Milan continued to grow, especially after 1559; Genoa flourished during the first half of the sixteenth century. By the end of the sixteenth century, Rome, Palermo, and Messina had also passed the 100,000 mark.

Rome and Naples   Rome, in particular, swelled dramatically from a city of less than 20,000 inhabitants at the beginning of the century to the 110,000 it counted during the pontificate of Clement VIII. Furthermore, the popes of the Counter-Reformation carried out a systematic beautification of Rome between 1565 and 1644, transforming it into one of the handsomest and most sumptuous cities in Europe. Lined with graceful boulevards studded with magnificent monuments and fountains, and dotted with luxurious palaces and churches, Rome became the showplace of Italy as well as the capital of the Catholic world. In their attacks on the growing problems of water supply, sanitation, housing, and the like, the Counter-Reformation popes also demonstrated their pioneering attention to matters of urban development.

The greatest impetus to city growth came from commerce, so it is not surprising to find that the coastal cities and those situated along well-traveled trade routes experienced the greatest expansion during the late sixteenth and

Naples in the sixteenth century, *showing the fortified harbor with the San Martin castle overlooking the beautiful bay. Along the beach at right fishing nets and cordage are drying in the sun.*

early seventeenth centuries. Such a city was Naples, the largest and busiest port in Italy. Ideally situated on the sheltered and graceful Bay of Naples, it had since ancient days been a busy port thriving on the commercial riches of the Mediterranean. Under Spanish control after 1504, it continued to prosper as a trading center, not only because it had the best Italian harbor on the Mediterranean but also because it received preferential attention from Spain. That attention resulted in exploitation, however, and, along with the burdensome influence of the Neapolitan nobility, led finally to great civil disorder and eventual decline.

Farther to the west, Marseille was profiting greatly from the Franco-Turkish commercial treaties as it began to rival Venice in the volume and value of its Levant trade. It was also the principal port of southern France and the entrance for Mediterranean products passing through the prosperous and growing city of Lyon, 200 miles up the Rhône. Mediterranean commerce, though, was on the decline by the later sixteenth century, and Marseille did not experience the degree of population growth that cities engaged in the Atlantic trade did. The same is true of Barcelona and Valencia, although the latter may have reached almost 100,000 by the beginning of the seventeenth century.

"The Busy Port of Seville" *is a painting, attributed to Claudio Coello, located in the Museo de América in Madrid. Dominating the skyline is the graceful Giralda and the great Gothic cathedral.*

Seville and Lisbon

The phenomenal blossoming of Seville as a result of the new Atlantic trade has already been noted. For nearly a century, it was the liveliest city in Spain and the port of entry for the wealth of the Indies. It was also an industrial center, famous for its silks, jewels, and ceramics, and attracted merchants and bankers from all over Europe, especially from Genoa. Five colleges, countless churches, and a tradition of music and dance made Seville an intellectual, cultural, and religious city as well. Sevillians do not forget that Velázquez and Murillo were both products of their Andalusian metropolis. However, the Thirty Years' War and the collapse of Spanish power saw the rapid decline of Seville both as a financial and a cultural center. Bankruptcy, inflation, and plague each took its toll.

Seville's twin city, in respect to overseas commerce and exotic prosperity, was Lisbon, which also surpassed the 100,000 mark by 1600. Like Naples, Lisbon was favored with an ideal natural harbor, which contributed immeasurably to its rise and prosperity. Standing at the mouth of the Tagus on the most westerly point of mainland Europe, it held a commanding position in the Atlantic trade and, even more important, in the trade with India and the East. Built on the hills overlooking the harbor (again like Naples), Lisbon was, and is, one of the most beautiful and charming of European cities. In its variety of goods and richness of trade, Lisbon was for a season the emporium of Europe and the crossroads of worldwide exchange.

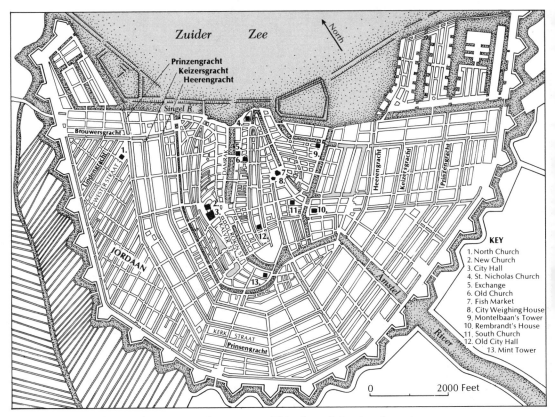

Amsterdam in the seventeenth century. *This plan of the city shows its waterways and concentric streets.*

On the map:
- Zuider Zee
- North
- Prinzengracht
- Keizersgracht
- Heerengracht
- Singel R.
- Brouwersgracht
- LINDEN STRAAT
- TWEIST STRAAT
- JORDAAN
- KROON'S
- KALVER ST.
- Heerengracht
- Keizersgracht
- Prinzengracht
- Amstel River
- KERK STRAAT
- Prinsengracht

KEY
1. North Church
2. New Church
3. City Hall
4. St. Nicholas Church
5. Exchange
6. Old Church
7. Fish Market
8. City Weighing House
9. Montelbaan's Tower
10. Rembrandt's House
11. South Church
12. Old City Hall
13. Mint Tower

0   2000 Feet

Amsterdam

In the seventeenth century, Lisbon's preeminence was taken over by Amsterdam, the Dutch city of canals that was destined to supersede all predecessors in wealth and power. Amsterdam became the financial heir of Antwerp after that great city succumbed to recurring siege and plunder during the war for Dutch independence. Amsterdam rose to prominence on a combination of Dutch sea power, marketing wizardry, and the financial organization of its merchant oligarchy. Amsterdam is a city standing on wooden piles driven through the flat mud estuary where the Amstel River joins the Zuider Zee (now the Ijsselmeer). For this reason, it has been referred to as an inverted forest where the trees grow down instead of up. From the beginning, canals were the avenues of transportation and trade. They were also the carriers of pollution and disease. The hub of the city was the Dam, or square, around which the canals and streets, with their docks, shops and homes, spread in concentric semicircles. In the center of the Dam was the Weigh House, the central market, surrounded by every variety of merchandising establishment imaginable, from fishmongers to silk merchants, with their accompanying restaurants, wine cellars, and brothels.

Seventeenth-century Amsterdam. *Busy Amsterdam harbor life is depicted in this painting by A. Storck Nieuwershuis. In the background is the Haringpakkerstoren Tower.*

Population pressure forced a major expansion of Amsterdam in the early seventeenth century under the supervision and guidance of the newly created "City Planning Board." Between 1612 and 1655, the area of the city was increased fourfold by clearing, draining, and reclaiming adjacent land and webbing it with a series of new interlinking canals. The enlarged city, with its designated areas for lower-, middle-, and upper-class dwellings, was enveloped by a semicircular wall with moats on both sides. Stone and brick structures now arose for the first time, with the picturesque step-gabled roofs giving the new city the appearance of a storybook town. More shipyards, docks, warehouses, packing sheds, guildhalls, and banks were built to accommodate the ever-widening world market that had its center in Amsterdam. Here, too, were located the offices and directors of the powerful East India Company and its sister corporation, the West India Company, as well as the Bank of Amsterdam. By 1650 Amsterdam had 200,000 residents and was by far the most cosmopolitan city in western Europe. Merchants, financiers, travelers, and scholars from all over the world made up its population, and Amsterdam presses, such as Jans and Elzevir, published books, pamphlets, news sheets, and tracts in every European language.

London
Amsterdam's rival across the channel was a much older city. Elizabethan London, which had surged from a medieval market town to a metropolis of nearly 250,000 inhabitants by 1600, was a city of contrasts, where the heights of splendor and the depths of squalor flourished side by side. The sixteenth-century growth of London followed the banks of the River Thames eastward beyond the Tower and westward to Charing Cross and thence south toward Westminster. By the time of the Civil War, it had expanded further in every direction, even enclosing Southwark and the Lambeth Marsh across the river. The growing pains of the city were felt in many ways, from overcrowded and dirty tenements to the swarms of people jostling one another for space and goods at Cheapside Market or Leadenhall. In sharp contrast to this squalor were the sumptuous palaces and wealthy homes, such as Somerset House, Arundel House, Essex House, and Bridewell, built along the northern bank. Others spread westward toward Saint James Palace from Covent Garden. Fear that the growing population outside the city walls would increase the danger of disease, crime, and riot inside led to frequent royal prohibitions against the building of houses surrounding the city, particularly lower-class dwellings, but it was a losing battle. The population continued to rise, due to immigration and trade, and as it did, the suburbs merged into the ever-widening bounds of greater London. By the time of the Great Plague and Fire of 1665–66, its population may have reached as high as 450,000.

London dominated the commercial and financial life of England. Its wealth was based on the woolen cloth trade, but during the Elizabethan Age and afterward, London merchants diversified their activities into additional fields. The construction of the Royal Exchange in 1566–67 marked the beginning point in the rise of London as a financial market, surpassing Antwerp in the 1580s and overtaking Amsterdam one hundred years later. It was Sir Thomas Gresham's idea to erect such an edifice, patterned after the familiar Antwerp Bourse, to serve as a clearinghouse for all commercial activities and a meeting place for merchants to negotiate, buy, and sell, or to exchange opinions about the state of affairs. The Exchange symbolized and aided the growing commercial activities of the London merchants as they extended their economic activities and financial influence throughout the world.

Paris
The greatest city of seventeenth-century Europe was Paris. Its population in 1600 may have reached half a million, and its political importance was commensurate with its size. The grace, elegance, and beauty that attracts modern visitors to Paris were largely absent in the sixteenth and seventeenth centuries. The Champs-Élysées, Invalides, Church of the Madeleine, Place de la Concorde, Panthéon, École Militaire, Arc de Triomphe, Opera House, Grand and

Petit Palais, Sacré-Coeur, Eiffel Tower, and the grand boulevards were all creations of a later day. The Paris of the Valois and early Bourbons was a congested "hodgepodge of stone and half-timbered buildings, all squeezed together ... The buildings seem piled on top of one another, teetering, out of proportion, unrepaired, situated at every angle, and walled in as if their builders were oblivious of their neighbors." Even then, Paris had its monuments and its glories. Notre Dame was one of the most graceful Gothic cathedrals in Christendom and was surrounded by other beautiful churches, from sparkling Sainte-Chapelle to the rich abbey church of Saint Germain-des-Prés. The Hôtel des Tournelles, Hôtel Saint-Paul, Francis I's Hôtel de Ville, and the Renaissance wings of the Louvre added regal splendor to the city, and these were augmented by Catherine de' Medici's Palace of the Tuileries with its elegant gardens.

Like the other cities that have been mentioned, the prosperity of Paris rested on trade. Located astride the Seine near its junctions with the Marne and the Oise, draining the entire fertile northern region of France and through their tributaries much of the south and east as well, Paris was ideally situated to dominate the inland trade west of the Rhine. Remnants of this flourishing trade may still be seen in the yearly Parisian Ham Fair, the Honeybread Fair, and the Scrap-Iron Fair. Yet Paris did not grow to such prominence as it held in the seventeenth century by trade alone. As capital of the largest monarchy in Europe, it occupied a political role equal, if not superior, to its economic importance. The patronage and wealth of the king, with all of the contingent benefits and evils, contributed greatly to the rapid growth and prestige of the city. Furthermore, Paris was a religious metropolis and a center of learning that attracted people from all over the Christian world. Second only to Rome in religious importance before the Reformation splintered the church, it was without peer in the prestige and power of its great university.

It may have been this volatile combination of aggressive guild tradesmen, haughty nobles and courtiers, quarrelsome clerics, contentious lawyers, and unruly students that made Paris such a disorderly city in the sixteenth and early seventeenth centuries, even defying the crown at times. Paris had frequently been on the verge of rebellion, but between 1560 and 1660, it was in political turmoil most of the time. The Saint Bartholomew's Day Massacre, the Day of the Barricades, and the Paris *Fronde* were only the extreme manifestations of a whole century of urban crises. Yet, given the religious fanaticism in Paris and the civil disturbances throughout France, the uncertainties and dangers of city life where disease and plague were a constant threat, the economic and social oppression of one class by another, and the general indifference of political and ecclesiastical authorities to these conditions, it is a wonder that riots were not even more frequent.

The problems of life in Paris were not entirely unique; similar difficulties arose in all of the rapidly growing cities of the time. The piling up of people multiplied the problems of food supply, health and sanitation, unemployment, corruption, and injustice; it aggravated social distinctions and rivalries, intensified economic burdens, and increased the incidence of lawlessness. These and many other issues were met or ignored with varying degrees of success and failure by most of the urban centers. Where these problems were added to larger political and religious conflicts, improvement was slow at best.

Some progress, however, was made in many of the cities. Fresh water was being piped to Paris by the 1590s; London launched a similar project in the early 1600s. A uniquely modern system of garbage collection was initiated in Valladolid, Spain, in the 1620s. Frequently, complaints about contamination and pollution prodded city councils or patricians (upper-class citizens) into ameliorating conditions. The political administration of some cities improved when rivalries between the urban nobility and the wealthy merchants were reduced, either by mutual agreements or by royal intervention. In Rome, both factions were tamed, and almost civilized, by a papacy that devoted more attention to urban matters as it lost influence in foreign affairs. Nevertheless, in most capital cities of the early seventeenth century, it was the social disruption caused by the influx of aristocratic courtiers and landed nobles that kept the cities in a state of uneasy tension, eased only by the occasional steadying influence of the monarch.

Society in Transition

The social hierarchy of late sixteenth- and early seventeenth-century Europe was in many ways as rigid as it had been in the Middle Ages. Class lines were as stratified as they had always been, and the entire social structure was formalized and hierarchical. In theory, at least, every rank of society had its formal functions and its accompanying place and privilege. Each had its own distinguishing status as well, from distinct dress style to mental attitudes and manner of speech. Civil, academic, and religious authorities were particularly conscious of the stratification of society into estates, ranks, and degrees, and their enforcement of sumptuary laws regulating personal behavior was intended to maintain that stratification. To live or dress above one's social station was a serious perversion of the natural order. Did not all nature, and heaven itself, bear witness to the universal hierarchy of which man is a part? Men and women, it was believed, must conform to the practices and performances of the station to which they were born.

This concept of rank was deeply rooted in medieval thought and practice, and was not consciously disturbed by sixteenth-century ideas. Luther believed the hierarchical order was divinely decreed, and Calvin was hardly less rigid in his social views. And yet, social mobility did exist. The desire to live and appear like a noble was always present among those of a lower rank, especially among the bourgeoisie who could afford it but were forbidden by custom and law to do so. Owning land, however, was not forbidden, and everyone who could held a plot of land. Nonetheless, in the transition from the Middle Ages to early modern times, from the agrarian subsistence economy of the tenth century to the commercial-agrarian-capitalist economy of the seventeenth century, social disparity had also become greater. Not only did social disparity increase, so did the gap between men and women, as political influence and economic power became more restrictive and gender became more important

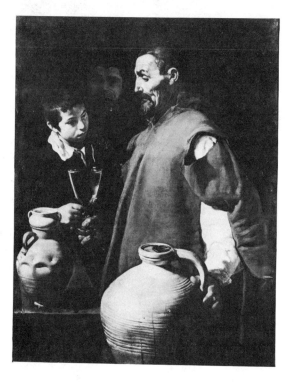

"The Water Carrier of Seville," *a penetrating picture of contrasting lives in affluent and poverty-ridden Seville, by Diego Velázquez.*

as a determining factor in discrimination. For the peasants, rural laborers, their urban counterparts, male and female, and the unnumbered homeless and propertyless vagabonds, life in 1600 was as comfortless and dreary as it had been in 1200, while the rich lived in the lap of luxury. The indulgence and extravagance of aristocratic life in the early seventeenth century was beyond even the imagination of medieval lords.

Noble status was achieved in seventeenth-century Europe by several routes: through the procession of law, through astute financial management, and through war. Probably the most common of these routes was through the purchase of landed estates and titles, a practice followed by a growing number of wealthy burghers and successful entrepreneurs who aspired to the life and status of aristocracy. Money gained in commercial and financial enterprises was frequently employed to purchase offices and titles or invest in land, where it could win social prestige even when it did not bring economic rewards. The buying of administrative offices and titled estates rose sharply during the first two decades of the seventeenth century. Yet ownership of land did not automatically mean a title. Nobility was an institutionalized system deriving from royal favor, which might or might not be associated with land. The king granted nobility for service accomplished or anticipated, and he was free to reward whomever he chose.

Another avenue of entry into the aristocracy was through marriage. Class lines were religiously adhered to in the matrimonial market, as in other enterprises, but there were always exceptions, and usually available opportunities for social progress to those who cultivated this promising field. The ambitious merchant or petty landowner who was blessed with attractive and talented daughters was particularly fortunate in this respect, since it was more likely that a nobleman's son would reach below his class to marry a wife (especially if her dowry was bulging) and raise her to nobility with him than for a titled lady to descend to "commonality" in order to marry a bourgeois husband. Horace Walpole's reference to the successful social climb of Bess of Hardwick suggests the varied possibilities for an ambitious woman:

> *Four times the nuptial bed she warm'd*
> *And every time so well perform'd*
> *That when death spoils each husband's billing*
> *He left the widow every shilling.*

Although perhaps not as easily as these lines suggest, Bess did promote the social interest of her family and rose from conspicuous nonimportance to become wife of the earl of Shrewsbury.

Social movement tended downward as well as upward. The proliferation of offices and titles, economic disasters resulting from the vicissitudes of war and inflation, poor management and lavish expenditure, and the changing patterns of political authority reduced many of the formerly haughty nobles to meaner status. A large percentage of the *hobereaux*, the lowest strata of the French nobility, arrived there from above rather than below. Yet, as a class, the aristocracy continued to play a key role in the political, economic, and cultural life of early modern times. And through the widespread system of patronage and clientage, the nobility sometimes offered a palliative to the rivalries and jealousies between social classes by maintaining links of local loyalty and service that overran the hierarchical structure. The top of that hierarchy was represented by the landed aristocracy living in their great country châteaux and manor houses with the pomp and display associated with aristocratic life. At the other extreme of the rural spectrum were the tenant farmers and propertyless farm laborers, whose life, little improved since medieval times, was arduous and dull.

With the growing sale of offices and estates in the early seventeenth century, it became increasingly common to see wealthy bourgeois gain positions of prestige and importance in society and in the government. The middle class dominated the law courts in Spain and France as well as in England, and municipal governments were always controlled by the well-to-do patricians. Trade had brought riches to the cities, but it had not altered the distribution of that wealth among the citizenry. The merchant class had grown in size and strength during the past 100 years, and offered a challenging threat to the politicoeconomic domination of the nobility, a threat that might have been more urgent had not so many of the rich bourgeoisie used their wealth to become landed nobles themselves, thus infusing new vitality into the nobility at a time when it was suffering from economic stress and political atrophy. The towns, like the country, had their own hierarchy of prestige and power, from governmental officers, lawyers, and financiers at the top, through the shopkeepers and artisans, to the unskilled dayworkers and unemployed at the bottom. As cities

grew in population and size, the problem of the urban jobless grew simultaneously. Life for the masses was still far from ideal, although it was generally
more hopeful than it had been two centuries earlier.

The Changing Family

The history of the family in the sixteenth and seventeenth centuries is still in
its infancy, but it is growing. The experts agree on some issues, but on many
more they are uncertain or continue to dispute. It is generally recognized, however, that this was a period of substantial change in both the structure and role
of the family in western Europe. The transformation did not occur suddenly
but was the result of gradually changing social conditions and new patterns of
thought. The increasing density of population in the sixteenth century, for example, and the growing complexity and organization of life, along with religious upheavals, greater social mobility, and the expanding power of the state
had profound effects upon the family and its relationship to other institutions.

In the first place, there seems to have been a decline in the responsibilities
and importance of the extended family, or kin groups (uncles, aunts, nephews,
nieces, cousins). Extended family responsibility for individual crimes (and benefits from individual accomplishment), such as was common in early Renaissance Italy, had died out in much of Europe by the end of the sixteenth century.
Even though hereditary officeholding continued in France for another two centuries, and kinship ties remained strong in certain commercial enterprises and
in local affairs in most of Europe, there was a notable decline in political and
military nepotism. Loyalties came to focus more on religious affiliations or
political associations, and there was a reduction in the social and economic
functions of the extended family. Public institutions, religious organizations,
private charities, and the state took over welfare and educational functions
that had previously been the responsibility of kin. Increasing geographic mobility and changes in values also caused loyalties to shift. This transfer was
primarily to the state and to the conjugal, nuclear family (husband, wife, and
children).

The increasing importance of the nuclear family as a focus of loyalty and
devotion was a major feature of early modern society. It is reflected in the legal
emphasis on primogeniture (the principle that the oldest child inherits the possessions of the parents) and in the increase of paternal authority. This trend is
particularly noticeable in Protestant areas, because the Reformation exalted
marriage and emphasized conjugal love and domestic virtues. Protestant (especially Calvinist) Bible reading and prayer tended to shift some of the religious focus from the church to the home. Paradoxically, this trend also reduced
women's role even further as they were subordinated to their husbands in the
hierarchically structured family. Puritan sermons emphasized the duty of wives
to be docile and submissive to their husbands. Yet then, as now, practice did
not always conform to theory.

The relationship of children to parents also underwent modification in this
period as a corollary to the new role of the family. Philippe Ariès's assertion

that parents in the Middle Ages were indifferent to children, and that "child-hood" was not discovered until the Renaissance, is an overstatement, but an overstatement that emphasizes the fact that children became "adults" very early in medieval society and were pretty much on their own to learn what they could about life through hard knocks and by imitating their parents. Es-pecially among the lower classes, children entered the adult world very young.

By the seventeenth century, a different situation existed, particularly in the middle classes. The family now became an institution for molding children into proper and productive adults. They were not part of adult society yet and needed to be not only coddled and played with as infants but also trained and educated during the years of childhood and adolescence. Sixteenth- and early-seventeenth-century parents seemed to take much greater interest in their chil-dren and their education. This view was reinforced by the schools and by the teachings of both Protestants and Catholics that parents were the guardians of these souls and responsible for their physical and spiritual growth.

This interest in children not only contributed to the growth of grammar-school education but also increased the parental obsession with discipline. The sixteenth century saw a remarkable increase in physical punishment of children in the home as well as in the schools. What we would now call child abuse was then considered necessary for proper growth and development. "Bow down his neck while he is young," wrote Thomas Becon in his 1550 catechism, "and beat him on his sides while he is a child, lest he wax stubborn and be disobedient to thee, and so bring sorrow to thy heart." Even princes were not exempt from harsh punishment, as this advice from Henri IV to the governess of his young son, the future King Louis XIII, reveals:

> I have a complaint to make: you do not send word that you have whipped my son. I wish and command you to whip him every time that he is obstinate or misbehaves, knowing well for myself that there is nothing in the world which will be better for him than that. I know it from experience, having myself profited, for when I was his age I was often whipped, that is why I want you to whip him and to make him understand why.

Calvinist stress on the sinfulness of children and their need for obedience must have strengthened parents' belief that to spare the rod would indeed spoil the child. The pressures of a hierarchical society to impress its members with the proper relationship between superiors and subordinates also reinforced the parental duty to repress their children and break their will to resist. Early sev-enteenth-century society was plagued by insubordination and insurrection. If these tendencies were not wiped out at an early age, it was argued, society itself would collapse. Children, like horses, had to be broken before they could become useful. Such breaking would also reduce the likelihood of resistance to the major decision that early modern society believed had to be made by par-ents, namely who the child should marry. Not surprisingly, the remedy did not always produce the desired result.

The children least subjected to parental abuse, or subjected to it for the least time, may have been the children of peasants and others of the lower classes, because their parents lacked many of the economic incentives of the bourgeoisie and because those children usually were sent away from home at a younger age to become servants or apprentices. Lower-class society remained less competitive and consequently internally more sociable.

Women in Post-Reformation Europe

Although the Reformation exalted the domestic role of women, it did nothing to change the stereotype of them as weak, unstable, emotional creatures who needed the steadying hand and constant leadership of men. Aristotle's opinion that women were unfinished or inchoate creatures was still widely held, and medical science taught that their dominant humors were cold and wet, which translated meant they were disposed to instability, vacillation, infidelity, and deception. Roman law added that women were also mentally inferior. These views were still widely held in the sixteenth century, and the arguments for men's domination over women increased after the Protestant Reformation. It was a basic assumption of Christian theology that Eve was responsible for the Fall of Adam, and consequently of all mankind, thus revealing women's weakness of character. And since "evidence" of women's inferiority could be found elsewhere in the Old Testament as well as in the injunctions of the Apostle Paul, it is not surprising that the intensified religious atmosphere actually increased the pious prejudice against women.

However they were perceived, the role of women did alter during and after the Reformation. As their public economic status declined, they found new ways to become involved in the economic life of their village and family. Indeed, their activity in family economics seems to have increased. Their religious participation, however, changed most of all, as they became increasingly involved in religious activities—with and without their husbands—that would have been unthinkable in previous centuries. Women were not always accepted in these roles—most often they were not—but many of them participated anyway and contributed much to the religious life of the time.

In Protestant areas it was not uncommon to see women preaching or prophesying against the municipal authorities, and in Catholic countries women's involvement in mysticism and ecstatic visions grew. The Protestant replacement of celibate priests with married pastors served to activate many capable wives, who, like Katherine Zell, Argula von Grumbach, Ursula Weide, and others, frequently became stalwart defenders of the faith. They were also called upon to manage households swollen by the influx of students and religious refugees. Wives and single women were also active in hospitals, orphanages, infirmaries, and other charitable institutions. These activities also flourished in Catholic areas, supervised or operated by female religious orders.

In the court society of the sixteenth and seventeenth centuries the role of women was also very important, for success, whether measured in marital alliances or the acquisition of estates, depended to a considerable extent upon

Women working in a hospital. *This picture of women caring for the sick in a Dutch hospital is part of a series by a Dutch Master depicting the seven acts of mercy.*

women's social skills. Many women moved upward on the social ladder by their feminine abilities, and some of them became effective administrators and rulers. Women also became more active in the professions as writers, teachers and scholars, and often spiritual leaders.

The conclusion seems obvious that the impact of the Reformation on women was both positive and negative. "Women were liberated as well as enslaved during the age of Reformation and Counter Reformation," writes Sherrin Marshall. "To the extent that they were forced to accept and fit into the stereotypes that shaped their behavioral options, women were confined. To the extent that they pursued—for themselves individually and collectively in the service of God—new activities and created definitions of spirituality not limited by gender, they were liberated." While constantly being reminded by Protestant pastors as well as Catholic priests of their proper behavior, subordinate role, and natural inferiority, many sixteenth-century women refused to be bound by convention, and staunchly, sometimes defiantly, demonstrated their moral courage and spiritual insight in the face of overwhelming opposition.

Suggestions for Further Reading

GENERAL ECONOMIC STUDIES

The most ambitious and successful account of early modern social and economic life is Fernand Braudel's impressive trilogy, *Civilization and Capitalism, 15th–18th Century,* tr. by Sian Reynolds (New York, 1982–84): vol. 1, *The Structure of Everyday Life: The Limits of the Possible;* vol. 2, *The Wheels of Commerce;* vol. 3, *The Perspective of the World.* This is a fitting sequel to his brilliant *The Mediterranean and the Mediterranean World in the Age of Philip II,* 2 vols. tr. by Sian Reynolds (New York, 1972). More controversial interpretations of early modern economic history are Immanuel Wallerstein, *The Modern World-System: Capitalist Agriculture and the Origins of the European World Economy in the Sixteenth Century* (New York, 1974); and *The Modern World-System: Mercantilism and the Consolidation of the European World Economy, 1600–1750* (New York, 1980). Wallerstein's thesis is challenged in T.H. Aston and C.H.E. Pilpin, eds., *The Brenner Debate: Agrarian Class Structure and Economic Development in Pre-Industrial Europe* (Cambridge, England, 1986). Also challenging is Peter Kriedte, *Peasants, Landlords, and Merchant Capitalists: Europe and the World Economy, 1500–1800* (New York and Cambridge, England, 1984). More general accounts are V.G. Kiernan, *State and Society in Europe, 1550–1650* (New York, 1980), and Geoffrey Parker, *Europe in Crisis, 1598–1648* (Brighton, England, 1980).

PRICES, BANKING, INDUSTRY, AND TRADE

Particularly interesting are Catharina Lis and Hugo Soly, *Poverty and Capitalism in Pre-Industrial Europe* (Hassocks, England, 1979); Daniel Hickey, *The Coming of French Absolutism: The Struggle for Tax Reform in the Province of Dauphiné, 1540–1640* (Toronto, 1986); Sharon Kettering, *Patrons, Brokers, and Clients in Seventeenth Century France* (New York and Oxford, 1988); Artur Attman, *The Struggle for Baltic Markets: Powers in Conflict, 1558–1618,* tr. by Eva and Allen Green (Göteborg, 1979); J.K. Fedorowicz, *England's Baltic Trade in the Early Seventeenth Century* (Cambridge, England, 1980); Eric Kerridge, *Textile Manufacturers in Early Modern England* (Manchester, England, 1985), and *Trade and Banking in Early Modern England* (New York, 1988). Peter Edwards, *The Horse Trade of Tudor and Stuart England* (New York and Cambridge, England, 1988) is enlightening. On the Dutch economy see Jan De Vries, *The Dutch Rural Economy in the Golden Age* (New Haven, 1974); D.W. Davies, *A Primer of Dutch Seventeenth Century Overseas Trade* (The Hague, 1961); Charles R. Boxer's classic, *The Dutch Seaborne Empire: 1600–1800* (New York, 1965); and especially Jonathan I. Israel's brilliant *Dutch Primacy in World Trade, 1585–1740* (New York and Oxford, 1989).

POPULATION AND CITIES

The best study of early modern demography is Michael W. Flinn, *The European Demographic System, 1500–1820* (Baltimore, 1981), which uses the latest statistical methods of demographic research from many countries to explain the dynamics of early modern population. Also see Theodore Rabb and Robert Rotberg, *Population and Economy* (New York and Cambridge, England, 1986), and E.A. Wrigley and R.S. Schofield, *The Population History of England, 1541–1871* (New York and Cambridge, England, 1989). On the effect of the plague see Paul Slack, *The Impact of Plague in Tudor and Stuart England* (London, 1985); Carlo M. Cipolla, *Fighting the Plague in Seventeenth-Century Italy* (Madison, 1981); and Clare Gittings, *Death, Burial and the Individual in Early Modern England* (London, 1984).

Jan De Vries, *European Urbanization, 1500–1800* (Cambridge, Massachusetts, 1984) is an impressive study. For others see Josef W. Konvitz, *Cities and the Sea: Port City Planning in Early Modern Europe* (Baltimore, 1978); Peter Clark and Paul Slack, *English Towns in Transition, 1500–1700* (London, 1976); John Patten, *English Towns,*

1500–1700 (Hamden, Connecticut, 1978); P. Butel and L.M. Cullen, eds., *Cities and Merchants: French and Irish Perspectives on Urban Development, 1500–1900* (Dublin, 1986). On individual cities see A.L. Beier and R. Finley, eds., *London, 1500–1700: The Making of the Metropolis* (London, 1986); Steve Rappaport, *Worlds Within World: The Structures of Life in Sixteenth-Century London* (New York and Cambridge, England, 1989); Jeffrey C. Smith, *Nuremberg, a Renaissance City, 1500–1618* (Austin, 1983); and Alexander F. Cowan, *The Urban Patriciate: Lubeck and Venice, 1580–1700* (Cologne, 1986).

URBAN AND RURAL SOCIETY

Two general accounts that can be recommended are Henry Kamen, *European Society, 1500–1700* (London, 1984), and George Huppert, *After the Black Death: A Social History of Early Modern Europe* (Bloomington, 1986). Also noteworthy is John Walter and Roger Schofield, eds., *Famine, Disease and the Social Order in Early Modern Society* (Cambridge, England, and New York, 1989). Class divisions and tensions in the towns are analyzed in a number of recent works, among the best are Philip Benedict, ed., *Cities and Social Change in Early Modern France* (London, 1989); Cissie Fairchilds, *Domestic Enemies, Servants and Their Masters in Old Regime France* (Baltimore, 1984); Robert Forster and Orest Ranum, eds., *Deviants and the Abandoned in French Society* (Baltimore, 1978), selections from *Annales;* James R. Farr, *Hands of Honor: Artisans and Their World in Dijon, 1550–1650* (Ithaca, 1989); Kathryn Norberg, *Rich and Poor in Grenoble, 1600–1814* (Berkeley, 1985); Susan Dwyer Amussen, *An Ordered Society: Gender and Class in Early Modern England* (New York, 1988); C.G.A. Clay, *Economic Expansion and Social Change: England, 1500–1700*, 2 vols. (Cambridge, England, 1984); A.L. Beier, *Masterless Men: The Vagrancy Problem in England, 1560–1640* (London, 1985); J.A. Sharpe, *Crime in Early Modern England, 1550–1750* (New York, 1984); and Linda Martz, *Poverty and Welfare in Habsburg Spain: The Example of Toledo* (New York and Cambridge, England, 1983).

The landed nobles constituted a significant and controversial element of early modern society. For a general view see Michael L. Bush, *The European Nobility, Vol. 1: Noble Privilege* (New York, 1983). For intriguing studies of one of the symbols of nobility see V.G. Kiernan, *The Duel in European History: Honour and the Reign of Aristocracy* (New York and Oxford, 1987), and François Billacois, *The Duel: Its Rise and Fall in Early Modern France* (New Haven, 1990). The latest in-depth study of the aristocracy in England is Lawrence Stone and Jeanne C. Fawtier Stone, *An Open Elite: England, 1540–1880* (New York and Oxford, 1984), which has been called the most important book on the English aristocracy since Stone's *The Crisis of the Aristocracy* (1965). A fresh and revealing look at the French nobility is provided by Ellery Schalk in *From Valor to Pedigree: Ideas of Nobility in France in the Sixteenth and Seventeenth Centuries* (Princeton, 1986), which argues that in the late sixteenth century the perception of the noble changed dramatically, from a deserving military professional to an inherited birthright.

On the rural lower classes see Emmanuel Le Roy Ladurie, *The French Peasantry, 1450–1660* (Berkeley, 1987), and Sheldon J. Watts, *A Social History of Western Europe, 1450–1720: Tensions and Solidarities Among Rural People* (London, 1984). Popular protest and rebellion are examined in Perez Zagorin, *Rebels and Rulers, 1500–1600, Vol. 1: Society, States, and Early Modern Revolution: Agrarian and Urban Rebellions; Vol. 2: Provincial Rebellion: Revolutionary Civil Wars, 1560–1660* (New York and Cambridge, England, 1982); Paul Slack, ed., *Rebellion, Popular Protest, and the Social Order in Early Modern England* (New York and Cambridge, England, 1984); Emmanuel Le Roy Ladurie, *Montaillou: The Promised Land of Error*, tr. by Barbara Bray (New York, 1978), and *Carnival: A People's Uprising at Romans, 1579–80*, tr. by M. Feeney (London, 1980). On popular culture see Robert Muchembled, *Popular Culture and Elite Culture in France, 1400–1750* (Baton Rouge, 1985).

WOMEN AND THE FAMILY

Helga Mobius, *Women of the Baroque Age* (Totowa, New Jersey, 1984) has some good insights. On women and the perception of them in England see Margaret O. Thickstun, *Fictions of the Feminine: Puritan Doctrine and the Representation of Women* (Ithaca, 1988); Linda Woodbridge, *Women and the English Renaissance: Literature and the Nature of Womankind, 1540–1620* (Urbana, Illinois, 1984); Mary Prior, ed., *Women in English Society, 1500–1800* (New York, 1985); Kathy Lynn Emerson, *Wives and Daughters: The Women of Sixteenth Century England* (Troy, New York, 1984); and Margaret George, *Women in the First Capitalist Society: Experiences in Seventeenth-Century England* (Urbana, Illinois, 1988). Women's work and working women are studied in Barbara A. Hanawalt, ed., *Women and Work in Preindustrial Europe* (Bloomington, Indiana, 1986), and Merry E. Wiesner, *Working Women in Renaissance Germany* (New Brunswick, New Jersey, 1986), a very penetrating study. Thomas M. Safley, *Let No Man Put Asunder: The Control of Marriage in the German Southwest, 1550–1600* (Kirksville, Missouri, 1984) looks at the tighter control of marriage by the magistrates as a result of the Reformation.

Changes in the family and family relationships are reviewed over a long period in Michael Mitterauer and Reinhard Sieder, *The European Family: Patriarchy to Partnership from the Middle Ages to the Present*, tr. by Karla Oosterveen and Manfred Horzinger (Chicago, 1982). Marriage and family are carefully studied in Jack Goody, *The Development of the Family and Marriage in Europe* (Cambridge, England, 1984); R.B. Outhwaite, ed., *Marriage and Society: Studies in the Social History of Marriage* (London, 1981); as well as Theodore Rabb and Robert Rotberg, eds., *Marriage and Fertility: Studies in Interdisciplinary History* (Princeton, 1980). Other probing studies are Margaret J.M. Ezell, *The Patriarch's Wife: Literary Evidence and the History of the Family* (Chapel Hill, 1987); Andrejs Plakans, *Kinship in the Past: An Anthropology of European Family Life, 1500–1900* (New York, 1984); John W. Shaffer, *Family and Farm: Agrarian Change and Household Organization in the Loire Valley, 1500–1900* (Albany, 1982); Ralph A. Houlbrooke, *The English Family, 1450–1700* (White Plains, New York, 1984); Hermann Rebel, *Peasant Classes: The Bureaucratization of Property and Family Relations under Early Habsburg Absolutism, 1500–1636* (Princeton, 1983). On the Dutch family see Sharrin Marshall, *The Dutch Gentry, 1500–1650: Family, Faith, and Fortune* (Westport, Connecticut, 1987). Children are the subject of C. John Sommerville's *The Rise and Fall of Childhood* (Beverly Hills, 1982), Linda A. Pollock, *Forgotten Children: Parent-Child Relations from 1590–1900* (New York and Cambridge, England, 1984), and Carmen Luke, *Pedagogy, Printing, and Protestantism: The Discourse on Childhood* (Albany, New York, 1989), which disagrees with many assertions of Philippe Aries.

11 | THE SCIENCE AND CULTURE OF POST-REFORMATION EUROPE

S EVERAL KINDS OF REVOLUTIONS WERE TAKING PLACE IN THE LATE SIX-
teenth and early seventeenth centuries. One of these was a revolutionary
fascination with nature that resulted in a new outlook on the physical
universe. People had become accustomed to defying political and ecclesiastical
control, and were rapidly losing their reverence for intellectual authority as
well. The nineteen centuries of Aristotelian domination of natural thought
were coming to an end. Innovation and experimentation were affecting
thought and transforming natural philosophy into the science of nature.

Not unexpectedly, the cultural manifestations of the early decades of the
seventeenth century also reflected the tumult of the times. The rise of the early
modern state, with its growth of absolutism in government, the response of
revolutionary political and social movements, civil and international war, and
the development of new ideas about the physical universe all had an impact
on thought and culture. The challenge to traditional values and modes of
thought by these new ideas resulted in a burst of creative energy that can be
interpreted as the final phase of the Renaissance in Europe.

A Revolution in Scientific Thought

In the sixteenth century, scientific thought had not yet separated itself from
philosophy and was scarcely distinguished from theology. Thus, speculation
about the character and quality of the cosmos was indivisible from conjecture
about God and his creations.

Copernicus

Nicolaus Copernicus (1473–1543) grew up in Poland, where he received an education in theology and
law at the University of Cracow. His real interest,
however, was science and mathematics, especially astronomy, which he pursued in Italy. For ten years he threw himself into the study of Greek, mathematics, law, and astronomy at Bologna, canon law at Ferrara, and medicine at
Padua, before returning to his native land. The last thirty years of his life were

devoted to stellar observations, mathematical calculations, and contemplation. His magnum opus, *De revolutionibus orbium coelestium* (The Revolution of the Celestial Sphere), was completed in 1530 but not published until the month of his death in 1543. In this work Copernicus hypothesized that the earth revolved in a circle about the sun, while at the same time rotating on its own axis every 24 hours. The planets, he proposed, also rotated in their crystalline spheres around the sun, whose mystical importance required that it occupy the central position.

Copernicus had no intention of upsetting the Aristotelian world-view. He merely wanted to simplify the explanation of planetary motion, reducing it to more manageable mathematics, and offering the formula to Pope Paul III as a means to facilitate calendar reform. He hoped to preserve the Aristotelian system by rectifying some of the later celestial mechanics postulated in the second century A.D. by the Greek astronomer Ptolemy. All Aristotelian elements and conditions remained the same: the circular and uniform motion of the planets in crystalline spheres; the teleological assumptions of the church; the nature of the rotational force. By his simple transposition of earth and sun, Copernicus sought to reduce the number of epicycles and eccentrics that Ptolemy had needed to explain planetary motion, thus satisfying his Platonic urge for simplicity and harmony, while at the same time retaining the nobility and aesthetics of sphericity and circular motion. Actually, it was hardly more accurate in explaining the motions of the sun and stars than Ptolemy's had been, and still left other problems unsolved, but it was a move in a direction that would lead to further speculation and progress.

Copernicus worried about how his astronomical principles would be accepted by the religious community, and prefaced his *De Revolutionibus* with an apologetic dedication to Pope Paul III. Luther retorted, "That fool [Copernicus] will upset the whole science of astronomy, but the Holy Scripture shows it was the sun not the earth that Joshua ordered to stand still." Clearly, the time had not arrived for scientific investigation to be conducted independently of religious ideas. Indeed, the inflaming polemics of the Reformation increased the touchiness of all sects and made them fearful of any new ideas that might discredit their particular faith or undermine respect for the Bible. Nevertheless, the Reformation had also implicitly legitimized rebellion and thus unwittingly opened the way to further intellectual dissension and speculation.

Telesio, Bruno, Campanella   One of those who questioned the traditional theological interpretation of nature and spoke strongly against the Aristotelian theory of matter and form was Bernardino Telesio (1508–88) of Cosenza in southern Italy. He opposed Aristotle on two counts: his lack of piety and his explanation of nature by abstract reason rather than by its own principles from observation and experience. According to Telesio, the entire process of nature is self-contained and self-sufficient, working according to laws instead of by divine intervention. This philosophy did not set well with the church, and his book was soon placed on the Index. Telesio remained a devout Catholic, but he was also a bold innovator, anticipating much of what later scientists would proclaim and establishing one of the foundations of modern scientific method by his insistence upon observation and experimentation.

Even more daring, and harder to assess, is another sixteenth-century Italian whose indiscreet disdain of the church cost him his life. In his intellectual curiosity and reckless neglect of personal safety, Giordano Bruno (1548–1600) paralleled the life and death of Michael Servetus, who was burned at the stake in Geneva when Bruno was five years old. A native of Nola, near Naples, Bruno entered the Dominican order when he was sixteen to satiate his thirst for knowledge. He worked hard, mastered the poets and philosophers, and achieved the doctorate of theology in 1575. The breadth of his studies and the restlessness of his mind caused him to question and attack many of the tenets of the church, and to become involved in pantheism and the mystical philosophy of Hermetism (from the *Hermetica,* composed of ancient texts on Hellenistic magic and the occult). The Inquisition interceded. To escape its grasp, he abandoned the habit of his order and fled northward. For the next sixteen years his wanderings took him to Switzerland, France, England, and Germany. In 1591, at the invitation of a Venetian noble who admired Bruno's writings, he returned to Venice. There was obvious danger in this move, but secure in the knowledge of Venice's aloofness from Rome and happy at the prospect of returning to his Italian homeland where "bloomed the culture that was the finest flower of humanity," he accepted the invitation. A few months later, his host denounced him to the Holy Office and he was immediately imprisoned. For almost eight years, he languished in the squalid jails of Venice and Rome before he was finally sentenced to death by burning.

Bruno was the first philosopher of note to accept Copernicus's heliocentricity theory, not just as a mathematical hypothesis but as a fact. Furthermore, he went beyond Copernicus in applying the theory to a broader and more radical cosmology. He abandoned Copernicus's and Ptolemy's theory of crystalline spheres, conceiving instead an infinite universe without end or bounds, without center or circumference, capable of maintaining innumerable earths, planets, and suns. From this conviction of infinitude grew his conception of God, life, force, causation, and the imperishability of matter.

Another venturesome prelate who helped bring about a revolution in thinking was Tommaso Campanella (1568–1639). Like Telesio and Bruno, Campanella was a native of southern Italy, where he, too, entered the Dominican order at an early age. In the course of his religious-philosophical education, he become dissatisfied with the rigid Aristotelianism of the order, preferring instead the naturalism of Telesio, whom he vigorously defended. He likewise supported the heliocentric system of Copernicus and spoke favorably of Bruno. In 1616, from a dismal Neopolitan dungeon, he wrote a courageous *Defense of Galileo* when Galileo was on trial for his Copernican views. Campanella's twenty-seven years of imprisonment began in 1599, following a charge of "heresy and conspiracy" brought by the Inquisition. Despite his captivity, Campanella remained a faithful Catholic and continued to write about nature, philosophy, and politics. Finally released, due in part to the sympathy of Pope Urban VIII, Campanella spent the last five years of his life at the priory of Saint-Jacques in Paris.

Devoted as he was to the church, and convinced of its divine role of leadership, Campanella was equally convinced that God revealed himself to man in nature as well as in Scripture and the church. Like Telesio, he believed that knowledge came through investigation, experimentation, and perception just as well as by faith. Campanella believed the scientific discoveries and speculations of his day were as much a part of God's workings through man as were his directives to the popes or his revelations to the ancient Hebrew prophets. Not since Pico della Mirandola and other humanists of the High Renaissance had anyone tried so hard to reconcile traditional scholastic theology with the new ideas of his time. The dichotomy of his crusadelike support of papal supremacy and his espousal of complete freedom of thought—each advocated with equal fervor in his *City of the Sun*—testify to the synthesizing nature of his thought.

By the last quarter of the sixteenth century, more people were becoming interested in the stars and planets, and in observing their movements and speculating about their interrelationship. Copernicus's theories were finally being discussed in the universities, and several new theories were advanced to better explain the stellar movements. One of the greatest stimulations to this interest in astronomy was the appearance of a brilliant new star in the heavens in 1572–73. To most of those who observed it—and everyone did, since it was brighter than anything else in the evening sky except the moon—it was a divine omen, sent to portend some momentous event or catastrophe. For sixteenth-century scientists, this supernova (an exploding star that gives off intense light), located in the constellation Cassiopeia, was very disturbing. Conditioned to believe the heavens were perfect and therefore unchanging, the scientists were hard pressed to explain this strange phenomenon; yet there it was, defying human reason and almost contemptuously changing colors from white to orange to red (as its explosive gases cooled), as if to mock mortal attempts to explain it. No sooner had the new star disappeared when another astronomical phenomenon occurred. In 1577 a new comet appeared, cutting across the ethereal heavens in defiance of the crystalline spheres.

Tycho Brahe and Kepler

Among those whose study of astronomy was greatly intensified by these marvels was a young Danish nobleman-scholar named Tycho Brahe (1546–1601). His minute observations of the 1572 supernova resulted in a book, *On the New Star,* which quickly caught the attention of the Danish king, Frederick II, who rewarded Tycho with the lordship of the island of Hven. Here he built the fabulous Uraniborg castle, which he equipped with libraries, laboratories, observatories, and the most elaborate instruments for astronomical observation. With these facilities and his own keen eyesight and meticulous patience, Tycho Brahe made the most accurate and detailed astronomical computations up to that time. From these observations, he became convinced of the inadequacy of the Aristotelian-Ptolemaic system, but was equally dissatisfied with the Copernican. He boldly denied the reality of the crystalline spheres after observing the path of the 1577 comet, and declared that the Ptolemaic system was cumbersome and impossible. At the same time, he was doubtful that the massive earth could actually rotate, as required by the Copernican system, since that seemed contrary to sound principles of physics. Besides, the notion was also contrary to the Bible, and that offended his Lutheran orthodoxy. He concluded, therefore, that both theories were in error and substituted a system of his own.

In Tycho's solar system, the other planets all revolve about the sun, while the sun, accompanied by the planets and the moon, revolves about the earth— just as they appear to do. The Tychonic system was mathematically comparable to the Copernican and had the advantage of not requiring the massive earth to move. It allowed people to retain their confidence in an earth-centered universe while accounting for the apparent movement of the other heavenly bodies. As Tycho observed, his system agreed with both mathematics and physics, accorded with appearances, and avoided theological censure.

The astronomical data amassed by Tycho Brahe passed on to his most promising pupil, Johannes Kepler (1571–1630), a brilliant mathematician-mystic from the German duchy of Württemberg. Kepler was educated at the University of Tübingen, where he came under the tutelage of Michael Maestlin, the most celebrated astronomer in Germany. Before leaving Tübingen, Kepler was already an enthusiastic Copernican, as well as a passionate astrologist. He was also a mathematical genius, fascinated by the mystery of planetary motion and by the "harmony of the stars." In 1596 he published his theory of the mathematical relationships of the planetary orbits, the *Mysterium Cosmographicum*, which he promptly sent to all astronomers, mathematicians, and princes of Europe. This gesture won him an invitation from Tycho Brahe to become his assistant at Uraniborg. Kepler refused, but a few years later, when religious persecution forced him to leave Graz, he applied to join Tycho's staff at Prague, where Emperor Rudolf II had established an observatory for Tycho in 1599. Kepler worked with the master observer for less than a year before Tycho died, whereupon Kepler received custody of all Tycho's papers and succeeded to his post as imperial mathematician.

Kepler continued the compilation of Tycho Brahe's planetary tables, which he published in 1627 as the *Rudolphine Tables*, and added some new observations to Tycho's logs, although Kepler's eyesight was too poor for him to become primarily an observer. It was as a theoretical astronomer that Kepler made his imprint on history, "reducing to order the chaos of data" left by Tycho Brahe. Kepler's enormously complex calculations—especially impressive because he did not have the aid of modern calculus—resulted in the elaboration of three important laws of planetary motion, further modifying and expanding the Copernican system. The most revolutionary of these was the pronouncement that the orbits of the planets around the sun are elliptical rather than circular, and that the sun's position is at one focus of the ellipse rather than at the center. His second calculation was that an imaginary line from any planet to the sun sweeps out equal areas in equal intervals of time. In other words, the speed of the planet is greater when it is closer to the sun and slower when it is farther away. Kepler's third law states that the squares of the periods of revolution of the planets around the sun are proportional to the cube of their mean distances from the sun. In lay terms, this means that the planets with larger orbits revolve at a slower average velocity than those with smaller orbits. By these computations, Kepler established a new vision of the solar system and described the mathematical relationships of its various parts.

By the beginning of the seventeenth century, it was becoming apparent that a new spirit of scientific inquiry was taking hold in Europe. One of the features of this attitude was its disrespect for Aristotle and its conscious undermining of Aristotelian principles of physics and astronomy, which had described the natural world in essentially qualitative terms. Much greater stress was now being laid on quantitative investigation and on the practical application of mathematics to solving physical problems. This process was facilitated by John Napier's invention of logarithms, whereby the extraction of square roots could be reduced to simple division and multiplication. A short time later, René Descartes applied the analytical method to solving geometric problems, and in so doing originated analytical geometry.

Galileo and the Advance of Science and Mechanics

One of the most alert mathematicians and perceptive scientists of the late sixteenth and early seventeenth centuries was Galileo Galilei (1564–1642), son of a minor Florentine nobleman turned cloth merchant who provided the best education he could afford for his son. Galileo was a gifted young man, brilliant in mathematics, an accomplished musician, and skillful as an artist and author. He was also contentious and self-assertive. He began the study of medicine at Pisa, where he was born, but abandoned it for other pursuits, winning for himself a reputation as a gadfly. He later taught mathematics at the University of Pisa and for eighteen years occupied the chair of mathematics at the renowned University of Padua. There he established his reputation as a scientist and inventor, and became a popular lecturer. Early in 1609, during his seventeenth year at Padua, Galileo learned of a lens grinder in Flanders who had invented a "spyglass" through which distant objects were made to appear close. From a written description of it, Galileo proceeded to construct a similar instrument himself.

The most significant feature of Galileo's telescope was the use to which he put it. Galileo was the first person to turn this new instrument toward the heavens, thereby opening a new era in astronomical observation. He had already been converted to the Copernican system and now was able to substantiate his belief. With his telescope, he identified the shadows on the surface of the moon as mountains, valleys, and plains, making this heavenly sphere seem remarkably like the earth. And since the moon obviously moves, why not the earth? He discovered that Venus, like the moon, changes phases as its position vis-à-vis the earth and the sun alters. He further showed that the sun turns on its own axis and that Jupiter has moons of its own that revolve about that

Galileo Galilei. *A crayon sketch by Ottavio Leoni, made in 1624 when Galileo was in Rome.*

planet while it in turn moves around the sun. Other remarkable things were revealed by Galileo's telescope. It showed the vast difference in the size and distance between the planets and the fixed stars, and confirmed that there were many times more stars than could be seen with the naked eye, suggesting a far more immense universe than anyone had imagined.

Suddenly Galileo was catapulted into the limelight. In 1610, less than a year after his first observations, he published the *Siderius Nuncius* (Starry Messenger), describing his new optical marvel and what he had seen with it. Many scoffed and ridiculed, but some listened. Galileo accepted a new position as philosopher and mathematician to Grand Duke Cosimo II of Florence and in 1611 traveled to Rome to explain to the leaders of the church the validity and value of his discoveries. The fathers at the Jesuit College in Rome were impressed; some accepted his discoveries with enthusiasm, others with guarded interest. The venerable Father Clavius, head mathematician of the Jesuits and leading proponent of the calendar reform under Pope Gregory XIII, praised Galileo for being the first to make such important observations. The head of their college, Cardinal Robert Bellarmine, was cordial; Pope Paul V assured Galileo of his good will; Maffeo Barberini, the future Pope Urban VIII, became Galileo's staunch friend. The Lyncean Academy—an association recently founded in Rome for the study of science—elected Galileo a member. Galileo was feted by cardinals, princes, and scholars, and he returned to Florence a conquering hero. "Were we still living under the ancient Republic of Rome," reported Cardinal del Monte, "I verily believe that a column would have been erected on the Capitol in his honor."

Galileo, however, had two powerful enemies working against him: one was the hard core of Aristotelian theologians who refused to tolerate any radical reforms in their cosmological system; the other was Galileo himself. He might have continued to study, observe, write, and teach Copernicanism as a theory had he not insisted upon carrying the fight to the enemy and thereby precipitating a confrontation. Like Luther, he seemed to enjoy baiting his opponents and ridiculing anyone who disagreed with him. His opponents did likewise. By 1616 they had become numerous, and some had influence in high places. Early in that year, Galileo was denounced to the Roman Inquisition. A committee of the Holy Office admonished him to abandon and cease to defend and teach as a physical fact the opinion that the sun is the center of the universe and that the earth moves around it. The decree implied, and was clarified in a subsequent affidavit from Cardinal Bellarmine, that Galileo could hold Copernicanism as a mathematical hypothesis as long as he did not assert it as a fact.

Telling Galileo to be quiet was like ordering the sea to be still. The appearance of three new comets in 1618 brought forth a barrage of polemical writing, including a treatise by the Jesuit, Orazio Grassi, that threw Galileo into a rage. He answered Grassi's tract with his own *Discourse on the Comets* (1619), followed four years later by what some have called the greatest polemic ever written on physical science. It was called *Il Saggiatore* (The Assayer) and contains what might be termed the manifesto of the scientific revolution, the declaration that knowledge of nature is acquired by observation and mathematics, not by reading ancient authorities.

Coinciding with the publication of this book was the election of Galileo's friend and admirer, Maffeo Barberini, as Pope Urban VIII (1623–44). Galileo dedicated the book to the new pope with flowery words and a petition for his continued favor and patronage. Galileo's star seemed again to be on the ascent. Pope Urban granted him audience, extolled him as a "great man whose fame shines in the heavens and goes far and wide on earth," presented him with costly gifts and apparel, and awarded him a pension for the support of his illegitimate son. Indeed, the pope blessed him with every favor he might wish, except the one thing Galileo desired most: repeal of the 1616 Holy Office decree; this, Urban would not do. Instead, he advised Galileo to be content with treating Copernicanism as a convenient mathematical postulate rather than as a physical fact, and admonished him to avoid theological and scriptural arguments.

Galileo returned to Florence and began the composition of his most famous and most fateful book, *Dialogue Concerning the Two Chief World Systems, Ptolemaic and Copernican,* wherein he openly defended the Copernican system. In January 1630 the manuscript was completed and Galileo initiated steps to have it approved and published in Rome. Several circumstances, including mounting opposition from the formerly sympathetic Jesuits, an outburst of the plague, and the death of Galileo's principal advocate in Rome, persuaded him to have the book published in Florence instead. The decision was unfortunate, for it required that Galileo resort to some rather underhanded means to bypass the Holy Office and obtain the imprimatur from under their noses. Early in 1632 the *Dialogue* emerged from the Landini press in Florence. The Holy Office was enraged and Urban VIII took Galileo's action as a direct insult to him.

The sick and aging Galileo was summoned before the Inquisition in Rome where, between 12 April and 21 June 1633, he was interrogated three times as to his opinions expressed in the *Dialogue*. Galileo finally recanted by declaring that he had rejected Copernicanism in 1616 and never again advocated it, and that upon rereading his *Dialogue* he could see how it was mistakenly seen as a defense of Copernicus. Galileo was required by the Holy Office to sign an abjuration of those heretical views, to refrain from raising the Copernican question again, or saying or writing anything "that might furnish occasion for a similar suspicion," to retire to his home under the surveillance of the Holy Office, and to recite the seven penitential psalms once a week for the next three years.

Despite his restriction and growing feebleness, Galileo soon regained his spirit and resumed his scientific writings, returning now to the studies of mechanics that had interested him so much as a youth. His final book, *Dialogues Concerning Two New Sciences*, dealing with the two branches of mechanics— statics and dynamics—was published by Elzevir in Leiden in 1638. Galileo considered it to be the best of all his writings. Even after he became totally blind, he continued scientific investigations until his death in January 1642.

It is unfortunate that the drama and emotion of Galileo's encounter with the Inquisition over his Copernican views has tended to obscure the true significance of his impact on the development of science. His greatest contribution was not to astronomy, although he did open important new dimensions in that field through his telescope. Of greater importance were his contributions to physics, particularly to the science of mechanics. As early as his first years at Pisa, Galileo had observed and studied the characteristics of motion, and he continued his experiments during his years at Padua. He discovered the law of the pendulum—that is, when a suspended weight is set into motion, its oscillations are traversed in equal times regardless of the length of arc—and applied this principle to measuring time. Tradition has it that Galileo first noted this phenomenon by observing the movements of a lamp suspended from the cupola of the cathedral in Pisa.

Of even more questionable authenticity is the story, first mentioned years later by Vincenzio Viviani, of Galileo's dropping weights from the top of the leaning bell tower at Pisa to determine their rates of fall. Simon Stevin and Jean Grotius did perform an experiment similar to this in the Netherlands, using weights dropped from about 30 feet, and declared (as did Galileo, and also J. B. Beneditti, Cardano, and Leonardo da Vinci before him) that bodies fall at a uniform rate of acceleration regardless of their weight. In addition to describing this "law" of falling bodies, Galileo showed that the movement of a body may be composed of more than one motion at a time. The path of a projectile, for example, combines a uniformly decelerating forward motion with a uniformly accelerating falling motion. He also declared that a moving body will continue in motion in a straight line at a uniform speed unless it is acted upon by another force to alter its direction or speed. This denied Aristotle's contention that the "natural" state of a body is rest, and anticipated Sir Isaac Newton's law of inertia.

Galileo contributed countless other discoveries, including the dynamics of impact; the theory of virtual velocities; experiments in sound, light, and magnetism; work on the strengths of different materials; the use of the screw as a machine; the analysis of alloys; the weight of air; and many more. He was greatly interested in hydrostatics and invented the thermoscope, and the hydrometer for measuring specific gravity. His pupil, Torricelli, invented the barometer. No one since Leonardo da Vinci had possessed such curiosity about the mechanics of the world, and unlike his artistic compatriot of a hundred years earlier, Galileo followed through on most of his observations and experiments, bringing to light new knowledge about the physical world and applying that knowledge to further discovery. He also advocated and applied the experimental method, showing the way for all future advance in scientific knowledge.

The Scientific Method: Bacon and Descartes

Despite the great advances made in scientific discovery by the 1630s, a complete break with the ancient world view had not yet been made, nor would it be until the remaining problems of physical motion were understood. Kepler accurately described the nature of planetary motion, but he could not explain why the planets moved in that manner, other than to provide harmonious celestial music. His rejection of uniform circular motion, which had been fundamental to all explanations of the universe before his time, called for a totally new conception of motion. Galileo provided many of the keys to the solution of this problem. He lacked only an accurate theory of acceleration to complete the puzzle. This was provided half a century later by Sir Isaac Newton who, by his theory of universal gravitation, finally put an end to the cosmological chaos of the early seventeenth century by providing a harmonious explanation of both planetary and terrestrial motion.

In the meantime, a sound methodological structure for scientific discovery was being shaped by two intellectual giants of the early seventeenth century. The respective methods of Francis Bacon and René Descartes were almost opposite; but when combined and appropriately applied, they became powerful tools for discovering and understanding the physical world. Bacon's approach was essentially empirical, what he called inductive, while Descartes's was primarily deductive. Neither method was new in the seventeenth century, but no one had ever advocated them as consistently and systematically as these two did, nor had anyone before them prefaced their constructive thought with such a thorough critique of previous errors and myths.

Sir Francis Bacon. *Painting by John Vanderbank after a portrait of 1618.*

Francis Bacon

Francis Bacon (1561–1626) was an ambitious man whose political skill and aspirations carried him to the pinnacle of power in Jacobean England as lord chancellor, only to dash him to the ground again in disgrace and dishonor. He was born at York House in London, the second son of Lady Anne and Sir Nicholas Bacon, lord keeper of the Great Seal, just three years after Queen Elizabeth ascended the throne of England. As a precocious youth, he amazed the court and delighted the queen with his spirited and sagacious conversation. At the age of twelve, he entered Trinity College, Cambridge, and began to study the classical philosophers. It was here that he first acquired his life-long distaste for Aristotelianism, not for Aristotle as a man but for his philosophy, which according to Bacon, is "barren of the production of works for the benefit of the life of man." Bacon did not quarrel with Aristotle on metaphysical grounds but disdained his irrelevance. The young Cambridge undergraduate believed that natural philosophy, indeed all education, ought to increase one's mastery over nature for the purpose of improving human existence. This idea became the great preoccupation of Bacon's life, "to reconstitute man's knowledge of nature in order to apply it to the relief of man's estate."

Bacon's chief contributions to scientific thought and method are contained in his *Advancement of Learning* and the *Novum Organum* (New Method), both constituting parts of his ambitious *Great Instauration,* in which he aspired to nothing less than systematizing and organizing all scientific knowledge, and applying it to the betterment of mankind.

Such a goal required a plan and a method, which Bacon provided. The first step in his instauration (renovation) was the recognition of the almost total defectiveness of the current state of knowledge. He attributed this to four "idols," or prejudices: (1) idols of the tribe, or the prejudices inherent in human nature; (2) idols of the den, meaning individual prejudices that alter truth to fit personal desires; (3) idols of the marketplace, by which he meant the careless and incorrect use of words so that many different meanings are conveyed by the same terms; and (4) idols of the theater, or the influence of other people's erroneous ideas. Once having smashed these idols of ignorance clothed in pseudoknowledge, the mind would be ready to attack the formidable task of advancing true knowledge.

Bacon outlined his method of acquiring truth in the *Novum Organum.* It is a technique of inductive thought by which a multitude of single facts or sense evidences are analyzed in several stages to arrive at a general principle. First comes tabulating all observed cases in which a certain phenomenon occurs, then listing all similar cases in which the phenomenon does not occur and other cases where it occurs in a modified form. This is followed by the exclusion of all uncommon factors and the isolation of the common ones, then the formulation of a principle or hypothesis expressing the inherent qualities found. This hypothesis is in turn verified to assure its validity.

Bacon's method contributed to scientific thought by starting from scratch, so to speak, by discarding old prejudices and adopting a fresh approach. It also placed a high premium on the observation of nature and arrived at conclusions only after careful examination of evidence. Bacon had an aggressive confidence in the reliability of this method and depicted in his *New Atlantis* the ideal society benefiting from the fruits of this applied science.

Nevertheless, Bacon's method is far from infallible. For one thing, it depends too heavily on what he called the form, or cause, of things and relies upon the ability of facts to speak for themselves more than they are likely to do. It also depends too much on the appearance of things and on the reliability of sense perceptions, ignoring quantitative data almost entirely. Herein lies Bacon's principal shortcoming as a philosopher of science: his neglect of mathematics. He failed to perceive the significance of mathematical formulation in the study of the physical world just as he failed to appreciate the meaning and growth of parliamentary government in the political world. The one kept him from recognizing and appreciating the work of contemporaries like Galileo, Kepler, Gilbert, and Harvey. The other led to his personal disgrace.

Yet Bacon played an important role in the advancement of learning even though he pioneered no new field of research and discovered no new laws of nature. As a philosopher of science, he saw and emphasized the role of science in human life. He envisioned the human power that could be realized through understanding nature and learning to control it.

René Descartes   Bacon's opposite in almost every way was the French philosopher-mathematician, René Descartes (1595–1650). Whereas Bacon was an extrovert, involved in public affairs and worldly honors, Descartes was an introvert, almost a recluse, who abandoned the active life in favor of seclusion and contemplation. Bacon was a social materialist; Descartes was a metaphysician. Although critical of the practical attainments of past knowledge, Bacon was still historically oriented. Descartes, on the other hand, was totally unhistorical, searching for and establishing his canons of truth philosophically, by reason alone.

Descartes was born at La Haye, near Poitiers, in the French province of Touraine. His father belonged to the ancient nobility of the sword and could afford to provide his son the best education. At the age of eight, Descartes was sent to the new Jesuit Collège de La Fleche in neighboring Maine, where he was introduced to all the scholastic arts and philosophies. He remained there eight years, showing a great affinity to mathematics and establishing a lifelong friendship with many of the Jesuit fathers. Nevertheless, he grew dissatisfied with the uncertainty of everything he was taught and determined to educate himself from "the great book of the world." First he traveled to Paris, then to the Netherlands, where he enlisted for a short period in the army of Maurice of Nassau during the first months of the Thirty Years' War. He wandered about northern Europe between 1619 and 1628 before deciding to retire to some secluded spot in Holland where he could meditate and write.

René Descartes. *This Frans Hals portrait was painted after Descartes adopted Holland as his home.*

Already, before retiring to the Low Countries, he had concluded that the learning of the schools was invalid, that former systems of thought were false, and that true knowledge must be founded on a skeptical rejection of all pseudoknowledge. The formulation of the famous Cartesian aphorism, *cogito ergo sum* ("I think, therefore I am"), was simply his way of expressing this method of rejecting all supposed truths except that which is manifestly true. All else could be questioned and doubted except the act of thinking itself, and since that must require a thinker, the reality of the thinker is established.

By the same rational method, and rejecting the untrustworthy sensory perceptions of Bacon's method, Descartes arrived at a belief and trust in God, the supreme essence:

> But these properties [of God, that is, infinite, independent, all-knowing, all-powerful, and so forth] are so great and excellent, that the more attentively I consider them the less I feel persuaded that the idea I have of them owes its origins to myself alone. And thus it is absolutely necessary to conclude, from all that I have before said, that God exists: for though the idea of substance be in my mind owing to this, that I myself am a substance, I should not, however, have the idea of an infinite substance, seeing I am a finite being, unless it were given me by some substance in reality infinite.

It is fundamental to Cartesian thought, as Alexandre Koyré has pointed out, that it "starts with the infinite, the perfect. It conceives infinite space before it inscribes figures in it. It conceives God before proceeding to understand man." In other words, it proceeds from the general to the specific, deducing the latter from the former.

From such "primary and clear evidences" as the existence of God, self, and the external world, arrived at intuitively by mental process rather than by experience, Descartes deduced the entire chain of truths, using as a general rule the principle that "all the things which we very clearly and distinctly conceive are true." Reason thus became for Descartes the only instrument of knowing truth, the supreme judge of reality for all things. Experiences based on the sensory perceptions of sight, hearing, touch, and smell vary with each individual and are therefore unreliable. Even for the same person, sensations may easily distort and falsify reality. Yet reason, said Descartes, is identical in all people and will give uniform and universal answers to everyone.

The Cartesian method, like the Baconian, is not without shortcomings and pitfalls. In the first place, it requires the impossible at the outset, namely, that the mind be cleansed of all previous ideas, that all opinions be renounced and all accepted traditions and authorities be rejected before the step-by-step acquisition of truths can begin. To presume to erase all mental inscriptions and frames of reference and make the mind a total void preparatory to embarking on the quest for knowledge is as faulty as the Baconian method. The presumption that pure reason is infallible is itself untrue. Furthermore, the Cartesian obsession with certainty might easily tempt a lazy mind (the kind most of us have) to take mental shortcuts in order to arrive more quickly at a desired goal.

Nevertheless, Descartes did provide an orderly and systematic method of thought that could be relied upon to arrive at truth more consistently than with the Scholastic method and much more consistently than with no method at all. He knew that science is not the result of an accumulation of facts, since facts always imply concepts. By basing his method on clear and indisputable concepts, and by reasoning in orderly steps from precise definitions based on common sense, Descartes helped liberate the human mind from its narrow shackles and direct it toward the ensuing Age of Reason. "We hold these truths to be self-evident," is an expression of the Cartesian concept of the clarity of reality and truth.

Science or Magic?

The line separating science from magic was very fine in the sixteenth and seventeenth centuries. To the popular mind, it was difficult to distinguish between the work of the chemist and the alchemist, the astronomer and the astrologer. They were usually the same person and dealt with mysteries of nature that were beyond the comprehension of the average person. It was no easier to believe that a compass needle pointed north because of its peculiar attraction to the force field set up between the two polar regions of the earth than that it was directed by the "spirits" within the needle. Science was and is mysterious to all who do not understand it.

Early modern scientists did not distinguish between science and magic. In Paracelsus (1493–1541) the two were so intermingled that it is impossible to separate them. Yet why should they be separated? Paracelsus's achievements were real regardless of how he is classified. Like his contemporaries, Paracelsus was trying to learn about nature and apply his findings in as many ways as possible. In his *De occulta philosophia* (On Occult Philosophy), Henry Cornelius Agrippa of Nettesheim (1486–1535) defended any magic by which "men may come to a knowledge of nature and of God." Dr. John Dee, the leading mathematician of Elizabethan England, participated in seances for the purpose of conversing with departed (therefore more experienced) spirits in order to gain further knowledge about nature. His friend, Leonard Digges, provided predictions of future events and conditions based on his mathematical calculations of planetary conjunctions and eclipses. In one form or another, astrology was believed in and practiced by every astronomer of the time, including Tycho Brahe, Kepler, and Galileo. Giordano Bruno contributed to the hermetic or occult tradition by his practice of mnemonics—the science, or magic, of memory improvement.

There is obviously a difference between this kind of "supernatural" science (what contemporaries called "Natural Magick"), however, and demonic intercourse for base or mischievous purposes. Giambattista della Porta (1538–

1615) wrote of the two kinds of magic in his 1558 *Magia Naturalis*. "The one is infamous, and unhappy, because it hath to do with foul spirits, and consists of Enchantments and wicked Curiosity; and this is called Sorcery. . . . The other Magic is natural; which all excellent wise men do admit and embrace." The investigation of the unusual characteristics of stones and crystals, the strange phenomenon of magnetic attraction, the medicinal properties of herbs and plants, and various optical illusions and refractions of light are all part of what Porta and Dee meant by natural magic. Porta's *Magia Naturalis* reads like an encyclopedia of scientific facts—treating such subjects as astronomy, biology, cryptography, distillation, hydraulics, magnetism, medicine, metallurgy, and refraction—along with discourses on the transmutation of plants, "love philters," magic lamps, and sleep potions. Even Gilbert's *De Magnete* (On the Magnet), one of the treatises used to illustrate the beginning of modern experimental science, was at the same time a work on natural magic, written to illustrate some of the supernatural forces of nature. The conclusion might be drawn that although all magicians of the sixteenth and early seventeenth centuries were not scientists, all scientists of the time were to some degree magicians.

Witchcraft   Although Porta and others distinguished between "Natural Magic" and sorcery, the two were not so easily separated in the popular mind. One of the credulities to arouse and infect European society at the very time of the scientific revolution was witchcraft. Belief in witches and incantations is an old phenomenon. It existed in all ancient societies and had been prevalent in western Europe during the Middle Ages. Yet instead of gradually dissolving in the light of new knowledge and science, the belief in sorcery and fear of witches became an obsession in the sixteenth and seventeenth centuries. Christianity had linked witchcraft with heresy and the Devil; with these potent and highly inflammable ingredients added to fear, superstition, and ignorance, simple witchcraft was converted into a systematic demonology, resulting in an epidemic of witch trials and burnings. The more people were burned as witches, the more numerous "witches" became. Denouncing people as witches became the most sinister form of witchcraft itself, as fear led to frenzy and common sense gave way to superstition and widespread persecution.

Many explanations have been offered for the witch-hunting epidemic that swept Europe. Most of these explanations contain important ingredients but never provide a complete answer to the persistent question of why the witch craze took place. Much recent scholarship emphasizes the role played by popular culture, with its built-in belief in magic and spirits. The essence of this culture is masterfully described here by the French social historian Robert Muchembled:

> Popular culture, then, found expression in rural society in a vision of the world that was superficially Christianized but fundamentally magical. Transmitted in the main by women, this philosophy made no strict

distinction between life and death. In it neither sickness nor death seemed natural or normal events, but seemed to be caused by the omnipresent action of superhuman forces. The world was full of forces, full of a mysterious and a priori dangerous vital energy. The souls of the dead penetrated this imprecise and invisible space and could just as easily bring serious harm to the living as defend them against all dangers. . . . Everything depended on a system of rites and taboos that man could use to deal with these powers: to protect himself against them, to bring harm to others, or to obtain what he desires. Everyone was thus to some extent a sorcerer in his relations with these terrifying powers. The true sorcerer, who was often a woman, simply held more trump cards than an ordinary human in this ritual game.

The witch hunt was undoubtedly based on fear, and may have been triggered by the attempts of those in authority to oppose popular culture, or at least control those aspects of peasant and commoner belief that they feared were a threat to themselves. It was not that the educated did not believe in the magical aspects of the universe, but they feared they might lose control to those unseen forces. The clergy especially were fearful of finding themselves at the mercy of the sorcerers, who, as has been noted, were mainly women. To many church officials, witchcraft, like Carnival, represented a reversal of the normal order of the universe, an attempt by women to subvert patriarchal authority. That is why it had to be attacked so vigorously.

Witchcraft had two meanings for people in early modern Europe. One was the practice of harmful magic, *maleficia* (evildoing) of some sort against someone, such as inflicting disease, bodily injury, or death by means of occult or supernatural powers. These deeds of sorcery might be performed by the use of some manipulative process or paraphernalia like potions, spells, or charms, or they might be more subtle kinds of incantations. The other activity of witchcraft had to do with relationship with the Devil, for witchcraft also implied Devil worship. This satanism was closely related to *maleficia* because it was believed that the power of witches to harm people came from their liaison with the Devil. The main elements of this liaison were a pact with Satan and repudiation of Christ; the ride by night to a secret rendezvous called the Witches' Sabbath, where the witches engaged in a variety of practices including gluttony, desecration of the Eucharist, and intercourse with the Devil; and the practice of infanticide and cannibalism.

The sharp increase in the preoccupation with witchcraft seems to have been stimulated, in part at least, by the publication in 1486 of the *Malleus Maleficarum* (Hammer of the Witches)—the first printed encyclopedia of demonology—and the issuance of the papal bull of 1484 authorizing the Dominicans to wipe out witchcraft in the Holy Roman Empire. Yet it was not until almost a century later that most of the great witchcraft trials took place. In the popular mind, sorcery was closely associated with heresy and with any kind of social eccentricity or nonconformity. Once started, the witch hunting spread until it grew into a terrifying hysteria. In 1623, at the height of the witch craze,

Witches' Sabbath. *A woodcut by Hans Baldung-Grien shows witches brewing a heady potion to harm their victims. Many accoutrements of their trade are depicted, with the Devil lurking nearby.*

Pope Gregory XV commanded that anyone who made a pact with the Devil or who practiced black magic that had caused the death of another, should be surrendered to the secular court and put to death. The systematization of witchcraft was largely the result of judicial torture and forced confessions put into the mouths of victims by their fastidious interrogators. Nevertheless, many accused witches' confessions were given without torture and contained the same esoteric details of Witches' Sabbaths and diabolic visitations.

The seriousness with which people took witchcraft in the sixteenth and seventeenth centuries was due in part to this heretical perversion of the Christian faith, and thus a direct and deliberate threat to society. Popular belief was that there were upward of two million witches at large at the end of the sixteenth century. The latest and most reliable modern studies estimate that at least 110,000 persons, mostly women, were tried for witchcraft throughout Europe between 1450 and 1750. Of these, some 60,000 were executed. The majority of the prosecutions appear to have been in Germany, followed by the lands adjacent—Poland, Bohemia, Switzerland, and France. Fewer prosecutions occurred in the Low Countries and in the British Isles (more than half of which were in Scotland), and fewer still in Italy and Spain.

Jean Bodin, the French jurist and great political theorist of the late sixteenth century, was an outspoken advocate of witch trials. Johann Weyer, physician to the duke of Cleves, on the other hand, argued that pacts with the Devil were frauds and that witches were harmless old women suffering from physical or mental disorders. For most people, it was difficult to distinguish between demonic sorcery and supernatural science. Galileo's guarantee that the earth did in fact revolve around the sun was no easier to comprehend than the Aristotelian assurance that it did not. The scientific revolution, like other revolutions, stirred up controversy and produced uncertainty. In that climate of divergence, credulity and confusion continued. Until the scientific principles and understanding of Kepler, Galileo, and Newton were understood, or at least trusted, witchcraft and demonology would continue to plague the western world and flourish side by side with growing knowledge and reason—one of the many paradoxes of Renaissance and Reformation Europe.

Religious Thought and Controversy

Tradition has it that the rise of scientific thought resulted in the erosion and decline of religion. Perhaps a more accurate way to describe the impact of science upon religion is that it caused a reorientation and redefinition of religion for many people, and a reevaluation of the role of the church in European society. The bitter confrontation of science and traditional religion came later. For now, the greatest minds tried earnestly to reconcile and harmonize the two. Reconciliation, however, is easier said than done. The main difficulty in harmonizing scientific with religious thought was the wide divisions and discrepancies within Christianity itself. Every attempt at religious reconciliation was thwarted by sectarian jargon or by dogmatic dissension of one kind or another.

First, there was the continuing schism within Christianity itself, opened by Luther and widened by successive reformers and counterreformers. As long as Christians placed a higher value on theological distinctions than on moral behavior, the breach would continue to widen. Doctrinal differences had become so rigid by the time of the Thirty Years' War, and so interwoven with political rivalries, as to make conflict almost inevitable. Yet Hugo Grotius, the great Dutch writer on international law, could counsel his countrymen in 1627 to make religious reconciliation through Christian piety the basis of Europewide peace. Many would listen to and agree with Grotius, but no one could stop the momentum of confessional competition and dynastic hostility.

Protestant Disputes Even within the sectarian alignments, there was discord and dispute over the doctrine of salvation and other issues. Lutherans, for example, divided sharply after Luther's death. One faction, following Philipp Melanchthon, centered at Wittenberg and known as Philippists, was willing to allow that a degree of free will was involved in salvation and that *some* good works might help to effect it. The Philippists were strongly opposed by the Gnesio-Lutherans, headed by Matthias Flacius Illyricus (1520–75) of Magdeburg, who accused Melanchthon of betraying the true gospel in order to accommodate the Catholics on the free will/good works issue. The Gnesio-Lutherans rigidly held the view of salvation by grace alone, denying totally the efficacy of good works. The

disputes continued to plague Lutheranism in the Empire until late in the century when a *Formula of Concord* was finally worked out, combining the acceptable confessions, and was subscribed to by eighty-six of the princes and imperial cities.

Calvinists had even more difficulty agreeing with one another on the doctrines of salvation. The middle-of-the-road Heidelberg Confession was rejected by Calvinists outside the Palatinate, and each nation soon published its own creed. The bitterest controversy among Calvinists took place in the Netherlands, where Arminians (who accepted free will) and Gomarists (who held to a strict predestinarianism) anathematized and killed one another during the first two decades of the seventeenth century. In England Calvinism took a distinct form under the general rubric of Puritanism. Most of the Puritans followed basic Calvinist doctrines, believed in predestination, held high moral values, and accepted Calvinist principles of discipline. Some, however, preferred the presbyterian form of church organization favored by the Scottish Calvinists, while the more radical and powerful faction abandoned the territorial system of organization and adopted the principle of congregationalism.

"Fishing for Souls" *represents the Protestants' successfully rescuing "lost" souls, while the Catholics' rescue attempt is about to result in a disaster. Painting by Adriaen Pietrszoon, 1614.*

This opened the way to a variety of forms of worship and more doctrinal disagreements.

Catholic Conflicts

Catholics were not free from controversy, either, as they groped for a common definition of orthodoxy. For them the dispute developed in three stages, lasting from the 1580s to the mid-seventeenth century, and even beyond. It began with the mounting Dominican-Jesuit rivalry as the dynamic young Society of Jesus encroached more and more on the bailiwick of the Dominicans. The Jesuits were upstart "modernists" who challenged the Dominican establishment on many counts. In the endeavor to present Catholicism in the most favorable light, Jesuits held that God in his mercy would take into account the frailties of human nature when pronouncing judgments. Some of the principles they employed as guidelines in the confessional were *probabilism* (allowing the confessor to make allowances for probable extenuating circumstances), *laxism* (limiting the number of mortal sins to infractions of major laws only), and *intentionalism* (taking into account the penitent's intention). Dominican reaction to this casuistry was vigorous and bitter, accusing the Jesuits of condoning and encouraging sin.

In the year of the Armada, 1588, a Spanish Jesuit named Luis de Molina (1535–1601) published a book entitled *Concordia Liberi Arbitrii cum Gratiae Donis* (Harmony of Free Will with Grace), in which he tried to reconcile the paradox of free will and grace by maintaining that grace operates only after the application of free will; that is, God's grace is rendered efficacious only by the actual consent of the human will. This doctrine, called Congruism but more widely known as Molinism, was naturally anathema to Protestants, and even seemed strange to many Catholics, who felt it overemphasized human will at the expense of divine grace. Dominicans took for their champion against Molina the Dominican professor of theology at the University of Salamanca, Domingo Báñez (1528–1604), confessor and spiritual advisor to Saint Teresa of Avila. Báñez's countertheory was that works are of no value unless performed while in a state of grace, and that grace itself is intrinsically efficacious with or without works. Thus, the Dominicans emphasized the will and grace of God, while the Jesuits stressed the will of the human being. The latter's practical, empirical theology was well adapted to the needs and uses of their missionary order in Christianizing the heathen and restoring Catholicism in Europe.

Jansenism   The most extreme Catholic opposition to Jesuit theology was initiated in the early seventeenth century by theologians from the University of Louvain. The most important of these was the Fleming, Cornelius Jansen (1585–1638), who not only reflected the strong anti-Jesuit attitude long prevalent at Louvain but also an Augustinian bent acquired from a lifelong reading of Saint Augustine. According to Jansen, there are two kinds of grace, one given to all men enabling them to do good, and another, higher grace, given only to the predestined elect. Christ's atonement was only for the latter. Jansen's influence was not strongly felt until after his death, when his writings were published in France under the title *Augustinus*. A coterie of dedicated friends, centered at the convent of Port Royal near Paris, constituted the nucleus of the vigorous Jansenist movement. Jansenism provided an organized opposition to Jesuit casuistry and free-will Molinism with a Catholic brand of determinism.

The most vitriolic stage of the Jesuit-Jansenist dispute came in the 1640s, after the publication of the *Augustinus* (1640) and Antoine Arnauld's *De la fréquente communion* (On the Frequency of Communion) in 1643. Despite Pope Innocent X's condemnation of it, Jansenism continued to flourish in France, especially with the strong support of such a unique and powerful thinker as Blaise Pascal (1623–62), and spread to Spain, Italy, Germany, and Poland. Pascal's *Provincial Letters,* a blistering but eloquent attack on Jesuit theology, helped keep Jansenism alive in France, and effectively damaged Jesuit credibility by showing how casuistry was a cover-up for moral laxity. A hundred years later, Jansenists were still around and active in the movement that led to the expulsion of the Jesuits from France in 1762.

Meanwhile, in early seventeenth-century France, the established church was experiencing its greatest period of vitality and growth. This was not just an outward show of strength, but a genuine spiritual revival of the Gallican church, a late flowering of the Counter-Reformation in France following its devastating religious wars. It was accompanied by increased devotional manifestations. In 1611 Cardinal Bérulle founded the French Oratory, which was devoted to infusing a new spirituality into the life of the clergy. His wide range of associations and contacts had a profound effect on the spread of mysticism in France, and stimulated Saint Francis de Sales (1567–1622), the saintly Savoyard humanist who devoted his energies to missionary labors among the Calvinists.

The outstanding seventeenth-century example of mystic devotion harmonized with an active life was Saint Vincent de Paul (1576–1660). His motto was that the only way to feel like a Christian was to live like one, and the best way to live as a Christian was to work like one. For a time he was chaplain in the galley fleet, after serving as a galley slave himself, and then chaplain to the powerful Gondi family. Subsequently, as a parish priest in the village of Châtillon-sur-Lombes, he became acutely aware of the physical and spiritual poverty of the peasants. To help remedy this, he founded a missionary order, known as the Lazarists (after Saint-Lazare, where they had their beginning), to travel throughout the country teaching the poor. Service to the needy was the key to Saint Vincent de Paul's activities. His principal supporter in that effort was Louise le Gras, who founded the Sisters of Charity.

Education and the Transmission of Knowledge

In the Middle Ages, education had been almost totally a function of the church. By the seventeenth century, it still had a predominantly religious orientation and was dominated by religious organizations. Nevertheless, under the influence of humanism, the Reformation, and the rise of scientific thought, many changes had taken place and new educational "systems" were in the making.

Humanism had greatly affected the scope and content of education in Europe, yet despite the lofty goals and noble manners of Castiglione, Erasmus, and Vives, the humanists' educational philosophy applied almost entirely to the well-to-do or intellectual elite, not to the masses, and it was the noble class that profited most from their influence. Especially in Elizabethan England, the humanists' sentiments took root and flourished among the aristocracy, where there was a growing demand for education to prepare young noblemen for the duties of court and state. Thomas Elyot's advice on the moral and cultural education of a ruler was generalized into the educational philosophy "to fashion a gentleman or noble person in virtuous and gentle discipline." Similarly, Roger Ascham's *The Schoolmaster* (1570) was aimed at training youth for service to the state.

The impact of the Reformation on early modern education was as great as that of humanism, and helped make schools more sectarian, polemical, and widespread. In Protestant countries, for example, there was a strong impulse to educate young people, train them to become good Christians and obedient subjects, and prepare some of them to become leaders of the church. The Reformation, however, also placed more emphasis on theological dispute and confessional conformity, and teaching and reciting catechisms became an integral part of sixteenth-century Protestant education. Still, the impetus given by Luther, Melanchthon, and Sturm bore fruit in the quality and quantity of grammar schools in Germany and in defining the responsibility of secular authorities for maintaining those schools. In Catholic countries the greatest stimulus to good schooling came from the Jesuits, who from their very beginning emphasized education.

In the meantime, mounting criticism of traditional education gave rise to a number of individual reformers. In France, Pierre Ramée (latinized as Peter Ramus, 1515–72) and Michel de Montaigne, in particular, disturbed the educational tranquility of their times by advocating radical changes. Ramus's reform proposals were based on the idea that experience, not authority, is the source of all knowledge. And Montaigne, who also took a pragmatic view of education, believed that learning results from establishing good habits in early childhood. He advised learning from other people, from nature, and from travel, because learning is an active and continuing process, not a one-time accomplishment. Education is attaining true wisdom rather than simple knowledge.

The base of English education was broadened by the writings and example of Richard Mulcaster (ca. 1530–1611), who believed in universal, compulsory schooling in reading, writing, drawing, and music for all children, rich or poor, boys and girls, up to the age of twelve. Beyond that age, the student's potential and the needs of the state should determine whether or not he or she should go on to more advanced study. Mulcaster's influence was particularly strong on the educational views of Francis Bacon. Above all, Bacon advocated the systematic study of nature by the inductive method, and pointed out the practicality of education. In *The Advancement of Learning* (1605), he equated knowledge with power, emphasizing the need to know the physical world and to convert that knowledge into practical purposes.

The fullest results of the influence of scientific methodology on education were seen in Johann Amos Comenius (1592–1670), the greatest pedagogical reformer of early modern times. This Czech theologian, scholar, and educator (born Jan Komensky, at Nivnitz, in Moravia) was a member of the religious community known as the *Unitas Fratrum,* or Unity of Brethren, which dated back to early Hussite times. Forced by the eruption of the Thirty Years' War to flee his native country, Comenius attained wide renown as a pastor, teacher, lexicographer, and humanitarian while living as an exile in Hungary, Poland, Sweden, Germany, and England. His greatest educational legacy was a book called *The Great Didactic* (1628 in Czech, 1657 in Latin), setting forth his ideas and methodology of education. It was a grandiose proposal, like Bacon's *Great Instauration,* worthy of the ambitious Baroque age in which it was born. "We venture to promise," Comenius wrote in his introduction, "a great didactic, that is to say, the whole art of teaching all things to all men, and indeed of teaching them with certainty, so that the result cannot fail to follow." The aims of life, he ventured, are learning, virtue, and piety, all of which can be attained or enhanced through education. He proposed educating girls as well as boys, of all social classes, in common schools. He also advocated teaching useful subjects, and in the proper sequence, in order that they might build upon previous studies and lead logically to more advanced learning in the universities.

Universities   In the meantime, university education had expanded so dramatically during the sixteenth century that the expression "educational revolution" has been applied to the phenomenon. This expansion not only consisted in the founding of many new universities but also, more significantly, in the increased importance placed on university education and consequently in an unprecedented number of university students and graduates. The church (both Protestant and Catholic) demanded increasing numbers of educated people, as did the other professions, especially the bureaucratic governments. The "new monarchies" of France, Spain, England, and Sweden gave impetus to university education, and particularly to the study of law, as these governments required well-trained lawyers, financiers, and administrators to operate the machinery of modernizing bureaucracies. In order not to be left too far behind, even the old nobility of the sword and the upper aristocracy gradually came to recognize the need for education, which they acquired either in the universities or in other more exclusive academies. Education was proving to be the road to power and wealth. In the course of the seventeenth century, however, partly because of the social disruption that resulted from the Thirty Years' War and the tendency of the new nobility to acquire land and titles and revert to the ways of the old, but especially due to the heavy hand of government domination, the momentum of university education declined and the European universities entered a period of recession and decay.

Printing   Much of the sixteenth-century advance in educational opportunity and incentive was due to the ever-widening impact of the printed book. The amount and diversity of printing was phenomenal and had a profound effect upon education and learning. In Venice the Aldine Press continued to publish books of great quality and quantity, not only for the learned but also inexpensive editions for the popular market. By the second half of the sixteenth century and during most of the seventeenth, the center of European printing was in the Low Countries. Literally hundreds of printers there produced thousands of books on every subject imaginable. The leaders of this industry were Christophe Plantin, a publisher-printer of Antwerp, and the Elzevir family of Leiden.

Plantin was actually French, born in Tours in 1520; he set up his first printing press in Paris, where the successful firm of the prominent printer and lexicographer Robert Estienne dominated the publishing world. In 1548 Plantin established himself in the flourishing city of Antwerp, which already

A sixteenth-century French printer. *This miniature from the* Chants Royaux sur la Conception *shows some of the activities of a busy printing establishment, from preparing the ink to proofreading final copy.*

boasted fifty-six active printing houses. He began as a bookseller, then became a binder and publisher, and finally, by 1555, began printing as well. Soon he established a reputation as a shrewd businessman, selling large editions of profusely illustrated books. He was a pioneer in the printing of copper engravings and etched drawings, and in 1570 became royal printer to Philip II of Spain. His famous eight-volume Polyglot Bible is one of the products of this association. After Plantin's death, the printing establishment passed to his son-in-law, Jan Moretus, and it continued as a family firm until 1875, when it was purchased by the city of Antwerp and converted into the justly famous Plantin-Moretus Museum of Printing.

The Elzevir publishing enterprise was founded by Louis Elzevir (ca. 1546–1617) in 1583. As official publisher to the newly founded University of Leiden and an enterprising searcher for valuable manuscripts, Elzevir laid the foundation for the most extensive publishing business of early modern Europe. By the time of his death, he had published over 100 scholarly works. His sons added a printing press in 1618 and began to print their famous small-format editions of the classics. Branches of the family business were established in The Hague, Utrecht, and Amsterdam. By the end of the Elzevir dynasty in 1712, the house had published over 1,600 separate titles, mostly Latin classics, theology, history, medicine, and other scholarly works.

Historical and Political Scholarship

The influence of religious controversy and the conjunction of scholarly stimulation associated with the expansion of printing and the enlarged availability of documents gave a positive impulse to scholarly production of all kinds, especially to the writing of history. John Knox's *History of the Reformation of Religion Within the Realm of Scotland* and John Foxe's *Book of Martyrs* illustrate the polemical extremes aroused in the partisans of the Reformation. Matthias Flacius Illyricus and his collaborators were responsible for the first comprehensive Protestant interpretation of church history, a thirteen-volume compilation of sources and biased commentary known as the *Magdeburg Centuries,* published between 1559 and 1574. The Catholic response was provided by the Vatican librarian and confidant of Pope Clement VIII, Cardinal Caesar Baronius (1538–1607), in his equally biased *Ecclesiastical Annals* (1588–1607). Baronius made good use of the valuable Vatican collections, however, and provided many facsimiles of documents, inscriptions, and coins. The fallacies in Baronius's *Annals* were revealed by the French humanist, Isaac Casaubon (1559–1614), and skillfully refuted in his *Exercitationes in Baronium.* The most controversial historical polemicist at the turn of the century was the brilliant Venetian, Pietro Paolo Sarpi, who was one of the best educated and most universal minds of the day. He thought of himself as a loyal Catholic, but as a patriotic Venetian he was sharply critical of papal pretensions. In his *History of the Council of Trent* (1619), he accused the papacy of deepening, rather than ending, the religious schism.

The best example of critical method and objectivity in historical scholarship came from the French Huguenot, Lancelot du Voisin de La Popelinière (1541–1608). The impartiality of La Popelinière's *Histoire de France,* which dealt with the passionate civil war period, is all the more remarkable because the author was a participant himself. His belief in and practice of historical objectivity was a beacon to future scholars. La Popelinière's works reflect the changes that were taking place as empiricism slowly replaced polemics in the writing of history, and more attention was given to the critical use of historical documents. In this connection, the work of the Bollandist Fathers, a group of Jesuit scholars in the Spanish Netherlands who collected and edited source materials for a more critical approach to the lives of the saints, was of immense importance. Their monumental *Acta Sanctorum* (Lives of the Saints) began publication in 1643 and is still in progress.

The cultivation of the auxiliary sciences of paleography and diplomatics (the study of ancient documents) and numismatics (the study of medals and coins) further promoted sound historical scholarship. Bacon added his philosophical perspective as he advocated the same critical approach to historical knowledge that he did for the study of nature. Unfortunately, he did not follow his own advice very closely in his *History of Henry VII.* Others did, however, and with the coming of philosophical approaches to the past, such as Jean Bodin's *Method for Easily Understanding History* (1566), the writing of history became more thoughtful as well as more accurate.

Political Thought   Theories of historical causation found their most immediate application in political thought. The twin but contradictory concepts of natural law and social contract dominated the political thinking of the post-Reformation era. Both were strongly present in the political theory of the Huguenots; Bodin saw the law of nature and God as the only limitation upon the sovereignty of the monarch, while Richard Hooker based his rational policy on the harmony of natural law. In the early seventeenth century, the Dutch experience produced considerable raw material for political speculation and several remarkable political thinkers, including Johannes Althusius (1557–1638) and Hugo Grotius (1583–1645).

Although he was born in Germany, Althusius's contributions to political thought were largely a result of his service to the Dutch republic. Strongly influenced by the Huguenot identification of natural law with the law of God (Althusius was a Calvinist himself), he combined this with his belief in a theory of contract that binds all the social groups together and forms the foundation of the state. Althusius saw the state as a corporation composed of individuals and groups possessing sovereignty themselves, which they delegate to the government by contract. If the governmental administrators fail to live up to their contract, their delegated sovereignty reverts to the people. The details of Althusius's views are worked out in his *Politica methodiae digesta* (Digest of Political Method), a work that is particularly important in the history of political thought for its advocacy of "federalism"—that is, a balanced distribution and exercise of power among the component parts of the body politic.

A large step in the separation of political thought from theology and the promotion of reason in the conduct of government was taken by Grotius, particularly in his *De iure belli et pacis* (The Law of War and Peace, 1625). Rationally and systematically reexamining the law of nature and of nations in terms of the political realities of his day, Grotius affirmed that war, as well as peace, was subject to general rules and laws that every nation must observe. After restating the legal arguments of his predecessors, Francisco Vitoria and Alberico Gentilli, Grotius added to them the strength of reason and logic for the purpose of achieving a less violent and more humane existence (a kinder, more gentle world). In this he was totally unsuccessful, but it was a commendable step in the right direction.

John Milton's bold declaration in favor of constitutionalism and freedom in his *Areopagitica* (1644) breathes the same humanistic idealism. Yet the dissensions and upheavals of early seventeenth-century England gave rise to other manifestations of political opinion. Thomas Hobbes (1588–1679) is the best representative of the reaction against both disorder and the constitutionalism of the time. In Hobbes the secularization of political thought reached its climax and with it the exaltation of the absolute state. According to Hobbes, to maintain order and stability, all of the administrative, judicial, military, and ecclesiastical power had to be centered in a strong, monarchical government. In the *Leviathan* (1657) he expressed the rigid contract theory that the people, for their own preservation and prosperity, abandoned all political rights and authority to the sovereign state, which is responsible to no one and whose power is irresistible. Yet for all of his rationalization and justification of power, Hobbes held that the absolute monarch was still bound by the laws of nature, and moral norms were still based on Christian traditions, just as they were for Althusius, Grotius, and Milton.

The Literary World of Early Modern Europe

The term traditionally used to characterize the art of the seventeenth century, and is increasingly applied to the literature and music as well, is *Baroque*. The expression itself is more widely used than defined, and like many stylistic locutions, is likely to mean something different each time it is used. Still, in a general sense, it might safely be taken to signify the exuberant action and intense feeling in the literature and music of the time, especially as expressed in drama (both literary and musical) and in the embellishments of poetic frills and harmonic counterpoint.

The European literature of the late sixteenth and early seventeenth centuries was understandably varied and uneven. In Italy the literary Renaissance had long since burned out, although the afterglow of that glorious age was still reflected in the poetic charm of Torquato Tasso's (1544–95) pastoral romance *Aminta* and particularly in his heroic epic *Gerusalemme liberata* (Jerusalem Liberated), the story of the Christian capture of Jerusalem in the First Crusade. Although medieval in theme, the poem's mingling of strong elements of classical form and late-Renaissance vigor give it a deserved place in the Italian literary tradition. In its time it was also extremely popular in France, Spain, and England. The more lasting literary legacy from Italy, however, was the continuing devotion to the theater, especially the professional, improvised, and satirical plays of the *Commedia dell'Arte*. Italian *commedias* were familiar in every country of Europe, and the more they were excoriated by the church as immoral and scandalous, the more popular they became. Machiavelli would have smiled knowingly.

Drama

The golden age of literature dawned in Spain before it set in Italy. The outburst of Spanish literary vigor was most pronounced in drama. The theater was already popular in Spain by the last quarter of the sixteenth century, and under the impact of its greatest dramatists, it dominated the literary scene during the first half of the seventeenth century, the great age of European drama. Lope de Vega (1562–1635) reveled in witty, light-hearted, and satirical plays that emphasized the vanity and dichotomy of human existence. Occasionally he probed deeper into the nature of man and struggled with the dilemmas of honor and moral right, and he was particularly adept at portraying the virtues and vices of Spanish character. The mid-seventeenth-century theater was dominated by the soldier-priest, Pedro Calderón de la Barca (1600–1681), whose *Autos sacramentales* (humanized allegorical plays) were very popular. Calderón was a deeply religious man who exalted honor above all other virtues, although he recognized the painful dilemma people face when honor conflicts with religion, justice, or compassion. His *La vida es sueño* (Life Is a Dream) grapples with many of the profound problems of life and human destiny.

The impact of Spanish drama was felt in all of the surrounding countries by the early seventeenth century. The most skillful French dramatist of the period, Pierre Corneille (1606–84), was strongly influenced by it, particularly its depiction of conflicts of honor. Not only did Corneille found French tragedy on a Spanish format, his most important play, *Le Cid*, was based on a previous play by Guillén de Castro and adopted its principal character from medieval Spanish history. Likewise, Corneille's single comedy, *Le menteur* (The Liar), was based on Alarcón's *Verdad sospechosa* (Suspected Truth). Corneille's use of precise and highly ornamental language, although not as excessive or extreme as Góngora's, also discloses his Baroque roots, and provided a target for Molière's later lampoons.

Further evidence that the age of Baroque was also the age of drama is provided by the late flowering of dramatic poetry in the Netherlands. The greatest of the Dutch dramatists was Joost van den Vondel (1587–1679) who, because of the majesty of his language, has been called "the perfect Baroque poet." Vondel decried the religious intolerance of his Calvinist compatriots, and in his masterpiece, *Lucifer*, emphasized the free agency and power of man. Vondel's influence was especially strong on the bombastic Andreas Gryphius (1616–64), the poet *par excellence* of the Thirty Years' War, although on the whole, the German literature of that period was mediocre.

In England, on the other hand, the exuberant spirit of drama reached its climax with Shakespeare (see pages 331–334) and continued to flourish for another generation until the theaters were closed by parliamentary decree in 1642. Ben Jonson (1573–1637) wrote many lusty plays, masques, and poems. Trained at Westminster School by the historian-teacher William Camden, Jonson later followed the uncertain career of acting before he became a playwright and close friend of Shakespeare. *The Alchemist*, which shows Jonson's vigorous and vivid writing, is perhaps his best play. Less colorful but more profound was John Milton (1608–74), whose masterful blank-verse religious epic *Paradise Lost* is the epitome of the Baroque fascination with human passions, supernatural powers, and majestic settings. This dramatic allegory of Satan, sin, and death was composed after the poet became blind. His avowed purpose was to "justify the ways of God to men" and symbolizes the continuing concern for religious expression yet without the narrow sectarianism of the previous age.

Music Perhaps the most dramatic manifestation of the age was expressed in music. Characteristic forms of early Baroque music were oratorios, concertos, cantatas, chorales, and, above all, the beginning of opera. Musical drama reached its crowning glory in the operas of Claudio Monteverdi (1567–1643) in which singing, acting, dancing, and instrumental music were combined with elaborately designed stage sets to make a harmonious display of all the arts and reflect the creative energy of the time. Monteverdi's first opera, *Orpheus*

(1607), was followed by other grandiose productions filled with both illusion and reality. Usually performed in the open air in conjunction with the great religious festivals, Italian opera became popular throughout the peninsula and gradually gained acceptance north of the Alps. Monteverdi also developed the madrigal to its most dramatic level between 1590 and 1640.

Opera's religious counterpart, the oratorio (a choral rendition of a scriptural text with recitatives and arias as well as chorus), was another musical form greatly admired in Italy and the rest of Europe. It grew out of the desire to give a musical setting to religious drama and was closely related to the cantata, another religious choral composition consisting of choruses, solos, and recitatives, usually accompanied by organ. Like the opera, the masters of oratorio and cantata were Italians. The greatest organist and composer of instrumental and organ music in this period was the worthy successor of Palestrina as papal organist, Girolamo Frescobaldi (1583–1643), whose music has been compared with the bubbling waters of a Bernini fountain.

Outside of Italy the most important musical development came in Germany, where it was closely associated with the Lutheran church service. There the chorale, a hymn sung in church to a traditional or specifically composed melody, reached its most eloquent and expressive form in the works of the composer-musicians Heinrich Schütz and Paul Gerhardt.

The Beginning of Baroque Art

Underlying Baroque art is a great craving for the classical harmony and balance of the High Renaissance, yet overriding it is a sense of dramatic action and movement that belie its classical roots. This dichotomy may be seen in the swirling lines and busy figures superimposed on a classical column, like frosting on a cake, or in the restless movement of a biblical painting, just as it is in the musical variations on a simple melody, or in the verbal embellishment of a Góngora poem. In each of these examples, the excitement and splendor of the artistic ornamentation, whether poetic, musical, linear, or architectural, all but hide its underlying, classical form. This paradox in the Baroque style is also revealed in the striving for spiritual expression while still being strongly attracted to earthy realism.

The characteristics of Baroque art vary with the artist and the medium, but several features occur frequently enough to be called typical. One of these is the tendency toward display, ostentation, and sensuousness exhibited in abundant ornamentation and the piling on of material. Baroque art was intended to appeal to the emotions of the spectator, and many techniques of illusion and effect were employed to heighten that emotional impact, such as the dramatic use of light and shade *(chiaroscuro)*, the depiction of intense and often violent action, and the employment of natural elements (light, water, setting) to intensify the dramatic effect. A third characteristic is the unrestrained use of space and the integrated relationship between space and solid. The figures in Baroque paintings reach out and move into space, unconfined by frame or boundary, almost making the spectator part of the picture.

Baroque ceiling decoration.
Pietro da Cortona's "The Triumph of Divine Providence," on the ceiling of the Gran Salone in the Palazzo Barberini, is a dynamic propaganda presentation of Pope Urban VIII as the agent of Divine Providence.

Painting

Baroque painting, like Baroque music, had its birth in Italy near the end of the sixteenth and beginning of the seventeenth centuries. Its earliest representatives were the Carracci brothers, Agostino and Annibale (1560–1609), and the indomitable Caravaggio (1573–1610). The Carracci ceiling frescoes in the Palazzo Farnese in Rome became the models of subsequent decorative painting for half a century or more. Grandiose and dramatic, these frescoes portray the Roman gods and goddesses in vivid color and elegant movements. The unorthodox Caravaggio, on the other hand, depicted both saints and sinners in stark realism as he pushed to its zenith the realistic representation of the human figure. Caravaggio was criticized because his Madonnas looked like the women one would have seen any day of the week, his youthful Christs like the boys who ran up and down the streets of Rome. Realism and emotional intensity were heightened by Caravaggio's bold use of light to dramatize his subjects. Backgrounds were darkened in order to spotlight the principal figures and action. Caravaggio's series of three canvases on the *Life and Martyrdom of Saint Matthew,* as well as his painting of the *Conversion of Saint Paul* and the *Crucifixion of Saint Peter,* vividly reveal the dramatic effectiveness of his *chiaroscuro* technique. The direction that was pointed to by the Carracci brothers

Caravaggio's "Crucifixion of St. Peter" *shows the gripping realism of Caravaggio's Baroque style and his dramatic use of light and shadow.*

Peter Paul Rubens, Self-Portrait. *This monumental portrait reveals the power and sweep of the great Baroque painter, restlessly anticipating his next triumph.*

and by Caravaggio was later followed by many painters of early seventeenth-century Italy.

In the meantime, the most prolific of the Baroque painters, Peter Paul Rubens (1577–1640) of Antwerp, was independently disseminating his flamboyant art throughout Europe. The most illustrious and unique of a long line of Flemish artists, Rubens painted in every form, including religious, mythological, historical, genre scenes (depicting scenes or events from everyday life), and landscapes, as well as portraits and political propaganda. His paintings are noted for their massive, rounded forms and dramatic action. Rubens's subjects twist and surge in a continuous panorama of movement as they mix and merge into one another, having no single focus and giving no rest to the eye. Violence and sensuality are keynotes of his huge canvases, just as grandeur and vitality characterize all of his work. Yet Rubens was a man of great affection and charm, and many of his portraits reflect this warmth. The disciples of Rubens, especially Jacob Jordaens (1593–1678) and Anthony Van Dyck (1599–1641), continued the Baroque tradition of richness and splendor but added their own individual qualities: Jordaens a bourgeois vitality and realism, Van Dyck an elegance and sensitivity to character. The latter's portraits of King Charles I and other English royalty are penetrating portrayals of personality, mood, and bearing.

The most varied expressions of Baroque painting appeared in Spain, where the influence of Flemish art had long been felt and the Italian impact was equally great. Yet the greatness of Spanish art resulted from its unique fusion of foreign influences with a native tradition that included deep religious feeling and vivid realism. José de Ribera (1591–1652) was a gifted painter who settled in Naples after 1616 and spent the rest of his life there, part of the time as court painter to the Spanish viceroys of Naples. His paintings, like Caravaggio's, featured sharply contrasting *chiaroscuro* along with vigorous and sometimes cruel realism. Unlike Caravaggio, though, Ribera was able to express deeply felt human emotions, from simple humility and compassion to triumphant glory. More religious were the works of Francisco de Zurbarán (1598–1664), who dramatically employed light and shade to heighten the devotional or spiritual impact of his paintings. His figures also possess a modeled, sculptured quality that gives them a reality that further emphasizes the direct communication between body and spirit, human beings and God.

The greatest of the Spanish masters was Diego de Velázquez (1599–1660), student and son-in-law of Francisco Pacheco, and during the last thirty-seven years of his life, official court painter to Philip IV. Velázquez was born and reared in Seville, where he soon established his reputation as an artistic prodigy, painting scenes of daily life and of people and things he saw in the streets. At the age of twenty-three, he was invited to Madrid, where he entered a new career as the painter of the royal family and of life at court. Six years later, he was induced by Rubens to visit Italy, where he spent a stimulating year and a half in Genoa, Venice, Rome, and Naples. Velázquez's works have been described as "the poetic transformation of reality." He was, indeed, a reflective, careful observer of nature, and through the application of his own poetic in-

Velázquez, "Old Women Cooking Eggs" (1628). *This remarkable oil painting reveals Velázquez's early interest in representing common objects and people in a realistic way.*

sight, was able to inject life and texture into whatever he painted, whether it was an egg frying sunny side up in an earthen pan, a humble water carrier (see page 366), or a portrait of the king of Spain or his minister (see page 453). His works are imaginative and ideal, yet always strikingly real, with a range and variety of color worthy of Titian. He was a master in the effective use of light and shade, and of balancing the relationship of light, color, and space to produce the visual yet intangible illusion of atmosphere. His art glorifies the grandeur that once was Spain's but was even then passing to other hands (see page 470).

The Baroque style was slower to develop in France, and even when it did, in the third and fourth decades of the seventeenth century, it was much more tranquil and subdued than elsewhere and maintained its preponderantly classical features throughout the century. Georges de La Tour (1593–1652) employed *chiaroscuro* more for realistic than for dramatic effect. In his paintings

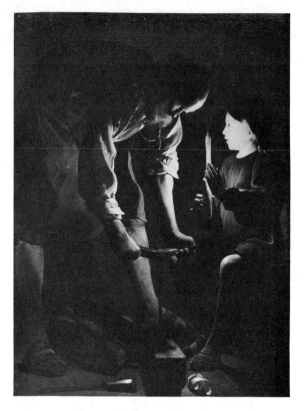

Georges de la Tour's "Saint Joseph, Carpenter" *shows the boy Jesus holding a candle for his father. Admiration and love are reflected in the boy's eyes. The dramatic lighting effect is typical of the Baroque style.*

of *Saint Joseph, Carpenter* (Louvre), and others, La Tour employed the internal, localized light of a candle to define and limit the relevant picture space and to focus on the meaning of the scene produced by this warm glow of light. His paintings are deeply moving, not in the dynamic sense of a Rubens but in a quiet, reflective, religious sense. Complementing La Tour were Louis Le Nain (1593–1648) and his brothers Antoine and Mathieu, whose peasant scenes glow with more subdued but luminous hues of browns, greys and greens, realistic yet detached, and classically calm and dignified. The zenith of early seventeenth-century French painting was reached with Nicolas Poussin (1594–1665), who bathed classical compositions in luminosity and reestablished the delicate balance between illusion and idealized truth that the Baroque had almost overthrown.

The final flowering of Baroque painting took place in the northern Netherlands, where it blended with a popular devotion to landscape and realistic "daily life" scenes to produce the greatest artistic outpouring of early modern times. Dutch painting of the seventeenth century had a very different purpose and flavor than that of Catholic Flanders, France, Spain, and Italy. It was not courtly art, nor did it emphasize either religious or classical themes. Instead it was primarily concerned with memorializing people, recording the circumstances of everyday life, and depicting the scenery of the seventeenth-century Lowlands. Its clientele were the merchants and burghers of that increasingly affluent society. Outside of a Baroque fascination with light and shade, Dutch

Pieter de Hooch, "Backyard in Delft." *The peace and tranquility of seventeenth-century Dutch landscape and genre paintings contrast strikingly with the activities of the seamen and warriors who were at the time creating a Dutch empire.*

paintings had little resemblance to the aristocratic, majestic art of the south. But still they were related.

The first of the Dutch masters was Frans Hals (ca. 1581–1666), the most expressive portraitist of the age and the most Baroque in his vigorous and dynamic early style. His later paintings became more subdued and dignified (see page 387). Hendrick Terbrugghen (1588–1629) and Gerard van Honthorst (1590–1656) of Utrecht also painted portraits, genre, and historical scenes in a remarkably Caravaggiesque style, with effective use of intense internal lighting. More characteristic of the seventeenth-century Netherlands, however, were the Haarlem landscape painters, Jan van Goyen, Salomon van Ruysdael, and Aert van der Neer, and the later "photographic" genre scenes of Jan Steen, Pieter de Hooch, and Jan Vermeer.

Rembrandt's "Christuskopf" (the Head of Christ) *is more than a portrait: it is a penetrating study of inner character and feeling.*

By common consent, the greatest of the Dutch painters was Rembrandt van Rijn (1606–69). The range and variety of his works was remarkable even in that age of prodigious productivity. Many of his canvases reflect a Baroque intensity of action—like *The Sacrifice of Abraham* (Hermitage Museum, Leningrad), *Belshazzar's Feast* (National Gallery, London), and *The Blinding of Samson* (Städelsches Kunstinstitut, Frankfurt)—and he continually explored the dramatic use of lighting in *The Anatomy Lesson of Dr. Tulp* (Mauritshuis, The Hague), *Descent from the Cross* (National Gallery of Art, Washington, D.C.), *The Presentation in the Temple* (Mauritshuis, The Hague), and the *Night Watch* (Rijksmuseum, Amsterdam), his most exciting group portrait. Rembrandt's greatest achievement, however, was the versatility and freedom of his painting technique and the insightful penetration of inner consciousness and character revealed in his many portraits and self-portraits.

Architecture and Sculpture

The magnificence and grandeur of the Baroque is best represented in the architecture and sculpture of early seventeenth-century Rome, which, under the auspices of the Counter-Reformation papacy, became the main force of artistic patronage in Italy. The Baroque rebuilding of the Eternal City was part of the papal yearning to revive the grandiose style of ancient Rome. The first Baroque building was the Jesuit church in Rome, *Il Gesù*, whose façade was completed by Giacomo della Porta in 1575. Surprisingly plain in comparison with the interior, the façade nevertheless reflected the Baroque spirit in its modeled pilasters and pediments, which were intended to give it a dynamic effect. Carlo Maderno's (1556–1629) Santa Susanna (constructed between 1597 and 1603) goes further toward an overall integration of line and space and more dramatic variations in relief. Between 1607 and 1612, Maderno also completed the façade of Saint Peter's Basilica, with its massive portico columns and giant pilasters at each end. Another notable work is Francesco Borromini's (1599–1667) façade of Sant'Agnese in the Piazza Navona, the concave center and extended flanks of which give an undulating effect to the surface and present a dramatic interplay of light and shadow. Inside, the full impact of the Baroque is felt in the integrated space, classic columns overrun with decorative ornamentation, and the fusion of architecture, sculpture, and painting.

The best illustration of this fusion, and of the work of the brilliant artist most closely associated with it—Gianlorenzo Bernini (1598–1680)—is the interior of Saint Peter's. Here, Bernini's dynamic sculptures strike the keynote of the Baroque. Action, splendor, profusion, and exuberance mark the interior decoration, from the gilded bronze, ninety-five-foot-tall, spiral-columned *Baldacchino* (canopy) over the high altar and tomb of Saint Peter, to the *Cathedra Petri* (Peter's Chair). Similarly, the statue-tombs of popes Urban VIII and Alexander VII, and the huge statue of Saint Longinus, along with many other tombs, statues, balconies, altars, and decorations, make the interior of Saint Peter's a showplace of Bernini's art. Outside, enclosing the vast piazza, Bernini symbolically extended the arms of the church in the encompassing embrace of a giant colonnade composed of 284 massive columns crowned with ninety-six double-sized statues of saints and martyrs.

Bernini's genius was not short of Michelangelo's, and in his virtuosity, he might be considered the last "Renaissance man." His works in Rome are almost numberless and include such magnificent and moving statues as the *Ecstasy of Santa Teresa* (which makes use of natural light and gilded sun lines to heighten the emotional impact), an intensely realistic *David*, the encounter of *Habakkuk and the Angel*, and the graceful *Apollo and Daphne;* fountains, including the *Fountain of the Four Rivers* in the Piazza Navona, the *Triton* fountain in the Piazza Barberini, and the *Barcaccia* at the foot of the Spanish steps; and splendid buildings like the Sant'Andrea al Quirinale church. He also produced no fewer than thirty-three lifelike marble portrait busts of many of his patrons, from Pope Urban VIII and Cardinal Scipione Borghese to Francesco d'Este, duke of Modena, and the Sun King himself, Louis XIV of France.

The impulse given to Baroque architecture and sculpture by Rome—and particularly Bernini—carried throughout Europe. In Spain it was especially popular in elaborate altarpieces and in the emotion-wrenching polychrome sculptures of Gregorio Fernández. The most decorative Baroque façades, however, appeared in Spanish churches and cathedrals in the New World. Another direct inheritor of Baroque architecture was southern Germany and Austria, where it spread after the termination of the Thirty Years' War. The Baroque embellishment of Salzburg, however, began much earlier, when three of its

Bernini, "Ecstacy of Saint Teresa." *The majestic conception and dramatic rendition of Baroque sculpture is revealed in this Bernini monument located in the Cornaro Chapel of Santa Maria della Vittoria in Rome.*

more flamboyant archbishops, Wolf Dietrich (1587–1612), Marcus Sitticus (1612–19), and Paris Lodron (1619–33) endeavored to make their city a northern Rome. The Baroque cathedral and square, the Residenz fountain, the archepiscopal palace, and even the waterworks at Hellbrunn witness their partial success and paved the way for the masterpieces of the later Baroque builder Fischer von Erlach: Architecture in France showed a much closer conformity to classical lines, although the monumentality of François Mansart's designs for the Louvre façade and the Orléans wing of the château of Blois reflect an exuberance that is not entirely subdued. The church of the Sorbonne (1635) is another example of the dynamism yet restraint of French architecture. In the Netherlands and England, an even more sober classicism prevailed in the buildings of Jacob van Campen and Inigo Jones that suggests a partial fulfillment of Renaissance ideals.

Suggestions for Further Reading

SCIENCE AND THOUGHT

Useful introductions to the age are P. M. Harmon, *The Scientific Revolution* (London, 1983), which complements Robert Mandrou, *From Humanism to Science, 1480–1700,* tr. by Brian Pearce (Hammondsworth, 1978), and Hugh Kearney, *Science and Change, 1500–1700* (New York, 1971). Also see John Redwood, *European Science in the Seventeenth Century* (New York, 1977), and Christopher Lewis, *The Merton Tradition and Kinematics in Late Sixteenth and Early Seventeenth Century Italy* (Padua, 1980). For England see Mordechai Feingold, *The Mathematicians' Apprenticeship: Science, Universities and Society in England, 1560–1640* (New York and Cambridge, England, 1984); Nicholas H. Clulee, *John Dee's Natural Philosophy, Between Science and Religion* (New York, 1990); and Georgia B. Christopher, *Milton and the Science of the Saints* (Princeton, 1982).

SCIENTISTS FROM COPERNICUS TO GALILEO

Two excellent accounts are Edward Rosen, *Copernicus and the Scientific Revolution* (Malabar, Florida, 1984), and *Three Imperial Mathematicians: Kepler Trapped between Tycho Brahe and Ursus* (New York, 1986), by the same author, who tells much of the story in the words of the participants. The text of Kepler's treatise is provided, with commentary and essays, by Nicholas Jardine, *The Birth of History and Philosophy of Science: Kepler's 'A Defense of Tycho Against Ursus,' with Essays on its Provenance and Significance* (New York and Cambridge, England, 1984). J.V. Field, *Kepler's Geometric Cosmology* (Chicago, 1988) locates Kepler's work within the history of science. The best analysis of Tycho's life and work is Victor E. Thoren, *The Lord of Uraniborg: A Biography of Tycho Brahe* (New York and Cambridge, England, 1990). On Galileo see Stillman Drake, *Galileo at Work: His Scientific Biography* (Chicago, 1978), *Galileo* (New York, 1980), and *Galileo: Pioneer Scientist* (Toronto, 1990), fascinating books by the leading Galilean authority; Maurice A. Finocchiaro, *Galileo and the Art of Reasoning: Rhetorical Foundation of Logic and Scientific Method* (Boston, 1980); W.A. Wallace, *Galileo and His Sources* (Princeton, 1984); and Pietro Redondi, *Galileo, Heretic*, tr. by Raymond Rosenthal (Princeton, 1987), which argues that Galileo was not condemned for his heliocentrism but for his support of atomism, which threatened to undermine the Catholic doctrine of transubstantiation.

BACON AND DESCARTES

The life of Bacon is updated in John Russell, *Francis Bacon* (Oxford, 1979), and Jean Overton Fuller, *Francis Bacon: A Biography* (London, 1981). Also see Peter Urbach, *Francis Bacon's Philosophy of Science: An Account and Reappraisal* (LaSalle, Illinois, 1987); Jerry Weinberger, *Science, Faith, and Politics: Francis Bacon and the Utopian Roots of the Modern Age* (Ithaca, 1985), a perceptive commentary on Bacon's *Advancement of Learning;* and Charles Whitney's provocative *Francis Bacon and Modernity* (New Haven, 1986). Still very useful is Paolo Rossi, *Francis Bacon: From Magic to Science*, tr. by Sacha Rabinovitch (Chicago, 1968). The most recent study of Descartes is Marjorie Grene, *Descartes* (Minneapolis, 1985), but also see Anthony Kenny, *Descartes* (New York, 1968), and J.F. Scott, *The Scientific Work of René Descartes* (London, 1952).

MAGIC AND OCCULT

Excellent as introductions to the role of magic in early modern science are Charles Webster, *From Paracelsus to Newton: Magic and the Making of Modern Science* (New York and Cambridge, England, 1982), and the essays in Brian Vickers, ed., *Occult and Scientific Mentalities in the Renaissance* (New York and Cambridge, England, 1984), which show the contribution of "occult sciences" such as alchemy and astrology to the scientific revolution. Patrick Curry focuses on astrology in *Prophecy and Power: Astrology in Early Modern England* (Princeton, 1989). Wayne Shumaker, *The Occult Sciences in the Renaissance: A Study in Intellectual Patterns* (Berkeley, 1979) is also a useful and thought-provoking study, as is Francis A. Yates, *The Occult Philosophy in the Elizabethan Age* (Boston, 1979). Other important works are E. William Monter, *Ritual, Myth and Magic in Early Modern Europe* (Athens, Ohio, 1984); Ioan P. Couliano, *Eros and Magic in the Renaissance,* tr. by Margaret Cook (Chicago, 1987) sees Renaissance magic as a way to manipulate people by appealing to sexual imagination; and Paul Barber's fascinating *Vampires, Burial, and Death: Folklore and Reality* (New Haven, 1988). The classic study of the relationship between magic and religion is Keith Thomas, *Religion and the Decline of Magic* (New York, 1971).

WITCHCRAFT

The literature on witchcraft has greatly increased in the last decade, much of it very penetrating and revealing. For general accounts see especially Brian P. Levack, *The Witch-Hunt in Early Modern Europe* (New York, 1987); Julio Caro Baroja, *The World of the Witches,* tr. by O.N.V. Glendinning (Chicago, 1987); Brian Easlea, *Witch Hunting, Magic and the New Philosophy: An Introduction to Debates of the Scientific Revolution, 1450–1750* (Brighton, England, 1980); Joseph Klaits, *Servants of Satan: The Age of the Witch Hunts* (Bloomington, 1985); Geoffrey Scarre, *Witchcraft and Magic in Sixteenth- and Seventeenth-Century Europe* (Atlantic Highlands, New Jersey, 1987), a brief, somewhat sensationalist survey; and Charles A. Hoyt, *Witchcraft* (Carbondale, Illinois, 1981). Good regional studies include H.C. Erik Midlefort, *Witchhunting in Southwestern Germany, 1562–1684* (Stanford, 1972); E. William Monter, *Witchcraft in France and Switzerland* (Ithaca, 1976); D. P. Walker, *Unclean Spirits: Possession and Exorcism in France and England in the Late Sixteenth and Early Seventeenth Centuries* (Philadelphia, 1981); Christina Larner, *Enemies of God: The Witch-Hunt in Scotland* (Baltimore, 1981), and *Witchcraft and Religion: The Politics of Popular Belief* (New York and Oxford, 1984); J. Fauret-Saadra, *Deadly Words: Witchcraft in the Bocage* (Cambridge, England, 1980); Michael Kunze, *Highroad to the Stake: A Tale of Witchcraft,* tr. by William E. Yuill (Chicago, 1987), an account of a single case in Bavaria in its entire social and intellectual context; Gustav Henningsen, *The Witches' Advocate: Basque Witchcraft and the Spanish Inquisition, 1609–1614* (Reno, 1980); Ruth Martin, *Witchcraft in Venice, 1550–1650* (New York, 1988); and Carlo Ginzburg's *The Night Battles: Witchcraft and Agrarian Cults in the Sixteenth and Seventeenth Centuries,* tr. by John and Anne Tedeschi (Baltimore, 1984), tracing the transformation and manipulation of popular notions of witchcraft. The role of the witch in art, society, and religion is discussed in Jane P. Davidson, *The Witch in Northern European Art, 1470–1750* (Freren, Germany, 1987).

RELIGIOUS THOUGHT

Religious controversy continued to occupy a large share of the intellectual activity of the late sixteenth and early seventeenth centuries. See in particular Robin B. Barnes, *Prophecy and Gnosis: Apocalypticism in the Wake of the Lutheran Reformation* (Stanford, 1988); Kaspar von Greyerz, ed., *Religion and Society in Early Modern Europe, 1500–1800* (London, 1984); Edmond Leites, ed., *Conscience and Casuistry in Early Modern Europe* (New York and Cambridge, England, 1988); Carter Lindberg, *The Third Reformation? Charismatic Movements and the Lutheran Tradition* (Macon, Georgia, 1983); Jill Raitt, ed., *Shapers of Religious Traditions in Germany, Switzer-*

land, and Poland, 1560–1600 (New Haven, 1981); Nichlas Tyacke, *Anti-Calvinists: The Rise of English Arminianism, c. 1590–1640* (New York and Oxford, 1987); Derk Visser, *Zacharias Ursinus, the Reluctant Reformer: His Life and Times* (New York, 1983), and *Controversy and Conciliation: The Reformation and the Palatinate, 1559–1583* (Allison Park, Pennsylvania, 1986). The transformation of Reformed theological thinking is studied in David A. Weir, *The Origins of the Federal Theology in Sixteenth-Century Reformation Thought* (New York and Oxford, 1990).

Other studies are Alexander Sedgwick, *Jansenism in Seventeenth-Century France* (Charlottesville, Virginia, 1977); David Stevenson, *The Origins of Freemasonry: Scotland's Century, 1590–1710* (New York and Cambridge, England, 1988); Lorna Jane Abray, *The People's Reformation: Magistrates, Clergy, and Commons in Strasbourg, 1500–1598* (Ithaca, 1985); R. Po-Chia Hsia, *Society and Religion in Münster, 1535–1618* (New Haven, 1984); Elizabeth G. Gleason, ed., *Reform Thought in Sixteenth Century Italy* (Chico, California, 1981); Christopher F. Black, *Italian Confraternities in the Sixteenth Century* (New York and Cambridge, England, 1989); and Carlo Ginzburg, *The Cheese and the Worms: The Cosmos of a Sixteenth-Century Miller*, tr. by John and Anne Tedeschi (Baltimore, 1980).

EDUCATION AND PRINTING

For important developments in early modern education see especially Anthony Grafton and Lisa Jardine, *From Humanism to the Humanities: Education and the Liberal Arts in Fifteenth and Sixteenth-Century Europe* (Cambridge, Massachusetts, 1986); Rosemary O'Day, *Education and Society, 1500–1800* (New York, 1982); George Huppert, *Public Schools in Renaissance France* (Urbana, 1984); Jay P. Anglin, *The Third University: A Survey of Schools and School Masters in the Elizabethan Diocese of London* (Norwood, Pennsylvania, 1985); J.M. Blom, *The Post-Tridentine English Primer* (London, 1982); and R.A. Houston, *Literacy in Early Modern Europe: Culture & Education, 1500–1800* (White Plains, New York, 1988). On the Jesuit schools see Aldo Scaglione, *The Liberal Arts and the Jesuit College System* (Philadelphia, 1986). J. R. Brink, *Female Scholars, a Tradition of Learned Women before 1800* (Montreal, 1980) is a timely study. Also see David Cressy, *Literacy and the Social Order: Reading and Writing in Tudor and Stuart England* (New York and Cambridge, England, 1980). On the universities outside of Italy see the essays in James M. Kittelson and Pamela J. Transue, eds., *Rebirth, Reform and Resilience: Universities in Transition, 1300–1700* (Columbus, 1984). Also see Christopher Brooke and Roger Highfield, *Oxford and Cambridge* (New York and Cambridge, England, 1988), James McConica, ed., *The History of the University of Oxford, Vol. III: The Collegiate University* (New York and Oxford, 1986), and Damien R. Leader, *A History of the University of Cambridge, Vol. I: The University to 1546* (New York and Cambridge, England, 1989).

Some of the variety of works on early modern printing stimulated by Elizabeth L. Eisenstein's monumental *The Printing Press as an Agent of Change*, 2 vols. (Cambridge, England, and New York, 1979) may be seen in the following: Roger Chartier, *The Cultural Uses of Print in Early Modern France*, tr. by Lydia G. Cochrane (Princeton, 1987), by the leading French scholar of the book; Roger Chartier, ed., *The Culture of Print: Power and the Uses of Print in Early Modern Europe*, tr. by Lydia Cochrane (Princeton, 1989), containing some excellent essays; and Gerald P. Tyson and Sylvia S. Wagonheim, eds., *Print and Culture in the Renaissance: Essays on the Advent of Printing in Europe* (Newark, 1986). Miriam U. Chrisman, *Lay Culture, Learned Culture: Books and Social Change in Strasbourg, 1480–1599* (New Haven, 1982) is an important study. Also see Sandra Hindman, ed., *The Early Illustrated Book: Essays in Honor of Lessing J. Rosenwald* (Washington, D.C., 1982); Bernard Capp, *Astrology and the Popular Press: English Almanacs, 1500–1800* (London, 1979), an authoritative guide to early almanacs; and Alison Saunders, *The Sixteenth Century French Emblem Book* (Geneva, Switzerland, 1988). A penetrating study of the English broadside ballad and chapbook is Tessa Watt, *Cheap Print and Popular Piety, 1550–1640* (New York and Cambridge, England, 1991). The importance of pamphlets is illustrated in Marie-Hélène Davies, *Reflections of Renaissance England: Life, Thought and Religion Mirrored in Illustrated Pamphlets, 1535–1640* (Allison Park, Pennsylvania, 1986); and Craig E. Harline, *Pamphlets, Printing, and Political Culture in the Early Dutch Republic* (Dordrecht, the Netherlands, 1987), which studies Dutch pamphlet literature and its environment between 1565 and 1648. On individual printers see William A. Pettas, *The Giunti of Florence: Merchant Publishers of the Sixteenth Century* (San Francisco, 1980); Elizabeth Armstrong, *Robert Estienne, Royal Printer: An Historical Study of the Elder Stephanus* (Abington, England, 1986); and Clive Griffin, *The Crombergers of Seville: The History of a Printing and Merchant Dynasty* (New York and Oxford, 1988).

HISTORIOGRAPHY AND POLITICAL SCIENCE

Donald J. Wilcox, *The Measure of Times Past: Pre-Newtonian Chronologies and the Rhetoric of Relative Time* (Chicago, 1987) is a sophisticated but not entirely convincing study of the philosophy of history from an unusual perspective. J.G.A. Pocock, *The Ancient Constitution and the Feudal Law: A Study of English Historical Thought in the Seventeenth Century,* 2nd ed. (New York and Cambridge, England, 1987) is an update and retrospect of his earlier book. A more traditional approach to English historiography is Joseph M. Levine, *Humanism and History: Origins of Modern English Historiography* (Ithaca, 1987), which argues that the effect of humanism on historiography was significant but not complete. Heather Dubrow and Richard Strier, eds., *The Historical Renaissance: New Essays on Tudor and Stuart Literature and Culture* (Chicago, 1988) shows the interplay of historical scholarship, literature, and politics, while Judith Anderson analyzes the depiction of historical figures in *Biographical Truth: The Representation of Historical Persons in Tudor-Stuart Writing* (New Haven, 1984). Also see D.R. Woolf, *The Idea of History in Early Stuart England* (Toronto, 1990). Finally, three other important studies are Ingeborg B. Vogelstein, *Johann Sleiden's Commentaries: Vantage Point of a Second Generation Lutheran* (Lanham, Maryland, 1986); Lynn S. Joy, *Gassendi the Atomist: Advocate of History in an Age of Science* (Cambridge, England, and New York, 1987); and Orest Ranum, *Artisans of Glory: Writers and Historical Thought in Seventeenth-Century France* (Chapel Hill, 1980).

A brief but tantalizing account of early modern political thought is Paul Avis, *Foundations of Modern Political Thought: From Machiavelli to Vico* (Dover, New Hampshire, 1987). Also see Gerhard Oestreich, *Neostoicism and the Early Modern State,* tr. by David McLiatock (New York and Cambridge, England, 1980); J.G.A. Pocock, *Politics, Language, and Time: Essays on Political Thought and History* (Chicago, 1989); and the essays in Anthony Pagden, ed., *The Languages of Political Theory in Early Modern Europe* (New York and Cambridge, England, 1987). A very penetrating study of social thought is Robert Brown, *The Nature of Social Laws: Machiavelli to Mill* (New York and Cambridge, England, 1984). The most recent study of Grotius's contributions to international relations is Hedley Bull, et al., eds., *Hugo Grotius and International Relations* (New York and Oxford, 1990). For some unique characteristics of political thought in France, Spain, and England see N.O. Keohane, *Philosophy and the State in France from the Renaissance to the Enlightenment* (Princeton, 1980); J.A. Fernández-Santamaría, *Reason of State and Statecraft in Spanish Political Thought, 1595–1640* (Lanham, Maryland, 1983); Martin N. Raitiere, *Faire Bitts; Sir Philip Sidney and Renaissance Political Theory* (Pittsburgh, 1984); and Stevie Davies, *Images of Kingship in Paradise Lost: Milton's Politics and Christian Liberty* (Columbia, Missouri, 1983).

THE BAROQUE AGE: LITERATURE

Good beginning points are Peter N. Skrine, *The Baroque: Literature and Culture in Seventeenth-Century Europe* (New York, 1978), and Basil Willey's re-issued classic, *The Seventeenth Century Background: Studies in the Thought of the Age in Relation to Poetry and Religion* (Henley-on-Thames, 1979). A very interesting approach to the literature of the period is Peter M. Daly, *Literature in the Light of the Emblem* (Toronto, 1979), which analyzes the structural parallels between emblems and literature. English literature is well represented in Murray Roston, *Milton and the Baroque* (Pittsburgh, 1980); John Carey, *John Donne: Life, Mind, and Art* (New York and Oxford, 1981); and Leah S. Marcus, *The Politics of Mirth: Jonson, Herrick, Milton, Marvell, and the Defense of Old Holiday Pastimes* (Chicago, 1986). An important work on women and literature is Linda Woodbridge, *Women and the English Renaissance: Literature and the Nature of Womankind, 1540–1620* (Urbana, Illinois, 1984), also Katharina M. Wilson, ed., *Women Writers of the Renaissance and Reformation* (Athens, Georgia, 1987). On Spanish literature see B.W. Ife, *Reading and Fiction in Golden Age Spain: A Platonist Critique and Some Picaresque Replies* (New York and Cambridge, England, 1985); D. Gareth Walters, *Francisco de Quevedo: Love Poet* (Washington, D.C., 1985); and Thomas R. Hart, *Cervantes and Ariosto: Renewing Fiction* (Princeton, 1989), an arresting comparison of *Don Quixote* and *Orlando Furioso*.

MUSIC AND THEATER

A remarkably good overview is Lorenzo Bianconi, *Music in the Seventeenth Century*, tr. by David Bryant (New York and Cambridge, England, 1987). H.F. Cohen, *Quantifying Music: The Science of Music at the First Stage of the Scientific Revolution, 1580–1650* (Boston, 1984) is very technical. On the beginning of opera see Barbra R. Hanning, *Of Poetry and Music's Power: Humanism and the Creation of Opera* (Ann Arbor, 1980), and Gary Tomlinson, *Monteverdi and the End of the Renaissance* (Berkeley, 1987), a carefully documented study of the meaning of Monteverdi's secular works. For a different mode see Jerome Roche, *North Italian Church Music in the Age of Monteverdi* (New York and Oxford, 1984), and Frederick Hammond, *Girolamo Frescobaldi* (Cambridge, Massachusetts, 1983). The definitive work on the music of Ferrara is Anthony Newcomb, *The Madrigal at Ferrara, 1579–1597*, 2 vols. (Princeton, 1980).

The flowering of drama in England and Spain is described in John Loftis, *Renaissance Drama in England and Spain* (Princeton, 1987) and Walter Cohen, *Drama of a Nation: Public Theater in Renaissance England and Spain* (Ithaca, 1988). Further analyses of English drama are S. Gorley Putt, *The Golden Age of English Drama: Enjoyment of Elizabethan and Jacobean Plays* (Totowa, New Jersey, 1981); Albert H. Tricomi, *Anticourt Drama in England, 1603–1642* (Charlottesville, Virginia, 1989); Maria Lomax, *Stage Images and Tradition: Shakespeare to Ford* (New York and Cambridge, 1987); Margot Heinemann, *Puritanism and Theatre: Thomas Middleton and Opposition Drama under the Early Stuarts* (New York and Cambridge, England, 1980); and Jean-Christophe Agnew, *Worlds Apart: The Market and the Theater in Anglo-American Thought, 1550–1750* (New York and Cambridge, England, 1986).

For other theater see Michael D. McGaha, ed., *Approaches to the Theater of Calderón* (Washington, D.C., 1982), and James A. Parente, Jr., *Religious Drama and the Humanist Tradition: Christian Theater in Germany and in the Netherlands, 1500–1680* (Leiden, 1987).

PAINTING

Baroque painting began in Italy with the Carracci brothers and Caravaggio. See especially Charles Dempsey, *Annibale Carracci and the Beginning of Baroque Style* (Locust Valley, New York, 1977); Carl Goldstein, *Visual Facts over Verbal Fiction: A Study of the Carracci and the Criticism, Theory and Practice of Art in Renaissance and Baroque Italy* (New York and Cambridge, England, 1988); S.J. Freedberg, *Circa 1600: A Revolution of Style in Italian Painting* (Cambridge, Massachusetts, 1983); and Richard E. Spear, *Caravaggio and His Followers* (New York, 1975). On art patronage see Francis Haskell, *Patrons and Painters: Art and Society in Baroque Italy*, rev. ed. (New Haven, 1980).

Flemish painting was dominated by Rubens. Recent updates of his life and work include Christopher White, *Peter Paul Rubens, Man and Artist* (New Haven, 1987); Lisa Vergara, *Rubens and the Poetics of Landscape* (New Haven, 1982); and Jeffrey M. Muller, *Rubens: The Artist as Collector* (Princeton, 1989). Also see Zerka Z. Filipezak, *Picturing Art in Antwerp, 1550–1700* (Princeton, 1987), which reveals the attitudes of Antwerpers, laypeople and artists, toward art and artists. Even though there were ties between Flanders and Spain, Spanish painting had characteristics setting it apart from Flemish art. See especially Jonathan Brown's sumptuously illustrated *Velázquez: Painter and Courtier* (New Haven, 1986), and *The Golden Age of Painting in Spain* (New Haven, 1991). Also Richard L. Kagan, ed., *Spanish Cities of the Golden Age: The Views of Anton Van den Wyngaerde* (Berkeley, 1988), containing contemporary drawings of some 60 Spanish cities. Court painting in Habsburg Prague is analyzed in Thomas D. Kaufmann, *The School of Prague: Painting at the Court of Rudolf II* (Chicago, 1988).

Dutch painting was a dominant feature of seventeenth-century art. It is studied in Madlyn M. Kahr, *Dutch Painting in the Seventeenth Century* (New York, 1978); Peter C. Sutton, *Masters of 17th Century Dutch Landscape Painting* (Philadelphia, 1988); M. Russell, *Visions of the Sea: Hendrick C. Vroom and the Origins of Dutch Marine Painting* (Leiden, 1983); and John M. Montias, *Artists and Artisans in Delft: A Socio-Economic Study of the Seventeenth Century* (Princeton, 1982). On Vermeer see John M. Montias, *Vermeer and His Milieu: A Web of Social History* (Princeton, 1989); Edward A. Snow, *A Study of Vermeer* (Berkeley, 1979); John M. Nash, *The Age of Rembrandt and Vermeer: Dutch Painting in the Seventeenth Century* (London, 1979). Another fine survey is Roland Fleischer and Susan Munshower, *The Age of Rembrandt: Studies in Seventeenth-Century Dutch Painting* (University Park, Pennsylvania, 1988). On Rembrandt's unique art see H. Perry Chapman, *Rembrandt's Self-Portraits: A Study in Seventeenth-Century Identity* (Princeton, 1990), and Svetlana Alpers, *Rembrandt's Enterprise: The Studio and the Market* (Chicago, 1988), a very small but provocative book.

ARCHITECTURE AND SCULPTURE

The standard account of Roman Baroque art is now Torgil Magnuson, *Rome in the Age of Bernini*, 2 vols. (Atlantic Highlands, New Jersey, 1982–86), but the most penetrating and insightful is Jennifer Montagu, *Roman Baroque Sculpture: The Industry of Art* (New Haven, 1989). On Bernini himself see Rudolf Wittkower, *Gian Lorenzo Bernini: The Sculpture of the Roman Baroque*, 3rd ed. (Oxford, 1981); Irving Lavin, *Bernini and the Unity of the Visual Arts*, 2 vols. (New York and Oxford, 1980); Irving Lavin, ed., *Gianlorenzo Bernini: A New Aspect of His Art and Thought* (University Park, Pennsylvania, 1985), a "critical anthology" of widely varying essays; and Cecil Gould, *Bernini in France: An Episode in Seventeenth-Century History* (Princeton, 1982). Other Baroque artists are studied in Anthony Blunt, *Borromini* (London, 1979); Joseph Connors, *Borromini and the Roman Oratory: Style and Society* (Cambridge, Massachusetts, 1980); Charles Avery, *Giambologna: The Complete Sculpture* (Mt. Kisco, New York, 1987); and Edward L. Goldberg, *After Vasari: History, Art, and Patronage in Late Medici Florence* (Princeton, 1989), which focuses on Filippo Baldinucci, curator of Leopoldo de Medici's collections. A brilliant work on Spanish Baroque architecture and history is Jonathan Brown and J.H. Elliott, *A Palace for a King: The Buen Retiro and the Court of Philip IV* (New Haven, 1980).

12 | AN AGE OF ABSOLUTISM AND UPHEAVAL

T HE FIRST FEW DECADES OF THE SEVENTEENTH CENTURY WERE TIMES OF political retrenchment and mounting absolutism in most of Europe. The revolutionary movements and civil disorders in France, the Netherlands, Scotland, England, and even Spain left a deep longing for stability and order. The victory of the *politiques* in France over both Protestant and Catholic extremists opened the way for a political absolutism there and indicated the tendency of the times in other countries as well.

Yet the trend toward authoritarianism did not go unchallenged. This was also the time when constitutionalism began to be a force in the political life of Europe. And discontent among all classes of society erupted in riots, rebellions, and civil war. This age was one of upheaval as well as absolutism.

Princes, Parliaments, and Rebellious Subjects

Absolute monarchy in the late sixteenth and early seventeenth centuries was based on the belief in a ruler with sovereign authority. It was the duty of this sovereign to make laws, to judge all but be judged by none. This aspect of sovereignty was expressed by Jean Bodin in 1576 and echoed a generation later by James I of England. James maintained that the monarch's power was, like God's, absolute, inalienable, and not subject to limitations or resistance. Even a tyrant must be unconditionally obeyed, because to act otherwise was to defy both nature and God. Not everyone agreed with James's declarations of divine sanction, but very few doubted the legitimacy of monarchy itself.

Nevertheless, as the power and majesty of the rulers increased so did their tendency to delegate or resign their authority to lesser courtiers and personal favorites. The first half of the seventeenth century was the heyday of the favorite, who ruled with delegated authority unmatched by anyone else in the kingdom. Not all of the royal favorites were of equal caliber, but the age produced a handful of ministers who were unusually capable and who enjoyed a maximum of royal favor and authority. Of these, Sully in France, Oxenstierna in Sweden, and Olivares in Spain achieved partial success in their political and economic schemes. Above them all stands the towering figure of Cardinal Richelieu and his somewhat less imposing disciple and successor, Mazarin. Together these two statesmen translated the theory of French absolutism into semireality.

Absolute monarchy cannot be understood unless one recognizes that there were still many practical limitations upon the king's power. European society was composed of corporate orders and interest groups clinging jealously to their various privileges and immunities and vying with one another, and with the crown, for prestige and power. The church was such a corporation, although its potency had been reduced, and so were the chartered towns, princes of the blood and the great nobles, officeholders at every level, and provincial governors and estates. Each of these constituted some actual or potential limitation upon the power of the king.

Next to the church, the most organized of these bodies were the various representative institutions that had been functioning in every major country of Europe since the late Middle Ages. England had its Parliament, subordinated to the royal will by the strong Tudor monarchs but still possessing vital powers over revenue. France had its provincial estates as well as a national Estates General, summoned frequently in the late sixteenth century, and notable for its independent and pugnacious attitude toward the crown. Spain had *Cortes* in Castile, Aragon, Catalonia, Valencia, and Navarre. The *Parlamento* of Sicily was active and not fully tamed. Sweden's *Riksdag* elected and deposed kings; the *Landtags* of Brandenburg, Saxony, Hesse, the Rhineland, and Bavaria were constant menaces to the German princes. And, although the imperial Diets offered less opposition to the Holy Roman emperor than they had in the 1530s and 1540s, the Bohemian parliament forced him in 1609 to concede a wide range of financial and religious powers. By 1609 the States General of the Netherlands had taken over sovereign power itself.

In their medieval origins, the parliaments had been used by the kings to counterbalance the great nobles with representatives of the towns and lesser nobility. By the sixteenth century, the functions of parliaments had increased in some areas and decreased in others but usually included petitions and complaints, prevention of misuse of revenues, voting taxes, and consent to laws decreed by the king. Yet it was becoming increasingly difficult to define these spheres of jurisdiction. While crown and court wrangled with the parliaments to mark off their respective powers, many people took the law into their own hands.

The rash of rebellions between the 1580s and the 1650s was caused by more than religious zeal and political dissatisfaction. The addition of serious economic and social crises resulting from oppressive taxes, poor harvests, the devastations of war, and lurching famine triggered popular rebellion in Naples in 1585; the *Croquants* ("clodhoppers") uprising of downtrodden peasants in central and southern France in 1593–95; a serious peasant revolt in Upper Austria from 1595 to 1597; another in Hungary in 1597, followed in 1604–07 by a broader rebellion against Habsburg rule there. In the 1620s and 1630s, another wave of uprisings shocked the European monarchs: in Austria, 1626–

27; England, 1628–31; Hungary, 1631–32; Austria again in 1632–36; Bavaria, 1633–34; the French *Croquants* once more in 1636–37, and the *Nu-Pieds* (barefooted ones) in Normandy in 1639. The 1640s and 1650s witnessed even greater upheavals as the Catalans and Portuguese revolted against Castilian rule in 1640; Palermo and Naples followed suit in 1647–48; Granada in 1648; and Seville and Córdoba in 1652. Russia was shaken by devastating urban uprisings in 1641, 1645, and 1648; Poland in 1651; and Switzerland was struck by peasant war in 1653.

To try to maintain order and enforce the decrees of absolutism, monarchs and their ministers contributed to the increasing impersonality of the state by enlarging the bureaucracy and expanding the function of government through new controls over people's lives. The *ad hoc* sale of offices in France, for example, resulted in a proliferation and superimposition of officials at certain levels. The chaotic overlapping of both financial and judicial responsibilities led to inefficiency and injustice and encouraged favoritism, corruption, and graft. Still, the system of venality made the bourgeoisie an active component of the state and helped make it more loyal to the crown than it had been since the Wars of Religion.

International Relations and Diplomacy

The century from 1560 to 1660 saw the erratic but continuous development of international diplomacy from a limited instrument of alliance and negotiation to a permanent system of interstate communications. From a European point of view, this was a time of recurring civil and international war, a period of religious and dynastic adjustment. The intensity of religious rivalry, added to older dynastic and newer national interests, also made this a crucial time in the development of the theory and practice of international relations.

The "Christian Commonwealth" was gone. Europe was now represented by autonomous national monarchies. For practical purposes, these monarchs needed accurate information, trustworthy negotiation, and reliable representation. The system of continuous diplomatic relations established and carried out through resident embassies, supplemented by special *ad hoc* legations, had been found most valuable in supplying information for the conduct of foreign policy. By the outbreak of the Thirty Years' War in 1618, every ruler of western Europe had resident ambassadors at the courts of both rival and friendly states. Many eastern monarchs were also represented. The system did not always function well, however. Problems of diplomatic immunity, exterritoriality, finances, precedence, and communication constantly plagued the operation of early modern diplomacy. In spite of shortcomings, resident diplomacy proved to be too valuable an instrument to abandon. No monarch liked the idea of foreign subjects nosing about his court and town, sniffing out news to be relayed to their masters. Yet that was the price he had to pay to secure the same opportunity for his own representatives abroad. During times of extreme unrest and ideological war, as in the last three decades of the sixteenth century, diplomacy was strained to its limits. Many embassies were closed, others sank

The Ambassadors. *This famous Hans Holbein double portrait representing the French ambassadors Jean de Dinteville and Georges de Selve also depicts symbols of the sciences, meditation on the vanity of worldly things, and a curious play with perspective.*

to mere spying. Civil war and rebellion compounded the difficulties by increasing the hazards and expenses of legation. But for better or for worse, the system of formal diplomatic relations among states was here to stay.

The proven usefulness of resident ambassadors, and the general acceptance of the methods and purposes of permanent diplomacy by the beginning of the seventeenth century, is reflected in the surge of literature about ambassadors. These treatises on the art of diplomacy appeared during a period when international affairs were becoming the center of thought and discussion, when problems of sovereignty, war and peace, neutral rights, and the law of nations were being examined and reexamined by the best minds of the day. Yet neither the theorists nor the practitioners of diplomacy were able to alter the tide of war that was moving steadily toward its peak in the early years of the seventeenth century.

Religious allegiances still counted for much of the justification, and some of the motivation, of foreign affairs. The creation of the Protestant and Catholic Leagues in 1608–09 indicates the religious polarity of the international scene by that time. Religious zeal helped motivate the Danish and Swedish interventions in the Thirty Years' War. It also determined the direction of Spanish assistance to the Empire in 1618–21. Certainly Ferdinand II's policies in Germany were dictated by religious as well as dynastic considerations. No government relied more on papal support than did Richelieu's France, even as it pursued a vigorous war against Spain. Dynastic-nationalist considerations, however, were equally vital to France. German princes were also solicitous of their family fortunes as they jockeyed for position in the Empire. Finally, considerations by the "absolute" monarchs for the protection and preservation of their sovereignty weighed heavily among the factors determining the direction and character of international affairs.

Yet despite the apparent anarchy of international relations, the community of Europe was neither entirely abandoned nor forgotten. Europe was no longer the religious entity it was conceived to be in the Middle Ages. Yet there remained a sense of community in diversity, a feeling of political maturity in the collective rejection of papal administration, and a tacit recognition of the natural laws of reciprocity in the functioning of interstate relations. Richelieu, symbol of the age of absolutism and power politics, put it this way:

> Kings should be very careful with regard to the treaties they conclude, but having concluded them they should observe them religiously, . . . I maintain that the loss of honor is worse than the loss of life itself. A great prince should sooner put in jeopardy both his own interests and even those of the state than break his word, which he can never violate without losing his reputation and by consequence the greatest instrument of sovereigns.

Richelieu and the Revival of France

The assassin's knife that ended Henri IV's brief reign in 1610 also cut the tenuous cords of communication between the French people and the crown, exposing the country to a new surge of aristocratic disorder. Led by the princes of the blood, the restless French nobility resumed its role of disruption and disturbance.

Little cause existed for confidence in the government of the widowed Marie de' Medici, regent now during the minority of the child-king Louis XIII. A coarse, self-indulgent woman, Marie de' Medici had little grasp of statesmanship. Her rule was weak, as well as corrupt, and gave encouragement to the more opportunistic of the nobles. She exhausted the treasury left by Sully in bribes and subsidies to the lords and in favors to her minions. Nevertheless, she bought time, and time was on her side. Fortunately for France, Marie de' Medici adopted a more cautious foreign policy than her husband had pursued. She sought peace with Spain by a double Habsburg-Bourbon marriage between Louis XIII and Anna, the daughter of Philip III of Spain; and between Louis's sister, Elizabeth, and the future Philip IV. She also showed some political wisdom in her selection of Armand du Plessis, the future Cardinal Richelieu, as secretary minister to handle foreign matters.

By 1614, however, the domestic situation was so bad that the queen regent was forced to summon the Estates General. From the outset, the assembly was

Cardinal Richelieu. *The great statesman is shown full length in his religious robes by Philippe de Champaigne.*

hopelessly divided. The third estate (the representatives of the middle and lower classes) avowed the absolute sovereignty of the king; the second estate (the nobles) proclaimed their own authority to rule; and the first estate (the clergy) declared the supremacy of God and the papacy. After four months of wrangling, the Estates General was dissolved, not to meet again for 175 years. The centrifugal forces had all but reduced France to a jumble of rival principalities by 1617 when the young king (now sixteen years of age), with the aid of his favorite, the duc de Luynes, seized control of the government and sent the queen mother and the rest of her court into exile. Yet intrigue, confusion, and vacillation continued for another seven years under the misrule of Luynes and his successor, La Vieuville. In 1624 Louis XIII was reconciled with his mother and admitted the talented Cardinal Richelieu to the royal council. A new day was dawning for France.

Immediately Louis XIII and Richelieu formed a partnership that was to prove profitable to each and ultimately advantageous to France. Louis XIII was a man of high intelligence but limited political ability. He was also neurotic and incapable of making great decisions of state. Yet he was aware of his own limitations and acknowledged the need for an able minister to conduct the affairs of government. He recognized Richelieu's abilities and allowed him almost total freedom to pursue his policies of state with the authority of the crown to back him up.

Richelieu was born in 1585 of a noble family of Poitou. He studied at the Collège de Navarre before graduating from the military academy. When his brother decided to give up a church career, Richelieu condescended to take his place "for the good of the Church and the glory of our house." He was rewarded with the bishopric of Luçon, and quickly began his climb to fame and success. He acted as spokesman for the clergy at the Estates General of 1614, winning the regent's attention by his clear elucidation of the current political problems. For the next ten years, his star rose and fell according to the fortunes of his matron. From the beginning, Richelieu was a ruthless, ambitious man who possessed willpower and determination. He also had intellectual ability, a quick and penetrating mind, and great powers of concentration and memory. At the same time, he was a man of action, with a zest for hard work down to the minutest detail.

The prime objectives of Richelieu's policy were the achievement of royal absolutism in France and the establishment of French power abroad. The cardinal's first crusade was against the Huguenots, who had already taken up arms and been defeated in 1622. Two years later, they rebelled again, and Richelieu, determined to destroy their ability to resist, laid siege to La Rochelle. For more than a year, the stalwart citizens held out but were finally reduced to such starvation and disease that they were forced to surrender, relinquishing as they did their former autonomy and privileges.

In the meantime, Richelieu had already started to crack down on the nobility. In 1626 a plot to overthrow the government and kill Richelieu was uncovered. Its instigator was the king's brother, Gaston, duc d'Orléans. The cardinal moved quickly. Gaston and his mother were sent into exile after an abortive *coup,* known as the Day of Dupes; a short time later, young Montmorency-Bouteville was hanged for fighting a duel in defiance of the royal order. In 1632 Richelieu put to death the disobedient governor of Languedoc. To break the power of the nobles and make the king absolute ruler, Richelieu strengthened and expanded the royal bureaucracy, making it an instrument of the crown rather than an asylum of privilege and vested interest. He reorganized the royal council, reducing its numbers and providing lesser councils for executive details. The great nobles, who were the governors of provinces, were gradually replaced by crown appointees. To strengthen royal control, he reactivated the office of *intendant,* a crown-appointed officer sent into the provinces to supervise the courts and the royal administration.

In financial matters Richelieu was not particularly innovative. With the exception of the supervisory role of the *intendants,* tax collection in France remained antiquated and wasteful, as it had been for centuries. Many of the taxes were still farmed out. The *taille* was irregularly assessed and inefficiently collected, with those who were most able to pay enjoying partial or complete exemption. Oblivious to its long-term effects, Richelieu recklessly expanded the sale of offices in order to acquire more money for France's military strength. His only other scheme for increasing revenues was to raise taxes. Yet he still spent more than the royal treasury received, and deficits swelled the debt ten-fold during the period of his ministry. To challenge and surpass Habsburg power, Richelieu saw only that money must be spent, armies created, and fortifications strengthened. It was up to Claude Bullion and successive *surintendants de finance* to provide the means.

Although he concentrated on building a land army, Richelieu did not neglect the sea. In his first year of power, he created a Council of the Marine, and a year later made himself grand master and superintendent general of navigation and commerce. Soon the Normandy ports were buzzing with activity. Shipbuilding took on a new priority; arsenals were established; schools of navigation and seamanship were founded. By 1635 the French Atlantic Fleet had been increased to more than thirty fighting vessels, and the Mediterranean galleys were almost as numerous.

The new navy was not only a weapon for defending French coasts and attacking Spanish shipping but also a means of providing protection for an accelerated program of commerce and colonization. Richelieu had hopes of making France the center of European trade. Joint-stock trading companies were organized for commercial colonization in America. Eager explorers, trappers, and merchants followed up Samuel de Champlain's Canadian explorations of 1605–09 and began harvesting a wealth of furs in the American northeast, known then as New France. At the same time, the French began showing persistent interest in the West Indies and its sugar trade, acquiring the fertile islands of Martinique and Guadeloupe in 1636.

Yet surpassing his interest in commerce and colonization was Richelieu's obsession for foreign affairs; his goal was to outmaneuver and outstrike the Habsburg enemies who encircled France. In 1625, long before he was militarily ready for a showdown with Spain, Richelieu quietly sent an army into the Alps and seized the Valtelline, that vital pass running from the north end of Lake Como, in Italy, eastward along the River Adda to Austria. The Valtelline was normally controlled by the Protestant Grisons, the mountain communities of southeastern Switzerland that were attached to, but not part of, the Swiss Confederation. The genius of Richelieu's strike is obvious. The Valtelline was the pass through which Spanish troops and supplies moved northward into Germany to add their strength to the Habsburg cause. Richelieu followed this coup with another in Mantua where he succeeded, against the claims of Savoy and the threats of Spain and Austria, in securing the Mantuan succession for the duke of Nevers, and with it a strong French base of support in northern Italy. In the meantime, Richelieu's diplomacy paid off in the north as he persuaded the Swedish king, Gustavus Adolphus, to lead an army into Germany against the Habsburgs. Then four years later, France itself entered the war as an open belligerent.

Mazarin and the Fronde

Richelieu's involvement in the Thirty Years' War led to new unrest and rebellion at home. In December 1642 Richelieu died, followed to the grave five months later by the king. Rebellion and disorder erupted again. The scepter of power passed to Richelieu's chosen successor, Cardinal Giulio Mazarini (gallicized as Mazarin), a suave Neapolitan diplomat who carried on Richelieu's policies for the next eighteen years during the minority of Louis XIV. Mazarin was intelligent and capable, but he did not possess either the willpower or the ruthless dedication of his mentor. Furthermore, he was a foreigner, Italian by birth and Spanish by culture, who could never hope to win the devotion or respect of the majority of the French people.

In one last effort to resist the growth of absolutism, civil war, known as the *Fronde,* erupted in 1648. It was led by the Parlement de Paris in a desperate demonstration against the arbitrary acts of the crown, especially in matters of finance. Claiming the power of the purse in the absence of the Estates General and seeking to secure some measure of general protection against the dreaded *lettres de cachet* (royal orders for arbitrary arrest), the Parlement demanded a reduction of the *taille* and alterations in its method of collection, the recall of the *intendants,* and an end to the venality of offices. In May and June 1648, an assembly of deputies from the Parlement and the sovereign courts proposed a major reform of the government, demanding not only an overhaul of the financial administration but also the right of *habeus corpus* (the right to a speedy trial) against arbitrary arrest.

The government reacted by arresting Pierre Broussel and other leaders of Parlement. Immediately the barricades went up, and civil war began. By October the government was forced to release Broussel and accept the Parlement's demands. The queen regent and the young king fled for safety to Saint Germain. As they did, the prince of Condé and his army were summoned to put down the rebellion in Paris. For three months Condé besieged the city, laying waste the surrounding countryside and cutting off all routes of supply or support. Resistance, however, was defiant. The *frondeurs* would not give up. Finally a negotiated settlement was reached in April 1649, ending the parlementary *Fronde.*

No sooner was the bourgeois rebellion over than a new crisis was created by the ambitious nobility. Condé, as prince of the blood and victorious general, demanded new honors and offices. So did others. In January 1650, after failing in an attempt to replace Mazarin, Condé, his brother, and his brother-in-law were arrested and imprisoned in the fortress of Vincennes. This act became the rallying point for other nobles and malcontents, and precipitated a new uprising, *la Fronde de la noblesse* (the revolt of the nobles).

The motley combination of landed nobles, *parlementaires,* and soldiers of fortune had little in common other than jealousy of one another and hatred of Mazarin, who now fled Paris to save his life. The *frondeurs* might have found a unifying leader in Gaston d'Orléans, the king's nefarious uncle, but he lacked both courage and conviction; or in the ambitious Cardinal de Retz, uncrowned king of Paris, but he was too personally ambitious to reconcile the divergent elements into a party of constitutional reform. By September 1651, enough friction had been created between Condé and the other nobles that he left Paris to join Spanish forces in the north. At the same time Mazarin succeeded in having Louis XIV declared of age, thus undercutting Gaston's pretentions to the throne. By the end of 1652 the *Fronde* had burned itself out.

Once more the task of recovery was resumed. The collapse of the *Fronde* brought discredit as well as defeat to those who had been a part of it and cleared the way for the final stage in the development of absolutism in France. The great nobles were disgraced; the Parlement de Paris was debarred from political and financial affairs; Paris was disenfranchised. For the next eight years, king and cardinal worked together to reestablish the credibility and power of the crown and restore peace to the realm. The war with Spain was brought to a favorable conclusion in the Peace of the Pyrenees in 1659, sealed by the marriage of Louis XIV to the *infanta* (daughter of the king) of Spain, Maria Teresa. When Mazarin died in March 1661, all of Richelieu's political objectives had been realized. The king was supreme in France; France was supreme in Europe.

English Absolutism and Overseas Expansion

James I (1603–25) ascended the throne of England (after reigning twenty-three years as King James VI of Scotland) at an inopportune time. Problems of finance, constitution, and religion, which had long been postponed or ignored, could no longer be neglected. Some of the same conditions and tensions that brought civil war to France forty years earlier now threatened the tranquility of England. The situation called for intelligence, statesmanship, and moderation, but the Stuarts were not overly gifted with any of these traits. The new English king, the thirty-seven-year-old son of Mary Queen of Scots, was, like his mother and his son, a tragic individual. He was well-meaning, temperate, reasonably tolerant (for an age of unbounded intolerance), well-schooled, and a devotee of peace. He was also pedantic and impractical. The logic of his political writings was sound but their wisdom was questionable. James believed in the divine right of kings, that monarchs are subject to no authority save God, and are unrestrained by human laws or sociopolitical interests. They are, in fact, James said, "breathing images of God on earth. . . . [Kings] are not only God's lieutenants upon earth and sit upon God's throne, but even by God himself they are called God." To James, church, Parliament, and common law courts were service organizations of the crown, not sharers of its sovereignty.

Antagonism between the king and Parliament began as soon as James reached London in 1603. In its very first session, Parliament began to assert its own claims to financial and legislative supremacy. The Commons, especially, were outspoken against the pretensions of the king. Parliament based its claim of authority on rather shaky historical precedents, but it refused to back down. In one issue after another, king and Parliament locked horns in dispute. Impasse followed, and in 1611 James dismissed the assembly.

The king's relationship with dissenting religious groups was no less stormy. Both Calvinists and Catholics were hopeful that the new regime would be more favorable to them than Elizabeth's had been. Puritans believed that the new king, coming from Calvinist Scotland, would patronize their religious views and support their social ethics. Catholics, on the other hand, expected James to be more sympathetic to their faith, probably because it was the faith of his

James I of England. *The first Stuart king's aloofness and reserve are emphasized in this well-known painting by Daniel Mytens.*

mother. Both were mistaken. At the Hampton Court Conference in 1604, James made it clear that he would tolerate no nonsense from the Puritans. He disliked Scottish Presbyterianism in the first place, and he was alarmed by a Puritan plea, known as the Millenary Petition, for major alterations in the Anglican service. He followed his threat, to "harry them out of the land" if they did not conform, with the dismissal of some 300 clergymen who had Puritan leanings. His treatment of the dissenters added to the growing body of opposition in the House of Commons, since the Puritan gentry now formed a substantial part of that body.

James's policy toward the Catholics seems at first to have been more understanding. He lifted some of the bans against Catholics in England, remitted recusancy fines (levied against those who refused to attend Anglican services), and proposed a plan to allow them private exercise of religion. However, alarmed by the sudden growth of the Catholic congregations, James not only reversed his decision but also ordered the immediate expulsion of all Catholic priests. In the summer of 1605, several of the priests who did not leave were arrested and peremptorily hanged. Anti-Catholic feeling reached a crescendo in December when a Catholic plot to blow up the houses of Parliament while Parliament was in session was discovered. Guy Fawkes (who, along with certain Jesuit and Catholic leaders, was arrested and executed) and the Gunpowder Plot quickly became the symbol of Catholic treachery and the justification for the resumption of vigorous anti-Catholic repression.

English foreign policy under James was dedicated to establishing and maintaining peace. The first step in that policy was a settlement with Spain in 1604. Peace was unpopular, yet it did allow a military respite that the nation could sorely use. Yet England could not remain aloof from the diplomatic power struggle that was taking place in Europe. In 1610 James joined the Protestant Union, formed in 1608 among the Protestant states of Germany, and married his daughter to Frederick, Count Palatine of the Rhine, the militant leader of the Union in Germany. Nevertheless, James hesitated to take further steps toward a commitment to Protestant Europe. He fancied himself a peacemaker, a mature mediator, who was not only anxious to stay out of war but also hoped to prevent one from beginning. He believed that an alliance between England and Spain would have the effect of curbing Spanish military threats, thus avoiding a possible conflict between Catholic and Protestant powers on the continent.

He was encouraged in this line of thought by the astute Spanish ambassador, Diego Sarmiento de Acuña, count of Gondomar. Gondomar was sent to England in 1614 for the express purpose of keeping that country neutral in any European conflict, and to prevent English pirates from harassing Spanish trade in America. By playing on James's desire for peace, Gondomar was able to attain most of his goals, climaxing his embassy in 1618 with the execution of Sir Walter Raleigh for molesting Spanish settlements in Guiana.

The keystone of James's policy was to have been a marriage alliance between his son Charles and the Spanish *infanta*. Negotiations for the match were carried on intermittently for eight years, but in the end the high Spanish price and growing anti-Spanish feeling in England prevented its conclusion. Even after the outbreak of the Thirty Years' War and his son-in-law's intervention and disaster in Bohemia, James persisted in his marriage negotiations with Spain, hoping thereby to prevent an escalation of the conflict. His efforts were futile, however, both in obtaining a Spanish bride for his son and in deterring the spread of war. By 1624, Puritan pressures to aid the Dutch, and the danger of new Spanish victories in the Lowlands, forced James to intervene with a military force.

English Colonization in America   In the meantime, the first English penetration of the Spanish colonial monopoly launched English colonizing ventures in America. More in spite of James I than through his support, London merchants organized a colonizing company for settling and trading in Virginia. In 1607 its first expedition planted a colony upriver from the Chesapeake Bay, naming it Jamestown in honor of the king. Difficult weather, lack of food and little desire to grow their own, harassment by Indians, and rampant disease almost destroyed the colony. Most of the settlers died within the first two years. Reinforcements from the newly chartered Virginia Company, the gradual realization that any wealth acquired would have to come from sweat and toil rather than from picking up gold nuggets, and the introduction of tobacco cultivation, combined to salvage the colony and eventually make it a successful enterprise.

The second permanent English settlement was the Plymouth Colony, established in 1620 by the Pilgrims, a voluntary joint-stock company composed of religious separatists from London, Southampton, and Leiden, Holland. It was later annexed to the larger Massachusetts Bay Colony, founded a few years later by other Puritans from England. Neither colony produced the economic wealth that it expected to, but they did plant a legacy of representative self-government in the colony with the Mayflower Compact, by which its signatories agreed to unite in a political-religious society and obey the laws that would subsequently be made.

From an economic point of view, other ventures were proving to be more profitable. This period was one of commercial expansion for England as well as for France and the Netherlands. The American colonies were only a small part of that activity. The Spanish monopoly in the West Indies was penetrated by English seamen and merchants in the first three decades of the seventeenth century. Saint Kitts was settled in 1624, and shortly afterward Nevis, Montserrat, Antigua, Trinidad, and Tobago. Barbados, that hidden jewel of the Caribbean, was claimed in 1625 and soon provided shelter for thousands of English colonizers who believed that England had become overpopulated. It also produced quick wealth from the sale of cotton, tobacco, and sugar.

In the Levant and the Near East, English merchants made serious inroads into the Portuguese empire. Pepper from the Malabar Coast was brought to London in the English ships of the Levant Company and its successor, the newly chartered (1600) joint-stock East India Company. The latter also brought cotton from Surat and Gujarat in northwestern India, as well as sugar, saltpeter, and great amounts of valuable indigo. Persian silks were imported after 1617. These were exchanged for smaller quantities of English textiles, lead, and tin. Although modest in comparison with the Spanish, Portuguese, and Dutch, English shipping in the early seventeenth century laid the foundation for a worldwide commercial empire.

Charles I and the Parliamentary Revolt

The situation of England was not good in 1625 when James I died and was succeeded by his son, Charles, who inherited a full-scale war with Spain, a war the country could not afford to continue, much less win. In addition, James had agreed to pay for men to assist the Dutch in their campaigns against Spain, and for 7,000 Danish troops in Germany. A marriage alliance between Charles and Henrietta Maria of France further committed the nation to costly political involvements on the continent.

Charles I was not the ruler to lead England out of these difficulties. He was vain, stubborn, and uncompromising, with the same exalted view of kingship that his father had. Nevertheless, Charles was not a "bad" king. He was religious, generally intelligent, and in most things moderate. He felt the responsibility of his high station and brought dignity and propriety to it. He was well-meaning, in the broadest sense, without the ruthlessness and cruelty that marred the character of some of his predecessors. Having a taste for beauty, he became one of the greatest royal patrons of the arts. He was noble in the face of adversity and even death, but in life he was incapable of understanding the forces and the issues that divided England. In most aspects of character and personality, he was equal to his contemporaries, Louis XIII and Philip IV. However, Charles had no Richelieu at the helm. Charles's favorite, the duke of Buckingham, was handsome, adroit, and loyal, but totally incapable of managing the affairs of a nation; William Laud, archbishop of Canterbury, was an austere and vindictive religious reactionary; the earl of Strafford, the king's chief advisor after Buckingham's death, was domineering and ambitious.

Charles I's reign began in tragedy and ended in disaster. Parliament was summoned to grant money for the war with Spain. After the fiery opening session, in which the Commons demanded constitutional reforms and the redress of grievances before considering subsidies, Parliament reluctantly granted Tonnage and Poundage (custom duties usually assigned to the crown) for one year only, and agreed to a small additional grant for the war. When its members drafted letters of impeachment against Buckingham, Charles dissolved the Parliament. Three months later, word was received of the complete failure of the English expedition against Cadiz and its tragic voyage home. Soon England found itself also at war with France and licking wounded pride after Buckingham failed to relieve La Rochelle.

The Parliament that convened in 1628 was more disagreeable than previous ones had been. Instead of granting the king the financial subsidies he wanted, they passed the Petition of Right, which prohibited arbitrary taxation, arbitrary arrest and imprisonment, the billeting of soldiers in private homes, and the imposition of martial law in peacetime. The House of Commons followed this bill with a remonstrance against the abuses of both church and state, for which they held Archbishop Laud and Buckingham responsible, and another against the king for his illegal collection of Tonnage and Poundage. Charles adjourned Parliament for six months, but when its members returned in January 1629, they were even more outspoken than before. After a stormy session during which nine MPs were arrested, Charles dissolved the Parliament, and for the next eleven years ruled England as an absolute monarch, raising money by various expedients. The most hated of his taxes was Ship Money, a tax previously levied on seaboard towns to finance coastal defense, which Charles extended to the whole country. Furthermore, he used the money not for defense but to finance his government in the absence of Parliament.

As illegal and semilegal taxes made more and more of the middle class hostile to the crown, and the landed gentry was being disturbed by tenure fines, the religious schism continued to widen. Puritans were disturbed by the policies of Archbishop Laud, who made great use of the pulpit, ecclesiastical courts, and visitation to browbeat the clergy and the people. Distressed by government restrictions on the use of the press and the pulpit, Puritans became increasingly bitter and even hostile toward the government. Surreptitious attacks on High Church policies and on those responsible for the policies became more frequent. By 1640 the Puritans were almost completely estranged from the church, and due to the marriage of Anglicanism with the crown, dangerously hostile to the government of Charles I. Parliament had to be summoned again.

The Long Parliament, so-called because it continued to function in one form or another from November 1640 until March 1660, began its tempestuous life by impeaching both Strafford and Laud. Next it passed the revolutionary Triennial Act, requiring the convening of Parliament every three years, with or without the king's consent. This action was followed by the abolition of the Court of Star Chamber and the Court of High Commission. Strafford was convicted of high treason and executed on 12 May 1641. With his death died Charles's last chance for a royal victory like that of the king of France. By the end of the year Parliament was ready to present King Charles with the Grand Remonstrance, a summary of all the grievances held against him by Parliament and the people. The king responded by entering the House of Commons with an armed escort to arrest John Pym and four other parliamentary leaders. Warned of his intent, they took refuge elsewhere in London. Charles retired to York, where he was joined by most of the Lords and some sixty members of Commons. The remaining 150 members of Commons, mostly Puritans, led by Pym and a few peers, constituted themselves the Parliament of England and continued to meet at Westminster.

When, during the summer of 1642, Parliament placed the elderly earl of Essex in command of a motley army of 20,000 poorly trained and ill-equipped infantry, supported by some 4,000 cavalry, and the king presented his royal army at Nottingham, the constitutional phase of the English Revolution was over. The military phase now began.

Civil War and Revolution

The war was fought by two minorities. Most people's sympathies were divided and their enthusiasm for the war was slight. The main supporters of the royalist side, known as Cavaliers, were a majority of the peers and landed aristocracy, the Anglican clergy (and all those of any class who sought to defend the church), and a segment of the peasantry. Parliamentary supporters, known as Roundheads, included some of the great nobles, the depressed landed gentry, the merchants and tradesmen, and Puritans of various persuasions, from Presbyterians to Sectarians and Independents. The Roundhead ranks were also inflated with a cross-section of revolutionaries, malcontents, and dissenters, including some English Catholics. The majority of the people were uncommitted to either side of a conflict that seemed to promise only violence and loss no matter who won. The parliamentary forces, which occupied London and most

Oliver Cromwell. *This anonymous portrait reveals some of the vigorous determination of the Puritan leader, as well as his staunch devotion.*

of the south and southeast, had the advantage of money, seaports, and the fleet. Until the advent of Cromwell, however, they lacked both leadership and persuasive goals.

Oliver Cromwell emerged as the champion of the Roundheads in 1643. He had previously sat as a member of Parliament, and more recently served in the army of the earl of Essex. Cromwell was the leader of the Puritan laity in East Anglia. He belonged to the landed gentry and always retained the tastes and sentiments of a nobleman. He possessed both land and wealth, and opposed any social revolution, or leveling of the classes, as vigorously as he objected to the king's irresponsible imposition of taxes. Like many of his class, Oliver Cromwell was a Puritan—not the more conventional Presbyterian variety but instead a radical, dedicated crusader whose party was known as the Independents. He believed, and infused his followers with the faith, that they were fighting in the Lord's cause. This vibrant spirit pervaded all of Cromwell's thoughts and actions. His work was God's work. His battles were God's battles.

Cromwell scoured the eastern counties for the sturdy Puritan yeomen who made up the backbone of his "Ironsides," as his regiment was called. "I raised such men as had the fear of God before them," he proclaimed, believers who took a covenant to walk and fight with the Lord. For them the war was a crusade. Before crusading, however, he trained and drilled them until they could fight as a disciplined and dedicated army. The turning point came at the Battle of Marston Moor, in July 1644, when Cromwell's cavalry defeated

Prince Rupert, the royalists' general, and won the north for Parliament. A year later, the several parliamentary armies were consolidated and put under the supreme command of Lord Fairfax, with Cromwell as lieutenant general. These forces were formed into the New Model Army with Cromwell's cavalry regiments becoming its nucleus.

In June 1645 the king was decisively defeated at the Battle of Naseby and the royalist cause collapsed. Serious schisms, however, were now showing up in Parliament. Disagreements between the war party and the peace party, between Independents and Presbyterians, and between Parliament and the army, prolonged the negotiations with the captive king. When Parliament ordered the troops to disband without pay, Cromwell and the army marched on London. In the midst of this disorder, Charles fled to the Isle of Wight where he signed a secret treaty with the Scots to help restore him to the throne.

Early in 1648, Parliament, now dominated by Cromwell and the army officers, took the step it had hitherto been loath to take. It renounced its allegiance to the king. Few people outside the radical "Levellers" and "Diggers," who advocated abolition of monarchy altogether, had previously considered the expedient of republicanism. Even Parliament thought of itself as loyal to the principle of "King and Parliament." Almost everyone considered monarchy to be the only workable form of government. Parliament's protracted negotiations with Charles were based on the assumption that the king would continue to reign while allowing wide financial and political powers to the assembly. However, discovery of the latest "treason" of the king in calling in the Scots caused many to change their allegiance.

War broke out again with a rising in South Wales, followed by the royalist seizure of Berwick and Carlisle, and by uprisings in Kent and Essex. The Scottish invasion into Lancashire came in August 1648, too late to support the royalist rising, and Cromwell was able to annihilate the invading army at Preston. Triumphantly, the army now took matters into its own hands. Parliament was purged of all those who were known to favor the restoration of the king. The Rump Parliament, composed of the remaining sixty members of Commons and guided by Cromwell and the army, appointed a High Court of Justice to try the king for treason. Denying the authority or legitimacy of the court, Charles refused to answer its questions. The court found Charles guilty anyway and sentenced him to death. He was beheaded at Whitehall on 30 January 1649.

Cromwell and the Puritan Commonwealth

England was now a republic—or Commonwealth, as it was called—ruled by the small minority of the House of Commons that had been elected nine years before. The House of Lords, along with the monarchy, was abolished, and "the Commons of England, in parliament assembled, being chosen by, and representing the people, have the supreme power in this nation." This Parliament, about one-tenth the size of the original Long Parliament, conducted the affairs of England for four years, in precarious coalition with the army.

The first crisis of the new government was one common to all revolutions. How long and how far should it go; where should it stop? Among the more radical elements in the Commonwealth were the Levellers, followers of John Lilborne, who believed in freedom of speech, toleration, and a democratic republic based on the consent of all the people. Leveller ideas soon infiltrated the army and led to discontent and mutiny. Fearing that the revolution would be carried beyond the "respectable" goals of the ruling classes, Cromwell smashed the incipient movement by force. In the meantime, disorder and insurrection in Ireland forced him to lead an expedition into the difficult Emerald Isle and put the dissenters to the sword. After this bloody Irish campaign, Cromwell, now elevated to captain general and commander-in-chief, led an army into Scotland against the followers of the king's son, who was proclaimed Charles II by the rebel Scots. In a masterful campaign ending in the battle of Worcester, September 1651, Cromwell completely destroyed the Scottish resistance. Charles escaped to France, where he bided his time until a more favorable day.

In the meantime, growing friction between Parliament and the army led to a constitutional showdown. In 1653 Cromwell dismissed the Rump, dissolved the Council of State, and instituted the so-called Protectorate. A written constitution (England's first and last), known as the Instrument of Government, provided for a single executive body composed of the lord protector (Cromwell) and a cooperative council of twenty-one. Parliament was composed of 460 members who were to meet triennially in sessions of no less than five months. The new government was short-lived. Frequent clashes between Parliament and protector resulted in Cromwell's dissolving the Parliament entirely in January 1655 and governing without a legislative body until another Parliament could be elected twenty months later. This Parliament continued, under the lord protector's tutelage, for a year and a half. Seven months after its adjournment, Cromwell died.

It is not easy to assess Oliver Cromwell's place in history. Three hundred years later he is still a controversial figure. Above all, he was a religiously motivated man, convinced by his dedicated Calvinist ethic that he was serving God. There were obvious contradictions in his character, between his championing of toleration and his massacre of Irish Catholics, between his advocacy of parliamentary government and his authoritarian dismissal of Parliament. Yet the Puritan spirit of Cromwell's politics provided a kind of consistency that demands some respect despite its exacting dogmatism, for Cromwell was a man of action, translating his biblical fervor into political achievement or military power. He loved and believed in his country, yet he distrusted both king and people. He wanted freedom and tolerance, but recognized the dangers of disorder and anarchy.

He was, without doubt, a great military leader. His armies were small and his campaigns less than grandiose, but his organizing ability, disciplinary leadership, and keen tactical sense made him one of the great commanders of the age. He was less successful as a political leader, although here, too, his ideological zeal carried him through many crises that would have ended the career of a lesser man. He was a moral force through the vicissitudes of civil war and political upheaval. No great innovator, and without a preconceived plan for the government of England, he was nonetheless an astute political tactician who could make the best of a situation. He was responsible for some of the disorder of the 1640s, but he made the 1650s a less chaotic time than it might have been without him.

A year and a half after Cromwell's death, the monarchy was reestablished in England. However, it was no longer an absolute monarchy; that was forever destroyed. Charles II and all his successors had to recognize the fundamental role of Parliament in English government. Likewise all nations now had to recognize the role of England in world affairs. Cromwell's conduct of foreign affairs was bold, if not always wise, and placed England once and for all at the forefront of international affairs and established its claim as a leading power, both in Europe and overseas.

The United Netherlands

The third nation to marshal its human and natural resources and rise to leadership and power in the first half of the seventeenth century was the Netherlands. Like France and England, the Netherlands was an Atlantic power, illustrating the shift of the economic and political center of gravity from the Mediterranean to the Atlantic seaboard. The Dutch ascendance was directly linked with Mediterranean decline, especially with the Spanish eclipse and the stagnation of the Portuguese empire.

The political structure of the seven United Provinces of the Netherlands was a great anomaly. The long and chaotic war with Spain had resulted in the creation of an *ad hoc* state, republican in form yet quasimonarchical in principle. The revolt against Spain had been a conservative revolution, holding fast to ancient traditions and reluctant to experiment recklessly. The predominant Dutch notion of political freedom was medieval in both conception and scope: the guarantee of limited and specific privileges, exemption from overall laws, corporate and class exemption from certain economic burdens. The constitution of the Union was intended to guarantee these freedoms. It was a federal republic, in which a maximum of autonomy was preserved by the provincial states and a minimum allowed to the central organ, the States General. Inefficiency was also guaranteed by the requirement of unanimous approval of the states for any major action of the States General. This veto power made normal functioning of the assembly almost impossible.

The highest official in the federal government was the *stadtholder*, who represented to the states the sovereign power of the nonexistent king. The powers of the States General, provincial states, and stadtholder not only were ill-defined and overlapping but also conflicted frequently with the interests or ambitions of the nobles and of the towns. Further confusion resulted from the unequal position of Holland in the federation. With its wealthy cities of Dordrecht, Rotterdam, Leiden, Haarlem, The Hague, and especially Amsterdam, Holland exerted the greatest influence upon the States General. The central organs of government thus effectively cancelled one another out and left the exercise of responsibility to the individual states and the local towns, each of which was dominated by urban oligarchies and merchant guilds.

The weaknesses and contradictions of the government were clearly revealed between 1609 and 1621, during the truce with Spain. By 1607 Maurice of Nassau, prince of Orange and royal stadtholder after the death in 1584 of his father, William the Silent, led the northern states to military victory and successful independence from Spain, a fact the Spanish government was unwilling to recognize. Maurice capitalized on his own popularity and the prestige of the House of Orange to win the loyalty of the nobility and the support of the Reformed church. However, the disproportionate strength of Holland gave its advocate-general, Jan Oldenbarneveldt, a unique position in Dutch affairs. The 1609 truce, largely Oldenbarneveldt's work, was opposed by Maurice and by those who believed a continuation of the war would favor Dutch commercial interests.

The lines of disagreement between the war faction and the peace faction hardened even more over the serious religious split between the orthodox Calvinism of the Reformed church and advocates of greater religious toleration. The latter, known as Arminians—after the theologian, Jacob Arminius (1560–1609), who opposed strict Calvinist predestinarianism with belief in free will and taught that salvation might be earned through faith and good works—challenged the narrowly predestinarian church. Arminius held that justification was a cooperative venture between the human and divine, not a deterministic decree from an autocratic God. He taught further that "reason is a revelation from God, through which man's free will operates." Here was Erasmus speaking again. The split widened after 1610, when the Arminians issued a formal Remonstrance setting forth their humanistic views. This document (which gave its authors and supporters the name of Remonstrants) rejected predestination, irresistible grace, and other tenets of orthodox Calvinism, substituting for them personal piety and reason.

Oldenbarneveldt sided with the Remonstrants, advocating, in addition, a political system of provincial autonomy and local rule. This, of course, not only threatened the authority of the established church, it ran counter to the centralizing ambitions of the House of Orange. Maurice and the States General resolved to summon a national synod. The Remonstrants appealed to the provincial states of Holland, which stoutly maintained that a national synod would be an infringement of the religious rights of the provincial states. Maurice immediately took up arms in the name of union and forced the provincial states to agree to a synod. Arminianism lost and Oldenbarneveldt was doomed. The Synod of Dort, November 1618, upheld the strict Calvinism of the Reformed church, accepted the Dutch Confession, and declared Arminians heretics. Oldenbarneveldt was arrested and tried by an appointed commission. Accused of seeking to divide and dissolve the union, he was found guilty and beheaded on 13 May 1619.

The Synod of Dort. *An engraving by Claes Jansz Visscher shows the great assembly of Protestant theologians that met at Dordrecht in 1618.*

In 1621 the Twelve-Year Truce ended and the war with Spain was resumed. Now, however, it was a Europewide conflagration. Maurice had some success against the Spanish *tercios*, but not like his successes before 1609. The key city of Breda surrendered to Ambrosio Spinola in May 1625, just a month after Maurice died. He was succeeded as stadtholder, captain-general, and head of the Council of State by his brother, Frederick Henry, who proved to be almost as great a general as Maurice, and considerably more skillful as a politician. As the war united the people of the Netherlands against their common enemy, it also brought the prince of Orange into a position analogous to that of the monarchs of neighboring countries, despite the decentralization of Dutch politics. In the 1640s Frederick Henry hoped to further enhance his dynastic ambitions by conquering and partitioning the Spanish Netherlands between himself and France. At the same time he was assisting his Stuart relative, Charles I, to regain the throne of England.

In both endeavors Frederick Henry failed, but not without leaving his son, William II, a legacy of imperialism and centralization. William learned his lessons well. When he succeeded his father in 1647, he made no secret of his ambitions. Disapproving of the peace that ended the Thirty Years' War in 1648 because it reduced his military powers, he turned to a frontal attack on the States General and on those who spoke up for states' rights. On the verge of victory, William was struck down by smallpox, leaving behind a relieved States General and a pregnant wife, heavy with the son who would one day become ruler of both the Netherlands and England and defy the might of Louis XIV. In the meantime, the Dutch, under a new grand pensionary of Holland, Jan de Witt, were reaching the zenith of their naval and commercial power.

Dutch Economic Power

Dutch wealth began with fish. As early as the thirteenth century, herring fishing in the Baltic and North Seas provided an easily marketable product of Dutch trade with the Baltic countries of the north, and with France and Spain in the south. When opportunities appeared, as during the Hundred Years' War when French and English trade was reduced to a trickle, Dutch seamen and merchants were quick to take advantage of the situation. By the time the dukes of Burgundy became rulers of the Lowlands, prosperity was evident in many parts. The southern Netherlands had then become the leading producers of cloth, but it was the successful marketing of that cloth throughout Europe that brought the greatest promise for the future. Even during the terrible years of the duke of Alba, Dutch commerce expanded in both volume and diversity. By the end of the sixteenth century, Dutch ships were not only the leading carriers of European products but had also become the masters of world commerce. Trade with the Levant, Persia, India, and the East Indies added further wealth and preeminence.

Paradoxically, the Dutch prospered under an economic system that was considered antiquated in the sixteenth century and had been or was being abandoned by most other countries. Yet the absence of state interference in the expanding Dutch trade allowed maximum opportunity for the commercial elements, especially in the towns of Holland and Zeeland. These elements were also favored by the relative absence of competitors and by the crucial location of the Netherlands at the conjunction of the sea lanes and the continental waterways. All regions of the Netherlands were accessible to the coastal ports by river, sea, lake, and canal; they were also linked by the great river systems of the Maas, Scheldt, and Rhine to the heart of the European continent. Ocean vessels sailed all the way from Rotterdam to Basel, Switzerland, without transferring cargo or crossing a lock.

Although the development of Dutch commercial enterprise was accomplished by relatively few and simple commercial organizations, those that were created functioned effectively. After 1594, when four Dutch trading ships sailed to Java, encroachment into the Portuguese eastern empire became commonplace. By 1600 many Dutch fleets had completed the circuit to the Spice Islands and southeast Asia, and after establishing alliances and bases in Am-

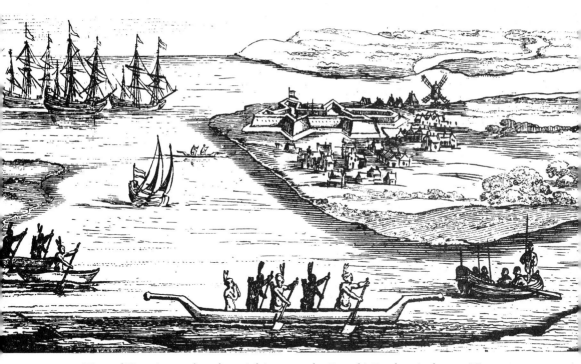

View of New Amsterdam *from Adriaen van der Donck's* Beschryvinghe van Nieuw-Nederlant *(1655). This remarkable earliest view of New York harbor shows lower Manhattan Island, Fort Amsterdam (now the Battery), New Jersey across the Hudson River, and the tip of Staten Island to the left.*

boyna, Ceram, Ternate, Bantam, and Mataram, returned with rich cargoes of pepper, cloves, nutmeg, mace, and cinnamon. To consolidate these gains and exploit the riches of the East, the joint-stock East India Company was formed in 1602. The new organization not only had a monopoly on all Asian trade but also held virtually sovereign powers, with the right to make war, sign treaties, appoint governors, judges, and military officials, and build and maintain fortifications. All officials were required to swear allegiance to the States General as well as to the company. No conflict of interest existed, however, since the same oligarchy of wealthy merchants who controlled the one also dominated the other. In a very brief time, the East India Company became the chief organ of Dutch imperialism in the East. One by one it took over most of the Portuguese bases, gaining almost complete control of the Spice Islands by 1618, taking Ceylon and Malacca and eventually Sumatra, and opening up trade with China and Japan.

A similar organization was the Dutch West India Company, founded in 1621 to help exploit the wealth of the New World. By mid-century the Dutch empire in America included Pernambuco and other parts of Brazil, the Caribbean Islands of Saint Eustace, Curaçao, Saba, and Saint Martin, and the mainland colony of New Netherland, extending northward from the mouth of the Hudson River as far as Fort Nassau (modern Albany, New York). Place names from Staten Island, Manhattan, Flushing, and Harlem, to Nyack, Orange

County, and the Catskills, are reminders of the Dutch foundations in the Hudson River Valley.

Yet the Dutch impact on the world cannot be measured in terms of economics and commerce alone. The half century of Dutch maritime predominance coincided with the Golden Age of Dutch urban culture, a culture that gave the world not only the thinking and writing of Grotius, Huygens, Spinoza, and Vondel, but, even more lasting, the great art of Franz Hals, Vermeer, Van Dyck, Ruisdael, and Rembrandt. The era of the Thirty Years' War was a time of consolidation and expansion for the Netherlands. A young nation, vigorous and optimistic, it prospered in time of war because it was able to comprehend its own role and purposes, and was determined not to be detracted from them toward some ephemeral objective. The Dutch went through crises just like everyone else. Yet the tranquility of Vermeer's paintings suggests that they saw meaning and purpose in their struggles and were able to profit from their adversities. Just as they harnessed the wind to fight the sea, so they tamed the impulses of war and directed them toward the creation of a united nation—united by particularism and by love of freedom rather than by the decrees of an absolute monarch.

Suggestions for Further Reading

GENERAL

The key arguments for and against the "general crisis" theory of early seventeenth-century history is adequately presented in Trevor Aston, ed., *Crisis in Europe 1560–1660: Essays from Past and Present* (New York, 1965; London, 1983), and Geoffrey Parker and Lesley M. Smith, eds., *The General Crisis of the Seventeenth Century* (London and Boston, 1985). Another collection, on the role of religion in rural rebellions around the world is Janos Bak and Gerhardt Benecke, eds., *Religion and Rural Revolt* (Dover, New Hampshire, 1984). The best studies of revolts and uprisings in this period are Yves-Marie Bercé, *Revolt and Revolution in Early Modern Europe: An Essay on the History of Political Violence*, tr. by Joseph Bergin (New York, 1987), and *History of Peasant Revolts: The Social Origins of Rebellion in Early Modern France*, tr. by Amanda Whitmore (Ithaca, 1990). Some significant comments are made about the politics and religion of the time in H.G. Koenigsberger, *Politicians and Virtuosi: Essays in Early Modern History* (London, 1986); also in Barbara C. Malament, ed., *After the Reformation: Essays in Honor of J.H. Hexter* (Philadelphia, 1980).

THE FRANCE OF LOUIS XIII

Two important works describing different aspects of French government are David Parker, *The Making of French Absolutism* (New York, 1983), and J. Russell Major, *Representative Government in Early Modern France* (New Haven, 1980). Also see Herbert H. Rowen's insightful *The King's State: Proprietary Dynasticism in Early Modern France* (New Brunswick, 1980). William Beik, *Absolutism and Society in Seventeenth-Century France: State Power and Provincial Aristocracy in Languedoc* (New York and Cambridge, England, 1985) is an outstanding study of the clash between central and provincial authority. Financial issues are central in Richard Bonney, *The King's Debts: Finance and Politics in France, 1589–1661* (Oxford, 1981) and James B. Collins, *Fiscal Limits of Absolutism: Direct Taxation in Early Seventeenth-Century France* (Berkeley,

1988). Tax reform in Dauphiné contributed to the increase of royal power, according to Daniel Hickey in *The Coming of French Absolutism: The Struggle for Tax Reform in the Province of Dauphiné, 1540–1640* (Toronto, 1986). The relationship of patrons and clients is carefully elucidated in Sharon Kettering, *Patrons, Brokers, and Clients in Seventeenth-Century France* (New York and Oxford, 1986). French institutions are scrutinized in Roland Mousnier, *The Institutions of France Under the Absolute Monarchy, 1598–1789, Vol. I: Society and the State*, tr. by Brian Pearce (Chicago, 1979), *Vol. II: The Organs of State and Society*, tr. by Arthur Goldhammer (Chicago, 1984). Also see David Parker, *La Rochelle and the French Monarchy: Order and Conflict in Seventeenth-Century France* (London, 1980), and Robin Briggs, *Communities of Belief: Cultural and Social Tension in Early Modern France* (New York, 1989). The upbringing of Louis XIII is examined through the journal of the king's doctor, Jean Heroard, in Elizabeth W. Marvick, *Louis XIII: The Making of a King* (New Haven, 1986). A careful study of the adult king is provided in A. Lloyd Moote, *Louis XIII, the Just* (Berkeley, 1989).

RICHELIEU AND MAZARIN

The early career of Richelieu is analyzed in light of his personality and childhood in Elizabeth W. Marvick, *The Young Richelieu: A Psychoanalytic Approach to Leadership* (Chicago, 1984). A more complete, and convincing, portrait is provided in Joseph Bergin, *The Rise of Richelieu* (New Haven, 1991), and *Cardinal Richelieu: Power and the Pursuit of Wealth* (New Haven, 1985). A concise and up-to-date assessment is A.J. Knecht, *Richelieu* (London and New York, 1991). A brilliant comparative analysis of Richelieu and his Spanish counterpart is provided in J.H. Elliott, *Richelieu and Olivares* (New York and Cambridge, England, 1984). Richard Bonney, *Society and Government in France under Richelieu and Mazarin, 1624–61* (New York, 1988) is a valuable study of the way French politics were managed by these two ministers. On Mazarin and the Fronde see A. Lloyd Moote, *The Revolt of the Judges: The Parlement of Paris and the Fronde, 1643–1652* (Princeton, 1971), and Richard M. Golden, *The Godly Rebellion: Parisian Curés and the Religious Fronde, 1652–62* (Chapel Hill, 1981).

EARLY STUART ENGLAND

Barry Coward, *The Stuart Age* (New York, 1980) is a convenient overview; another useful book is Robert Ashton, *The City and the Court, 1603–1643* (New York and Cambridge, England, 1979). Intellectual history and popular culture are examined in light of the civil upheaval in Hugh Trevor-Roper, *Catholics, Anglicans, and Puritans: Seventeenth Century Essays* (Chicago, 1987) and David Underdown, *Revel, Riot, and Rebellion: Popular Politics and Culture in England, 1603–1660* (New York and Oxford, 1985). The union of England and Scotland are put in context by Bruce Galloway in *The Union of England and Scotland, 1602–1608* (Edinburgh, 1986) and Brian P. Levack, *The Formation of the British State: England, Scotland, and the Union, 1603–1707* (New York and Oxford, 1987). On the internal politics of James I's reign see Linda Levy Peck, *Northampton: Patronage and Policy at the Court of James I* (London, 1982), and Roger Lockyear, *Buckingham: The Life and Political Career of George Villiers, First Duke of Buckingham, 1592–1628* (London, 1984).

CHARLES I AND PARLIAMENT

A convincing new biography of the tragic king is Pauline Gregg, *King Charles I* (Berkeley, 1984), which draws heavily on original sources. Also insightful is Charles Carlton,

Charles the First: The Personal Monarch (Boston, 1983), and L.J. Reeve, *Charles I and the Road to Personal Rule* (Cambridge, England, and New York, 1989). The absentee rule of Charles I in Scotland is skillfully portrayed in Maurice Lee, Jr., *The Road to Revolution: Scotland under Charles I, 1625–37* (Urbana, Illinois, 1985). A thoughtful comparison of Charles and Cromwell is provided by Maurice Ashley, *Charles I and Oliver Cromwell: A Study in Contrasts and Comparisons* (New York, 1987). The most detailed study of the late Jacobean and early Caroline parliaments is Conrad Russell, *Parliaments and English Politics, 1621–1629* (New York and Oxford, 1979, 1982). The early Stuart House of Lords is carefully analyzed in Elizabeth R. Foster, *The House of Lords, 1603–1649: Structure, Procedure, and the Nature of Its Business* (Chapel Hill, 1983). The crucial period of Charles I's rule without Parliament is studied by Esther S. Cope in *Politics Without Parliaments, 1629–1640* (Winchester, Massachusetts, 1987). Two of the leading personalities of the parliamentary revolution are examined in William W. MacDonald, *The Making of an English Revolutionary: The Early Parliamentary Career of John Pym* (Rutherford, New Jersey, 1982), and Charles Carlton, *Archbishop William Laud* (London, 1987).

THE ENGLISH REVOLUTION AND CIVIL WAR

The most probing account to date of the origins of the war is Conrad Russell, *The Causes of the English Civil War* (New York and Oxford, 1990), which looks carefully at the constitutional, religious, and economic issues. Mark Gould constructs a complex social theory of the English upheaval in *Revolution in the Development of Capitalism: The Coming of the English Revolution* (Berkeley, 1987). The beginning of hostilities is narrated quite effectively by Anthony Fletcher in *The Outbreak of the English Civil War* (London, 1981). A succinct political-religious-social overview of the war is provided in G.E. Aylmer, *Rebellion or Revolution? England, 1640–1660* (New York and Oxford, 1986). Ronald W. Harris, *Clarendon and the English Revolution* (Stanford, 1983) is useful, and David Underdown's classic, *Pride's Purge: Politics and the Puritan Revolution*, has been reissued in paperback (London, 1985). Valuable essays commemorating the work of Christopher Hill are collected in Geoff Eley and Willam Hunt, eds., *Reviving the English Revolution* (New York, 1989). Regional and thematic accounts include Ann Hughes, *Politics, Society and Civil War in Warwickshire, 1620–1660* (New York and Cambridge, England, 1987); Ronald Hutton, *The Royalist War Effort, 1642–1646* (New York, 1984); and Mark A. Kishlansky, *The Rise of the New Model Army* (New York and Cambridge, England, 1979).

The Puritan role in the English revolution and civil war is again receiving much attention. See in particular Michael G. Finlayson, *Historians, Puritanism, and the English Revolution: The Religious Factor in English Politics Before and After the Interregnum* (Toronto, 1983, 1985), and J.T. Cliffe, *Puritans in Conflict: The Puritan Gentry During and After the Civil Wars* (London, 1988), a meticulously documented study that argues for the importance of religion in the war. Other significant works are William Hunt, *The Puritan Moment: The Coming of Revolution in an English County* (Cambridge, Massachusetts, 1984); J.F. McGregor and B. Reay, eds., *Radical Religion in the English Revolution* (Oxford, 1984); William M. Lamont, *Richard Baxter and the Millennium: Protestant Imperialism and the English Revolution* (London, 1979); and two different views of the Ranters: J.C. Davis, *Fear, Myth and History: The Ranters and the Historians* (New York and Cambridge, England, 1986), and Jerome Friedman, *Blasphemy, Immorality, and Anarchy: The Ranters and the English Revolution* (Athens, Ohio, 1987). On the Puritan Commonwealth and Cromwellian Protectorate, see

Austin Woolrych, *Commonwealth to Protectorate* (New York and Oxford, 1982). On the role of the Cromwellian fleet see Bernard Capp, *Cromwell's Navy: The Fleet and the English Revolution, 1648–1660* (Oxford and New York, 1989).

THE NETHERLANDS

Still very useful is K.H.D. Haley, *The Dutch in the Seventeenth Century* (London, 1972), but many new insights are provided in Jonathan Israel, *The Dutch Republic and the Hispanic World, 1606–1661* (New York and Oxford, 1982), and *Dutch Primacy in World Trade, 1585–1740* (New York, 1989); Sherrin Marshall, *The Dutch Gentry, 1500–1650: Family, Faith and Fortune* (Westport, Connecticut, 1987); and especially Simon Schama, *The Embarrassment of Riches: An Interpretation of Dutch Culture in the Golden Age* (New York, 1987), which argues that the Dutch felt a "fundamental dichotomy between the pursuit and enjoyment of wealth and the shame and fear at its possession." A fresh perspective on humanism and religion in the Dutch theater is James A. Parente, Jr., *Religious Drama and the Humanist Tradition: Christian Theater in Germany and in The Netherlands, 1500–1680* (New York, 1987). Important insights into Dutch politics and culture may also be gained in Craig E. Harline, *Pamphlets, Printing and Political Culture in the Early Dutch Republic* (The Hague, 1987). On individual Dutch cultural and political leaders see C.S.M. Rademaker, *Life and Work of Gerardus Joannes Vossius, 1577–1649*, tr. by H.P. Doezema (Assen, the Netherlands, 1981); H. Quarles van Ufford, *A Merchant-Adventurer in the Dutch Republic: John Quarles and His Times, 1596–1646/7* (Amsterdam, 1983); and Herbert H. Rowen, *John de Witt, Grand Pensionary of Holland, 1625–1672* (Princeton, 1978). Also see Rowen's valuable *The Princes of Orange: The Stadholders in the Dutch Republic* (New York and Cambridge, England, 1985).

13 | The Era of the Thirty Years' War

RENAISSANCE CIVILIZATION HAD BEEN A MEDITERRANEAN PHENOMEnon. Italy was its geographic and cultural center as well as the economic focus of European industry and trade. Toward the east sprawled the territories and dominions of the powerful Ottoman Empire, ever threatening and ever encroaching upon Italy and the eastern Mediterranean. On the west was Spain, brought to its pinnacle of power by the conjunction of its largest parts, Castile and Aragon, and by the discovery and exploitation of the wealth of the New World. In the sixteenth century, the Mediterranean continued to hold the key to European power, even though by mid-century Italy had ceased to be the pivot of European political struggles. Spain ruled the western Mediterranean and controlled the sea-lanes to America, while the Turks vied for power over the eastern half.

However, the rise of the Atlantic powers of France, the Netherlands, and England marked the twilight of the Mediterranean Renaissance world. The catalyst in that transformation, though not its only cause, was the Thirty Years' War, which convulsed Europe from 1618 until 1648. Due to the dynastic ties of the House of Habsburg and the political interests of Spain in Bohemia, the Mediterranean decline and the upheavals in central and northeastern Europe are linked together in that tragic conflict.

Spain in Decline

Nowhere is the atrophy of the Mediterranean more clearly demonstrated than in the decline of Spanish importance in the seventeenth century. For some time, Spain itself had been turning away from the Mediterranean toward the Atlantic. During the last two decades of Philip II's reign, Atlantic trade—primarily in American silver, but also in the hides, dyes (cochineal, indigo, and dyewoods), and eastern silks reshipped from the Manila galleons—accounted for an ever-greater share of Spain's income. The first half of the seventeenth century, though, witnessed a steady attrition of bullion imports and a marked decline in total tonnage of trade. The recession was noticeable from 1611 on; by 1619–23 it had become critical.

The Reign of Philip III

Philip III (1598–1621), pious and procrastinating, tried to continue the authoritarianism of his father by identifying the requirements of religion and culture with the interests of Spain. Unlike Philip II, however, he resigned the ruling of his realms to court favorites who were incapable of coping with the mounting problems of imperial rule. Insufficient income, caused by agricultural crisis as well as by commercial recession, created serious economic problems at a time when political and military stresses were at their highest. A burdensome but inefficient tax structure aggravated both the economic and the political situations. So did the expulsion of the Moriscos in 1609. Uncontrollable graft stemming from the system of patronage and clientage; recurring separatist movements in Italy, Aragon, Catalonia, and even parts of Castile; and a decline in Spanish population all contributed to social unrest and eventually to revolt. The personal incompetence of the king and his *privado* (favorite), the duke of Lerma, did nothing to bolster confidence in the government.

At no time in Spanish history were paradoxes deeper or more apparent. Spaniards themselves took the lead in commenting on the absurdity of Europe's wealthiest and most powerful nation forced into bankruptcy and financial impotence by the bankers of Genoa, Amsterdam, and London. National anxiety was reflected in the writings of the *arbitristas*, public-minded men of Castile who spoke out on the economic and political ills of the time, offering remedies to the problems, as well as timely criticism. Many of the *arbitristas* made the sensible suggestion that the tax burden be more evenly distributed; others proposed that government expenditures be reduced; some recommended the resettlement and activation of depopulated areas of Castile. Yet all such proposals fell on deaf ears in Madrid, where the duke of Lerma and a coterie of court aristocrats satisfied themselves that the problems existed only in the minds of the critics. Many were willing to believe, like Don Quixote, that the reality of things was not in their appearance.

The beginning of the century did seem to usher in the Golden Age of Spain. Who could challenge her on land or on sea? Strangely enough, the peace settlements of 1598, 1604, and 1609 that heralded the *Pax Hispanica* were in fact each the result of Spanish defeat—by France, by England, by the Dutch— but a kind of defeat that could as easily be called victory. So for twenty more years, Spain basked in the illusion of military prowess. In time the Spanish nation itself came to believe this illusion. The fatigue and disillusionment of 1598 gave way, especially in the minds of many ambitious nobles, to renewed thoughts of grandeur and power. That is why so many in Spain ignored the prophetic warnings of the *arbitristas,* why they considered talk of economic weakness and decay to be only the babble of malcontents or outright traitors. It also explains why they rushed to defend Habsburg honor in Bohemia in 1618, and why they were so anxious to resume the war with the Dutch as soon as their truce expired in 1621.

The Count-Duke of Olivares,
*the principal minister of Spain
under Philip IV. Portrait by
Velázquez.*

**Philip IV
and Olivares**

The reign of Philip IV (1621–65) was a wartime regime. It was also a time of reform and revolt. The
lethargy of the early years of the century gave way to
activism and a new political dynamic. As the Spanish
awareness of vulnerability grew, the determination to resist decline also
mounted. The kingpin of the revitalization was Philip IV's capable minister,
Gaspar de Guzmán, count-duke of Olivares, son of Philip II's energetic ambassador to Rome in the 1580s. Olivares governed Spain from 1622 until his
fall from power in 1643. Unlike his immediate predecessors, Olivares saw the
urgent need to reform the government and economy if Spain were to retain its
predominance in Europe. His comprehensive program for the centralization of
the monarchy along the lines of the French state called for a drastic reduction
in the size of the bureaucracy and the expenditures of the court; a tax reform
that would help alleviate the stifling financial burden of the Castilian peasants
and villagers; the integration of the Spanish realms into a unified kingdom with
financial and military responsibilities in each area commensurate with those of
Castile; a national system of banks to assist the central government in financial
affairs; unification of the law systems; and a unified militia, manned and maintained on a proportional basis by all of the states in the monarchy.

Olivares's program encountered immediate and tenacious opposition.
The great nobles were alarmed. Aragon, Valencia, and Catalonia resisted the

conscription of soldiers for service outside their respective states. The Catalans refused even to contribute money to a common army and reacted with increasing vehemence against further "Castilianization" of Spain. The tradition of local and regional independence in the eastern kingdoms of Spain was too deeply felt even for Olivares to uproot. His attempted consolidation of power led directly to the Catalan revolt of 1640, which was preceded by rebellion in the Basque provinces and accompanied by disorders in Aragon and Andalusia. Olivares was dismissed in 1643, only two months after the death of his rival, Richelieu. The revolt of Catalonia was eventually suppressed but not without leaving deep and ugly scars. Barcelona did not submit until 1652, and fighting continued in the mountains until the Peace of the Pyrenees in 1659. Spanish particularism and decentralization continued for more than another half-century before Bourbon autocracy reduced the Spaniards to subservience. In the meantime, Portugal seized the opportunity presented by the Catalan revolt to follow suit and declare its own independence from Spain.

For all of its positive proposals, Olivares's reform program failed to recognize Spain's fundamental problem—its political, financial, and military overextension. Spanish resources were inadequate for Spain's immense involvement in Europe and overseas. Spanish participation in the Thirty Years' War was particularly costly, involving almost continuous military operations on at least three fronts and an enormous outlay of money and manpower. Yet Olivares and the majority of those in control vigorously advocated continued Spanish operations on every front.

Setback after setback followed the Dutch capture of the Spanish silver fleet in 1628. Between 1628 and 1631, Spain was embroiled with France in Mantua, followed shortly thereafter by a general declaration of war by France. French pressure on Catalonia was followed by intermittent invasion. Deeper involvement in Germany and in the Lower Palatinate hindered operations against the Dutch, who in 1639 inflicted a crushing defeat by destroying a Spanish fleet in the Downs. From 1640 until 1659 the bloodletting continued, with Spanish arms usually showing the valor and discipline that had made the *tercios* feared throughout Europe, but without the resources to match their will. The defeat of the Army of Flanders by the French at Rocroi in 1643 was largely due to its being unable to afford the purchase of horses for its Spanish cavalry. English entry into the war further harassed the Indies trade and constricted Spanish bullion imports to a trickle. The Peace of the Pyrenees, signed 7 November 1659, marked the end of Spanish domination in Europe. Physical, economic, and mental exhaustion had overtaken it. Only a remnant of Spanish Golden Age culture lingered a few more years in the rich and moving canvases of Bartolomé Estéban Murillo and the plays of Pedro Calderón de la Barca.

Baroque Italy

Spanish power was still a major factor in Italy, with unchallenged possession of Milan in the north and Naples and Sicily in the south. Throughout the Spanish period, Sicily retained a considerable degree of autonomy and inde-

pendence through the Sicilian *parlamento* and through the local civil and ecclesiastical officers. Nevertheless, Spanish control was effective enough in the
island to prevent its being plundered by the Turks—most of the time. In both
Sicily and Naples the king was represented by viceroys who functioned at the
apex of a fairly successful conciliar system. In Naples the Spanish presence was
greatly resented, but even there it was not until 1647, at a time when Spain's
whole world was falling apart, that insurrection erupted. In the duchy of
Milan, Spanish rule was more recent but no less forceful. An oft-quoted aphorism of the time noted that whereas in Sicily the Spaniards nibbled and in Naples they ate, in Milan they devoured.

In neighboring Genoa, a different situation existed. As an independent
power, Genoa declined rapidly in the early sixteenth century, ground between
the millstones of France and Spain. However, under the energetic leadership
of Andrea Doria and his nephew Gian Andrea Doria, who tied Genoese fortunes to the Spanish state, Genoa feasted on the fruits of Spanish success. Even
before Andrea Doria left the French service to become grand admiral of Spain,
bringing with him his powerful Mediterranean galley fleet, Genoese merchants,
bankers, and seamen were deeply embedded in Castilian overseas activities.
Christopher Columbus was only one of many enterprising Genoese to thus
capitalize on the Castilian expansion. Soon the Genoese came to dominate the
financial life of Spain, a domination that lasted at least a century. Yet even the
exploitation of New World wealth could not fully compensate the weakened
Genoese republic for its loss of Mediterranean trade.

Venice
Venetian decline was another symptom of the general
withering of the Mediterranean as the focus of European wealth and power. Venice succumbed to a
combination of pressures—economic, demographic, political, and psychological—which, in their total impact upon the Republic, were decisive. The erosion of Venetian commerce as a result of the encroachment of the French, English, and Dutch into the Mediterranean; the emigration of Venetian nobles to
the mainland; the menacing and destructive incursions of Barbary pirates and
other Mediterranean corsairs; and the long and costly rivalry with Rome all
had telling effects on the prestige and power of the proud Republic. The wonder is not Venice's eventual decline but its long and continuous existence as an
independent and respected state in the new age of monarchical powers.

However, Venice was not as vulnerable to the vicissitudes of European
politics and war as were neighboring Italian states, partly because the Republic
of Saint Mark had been able to maintain an active independence from the
dynastic quarrels of the non-Italian powers. That independence was threatened
in 1618 by a conspiracy, crudely concocted by the Spanish ambassador, the
viceroy of Naples, and others, to overthrow the Venetian government and turn
the city over to Spain. The plot, however, was uncovered in time. Several con-
spirators were executed and the duke of Bedmar, the Spanish ambassador, was
recalled to Madrid. From that time on, the Doge and senate were even more
careful to steer clear of the political alliances and alignments that sucked one

state after another into the Thirty Years' War. Fortunately, Venetian diplomacy still functioned efficiently and succeeded in avoiding many of the pitfalls that might have spelled complete ruin.

In the meantime, Venice remained the quintessence of grandeur and beauty, with its noble churches and gala palaces gracing the shores of the Grand Canal. And it contributed more than graceful buildings to early seventeenth-century culture. It was as choirmaster at Saint Mark's that Monteverdi composed many of his madrigals and in the nearby theater of San Cassiano that he staged some of his most famous operas. Here, too, Fra Pietro Paolo Sarpi, "the loftiest intellect that Venice ever produced," mastered the intricacies of mathematics, astronomy, physics, and philosophy while becoming the most respected theologian and priest in Venice. Sarpi's moderate, independent Catholicism and his proud aloofness toward the popes typifies the religious and cultural independence of seventeenth-century Venice.

Nevertheless, the glory of the proud island city was obviously past; its once-great commercial wealth had been reduced to modest merchandizing among the Italian cities and the coastal towns of the pirate-infested Mediterranean. After 1645 the Turkish menace returned. Venetian fortitude and valor again recalled its heroic past, but the drain of men and resources, not relieved now by help from Spain or Rome as in the days of Lepanto, was more than the Republic could sustain. Its political and economic decline was slow and stately, but it was irreversible.

The Papacy   There was no love lost in Rome over the recession of Venice; indeed, the papacy had done its share to accelerate the process. Since early Renaissance times, Venice, as next-door neighbor to the Papal States, had been a thorn in the side of the popes, especially those with political ambitions, even during the time of their "holy" leagues against the Turks.

Rome alone among all the Italian states experienced a resurgence of self-confidence and vigor, if not of prestige or actual power, in the late sixteenth and early seventeenth centuries. The Counter-Reformation restored the papacy to the spiritual leadership of Catholic Europe and produced a vigorous offensive against the political dilly-dallying of Catholic states that failed to live up to the evangelical spirit of the Council of Trent. During the pontificate of the autocratic and politically aggressive Pope Sixtus V (1585–90), strong disagreements occurred between the Holy See and the Spanish monarch over the leadership of Christendom. The pontiff was no better disposed toward Henri III, and was heard to remark that France would be better off with Elizabeth Tudor on the throne than the decadent Valois. The pope's admiration for Henri of Navarre stopped only at the Huguenot chieftain's refusal to become a Catholic. Sixtus's successor lived to receive Navarre's reconciliation and to sanctify his coronation as Henri IV. But Clement VIII's (1592–1605) active absorption in foreign affairs and diplomacy lost him more friends than it won.

Pope Paul V (1605–21) renewed the papal vendetta with Venice with the exclamation, "I am pope, and demand nothing but obedience!"—a declaration that he followed with that once-mighty weapon of the Middle Ages, the papal interdict. Venice stood firm, and the pope was eventually forced to retreat, but not before he had thoroughly demonstrated the political bankruptcy of the papacy. Pope Paul's insistence on the prerogatives of his office and his rigorous enforcement of the decrees of the Council of Trent, however, are reminders that the papacy was not ready to concede its religious leadership to either the Protestants or the secular princes. That leadership was partly expressed in the powerful cultural flowering that made seventeenth-century Rome the capital of Baroque architecture, sculpture, and music. Paul V was a Borghese and, like other members of that illustrious family, a vigorous devotee of art. His nephew, Cardinal Scipione Borghese, created the beautiful Villa Borghese and endowed it with its richest art collections.

Another patron family of Roman art and letters, the Barberini, contributed the ablest pontiff in Maffeo Barberini, Pope Urban VIII (1623–44). Urban was the life-long friend and patron of Bernini, who created many of the Baroque adornments of Rome, including the Barberini Palace. He was also Borromini's and Frescobaldi's benefactor, and a sympathetic admirer of Galileo. Much of the artistic grandeur of Rome must be attributed to the Barberini pope.

Nevertheless, like so many of his predecessors, it was in the field of politics that Urban VIII hoped to make his greatest impact. He not only pictured himself as a defender of the church against heretics and infidels, a role in which he dreamed of leading a final crusade against the Turks, but also believed the papacy could still play a decisive part in the political affairs of Europe. His vision of the church militant included the fantasy of a papacy subduing the martial spirit of the princes and ushering in a new *Pax Romana* to war-torn Europe. Urban considered the Habsburgs to be the principal disturbers of the peace, and for that reason he generally supported Richelieu's anti-Habsburg policies. In the process he won both the hatred of the Habsburgs and the distrust of the Bourbons. For his more petty excursions into Italian politics, he also reaped the rancor of the lesser princes. Even in Rome itself, the city he had done so much to enhance, his name became an object of scorn. Urban raised taxes, ruled as an absolute monarch, and desecrated ancient monuments to build new ones. *"Quod non fecerunt barbari fecerunt Barberini"* ("What the barbarians did not do, the Barberini do"), was the unkind epithet his subjects used.

Tuscany and Savoy   Other Italian states experienced commensurate troubles. During the long rule of Duke Cosimo de' Medici (1537–74), the grand duchy of Tuscany was created out of the incorporation of Siena into the duchy of Florence. After consolidating his power and neutralizing his enemies, Cosimo ruled with such a skillful balance of the lion and the fox that his earlier compatriot Machiavelli would have been proud. Cosimo even added a cultural dimension to his rule by building the Ufizzi Gallery. Under the clever rule of Cosimo's grandson, Ferdinando (1587–1609), the grand dukes also became the wealthiest dynasty in Italy. Cosimo II (1609–20) added to Florentine intellectual renown by sponsoring the great Galileo. Yet in spite of its prosperous, absolutist, and cultured appearance, Medici rule in Tuscany survived only in the shadow, and by the grace, of France and Spain. Linked to France by family and strong diplomatic ties with Catherine de' Medici—reinforced after her death by the marriage of King Henri IV to Marie de' Medici, daughter of Grand Duke Francesco (Cosimo's son and successor)—and to Spain by the predominance of Spanish power in Italy, Tuscany remained a pawn in the politics of foreign princes.

Another, more successful, autocratic family ruled in Savoy, where Emanuele Filiberto (1553–80) and his son Carlo Emanuele (1580–1630) succeeded in making the most of their buffer location between France and Spanish Milan. Choosing the winning side in the Habsburg-Valois wars, the duke of Savoy not only won the continued support of Spain, thus ensuring the duchy against French aggression, but also strengthened his diplomatic ties by marrying Philip II's daughter, Caterina. This marriage further guaranteed Spanish support for possible Savoyard ambitions. Savoy's rulers, however, were usually content to dance to the Habsburg tune. For a while it appeared that nearby Mantua would succumb to the same music. In the war of the Mantuan succession (1627–31), however, the diversion of Spanish arms into Germany as a result of the Swedish invasion allowed the French duke of Nevers, with the support of Venice and the papacy, to control the Mantuan state.

The Ottoman Empire

Since the conquest of Adrianople in 1354, the Turks had been a chronic threat to the West, steadily extending and consolidating their dominions across Mediterranean Europe and up the Danube plain. Under Sultan Suleiman the Magnificent (1520–66) they had captured Rhodes, conquered Tripoli, raided Corfu and the entire southwestern coast of Italy, laid seige to Malta, and terrorized coastal towns from Ragusa to Valencia. Simultaneously they conquered Jedistan and Hungary, as well as the eastern marshes of Armenia to the Caspian Sea, and sent their janissaries to the very gates of Vienna.

Ottoman rule was absolutist in the extreme. The sultan, as military leader, lawgiver, and successor to the prophet Mohammed, was the supreme head of the Turkish state, to whom all Moslems owed unquestioned allegiance. Social and institutional limitations upon the power of the ruler, such as those exercised in western Europe by nobility, church, parliament, or cities, were unknown in the Ottoman Empire. The Ottoman system, based on military conquest and systematic slavery, generated neither a permanent landed aristocracy nor a rival dynasty to challenge the authority of the sultan. Since the governmental officials, from the grand vizier to the personal bodyguards, were usually slaves possessing no hereditary rights, and family ties were obviously weak (even the sultan was likely to be the son of a slave mother), little likelihood existed of organized opposition to the crown—except, that is, from the sultan's immediate kin. To avoid that threat, Suleiman executed all of his sons except the one he desired to succeed him. Each new sultan, upon reaching the throne, put any surviving brothers and their male children to the sword, thereby eliminating all question of succession.

Yet for all of its ruthlessness, the Ottoman Empire's dependence upon plunder, slaves, and new land made it a victim of its own needs. When the expansive thrust into Europe was stalemated after 1571–81, the supply of booty shriveled and the system of social and cultural renovation died. A time of troubles ensued, during which the Ottoman sultanate was confronted with disgruntled vested interests and frustrated "young Turks." In 1589 a massive janissary mutiny removed the grand vizier and other high officials. In 1622 rioting soldiers deposed and executed Sultan Osman II, and in 1648 they dealt similarly with Ibrahim I. The landowning class was everywhere in opposition to the bureaucracy that controlled the central power. Nevertheless, the sultanate survived and undiminished in authority, awaiting only the arrival of an occupant worthy of the name. A dynasty of grand viziers of the Kuprülü family revitalized the Ottoman government at mid-century, after the overthrow of Sultan Ibrahim I. Mohammed Kuprülü launched a new era of aggression that reached its climax, as far as the West was concerned, in the second siege of Vienna in 1683.

In the meantime, the Turks had stamped their imprint on Europe. Italy, especially, was affected by Turkish penetration in the Mediterranean, and in the peninsula no state was more directly involved than Venice. Venetian colonies and outposts in the Adriatic had been subject to Turkish attack since the fall of Constantinople, but not until the reign of Suleiman did the Turks make a serious bid for Mediterranean naval supremacy. Strangely, that bid was made with French help, as a result of the commercial-military arrangements between those two powers beginning in 1536. In that year Francis I received the first "capitulations" from the sultan granting favorable trading terms to the French and initiating a Franco-Turkish military alliance that brought questionable advantage to both partners. The commercial concessions to France were considerable, however, and the treaty was renewed in 1569, 1581, and again in 1604. By 1570 Turkish sea power was formidable and had succeeded in subduing many of the Venetian islands. Unable to confront the Turks head on, Venice was forced to combine naval experience with clever diplomacy in order to maintain its vital commerce with the Levant.

The naval victory of the Spanish-Venetian fleet at Lepanto in October 1571, with the French remaining neutral, might have ended the Turkish threat in the Mediterranean had it been followed by an immediate attack on Istanbul. Europe's resources, however, were already strained to the limit, and the risk involved in committing so many men and ships to such an extended war would have been unwise. In 1573 Venice withdrew from the Holy League (of Spain, Venice, and the papacy) and signed a separate peace with the Turks that recognized Ottoman control of Cyprus and all previous conquests. By the same treaty, commercial relations were resumed. The precarious peace lasted seventy years and helped delay the inevitable demise of the Venetian Republic.

The Habsburg Empire

The Spanish branch of the House of Habsburg constituted only part of the vast Habsburg empire. Philip II's Austrian cousins, Maximilian II and Rudolf II, reigned over more of Europe's surface than any other Christian prince except the king of Spain (with a population more than double that of Philip's European possessions), and as Holy Roman emperors, commanded the recognition, if not always the respect, of all Christendom. Yet even though he reigned, the Holy Roman emperor did not rule in the fragmented states of sixteenth-century Germany. Power lay in the hands of the local rulers—the Wettins in Saxony, the Wittelsbachs in Bavaria and later in the Palatinate, the Hohenzollerns in Brandenburg—and with the dukes, landgraves, and counts of over two hundred other rival political units.

Only in the hereditary Habsburg territories of Tyrol, Carinthia, Carniola, Styria, and Austria could Habsburg control be described as sovereign, and even there its effectiveness depended to a great extent on the external situation. Absolutism may have been a Habsburg dream but it was never a reality. In 1526 Charles V's brother, Ferdinand (1526–64), inherited the kingdom of Bohemia and part of Hungary, which he retained after he became emperor in 1558. In this polyglot inheritance, in which fourteen or fifteen separate languages were spoken, Ferdinand, his son Maximilian (1564–76), and his grandson Rudolf (1576–1612) tried to maintain a semblance of Habsburg hegemony. It was not an easy task, especially in the eastern territories.

The first fourteen years of Ferdinand's rule in Hungary were contested by the rival king John Zapolya, and later by the independent-minded nobles. In Bohemia and Moravia, religious heterodoxy was deeply implanted and nearly captured the mind of Emperor Maximilian II himself. In 1575 Maximilian openly allowed the practice of the Bohemian Confession throughout the Czech kingdom. Even his devoutly Catholic son, Rudolf II (who, through constant Habsburg intermarriage, was Philip II's brother-in-law as well as his nephew and cousin), that strange, pathologic astrologer-emperor, was cautious in his encouragement of the Jesuit missions to Austria and Bohemia. Only in the southern and western territories did Rudolf ruthlessly apply the religious decisions of the Peace of Augsburg and the Council of Trent. On the whole, Habsburg policy was meant to rock the boat as little as possible, preserving the tenuous balance within each of the various Habsburg domains while gradually building up strength against the ever-present threat of the Turks.

In Bohemia, to achieve even this stalemate would have been counted success. The determined Czech patriots, however, were no more willing to have Catholicism, or Lutheranism for that matter, foisted on them than they were to subordinate themselves to Habsburg domination. They resisted every attempt Rudolf II made to bring them into line. Forced to acknowledge complete Czech religious freedom in his Letter of Majesty of 1609, Rudolf laid the foundations for a struggle that would eventually draw all of Europe into war. Even Rudolf's moving his capital to Prague did not prevent Bohemia from becoming for the Austrian Habsburgs what the Netherlands had been for the Spanish.

The religious settlement at Augsburg (1555) had created a false picture of the confessional struggles in the Holy Roman Empire by shrouding the scene with a façade of agreement that was neither lasting nor true. The insertion of the "ecclesiastical reservation," declaring that the estates of ecclesiastical lords converted to Lutheranism should remain intact and that such persons should lose their offices and incomes, only increased the chances of conflict. The Rhineland soon became a seedbed of Calvinist activity and subversion as the doctrines of Reformed Protestantism spread through the lower and upper Palatinate into neighboring Nassau, Hesse, Anhalt, and even into Brandenburg. At the same time, a rekindled Catholicism, spearheaded by the Jesuits, returned many cities and provinces to Roman allegiance.

In 1609 the half-century of simmering peace in Germany was threatened by a serious crisis over the succession in Jülich-Cleves, duchies that were claimed by both the Protestant margrave of Brandenburg and the Catholic nephew of the former duke of Cleves. The volatile situation was made worse by the polarization of Germany into rival and aggressive politico-religious camps organized into the Protestant Union, led by Frederick Count Palatine of the Rhine, and the Catholic League headed by Duke Maximilian of Bavaria. These alliance clusters were soon enlarged and made more dangerous by the encouragement and association of France, England, and the Netherlands with the Protestant Union, and the adherence of Spain and the emperor to the Catholic League. In the early seventeenth century, the Empire was swaggering recklessly on the brink of war.

Northern and Eastern Europe

The northern neighbors of the Holy Roman Empire had not posed any particular problem for the Habsburg rulers in the past. When the Vasa dynasty was established in 1523, Sweden was still a peripheral European state with only occasional relations with southern powers or with European culture and thought. Gustavus Vasa (1523–60) created for the first time an independent kingdom that, although poor and underpopulated, was a unified and viable nation. However, under his three sons, who ruled from 1560 to 1611, Swedish autonomy was squandered in disastrous wars with Denmark (1563–70 and 1610–11); Poland and Russia (1570–83, 1590–95, and 1610–11); civil war among brothers for the throne; and religious fighting among Lutherans, Calvinists, and Catholics, ending in the irreversible dominance of Lutheranism.

Gustavus Adolphus (Gustav Adolf), who assumed the Swedish throne in 1611 at the age of sixteen, was most responsible for the rapid revival of Sweden as a major European power. Under his energetic leadership, and stimulated by the emotional excitement of the religious rivalries at home and abroad, Sweden emerged as the great Baltic power of the seventeenth century, threatening at one point to dominate the whole of northern Europe. Gustavus Adolphus was a stimulating leader, able to command the respect and support of nobles, burghers, and peasants alike, and capable of using their services to mold the hodgepodge of salt-water fishermen, tenant farmers, day laborers, clergymen, and petty nobles into an integrated, dynamic society and the leading military power in Europe. He was a statebuilder in the broadest sense, combining the dedicated care of a father with the organizational skill of a bureaucrat. Yet without the equally keen administrative ability of his chancellor, Axel Oxenstierna, Gustavus's task would have been much harder.

Sandwiched between the traditional foes of Russia to the east and Denmark on the west, with Polish belligerence frequently added, Sweden's survival was threatened more than once. Yet Sweden, like the Netherlands, prospered in time of war. In fact, under Gustavus Adolphus it thrived on war. Poor and underpopulated, Sweden nevertheless made the best of both its resources and the foreign entrepreneurs who were willing and able to develop them. Flemish industrialists and Dutch financiers, such as Louis de Geer, activated the Swedish metallurgical industry and helped make Sweden the leading exporter of copper and iron, and one of the main manufacturers of cannon and other arms. Direct subsidies from Richelieu's France also made up a large share of the Swedish income after 1631. In a few short years, Gustavus Adolphus had created a national war machine that catapulted Sweden into the front rank of European powers. As Sweden's military power grew, so did its political and economic involvement abroad, and with it a sophisticated diplomatic network extending across Europe.

The contrasting fortunes of Denmark make Sweden's supremacy more remarkable. Prosperous and more populous than Sweden, the kingdom of Denmark (which included the southern coastal area of modern Sweden from Göteborg to Kalmar, and all of Norway) was closely linked with northern Europe by economic and cultural ties as well as by bonds of dynastic matrimony. Christian IV (1588–1648) was the brother-in-law of James I of England and also the duke of Holstein, which made him a member of the Lower Saxon circle of the Holy Roman Empire, and a very interested participant in German affairs. Yet Denmark was an agricultural and pastoral land, unproductive of industrial wealth and not able to expand militarily as Sweden had done. Denmark's involvement in the Thirty Years' War, therefore, resulted in the end of its influence in Germany and the permanent passing of Danish supremacy in the Baltic.

Poland-Lithuania   Adjacent to the Habsburg Empire on the east lay the broad plains of Poland and Lithuania, where some 4 to 5 million people struggled with nature and each other for survival. Life there was dominated by the nobility, who not only ruled their serfs completely but were able to withstand every attempt by the monarchs to consolidate royal power. In 1560 the kingdom of Poland and the vast grand duchy of Lithuania, hitherto joined only in the person of a common monarch, forged a somewhat closer union called the commonwealth (*respublica*). When Sigismund II, last of the Jagiellonian dynasty, died in 1572, the commonwealth's nobles convened en masse and elected as their ruler a foreigner, Henri of Valois, brother of the king of France.

The Valois dynasty proved short-lived in Poland-Lithuania. From the outset, Henri found his new realm bleak and inhospitable, in spite of the considerable influence of the Italian Renaissance and the contributions to literature and thought of Polish humanists like Jan Kochanowski and Andrzej Frycz Modrzewski (Modrevius). Moreover, the nobility had imposed strict limitations on royal power in order to keep the monarchy relatively weak and to guarantee religious toleration, which the nobles had pledged in 1573 to observe among themselves. Henri chafed at these conditions, and little more than a year after his election, when news arrived of his brother's death, he sneaked out of Cracow by night and returned to France.

The Polish nobles chose as their next ruler Stephen Báthory (1576–86), prince of Transylvania and hero of the wars against the Turks. Báthory gave all the appearances of a vigorous and determined king, intent upon gaining meaningful, if not absolute, power in the commonwealth, expanding Lithuania's frontiers against the Russians, and ensuring Polish aid in Hungary's struggle for liberation from the Turks. His untimely death after a ten-year reign, however, boded ill for the future. The Catholic Sigismund Vasa (1587–1632) of Sweden was elected to succeed Báthory, and foreign wars, domestic insurrection, and growing social chaos marked his forty-five year reign.

Yet until the mid-seventeenth century, Poland-Lithuania preserved a greater measure of religious toleration than did most contemporary European states. Catholicism regained its position as the faith of the majority of the Polish nobility and peasantry during Sigismund's reign. In 1596 the Union of Brest brought a considerable number of Eastern Orthodox nobles and clergy in the Ukraine (then part of Poland) into obedience to the papacy, while leaving them free to use the traditional Orthodox liturgy, thus creating the *Uniat* (or Ukrainian Catholic) church that still exists in the western Ukraine. These Catholic advances owed much to the educational and political work of the Jesuits, as well as to the monarch's ability to use political patronage to reward conversions to Catholicism. Nevertheless, a vigorous, though divided, Protestant community remained in both Poland and Lithuania, and Orthodoxy also had powerful protectors among the nobility. The numerous and often prosperous Jewish communities likewise enjoyed a freedom from harassment unknown elsewhere.

Under these circumstances, radical Protestant doctrines that would have been repressed in other countries found open adherents in Poland-Lithuania. Most notable among these were the Socinians, the antitrinitarian movement organized by the exiled Italian Fausto Sozzini (1539–1604). An able and learned scholar, Sozzini sought to mold the conflicting antitrinitarian, Anabaptists, and pacifist currents of Polish religious radicalism into a consistent theology, at the same time urging his followers to obey the state insofar as conscience allowed.

Russia   Farther to the east, beyond the Dnieper, lay the endless expanse of Russia, where the grand dukes of Muscovy had successfully created a viable kingdom among the princedoms of Eurasia. Ivan IV, the Terrible (1533–84), declared himself tsar of all the Russias and proceeded to establish a regime that was expansive, autocratic, and incomparably cruel. Ivan extended the Muscovite

The Cathedral of Saint Basil *in Moscow, built by Ivan the Terrible between 1555 and 1561 to celebrate his victories over the Tartars.*

empire south into the Tartar khanates of Kazan and Astrakhan, and through the initiative and wealth of the powerful Stroganovs and their cossack mercenaries, made western Siberia part of the Muscovite domain.

The territorial expansion of Muscovy was accompanied by the systematic devastation of local institutional, aristocratic authority and the creation of a highly centralized regime. Like western monarchs of the early Renaissance, Ivan IV gained power and territory at the expense of the landed magnates. He converted the estates system into an instrument of his own control to reduce the independent authority of the *boyars* (landed aristocrats) and in turn attached many of them to his service. To do this he created a royal domain (*oprichnina*), comprising nearly half of the grand duchy of Muscovy, in which he could exercise absolute power. Estates of the former landowners within the *oprichnina* were confiscated by the tsar and supervised through a royal officialdom of secret police and a new service nobility. Many of the *boyars* were removed to distant regions while others, including many hapless bystanders, were ruthlessly killed. Thus securely established inside his own closed system, and deified by the cowed Orthodox Church, Ivan succeeded in establishing an absolutism that surpassed the wildest hopes of western monarchs.

The weakness of autocracy was quickly revealed, however, when Ivan died and was succeeded by his simple-minded son Fedor. Social, political, and economic upheaval ensued, a "Time of Troubles" that lasted until 1613. For thirty years, from 1584 to 1613, Russia was devastated by wars of succession as Boris Godunov, the pretender Dmitri Ivanovich, and others (including invading Poles and Swedes) fought for control of the Russian state. Civil war was accompanied by great social upheaval that saw many aristocratic families rise and fall, vast estates change hands many times, villages and the countryside pillaged and ruined, and the peasants reduced to legal and permanent serfdom. Over 2 million lives were spent in those upheavals. Finally, in 1613, the *boyar* Mikhail Fedorovich Romanov was elected tsar, inaugurating the dynasty that would rule Russia until 1917.

The rise of the Romanovs did not put a sudden end to the Russian crisis, but it did alter its nature and effect. Exhausted by the terrible Time of Troubles, most of Russian society lapsed into political and social passivity as the crown, aided by the clergy and not hindered by the national assembly *(Zemsky Sobor)* gradually regained the upper hand. Step by step, the Romanov tsars created an authoritarian monarchy whose autocratic power was not seriously challenged for three hundred years, although during the Thirty Years' War its permanence was successively threatened by Swedish attack, Polish invasion, marauding Tartars, and the possibility of war with the Ottoman Turks.

Even though the Russian experience closely resembled many events in the West during the same period, direct contacts between Muscovy and Europe were scattered and brief. In 1553 the English expedition of Richard Chancelor reached Moscow, opening a brief period of active commercial and diplomatic relations between Russia and England. Some contact was made with the French and Dutch during Ivan's rule, but it was not until the Romanovs came to power that more continuous channels of communication between East and West were initiated. In the meantime, Russian involvement in the Baltic brought the grand duchy into ever-more-frequent contact with Vasa Sweden, and it was Sweden that established the first resident embassy in Moscow.

The Outbreak of the Thirty Years' War

The great cataclysm that enveloped Europe in the third decade of the seventeenth century followed a brief period of relative and precarious peace. That peace had been formalized in the Treaty of Vervins (1598) between Spain and France; the Treaty of London (1604) between Spain and England; and the 1609 truce between Spain and the United Netherlands. Even then, the decade 1609–19 was more a period of jockeying for position and advantage among the great powers, resulting in a series of recurring international crises, than it was a time of real peace. In 1609–10 the crisis of the Jülich-Cleves succession brought Europe to the brink of war. It was averted only by the assassination in 1610 of the French king, Henri IV, who had assumed leadership of the anti-Habsburg alliance. The subsequent Treaty of Xanten, settling the disputed succession in the little marquisate of Montferrat, cradled between Savoy, Genoa, and Spanish Milan, almost ignited a Europewide conflagration before it was brought under control. Other crises developed and broke on the verge of catastrophe during that tension-charged decade. Some historians maintain that the hostilities of the so-called Thirty Years' War actually began in 1609 rather than 1618. And so they did, just as the hostilities of World War I began in 1905 with the first Moroccan crisis. Yet in the same way, a general war was avoided, or rather delayed, in both instances by the unwillingness of the great powers to be forced by an alliance system into a war not of their own choosing and possibly against their best interests. When the situation seemed more to their advantage, they displayed much less dedication to peace.

The crisis that developed in Bohemia after 1611, reaching its climax in 1618, resulted from a deep-seated social cleavage made worse by profound religious differences and triggered by the Habsburg play for tighter control of its troublesome territories. Archduke Matthias, with the approval of most of the Habsburg clan, forced his eccentric brother, Emperor Rudolf II, to abdicate the government of Bohemia. The Czech estates promptly elected Matthias their king and a few months later he succeeded Rudolf as Holy Roman emperor. Political disunity among the competing estates of Austria, Bohemia, Moravia, Silesia, Lusatia, and Hungary allowed the emperor to tighten his financial control of the eastern empire but did little to raise his political stature or improve the decaying relations between the Habsburgs and their subjects. The powerful Spanish party in Prague, led by Philip III's ambassador there, exploited the situation in order to enlarge Spanish interests and secure the election of a suitable successor to the childless and sickly Matthias.

Archduke Ferdinand of Styria, a capable and energetic cousin of the king, was the Habsburg choice. In 1618 Ferdinand did become king of Bohemia and a year later was elected Emperor Ferdinand II. Ferdinand was an arch-Catholic, determined to erase all religious concessions made in Bohemia by his predecessors. The Czechs rebelled; a diet of Protestant nobles assembled in Prague in the spring of 1618 to denounce Habsburg policy. Their determination was made more vivid by the famous "defenestration of Prague," when two of the Habsburg governors and a secretary were bodily thrown from an upper window of Hradcin castle into the dry moat some fifty feet below. Miraculously, all three escaped death but the incident marked a decisive break with Habsburg rule.

Rivals throughout Germany and all over Europe seemed anxious to fight. Only hours after the imperial diet had elected Ferdinand II, the revolutionary government in Prague deposed him as their king, and chose in his place young Count Frederick, Calvinist elector of the Palatinate and son-in-law of England's James I. The recreated Protestant Union, under Frederick, sent Count Mansfeld with a mercenary army to the Czech's aid. Others arrived from Silesia and Lusatia. The imperial forces and their allies in the Catholic League, however, soon swelled to enormous size. Maximilian of Bavaria took the field

The "Defenestration of Prague," *in which two Habsburg governors and their secretary were thrown from the window of the Hradcin castle (23 May 1618) by Czech patriots. It was the opening round of the Thirty Years' War.*

with 25–30,000 men under the command of Count Johannes von Tilly. Spain launched a simultaneous attack on the Palatinate with a veteran army from the Spanish Netherlands commanded by the Milanese general Ambrosio Spinola. The Bohemian uprising was crushed at the battle of White Mountain, outside of Prague, on 8 November 1620. Frederick, the "Winter King," lost the Palatinate as well as the Bohemian throne and fled into exile in Holland.

Once started, the war was impossible to stop. There were too many possibilities for material gain in the conglomeration of German states. Protestants hoped to extend their control over Germany; Catholics were determined to roll back the Reformation and wipe out heresy. Maximilian of Bavaria intended to promote the fortunes of the Wittelsbachs—to match, if not exceed, the power of the Habsburgs. The margrave of Baden, in the meantime, wanted Württemberg, while the landgrave of Hesse eyed western Würzburg. The elector of Saxony had designs on neighboring Lusatia and Silesia, and Brandenburg sized up the duchy of Mecklenburg. Emperor Ferdinand hoped all the time to consolidate Habsburg lands as best he could and establish a meaningful rule in Germany.

Throughout the Empire, unscrupulous soldiers of fortune stepped forward to promote their own interests and prolong the military bloodletting. Mansfeld, who sold his services and his army to the highest bidder on either side, was soon joined by other *condottiere*-type captains, including Hans Georg von

Wallenstein. *A portrait by Anthony Van Dyck of the brilliant and enigmatic commander of the imperialist army during the early phases of the Thirty Years' War.*

Arnim (a Brandenburg Protestant who fought on the Catholic side much of the time), and the most ambitious, talented, and successful opportunist of them all, Albrecht von Wallenstein, a Bohemian nobleman and Protestant who served himself handsomely as commander-in-chief of the Catholic imperial army. Wallenstein (1583–1634), like the Baroque style he personified, was, in Karl Friedrich's phrase, a man "combining medieval faith and superstition with a renaissance sense of power and artistic performance." His tragic murder in 1634 only heightened the dramatic impact of his contradictory personality on history.

Foreign motives for involvement in the Empire were no more altruistic. The sultan used the German diversion to strike at Poland, inflicting a major defeat on the Poles at Jassy; the sultan's vassal, Bethlen Gabor of Transylvania, occupied more of Hungary and coerced the estates into electing him king of Hungary. The Polish monarch, Sigismund III, asserted his claim to the throne of Sweden, while his cousin, Gustavus Adolphus, the incumbent king, tried to cajole Moscow into a joint Swedish-Russian attack on Poland. When that failed, he cast his eyes on the political vacuum in northern Germany. King Christian of Denmark saw the same advantages there for himself and for Protestantism. Maurice of Nassau and the Dutch states, meanwhile, hoped to profit from the diversionary Bohemian affair to fortify themselves against the inevitable renewal of their war with Spain, while James I tried to play Elizabeth's game of "now I'm for you, now I'm not" with both the Dutch and the Spanish. France, floundering in civil disorder during the minority of Louis XIII, soon emerged under Cardinal Richelieu to renew the challenge against Habsburg Spain, whose interests were intricately involved due to its many commitments throughout the continent.

War to Exhaustion

It is unnecessary to follow the ebb and flow of the countless campaigns of the next three or four decades, or dwell on the brutality and butchery of battles and sieges, in order to discern the consequences and meaning of this first "World War." Its results were progressively manifested in its prolongation and in its Europewide involvement.

After the Spanish-imperial victories of the first five years of war—during which Bohemia was subdued, the Palatinate devastated, and the Netherlands south of the Maas River overrun by Spinola's army following his capture of Breda—Christian IV of Denmark personally intervened at the head of a Danish and German mercenary army to give the Protestant cause a leader and a new lease on life. It was soon evident, however, that Christian was outclassed as a military commander by Wallenstein and Tilly, who led the imperial forces to repeated victories and the eventual subjugation of all of northern Germany as far as Jutland itself.

At the height of the Catholic-imperial tide, Emperor Ferdinand issued the Edict of Restitution in March 1629. Catholic properties taken by Protestant princes or cities during the past seventy-five years were restored; sequestered bishoprics were reinstated; Calvinist worship was prohibited. Ferdinand rankled many of the German princes, however, by his elevation of Maximilian of Bavaria to the rank of elector, while giving the lands and title of the duke of Mecklenburg to Wallenstein. The electors trimmed Ferdinand's sails a little at the Diet of Regensburg, June–August 1630, forcing him to dismiss Wallenstein from military command and confiscating much of his wealth. At the climax of his sudden humiliation, Ferdinand was faced with a new invasion from the north.

The leadership of the Nordic resurgence had now passed to Gustavus Adolphus who, at age thirty-five, had already ruled Sweden for nineteen years. Most of these years had been spent in long and successful wars against his Baltic neighbors. As a warrior-king, Gustavus Adolphus was without peer in his leadership of men, and proved early in his career to be a tactician of unusual caliber. In July 1630 he landed in Pomerania at the head of a disciplined and well-equipped Swedish army, the first and only national army in the war. Under the military genius of the Swedish king, the tide began to turn. First Pomerania, followed by Mecklenburg and Brandenburg, then Magdeburg, Hesse-Cassel, and Saxony were swept into the Swedish alliance. A diplomatic entente with France produced money to finance the Swedish invasion. Fourteen months after his first landing, Gustavus Adolphus stood near Breitenfeld, just

"The Surrender of Breda," *1625. This striking painting by Velázquez (1635) shows Justin of Nassau giving the keys of the city to Ambrosio Spinola, commander of the Spanish army.*

north of Leipzig, with 40,000 men, mostly Swedes and Saxons, facing an imperial army of equal numbers under Tilly. Gustavus's brilliant victory, after his Saxon allies had been routed, proved the superiority of his tactics and generalship. The victorious Swedish army advanced across Thuringia to the Rhine, then moved eastward toward Nuremberg and south into the heart of Bavaria.

In the meantime, Wallenstein was recalled and given command of an imperial army that now drove the Saxons out of Bohemia and intercepted Gustavus Adolphus near Leipzig as he returned north to rescue his allies. In the battle of Lützen that followed, Wallenstein was forced to break off the fight and withdraw again into Bohemia. The Swedish victory was illusory, however, for Gustavus Adolphus was mortally wounded. Oxenstierna, who possessed the same religious motivation and dedication as the king, was acquainted with every aspect of Swedish policy and continued to promote that policy after Gustavus's death. A short time later, Wallenstein was murdered by one of his Irish captains, and the conflict took on new dimensions.

Gustavus Adolphus at the Battle of Lützen. *This realistic painting by Jan Asselyn shows the Swedish king leading a cavalry charge shortly before he was killed.*

Historians have long noted that the entrance of France in 1635 opened a new phase in the Thirty Years' War. Yet it was only French methods, not motives, that changed. Since Henri IV's abortive alliance system of 1610, France had been an active thorn in the Habsburg side. Richelieu was a key agent in the Danish invasion, and since 1631 had been the principal paymaster of the Swedish army. It must also be remembered that there was more than one war going on. In addition to the central front in Germany and Bohemia, and the western front in the Rhineland and the Netherlands, war flared up also on the eastern periphery of the Empire, influencing some of the decisions in the west. The Smolensk War, as it was called, between Russia and Poland, drew off enough of the Swedish forces to make their encounter with the Spanish-imperial army at Nördlingen (September 1634) a major disaster for Sweden. The outcome of the battle of Nördlingen, which guaranteed that southern Germany would remain Catholic, was also influenced by the addition of some 8,000 to 10,000 fresh Spanish and Italian troops brought through the Valtelline Pass in the summer of 1634 by Philip IV's brother, the cardinal-infante of Spain.

Since 1622, when the count-duke of Olivares became Philip IV's minister, Spain had pursued a systematic encirclement of northern and eastern France, which Richelieu now helped to turn into a major confrontation. Richelieu's administration as chief minister in France coincided almost identically with Olivares's in Spain. Both men were ambitious, confident, and capable. Olivares headed a state whose effective armies and strategic footholds were the envy of all Europe, but whose economic base was both weak and precariously

471

overextended. Richelieu's France, on the other hand, had little external prestige but was gradually putting its domestic house in order following the long civil wars and the relapse that followed the assassination of Henri IV. French economic recovery was well under way when Richelieu began muddying Habsburg waters. Through diplomatic and military intercession, he reversed the allegiances of Savoy and the Grisons. By direct intervention, he won the dispute over the Mantuan succession in 1627–31. At the same time, he subsidized the Dutch in their war with Spain and kept the emperor from entering that war by sponsoring the Swedish invasion of Germany.

After the Swedish defeat at Nördlingen, Richelieu openly entered the arena against the Habsburgs, with the blessings of Pope Urban VIII. First the war went poorly, almost disastrously, for France. Then the tide began to turn. A Franco-Dutch campaign against the Spanish Netherlands took Artois, occupied the Generalité (south of the Meuse), and reconquered Breda. In 1639 the Dutch destroyed a Spanish fleet in the English Channel while French mercenaries cut off the Rhine supply line at Breisach. At that moment, internal convulsions in Catalonia and Portugal further paralyzed the Spanish war effort and brought the downfall of Olivares. In 1642 France occupied Roussillon, and a year later at Rocroi, just south of the southern tip of the bishopric of Liège, 22,000 French troops, commanded by the prince of Condé, crushed a larger Spanish army that was composed of the cardinal-infante's hitherto-undefeated infantry. Still, the war dragged on for another five years before the haggling of negotiators at Münster (where France negotiated with the Empire and the Catholic states and cities of Germany, and Spain with the Netherlands) and at Osnabrück (where Swedish, Danish, and delegates of the Protestant states met with the imperial representatives) could conclude a series of agreements collectively known as the Peace of Westphalia.

The Peace of Westphalia

By the terms of the 1648 peace, a major territorial and religious settlement was made for central Europe. The western area of conflict, however, between France and Spain, was not concluded until eleven years later, with the Peace of the Pyrenees. By that time, a new war had broken out in the north between Sweden, Poland, and Russia, which was soon joined by Brandenburg and France on one side, and strangely by Austria, Spain, Denmark, and the Netherlands on the other. Eventually, settlements were made between Sweden and Denmark in 1658 and 1660, between Sweden and Poland in 1660, and between Russia and Poland in 1667.

Taken together, the peace settlements of the two decades 1648–67 recognized and formalized a major turning point in European history. Discounting some reversals and exceptions, the heaviest losers in the war were Spain, Austria, Poland, and Denmark, while the chief beneficiaries were France, Sweden, and the United Netherlands. There may be some substance to J.V. Polišenský's claim that the war resulted in the defeat of the medieval ruling aristocracy by the "new nobility" (the bourgeois capitalists). Such a generalization, however,

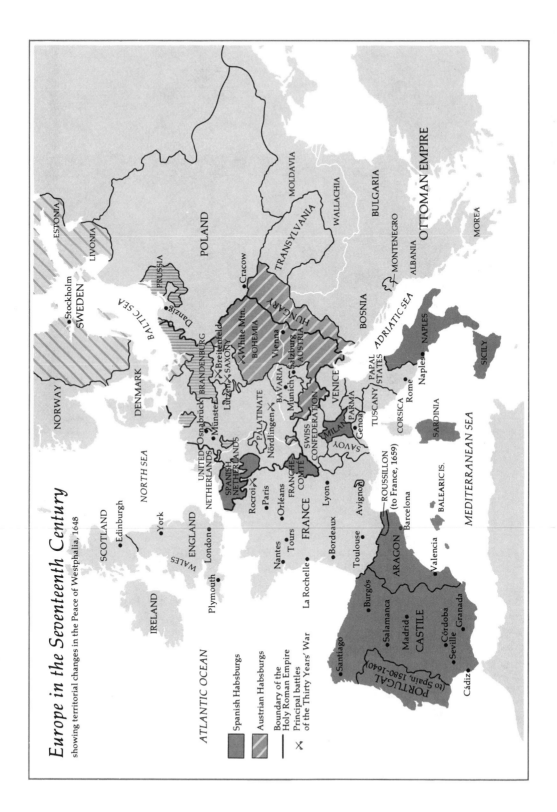

Europe in the Seventeenth Century
showing territorial changes in the Peace of Westphalia, 1648

Spanish Habsburgs

Austrian Habsburgs

— Boundary of the Holy Roman Empire

✕ Principal battles of the Thirty Years' War

ATLANTIC OCEAN

IRELAND

SCOTLAND
•Edinburgh

•York

WALES

ENGLAND
London•

Plymouth•

NORTH SEA

NORWAY

DENMARK

BALTIC SEA

SWEDEN
•Stockholm

NORWAY

ESTONIA

LIVONIA

PRUSSIA

•Danzig

POLAND

•Cracow

MOLDAVIA

TRANSYLVANIA

WALLACHIA

BULGARIA

OTTOMAN EMPIRE

MOREA

ALBANIA

MONTENEGRO

BOSNIA

ADRIATIC SEA

UNITED NETHERLANDS
SPANISH NETHERLANDS

Osnabrück
Münster

BRANDENBURG

Breitenfeld✕
Lützen✕ SAXONY
✕White Mtn
BOHEMIA
Vienna•
Salzburg
AUSTRIA
HUNGARY

PALATINATE

BAVARIA
Munich•

Nördlingen✕

SWISS CONFEDERATION

FRANCHE-COMTÉ

Rocroi✕
•Paris
•Orléans

FRANCE

Nantes•
Tours•

La Rochelle•

•Bordeaux

•Lyon

Toulouse•

ROUSSILLON
(to France, 1659)

SAVOY

MILAN
Genoa•

PARMA

VENICE

TUSCANY

PAPAL STATES
Rome•

CORSICA

SARDINIA

Naples•
NAPLES

SICILY

MEDITERRANEAN SEA

Avignon

Barcelona•

ARAGON

BALEARIC IS.

Valencia•

PORTUGAL
(to Spain, 1580–1640)

•Burgós

•Salamanca
Madrid•
CASTILE

•Córdoba
Seville•
Granada•

•Cádiz

•Santiago

The Treaty of Westphalia.   *This painting by Gerard Ter Borch shows the Dutch and Spanish delegates at Münster swearing the oath of ratification to the treaty. The Dutch representatives have their hands raised, while the Spanish have their hands on a Bible.*

runs into as many difficulties as the older view that the two opposing forces were simply Catholicism and Protestantism. The social, economic, administrative, and religious structure of France was closer to the Spanish system than to that of either the Dutch or the Swedish. Yet throughout the period France fought with and financed the latter, not Spain.

Near the beginning of the war, there was a distinguishable ideological division of Europe along confessional lines, not a new polarization but an old one, remaining from the religious wars of the sixteenth century. To this division were added other causes of war: personal and territorial aggrandizement, economic advantage, dynastic rivalry (especially strong between Habsburg and Bourbon), social struggles, and even petty personal jealousy. Sometimes these ingredients lined up evenly on either side; more often they crossed lines to add greater confusion to the situation. To reduce the causes or the consequences of this complex international upheaval to the simple polarities of class struggle, or to feudalism versus modernism, or to court against country, absolute mon-

Executions during the Thirty Years' War, *from the series on the* Misères de la guerre *(the Miseries of War) by Jacques Callot.*

archy against representative government, Mediterranean world against the Baltic, or Catholicism against Protestantism, is to ignore the variety of motivations that spawned and prolonged it. By the time of the Peace of Westphalia, many of the religious motivations that had dominated at the beginning of the war no longer prevailed, although the separate Catholic-Protestant negotiations at Münster and Osnabrück are evidence that strong religious feelings still existed. Political decisions were less frequently made for religious reasons now, and the stipulations that were made concerning religion were clearly separated from political and economic matters.

France emerged as the dominant power in Europe. By treaty arrangement, it was recognized as sovereign over Metz, Toul, and Verdun, as well as Pignerol, Breisach, most of Alsace, and the city of Philippsburg. In the Peace of the Pyrenees, France received Roussillon, Artois, Cambrai, and a claim to the Spanish succession through the marriage of Louis XIV to Philip IV's daughter Maria Teresa. Swedish supremacy in the Baltic was ensured by the acquisition of the southern end of the Swedish peninsula, western Pomerania, the bishoprics of Bremen and Verden (with three votes in the imperial diet), the city of Wismar, and a cash indemnity. The complete independence of the United Netherlands was recognized. What France, Sweden, and the Netherlands won, the Habsburgs lost. Within the Empire, the territorial independence and sovereignty of each of the states was recognized, thereby all but ending the Holy Roman Empire as a political entity. Furthermore, the religious peace of Augsburg was reaffirmed, with Calvinism given an equal legal position in all imperial affairs, and the ecclesiastical reservation acknowledged.

As far as the economic and social impact of the war upon Germany is concerned, the arguments go on. By the careful use of selected sources, it is possible to prove that the war either paralyzed German growth for the next two centuries, killing two-thirds of the population and crippling agriculture, industry, and commerce, or that it had a relatively slight long-range effect on either the economy or the social life. Both claims may be right. In some areas all of the horrible and devastating effects of war at its worst were experienced, yet other regions remained relatively free from destruction, and some even enjoyed economic growth. What is true of the war's impact on Saxony does not hold for Baden. This was a seventeenth-century world war, "morally subversive, economically destructive, socially degrading," but it was not total war in the twentieth-century sense. It was only as total as the technology of the time could make it. It was enough, however, to result in the most destructive conflict in European history up to that time.

Epilogue: Legacy of the Reformation Age

The confessional conflicts that emerged from the sixteenth-century Reformation, though not caused by the Reformation alone, seem to have culminated by the middle of the seventeenth century. Wars did not cease after the Peace of Westphalia, but for a time at least they appear to have been less passionately fought. The desire for stability and equilibrium came to prevail over the demand for religious conformity. For most Europeans, heterodoxy was becoming more acceptable than it had been during the religious conflicts of the previous one hundred years. At least it was preferred to mutual destruction. Many came to see that compromise—that most feared word during the religious wars— was not always synonymous with dishonor, and that partial success might be more satisfactory than the risk of total defeat in the pursuit of total victory. Exhausted from the bloodletting of those ideological struggles, Europeans slowly came to accept the reality and permanence of the Reformation when they realized that ideas could be transformed, but not destroyed.

The immediate legacy of the Reformation era was an increase in fear, hate, intolerance, and bloodshed. Yet this age of reform and revolution included many constructive features that in time provided a healthier heritage. Hardly an area of human endeavor was unaffected by the prolonged religious upheaval—church, government, economy, education, culture—but it seems unwise to attempt to attribute every aspect of the modern world to some feature of the Reformation or to allocate praise and blame in the way many have done. Such sweeping claims have done more to damage historical understanding than to enhance it. Nevertheless, the post-Reformation world *was* different, and some of that difference was due to ideas, institutions, and events set in motion by the religious schism of the sixteenth century.

The most obvious legacy was the replacement of the monolithic church of the pre-Reformation era by a multitude of evangelical, reformed, and "revealed" churches, coexisting with a trimmed-down and revitalized Roman Catholic church that was still influential but held only a vestige of its previous power. A result of this fragmentation was an eventual decrease in religious intensity. The period set a pattern for resistance to tyranny and opened the door to greater freedom. Religious tolerance did not yet mean the freedom to *worship* freely when, where, and how one desired, but it did promote a growing freedom of conscience, to *believe* as one desired. Worship was still prescribed in most of Europe, although in a few places laws against dissenters were less rigorously applied. Deference had to be paid to the state church, although other religions were often allowed to function if they did not cause trouble. Even witch-hunting declined by the mid-seventeenth century, as did the use of judicial torture; and that most infamous instrument of mental tyranny, the Spanish Inquisition, was in remission.

The legacy of lowered religious intensity and the spread of pluralism was also accompanied by a rise in political demands. As the state was freed from the active control of the church, a new relationship not only emerged between church and state but also between people and the state. As governments became more independent and secular they also became more absolute. It has been observed that the search for divine truth that obsessed Martin Luther was replaced a century later by the search for power. This new passion for power found its fullest expression in the growth of the absolute monarchy. Governments became more effectively organized and more economically stable, and they demanded higher taxes and wider allegiance. The future would lie not with multinational empires, such as the papacy and the Holy Roman Empire, but with the national state.

The proliferation and personalization of religion that began with the Reformation was accompanied by a secularization of life—private, public, and political. That secularization began with some of the reformers themselves, as they relinquished ecclesiastical jurisdiction to civil authorities, but became more pronounced in the seventeenth century when reaction to religious dogmatism and fanaticism set in. The disenchantment with religion contributed to the social and political alienation of the poor as social services that had formerly been the province of the religious now fell under the impersonal control of the state. It may also be, as Lewis Spitz has suggested, that this reaction reinforced the growing interest in science because religious controversy made the study of nature seem safer and less controversial. It likewise contributed to the creation of a scientific elite and the separation of "science" from "magic."

Secularization affected cultural change as well, as the growing emphasis on power was translated into visual and auditive images. Although Baroque art and music evoked powerful religious emotions, they also dramatized secular tensions and strengths, and tended further to separate elite from popular culture. It was increasingly difficult for common people to understand the art of the aristocracy. Opera and the oratorio were not for the masses, nor were Rubens's paintings. And the patrons of "high culture" had little interest either in making their civilization comprehensible to the lower classes or in appreciating the value of peasant music, dance, or art. Traditionally the common ground for all classes, of Christian society anyway, was the church. Yet even the church was different for an aristocrat than for a peasant, and the Reformation added innumerable other distinctions. The post-Reformation world was pluralistic to a degree unimaginable earlier, and continued to separate and individualize at the same time that it consolidated and expanded.

Obviously, not everything that took place in the seventeenth century, or since, was caused by the Reformation. Yet that movement, with its fragmentation of Christianity, attendant strengthening of the national state, and permeation of secularism, did set in motion a sequence of events and a production of ideas that have had a continuing impact on the world in which we live.

Suggestions for Further Reading

SPAIN IN DECLINE

A very useful introduction to seventeenth-century Spain is R.A. Stradling, *Europe and the Decline of Spain* (London, 1981). Also see his *Philip IV and the Government of Spain, 1621–1665* (New York and Cambridge, England, 1988). The definitive biography of Philip IV's minister and favorite is J.H. Elliott, *The Count-Duke of Olivares: The Statesman in the Age of Decline* (New Haven, 1986), based on a wide reading of primary and secondary sources. Also of value are several essays in his *Spain and Its World, 1500–1700* (New Haven, 1989). For a different perspective on Philip IV, see Jonathan Brown and J.H. Elliott, *A Palace for a King: The Buen Retiro and the Court of Philip IV* (New Haven, 1980). Spanish political thought is carefully analyzed in J.A. Fernández-Santamaría, *Reason of State and Statecraft in Spanish Political Thought, 1595–1640* (Lanham, Maryland, 1983). On Valencia see James Casey, *The Kingdom of Valencia in the Seventeenth Century* (New York and Cambridge, England, 1979).

Social and economic issues are featured in James S. Amelang, *Honored Citizens of Barcelona: Patrician Culture and Class Relations, 1490–1714* (Princeton, 1986); David R. Ringrose, *Madrid and the Spanish Economy, 1560–1850* (Berkeley, 1983); and Carla R. Phillips, *Ciudad Real, 1500–1750* (Cambridge, Massachusetts, 1979). A productive new approach to Spanish imperial history is taken in Carla Phillips' magnificent *Six Galleons for the King of Spain: Imperial Defense in the Early Seventeenth Century* (Baltimore, 1986). The role of lawyers, bankers, and inquisitors is investigated in Richard L. Kagan, *Lawsuits and Litigants in Castile, 1502–1700* (Chapel Hill, 1981); James C. Boyajian, *Portuguese Bankers at the Court of Spain, 1626–1650* (New Brunswick, 1983); and Henry Kamen, *Inquisition and Society in Spain in the Sixteenth and Seventeenth Centuries* (Bloomington, 1985).

ITALY AND THE OTTOMAN EMPIRE

Carlo M. Cipolla, *Fighting the Plague in Seventeenth-Century Italy* (Madison, 1981) looks at one of the factors in the decline of the Italian states. On Venice Richard T. Rapp, *Industry and Economic Decline in Seventeenth Century Venice* (Cambridge, Massachusetts, 1976) is valuable. The historiography on Tuscany (Florence) during the seventeenth century is more extensive. See in particular Carlo M. Cipolla, *Money in Sixteenth-Century Florence* (Berkeley, 1989); *Faith, Reason, and the Plague in Seventeenth-Century Tuscany* (Ithaca, 1979); and Giulia Calvi, *Histories of a Plague Year: The Social and the Imaginary in Baroque Florence*, tr. by Dario Biocca and Bryant T. Ragan, Jr. (Berkeley, 1988). The best general account of Florence is Eric Cochrane, *Florence in the Forgotten Centuries, 1527–1800: A History of Florence and the Florentines in the Age of the Grand Dukes* (Chicago, 1973). Also see his posthumous *Italy, 1530–1630*, ed. by Julius Kirshner (New York, 1988), and on post-Renaissance Florentine art Edward L. Goldberg, *After Vasari: History, Art and Patronage in Late Medici Florence* (Princeton, 1988).

On the Ottoman Turks see Cornell H. Fleischer, *Bureaucrat and Intellectual in the Ottoman Empire: The Historian Mustafa Ali* (Princeton, 1986); Suraiya Faroqui, *Towns and Townsmen of Ottoman Anatolia: Trade, Crafts and Food Production in an Urban Setting, 1520–1650* (New York and Cambridge, England, 1984); Bruce McGowan, *Economic Life in Ottoman Europe: Taxation, Trade, and the Struggle for Land, 1600–1800* (New York and Cambridge, England, 1981); and most recently, Daniel Goffman, *Izmir and the Levantine World, 1550–1650* (Seattle, 1990).

HOLY ROMAN EMPIRE AND EASTERN EUROPE

R.J.W. Evans, *Rudolf II and His World: A Study in Intellectual History, 1576–1612* (Oxford, 1973) is a good starting point. Also see Thomas M. Barker, *Army, Aristocracy, Monarchy: Essays on War, Society, and Government in Austria, 1618–1780* (Boulder, Colorado, 1982); Orest Subtelny, *Domination of Eastern Europe: Native Nobilities and Foreign Absolutism, 1500–1715* (Toronto, 1986); and Frank Sysn and Ivo Banac, eds., *Concepts of Nationhood in Early Modern Eastern Europe* (Cambridge, England, 1986). Hungarian society is surveyed in Vera Zimányi, *Economy and Society in Sixteenth-Seventeenth Century Hungary, 1526–1650,* tr. by Matyas Esterhazy (Budapest, 1987).

On Scandinavia see David Kirby, *Northern Europe in the Early Modern Period: The Baltic World 1492–1772* (New York, 1990) for a broad coverage; Göran Rystad, ed., *Europe and Scandinavia: Aspects of the Process of Integration in the Seventeenth Century* (Solna, Sweden, 1983); Michael Roberts, *The Early Vasas: A History of Sweden, 1523–1611* (New York and Cambridge, England, 1986), and *Gustavus Adolphus and the Rise of Sweden* (Mystic, Connecticut, 1973). Michael F. Metcalf, *The Riksdag: A History of the Swedish Parliament* (Stockholm, 1987) is an important study of the Riksdag from its beginning in the fifteenth century to the present. Also see Kurt Johannesson, *The Renaissance of the Goths in Sixteenth-Century Sweden: Johannes and Olaus Magnus as Politicians and Historians,* tr. by James Larson (Berkeley, 1991).

A good overview of Poland is Norman Davies, *God's Playground: A History of Poland, Vol. I: Origins to 1795* (Oxford, 1981). More specialized is David A. Frick, *Polish Sacred Philology in the Reformation and the Counter-Reformation (1551–1632)* (Berkeley, 1989). For Russia see Robert O. Crummey, *The Formation of Muscovy, 1304–1643* (London, 1987); Linda Gordon, *Cossack Rebellions: Social Turmoil in the Sixteenth-Century Ukraine* (Albany, 1983); Francis Carr, *Ivan the Terrible* (Totowa, New Jersey, 1981); Maureen Perrie, *The Image of Ivan the Terrible in Russian Folklore* (New York and Cambridge, England, 1987). The breakdown of Ivan's empire is described in Ruslan G. Skrynnikov, *Boris Godunov* (Gulf Breeze, Florida, 1982), and *The Time of Troubles: Russia in Crisis, 1604–1618,* both tr. by Hugh F. Graham (Gulf Breeze, Florida, 1988). The development of a more European-style monarchy under the Romanovs is outlined in Paul Dukes, *The Making of Russian Absolutism, 1613–1801* (New York, 1982). Also see Paul Buchkovitch, *The Merchants of Moscow, 1580–1650* (New York and Cambridge, England, 1980), and Richard Hellie, *Slavery in Russia, 1450–1725* (Chicago, 1982).

THE THIRTY YEARS' WAR

The most penetrating study to date on the war is Geoffrey Parker, *The Thirty Years' War* (Boston, 1984). Although broader in scope and much smaller, M.S. Anderson's

War and Society in Europe of the Old Regime, 1618–1789 (Leicester, England, 1988) has some perceptive comments on the Thirty Years' War. More traditional is David Maland, *Europe at War, 1600–1650* (Totowa, New Jersey, 1980), and the works by J.V. Polišenský, *The Thirty Years' War* (Berkeley, 1971) and *War and Society in Europe, 1618–1648* (New York, 1978), are also useful. Christopher R. Friedrichs, *Urban Society in an Age of War* (Princeton, 1979) is an interesting study of the city of Nördlingen between 1580 and 1720. The latest perceptions of military changes during the early modern period can be found in Geoffrey Parker, *The Military Revolution: Military Innovation and the Rise of the West, 1500–1800* (New York and Cambridge, England, 1988).

APPENDIX I

Chronology of Important Events

1500 Treaty of Granada. Birth at Ghent of the future Emperor Charles V. Erasmus's *Adages* published. Benvenuto Cellini born.

1501 First African slaves imported to Hispaniola. Prince Arthur marries Catherine of Aragon.

1502 Spanish consolidate power in Naples. University of Wittenberg founded. Prince Arthur dies.

1503 Fall of Cesare Borgia. Erasmus's *Enchiridion* published.

1504 Thomas More elected to Parliament. Death of Queen Isabel of Castile.

1505 Luther enters Augustinian cloister at Erfurt. John Knox born.

1506 Zwingli at Glarus. Reuchlin publishes Latin-Hebrew grammar. Massacre of Jews in Lisbon. Death of Columbus. Francis Xavier born.

1507 Luther ordained. Pope Julius II promulgates indulgences for rebuilding St. Peter's. Margaret of Austria named regent of the Low Countries.

1508 Luther at Wittenberg. League of Cambrai against Venice.

1509 Accession of Henry VIII. John Calvin born. Erasmus publishes *The Praise of Folly*. University of Alcalá founded.

1510 Reuchlin-Pfefferkorn controversy begins. Luther visits Rome.

1511 Holy League against France. Council of Pisa. Erasmus at Cambridge. Birth of Michael Servetus.

1512 Lateran Council begins. Henry VIII invades France. Ferdinand of Aragon conquers Navarre. Luther completes doctorate.

1513 English victory over Scots at Flodden Field. Death of James IV. Battle of the Spurs. Machiavelli writes *The Prince*. Leo X becomes pope.

1514 Wolsey becomes archbishop of York. *Letters of Obscure Men* published. Andreas Vesalius born.

1515 Accession of Francis I. Battle of Marignano. Treaty of Fribourg. St. Teresa of Avila and St. Philip Neri born.

1516 Concordat of Bologna. Erasmus's *New Testament* published. Sir Thomas More's *Utopia* published. Charles I becomes king of Castile and Aragon.

1517 Luther's *Ninety-Five Theses*. Oratory of Divine Love founded. Sultan Selim I conquers Egypt. Lateran Council ends.

1518 Zwingli at Zürich. Peace of London. Wolsey appointed papal legate *a latere* in England. Thomas More joins king's Council.

1519 Charles V elected Holy Roman emperor. Leipzig Debate. Zwingli begins preaching in Zürich.

1520 Luther's Three Treatises. Papal bull *Exsurge domine*. Meeting at the "Field of Cloth of Gold." Revolt of the *Comuneros*. "Bloodbath of Stockholm." Gustavus Vasa leads rebellion against Denmark. Suleiman the Magnificent becomes Ottoman sultan.

1521 Diet and Edict of Worms. First Habsburg-Valois war. French besiege Pamplona, Loyola wounded. Suleiman conquers Belgrade. Melanchthon's *Loci communes* published.

1522 Rhodes falls to the Turks. Luther's *New Testament* published. Henry VIII given title "Defender of the Faith." Adrian VI becomes pope.

1523 Christian II of Denmark deposed; Gustavus Vasa becomes king of Sweden.

Knights' Revolt crushed. Zwinglian reforms in Zürich. Lefèvre's *New Testament* published. Clement VII becomes pope.

1524   Peasants' Revolt in Germany. Francis I conquers Milan. Theatines established. Erasmus's *On the Freedom of the Will* published. Ronsard born. Council of the Indies formed.

1525   Battle of Pavia. German peasants defeated. Thomas Müntzer executed. First Anabaptist congregation at Zollikon. Luther's *On the Bondage of the Will* published. Tyndale's *New Testament* published. Luther marries Katharina von Bora.

1526   Treaty of Madrid. Battle of Mohács. Ferdinand becomes king of Bohemia and Hungary; John Zapolya of Turkish Hungary. League of Cognac. First Diet of Speyer.

1527   Sack of Rome. Beginning of Reformation in Sweden. First Anabaptist martyrs. Schleitheim Articles. University of Marburg founded. Philip II born. Death of Machiavelli.

1528   Basel, Bern, and Strasbourg join Reformation. Zwingli's *Commentary on the True and False Religion* published. Capuchin Order founded. Andrea Doria shifts allegiance from France to Spain. Hubmaier burned. Death of Dürer.

1529   Diet of Speyer and the "Protest." Marburg Colloquy between Luther and Zwingli. Fall of Wolsey; Thomas More becomes lord chancellor. Peace of Cambrai. Turks besiege Vienna.

1530   Diet of Augsburg and Augsburg Confession. Charles V crowned by pope in Bologna. Knights of St. John take Malta.

1531   Second Battle of Kappel; death of Zwingli. Ferdinand of Habsburg elected king of the Romans. Schmalkaldic League formed. Parliament recognizes Henry VIII as Supreme Head of the Church in England.

1532   Submission of English clergy. Thomas More resigns as lord chancellor. Turks invade Hungary.

1533   Henry VIII marries Anne Boleyn. Act of Appeals. Thomas Cromwell appointed secretary; Thomas Cranmer appointed archbishop of Canterbury. Elizabeth born. Montaigne born. Henri dauphin of France marries Catherine de' Medici.

1534   Anabaptists at Münster. Day of the Placards in France. Loyola founds the Society of Jesus. Act of Supremacy. Cartier explores eastern Canada. Paul III becomes pope.

1535   Massacre of Anabaptists at Münster. Execution of Sir Thomas More. Coverdale's Bible. Contarini made a cardinal. Charles V captures Tunis. Antonio de Mendoza first viceroy of New Spain.

1536   First edition of Calvin's *Institutes*. Franco-Turkish treaty. Third Habsburg-Valois war. Suppression of the monasteries. The Pilgrimage of Grace. Anne Boleyn beheaded. Death of Erasmus. Tyndale burned.

1537   Edward VI born; death of Jane Seymour. Civil war in Peru. First printing press in Mexico.

1538   Calvin and Farel expelled from Geneva. James V of Scotland marries Mary of Guise.

1539   Revolt of Ghent against Charles V. Strike of printers in Paris and Lyon. Second dissolution of monasteries in England. The *Six Articles* published. The Great English Bible published.

1540   Papal authorization of the Jesuits. Edict of Fontainebleau. Henry VIII marries Anne of Cleves, then Catherine Howard. Thomas Cromwell executed. Jews expelled from Naples.

1541   Diet of Regensburg. Calvin returns to Geneva, issues the *Ecclesiastical Ordinances*. Xavier embarks on mission to the Far East. El Greco born.

1542   Fourth Habsburg-Valois war. Catherine Howard beheaded. Scots defeated at Solway Moss; James V killed. Roman Inquisition established. *New Laws* promulgated by Charles V. San Juan de la Cruz born.

1543   Alliance between Charles V and Henry VIII against Francis I. Henry VIII marries Catherine Parr. Copernicus's *De Revolutionibus* and Vesalius's *Fabrica* published.

1544   Peace of Crépy between Charles and Francis. English invade Scotland. Torquato Tasso born.

1545   Opening of the Council of Trent. Silver discovered in Potosí, Bolivia. Don Juan of Austria born.

1546   Death of Luther. Schmalkaldic War begins. Tycho Brahe born. Anne Askew burned at the stake.

1547   Death of Henry VIII and Francis I. Battle of Mühlberg. Council of Trent moved to Bologna. Ivan IV proclaimed tsar. Cervantes born.

1548   Augsburg Interim proclaimed by Charles V. Loyola's *Spiritual Exercises* published. Giordano Bruno born.

1549   First English Prayer Book. Act of Uniformity. Kett's Rebellion. St. Francis Xavier in Japan. Death of Pope Paul III.

1550   Thomas Cranmer's *Defence of the True Doctrine of the Sacrament* published. Cardinal del Monte becomes Pope Julius III. Birth of John Napier.

1551   Second opening of the Council of Trent. Habsburg-Valois wars resumed. The Geneva Bible published. Duke of Northumberland overthrows Somerset. John Knox named court preacher in England. The Turks capture Tripoli.

1552   Second *Book of Common Prayer* and *Forty-Two Articles* published. Treaty of Passau. Alliance of Henri II with German Protestants. French take bishoprics of Metz, Toul, and Verdun. Charles V flees Innsbruck.

1553   Mary Tudor becomes queen of England; reintroduces Catholicism. Servetus executed in Geneva.

1554   Marriage of Mary Tudor and Philip of Spain. Wyatt's Rebellion. Mary of Guise becomes regent of Scotland. Walter Raleigh born.

1555   Diet of Augsburg. Religious Peace of Augsburg. Charles V abdicates sovereignty of the Netherlands to his son Philip. Cardinal Carafa becomes Pope Paul IV.

1556   Abdication of Charles V in the rest of his territories. Death of Loyola. Thomas Cranmer burned at the stake; Reginald Pole made archbishop of Canterbury.

1557   Bank failures and credit crisis. Spanish victory over French at St. Quentin. First Index of Prohibited Books issued by Pope Paul IV.

1558   Accession of Elizabeth I. French take Calais. Death of Charles V at Yuste. John Knox's *First Blast* published.

1559   Peace of Cateau-Cambrésis. Death of Henri II. Calvinist synod in Paris. Act of Uniformity and Supremacy in England. Rising of the Lords of the Congregation in Scotland. Pius IV becomes pope.

1560   Tumult of Amboise. Catherine de' Medici regent for Charles IX; issues edict of toleration. English intervention in Scotland. Treaty of Edinburgh. Death of Melanchthon.

1561   Colloquy of Poissy. Edict of January. Estates General meets at Orléans. Mary Stuart returns to Scotland. Francis Bacon born.

1562   Beginning of Wars of Religion in France following massacre at Vassy. Council of Trent reconvenes. Heidelberg Catechism. The Thirty-Nine Articles approved by Parliament. Lope de Vega born. French Huguenot settlement in Florida.

1563 End of the Council of Trent. Peace of Amboise ends first civil war in France.

1564 Death of Calvin. Death of Michelangelo. Peace of Troyes between England and France. Cardinal Granvelle dismissed. Shakespeare born. Galileo born. Maximilian II Holy Roman emperor.

1565 Conference of Bayonne. Turkish siege of Malta fails. St. Augustine, Florida, founded. Jesuits in Poland. Ivan IV sets up the *oprichnina*. Death of Pius IV.

1566 "The Beggars" resist the Spanish in the Netherlands; rebellion begins. David Riccio murdered. Second Helvetic Confession. *Roman Catechism* issued. Suleiman the Magnificent dies; succeeded by Selim II. Pius V elected pope.

1567 Revolt in the Netherlands. Duke of Alba arrives; Margaret of Parma resigns as governor. Second civil war in France. Lord Darnley murdered and Mary Queen of Scots forced to abdicate; she marries the earl of Bothwell.

1568 Execution of Egmont and Hoorn in Brussels. Third civil war in France begins. Morisco revolt in Granada. Jesuit seminary founded at Douai. Mary Queen of Scots flees to England. Hawkins and Drake ambushed at San Juan de Ulloa.

1569 Huguenots defeated at Jarnac. Rising of the Northern Earls. Cosimo de' Medici becomes first Grand Duke of Tuscany. Death of Pieter Bruegel.

1570 Peace of St. Germain ends third French civil war. Moriscos defeated in Spain. Turks attack Cyprus. Elizabeth I excommunicated.

1571 Battle of Lepanto, defeat of Turkish fleet. Ridolfi Plot uncovered; Duke of Norfolk beheaded. Kepler born. Death of Cellini.

1572 Massacre of St. Bartholomew; fourth French civil war begins. William of Orange chosen stadtholder of Holland. Sea Beggars capture Brill. Treaty of Blois. Death of John Knox. Gregory XII becomes pope.

1573 Alba recalled from the Netherlands; succeeded by Requesens. Henri of Anjou elected king of Poland. Compact of Warsaw. Venice makes peace with Turks. François Hotman's *Francogallia*.

1574 Henri of Anjou becomes king of France. Renewed civil war. Turks recapture Tunis. Tasso completes *Jerusalem Liberated*.

1575 Stephen Báthory elected king of Poland. Bohemian Confession. University of Leiden founded. Beza's *Life of Calvin* published. Philip II declares bankruptcy. Plague in Venice and northern Italy.

1576 "Spanish Fury" in Antwerp. Pacification of Ghent. Don Juan of Austria becomes governor of the Netherlands. Formation of the French Catholic League. Bodin's *République* published. Rudolf II becomes Holy Roman emperor.

1577 The sixth civil war in France. Drake begins memorable voyage of circumnavigation. John Dee's *The Art of Navigation* published. Rubens born.

1578 Duke of Parma becomes governor in the Netherlands following death of Don Juan. Duke of Anjou declared "Defender of Dutch Liberties." Sebastian of Portugal killed in North Africa.

1579 Union of Arras and Union of Utrecht split the Netherlands in two. *Vindiciae contra Tyrannos* published. Socinians in Poland. English Jesuit college founded in Rome. Rebellion in Ireland.

1580 Drake completes circumnavigation of globe. Philip II takes over Portugal. France bankrupt. Seventh civil war. *Formula of Concord* published. Montaigne's *Essays* published. Plague in Lisbon.

1581 Union of Utrecht. Act of Abjuration in northern Netherlands renounces allegiance to Spain. William of Orange accepts sovereignty. Galileo enters University of Pisa. Poland invades Russia.

1582 Pope Gregory XIII institutes Gregorian calendar. John Whitgift Archbishop of Canterbury. Jesuit missionaries in China.

1583 "French Fury" in Antwerp. Throckmorton Plot uncovered. Hugo Grotius born. Galileo discovers principle of the pendulum. Santa Cruz defeats French fleet in the Azores.

1584 William of Orange assassinated. Death of the duke of Anjou. Catholic League reorganized in France. Treaty of Joinville between Spain and the Catholic League. Death of Ivan the Terrible.

1585 Treaty of Nemours. War of the Three Henries (8th civil war in France). Treaty of Nonesuch. Leicester sent to the Netherlands. Spanish take Antwerp and Brussels. Shakespeare arrives in London. Richelieu's birth.

1586 Leicester forced to resign as governor of Netherlands. Babington Plot uncovered. Treaty of Berwick between Elizabeth and James VI. Death of Philip Sidney.

1587 Mary Queen of Scots beheaded. Drake raids Cádiz. Henri of Navarre defeats royal army at Coutras.

1588 "Day of the Barricades" in Paris. Defeat of the Spanish Armada. Estates General meets in Blois; duke and cardinal of Guise assassinated. Hobbes born.

1589 Death of Catherine de' Medici. Assassination of Henri III. Battle of Arques. The "English Armada." Diego Ribera born.

1590 Battle of Ivry. Siege of Paris. The Dutch take Breda. Gregory XIV pope.

1591 Reign of terror in Paris. Rebellion in Aragon surpressed. Innocent IX pope.

1592 Clement VIII elected pope. Sigismund king of Sweden. Death of Montaigne.

1593 Henri IV accepts Catholicism. *Croquants* uprising. Louis Le Nain born. Christopher Marlowe dies.

1594 Henri IV enters Paris, is crowned king of France. Jesuits expelled from France. Rebellion in Ireland. Antonio Pérez's *Relaciones*.

1595 Henri IV absolved by Pope Clement VIII. France declares war on Spain. Descartes born. Dutch begin colonization of East Indies.

1596 Alliance of England, France, and Netherlands against Spain. Shakespeare's *Romeo and Juliet*. Death of Sir Francis Drake.

1597 Third Spanish Armada fails. Hooker's *Laws of Ecclesiastical Polity* published. Death of Peter Canisius.

1598 Edict of Nantes. Peace of Vervins. Death of Philip II. Southern Netherlands assigned to Albert and Isabel. Boris Godunov becomes tsar. Bernini born.

1599 Sigismund deposed by Swedes. Oliver Cromwell born. Velázquez born. Truce with Irish rebels. Shakespeare's *Julius Caesar*.

1600 English East India Company chartered. Henri IV marries Marie de' Medici. Giordano Bruno burned in Rome.

1601 Earl of Essex executed. Elizabethan Poor Law. Matteo Ricci arrives at the Chinese court. Birth of future Louis XIII. Death of Tycho Brahe.

1602 Dutch East India Company chartered. Shakespeare's *Hamlet*. Tax revolts in France. Plague in London.

1603 Death of Elizabeth; accession of James I. Raleigh imprisoned for treason. Jesuits return to France. Champlain in Canada. Hotman's *The Ambassador*.

1604 Hampton Court Conference. Treaty of London ends Anglo-Spanish war. Shakespeare's *Othello*. The *paulette* instituted in France.

1605 Gunpowder Plot uncovered. Paul V elected pope. Cervantes publishes *Don*

Quixote, Pt. I. Bacon's *Advancement of Learning* published. Jesuits in Paraguay. Death of Boris Godunov.

1606 Shakespeare's *King Lear*. Rembrandt born.

1607 Settlement of Jamestown. Violence at Donauwörth. Shakespeare's *Macbeth*.

1608 German Protestant Union formed. Emperor Rudolf cedes Austria, Hungary, and Moravia to Matthias. Champlain founds settlement at Quebec. Milton born.

1609 Catholic League. Succession question in Cleves-Jülich. Twelve Years' Truce between Spain and United Netherlands begins. Moriscos expelled from Spain. Bank of Amsterdam founded.

1610 Henri IV assassinated. Galileo constructs telescope, publishes the *Starry Messenger*. Death of Robert Parsons, S.J.

1611 Rudolf resigns throne of Bohemia to Matthias. Gustavus Adolphus becomes king of Sweden. War with Denmark. King James Bible published. Amsterdam bourse established.

1612 Death of Rudolf II; Matthias I becomes Holy Roman emperor. Alliance between the Protestant Union and England. Champlain governor of New France.

1613 Alliance of Protestant Union with the Netherlands. Michael Romanov elected tsar.

1614 Treaty of Xanten. Rebellion of Condé in France. Estates General meets.

1615 Dutch seize the Moluccas. Harvey's first lectures on circulation of the blood. Camden's *Annales* published.

1616 Huguenot uprising in France. Galileo ordered to cease and desist. Campanella writes defense of Galileo. Cervantes and Shakespeare die.

1617 Counter-Remonstrants against Oldenbarneveldt. Concini murdered. Raleigh sails for Guiana.

1618 Defenestration of Prague and outbreak of the Thirty Years' War. Sir Walter Raleigh executed. Synod of Dort begins.

1619 Frederick of Palatinate elected king of Bohemia. Ferdinand II becomes Holy Roman emperor. Oldenbarneveldt executed. Ben Jonson born.

1620 Battle of White Mountain. *Mayflower* sails to America. African slaves imported into Jamestown. Bacon's *Novum Organum* published.

1621 End of Twelve Years' Truce; war resumed between Spain and the Netherlands. Dutch West India Company founded. Philip IV king of Spain. War between Poland and Sweden. Bacon's *New Atlantis* published.

1622 Count-duke of Olivares chief minister in Spain. Richelieu created cardinal. Sultan Osman II deposed and executed.

1623 Urban VIII becomes pope. Galileo publishes *The Assayer*. Pascal born. Maximilian of Bavaria made elector.

1624 Richelieu becomes chief minister. French occupy the Valtelline. England declares war on Spain. Dutch settlement at New Amsterdam.

1625 Christian IV of Denmark enters war in Germany. Wallenstein commands imperial forces. Tilly invades Lower Saxony. Spanish capture Breda. Charles I succeeds James I in England. Grotius's *De jure belli et pacis* published.

1626 Tilly defeats Christian IV at Lutter. Peace of La Rochelle between French crown and Huguenots. St. Peter's basilica completed. Dutch purchase Manhattan Island from Indians.

1627 England and France at war. Huguenot rising; siege of La Rochelle begins. French bankruptcy. Mantuan succession crisis. Kepler's *Rudolfine Tables* published.

1628   Richelieu takes La Rochelle. Dutch seize Spanish silver fleet. Petition of Right. Buckingham assassinated. Comenius's *The Great Didactic* published. War of Mantuan succession.

1629   Edict of Restitution. Peace of Lübeck. Christian IV withdraws from Germany. Charles I dissolves Parliament. Massachusetts Bay Company chartered.

1630   Gustavus Adolphus invades Germany. Wallenstein dismissed. French occupy Savoy. "Day of Dupes" in France. Velázquez paints *Forge of Volcan*.

1631   Battle of Breitenfeld; Swedish victory. Prague taken by Saxon troops. End of the Mantuan war.

1632   Wallenstein recalled. Battle of Lützen; death of Gustavus Adolphus. Smolensk war. Galileo's *Dialogue* published. Birth of John Locke and Christopher Wren.

1633   Heilbronn Confederation. Laud becomes archbishop of Canterbury.

1634   Wallenstein assassinated. Battle of Nördlingen. Alliance between France and Sweden. Dutch capture Curaçao.

1635   Peace of Prague. France declares war on Spain. French occupy Valtelline again. Velázquez's *Surrender of Breda*. Founding of French Academy.

1636   Spanish troops invade France.

1637   Dutch expel Portuguese from Gold Coast. Descartes's *Discourse on Method* published. Ferdinand III Holy Roman emperor.

1638   Siege of Breisach. French take Roussillon. Dutch given trading rights in southern India. Galileo's *Dialogue Concerning Two New Sciences* published.

1639   Dutch sink Spanish fleet off the Downs. *Nu-pieds* uprising in Normandy. French invade Alsace.

1640   Catalan Revolt. Portuguese Revolt. Scots invade England. Long Parliament convenes. Archbishop Laud impeached. Janson's *Augustinus*.

1641   Strafford executed. Grand Remonstrance. Irish rebellion. Dutch capture Malacca.

1642   English civil war begins. Death of Richelieu; Mazarin becomes chief minister. New Zealand and Tasmania discovered. Rembrandt's *The Night Watch*. Newton born.

1643   French victory over Spanish at Rocroi. Fall of Olivares. Sweden invades Denmark. Louis XIV becomes king of France.

1644   Cromwell's victory at Marston Moor. Innocent X succeeds Urban VIII as pope. Milton's *Areopagitica* published.

1645   Archbishop Laud executed. New Model Army formed. Parliamentary victory at Naseby. Peace negotiations begin at Münster and Osnabrück. Revolt in Naples.

1646   Swedish forces take Prague. Charles I surrenders.

1647   Charles I escapes and is recaptured. Rebellion in Naples. Rembrandt's *Holy Family*.

1648   Peace of Westphalia ends Thirty Years' War. Outbreak of the *Fronde* in France. Pride's Purge in the House of Commons. Uprising in Granada.

1649   Execution of Charles I. Serfdom in Russia.

1650   Charles II lands in Scotland. Death of William II: republic in the Netherlands.

1651   Cromwell defeats Charles II at Worcester. English Navigation Act. Condé enters Paris.

1652   England declares war on Netherlands. Cromwell issues Act of Settlement for Ireland. Disturbances in Seville and Córdoba.

1653   End of the *Fronde*. Pascal joins Jansenists at Port-Royal. Parliament dissolved by Cromwell, who becomes lord protector.

1654   Treaty of Westminster ends Anglo-Dutch war. Louis XIV crowned king of France.

1655   Jan de Witt, Grand Pensionary of Holland. Charles X of Sweden invades Poland. Alexander VII becomes pope.

1656   France and England at war with Spain. Rembrandt's *Blessing of Abraham.*

1657   Anglo-French Treaty of Paris. Hobbes's *Leviathan* published.

1658   Death of Cromwell. Denmark and Sweden at war. Leopold I becomes Holy Roman emperor.

1659   Peace of the Pyrenees ends war between France and Spain.

1660   Charles II restored to English throne. Peace of Oliva ends war between Austria, Brandenburg, Poland, and Sweden. Treaty of Copenhagen ends war between Denmark and Sweden. Death of Velázquez.

APPENDIX II

Rulers of European States

The Papacy

1503–1513	Julius II (Giuliano della Rovere)
1513–1521	Leo X (Giovanni de' Medici)
1522–1523	Adrian VI (Adrian Dedel of Utrecht)
1523–1524	Clement VII (Giulio de' Medici)
1534–1549	Paul III (Alessandro Farnese)
1550–1555	Julius III (Giovanni del Monte)
1555	Marcellus II (Marcello Cervini)
1555–1559	Paul IV (Gian Pietro Carafa)
1559–1565	Pius IV (Giovanni Angelo de' Medici)
1566–1572	Pius V (Michele Ghislieri)
1572–1585	Gregory XIII (Ugo Buoncompagni)
1585–1590	Sixtus V (Felice Peretti)
1590	Urban VII (Giambattista Castagna)
1590–1591	Gregory XIV (Niccolò Sfondrati)
1591	Innocent IX (Giovanni Antonio Facchinetti)
1592–1605	Clement VIII (Ippolito Aldobrandini)
1605	Leo XI (Alessandro de' Medici)
1605–1621	Paul V (Camillo Borghese)
1621–1623	Gregory XV (Alessandro Ludovisi)
1623–1644	Urban VIII (Maffeo Barberini)
1644–1655	Innocent X (Giambattista Pamfili)
1655–1667	Alexander VII (Fabio Chigi)

France

HOUSE OF VALOIS

1515–1547	Francis I
1547–1559	Henri II
1559–1560	Francis II
1560–1574	Charles IX*
1574–1589	Henri III

HOUSE OF BOURBON

1589–1590	Charles X**
1589–1610	Henri IV
1610–1643	Louis XIII
1643–1715	Louis XIV

---

*Catherine de' Medici regent, 1560–1565
**Recognized only by the Catholic League

England

HOUSE OF TUDOR

1509–1547   Henry VIII
1547–1553   Edward VI
1553–1558   Mary I
1558–1603   Elizabeth I

HOUSE OF STUART

1603–1625   James I (James VI of Scotland)
1625–1649   Charles I (Charles I of Scotland)
1649–1660   Commonwealth and Protectorate

Scotland

HOUSE OF STEWART (STUART)

1488–1513   James IV
1513–1542   James V
(1513–1528) Regency
1542–1567   Mary Queen of Scots
(1542–1560) Regency
1567–1625   James VI (James I of England)
(1567–1580) Regency
1625–1649   Charles I (Charles I of England)

Spain

HOUSE OF HABSBURG

1516–1556   Charles I (Emperor Charles V)
1556–1598   Philip II
1598–1621   Philip III
1621–1665   Philip IV

Portugal

HOUSE OF AVIS

1495–1521   Manoel I
1521–1557   João III
1557–1578   Sebastian
1578–1580   Cardinal Henry

HOUSE OF HABSBURG

1580–1598   Philip I (Philip II of Spain)
1598–1621   Philip II (Philip III of Spain)
1621–1640   Philip III (Philip IV of Spain)

HOUSE OF BRAGANZA

1640–1656   João IV
1656–1667   Afonso VI

The Netherlands

HOUSE OF ORANGE

1581–1584	William I, the Silent
1584–1625	Maurice
1625–1647	Frederick Henry
1647–1650	William II
1650–1672	Republic

Denmark and Norway

HOUSE OF OLDENBURG

1513–1523	Christian II (also king of Sweden)
1523–1533	Frederick I
1533–1559	Christian III
1559–1588	Frederick II
1588–1648	Christian IV
1648–1670	Frederick III

Sweden

HOUSE OF VASA

1523–1560	Gustavus I
1560–1568	Eric IV
1568–1592	John II
1592–1604	Sigismund (King of Poland, 1587–1632)
1604–1611	Charles IX
1611–1632	Gustavus Adolphus (Gustav II Adolf)
1632–1654	Christina
1654–1660	Charles X Gustavus

Holy Roman Empire

HOUSE OF HABSBURG

1493–1519	Maximilian I
1519–1556	Charles V (King of Castile and Aragon, 1516–1556)
1558–1564	Ferdinand I (King of Bohemia and Hungary, 1526–1564)
1564–1576	Maximilian II (King of Bohemia and Hungary)
1576–1612	Rudolf II (King of Bohemia, 1576–1611; King of Hungary, 1576–1608)
1612–1619	Matthias (King of Bohemia, 1611–1619; King of Hungary, 1608–1619)
1619–1637	Ferdinand II (King of Bohemia and Hungary)
1637–1657	Ferdinand III (King of Bohemia and Hungary)

Bohemia

1471–1516	Vladislav II (Jagiellonian; Ladislas II of Hungary)
1516–1526	Louis II (Jagiellonian; also king of Hungary)
1526–1564	Ferdinand I (Habsburg; king of Hungary and Holy Roman Emperor, 1558–1564)
1564–1576	Maximilian (Habsburg; king of Hungary and H.R.E.)

1576–1611   Rudolf II (Habsburg; king of Hungary and H.R.E.)
1611–1619   Matthias (Habsburg; king of Hungary and H.R.E.)
1619–1620   Frederick (Count Palatine of the Rhine; the "Winter King")
1619–1637   Ferdinand II (Habsburg; king of Hungary and H.R.E.)
1637–1657   Ferdinand III (Habsburg; king of Hungary and H.R.E.)

Hungary

1490–1516   Ladislas II (Jagiellonian; Vladislav II of Bohemia)
1516–1526   Louis II (Jagiellonian; also king of Bohemia)
1526–1564   Ferdinand I (Habsburg; king of Bohemia and H.R.E., 1558–1564)
1526–1540   John Zapolya (rival claimant)
1564–1576   Maximilian (Habsburg; king of Bohemia and H.R.E.)
1576–1608   Rudolf (Habsburg; king of Bohemia and H.R.E.)
1608–1619   Matthias (Habsburg; king of Bohemia and H.R.E.)
1619–1637   Ferdinand II (Habsburg; king of Bohemia and H.R.E.)
1637–1657   Ferdinand III (Habsburg; king of Bohemia and H.R.E.)

Poland

1492–1501   John Albert (Jagiellonian)
1501–1506   Alexander (Jagiellonian)
1506–1548   Sigismund I (Jagiellonian)
1548–1572   Sigismund II Augustus (last Jagiellonian)
1573–1574   Henri of Valois (King of France, 1574–1589)
1576–1586   Stephen Báthory (of Transylvania)
1587–1632   Sigismund III (Vasa; king of Sweden, 1592–1604)
1632–1648   Władysław IV (Vasa)
1648–1668   John II Casimir (Vasa)

Russia

1462–1505   Ivan III, the Great
1505–1533   Vassili III
1533–1584   Ivan IV, the Terrible
1584–1598   Fedor I
1598–1605   Boris Godunov
1605   Fedor II
1605–1606   Pseudo-Dimitri I
1606–1610   Vassili IV   } Time of Troubles
1607–1610   Pseudo-Dimitri II
1610–1613   Władysław of Poland
1613–1645   Michael (Romanov)
1645–1676   Alexis (Romanov)

Ottoman Turks

1512–1520   Selim I
1520–1566   Suleiman I, the Magnificent
1566–1574   Selim II, the Sot
1574–1595   Murad III
1595–1603   Mohammed (Mahmet) III
1603–1617   Ahmed I

1617–1618   Mustafa I
1618–1622   Osman II
1622–1623   Mustafa I (restored)
1623–1640   Murad IV
1640–1648   Ibrahim I
1648–1687   Mohammed (Mahmet) IV

APPENDIX III
Genealogical Charts

VALOIS AND BOURBON

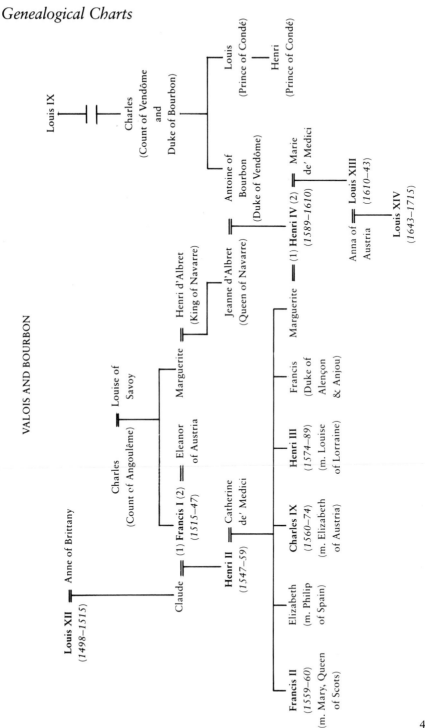

TUDORS AND STUARTS

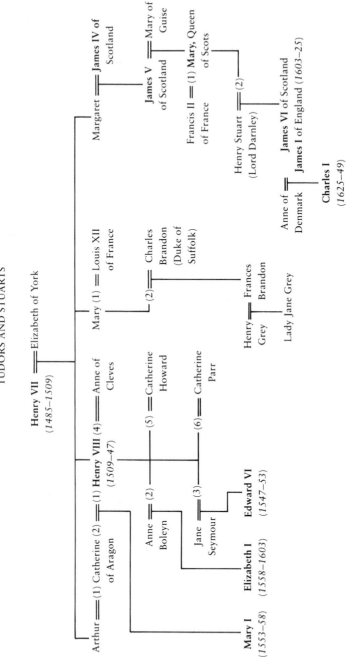

SPANISH HABSBURGS

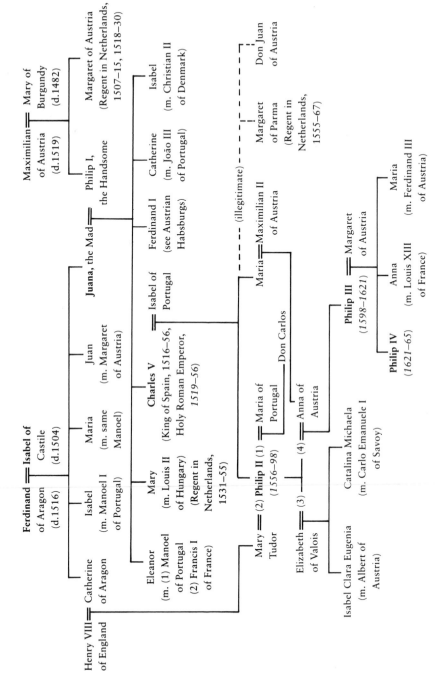

497

Maximilian I of Austria (Emperor) (d.1519) = Mary of Burgundy (d.1482)

Ferdinand of Aragon (d.1516) = Isabel of Castile (d.1504)

Philip, the Handsome (d. 1506) = Juana, the Mad

Margaret (m. (1) Juan of Spain (2) Philibert of Savoy)

Eleanor (m. (1) Manoel I of Portugal (2) Francis I of France)

Juan (m. Margaret of Austria)

Isabel (m. Manoel I of Portugal)

Catherine of Aragon (m. Henry VIII)

Charles V (Holy Roman Emperor, 1519–56) (see Spanish Habsburgs)

Ferdinand I (Holy Roman Emperor, 1558–64) = Anna of Bohemia and Hungary

Mary (m. Louis II of Hungary)

Catherine (m. João III of Portugal)

Isabel (m. Christian II of Denmark)

Maria of Spain = Maximilian II (Emperor, 1564–76)

Ferdinand (Count of Tyrol)

Mary (m. William V of Cleves)

Joanna (m. Francesco of Tuscany)

Anna = Albert II of Bavaria

Mary = Charles of Styria

Philip II = Anna of Spain

Rudolf II (Emperor, 1576–1612)

Elizabeth (m. Charles IX of France)

Matthias (Emperor, 1612–19)

Maximilian II (Emperor, 1564–76)

Ernest (Governor of the Netherlands, 1594–95)

Albert (m. Isabel Clara Eugenia of Spain)

Anna (m. Sigismund III of Poland)

Maria (m. Sigismund Bathory of Transylvania)

Maria Anna of Bavaria = Ferdinand II (Emperor, 1619–37)

Margaret (m. Philip III of Spain)

Leopold (m. Claudia of Tuscany)

Maria Magdalena (m. Cosimo II of Tuscany)

Ferdinand III (Emperor, 1637–57)

Photo Credits

Chapter 1   p. 11, by permission of the Houghton Library, Harvard University; p. 12, The Pierpont Morgan Library, New York, M399, f.12v; p. 15, Bibliothèque Municipale de Rouen; p. 17, Alinari/Art Resource, N.Y.; p. 20, courtesy of Biblioteca San Marco, Venice; p. 21, Giraudon/Art Resource, N.Y.; p. 23, Alte Pinakothek, Munich; p. 25, Giraudon/Art Resource, N.Y.; p. 26, Giraudon/Art Resource, N.Y.; p. 30, copyright reserved to Her Majesty, Queen Elizabeth II; p. 33, Alte Pinakothek, Munich; p. 38, courtesy of the Courtauld Institute of Art, London; p. 41, Alinari/Art Resource, N.Y.

Chapter 2   p. 55, City Museum and Art Gallery, Bristol; p. 58, The Bettmann Archive, Inc.; p. 69, reproduced by courtesy of the Trustees of the British Library; p. 74, Alinari/Art Resource, N.Y.; p. 76, Germanisches Nationalmuseum, Nuremberg; p. 79, Germanisches Nationalmuseum, Nuremberg; p. 83, Alinari/Art Resource, N.Y.; p. 87, Derechos Reservados © Museo del Prado, Madrid.

Chapter 3   p. 95, Statens Museum for Kunst, Copenhagen; p. 100, courtesy of Swiss National Museum, Zürich; p. 102, from the Department of Prints and Drawings of the Zentralbibliothek, Zürich; p. 106, courtesy of Kunstmuseum Basel, Kupferstichkabinett; p. 111, The Beinecke Rare Book and Manuscript Library, Yale University; p. 116, reproduced by courtesy of the Trustees of the British Museum.

Chapter 4   p. 131, Giraudon/Art Resource, N.Y.; p. 135, reproduced by courtesy of the Trustees of the British Library; p. 136, Bernisches Historisches Museum, Bern; p. 143, Swiss National Tourist Office, Zürich; p. 150, Giraudon/Art Resource, N.Y.; p. 155, provided by author.

Chapter 5   p. 165, National Portrait Gallery, London; p. 166, Kunsthistorische Museum, Vienna; p. 167, National Portrait Gallery, London; p. 170, reproduced by courtesy of the Trustees of the British Museum; p. 175, National Portrait Gallery, London; p. 179, National Portrait Gallery, London; p. 180, National Portrait Gallery, London; p. 181, The Fotomas Index; p. 185, Alinari/Art Resource, N.Y.

Chapter 6   p. 195, Alinari/Art Resource, N.Y.; p. 201, University Chapel, Seville; p. 205, reproduced by courtesy of the Trustees of the Chester Beatty Library, Dublin; p. 210, Alinari/Art Resource, N.Y.; p. 216, reproduced by courtesy of the Trustees of the British Museum; p. 219, Alinari/Art Resource, N.Y.; p. 222, Alinari/Art Resource, N.Y.; p. 223, Foto Marburg/Art Resource, N.Y.

Chapter 7   p. 232 (top), by permission of the Houghton Library, Harvard University; p. 232 (bottom), Kunsthistorische Museum, Vienna; p. 233, Giraudon/Art Resource, N.Y.; p. 234, collection of Musée Jacquemart-Andre, Paris; p. 242, Bibliothèque Nationale, Paris; p. 247, Musée de Grenoble; p. 255, Giraudon/Art Resource, N.Y.; p. 257, Foto Marburg/Art Resource, N.Y.

Chapter 8   p. 265, Derechos Reservados © Museo del Prado, Madrid; p. 273, Historical Pictures Service, Chicago; p. 279, Bildarchiv der Österreichischen Nationalbibliothek, Vienna; p. 280, The National Maritime Museum, London; p. 284, Kunsthistorische Museum, Vienna; p. 285, Rijksmuseum, Amsterdam; p. 288, Gemeentelijke Archiefdienst; p. 290, Musées Royaux des Beaux-Arts de Belgique; p. 297, The Metropolitan Museum of Art, bequest of Mrs. H. O. Havemeyer, 1929. The H. O. Havemeyer Collection, 1929 (29.100.6).

Chapter 9   p. 304, Alinari/Art Resource, N.Y.; p. 316, National Portrait Gallery, London; p. 319, Bibliothèque Nationale, Paris; p. 323, National Portrait Gallery, London; p. 327, The National Maritime Museum, London; p. 333, by permission of the Folger Shakespeare Library.

Chapter 10   p. 342, The Pierpont Morgan Library, New York, M399, f.5v; p. 346, Museum Boymans-van Beuningen, Rotterdam; p. 349, Hamburger Kunsthalle; p. 359, by permission of the Houghton Library, Harvard University; p. 360, Giraudon/Art Resource, N.Y.; p. 362, Giraudon/Art Resource, N.Y.; p. 366, from the Wellington Museum, by courtesy of the Board of Trustees of the Victoria and Albert Museum; p. 371, Rijksmuseum Twenthe, Lasondersingel 129–131, 7514 BP Enschede, The Netherlands.

Chapter 11   p. 381, Giraudon/Art Resource; p. 385, National Portrait Gallery, London; p. 387, Giraudon/Art Resource, N.Y.; p. 392, from the Berlin-Dahlem Museen, photograph by Joachim Blauel/Artothek; p. 394–95, Rijksmuseum, Amsterdam; p. 400, Giraudon/Art Resource, N.Y.; p. 406, Scala/Art Resource, N.Y.; p. 407 (top), Alinari/Art Resource, N.Y.; p. 407 (bottom), Giraudon/Art Resource, N.Y.; p. 409, The National Gallery of Scotland; p. 410, Giraudon/Art Resource, N.Y.; p. 411, reproduced by courtesy of the Trustees, The National Gallery, London; p. 412, Gemäldegalerie, Staatliche Museen Preussischer Kulturbesitz, Germany; p. 414, Art Resource, N.Y.

Chapter 12   p. 426, reproduced by courtesy of the Trustees, The National Gallery, London; p. 428, Giraudon/Art Resource, N.Y.; p. 433, National Portrait Gallery, London; p. 438, National Portrait Gallery, London; p. 443, Rijksmuseum, Amsterdam; p. 445, courtesy of The New York Historical Society, N.Y.

Chapter 13   p. 453, courtesy of The Hispanic Society of America, N.Y.; p. 464, Culver Pictures, N.Y.; p. 467, Bildarchiv der Österreichischen Nationalbibliothek, Vienna; p. 468, Bayerisches Nationalmuseum, Munich; p. 470, Derechos Reservados © Museo del Prado, Madrid; p. 471, Herzog Anton Ulrich Museum, Braunschweig; p. 474, reproduced by courtesy of the Trustees, The National Gallery, London; p. 475, reproduced from the collections of the Library of Congress.

INDEX